CRIMINAL JUSTICE
A Brief Introduction

SECOND EDITION

Frank Schmalleger, Ph.D.

Prentice Hall, Upper Saddle River, New Jersey 07458

Library of Congress Cataloging-in-Publication Data

Schmalleger, Frank.
    Criminal justice : a brief introduction / by Frank
Schmalleger.
       p. cm.
    Includes bibliographical references and index.
    ISBN 0-13-396731-X
    1. Criminal justice. Administration of — United States. I. Title.
HV9950.S34 1997
364.973—dc20   95–50986
                                              CIP

Production Editor: *Adele Kupchik*
Managing Editor: *Mary Carnis*
Acquisitions Editor: *Robin Baliszewski/Neil Marquardt*
Editorial Assistant: *Rose Mary Florio*
Director of Manufacturing & Production: *Bruce Johnson*
Manufacturing Buyer: *Ed O'Dougherty*
Marketing Manager: *Frank Mortimer, Jr.*
Copy Editor: *Robert Fiske*
Formatting/page make-up: *Adele Kupchik*
Printer/Binder: *Banta Company*
Interior Design: *Sheree Goodman*
Cover Design: *Bruce Kenselaar*
Cover Illustration: *Pierre Fortin*

©1997, 1994 by Prentice-Hall, Inc.
A Simon & Schuster Company
Upper Saddle River, New Jersey 07458

Printed in the United States of America

10 9 8 7 6 5 4 3

ISBN 0-13-396731-X

Prentice-Hall International (UK) Limited, *London*
Prentice-Hall of Australia Pty. Limited, *Sydney*
Prentice-Hall Canada Inc., *Toronto*
Prentice-Hall Hispanoamericana, S.A., *Mexico*
Prentice-Hall of India Private Limited, *New Delhi*
Prentice-Hall of Japan, Inc., *Tokyo*
Simon & Schuster Asia Pte. Ltd., *Singapore*
Editora Prentice-Hall do Brasil, Ltda., *Rio de Janeiro*

For

NICOLE "ARIEL" SCHMALLEGER,

who has always been the apple of her father's eye

Contents

Preface

Criminal justice is a dynamic and fluid field of study. Ever-changing crime statistics, newsworthy events involving American law enforcement, precedent-setting U.S. Supreme Court decisions, and rapidly breaking changes in correctional practice all challenge professors and students alike to keep pace with the field as it undergoes constant modification.

Criminal Justice: A Brief Introduction results from the realization that today's justice professionals need to have the latest information available to them in a concise and affordable source. The paperback format of this book has made it possible to translate quickly the latest happenings in the justice field into a pragmatic textbook which is both inexpensive and easily read. *Criminal Justice: A Brief Introduction* focuses directly on the crime picture in America and the three traditional elements of the criminal justice system: police, courts, and corrections. The text is enhanced by the addition of career boxes that can assist today's pragmatically minded students in making appropriate career choices. Photographs, charts, graphs, and other visual aids help keep student attention and add variety to the text itself.

As the 21st century nears, it is appropriate that a streamlined and up-to-date book such as this should be in the hands of students. The "information age" is truly upon us, and the quick dissemination of information has become a vital part of contemporary life. No doubt new technologies will facilitate even faster information transfer in the near future. Many of them—including online data retrieval, electronic updates, computer publishing, and the Internet's World Wide Web—are already at work behind the scenes in the molding of *Criminal Justice: A Brief Introduction.*

As the author of numerous texts on the criminal justice system, I have often been amazed at how the end result of the justice process is sometimes barely recognizable to anyone involved in the process as "justice" in any practical sense of the word. It is my sincere hope that the technological and publishing revolutions now upon us will combine with a growing social awareness to facilitate needed changes in our system—supplanting what have at times appeared as self-serving system-perpetuated injustices with new standards of equity, compassion, understanding, fairness, and heartfelt justice for all.

FRANK SCHMALLEGER, PH.D.
THE JUSTICE RESEARCH ASSOCIATION
JUNE 1996

cknowledgments

Many thanks go to all who assisted in so many different ways in the development of this textbook. The manuscript reviewers, Joan Luxenburg at the University of Central Oklahoma, Gary J. Prawel at Monroe Community College, Carl E. Russell at Scottsdale Community College, and Kevin M. Thompson at North Dakota State University, should know how grateful I am to them for their helpful comments and valuable insights. A heartfelt "thank you" is due my good friend

Gordon Armstrong, who always comes through when the chips are down. The efforts of Prentice Hall editor Neil Marquardt, production editor Adele Kupchik, managing editor Patrick Walsh, copy editor Robert Fiske, and editorial assistant Rose Mary Florio, are all recognized and appreciated. Special thanks go to Robin Baliszewski, who is that perfect combination of editor, friend, and marketing executive, and to my wife, Harmonie Star-Schmalleger, for the personal support she has so lovingly and consistently offered. Thank you, also, to my beautiful daughter, Nicole, to whom this book is dedicated, for her support and encouragement as writing progressed.

Frank Mortimer deserves special recognition for his vision, insight, and downright hard work in bringing both this book and its larger sibling, *Criminal Justice Today,* to fruition. As he would say: "Thank you, Frank. Thank you very much."

About the Author

Frank Schmalleger, Ph.D. is Director of the Justice Research Association, a private consulting firm and "think-tank" focusing on issues of crime and justice. The Justice Research Association, which is based in Hilton Head Island, South Carolina, serves the needs of the nation's civil and criminal justice planners and administrators through workshops, conferences, and grant-writing and program evaluation support.

Dr. Schmalleger holds degrees from the University of Notre Dame and the Ohio State University, having earned both a master's (1970) and doctorate in sociology (1974) from Ohio State University with a special emphasis in criminology. From 1976 to 1994, he taught criminal justice courses at Pembroke State University, a campus of the University of North Carolina. For the last 16 of those years, he chaired the university's Department of Sociology, Social Work, and Criminal Justice. As an adjunct professor with Webster University in St. Louis, Missouri, Schmalleger helped develop the university's graduate program in security administration and loss prevention. He taught courses in that curriculum for more than a decade. Schmalleger has also taught in the New School for Social Research's online graduate program, helping build the world's first electronic classrooms in support of distance learning through computer telecommunications.

Frank Schmalleger is the author of numerous articles and many books, including the widely used *Criminal Justice Today* (Prentice Hall, 1997); *Criminology Today* (Prentice Hall, 1996); *Computers in Criminal Justice* (Wyndham Hall Press, 1991); *Career Paths: A Guide to Jobs in Federal Law Enforcement* (Regents/Prentice Hall, 1994); *Criminal Justice Ethics* (Greenwood Press, 1991); *Finding Criminal Justice in the Library* (Wyndham Hall Press, 1991); *Ethics in Criminal Justice* (Wyndham Hall Press, 1990); *A History of Corrections* (Foundations Press of Notre Dame, 1983); and *The Social Basis of Criminal Justice* (University Press of America, 1981).

Schmalleger is also founding editor of the journal *The Justice Professional*. He serves as editor for the Prentice Hall series *Criminal Justice in the Twenty-First Century*, and as Imprint Advisor for Greenwood Publishing Group's criminal justice reference series. His most recent project involves development of an encyclopedia on crime and justice for Greenwood Publishing Group, for which he serves as editor in chief.

Schmalleger's philosophy of both teaching and writing can be summed up in these words: "In order to communicate knowledge we must first catch, then hold, a person's interest—be it student, colleague, or policy maker. Our writing, our speaking, and our teaching must be relevant to the problems facing people today, and they must—in some way—help solve those problems."

CRIMINAL JUSTICE

A Brief Introduction

Injustice anywhere is a threat to justice everywhere.

–Martin Luther King, Jr.

Crime in America

INDIVIDUAL RIGHTS VERSUS SOCIAL CONCERNS

Goals of the Criminal Justice System

Common law, constitutional, statutory,
and humanitarian rights of the accused:

Justice for the Individual
Personal Liberty
Dignity as a Human Being
The Right to Due Process

The individual rights listed must be effectively balanced against
these community concerns:

Social Justice
Equality Before the Law
The Protection of Society
Freedom from Fear

How does our system of justice work toward balance?

The will of the people is the best law.

The great American statesman and orator Daniel Webster (1782–1852) once wrote: "Justice is the great interest of man on earth. It is the ligament which holds civilized beings and civilized nations together." Although Webster may have lived in a relatively simple time with few problems and many shared rules, justice has never been easily won. Unlike Webster's era, society today is highly complex and populated by groups with a wide diversity of interests. It is within that challenging context that the daily practice of American criminal justice occurs.

The criminal justice system has three central components: police, courts, and corrections. The activities and the legal environment surrounding the police are discussed in Part II of this book. Part III describes courts and sentencing, and Part IV deals with prisons, probation, parole, and community corrections. We begin here in Part I, however, with an overview of that grand ideal that we call *justice*—and we consider how the justice ideal relates to the everyday practice of criminal justice in the United States today. To that end, in the three chapters that compose this section, we will examine how and why laws are made. We will look at the wide array of interests that impinge upon the justice system, and we will examine closely the dichotomy that distinguishes citizens who are primarily concerned with individual rights from those who emphasize the need for individual responsibility and social accountability. In the pages that follow, we will see how "justice" can mean protection from the power of the state to some, and vengeance to others. In this first section, we will also lay the groundwork for the rest of the text by painting a picture of crime in America today, suggesting possible causes for it, and showing how policies for dealing with crime have evolved.

As you read about the complex tapestry that is the practice of criminal justice in America today, you will see a system in flux, perhaps less sure of its values and purpose than at any time in its history. You may also catch the sense, however, that very soon a new and reborn institution of justice may emerge from the ferment that now exists. Whatever the final outcome, it can only be hoped that "justice," as proffered by the American system of criminal justice, will be sufficient to hold our civilization together—and to allow it to prosper well into the next century.

CHAPTER 1

What Is Criminal Justice?

—Photo by Ron Jenkins/Fort Worth Star Telegram

*C*rime does more than expose the weakness in social relationships; it undermines the social order itself, by destroying the assumptions on which it is based.[1]

—CHARLES E. SILBERMAN

*V*iolent crime and the fear it provokes are crippling our society, limiting personal freedom, and fraying the ties that bind us.

—PRESIDENT BILL CLINTON
1994 STATE OF THE UNION ADDRESS

*W*e are sick and tired of playing games where innocent people are killed because we can't figure out an inexpensive, common sense method of enforcing law and order.

—HOUSE SPEAKER NEWT GINGRICH[2]

KEY CONCEPTS

crime	social control	justice
public order advocates	individual rights	booking
social justice	criminal justice	due process
consensus model	conflict model	criminal justice system
probable cause	warrant	individual rights advocates
bail	preliminary hearing	grand jury
indictment	arraignment	trial by jury
consecutive sentence	concurrent sentence	criminology
crime control model	due process model	

Justice and Criminal Justice

Late at night, on the evening of February 27, 1995, teenage neo-Nazi skinhead brothers Bryan and David Freeman bludgeoned their parents and younger brother to death with baseball bats in the family's Allentown, Pennsylvania, home.[3] David was 15 years old at the time of the killings, Bryan was 17. The first to be killed was probably their 48-year-old mother, Brenda, who suffered massive head injuries and stab wounds. Investigators theorize that their mother confronted the boys after their noisy late night return home, and was arguing with them when at least one son attacked her, smashing her skull with a club. She fell face down onto the carpeted hallway outside the bedroom her sons shared, trying to protect her head with her hands. One of the boys then jumped on his mother and stabbed her repeatedly in the back. After what may have been a brief conference, the brothers then made their way upstairs to their parents' bedroom, where their 54-year-old father, Dennis, was sleeping. There, they cut their father's throat and clubbed him to death before he could leave the bed. Next, they moved on to the bedroom of their 11-year-old brother, Eric, crushing his skull with a hammer as he slept. Viewing the murder scene the next day, Lehigh County coroner Wayne Snyder called the slayings, "the most savage, brutal, cowardly acts of murder I've ever seen."[4]

Although the murders shocked many people in the Lehigh Valley area, they didn't surprise everyone. The Freeman brothers had long been vowing to kill their strict but loving Jehovah's Witnesses parents. The Friday before the killings, Mrs. Freeman told a sister-in-law that her sons were threatening to kill her. The brothers' skinhead lifestyle did not sit well with the older Freemans, who constantly tried to regain control over their sons. In response, the boys threatened their parents, saying they would kill them if they did not allow them the freedom to do what they wanted. On at least one occasion, prior to the murders, Bryan pinned his mother to the floor and raised a hatchet over her head, threatening to kill her until she was able to talk herself free.

Mustering what strength they could, Dennis and Brenda Freeman prayed, sought counseling, and had their sons hospitalized, hoping to save the family. They also talked with officials at Salisbury Township High School, sought help from a local Toughlove International parenting group, discussed their plight with the Allentown police, and even consulted the Pennsylvania Human Relations Commission—which put them in contact with the Philadelphia B'nai B'rith Anti-Defamation League, an organization that tracks hate groups and recommends strategies for combating prejudice. Leaving no stone unturned in efforts to help her sons, Mrs. Freeman also contacted a gang prevention specialist in her hometown and a former white supremacist living in Ithaca, New York, for clues on how to get her sons back under control. Few efforts did any good, and at least once during a counseling session, Bryan attacked his father and had to be physically restrained.

By all accounts, the young Freeman brothers had normal childhoods. Then, about two years prior to the murders, they began to change. The changes were gradual at first, but soon became more pronounced. The boys fell in with a rebellious crowd, took to drinking, and experimented with drugs.[5] Soon they stopped regular school attendance, shaved their heads, began body-building, and paid for a series of garish tattoos to cover their arms and torsos. They began attending white supremacist meetings and collected fascist paraphernalia, including knives. Two weeks before killing their parents, they paid to have their foreheads tattooed; Bryan with "Berserker," and David with "Seig Heil." Run-ins with the police had become routine, and, authorities believe, when their parents took away the boys' car and threatened to have them reinstitutionalized, the killings took place.

After the murders, the brothers took their mother's car and fled. They were arrested two days later in an abandoned house in Michigan, where they had fled with a skinhead cousin, Nelson Birdwell. Birdwell admitted to police that he had

been present in the Freeman home at the time of the killings, but claimed that he had hidden in a closet to avoid becoming involved. In early 1996 both David and Bryan pled guilty to first degree murder. They were sentenced to life in prison without possibility of parole.

The Freeman killing seemed to usher in a spate of parricide (parent-killings) cases in the Allentown area and elsewhere. On the day following arrest of the Freeman brothers, George and Susan Howorth were found dead in their Fogelsville, Pennsylvania, home by their older son, Stephen—alleged victims of their younger son, Jeffrey, 16, who sprang from hiding and shot his parents as they returned home after work. Susan, 48, was shot nine times with her son's .22-caliber rifle; her 46-year-old husband, five times. Neither had time to take off the heavy coats they were wearing that cold March afternoon. A rambling note found on a desk in Jeffrey's bedroom told of his intention to commit the murders, in part because of his parent's disappointment at his academic performance and low SAT scores that had just arrived in the mail. Part of the note, addressed to his brother, read, "I told you I would do it, Steve. You can't say I didn't warn you."[6] Jeffrey was arrested a few days later in Missouri, when the car he was driving ran out of gas along Interstate 70.

A couple of days after the Howorth killings, in what may have been a copycat crime, 15-year-old Jason Lewis of suburban Atlanta, Georgia, was charged with shooting both of his parents with a 12-gauge shotgun as they watched television in the family's mobile home. Although Jason did not mention the Pennsylvania killings, letters he wrote to friends said that he wanted to live out the story of "Natural Born Killers," the Oliver Stone movie about a couple who goes on a killing spree.[7]

Experts doubt whether the United States is about to experience an epidemic of parricide cases, but crimes like those described here dramatically highlight the recent rise in violent crime among teenagers and enhance the fear of **crime** so many Americans have come to feel. They also challenge long-cherished beliefs about the extent of **social control** in American society and call into question a number of basic values centered on the family, children, violence in the media, and child-rearing practices. The spate of parent-killings sent chills up the spines of many mature Americans who asked themselves how the nation and its youth had strayed so far from what otherwise seemed like simple standards of decency and responsibility. Previously accepted arguments that poverty, lack of proper

*C*rime. Behavior in violation of the criminal laws of a state, the federal government, or a local jurisdiction which has the power to make such laws.

*S*ocial Control. The use of sanctions and rewards available through a group to influence and shape the behavior of individual members of that group. Social control is a primary concern of social groups and communities, and it is the interest that human groups hold in the exercise of social control that leads to the creation of both criminal and civil statutes.

socialization, and society in general are the causes of crime seemed especially ineffective explanations for the killings committed by Bryan and David Freeman and Jeffrey Howorth since all three had grown up in almost model and intact families, with parents who held strong Christian convictions and apparently worked hard to raise their children in ways they thought proper.

But crimes come and go. A few months later, the Pennsylvania killings were nearly forgotten, and the nation's attention, fed by the media, turned to other spectacular crimes. In 1995, the murder trial of former football superstar and media personality O. J. Simpson received much national exposure, with daily reports on the trial appearing on television and in newspapers throughout the country. Simpson, who stood accused of brutally murdering his ex-wife Nicole, and her associate Ronald Goldman, hired a team of lawyers whom some referred to as "the million dollar defense"—an action that, following acquittal, many saw as akin to buying justice.

Perhaps no one criminal incident gripped the psyche of the American people, and was to later galvanize the policy-making efforts of legislators, more than the 1995 bombing of the Alfred P. Murrah Federal Building in Oklahoma City by right-wing extremists. Nearly 170 people died in the bombing, 19 of them children. Hundreds more were wounded, and millions of dollars worth of property damage occurred. The bombing had the added impact of demonstrating just how vulnerable the United States is to terrorist assault. Following the attack, many realized that the very freedoms that allow America to serve as a model of democracy to the rest of the world make it possible for terrorist or terrorist-affiliated groups to operate within the United States relatively unencumbered.

O. J. Simpson, with his lawyers, in court to face double-murder charges. In the many months of the trial, the public followed the case as though it were a soap opera. The trial brought up many issues about crime and the criminal justice process that had not been discussed publicly before. Photo courtesy of Sygma.

Crimes like these have changed the mood of the nation, or, perhaps more accurately, have accelerated what was an already changing mood. For many Americans, concerned with crime and justice, and clinging to heartfelt standards of right and wrong, it is as though an age of innocence has ended. The Reverend Robert Wright, in a memorial service for the Howorths, put it well when he said: "Something inside so many of us was murdered that night. We will not be the same."[8] Reverend Wright's words seem to apply equally well to Nicole Brown Simpson, Ronald Goldman, the Freemans, and all the victims of the Oklahoma City bombing.

The Focus of This Book—Individual Rights and Public Order

This book, which is about the American system of criminal justice and the agencies and processes that constitute it, has an orientation that we think is especially valuable for studying criminal justice today. For many years, the dominant philosophy in American criminal justice has focused on guaranteeing the rights of criminal defendants while seeking to understand the root causes of crime and violence. Recently, however, a growing conservative emphasis has focused on the rights and interests of crime victims, and has called into question some of the fundamental premises upon which the American system of criminal justice has been built. The materials presented in this text are in keeping with that realization and are built around the following theme:

> There is a new recognition in contemporary society of the need to balance (1) the respect accorded the rights of individuals faced with criminal prosecution against (2) the valid interests of society in preventing future crimes and in reducing the harm caused by criminal activity. Although the personal freedoms guaranteed to criminal suspects by the Constitution must be closely guarded, so too the urgent social needs of local communities for controlling unacceptable behavior and protecting law-abiding citizens from harm must be recognized. Still to be adequately addressed are the interests of victims and the fear of crime now so prevalent in the minds of many law-abiding citizens.

Most people today who intelligently consider the criminal justice system assume either one or the other of these two perspectives. We shall refer to those who seek to protect personal freedoms and civil rights within the criminal justice process as **individual rights advocates.** Those who suggest that, under certain circumstances involving criminal threats to public safety, the interests of society (especially crime control) should take precedence over individual rights will be called **public order advocates.** In this book, we seek to look at ways that the individual rights and the public order perspectives can be balanced to serve both sets of needs.

Both points of view have their roots in the values that formed our nation. However, the past 30 years have been especially important in clarifying the differences between these points of view. The last few decades have seen a burgeoning concern with the rights of ethnic minorities, women, the physically and mentally challenged, and many other groups. The civil rights movement of the 1960s and 1970s emphasized equality of opportunity and respect for individuals regardless of race, color, creed, or personal attributes. As new laws were passed and suits filed, court involvement in the movement grew. Soon a plethora of hard-won individual rights and prerogatives, based on the U.S. Constitution and the Bill of Rights, were recognized and guaranteed. By the 1980s, the rights movement had profoundly affected all areas of social life—from education, through employment, to the activities of the criminal justice system.

This emphasis on **individual rights** was accompanied by a dramatic increase in criminal activity. "Traditional" crimes such as murder, rape, and assault, as reported by the FBI, increased astronomically during the 1970s. Many theories were advanced to explain this virtual explosion of observed criminality. A few doubted the accuracy of "official" accounts, claiming that any actual rise in crime was much less than that portrayed in the reports. Some analysts of American culture, however, suggested that

Individual Rights Advocates. Those who seek to protect personal freedoms within the process of criminal justice.

Public Order Advocates. Those who suggest that, under certain circumstances involving criminal threats to public safety, the interests of society should take precedence over individual rights.

Individual Rights. Those rights guaranteed to criminal defendants by the U.S. Constitution (especially as found in the first ten amendments to the Constitution, known as the Bill of Rights) when facing formal processing by the criminal justice system. The preservation of the rights of criminal defendants is important to society because it is through the exercise of such rights that the values of our culture are most clearly and directly expressed.

increased criminality was the result of newfound freedoms that combined with the long pent-up hostilities of the socially and economically deprived to produce social disorganization.

By the mid-1980s, popular perceptions identified one particularly insidious form of criminal activity—the dramatic increase in the sale and use of illicit drugs—as a threat to the very fabric of American society. Cocaine, in particular, and later laboratory-processed "crack," had spread to every corner of America. The country's borders were inundated with smugglers intent on reaping quick fortunes. Large cities became havens for drug gangs, and many inner-city areas were all but abandoned to highly armed and well-financed racketeers. Some famous personalities succumbed to the allure of drugs, and athletic teams and sporting events became focal points for drug busts. Like wildfire, drugs soon spread to younger users. Even small-town elementary schools found themselves facing the specter of campus drug dealing and associated violence.

Worse still were the seemingly ineffective governmental measures to stem the drug tide. Drug peddlers, because of the huge reserves of money available to them, were often able to escape prosecution, or wrangle plea bargains and avoid imprisonment. Media coverage of such "miscarriages of justice" became epidemic, and public anger grew.

By the close of the 1980s, neighborhoods and towns felt themselves fighting for their communal lives. City businesses faced dramatic declines in property values, and residents wrestled with the eroding quality of life. Huge rents had been torn in the national social fabric. The American way of life, long taken for granted, was under the gun. Traditional values appeared in danger of going up in smoke along with the "crack" now being smoked openly in some parks and resorts. Looking for a way to stem the tide, many took up the call for "law and order." In

A firefighter cradles a child rescued from the Alfred P. Murrah Federal Building in Oklahoma City after a terrorist bombing there in 1995. Recent acts of domestic terrorism have raised the stakes in the battle to defend civil liberties and personal freedoms in the face of growing demands to make America safe. The child shown here later died. Photo by Charles H. Porter, 4th, courtesy of Sygma.

response, President Reagan initiated a "War on Drugs" and created a "drug czar" cabinet-level post to coordinate the war. Careful thought was given at the highest levels to using the military to patrol the sea lanes and air corridors through which many of the illegal drugs entered the country. President Bush, who followed President Reagan into office, quickly embraced and expanded the government's antidrug efforts.

The 1990s began with a focus on police brutality and management effectiveness. In 1992, the videotaped beating of Rodney King, a black motorist, at the hands of Los Angeles area police officers, splashed across TV screens throughout the country and reintroduced the nation to the concerns of what sociologists now call "underrepresented groups." As the King incident seemed to show, when members of such groups come face to face with agents of the American criminal justice system, something less than justice may be the result. Although initially acquitted by a California jury that contained no black members, two of the officers who beat King were convicted in a 1993 federal courtroom of violating his civil rights.[9]

The year 1993 saw an especially violent encounter in Waco, Texas, between agents of the Bureau of Alcohol, Tobacco, and Firearms, the FBI, and members of cult leader David Koresh's Branch Davidian. The fray, which began when ATF agents assaulted Koresh's fortresslike compound, leaving 4 agents and 6 cultists dead, ended 51 days later with the fiery deaths of Koresh and 71 of his followers. Many of them were children. The assault on Koresh's compound led to a congressional investigation and charges that the ATF and FBI had been ill-prepared to deal successfully with large-scale domestic resistance and had reacted more out of alarm and frustration than wisdom. Janet Reno, attorney general under President Clinton, refused to blame agents for misjudging Koresh's intentions although 11 Davidians were later acquitted of charges they murdered the agents.

By the mid-1990s, however, a strong shift away from the claimed misdeeds of the criminal justice system began, and a newfound emphasis on individual accountability arose among an American public fed up with crime and fearful of its own victimization. Growing calls for enhanced responsibility began to quickly replace the previous emphasis on individual rights. As a juggernaut of conservative opinion made itself felt on the political scene, Texas Senator Phil Gramm observed that the public wants to "grab violent criminals by the throat, put them in prison (and) stop building prisons like Holiday Inns."[10]

It was probably the public's perception of growing crime rates, coupled with a belief that offenders frequently went unpunished, or that many received only judicial slaps on the wrist, that led to the burgeoning emphasis on responsibility and punishment. However, a few spectacular crimes that received widespread coverage by the news media heightened the public's sense that crime in the United States was out of hand and that new measures were needed to combat it. In 1993, for example, James Jordan, father of Chicago Bulls basketball superstar Michael Jordan, was killed in a cold-blooded robbery by two young men with long criminal records. Jordan's death, which seemed the result of a chance encounter, helped rivet the nation's attention on what appeared to be the increasing frequency of random and senseless violence.

In that same year, a powerful bomb ripped apart the basement of one of the twin World Trade Center buildings in New York City. The explosion, which killed five and opened a 100-foot crater through four sublevels of concrete, displaced 50,000 workers, including employees at the commodities exchanges that handle billions of dollars worth of trade in oil, gold, coffee, and sugar. The product of terrorists with foreign links, the bombing highlighted the susceptibility of the American infrastructure to terrorist activity.[11]

Similarly, in 1993, the heart-wrenching story of Polly Klaas splashed across the national media. Twelve-year-old Polly was kidnapped from a slumber party at her home while her mother and little sister slept in the next room. Two other girls were left bound and gagged after a bearded stranger broke into the Klaas home in

Petaluma, California. Despite efforts by hundreds of uniformed officers and 4,000 volunteers, attempts to find the girl proved fruitless. Nine weeks later, just before Christmas, an ex-con named Richard Allen Davis was arrested and charged with Polly's murder. Investigators found that Davis's life read like a litany of criminal activity, and that Polly's death was due at least partially to failure of the criminal justice system to keep a dangerous Davis behind bars.

In 1994, the attention of the nation was riveted to proceedings in the Susan Smith case. Smith, a South Carolina mother, confessed to drowning her two young boys (ages 1 and 3 at the time) by strapping them into child safety seats and rolling the family station wagon off a pier and into a lake. Smith, who appears to have been motivated by the demands of an extramarital love affair, had originally claimed a black man carjacked her vehicle with the boys still inside.

Senseless violence linked to racial hatred stunned the nation during the 1995 trial of Colin Ferguson. Ferguson, who was eventually convicted of killing 6 passengers and wounding 19 others during what prosecutors claimed was a racially motivated shooting rampage on a Long Island Railroad commuter train in 1993, maintained his innocence throughout the trial even though he was identified by more than a dozen eyewitnesses, including some he had shot. "This is a case of stereotyped victimization of a black man and subsequent conspiracy to destroy him—nothing more," Ferguson told the jury. Many were offended that Ferguson declared himself the victim when the real victims were either dead or seriously injured. Famed defense attorney William Kunstler suggested that Ferguson plead not guilty by reason of insanity, which, Kunstler argued, had been caused by "black rage" at racial injustice in America. Instead, Ferguson claimed that he had dozed off on the train and that a white man had stolen his gun and shot the passengers. Public backlash at the increasing willingness of defense attorneys to use an "offender as victim" defense contributed to growing disgust with what many saw as a hamstrung and ineffective criminal justice system.

Recently, a landslide of conservative sentiment was ushered in by growing public frustration with the apparent inability of our society and its justice system to prevent crimes, and to hold offenders who are identified and then arrested to heartfelt standards of right and wrong. That landslide, when it came in the form of a Republican sweep of congressional elections in 1994, targeted seemingly ineffective social programs and the liberal agendas that had built them. Sweeping changes in attitudes toward crime and criminal offenders were reflected in other areas of society as well. Affirmative action, welfare, and other social programs that had first been promulgated under the banner of individual rights, came under increasing fire in both national and state arenas. Many newly elected public officials stopped asking what society could do to protect individuals accused of crimes and demanded to know instead how offenders could effectively be held accountable for violations of the criminal law. The mood of the nation was well summarized in a postelection statement by Paul McNulty, a former Justice Department official: "They want punishment and they want it badly."[12]

Perspectives on Criminal Justice and the Theme of This Book

Realistically, although conservative sentiments still very much influence public policy, it is important to recognize that national feelings, however strong, have historically been somewhat akin to the swings of a pendulum. Hence, although the emphasis on individual rights that rose to ascendancy a few decades ago, now appears to have been eclipsed by calls for social and individual responsibility, the tension between the two perspectives still forms the basis for most policy-making activity in the criminal justice arena. Rights advocates continue to carry on the fight for an expansion of civil and criminal rights, seeing both as necessary to an equitable and just social order. The treatment of the accused, they argue, mirrors basic cultural values. The purpose of any civilized society, they claim, should be to secure rights and

Theory into Practice: Individual Rights Versus Group Interests—Megan's Law

The recent rise of conservative social policies and their effect on the practice of American criminal justice can be seen in the passage of new statutes such as New Jersey's "Megan's Law." Megan's law was enacted by the New Jersey state legislature on October 31, 1994, and requires community notification whenever an imprisoned sex offender is scheduled to be released. The law was named after 7-year-old Megan Kanka, who was brutally attacked and killed by a paroled sex offender living across the street from her home. The information required to be released to the public under Megan's Law includes the offender's name, a recent photograph, physical description, a list of the offenses for which he or she was convicted, current address, place of employment or school, and the offender's automobile license plate number.

New Jersey and 38 other states now require released sex offenders to register with authorities. In passing Megan's Law, however, New Jersey joined 12 states whose laws provide for some form of public notification when sex offenders are about to be released from confinement. As this book goes to press, Pennsylvania and a number of other jurisdictions are in the process of enacting their own versions of such laws supported, in part, by a federal initiative advocating notification legislation.

One of the first court tests of New Jersey's law came on February 28, 1995, when U.S. District Judge Nicholas H. Politan ruled that the community notification provision of Megan's Law was unconstitutional. A notification requirement, ruled Judge Politan, amounted to a second form of punishment—one to which the offender had not been sentenced. The judge, however, upheld New Jersey's requirement that sex offenders must register with local authorities in areas where they reside.

According to the American Civil Liberties Union, notification rules similar to New Jersey's have been thrown out by state judges in Alaska, Arizona, California, Illinois, Louisiana, and New Hampshire. Recently, however, the Supreme Court of the state of Washington upheld a statute almost identical to Megan's Law, ruling that it was a regulatory measure and not a cloaked punitive device.

The New Jersey ruling against Megan's Law provisions came in the case of 49-year-old Alexander A. Artway, who was convicted in 1965 of statutory rape and of sodomizing a 21-year-old woman in 1971. The state had been supported in arguing the legitimacy of the law by the U.S. Justice Department. U.S. Attorney General Janet Reno depicted the issues involved in the case this way: "I think we have got to balance the interests (of the public and released prisoners), and we have received studies...that there is at least a 40 percent recidivism rate among child sex offenders." "We understand," Reno said, "the necessity for striking that balance and making sure the public is protected."

Judge Politan's action led to a war of words between advocates on both sides of the issue. The judge enraged Megan's Law supporters when he asked whether requiring public notification upon the release of sex offenders was similar to the Nazi practice of making Jews wear a Star of David during the Second World War. Supporters countered that though innocent people were forced to wear the yellow star, Artway's right to privacy ended when he committed his crimes.

Reaction from Artway himself was quick in coming. "My reaction is 'Yahoo,'" Artway said outside the courtroom building. "I jump in the air and click my heels. I can now move to another area if that becomes necessary for my protection." Artway seemed to be referring, at least in part, to the fact that a New Jersey man who had been mistaken for a released sex offender had previously suffered a beating at the hands of two men.

Megan's mother called the judge's decision "a slap in the face," saying that it "clearly puts the pedophile above our children." The New Jersey state Supreme Court later upheld the law although its future will likely be decided on appeal to federal courts.

QUESTIONS FOR DISCUSSION

1. What rights should an offender have in cases such as those addressed by Megan's Law?

2. What rights should the community have?

3. Whose rights should be most closely guarded if a clash of interests arises? Why?

SOURCES: Michael Kirkland, "U.S. Defends N.J. Sex Offender Law," United Press International online, northeastern edition, February, 9, 1995; Henry Stern, "Megan's Law," The Associated Press online, northern edition, February 16, 1995; and Jeffrey Gold, "Megan's Law," The Associated Press online, March 1, 1995.

freedoms for each of its citizens—including the criminally accused. Rights advocates fear unnecessarily restrictive government action and view it as an assault upon basic human dignity and individual liberty. In defense of their principles, criminal rights activists tend to recognize that it is sometimes necessary to sacrifice some degree of public safety and predictability in order to guarantee basic freedoms. Hence, rights advocates are content with a justice system that limits police powers and that holds justice agencies accountable to the highest evidentiary standards. An example of the kind of criminal justice outcome feared by individual rights advocates can be had in the case of James Richardson, who served 21 years in a Florida prison for a crime he did not commit.[13] Following perjured testimony, Richardson was convicted in 1968 of the poisoning deaths of his seven children. He was released in 1989 after a babysitter confessed to poisoning the children's last meal because of personal jealousies. The criminal rights perspective allows that it is necessary to see some guilty people go free in order to reduce the likelihood of convicting the innocent.

In the present conservative environment, however, calls for system account-ability are often tempered with new demands to unfetter the criminal justice sys-tem in order to make arrests easier and punishments swift and harsh. Advocates of law and order, wanting ever-greater police powers, have mounted an effective drive to abandon some of the gains made in support of the rights of criminal defendants during the civil rights era. Citing high rates of recidivism, uncertain punishments, and an inefficient courtroom maze, they claim that the criminal justice system has coddled offenders and encouraged continued law violation. Society, they say, if it is to survive, can no longer afford to accord too many rights to the individual or place the interests of any one person over that of the group.

As we near the start of the 21st century, the trick, it seems, will be to balance indi-vidual rights and personal freedoms with social responsibility and respect for author-ity. At a recent conference sponsored by the *New York Post*, New York City Mayor Rudolph W. Giuliani identified the tension between personal freedoms and individual responsibilities as the crux of the crime problem facing his city and America today. We mistakenly look to government and elected officials, Giuliani said, to assume respon-sibility for solving the problem of crime when, instead, it is each individual citizen who must become accountable for fixing what is wrong with our society. In the mayor's words: "We only see the oppressive side of authority…What we don't see is that free-dom is not a concept in which people can do anything they want to, be anything they can be. Freedom is about authority. Freedom is about the willingness of every single human being to cede to lawful authority a great deal of discretion about what you do."

This text has two basic purposes: (1) to describe in detail the criminal justice system while (2) helping students develop an appreciation for the delicacy of the balancing act now facing it. The question for the future will be how to ensure the existence of, and effectively manage, a justice system that is as fair to the individ-ual as it is supportive of the needs of society. Is "justice for all" a reasonable expec-tation of today's system of criminal justice? As the book will show, this question is complicated by the fact that individual interests and social needs frequently diverge, whereas, at other times, they parallel each other.

Social Justice

Justice. The principle of fairness; the ideal of moral equity.

The well-known British philosopher and statesman Benjamin Disraeli (1804–1881) once defined **justice** as "truth in action." One popular dictionary defini-tion of justice says that it is "the principle of moral rightness, or conformity to truth."[14] Justice, in the truest sense of the word, is the ultimate goal of criminal justice.

Social Justice. An ideal which embraces all aspects of civilized life and which is linked to fundamental notions of fairness and to cultural beliefs about right and wrong.

Criminal justice and civil justice are both aspects of a wider form of equity termed **social justice.** Social justice is a concept that embraces all aspects of civi-lized life. It is linked to notions of fairness and to cultural beliefs about right and wrong. Questions of social justice can be asked about relationships between indi-viduals and between parties (such as corporations and agencies of government), between the rich and the poor, between the sexes, between ethnic groups and minorities, and about social linkages of all sorts. In the abstract, the concept of social justice embodies the highest personal and cultural ideals.

Civil justice concerns itself with fairness in relationships between citizens, government agencies and businesses in private matters involving contractual obligations, business dealings, hiring, equality of treatment, and so on. **Criminal justice,** in its broadest sense, refers to those aspects of social justice that concern violations of the criminal law. Community interests demand apprehension and punishment of law violators. At the same time, criminal justice ideals extend to the protection of the innocent, the fair treatment of offenders, and fair play by the agencies of law enforcement, including the courts and correctional institutions.

Reality, however, typically falls short of the ideal and is severely complicated by the fact that justice seems to wear different guises when viewed from diverse social vantage points. To many people, the criminal justice system and criminal justice agencies often seem biased in favor of the powerful. The laws they enforce seem to emanate more from well-financed, organized, and vocal interest groups than they do from an idealized sense of social justice. Disenfranchised groups, those who do not feel as though they share in the political and economic power of society, are often wary of the agencies of justice, seeing them more as enemies than as benefactors.

On the other hand, justice practitioners, including police officers, prosecutors, judges, and correctional officials, frequently complain of unfair criticism of their efforts to uphold the law. The "realities" of law enforcement, they say, and of justice itself, are often overlooked by critics of the system who have little experience in dealing with offenders and victims.

Whichever side we choose in the ongoing debate over the nature and quality of justice in America, we should recognize that the process of criminal justice is especially important in achieving and maintaining social order. From the perspective of social order, law is an instrument of control. Laws set limits on behavior and define particular forms of social interaction as either acceptable or unacceptable. Laws, including whatever inequities they may embody, are a primary device for order creation in any mature society.

Criminal Justice. The criminal law, the law of criminal procedure, and that array of procedures and activities having to do with the enforcement of the criminal law. Criminal justice cannot be separated from social justice because the kind of justice enacted in our nation's criminal courts is a reflection of basic American understandings of right and wrong.

The Justice Ideal: A Modern Conflict

Most of us agree that laws against murder, rape, assault, and other serious crimes are necessary. Certain other laws, such as those against marijuana use, prostitution, gambling, and some "victimless crimes" rest on a less certain consensus.

Where a near-consensus exists about the legitimacy of a particular statute, questions may still be raised about how specific behavior fits the law under consideration. Even more fundamental questions can center on the process by which justice is achieved. Two cases that received much media attention in recent years illustrate these points. One involved the "subway gunman," Bernhard Goetz.[15] Goetz, a 39-year-old electronics specialist, admitted shooting four young men who, he said, approached him in a threatening manner. Goetz had been mugged previously and carried a concealed weapon.

Few would disagree that mugging is wrong, and most would grant that some form of self-defense is justifiable under certain circumstances, including robbery. The Goetz situation, however, was complicated by many things, among them the fact that Goetz was white, the muggers black; Goetz fled after the shootings; he shot one of the men twice—after telling him, "You don't look too bad. Here's another"; and it was later shown that some of the young men had committed crimes both before and after the subway incident. Although no one died, one of the people shot was permanently paralyzed. Bernhard Goetz finally was convicted of a firearms violation and received a sentence of six months in prison. He was also ordered to undergo psychiatric treatment, placed on five years' probation, fined $5,000, and made to perform 280 hours of community service.

The other case (which is discussed in greater detail in Chapter 3) involved Daimion Osby, a black killer of a few years ago. Osby's courtroom encounter ended in a mistrial after lawyers claimed that his spontaneous shooting of two black Fort Worth, Texas, men in a parking lot resulted from "urban survival syndrome." Osby's attorneys had argued that urban survival syndrome may lead to homicide through years of exposure to the realities of inner-city life, which desensitizes people to crime and violence. One expert witness successfully testified that Osby should be excused from shooting the two because he killed only after having been "threatened by young black men who fit the profile of the most dangerous men in America."[16]

To most people, the law was clear in both cases. Neither Goetz nor Osby should have been carrying a concealed weapon. They should not have shot anyone unless there was an immediate, serious, and demonstrable threat to their safety. Yet though a considerable consensus existed on the law and on the facts of each case, actors in the criminal justice system found themselves embroiled in a raging debate about what an appropriate outcome should be. One famous legal scholar, for example, analyzing the Goetz case relative to the social context of the times, referred to Goetz's actions as "a crime of self-defense."[17]

Basic to both cases was the belief, held by some, including many members of the black community, that minorities historically have been both victimized by society and unfairly represented in the justice process. The fact that black men approached a white in New York's subways was said to be automatically interpreted much differently than if the races involved had been reversed. Other critics said that both the Goetz and Osby incidents reflected the system's devaluation of the life of a black man.

Whatever one's opinion of these cases, both illustrate the fact that any formal resolution of law violations occurs through an elaborate process. Justice, although it can be fine-tuned in order to take into consideration the interests of ever-increasing numbers of people, rarely pleases everyone. Justice is a social product, and, like any product that is the result of group effort, it is a patchwork quilt of human emotions, reasoning, and concerns. One of the major challenges faced by the justice system today comes in the form of disenfranchised groups who are not convinced that they receive "justice" under current arrangements. Was justice done in the Osby or the Goetz case? The question will be debated for years, but it is doubtful whether an answer acceptable to everyone will ever be found.

Darrel Frank, the founder of Dead Serious, Incorporated, shown with the organization's official vehicle. Reflecting the "get tough" on crime and criminals attitude now so prevalent in American society, Dead Serious offers a $5,000 reward to members who legally kill a criminal. Photo courtesy of Fort Worth Star-Telegram.

Theory into Practice: Celebrity Justice— The Double-Murder Trial of O. J. Simpson

In the early morning hours of June 13, 1994 a man alerted by a barking dog discovered two bodies in West Los Angeles. Dead was the beautiful white wife of black Heisman Trophy winner and football great, Orenthal James Simpson. Killed along with her, in a savage knife attack, was handsome Ronald Goldman, an aspiring young actor and waiter. The murders occurred at 875 South Bundy Drive, in the exclusive Brentwood section of the city. Police investigators quickly found enough evidence, including 19 prior incidents of spousal abuse, for them to focus on Simpson as their only suspect.

The lead homicide investigator in the case, Detective Philip Vannatter, told CBS news that in 30 years of investigating crime scenes he had never seen a case with more conclusive evidence. There could be no doubt in the mind of anyone who had access to all the evidence and who viewed it objectively, said Vannatter, that O. J. Simpson was the killer.

Under the American system of justice, however, it is not enough that the police are convinced of who the perpetrator is. The system requires that police investigators convince prosecutors that sufficient evidence is at hand for a trial, and then it becomes the job of prosecuting attorneys, who work for the state or federal government, to take a case to trial and to attempt to convince a jury that the defendant is guilty. If even one juror remains unconvinced, the defendant may go free. Because the jury is critical to the outcome of any criminal case, jury selection can be an involved and time-consuming process. Before 12 jurors and 12 alternates had been selected in the Simpson trial, 5,000 notices were sent to potential jury pool members in the Los Angeles area. Members of the pool were each asked to complete a 72-page questionnaire, and expert jury consultants for both sides scrutinized the thousands of returned questionnaires.

But the O. J. Simpson case was atypical from the start. Not only were the victims white and the alleged assailant black, the defendant was also a wealthy man, a sports hero turned movie star, with wide public recognition and a large number of fans. Instead of a court-appointed lawyer, made available to the majority of murder suspects in Los Angeles, Simpson quickly hired some of the most expensive and best-known defense attorneys in the country. The Simpson high-powered defense team came to include legendary lawyer F. Lee Bailey, the up-and-coming Johnnie Cochran, legal mastermind Alan Dershowitz, and scrappy Robert Shapiro. Each was a specialist in different aspects of the criminal law, and every one had a lengthy record of representing celebrated defendants with much success.

Even before the trial began, the Simpson case received daily attention from the national media. Near its finish, media watchers declared that the Simpson trial had received more coverage than any other single event in the history of television—with networks and cable channels broadcasting thousands of hours of courtroom testimony, talk show interviews with key personnel, and expert commentary.

During the trial, which was expected to last nearly a year, every item of evidence presented by the prosecution was examined and reexamined in minute detail by defense attorneys, and each prosecution witness was subjected to rigorous cross-examination. By its seventh month, the trial had already cost California taxpayers more than $5 million.

Lost in the media blitz surrounding the Simpson trial, however, was the fact that on the day Nicole Simpson and Ron Goldman died, four other homicides were recorded in Los Angeles County. Of the four others, three died from gunshots, and at least three knew their killers. All the victims were from relatively poor families, and all the killings happened in seedy city neighborhoods. Each of the victims, save one, was black or Hispanic, and all appear to have been killed by minorities. With the exception of the Simpson killings, it was a typical day, statistically speaking, in a county where, on average, five people are murdered every day. Chances are, however, that you've never heard the names of those other Los Angeles homicide victims, killed on June 12, 1994. Names like rap promoter David Abraham, shot twice by a robber and found face down in an alley, and who left behind a young wife and an infant son; Jaime Moreno, who was 26-years-old when he was knifed by his brother-in-law during a fight; Cynthia Siegfried, a 30-year-old mother of two who died from a bullet meant for a friend while riding through the South Coast community of Lomita at 1:30 A.M.; and young Trinidad Velasquez, whose short life was apparently filled with brutality, most of it inflicted by a jealous husband who beat her, cut off a finger, then shot her three times in the face—angry that she had worn revealing shorts.

Surviving family members of these forgotten victims fret that the Simpson trial took resources away from what might otherwise have been productive investigations into the deaths of their loved ones. Jamie Moreno's death was quickly ruled "justifiable homicide" even though his killer used a knife and Moreno was unarmed. David Abraham's killer was never found, and his wife worries that police technicians botched the job of gathering evidence. "I get so

(Continued on next page)

frustrated," says Phyllis Abraham. "They spend all this money on the DNA tests (in the Simpson trial), and all I want to know is what happened to the fingerprints on my husband's car." Police say nothing was found on the car.

The man who killed Cynthia Siegfried copped a plea and drew a 17-year sentence for manslaughter (which would have been reduced still further, except for a previous conviction on charges of armed robbery). Police are still looking for Trinidad Velasquez's killer, who fled the scene. "They took a report, and that's it," says her sister, Catalina. "They don't care about Hispanic people," she claims. Velasquez's brother, Pedro, shares some of his sister's feelings. "They stopped looking," he says. "I would tell the Goldmans and Browns to be grateful for police and a trial. We didn't get that."

*A*merican Criminal Justice: The System

The Consensus Model

The Criminal Justice System. The aggregate of all operating and administrative or technical support agencies that perform criminal justice functions. The basic divisions of the operational aspects of criminal justice are law enforcement, courts, and corrections.

To this point, we have described the agencies of law enforcement, the courts, and corrections as a **system of criminal justice.**[18] Those who speak of a system of criminal justice usually define it as consisting of the agencies of police, courts, and corrections. Each of these agencies can, in turn, be described in terms of their subsystems. Corrections, for example, includes jails, prisons, community-based treatment programs such as "halfway houses," and programs for probation and parole. Each subarea contains still more components. Prisons, for example, can be described in terms of custody levels, inmate programs, health care, security procedures, and so on. Some prisons operate as "boot camp" facilities, designed to "shock" offenders into quick rehabilitation, whereas others are long-term confinement facilities designed for the most hard-core criminals who are likely to return to crime quickly if released. Students of corrections also study the process of sentencing, through which an offender's fate is decided by the justice system, and examine the role of jails in holding prisoners prior to conviction and sentencing.

The system's model of criminal justice is characterized primarily by its assumption that the various parts of the justice system work together by design in order to achieve the wider purpose we have been calling "justice." Hence, the system's perspective on criminal justice generally encompasses a larger point of view called the **consensus model**. The consensus model assumes that all the components of the criminal justice system strive toward a common goal and that the movement of cases and people through the system is smooth because of cooperation among the various components of the system.

Consensus Model. A perspective on the study of criminal justice which assumes that the system's subcomponents work together harmoniously to achieve that social product we call "justice."

The system's model of criminal justice, however, is more an analytical tool than it is a reality. Any analytical model, be it in the so-called hard sciences or in the social sciences, is simply a convention chosen for its explanatory power. By explaining the actions of criminal justice officials (such as arrest, prosecution, and sentencing) as though they are systematically related, we are able to envision a fairly smooth and predictable process (described in more detail later in this chapter). The advantage we gain from this convention is a reduction in complexity that allows us to describe the totality of criminal justice at a conceptually manageable level.

The system's model has been criticized for implying a greater level of organization and cooperation among the various agencies of justice than actually exists. The word *system* calls to mind a near-perfect form of social organization. The modern mind associates the idea of a system with machinelike precision in which wasted effort, redundancy, and conflicting actions are quickly abandoned and their causes repaired. The justice system has nowhere near this level of perfection, and the system's model is admittedly an oversimplification that is primarily useful for analytical purposes. Conflicts among and within agencies are rife, immediate goals are often not shared by individual actors in the system, and the system may move in different directions depending on political currents, informal arrangements, and personal discretionary decisions.

The Conflict Model

The **conflict model** provides another approach to the study of American criminal justice. The conflict model says that criminal justice agency interests tend to make actors within the system self-serving. Pressures for success, promotion, pay increases, and general accountability, according to this model, fragment the efforts of the system as a whole, leading to a criminal justice *non*system.[19]

Jerome Skolnick's classic study of clearance rates provides support for the idea of a criminal justice nonsystem.[20] Clearance rates are a measure of crimes solved by the police. The more crimes the police can show they have solved, the happier is the public they serve.

Skolnick discovered an instance in which an individual burglar was caught red-handed during the commission of a burglary. After his arrest, the police suggested that he should confess to many unsolved burglaries that they knew he had not committed. In effect, they said, "Help us out, and we will try to help you out!" The burglar did confess—to more than 400 other burglaries. Following the confession, the police were satisfied because they could say they had "solved" many burglaries, and the suspect was pleased because the police had agreed to speak on his behalf before the judge.

Both models have something to tell us. Agencies of justice with a diversity of functions (police, courts, and corrections), and at all levels (federal, state, and local), are linked closely enough for the term system to be meaningfully applied to them. On the other hand, the very size of the criminal justice undertaking makes effective cooperation between component agencies difficult. The police, for example, may have an interest in seeing offenders put behind bars. Prison officials, on the other hand, may be working with extremely overcrowded facilities. They may desire to see early release programs for certain categories of offenders such as those who are judged to be nonviolent. Who wins out in the long run could be just a matter of internal politics. Everyone should be concerned, however, when the goal of justice is affected, and sometimes even sacrificed, because of conflicts within the system.

*C*onflict Model. A perspective on the study of criminal justice which assumes that the system's subcomponents function primarily to serve their own interests. According to this theoretical framework, "justice" is more a product of conflicts among agencies within the system than it is the result of cooperation among component agencies.

*A*merican Criminal Justice: The Process

Structurally, as we have seen, the criminal justice system can be described in terms of its component agencies: police, courts, and corrections. Functionally, the components of the "system" may work together well, or they may be in conflict. Whether system or nonsystem, however, the agencies of criminal justice must process cases that come before them. An analysis of case processing within the system provides both a useful guide to this book and a "road map" to the criminal justice system itself. Beginning with the investigation of reported crimes, Figure 1-1 diagrams the processing of a criminal case through the federal justice system.

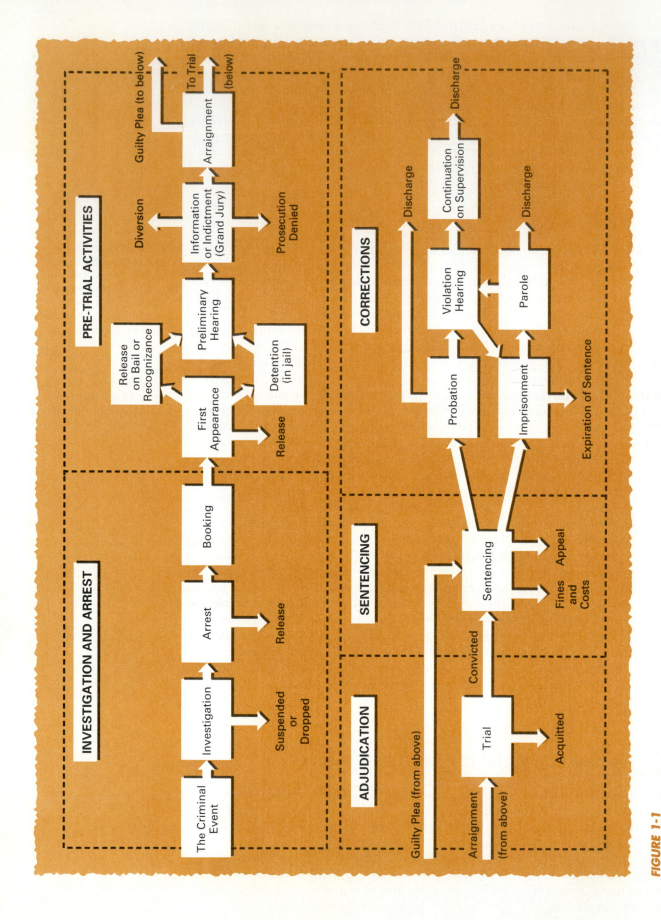

INVESTIGATION AND ARREST

The Criminal Event → Investigation → Arrest → Booking

Investigation → Suspended or Dropped

Arrest → Release

PRE-TRIAL ACTIVITIES

First Appearance → Release on Bail or Recognizance → Preliminary Hearing → Information or Indictment (Grand Jury) → Arraignment

First Appearance → Release

First Appearance → Detention (in jail)

Information or Indictment (Grand Jury) → Diversion

Information or Indictment (Grand Jury) → Prosecution Denied

Arraignment → Guilty Plea (to below)

Arraignment → To Trial

Arraignment → (below)

ADJUDICATION

Guilty Plea (from above)

Arraignment (from above) → Trial

Trial → Convicted

Trial → Acquitted

SENTENCING

Sentencing → Fines and Costs

Sentencing → Appeal

CORRECTIONS

Probation → Violation Hearing

Imprisonment → Parole

Probation → Discharge

Violation Hearing → Continuation on Supervision → Discharge

Parole → Discharge

Imprisonment → Expiration of Sentence

FIGURE 1-1

Criminal Case Processing. Source: Adapted from U.S.Department of Justice, Compendium of Federal Justice Statistics, 1989 (Washington, D.C.: Bureau of Justice Statistics, 1992), p. 3.

18

Theory into Practice: Japanese Say No to Crime

Whereas American society emphasizes individual rights, Japanese culture has long given primacy to group concerns and social order. The impact that such a cultural emphasis has had on crime rates in Japan is eye-opening, as the following table shows:

Crime Statistics
Rate per 100,000 persons

	Japan	United States
Murder	0.98	9.5
Robbery	1.75	255.8
Arson	1.13	45.9
Burglary	186.9	1,099.0
Aggravated assault	5.4	440.0

Japanese society ostracizes offenders, demanding that they be caught, show remorse, and confess. Japanese prisons are harsh places where communication between inmates is not permitted and hard work is required. Japanese police have sweeping powers, and civil liberties in the sense of American due process, are far less pervasive in Japan than in the United States. Police in Japan may detain suspects for up to 21 days before a judicial hearing, and they operate free of *Miranda* requirements, often pressuring suspects into confessions.

But the one thing that, more than any other, may account for low rates of crime in Japan, is a sense of personal honor and responsibility that makes up the Japanese national character. Symptomatic of the interpersonal trust that underlies social relationships in Japan is a police-run program that allows anyone to go to a police station or police call box and borrow money (usually $10–$20) at any time on the honor system. "We can't ask them for I.D. because usually the reason they need to borrow cash is that they've lost their wal-

let," says Tokio Kunichika, chief of police for the Tokyo subway system. It surprises Americans to learn that almost all the borrowed money is quickly returned.

Other differences are noteworthy between America and Japan that may bear on the incidence of crime. In the United States, more than 30 percent of children are born to unwed mothers. In Japan, the figure is around 1 percent. Furthermore, few Japanese citizens own guns. Official statistics show 425,000 gun owners in Japan (though the figure includes air rifles and BB guns), whereas as many as 200 million guns are in private hands in the United States. Most important of all may be the fact that Japanese children are taught strict values from an early age. As one author puts it, "What Americans call 'family values' are rigorously inculcated in Japan. The value of good behavior, of fitting into a common society, is drummed into children from the moment they set off to first grade in identical school uniforms."

Not everyone, however, agrees that low crime rates are worth the social cost. "I think that there is a lot that Japan has sacrificed for safety," says Koichi Miyazawa, a professor at Keio University in Tokyo. "Safety has been achieved at the expense of freedom," Miyazawa adds.

QUESTIONS FOR DISCUSSION

1. Do you agree with Professor Miyazawa that Japan has paid too high a price for reduced rates of crime? Why or why not?

2. Will American society ever be able to reduce crime as the Japanese have? If so, how might that be accomplished?

SOURCES: Nicholas D. Kristof, "Japanese Say No to Crime: Tough Methods, at a Price," *The New York Times,* May 14, 1995, p. 1A, and "Japan Hangs Three Death Row Convicts," Reuters online, May 26, 1995.

Investigation and Arrest

The modern justice process begins with investigation. When a crime has been committed, it is often discovered and reported to the police. On occasion, a police officer on routine patrol discovers the crime while it is still in progress. Evidence will be gathered on the scene when possible, and a follow-up investigation will attempt to reconstruct the likely sequence of activities. A few offenders are arrested at the scene of the crime, and some are apprehended only after an extensive investigation. In such cases, arrest **warrants** issued by magistrates or other judges provide the legal basis for an apprehension by police.

An arrest involves taking a person into custody and limits his or her freedom. Arrest is a serious step in the process of justice and involves a discretionary decision made by the police seeking to bring criminal sanctions to bear. Most arrests

Warrant. Any of a number of writs issued by a judicial officer, which direct a law enforcement officer to perform a specified act and affords protection from damages if he or she performs it.

are made peacefully, but some involve force when the suspect tries to resist. Only about 50 percent of all persons arrested are eventually convicted, and of those, only about 25 percent are sentenced to a year or more in prison.

During arrest and prior to questioning, defendants are usually advised of their constitutional rights as enumerated in the famous Supreme Court decision of *Miranda* v. *Arizona*.[21] Defendants are told:

> (1) "You have the right to remain silent." (2) "Anything you say can and will be used against you in court." (3) "You have the right to talk to a lawyer for advice before we ask you any questions, and to have him with you during questioning." (4) "If you cannot afford a lawyer, one will be appointed for you before any questioning if you wish." (5) "If you decide to answer questions now without a lawyer present, you will still have the right to stop answering at any time. You also have the right to stop answering at any time and may talk with a lawyer before deciding to speak again." (6) "Do you wish to talk or not?" and (7) "Do you want a lawyer?"[22]

It is important to realize that although popular television programs almost always show a rights advisement at the time of arrest, the Miranda decision only requires police personnel to advise a person of his or her rights prior to questioning. An arrest without questioning can occur in the absence of any warning. When an officer interrupts a crime in progress, public safety considerations may make it reasonable for the officer to ask a few questions prior to a rights advisement. Many officers, however, feel on sound legal ground only by immediately following arrest with an advisement of rights. Investigation and arrest are discussed in detail in Chapter 5, "Policing: Legal Aspects."

Booking

Booking. A law enforcement or correctional administrative process officially recording an entry into detention after arrest, and identifying the person, place, time, and reason for the arrest, and the arresting authority.

During the arrest process, suspects are booked: Pictures are taken; fingerprints are made; and personal information, such as address, date of birth, weight, and height, are gathered. Details of the charges are recorded, and an administrative record of the arrest is created.

During booking, suspects are again advised of their rights and are asked to sign a form on which each right is written. The written form generally contains a statement acknowledging the rights advisement and attesting to the fact that the suspect understands them.

First Appearance

Bail. The money or property pledged to the court or actually deposited with the court to effect the release of a person from legal custody.

Within hours of arrest, suspects must be brought before a magistrate, a judicial officer, for a first or initial appearance. The judge will tell them of the charges against them, will again advise them of their rights, and may sometimes provide the opportunity for **bail.**

Most defendants are released on recognizance (into their own care or the care of another) or given the chance to post bond during their first appearance. A bond may take the form of a cash deposit or a property bond in which a house or other property can serve as collateral against flight. Those who flee may be ordered to forfeit the posted cash or property. Suspects who either are not afforded the opportunity for bail because their crimes are very serious or do not have the needed financial resources are taken to jail to await the next stage in the justice process.

If a defendant doesn't have a lawyer, one will be appointed at the first appearance. The defendant may actually have to demonstrate financial hardship or be ordered to pay for counsel. The names of assigned lawyers are usually drawn off the roster of practicing defense attorneys in the county. Some jurisdictions use public defenders to represent indigent defendants. All aspects of the first appearance, including bail bonds and appointed counsel, are discussed in detail in Chapter 7, "The Courts."

Preliminary Hearing

The primary purpose of a **preliminary hearing,** also sometimes called a preliminary examination, is to establish whether or not sufficient evidence exists against a person to continue the justice process. At the preliminary hearing, the hearing judge will seek to determine whether there is **probable cause** to believe that (1) a crime has been committed and (2) the defendant committed it. The decision is a judicial one, but the process provides the prosecutor with an opportunity to test the strength of evidence at his or her disposal.

The preliminary hearing also allows defense counsel the chance to assess the strength of the prosecution's case. As the prosecution presents evidence, the defense is said to "discover" what it is. Hence, the preliminary hearing serves a *discovery* function for the defense. If the defense attorney thinks the evidence is strong, he or she may suggest that a plea bargain be arranged. Indigent defendants have a right to be represented by counsel at the preliminary hearing.

Information or Indictment

In some states, the prosecutor may seek to continue the case against a defendant by filing an "information" with the court. An information is filed on the basis of the outcome of the preliminary hearing.

Other states require an **indictment** be returned by a **grand jury** before prosecution can proceed. The grand jury hears evidence from the prosecutor and decides whether a case should go to trial. In effect, the grand jury is the formal indicting authority. It determines whether or not probable cause exists to charge a defendant formally with a crime. Grand juries can return an indictment on less than a unanimous vote.

The grand jury system has been criticized because it is one-sided. The defense has no opportunity to present evidence; the grand jury is led only by the prosecutor, often through an appeal to emotions or in ways that will not be permitted in a trial.

At the same time, the grand jury is less bound by specific rules than a jury in a trial. For example, one member of a grand jury related to the author that a rape case had been dismissed because the man had taken the woman to dinner first. Personal ignorance and subcultural biases are far more likely to be decisive in grand jury hearings than in criminal trials.

In defense of the grand jury, however, we should recognize that defendants who are clearly innocent will likely not be indicted. A refusal to indict can save considerable time and money by diverting poorly prepared cases from further processing by the system.

Arraignment

At **arraignment,** the accused stands before a judge and hears the information or indictment against him or her as it is read. Defendants will again be notified of their rights and will be asked to enter a plea. Acceptable pleas generally include (1) not guilty, (2) guilty, and (3) no contest (*nolo contendere*), which may result in conviction but which can't be used later as an admission of guilt in civil proceedings. Civil proceedings, though not covered in detail in this book, provide an additional avenue of relief for victims or their survivors. Convicted offenders increasingly find themselves facing suits brought against them by victims seeking to collect monetary damages.

Federal rules of criminal procedure specify that "arraignment shall be conducted in open court and shall consist of reading the indictment or information to the defendant or stating to him the substance of the charge and calling on him to plead thereto. He shall be given a copy of the indictment or information before he is called upon to plead."[23]

Preliminary Hearing. The proceeding before a judicial officer in which three matters must be decided: whether a crime was committed; whether the crime occurred within the territorial jurisdiction of the court; and whether there are reasonable grounds to believe that the defendant committed the crime.

Probable Cause. A legal criterion residing in a set of facts and circumstances which would cause a reasonable person to believe that a particular other person has committed a specific crime. Probable cause refers to the necessary level of belief which would allow for police seizures (arrests) of individuals and searches of dwellings, vehicles, and possessions.

Indictment. A formal, written accusation submitted to the court by a grand jury, alleging that a specified person(s) has committed a specified offense(s), usually a felony.

Grand Jury. A body of persons who have been selected according to law and sworn to hear the evidence against accused persons and determine whether there is sufficient evidence to bring those persons to trial, to investigate criminal activity generally, and to investigate the conduct of public agencies and officials.

Arraignment. The hearing before a court having jurisdiction in a criminal case, in which the identity of the defendant is established, the defendant is informed of the charge(s) and of his or her rights, and the defendant is required to enter a plea. In some usages, an arraignment is any appearance in court prior to trial in criminal proceedings.

Guilty pleas are not always accepted by the judge. If the judge feels a guilty plea was made under duress, or because of the defendant's lack of knowledge, the plea will be rejected, and a plea of not guilty will be substituted for it. Sometimes defendants "stand mute"; that is, they refuse to speak or enter a plea of any kind. In that case, the judge will enter a plea of not guilty on their behalf. The arraignment process, including pretrial motions made by the defense, is discussed in detail in Chapter 7, "The Courts."

Trial

Trial by Jury. The examination in a court of the issues of fact and law in a case, for the purpose of reaching a judgment of conviction or acquittal of the defendant(s).

Every criminal defendant has a right under the Sixth Amendment to the U.S. Constitution to a **trial by jury.** The U.S. Supreme Court, however, has held that petty offenses are not covered by the Sixth Amendment guarantee and that the seriousness of a case is determined by the way in which "society regards the offense." For the most part, "offenses for which the maximum period of incarceration is six months or less are presumptively petty."[24] In *Blanton* v. *North Las Vegas* (1989),[25] the Court held that "a defendant can overcome this presumption, and become entitled to a jury trial, only by showing that...additional penalties [such as fines and community service] viewed together with the maximum prison term, are so severe that the legislature clearly determined that the offense is a serious one." The *Blanton* decision was further reinforced in the case of *U.S.* v. *Nachtigal* (1993).[26]

In most jurisdictions, many criminal cases never come to trial. The majority are "pled out" (that is, dispensed of as the result of a bargained plea) or dismissed for a variety of reasons. Some studies have found that as many as 82 percent of all sentences are imposed in criminal cases because of guilty pleas rather than trials.[27]

In cases that do come to trial, the procedures that govern the submission of evidence are tightly controlled by procedural law and precedent. Procedural law specifies what type of evidence may be submitted, what the credentials of those allowed to represent the state or the defendant must be, and what a jury is allowed to hear.

Precedent refers to understandings built up through common usage and to decisions rendered by courts in previous cases. Precedent in the courtroom, for example, requires that lawyers request permission from the judge before approaching a witness. It also can mean that excessively gruesome items of evidence may not be used or must be altered in some way so that their factual value is not lost in the strong emotional reactions they may create.

Some states allow trials for less serious offenses to occur before a judge if defendants waive their right to a trial by jury. This is called a bench trial. Other states require a jury trial for all serious criminal offenses.

Trials are expensive and time consuming. They pit defense attorneys against prosecutors. Regulated conflict is the rule, and juries are required to decide the facts and apply the law as it is explained to them by the judge. In some cases, however, a jury may be unable to decide. In such cases, it is said to be deadlocked, resulting in a mistrial being declared. The defendant may then be tried again when a new jury is impaneled. The criminal trial and its participants are described fully in Chapter 8, "The Courtroom Work Group and the Criminal Trial."

Sentencing

Once a person is convicted, it becomes the responsibility of the judge to impose some form of punishment. The sentence may take the form of supervised probation in the community, a fine, a prison term, or some combination of these. Defendants will often be ordered to pay the costs of court or of their own defense if they are able.

Prior to sentencing, a sentencing hearing may be held in which lawyers on both sides present information concerning the defendant. The judge may also request that a presentence report be compiled by a probation or parole officer. The report will contain information on the defendant's family and business situation, emotional state, social background, and criminal history. It will be used to assist the judge in making an appropriate sentencing decision.

Judges traditionally have had considerable discretion in sentencing although new state and federal laws now place limits on judicial discretion in some cases, requiring that a sentence "presumed" by law be imposed. Judges still retain enormous discretion, however, in specifying whether sentences on multiple charges are to run consecutively or concurrently. Offenders found guilty of more than one charge may be ordered to serve another sentence after one is completed (a **consecutive sentence**) or be told that their sentences will run at the same time (a **concurrent sentence**).

Many sentences are appealed. The appeals process can be complex, involving both state and federal judiciaries. It is based on the defendant's claim that rules of procedure were not properly followed at some earlier stage in the justice process or that the defendant was denied the rights accorded him or her by the U.S. Constitution. Chapter 9, "Sentencing," outlines modern sentencing practices and describes the many modern alternatives to imprisonment.

Corrections

Once an offender has been sentenced, the stage of "corrections" begins. Some offenders are sentenced to prison where they "do time for their crimes." Once in the correctional system, they are classified according to local procedures and assigned to confinement facilities and treatment programs. Newer prisons today bear little resemblance to the massive bastions of the past, which isolated offenders from society behind huge stone walls. Many modern prisons, however, still suffer from a "lock psychosis" among top- and mid-level administrators as well as a lack of significant rehabilitation programs. Chapter 11, "Prisons and Jails," discusses the philosophy behind prisons and sketches their historical development. Chapter 12, "Prison Life," portrays life on the inside and delineates the social structures that develop as a response to the pains of imprisonment.

Probation and Parole

Not everyone who is convicted of a crime and sentenced ends up in prison. Some offenders are ordered to prison only to have their sentences suspended and a probationary term imposed. They may also be ordered to perform community service activities as a condition of their probation. During the term of probation, these offenders are required to submit to supervision by a probation officer and to meet other conditions set by the court. Failure to do so results in revocation of probation and imposition of the original prison sentence. Other offenders, who have served a portion of their prison sentences, may be freed on parole. They will be supervised by a parole officer and assisted in their readjustment to society. As in the case of probation, failure to meet the conditions of parole may result in parole revocation and a return to prison. Chapter 10, "Probation, Parole, and Community Corrections," deals with the practice of probation and parole and with the issues surrounding it.

ue Process and Individual Rights

Imposed upon criminal justice case processing is the constitutional requirement of fairness and equity. Guaranteed by the Fifth, Sixth, and Fourteenth Amendments to the U.S. Constitution, this requirement is referred to as **due process.** The due process clause of the U.S. Constitution is found succinctly stated in the Fifth Amendment, which reads "No person shall be...deprived of life, liberty,

Consecutive Sentence. A sentence that is one of two or more sentences imposed at the same time, after conviction for more than one offense, and which is served in sequence with the other sentences; or, a new sentence for a new conviction, imposed upon a person already under sentence(s) for previous offense(s), which is added to a previous sentence(s), thus increasing the maximum time the offender may be confined or under supervision.

Concurrent Sentence. A sentence that is one of two or more sentences imposed at the same time after conviction for more than one offense and to be served at the same time; or, a new sentence imposed upon a person already under sentence(s) for a previous offense(s) to be served at the same time as one or more of the previous sentences.

Due Process. A right guaranteed by the Fifth, Sixth, and Fourteenth Amendments of the U.S. Constitution, and generally understood, in legal contexts, to mean the due course of legal proceedings according to the rules and forms which have been established for the protection of private rights. Due process of law, in criminal proceedings, is generally understood to include the following basic elements: a law creating and defining the offense, an impartial tribunal having jurisdictional authority over the case, accusation in proper form, notice and opportunity to defend, trial according to established procedure, and discharge from all restraints or obligations unless convicted.

or property, without due process of law." The constitutional requirement of due process mandates the recognition of individual rights in the processing of criminal defendants when they are faced with prosecution by the states or the federal government. The guarantee of due process is found not just in the Fifth Amendment, but underlies the first ten amendments to the U.S. Constitution, which are collectively known as the "Bill of Rights." The Fourteenth Amendment is of special importance, however, for it makes due process binding upon the states—that is, it requires individual states in the union to respect the due process rights of U.S. citizens who come under their jurisdiction.

The fundamental guarantees of the Bill of Rights have been interpreted and clarified by courts (especially by the U.S. Supreme Court) over time. The due process standard became reality following a number of far-reaching Supreme Court decisions affecting criminal procedure that were made during the 1960s. The 1960s was the era of the Warren Court, led by Chief Justice Earl Warren, a Supreme Court that is remembered for its concern with protecting the innocent against the massive power of the state in criminal proceedings.[28] As a result of the tireless efforts of the Warren Court to institutionalize the Bill of Rights, the daily practice of modern American criminal justice is now set squarely on the due process standard. Due process requires that agencies of justice recognize these rights in their enforcement of the law, and under the due process standard, rights violations may become the basis for the dismissal of evidence or criminal charges, especially at the appellate level. Table 1-1 outlines the basic rights to which defendants in criminal proceedings are generally entitled.

The Role of the Courts in Defining Rights

Although the Constitution deals with many issues, what we have been calling "rights" are open to interpretation. Many modern rights, though written into the Constitution, would not exist in practice were it not for the fact that the U.S. Supreme Court decided, at some point in history, to recognize them in cases brought before it. The well-known Supreme Court case of *Gideon* v. *Wainwright* [29] (1963), for example (which is discussed in detail in Chapter 8) found the Court embracing the Sixth Amendment

TABLE 1-1

Individual Rights Guaranteed by the Bill of Rights

A RIGHT...

To Be Assumed Innocent Until Proven Guilty
Against Unreasonable Searches of Person and Place of Residence
Against Arrest Without Probable Cause
Against Unreasonable Seizures of Personal Property
Against Self-Incrimination
To Fair Questioning by the Police
To Protection from Physical Harm Throughout the Justice Process
To an Attorney
To Trial by Jury
To Know the Charges
To Cross-Examine Prosecution Witnesses
To Speak and Present Witnesses
Not to Be Tried Twice for the Same Crime
Against Cruel or Unusual Punishment
To Due Process
To a Speedy Trial
Against Excessive Bail
Against Excessive Fines
To Be Treated the Same as Others, Regardless of Race, Sex, Religious Preference, and Other Personal Attributes

guarantee of a right to a lawyer for all criminal defendants and mandating that states provide lawyers for defendants who are unable to pay for them. Prior to *Gideon*, court-appointed attorneys for defendants unable to afford their own counsel were practically unknown, except in capital cases and in some federal courts. After the *Gideon* decision, court-appointed counsel became commonplace, and measures were instituted in jurisdictions across the nation to fairly select attorneys for indigent defendants. Note, however, that though the Sixth Amendment specifically says, among other things, that "In all criminal prosecutions, the accused shall enjoy the right to...have the Assistance of Counsel for his defence," it does *not* say, *in so many words*, that the state is *required to provide* counsel. The U.S. Supreme Court, interpreting the Constitution, has said *that*.

Unlike the high courts of many other nations, the U.S. Supreme Court is very powerful, and its decisions often have far-reaching consequences. The decisions rendered by the justices in cases like *Gideon* become, in effect, the law of the land. In essence, such decisions often carry as much weight as legislative action. For this reason, some writers speak of "judge-made law" (rather than legislated law) in describing judicial precedents that affect the process of justice.

Rights that have been recognized by Court decision are often subject to continual refinement. New interpretations may broaden or narrow the scope of applicability accorded to constitutional guarantees. Although the process of change is usually very slow, we should recognize that any right is subject to continual interpretation by the courts—and especially by the U.S. Supreme Court.

Crime Control through Due Process

Two primary goals were identified at the start of this chapter: (1) the need to enforce the law and maintain social order and (2) the need to protect individuals from injustice. The first of these principles values the efficient arrest and conviction of criminal offenders. It is often referred to as the **crime control model** of justice. The crime control model was first brought to the attention of the academic community in Herbert Packer's cogent analysis of the state of criminal justice in the late 1960s.[30] For that reason, it is sometimes referred to as Packer's crime control model.

The second principle is called the **due process model** for its emphasis on individual rights. Due process is a central and necessary part of American criminal justice. It requires a careful and informed consideration of the facts of each individual case. Under the model, police are required to recognize the rights of suspects during arrest, questioning, and handling. Prosecutors and judges must recognize constitutional and other guarantees during trial and the presentation of evidence. Due process is intended to ensure that innocent people are not convicted of crimes.

Until now, we have suggested that the dual goals of crime control and due process are in constant and unavoidable opposition to each other. Some critics of American criminal justice have argued that the practice of justice is too often concerned with crime control at the expense of due process. Other conservative analysts of the American scene maintain that our type of justice coddles offenders and does too little to protect the innocent.

Although it is impossible to avoid ideological conflicts such as these, it is also realistic to think of the American system of justice as representative of *crime control through due process*. It is this model, of law enforcement infused with the recognition of individual rights, that provides a workable conceptual framework for understanding the American system of criminal justice—both now and into the future.

Crime Control Model. A criminal justice perspective that emphasizes the efficient arrest and conviction of criminal offenders.

Due Process Model. A criminal justice perspective that emphasizes individual rights at all stages of justice system processing.

Criminal Justice and Criminology

The study of criminal justice as an academic discipline began in this country in the 1920s when August Vollmer, the former police chief of Berkeley, California, persuaded the University of California to offer courses on the subject.[31] Vollmer was

Criminology. The scientific study of crime causation, prevention, and the rehabilitation and punishment of offenders.

joined by his student Orlando W. Wilson and by William H. Parker in calling for increased professionalism in police work through better training.[32] Early criminal justice education was practice oriented; it was a kind of extension of on-the-job training for working practitioners.

Whereas criminal justice was often seen as a technical subject, **criminology** had a firm academic base. Criminology is the study of the causes of crime and of criminal motivation. It combines the academic disciplines of sociology and psychology in an effort to explore the mind of the offender. The study of criminology is central to the criminal justice discipline, and courses in criminology are almost always found in criminal justice programs. Victimology is a subfield of criminology that seeks answers to the question of why some people are victimized, whereas others are not.

As a separate field of study, criminal justice had fewer than 1,000 students before 1950.[33] The turbulent 1960s and 1970s brought an increasing concern with social issues and, in particular, justice. Drug use, social protests, and dramatically increasing crime rates turned the nation's attention to the criminal justice system. During the period, Congress passed two significant pieces of legislation: (1) the Law Enforcement Assistance Act of 1965, which created the Law Enforcement Assistance Administration (LEAA), and (2) the Omnibus Crime Control and Safe Streets Act of 1968. Through LEAA, vast amounts of monies were funneled into fighting crime.

Law enforcement agencies received a great deal of technical assistance and new crime-fighting hardware. Students interested in the study of criminal justice often found themselves eligible for financial help under the Law Enforcement Education Program (LEEP).

LEEP monies funded a rapid growth in criminal justice offerings nationwide. In the first year of its existence, the LEEP program spent $6.5 million on 20,602 students in 485 schools around the country. By 1975, more than 100,000 students were studying criminal justice at 1,065 schools with assistance from LEEP. The federal government in that year spent in excess of $40 million on criminal justice education.[34]

LEEP funding began to decline in 1979. Meanwhile, criminal justice programs nationwide were undergoing considerable self-examination. The direction of justice studies and the future of the discipline were open to debate. The resultant clarification of criminal justice as a discipline, combined with the recent resurgence of federal funding initiatives through the Violent Crime Control and Law Enforcement Act of 1994, and the "block grants" and other programs it and later legislation provided, has made the field stronger and more professional than ever before.

Summary

In this chapter, we have described the process of American criminal justice and the agencies that contribute to it as a system with three major components: police, courts, corrections. As we have warned, however, such a viewpoint is useful primarily for the reduction in complexity it provides. A more realistic approach to understanding criminal justice may be the nonsystem approach. As a nonsystem, criminal justice is depicted as a fragmented activity in which individuals and agencies within the process have interests and goals that at times coincide, but often conflict.

Defendants processed by the system come into contact with numerous justice professionals whose duty it is to enforce the law, but who also have a stake in the agencies that employ them and who hold their own personal interests and values. As they wend their way through the system, defendants may be held accountable to the law, but in the process they will also be buffeted by the personal whims of "officials" as well as by the practical needs of the system itself. A complete view of American criminal justice needs to recognize that the final outcome of any encounter with the criminal justice system will be a consequence of decisions made not just at the legislative level, but in the day-to-day activities undertaken by everyone involved in the system. Hence, in a very real sense, justice is a product whose quality depends just as much on practical considerations as it does on idealistic notions of right and wrong.

An alternative way of viewing the practice of criminal justice is in terms of its two goals: crime control and due process. The crime control perspective urges rapid and effective law enforcement, and calls for the stiff punishment of law breakers. Due process, on the other hand, requires a recognition of the defendant's rights and holds the agents of justice accountable for any actions that might contravene those rights.

The goals of due process and crime control are often in conflict. Popular opinion may even see them as mutually exclusive. As we describe the agencies of justice in the chapters that follow, the goals of crime control and due process will appear again and again. As we shall see, the challenge of criminal justice in America is one of achieving efficient enforcement of the laws while recognizing the rights of individuals. The mandate of crime control through due process ensures that criminal justice will remain an exciting and ever-evolving undertaking.

Discussion Questions

1. What are the two models of the criminal justice process that this chapter describes? Which model do you think is more useful? Which is more accurate?
2. What have we suggested are the primary goals of the criminal justice system? Do you think any one goal is more important than the others? If so, which one? Why?
3. What do we mean when we say that the "primary purpose of law is the maintenance of order"? Why is social order necessary?
4. Do we have too many criminal laws? Too few? Do we have enough social order or too little? What more, if anything, needs to be changed?
5. What might a large, complex society such as our own be like without laws? Without a system of criminal justice? Would you want to live in such a society? Why or why not?
6. What do we, as individuals, have to give up to facilitate social order? Do we ever give up too much in the interest of social order? If so, when?

References

1. Charles E. Silberman, *Criminal Violence, Criminal Justice* (New York: Random House, 1978), p. 12.
2. "Gingrich Says Felons Should Be Tracked By Satellite," Reuters online, March 4, 1995.
3. Aminah Franklin, "Brutal, Cowardly Murder: Police Say Threats Preceded Slaying of Salisbury Family," *The Morning Call*, March 1, 1995, p. A1.
4. Ibid.
5. David Washburn, "Brothers Cultivated Defiant Attitude," *The Morning Call*, March 1, 1995, p. A4.
6. Aminah Franklin, "Police Scour Region for Teen Accused of Shooting Parents," *The Morning Call*, March 4, 1995, A3.
7. "Teen Held in Slaying of Parents," *The Morning Call*, March 7, 1995, p. A1.
8. Aminah Franklin, "A Search for Understanding: Loved Ones Gather in Howorths' Memory," *The Morning Call*, p 1A.
9. See, "Cries of Relief," Time, April 26, 1993, p. 18, and "King II: What Made the Difference?" *Newsweek*, April 26, 1993, p. 26.
10. Ibid.
11. "FBI: Definitely a Bomb," *USA Today*, March 1, 1993, p. 1A.
12. Sam Vincent Meddis, "Voters Say 'Get Tough,' But Answers Not So Simple," *USA Today*, November 16, 1994, p. 6A.
13. "A Free Man," *USA Today*, April 27, 1989, p. 13A.
14. *The American Heritage Dictionary on CD-ROM*, (Boston: Houghton Mifflin Company, 1991).
15. "The Subway Gunman," *Facts on File* (New York: Facts on File, 1987), p. 792.
16. For additional information on this case see, Jordan Bonfante, et al. "Oprah! Oprah in the Court!" *Time* online, May 29, 1994.
17. George P. Fletcher, *A Crime of Self-defense: Bernhard Goetz and Law on Trial* (New York: The Free Press, 1988).
18. The systems model of criminal justice is often attributed to the frequent use of the term *system* by the 1967 Presidential Commission in its report, *The Challenge of Crime in a Free Society* (Washington, D.C.: U.S. Government Printing Office, 1967).
19. One of the first published works to use the nonsystems approach to criminal justice was the American Bar Association's *New Perspective on Urban Crime* (Washington, D.C.: ABA Special Committee on Crime Prevention and Control, 1972).
20. Jerome H. Skolnick, *Justice Without Trial* (New York: John Wiley, 1966), p. 179
21. *Miranda* v. *Arizona*, 384 U.S. 436 (1966).
22. North Carolina Justice Academy, *Miranda Warning Card* (Salemburg, N.C.).
23. Fed. R. Crim. P. 10.
24. *Blanton* v. *North Las Vegas*, 489 U.S. 538 (1989).
25. Ibid.
26. *U.S.* v. *Nachtigal*, No. 92-609. Decided February 22, 1993.
27. Barbara Borland and Ronald Sones, *Prosecution of Felony Arrests*, 1981 (Washington, D.C.: Bureau of Justice Statistics, 1986).
28. For a complete analysis of the impact of decisions made by the Warren Court, see Fred P. Graham, *The Due Process Revolution: The Warren Court's Impact on Criminal Law* (New York: Hayden Press, 1970).

29. *Gideon* v. *Wainwright,* 372 U.S. 353 (1963).

30. Herbert Packer, *The Limits of the Criminal Sanction* (Stanford, Calif.: Stanford University Press, 1968).

31. For an excellent history of policing in the United States, see Edward A. Farris, "Five Decades of American Policing: 1932–1982," *The Police Chief,* November 1982, pp. 30–36.

32. Gene Edward Carte, "August Vollmer and the Origins of Police Professionalism," *Journal of Police Science and Administration,* Vol. 1, no. 1 (1973), pp. 274–281.

33. Larry L. Gaines, "Criminal Justice Education Marches On!" in Roslyn Muraskin, ed., *The Future of Criminal Justice Education* (New York: Criminal Justice Institute, Long Island University, C. W. Post Campus, 1987).

34. Ibid.

CHAPTER 2

The Crime Picture

—*Photo by Spencer Grant/Stock Boston*

*I*t may turn out that a free society cannot really prevent crime. Perhaps its causes are locked so deeply into the human personality, the intimate processes of family life, and the subtlest aspects of the popular culture that coping is the best that we can hope for...[1]

—JAMES Q. WILSON, UCLA

*N*o one way of describing crime describes it well enough.
—THE PRESIDENT'S COMMISSION ON LAW ENFORCEMENT
AND ADMINISTRATION OF JUSTICE

*W*e are the most violent and self-destructive nation on earth....In 1990, no nation had a higher murder rate than the United States. What is worse, no nation was even close.

—A REPORT RELEASED BY JOSEPH R. BIDEN, JR.
U.S. SENATE JUDICIARY COMMITTEE CHAIRMAN

KEY CONCEPTS

violent crime	property crime	Crime Index
clearance rate	murder	forcible rape
date rape	robbery	aggravated assault
burglary	larceny	motor vehicle theft
arson	hate crimes	organized crime

Introduction: Sources of Data

On Easter Sunday of 1992, three members of the Ewell family of Fresno, California, were gunned down in the entryway of their home as they returned from a visit to Santa Cruz.[2] Dead were 59-year-old Dale Ewell, his wife Glee, and their daughter, Tiffany, 24. Statistically, there was little to distinguish these murders from the 3,921 others that were recorded in California that year. The Ewells went down in the record books as three more homicides in a state already overburdened with news of drive-by shootings, gang-related killings, drug deals gone bad, and homicidal arguments fueled by liquor and lust.

But there is a story behind every crime statistic, and the Ewell's story is an interesting one. Dale Ewell was a self-made multimillionaire and owner of Western Piper Sales, a California airplane dealership. Glee Ewell, 57, was a pillar of high society, involving herself in everything from Republican campaigns to art festivals. Their daughter Tiffany was shy, but well liked by all who knew her. The Ewells also had a son, Dana—and in 1995 Dana Ewell was arrested by San Joaquin Valley authorities and charged with arranging the murders of his family.

Dana Ewell was described as "the clean-cut son who seemed to have the perfect alibi." On the day of the killings, he was 200 miles away with his girlfriend and her FBI-agent father. Dana, however, acted suspiciously. While in high school, years before the killings, he drove a gold Mercedes and wore expensive Armani suits. He bragged that he had made a fortune playing the stock market and running two small companies. A day after the funerals, rather than grieving, Dana took his friends water skiing with the family's boat. He assumed the helm of his father's business and, using the family fortune, bought a personal airplane.

Investigators say that Dana hired Joel Radovcich, 24, a fellow student at Santa Clara University, to kill his parents and sister. After Dana had established an alibi, say authorities, Radovcich—armed with a semiautomatic assault rifle—acted. He drove to the family's home on Park Circle Drive in Fresno and lay in the bushes waiting for the family to arrive. Worried they could all die in a plane crash, the Ewells traveled home separately. The mother and daughter arrived first by car. They were shot as they stepped onto the red tiles of their entry alcove, the mother dying first. Dale Ewell arrived by plane and drove to his house, strolling up the walkway shortly after the first killings. He was shot in the back as he drew near the door.

Dana Ewell is now seeking access to his family's fortune to pay legal fees, as he sits in jail without bond awaiting trial. Both Ewell and Radovcich, who face death sentences if convicted, claim innocence.

This chapter provides a statistical picture of crime in America today. It does so by examining information on reported crimes from the FBI's *Uniform Crime Reports* (UCR), as well as data from the door-to-door National Crime Victimization Survey (NCVS) conducted by the Bureau of Justice Statistics (BJS). While reading this chapter, however, keep in mind that statistical aggregates of reported crime, whatever their source, do not easily reveal the human suffering, cost in lost lives, lessened productivity, and reduced quality of life that crime causes. Although all murder victims, like the Ewells, for example, led an intricate life and had a family, dreams, and desires, their death at the hands of another person, is routinely recorded only as a numerical count in existing statistical reports. Such information does not contain details on the personal lives of crime victims but represents merely a numerical compilation of reported law violations.

Crime Data and Social Policy

Crime statistics do more than provide a picture of crime in this country. If used properly, they can provide one of the most powerful tools available to social-policy decision makers. Decision makers at all levels, including legislators, elected public officials, and administrators throughout the criminal justice system, rely on crime data to analyze and evaluate existing programs, fashion and design new crime control initiatives, develop funding requests, and plan new laws and crime control legislation. The "get tough" policies described in Chapter 1, for example, are in large part based on the public's perception of increasing crime rates and the measured ineffectiveness of existing programs to reduce the incidence of repeat offending.

Some, however, question just how "objective"—and therefore how useful—crime statistics are. Social events, including crime, are complex and difficult to quantify. Even the choice of which crimes should be included in statistical reports, and which should be excluded, is itself a judgment, reflecting the interests and biases of policy makers. The FBI, for example, classifies certain crimes as "Part I offenses," often called "major crimes." We'll be discussing each of these offenses in detail later in the chapter, but for now note that they include:

- Murder
- Forcible rape
- Robbery
- Aggravated assault
- Burglary
- Larceny
- Motor vehicle theft
- Arson

Part I offenses do not encompass most large-scale white-collar crimes, such as insider trading in securities, price fixing by corporate executives, and unfair business practices. Nor are statistics on "victimless" crimes (also called "social order crimes") included. Such crimes, however, probably result in far more monetary damage than most of the traditionally classified "major offenses."

Collecting Crime Data

Crime statistics are difficult to interpret because of the way in which they are collected. Most widely quoted numbers purporting to describe crime in America come from the FBI's *Uniform Crime Reports* (UCR) and depend on reports to the police by victims of crime. One problem with such summaries is that citizens do not always make official reports, sometimes because they are afraid to contact the police, or perhaps because they don't think the police can do anything about the offense. Even when reports are made, they are filtered through a number of bureaucratic levels. As Frank Hagan points out, quoting an earlier source, "The government is very keen on amassing statistics. They collect them, add to them, raise them to the *n*th power, take the cube root and prepare wonderful diagrams. But what you must never forget is that every one of these figures comes in the first instance from the *chowty dar* (village watchman), who puts down what he damn pleases."[3]

Another problem is the fact that certain kinds of crimes are rarely reported and are especially difficult to detect. These include "victimless crimes," or crimes that, by their nature, involve willing participants. Victimless crimes include such things as drug use, prostitution, and gambling. Similarly, white-collar and high-technology offenses such as embezzlement, computer crime, and corporate misdeeds, probably enter the official statistics only rarely. Hence, a large amount of criminal activity goes undetected in the United States, while those types of crimes that are detected may paint a misleading picture of criminal activity by virtue of the publicity accorded to them.

A second data collection format is typified by the Bureau of Justice Statistics' (BJS) National Crime Victimization Survey (NCVS). It relies on personal interpretations of what may (or may not) have been criminal events and on quasi-confidential surveys that may selectively include data from those most willing to answer interviewer's questions; it excludes information from less gregarious respondents. Some victims are afraid to report crimes even to nonpolice interviewers. Others may inaccurately interpret their own experiences or may be tempted to invent victimizations for the sake of interviewers. As the first page of the NCVS admits, "Details about the crimes come directly from the victims, and no attempt is made to validate the information against police records or any other source."[4]

Although the FBI's UCR and the BJS's NCVS are the country's major sources of crime data, other regular publications contribute to our knowledge of crime patterns throughout the nation. Available yearly is the *Sourcebook of Criminal Justice Statistics*, a compilation of national information on crime and on the criminal justice system. The *Sourcebook* is published by BJS through support provided by the Justice System Improvement Act of 1979. A less frequent, but more concise, document is the *Report to the Nation on Crime and Justice*, issued in updated editions every few years. The National Institute of Justice (NIJ), the primary research arm of the U.S. Department of Justice, along with the Office of Juvenile Justice and Delinquency Prevention (OJJDP), the Federal Justice Research Program, and the National Victim's Resource Center, provide still more information on crime patterns.

The Uniform Crime Reports

Development of the UCR Program

In 1930, Congress authorized the attorney general of the United States to survey crime in America, and the FBI was designated to implement the program. The Bureau quickly built upon earlier efforts by the International Association of Chiefs

Victimless crimes such as prostitution are rarely reported. As a consequence, they are likely to be seriously underrepresented in the FBI's Uniform Crime Reports. Here, teenage prostitutes solicit a "John." Photo by John Maher/Stock Boston.

of Police (IACP) to create a national system of uniform crime statistics. As a practical measure, IACP recommendations had used readily available information, and so it was that citizens' reports of crimes to the police became the basis of the plan.[5]

During its first year of operation, the UCR Program received reports from 400 cities in 43 states. Twenty million people were covered by that first comprehensive survey. Today, almost 16,000 law enforcement agencies provide crime information for the program, with data coming from city, state, and county departments. To assure uniformity in reporting, the FBI has developed standardized definitions of offenses and terminologies used in the program. A number of publications, including the *Uniform Crime Reporting Handbook* and *Manual of Law Enforcement Records*, are supplied to participating agencies, and training for effective reporting is made available through FBI-sponsored seminars and instructional literature.

Following IACP recommendations, the original UCR Program was designed to permit comparisons over time through construction of a **Crime Index**. The Index summed the total of seven major offenses—murder, forcible rape, robbery, aggravated assault, burglary, larceny-theft, and motor vehicle theft—and expressed the result as a crime rate based on population. In 1979, by congressional mandate, an eighth offense—arson—was added to the Index. Although UCR categories today parallel statutory definitions of criminal behavior, they are not legal classifications but only conveniences created for statistical reporting purposes.

Historical Trends

Since the UCR Program began, there have been two major shifts in crime rates. One occurred during the early 1940s, when crime decreased because of the large number of young men who entered military service during World War II. Young males compose the most "crime-prone" segment of the population, and their removal to the European and Pacific theaters of war did much to lower crime rates.

The other noteworthy shift in offense statistics—a dramatic increase in most forms of crime beginning in the 1960s—also had a link to World War II. With the end of the war, and the return of millions of young men to civilian life, birth rates skyrocketed during the period 1945–1955, creating a postwar "baby boom." By 1960, "baby boomers" were entering their teenage years. A disproportionate number of young people produced a dramatic increase in most major crimes.

Other factors contributed to the increase in reported crime during the same period. Modified reporting requirements, which reduced the stress associated with filing police reports, and the publicity associated with the rise in crime, sensitized victims to the importance of reporting. Crimes that may have gone undetected in the past began to figure more prominently in official statistics. Similarly, the growing professionalization of some police departments resulted in more accurate and increased data collection, causing some of the most progressive departments to appear to be associated with the largest crime increases.[6]

The 1960s were tumultuous years. The Vietnam war, a vibrant civil rights struggle, the heady growth of secularism, dramatic increases in the divorce rate, diverse forms of "liberation," and the influx of psychedelic and other drugs, all combined to fragment existing institutions. Social norms were blurred, and group control over individual behavior declined substantially. The "normless" quality of American society in the 1960s contributed greatly to the rise in crime. Crime rates continued their upward swing with a brief respite in the early 1980s when postwar boomers began to age out of the crime-prone years, and American society emerged from the cultural drift that had characterized the previous 20 years. About the same time, however, an increase in drug-related criminal activity led to heightened crime rates, especially in the area of violent crime. Crime rates peaked about 1991, with decreases in the rate of most major crimes now being reported.

Crime Index. An inclusive measure of the violent and property crime categories of the UCR, also known as "Part I offenses." The Crime Index has been a useful tool for geographic (state-to-state) and historical (year-to-year) comparative purposes because it employs the concept of a crime rate (the number of crimes *per* unit of population). However, the addition of arson, as an eighth index offense in recent years, and the new executive branch requirements with regard to the gathering of "hate crime" statistics have the potential to result in new crime index measurements which provide less than ideal comparisons.

UCR Terminology

Figure 2-1 shows the UCR crime clock, which is calculated yearly as a shorthand way of diagramming crime severity in the United States. Seven Part I offenses are listed in the right-hand margin of the figure. Arson has been temporarily excluded although it is now an eighth index offense.

The crime clock distinguishes between two general categories of crime: **violent (or personal) crime** and **property crime**. Violent crimes include murder, forcible rape, robbery, and aggravated assault. Property crimes, as the figure shows, are burglary, larceny, and motor vehicle theft. Other than for the use of such a simple dichotomy, UCR data do not provide a clear measure of the severity of the crimes they cover.

Crime clock data are based, as are most UCR statistics, on crimes reported to (or discovered by) the police. For a few offenses, the numbers reported are probably close to the actual number of occurrences. Murder, for example, is difficult to conceal because of its seriousness. Even when the crime of murder is not immediately discovered, the victim is often quickly missed by friends and associates, and a "missing persons" report is filed with the police.

Auto theft is another crime that is reported with a frequency similar to its actual rate of occurrence, probably because insurance companies require that a police report be filed before any claims can be collected. Unfortunately, most crimes other than murder and auto theft appear to be seriously underreported. Victims may not report for various reasons, including (1) the belief that the police can't do anything, (2) a fear of reprisal, (3) embarrassment about the crime itself, or a fear of being embarrassed during the reporting process, and (4) an acceptance of criminal victimization as a normal part of life.

UCR data tend to underestimate the amount of crime that actually occurs for another reason: built into the reporting system is the hierarchy rule—a way of "counting" crime reports such that only the most serious out of a series of events is scored. If a man and woman go on a picnic, for example, and their party is set upon by a criminal who kills the man, rapes the woman, steals the couple's car, and later burns the vehicle, the hierarchy rule dictates that only one crime will be reported in official statistics—that of murder. The offender, if apprehended, may later be charged with each of the offenses listed, but only one report of murder will appear in UCR data.

Most UCR information is reported as a *rate* of crime. Rates are computed as the number of crimes *per* some unit of population. National reports generally make use of large units of population, such as 100,000 persons. Hence, the rate of rape reported by the UCR for 1994 was 39.2 forcible rapes per every 100,000 inhabitants of the United States.[7] Rates allow for a meaningful comparison over areas and across time. The rate of reported rape for 1975, for example, was about 26 per 100,000.[8] We expect the number of crimes to increase as population grows, but rate increases are cause for concern because they indicate that crimes are increasing faster than the population is growing. Rates, however, require interpretation. Since the FBI definition of rape includes only female victims, for example, the rate of victimization might be more meaningfully expressed in terms of every 100,000 female inhabitants. Similarly, although there is a tendency to judge an individual's risk of victimization based on rates, such judgments tend to be inaccurate since they are based purely on averages and do not consider individual life circumstances, such as place of residence, wealth, and educational level. Although rates may tell us about aggregate conditions and trends, we must be very careful in applying them to individual cases. The crime clock, itself a useful diagrammatic tool, is not a rate-based measure of criminal activity and does not allow easy comparisons over time.

A commonly used term in today's UCRs is **clearance rate**. The clearance rate of any crime refers to the proportion of reported crimes that have been "solved." Clearances are judged primarily on the basis of arrests and do not involve judicial disposition. Once an arrest has been made, a crime is regarded as "cleared" for purposes of reporting in the UCR Program. Exceptional clearances (sometimes called

Violent Crime. An offense category which, according to the FBI's Uniform Crime Reports (UCR), includes murder, rape, aggravated assault, and robbery. Because the UCR depends on *reports* (to the police) of crimes, the "official statistics" on these offenses are apt to inaccurately reflect the actual incidence of such crimes.

Property Crime. An offense category which, according to the FBI's UCR program, includes burglary, larceny, auto theft, and arson. Since citizen reports of criminal incidents figure heavily in the compilation of "official statistics," the same critiques apply to tallies of these crimes as to the category of violent crime.

Clearance Rate. A traditional measure of investigative effectiveness that compares the number of crimes reported or discovered to the number of crimes solved through arrest or other means (such as the death of a suspect).

clearances by exceptional means) can result when law enforcement authorities believe they know who the perpetrator of a crime is but cannot make an arrest. The perpetrator may, for example, flee the country, commit suicide, or die.

For data-gathering and reporting purposes, the UCR Program divides the country into four geographic regions: the Northeast, West, South, and Midwest. Unfortunately, no real attempt has been made to create divisions with nearly equal populations or similar demographic characteristics, and it is difficult to meaningfully compare one region of the country with another. Table 2-1 summarizes UCR statistics for 1994.

Part I Offenses

Murder

Murder is the unlawful killing of one human being by another.[9] UCR statistics on murder describe the yearly incidence of all willful and unlawful homicides within the United States. Included in the count are all cases of nonnegligent manslaughter that have been reported or discovered by the police. Not included in the court are suicides, justifiable homicides (self-defense), deaths caused by negligence or accident, and attempts to murder. In 1994, some 23,305 murders came to the attention of police departments across the United States.[10] First degree murder is a term that describes criminal homicide that is planned or involves premeditation. Second degree murder is an intentional and unlawful killing, but one that is generally unplanned and that may happen "in the heat of passion."

Murder is the smallest numerical category in the Part I offenses. The 1994 murder rate was 9 homicides for every 100,000 persons in the country—a decrease of 5 percent over the previous year. Murder rates tend to peak annually in the warmest months. In many years, July and August show the highest number of homicides; typically, in 1994, the month of August showed the highest number of murders.

Geographically, murder is most common in the southern states. However, because these states are also the most populous, a meaningful comparison across regions of the country is difficult. Although the 1994 data show a one-year decline in the murder rate, ten-year trends show the 1994 rate was 14 percent higher than in 1985.

Murder. The unlawful killing of a human being. Murder is a generic term, which, in common usage may include first and second degree murder, as well as "manslaughter," "involuntary manslaughter," and other, similar kinds of offenses.

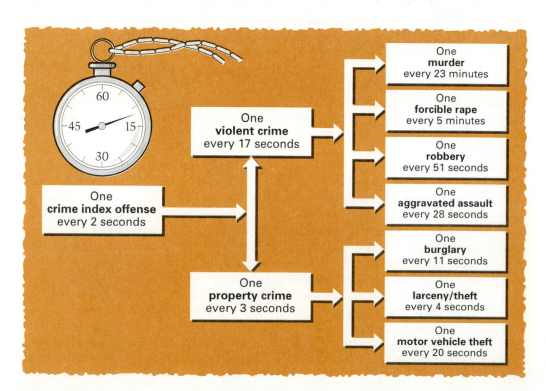

FIGURE 2-1
FBI Crime Clock 1994, showing the frequency of major crime commission. Source: Adapted from Federal Bureau of Investigation, Uniform Crime Reports for the United States, 1994 *(Washington, D.C.: U.S. Government Printing Office, 1995).*

Age is no barrier to murder. Statistics for 1994 reveal that 257 infants (under the age of 1) were victims of homicide, as were 434 persons aged 75 and over.[11] Persons aged 20–24 were the most likely to be murdered. Murder perpetrators also were most common in the 20- to 24-year-old age group.

Firearms are the weapon of choice in most murders. Ours is a well-armed society, and guns accounted for 70 percent of all killings in 1994. Handguns outnumbered shotguns by 12 to 1 in the murder statistics, whereas rifles were a distant third. Knives were used in approximately 15 percent of all murders. Other weapons included explosives; poisons; narcotics overdoses; blunt objects such as clubs; and hands, feet, and fists.

Few murders are committed by strangers. Only 13 percent of all murders in 1994 were perpetrated by persons classified as "strangers." In 40 percent of all killings, the relationship between the parties had not yet been determined. The largest category of killers was officially listed as "acquaintances," which probably includes a large number of former "friends." Arguments cause most murders (29 percent), but murders occur during commission of other crimes, such as robbery, rape, and burglary. Homicides that follow from other crimes are more likely to be impulsive than planned.

Murders may occur in sprees, which "involve killings at two or more locations with almost no time break between murders."[12] Mass murders entail "the killing of four or more victims at one location, within one event."[13] Serial murders happen over time and are officially defined to "involve the killing of several victims in three or more separate events."[14] Days, months, or even years may elapse between the murders. Serial killers have been frequently portrayed in the media. Some of the more infamous in recent years include Jeffrey Dahmer, who received 936 years in prison for the homosexual dismemberment murders of 15 young men (and who was himself later murdered in prison); Ted Bundy who killed many college-age women; Henry Lee Lucas, now on death row in Texas, who was convicted of 11 murders and linked to 140 others; Charles Manson, still serving time for ordering followers to kill 7 Californians, including famed actress Sharon Tate; and David Berkowitz, also known as the "Son of Sam," who killed 6 people and wounded 7 on lover's lanes around New York City.

Because murder is such a serious crime, it consumes substantial police resources. Consequently, over the years, the offense has shown the highest clearance rate of any index crime; 64 percent of all homicides were cleared in 1994. Figure 2-2 shows clearance rates for all Part I offenses.

TABLE 2-1

UCR Part 1 Offenses, 1994

Offense	Number	Rate per 100,000	Clearance Rate
PERSONAL OR VIOLENT CRIMES			
Murder	23,305	9.0	64%
Forcible rape	102,096	39.2	52
Robbery	618,817	237.7	24
Aggravated assault	1,119,950	430.2	56
PROPERTY CRIMES			
Burglary	2,712,156	1,041.8	13
Larceny	7,876,254	3,025.4	20
Motor vehicle theft	1,539,097	591.2	14
Arson[1]	102,139	—	15
U.S. total	14,093,814	5,374.4	21

1. Arson can be classified as either a property crime or a violent crime, depending on whether or not personal injury or loss of life results from its commission. It is generally classified as a property crime, however. Arson statistics are incomplete for 1994 and do not enter in the "total" tabulations.

SOURCE: Adapted from Federal Bureau of Investigation, *Uniform Crime Reports for the United States, 1994* (Washington, D.C.: U.S. Government Printing Office, 1995).

Theory into Practice: Guns, Crime, and Crime Control

The Second Amendment to the U.S. Constitution reads, "A well regulated Militia, being necessary to the security of a free State, the right of the people to keep and bear Arms, shall not be infringed." Constitutional guarantees have combined with historical circumstances to make ours a well-armed society. In a typical year, approximately 13,500 murders are committed in the United States with firearms—most with handguns. Handguns are also used in many other crimes. Approximately 1 million serious violations of the law—ranging from homicide, through rape, robbery, and assault—occur each year in which a handgun is used. Government statistics show:[1]

- Nonfatal handgun crimes average 4.5 offenses per year for every 1,000 people age 12 or over.
- Handguns are used in approximately 56 percent of all murders.
- Offenders armed with handguns commit one in every eight nonfatal violent crimes, such as rape, robbery, and assault.
- Young black males compose the group most victimized by handgun crime. Approximately 40 handgun crimes are committed yearly against every 1,000 black males age 16–19, a rate four times that for young white males.
- Offenders fire their weapons in 17 percent of all nonfatal handgun crimes, missing the victim four out of five times.
- About 21,000 victims a year are wounded by handguns.
- An average of 62,000 persons per year—about 1 percent of all violent crime victims—defend themselves with a firearm.
- Firearms are stolen in an estimated 340,000 crimes per year.

In 1994, in response to growing public concern over the easy availability of handguns, the U.S. Congress passed, and President Clinton signed, the Brady Handgun Violence Prevention Act. The law was named for Reagan-era press secretary James Brady, who was shot and severely wounded in an attempt on the president's life on March 30, 1981.

The Brady Law provides for a five-day waiting period before the purchase of a handgun, and for the establishment of a national instant criminal background checking system to be contacted by firearms dealers before the transfer of any firearm. Until the instant background checking system is in place, however, licensed gun dealers are required to notify the chief law enforcement officer in their area of all applications to purchase a handgun. Applications, made on a federally provided form, are to be checked by the

police who are required to "make a reasonable effort to ascertain within 5 business days whether receipt or possession [of a handgun] would be in violation of [federal, state, or local] law, including research in whatever State and local record-keeping systems are available and in a national system designated by the Attorney General." The law also provides that "If a chief law enforcement officer determines that an individual is ineligible to receive a handgun and the individual requests the officer to provide the reason for such determination, the officer shall provide such reasons to the individual in writing within 20 business days after receipt of the request."[2]

Once the national instant criminal background check system is established, a licensed importer, licensed manufacturer, or licensed dealer will be required to verify the identity of the purchaser using a valid photo ID (such as a driver's license), and to contact the system in order to receive a unique identification number authorizing the purchase before transfer of the handgun can be made.

The Violent Crime Control and Law Enforcement Act of 1994 further regulated the sale of firearms within the United States, banning the manufacture of 19 military-style assault weapons, including those with specific combat features, such as high-capacity ammunition clips capable of holding more than ten rounds. The 1994 law also prohibits the sale or transfer of a gun to a juvenile, as well as the possession of a gun by a juvenile, and it prohibits gun sales to, and possession by, a person subject to family violence restraining orders.

More government regulation of gun ownership is planned. In 1995, Housing and Urban Development Secretary Henry Cisneros said that the Clinton administration was considering a ban on firearms in public housing projects in order to reduce crime and improve the quality of life there.[3]

Not everyone agrees that gun sales and gun ownership should be subject to federal regulation. The National Rifle Association, the Citizens' Committee for the Right to Keep and Bear Arms, and other pro-gun ownership groups have filed lawsuits to derail enforcement of the Brady Act and the assault weapons provisions of the Violent Crime Control and Law Enforcement Act. The NRA, and some local sheriffs, maintain that many existing gun control laws violate the Constitution's Second Amendment. NRA attorneys also claim that the Tenth Amendment, which guarantees the rights of the states, means that "the federal government cannot make state officials the administrative agents of the federal government" and that local sheriffs (who are often the chief law enforcement officers in their areas) cannot be required to enforce the

(Continued on next page)

Brady Law. Similarly, the NRA criticizes the proposed ban on guns in housing projects, again citing the Second Amendment right to bear arms, and arguing that the ban would be "discriminatory" and would disarm and "single-out low-income citizens." As this book goes to press, NRA-sponsored efforts are underway in the House and Senate to repeal the ban on some military-style assault weapons.

In a potentially serious blow to federal efforts at gun control, the U.S. Supreme Court, in the case of *U.S. v. Alfonso Lopez, Jr.* (1995),[4] agreed with a lower court ruling that dismissed charges against a 12th-grade student who had carried a concealed .38 caliber handgun and five bullets into the Edison High School in San Antonio, Texas. The student was charged with violating the federal Gun-Free School Zones Act of 1990, which forbids "any individual knowingly to possess a firearm at a place that [he or she] knows...is a school zone." The law had been passed to assuage parents' concerns that their children might be in mortal danger because of the presence of guns in the hands of school-aged children and interlopers on school property.

Arguing that the federal government has the power to control commerce between the states (based on Article I, section 8, clause 3 of the U.S. Constitution, which delegates to Congress the power "to regulate Commerce with foreign Nations, and among the several States, and with the Indian Tribes"), government lawyers told the Court that it was necessary for the federal government to take steps intended to control violence in schools. "The occurrence of violent crime in school zones," they said, has brought about a "decline in the quality of education" that "has an adverse impact on interstate commerce and the foreign commerce of the United States." Although the Court agreed that this was a rational conclusion, it ruled that education, in the context of the law, was a local and not a national concern. Hence, said the Justices, "To uphold the Government's contentions here, we would have to pile inference upon inference...to convert congressional authority under the Commerce Clause to a general police power of the sort retained by the States." Unless the Court changes its mind, most effective gun-control legislation, beyond that already in place, may need to emanate from state- and local-level initiatives.

QUESTIONS FOR DISCUSSION

1. This box says that "Not everyone agrees that gun sales and gun ownership should be subject to federal regulation." How do you feel? Why?

2. Do you believe that regulating the sale of handguns will lower the crime rate in the United States? Why or why not?

1. Michael J. Sniffen, *"Handgun Crimes,"* The Associated Press online, May 15, 1994.

2. 18 U.S.C., Section 922(q)(1)(A).

3. *"Administration May Ban Firearms from Public Housing,"* United Press online, northern edition, February 5, 1995.

4. *U.S. v. Lopez,* 115 S. Ct. 1624, 131, L. ed. 2d 626 (1995).

Forcible Rape

Forcible rape is the least reported of all violent crimes. Typical estimates are that only one of every four forcible rapes that actually occur are reported to the police. An even lower figure was reported by a 1992 government-sponsored study that found that only 16 percent of rapes were reported.[15] The victim's fear of embarrassment has been cited as the reason most often given for nonreports. In the past, reports of rape were usually taken by seemingly hardened desk sergeants or male

*F*orcible Rape. Unlawful sexual intercourse with a female, by force and against her will, or without legal or factual consent. Statutory rape differs from forcible rape in that it involves sexual intercourse with a female who is under the age of consent— regardless of whether or not she is a willing partner. Date rape, or acquaintance rape, are subcategories of rape which are of special interest today.

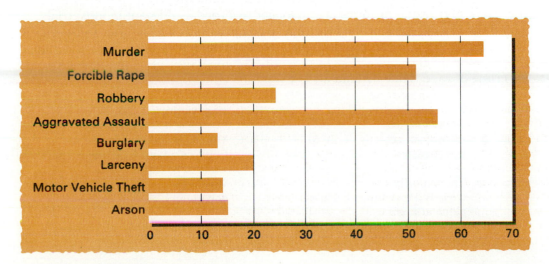

FIGURE 2-2
Crimes cleared by arrest, 1994. Source: Federal Bureau of Investigation, Crime in the United States, 1994 *(Washington D.C.; U.S. Department of Justice, 1995).*

detectives who may not have been sensitive to the needs of the victim. In addition, the physical examination that victims had to endure was often a traumatizing experience in itself. Finally, many states routinely permitted the woman's sexual history to be revealed in detail in the courtroom if a trial ensued. All these practices contributed to a considerable hesitancy among rape victims to report their victimizations.

The last decade has seen many changes designed to facilitate accurate reporting of rape and other sex offenses. Trained female detectives often act as victim interviewers, physicians have been better educated in handling the psychological needs of victims, and sexual histories are no longer regarded as relevant in most trials.

Rape is a complex crime involving strong emotions and injuries to the victim that often go beyond the physical. As a consequence, it is not a well-understood offense. Ronald Barri Flowers[16] has identified many cultural myths that surround the crime of rape. They include:

Fallacy 1: Rape cannot occur if the woman resists.

Fact: Most victims of rape do resist.

Fallacy 2: All women secretly desire to be raped.

Fact: Although some women may fantasize about rape, none actually want to be raped.

Fallacy 3: The majority of rapes are triggered by women being out alone at night.

Fact: Most rapes occur following social encounters, such as dates.

Fallacy 4: Rape is a victim-precipitated crime.

Fact: Rape is an offender-precipitated crime.

Fallacy 5:	Only young attractive women are raped.	Fact:	Women of all ages and appearances have been victims of rape.
Fallacy 6:	It cannot happen to me.	Fact:	Rape can happen to anyone.
Fallacy 7:	Rape is motivated by the need for sexual gratification.	Fact:	Most rapists appear to be motivated by the need to feel powerful.
Fallacy 8:	Most rapes are perpetrated by strangers.	Fact:	Most rapes are committed by acquaintances of the victim.
Fallacy 9:	The rapist looks the part.	Fact:	A rapist can be anyone.
Fallacy 10:	Rape is an impulsive act.	Fact:	Some rapes are impulsive, but many are planned.

UCR statistics show 102,096 reported rapes for 1994, a slight decrease over the number of offenses reported for the previous year. Rape is a crime that has shown a consistent increase in reporting even in years when other personal crimes have been on the decline (see Figure 2-3). By definition, rapes reported under the UCR Program are always of females. Homosexual rape is excluded from the count, as are instances of forced oral copulation, but attempts to commit rape by force or the threat of force are included. Statutory rape, where no force is involved, but the female is below the age of consent, is not included in rape statistics.

The offense of rape follows homicide in its seasonal variation. Most rapes in 1994 were reported in the hot summer months, whereas January, February, and December recorded the lowest number of reports. Most rapes are committed by acquaintances of the victims and often betray a trust or friendship. **Date rape**, which falls into this category, appears to be far more common than previously believed.

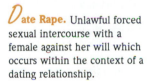

Date Rape. Unlawful forced sexual intercourse with a female against her will which occurs within the context of a dating relationship.

Rape is often a planned violent crime that serves the offender's need for power rather than sexual gratification.[17] It is frequently committed by a man known to the victim—as in the case of date rape. Victims may be held captive and subjected to repeated assaults.[18] In the crime of heterosexual rape, any female—regardless of age, appearance, or occupation—is a potential victim. Through personal violation, humiliation, and physical battering, rapists seek a sense of personal aggrandizement and feelings of dominance. In contrast, victims of rape often experience a lessened sense of personal worth; increased feelings of despair, helplessness, and vulnerability; a misplaced sense of guilt; and a lack of control over their personal lives.

Rape within marriage, which was not always recognized as a crime, is a growing area of concern in American criminal justice, and new laws are being written to sanction it. Some states have redefined their rape statutes to include homosexual

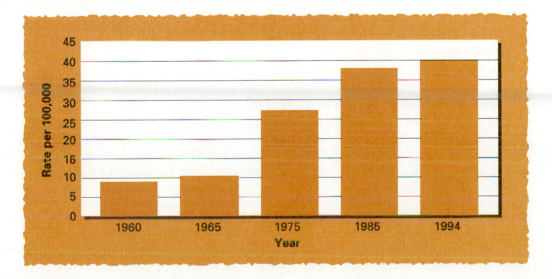

FIGURE 2-3
Rate of reported rape, 1960–1994. Source: Federal Bureau of Investigation, Crime in the United States *(Washington, D.C.: U.S. Government Printing Office, various years).*

rape and marriage rape although the latter is sometimes classified as sexual battery (indicating that force has been used), a lesser offense than the crime of rape.

Although UCR statistics report only the rape or attempted rape of females, some state statutes, by definition, allow for the rape of a male by a female—although such an offense, when it occurs, is typically of the statutory variety. In late 1993, for example, 24-year-old Fairfax County, Virginia, swimming coach Jean-Michelle Whitiak pleaded guilty to one count of statutory rape, admitting an affair with a 13-year-old boy. When the boy ended the relationship, Whitiak said, she had sex with two of his friends.[19]

Robbery

Robbery, sometimes confused with burglary, is a personal crime and involves a face-to-face confrontation between victim and perpetrator. Weapons may be used, or strong-armed robbery may occur through intimidation, especially where gangs threaten victims by sheer numbers. Purse snatching and pocket picking are not classified as robbery by the UCR Program, but are included under the category "larceny-theft."

In 1994, individuals (versus businesses and banks) were typical targets of robbers. Banks, gas stations, convenience stores, and other businesses were the second most common target of robbers, with residential robberies accounting for only 10.5 percent of the total. In 1994, 618,817 robberies were reported to the police, and 62 percent of them were highway robberies (meaning that they occurred outdoors, probably as the victim was walking) or muggings. Strong-armed robberies were the most common, accounting for 40 percent of total robberies reported. Guns were used in 42 percent of all robberies and knives in 10 percent.

Armed robbers are dangerous. Guns are actually discharged in 20 percent of all robberies.[20] Whenever a robbery occurs, the UCR Program scores the event as one robbery even though a number of victims may have been robbed during the event. With the move toward incident-driven reporting (discussed later in this chapter), however, the UCRs will soon make data available on the number of individuals robbed in each instance of robbery. Because statistics on crime show only the most serious offense that occurred during a particular episode, robberies are often hidden when they occur in conjunction with other, more serious, crimes. For example, in a recent year, 3 percent of robbery victims were also raped, and a large number of homicide victims were robbed.[21]

Robbery is primarily an urban offense, and most arrestees are young males who are members of minority groups. The robbery rate in large cities in 1994 was 877 (per every 100,000 inhabitants), whereas it was only 75 in rural areas. Ninety-two percent of those arrested in 1994 were male, 64 percent were under the age of 25, and 63 percent were minorities.[22]

Aggravated Assault

Assaults are of two types: aggravated and simple. Simple assaults may involve pushing and shoving or even fistfights. **Aggravated assaults** are distinguished from simple assaults by the fact that either they include the use of a weapon or the individual assaulted requires medical assistance. When deadly weapons are used, even though no injury may result, aggravated assaults may be chargeable as attempted murder.[23] Hence, because of their potentially serious consequences, the UCR Program scores some cases of attempted assault as aggravated assaults.

In 1994, 1,119,950 cases of aggravated assault were reported to law enforcement agencies in the United States. The summer months evidenced the greatest frequency of assault, whereas February was once again the month with the lowest number of reports. Most aggravated assaults were committed with blunt objects or objects near at hand (32 percent) though hands, feet, and fists were also commonly used (26 percent). Less frequent were knives and firearms (18 and 24 percent, respectively), as

---

Robbery. The unlawful taking or attempted taking of property that is in the immediate possession of another, by force or the threat of force. Armed robbery differs from unarmed or strong-armed robbery with regard to the presence of a weapon. Contrary to popular conceptions, highway robbery does not necessarily occur on a street—and rarely in a vehicle. Highway robbery is a term applicable to any form of robbery which occurs in a public place and out of doors.

Assault. The unlawful intentional inflicting, or attempted or threatened inflicting, of injury on the person of another. Historically, "assault" meant only the attempt to inflict injury on another person. A completed act constituted the separate offense of battery. Under most modern penal codes, however, attempted and completed acts are put together under the generic name, "assault." Although the names *aggravated assault* and *simple assault* are standard terms for reporting purposes, most state penal codes use labels such as "first degree" and "second degree" to make such distinctions.

Figure 2-4 shows. Because those who commit assaults are often known to those attacked, aggravated assaults are relatively easy to solve. Fifty-six percent of all aggravated assaults reported to the police in 1994 were cleared by arrest.

Burglary

Although it may involve personal and even violent confrontations, **burglary** is primarily a property crime. Burglars are interested in financial gain and usually fence (that is, illegally sell) stolen items in order to recover a small fraction of their cash value. About 3 million burglaries were reported to the police in 1994. Dollar losses to burglary victims totaled more than $3.6 billion, with an average loss per offense of $1,311.

Many people fear nighttime burglary of their residence. They imagine themselves asleep in bed as a stranger breaks into their home and then conjure up visions of a violent confrontation. Although such scenarios do occur, daytime burglary is more common. Many families now have two or more breadwinners, and since children are in school during the day, some homes—and even entire neighborhoods—are virtually unoccupied during daylight hours. This shift in patterns of social activity has led to a growing burglary threat against residences during daytime.

The UCR Program employs three classifications of burglary: (1) forcible entry, (2) unlawful entry where no force is used, and (3) attempted forcible entry. In most jurisdictions, force need not be employed for a crime to be classified as burglary. Unlocked doors and open windows are invitations to burglars, and the crime of burglary consists not so much in a forcible entry as it does in the intent of the offender to trespass and steal. In a ten-year period analyzed by the Bureau of Justice Statistics, 23 percent of all burglaries were unlawful entries, 69 percent were forcible entries, and 8 percent were attempted forcible entries.[24] The most dangerous burglaries were those in which a household member was home (about 10 percent of all burglaries).[25] Residents who were home during a burglary suffered a greater than 30 percent chance of becoming the victim of a violent crime.[26]

Property crimes generally involve low rates of clearance. Burglary is no exception. The clearance rate for burglary in 1994 was only 13 percent. Burglars are usually unknown to their victims, and even if known, they conceal their identity by committing their crime when the victim is not present.

Larceny

Larceny is another name for theft. Some states distinguish between simple larceny and grand larceny. Grand larceny is usually defined as theft of valuables in excess of a certain set dollar amount, such as $200. Categorizing the crime by dollar amount, however, can present unique problems, as during the high fiscal inflation

Burglary. The unlawful entry of any fixed structure, vehicle, or vessel used for regular residence, industry, or business, with or without force, with intent to commit a felony, or larceny. For UCR purposes, the crime of burglary can be reported if (1) an unlawful entry of an unlocked structure has occurred, (2) a breaking and entering (of a secured structure) has taken place, or (3) a burglary has been attempted.

Larceny. The unlawful taking or attempted taking of property other than a motor vehicle from the possession of another, by stealth, without force and without deceit, with intent to permanently deprive the owner of the property. Larceny is the most common of the eight major offenses although probably only a small percentage of all larcenies which occur are actually reported to the police because of the small dollar amounts involved.

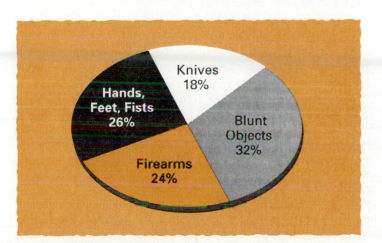

FIGURE 2-4
Aggravated assault—weapons used, 1994. Source: Federal Bureau of Investigation, Crime in the United States, 1994 *(Washington, D.C.: U.S. Department of Justice, 1995).*

Knives 18%

Hands, Feet, Fists 26%

Blunt Objects 32%

Firearms 24%

periods of the 1970s, when legislatures found themselves unable to enact statutory revisions fast enough to keep pace with inflation.

Larceny, as defined by the UCR Program, includes thefts of any amount. The reports specifically list the following offenses as types of larceny (listed here in order of declining frequency):

- ✔ Thefts from motor vehicles
- ✔ Shoplifting
- ✔ Thefts of motor vehicle parts and accessories
- ✔ Thefts from buildings
- ✔ Bicycle thefts
- ✔ Pocket picking
- ✔ Purse snatching
- ✔ Thefts from coin-operated machines

Thefts of farm animals (known as rustling) and thefts of most types of farm machinery also fall into the larceny category. In fact, larceny is such a broad category that it serves as a kind of catchall in the UCR. In 1995, for example, Yale University officials filed larceny charges against 25-year-old student Lon Grammer, claiming that he had fraudulently obtained university monies.[27] The university maintained that Grammer stole his education by forging college and high school transcripts and concocting letters of recommendation prior to admission. Grammer's alleged misdeeds—which Yale University officials said mislead them into thinking that Grammer, a poor student before attending Yale, had an exceptional scholastic record—permitted him to receive $61,475 in grants and loans during the time he attended the school. Grammer was also expelled.

Larceny is a kind of catchall category, and reported thefts can involve a wide diversity of materials with values that range anywhere from pocket change to the stealing of a $100 million aircraft. As a consequence, some state laws distinguish between grand theft (or grand larceny) and petty theft. Specifically excluded from the count of larceny for reporting purposes are crimes of embezzlement, con games, forgery, and worthless checks. Larceny has been traditionally thought of as a crime that requires physical possession of the item appropriated. Hence, most computer crimes, including thefts engineered through online access or thefts of software and information itself, have typically not been scored as larcenies—unless electronic circuitry, disks, or machines themselves were actually stolen. On the other hand, the crime of larceny may count other types of high-technology thefts. In 1995, for example, Dr. Ricardo Asch, a world-renowned fertility doctor working at the University of California-Irvine, was accused of stealing frozen human embryos and implanting them into infertile women.[28] California university police reported they were investigating the egg thefts, and Dr. Asch resigned from his position at the university's Center for Reproductive Health.

Reports to the police in 1994 showed 7,876,254 larcenies nationwide, with the total value of property stolen placed at $4 billion. The most common form of larceny in recent years has been theft of motor vehicle parts, accessories, and contents. The theft of tires, wheels, stereos, hubcaps, radar detectors, CB radios, cassette tapes, compact discs, and cellular phones account for many of the items reported stolen.

Larceny is the most frequently reported major crime according to the UCR. It may also be the UCR's most underreported crime category because small thefts rarely come to the attention of the police. The average value of items reported stolen in 1994 was about $505 per incident.

Motor Vehicle Theft

For record-keeping purposes, the UCR Program defines motor vehicles as self-propelled vehicles that run on the ground and not on rails. Included in the definition are automobiles, motorcycles, motorscooters, trucks, buses, and snowmobiles.

Excluded are trains, airplanes, bulldozers, most farm and construction machinery, ships, boats, and spacecraft—whose theft would be scored as larceny.[29] Vehicles that are temporarily taken by individuals who have lawful access to them are not scored as thefts. Hence, spouses who jointly own most property may drive the family car even though one spouse may think of the vehicle as his or her exclusive personal property.

As mentioned earlier, **motor vehicle theft** is a crime in which most occurrences are reported to law enforcement agencies. Insurance companies require police reports before they will reimburse car owners for their losses. Some reports of motor vehicle thefts, however, may be false. People who have damaged their own vehicles in solitary crashes, or who have been unable to sell them, may try to force insurance companies to "buy" them through reports of theft.

In 1994, more than 1.5 million motor vehicles were reported stolen. The average value per vehicle stolen was $4,940, making motor vehicle theft a $7.6 billion crime. The clearance rate for motor vehicle theft was only 14 percent in 1994. City agencies reported the lowest rates of clearance (13 percent), whereas rural counties had the highest rate (32 percent). Many stolen vehicles are routinely and quickly disassembled, with parts being resold through chop shops. Auto parts are, of course, much more difficult to identify and trace than are intact vehicles. In some parts of the country, chop shops operate like big business, and one shop may strip a dozen or more cars per day.

Motor vehicle theft can turn violent in cases of carjacking—a crime in which offenders force the occupants of a car onto the street before stealing the vehicle. In an incident that brought carjacking to national prominence a few years ago, Pamela Basu of Savage, Maryland, was dragged two miles to her death when she became entangled in her seat belt after being pushed from her car as the carjackers drove off. The thieves had to sideswipe a chain-link fence in order to finally dislodge her. Her 2-year-old daughter, still strapped into her carseat, was apparently later tossed from the vehicle. The FBI estimates that carjackings account for slightly more than 1 percent of all motor vehicle thefts.[30]

Arrest reports for motor vehicle theft show that the typical offender is a young male. Sixty percent of all arrestees in 1994 were under the age of 21, and 88 percent were male.

*M*otor Vehicle Theft. The unlawful taking or attempted taking, of a self-propelled road vehicle owned by another, with the intent to deprive him or her of it permanently or temporarily. The stealing of trains, planes, boats, construction equipment, and most farm machinery is classified as larceny under the UCR reporting program—*not* as motor vehicle theft.

A crime of theft? Dr. Ricardo Asch, the California physician accused in 1995 of stealing frozen human embryos and illegally transferring them to infertile couples. Crime today can take many forms that traditional laws may be hard-pressed to cover. Photo by Orange County Register/SABA Press Photos, Inc.

Arson

The UCR Program received crime reports from 16,314 law enforcement agencies in 1994.[31] Of these, only 9,409 submitted arson reports for all 12 months of the year. Few agencies provided complete data on the type of arson (nature of the item burned), the estimated monetary value of the property damaged, ownership of the property, and so on.

Current arson data include only those fires that, through investigation, are determined to have been willfully or maliciously set. Fires of unknown or suspicious origin are excluded from arson statistics.[32]

The intentional and unlawful burning of structures (houses, storage buildings, manufacturing facilities, and so on) was the type of **arson** most often reported in 1994 (43,870 instances). The arson of vehicles was the second most common category, with 21,261 such burnings reported. The average dollar loss per instance of arson in 1994 was $9,761, and total nationwide property damage was placed at more than $1 billion.[33] As with most property crimes, the clearance rate for arson was low—only 15 percent nationally.

The crime of arson exists in a kind of statistical limbo. In 1979, Congress ordered that it be added as an eighth Index offense. To date, however, the UCR Program has been unable to integrate statistics on arson successfully into the yearly Crime Index. The problem is twofold: (1) many law enforcement agencies have not yet begun making regular reports to the FBI on arson offenses that come under their jurisdiction, and (2) any change in the number of Index offenses produces a Crime Index that will not permit meaningful comparisons to earlier crime data.

The Crime Index is a composite offense rate that provides for useful comparisons over time and between jurisdictions so long as it retains definitional consistency. Adding a new offense to the Index, or substantially changing the definition of any of its categories, still provides a measure of "crime," but it changes the meaning of the term.

Some of these difficulties may eventually be resolved through the Special Arson Program, authorized by Congress in 1982. The FBI, in conjunction with the National Fire Data Center, now operates a Special Arson Reporting System that focuses on fire departments across the nation. The Arson Reporting System is designed to provide data that supplement yearly UCR arson tabulations.[34]

Arson. The burning or attempted burning of property with or without intent to defraud. Some instances of arson are the result of malicious mischief, whereas others involve attempts to claim insurance monies. Still others are committed in an effort to disguise other crimes such as murder, burglary, and larceny.

Part II Offenses

The Uniform Crime Reports also include information on what the FBI calls Part II offenses. Part II offenses are generally less serious than those that make up the Crime Index and include a number of social order, or so-called "victimless" crimes. The statistics on Part II offenses are for recorded arrests, not crimes reported to the police. The logic inherent in this form of scoring is that most Part II offenses would never come to the attention of the police were it not for arrests. Included in the Part II category are the crimes shown in Table 2-2, with the number of arrests reported in each category for 1994.

Part II arrests are counted each time a person is taken into custody. As a result, the statistics in Table 2-2 do not measure the number of persons arrested, but rather the number of arrests made. Some persons were arrested more than once.

Proposed Changes in the UCR

Changes are coming in the Uniform Crime Reports. From 1985 to 1992, the UCR Program was comprehensively evaluated under federal contract by ABT Associates, Inc., of Cambridge, Massachusetts. The final report of the UCR study

TABLE 2-2

UCR Part II Offenses, 1994

Offense Category	Number of Arrests
Simple assault	1,223,600
Forgery and counterfeiting	115,300
Fraud	419,800
Embezzlement	14,300
Stolen property (receiving, etc.)	164,700
Vandalism	323,300
Weapons (carrying, etc.)	259,400
Prostitution and related offenses	98,800
Sex offenses (statutory rape, etc.)	100,700
Drug law violations	1,351,400
Gambling	18,500
Offenses against the family (nonsupport, etc.)	117,200
Driving under the influence	1,384,600
Liquor law violations	541,800
Public drunkenness	713,200
Disorderly conduct	746,200
Vagrancy	25,300
Curfew/loitering	128,400
Runaways	248,800
All other violations of state and local laws (except traffic law violations)	3,743,200
Total	11,738,500

SOURCE: Adapted from Federal Bureau of Investigation, *Uniform Crime Reports for the United States, 1994* (Washington, D.C.: U.S. Government Printing Office, 1995).

group, entitled *A Blueprint for the Future of the Uniform Crime Reporting System*, recommended a number of sweeping changes. Among them are:

✔ Each category of offense should clearly distinguish statistics on attempts from actual commissions.

✔ The rape category should be broadened to include all forcible sex offenses. Sexual battery, sodomy, and oral copulation—accomplished through the use of force—should be counted.

✔ The "hierarchy rule" should be modified so as to count the most serious offense for *each individual victim* during an incident.[35]

✔ Crimes against individuals, households, and businesses should be more clearly distinguished in most categories.

✔ Aggravated assault should be more clearly defined in terms of the weapons used and the degree of injury suffered.

✔ A code of professional standards should be developed for reporting agencies and for the system as a whole.

✔ The UCR should be modified so as to permit easier and more meaningful comparisons with the NCVS and with Offender-Based Transaction Statistics (OBTS).

Whereas the original UCR system was "summary based," the new "enhanced" UCR, to be called the National Incident-Based Reporting System, or NIBRS, will be incident driven. The old system depended on statistical tabulations of crime data, which were often little more than frequency counts. Under the new system, many details will be gathered about each criminal incident. Included among them will be information on place of occurrence, weapon used, type and value of property damaged or stolen, the personal characteristics of the offender and the victim, the nature of any relationship between the two, nature of the disposition of the complaint, and so on. The new reporting system will replace the old Part I and Part II offenses with 22 general offenses, to include arson, assault, bribery, burglary, counterfeiting, vandalism, narcotic offenses, embezzlement, extortion, fraud, gambling, homicide, kidnapping, larceny, motor vehicle theft, pornography, prostitution, robbery, forcible sex offenses, nonforcible sex offenses, receiving stolen property, and weapons violations. Other offenses on which data will be gathered are bad checks, vagrancy, disorderly conduct, driving under the influence, drunkenness, nonviolent family offenses, liquor law violations, "peeping-Tom" activity, runaway, trespass, and a general category of all "other" criminal law violations. The FBI began accepting crime data in the NIBRS format in January 1989. The system is intended to be fully in place by 1999.

The 1990 Crime Awareness and Campus Security Act, which required college campuses to commence publishing annual "security reports" beginning in September 1992, has the potential to noticeably affect crime rates reported through the UCR Program. Although campuses are not required by law to share crime data with the FBI, many have begun doing just that—increasing the reported incidence of a variety of offenses.

A final change in reporting practices followed from the Hate Crime Statistics Act, signed into law by President Bush in April 1990. The act mandates a statistical tally of "hate crimes," and data collection under the law began in January 1991. **Hate crimes** are defined by statute as offenses in which there is "evidence of prejudice based on race, religion, sexual orientation, or ethnicity." In 1994, police agencies reported a total of 5,852 hate crime incidents, including nearly 20 murders, across the country. Eighteen percent of the incidents were motivated by religious bias, whereas 66 percent were caused by racial hatred. Twelve percent of all hate crimes were based on sexual orientation, and most of those were committed against males believed by their victimizers to be homosexuals.[36] Most hate crimes fell into the category of "intimidation" although vandalism, simple assault, and aggravated assault also accounted for a fair number of hate crime offenses. A few robberies and rapes were also classified under the hate crime umbrella in 1994.

 he National Crime Victimization Survey

As mentioned near the beginning of this chapter, a second major source of statistical data about crime in the United States is the National Crime Victimization Survey (NCVS), which is based on victim self-reports rather than police reports. The NCVS began operation in 1972 and built on earlier efforts by both the National Opinion Research Center and the President's Commission on Law Enforcement and the Administration of Justice in the late 1960s to uncover what some had been calling the "dark figure" (or unreported offenses) of crime.

Early data from the NCVS changed the way criminologists thought about crime in the United States. The use of victim self-reports led to the discovery that crime of all types was more prevalent than UCR statistics indicated. Many cities were shown to have victimization rates more than twice the rate of reported offenses. Others, such as St. Louis, Missouri, and Newark, New Jersey, were found to have rates of victimization that very nearly approximated reported crime. New York, often thought of as a "high-crime" city, was discovered to have one of the lowest rates of self-reported victimization.

NCVS data are gathered by the Bureau of Justice Statistics (BJS) through a cooperative arrangement with the U.S. Census Bureau.[37] NCVS interviewers work with a national sample of about 42,000 households, which are interviewed twice each year. Household lists are completely revised at the end of every three-year period. BJS statistics are published as research briefs called "Crime and the Nation's Households" and "Criminal Victimization" and annual reports entitled *Criminal Victimization in the United States*.

Using definitions similar to those used by the UCR Program, the NCVS includes data on the national incidence of rape, robbery, assault, burglary, personal and household larceny, and motor vehicle theft. Not included are murder, kidnapping, and victimless crimes. Commercial robbery and the burglary of businesses were dropped from NCVS reports in 1977. The NCVS employs a hierarchical counting system similar to that of the UCR: It counts only the most "serious" incident in any series of criminal events perpetrated against the same individual. Both completed and attempted offenses are counted although only persons 12 years of age and older are included in household surveys. Highlights of NCVS statistics for the early 1990s reveal that:

- ✔ Approximately 23 million American households per year are touched by crime—or 25 percent of all households.[38]
- ✔ Nearly 43 million victimizations are reported to the NCVS per year.
- ✔ City residents are about twice as likely as rural residents to be victims of crime.
- ✔ About half of all violent crimes, two-fifths of all household crimes, and slightly more than one-fourth of all crimes of personal theft are reported to police.[39]
- ✔ The total "personal cost" of crime to victims is about $13 billion per year for the United States as a whole.
- ✔ Victims of crime are more often men than women.
- ✔ Younger people are more likely than the elderly to be victims of crime.
- ✔ Blacks are more likely than whites or members of other racial groups to be victims of violent crimes.[40]
- ✔ Violent victimization rates are higher among people in lower-income families.
- ✔ Young males have the highest violent victimization rates; elderly females have the lowest.
- ✔ The chance of violent criminal victimization is much higher for *young* black males than for any other segment of the population. (The life chances of murder run from a high of 1 in 21 for a black male to a low of 1 in 369 for a white female.)[41]

Table 2-3 compares UCR and NCVS data for 1994.

Problems with the NCVS

Because most researchers believe that self-reports provide a more accurate gauge of criminal incidents than do police reports, many tend to accept NCVS data over that which is provided by the UCR program. The NCVS, however, is not without

TABLE 2-3

A Comparison of UCR and NCVS Data, 1994

Offense	UCR	NCVS[1]
VIOLENT CRIME		
Homicide[2]	23,305	—
Forcible Rape	102,096	316,000
Robbery	618,817	1,299,000
Aggravated Assault	1,119,950	2,478,000
PROPERTY CRIME		
Burglary	2,712,156	5,482,000
Larceny	7,876,254	23,765,000
Motor Vehicle Theft	1,539,097	1,764,000
Arson[3]	102,139	—
Total of all crimes recorded[4]		42,359,000

1. NCVS data covers "households touched by crime," not absolute numbers of crime occurrences. More than one victimization may occur per household, but only the number of households in which victimizations occur enter the tabulations.

2. Homicide statistics are not maintained by the NCVS.

3. Arson data are incomplete in the UCR and not reported by NCVS.

4. Includes other crimes not shown in the table.

SOURCES: Compiled from the U.S. Department of Justice, *Criminal Victimization 1994* (Washington, D.C.: Bureau of Justice Statistics, 1996); and Federal Bureau of Investigation, *Crime in the United States 1994* (Washington, D.C.: U.S. Government Printing Office, 1995).

its problems. Primary among them is the potential for false or exaggerated reports. False reports may be generated by overzealous interviewers or self-aggrandizing respondents and are difficult to filter out. There are no reliable estimates on the proportion of such responses that make up NCVS totals. Unintentional inaccuracies create other problems. Respondents may suffer from faulty memories, they may misinterpret events, and they may ascribe criminal intent to accidents and mistakes. Likewise, the lapse of time between the event itself and the conduct of the interview may cause some crimes to be forgotten and others to be inaccurately reported.

Redesign of the NCVS

Just as the Uniform Crime Reports are undergoing change, so too is the National Crime Victimization Survey. In 1995, the NCVS began reporting data from a redesigned questionnaire[42] intended to provide details on:

✔ Interaction between victim and offender
✔ Victims' crime deterrence efforts
✔ Perceived effectiveness of crime deterrence efforts
✔ Bystander behavior
✔ Perceived alcohol and drug use by offenders
✔ Suspected offender gang involvement

The redesigned questionnaire included changes to both the survey's content and procedures used in data gathering, including:

✔ Additional cues to help survey participants recall incidents
✔ Questions encouraging respondents to report victimizations that they themselves may not define as crimes
✔ More direct questions on rape, sexual assault, and other sexual crimes
✔ New material to measure victimization by nonstrangers, including domestic violence

Multiple questions and cues on crimes committed by family members, intimates, and acquaintances were added to the survey to explore domestic violence issues, and the new NCVS broadened the scope of covered sexual incidents beyond the traditional categories of rape and attempted rape to include sexual assault (other than rape), verbal threats of rape or sexual assault, and unwanted sexual contact without force but involving threats or other harm to the victim. The new questionnaire also allows for the classification of victimizations according to various life "domains," such as work or leisure, in which they occur. A 1994 NCVS report,[43] for example, showed that nearly 1 million people become victims of violent crime while at work—accounting for about 15 percent of all violent victimizations reported to surveyors. The same report said that more than 2 million personal thefts (about 25 percent of all such thefts) and more than 200,000 auto thefts (about 13 percent of the total number of cars stolen) occur annually while persons are at work.

The most recent NCVS data indicate that 13 percent of violent victimizations (murders, rapes, robberies, and assaults) are committed by intimates (spouses, exspouses, boyfriends, or girlfriends).[44] The huge majority of violent crimes committed by intimates are assaults (81 percent of all such crimes), whereas 15 percent of murders were committed by intimates. Thirty-three percent of victims of violent crimes believed their assailants to be under the influence of drugs or alcohol. In cases of rape, the proportion of assailants believed under the influence jumped to 45 percent, the highest reported by the survey. Seventy-one percent of violent crime victims reported taking some self-protective measure. Self-protective measures included struggling or fighting with the assailant, threats, running away, efforts at appeasement, or pleading. Sixty percent of victims who took self-protective measures reported that their actions reduced the severity of their victimization.

Justice agency response, as measured by the survey, shows that the police came to see the victim in 70 percent of violent crimes, 68 percent of household crimes (such as burglary and motor vehicle theft), and 51 percent of all larcenies. Police response was fastest in violent crimes, averaging under ten minutes, and slowest where household crimes were involved.

Comparisons of the UCR and NCVS

Table 2-4 summarizes the differences between the UCR and the NCVS. Both provide estimates of crime in America. Both are limited by the types of crimes they choose to measure, by those they exclude from measurement, and by the methods they use to gather crime data.

Crime statistics from the UCR and NCVS are often used in building explanations for criminal behavior. Unfortunately, however, researchers too often forget that statistics, which are merely descriptive, can be weak in explanatory power. For example, NCVS data show that "household crime rates" are highest for households (1) headed by blacks, (2) headed by younger people, (3) with six or more members, (4) headed by renters, and (5) in central cities.[45] Such findings, combined with statistics that show that most crime occurs among members of the same race, have led some researchers to conclude that values among certain black subcultural group members both propel them into crime and make them targets of criminal victimization. The truth may be,

TABLE 2-4

How Do the UCR and NCVS Compare?

	Uniform Crime Reports	National Crime Victimization Survey
Offenses measured	Homicide Rape Robbery (personal and commercial) Assault (aggravated) Burglary (commercial and household) Larceny (commercial and household) Motor vehicle theft Arson	— Rape Robbery (personal) Assault (aggravated and simple) Household burglary Larceny (personal and household) Motor vehicle theft
Scope	Crimes reported to the police in most jurisdictions; considerable flexibility	Crimes both reported and not reported to police; all data are available for a few large geographic areas
Collection method	Police department reports to FBI or to centralized state agencies that then report to FBI	Survey interviews; periodically measures the total number of crimes committed by asking a national sample of 49,000 households encompassing 101,000 persons age 12 and over about their experiences as victims of crime during a specified period
Kinds of information	In addition to offense counts, provides information on crime clearances, persons arrested, persons charged, law enforcement officers killed and assaulted, and characteristics of homicide victims	Provides details about victims (such as age, race, sex, education, income, and whether the victim and offender were related to each other) and about crimes (such as time and place of occurrence, whether or not reported to police, use of weapons, occurrence of injury, and economic consequences)
Sponsor	Department of Justice Federal Bureau of Investigation	Department of Justice Bureau of Justice Statistics

SOURCE: Bureau of Justice Statistics, *Report to the Nation on Crime and Justice*, 2nd ed. (Washington, D.C.: U.S. Department of Justice, 1988), p. 11.

however, that crime is more a function of geography (inner-city location) than of culture. From simple descriptive statistics, it is difficult to know which is the case.

merging Patterns of Criminal Activity

Planned revisions in both the NCVS and the UCR reflect the fact that patterns of criminal activity in the United States are changing. Georgette Bennett has termed the shift in crime patterns "crimewarps."[46] Crimewarps, says Bennett, represent major changes in both what society considers criminal and in who future criminal offenders will be. Some areas of coming change that she predicts are:[47]

✔ The decline of street crime
✔ The growth of white-collar crime
✔ Increasing female involvement in crime
✔ Increased crime commission by the elderly
✔ A shift in high crime rates from the "Frost Belt" to the "Sun Belt"
✔ Safer cities, with increasing criminal activity in rural areas
✔ The growth of high-technology crimes

The Fear of Crime

Although we may read in newspapers or in books like Georgette Bennett's that violent street crime is decreasing, we may not believe it. In fact, we may be just as afraid as ever. As Bennett has pointed out,[48] the fear of crime is often out of proportion to the likelihood of criminal victimization. Table 2-5 compares the chance of violent victimization with life chances of other serious events. For most people, the chance of accidental injury at work or at home is far greater than the chance of being criminally attacked.

The Bureau of Justice Statistics points out that "fear of crime affects many people, including some who have never been victims of crime."[49] Sources of fear are diverse. Some flow from personal experience with victimization, but most people fear crime because of dramatizations of criminal activity on television and in movies, and because of frequent newspaper and media reports of crime. Feelings of vulnerability may result from learning that a friend has been victimized or from hearing that a neighbor's home has been burglarized.

A recent survey of American voters, *The 1994 Battleground Survey*,[50] found that crime topped the list of citizens' concerns. In the words of the pollsters, "Americans say crime is the No. 1 problem facing the country today...." Crime was reported to be the respondent's "top concern" by 26 percent of all those participating in the survey—easily outdistancing reported concerns over the economy (9 percent), jobs (7 percent), unemployment (7 percent), and drugs (6 percent). Interestingly, respondents to *The 1994 Battleground Survey*, which attempts to identify "hot" political issues, appeared to separate drug-related crimes from the threat of more personal crimes such as murder, rape, and robbery. An independent *Washington Post* poll, conducted shortly after the Battleground Survey, confirmed the survey's findings, showing that 21 percent of Americans were more concerned about crime than about any other issue.[51]

Interestingly, the groups at highest risk of becoming crime victims are not the ones who experience the greatest fear of crime. The elderly and women report the greatest fear of victimization even though they are among the lowest-risk groups for violent crimes. Young males, on the other hand, who stand the greatest statistical risk of victimization, often report feeling the least fear.[52] Similarly, although people most fear violent victimization by strangers, many such crimes are committed by nonstrangers or by people known to victims by sight.

TABLE 2-5

Life Chances of Serious Events[1]—How Do Crime Rates Compare With the Rates of Other Life Events?

Events	Rate per 1,000 Adults per Year[2]
Accidental injury, all circumstances	242
Accidental injury at home	79
Personal theft	72
Accidental injury at work	58
Violent victimization	31
Assault (aggravated and simple)	24
Injury in motor vehicle accident	17
Death, all causes	11
Victimization with injury	10
Serious (aggravated) assault	9
Robbery	6
Heart disease death	4
Cancer death	2
Rape (women only)	2
Accidental death, all circumstances	0.5
Pneumonia/influenza death	0.3
Motor vehicle accidental death	0.2
Suicide	0.2
Injury from fire	0.1
Homicide/legal intervention death	0.1
Death from fire	0.03

1. These rates approximate your chances of becoming a victim of these events. More precise estimates can be derived by taking account of such factors as your age, sex, race, place of residence, and lifestyle.

2. These rates exclude children from the calculations (those under age 12–17, depending on the series). Fire injury/death data are based on the total population because no age-specific data are available in this series.

SOURCE: *Current Estimates from the National Health Interview Survey, United States, 1982,* National Center for Health Statistics; "Advance Report of Final Mortality Statistics, 1983." *Monthly Vital Statistics Report,* National Center for Health Statistics; *Estimates of the Population of the United States, by Age, Sex, and Race: 1980 to 1984.* U.S. Bureau of the Census; *The 1984 Fire Almanac,* National Fire Protection Association; and "Criminal Victimization 1984," *BJS Bulletin,* October 1985; Bureau of Justice Statistics, *Report to the Nation on Crime and Justice,* 2nd ed. (Washington, D.C.: U.S. Department of Justice, 1988), p. 24.

Women and Crime

Women Victims

Women are victimized far less frequently than are men in every major crime category other than rape.[53] When women are victimized, however, they are more likely than men to be injured.[54] Even though experiencing lower rates of victimization, it is realistic to acknowledge that a larger proportion of women than men make modifications in the way they live because of the threat of crime.[55] Reflecting the growing fear of crime now so pervasive in America, women, especially those living in cities, are increasingly careful about where they travel and the time of day they leave their homes—particularly if unaccompanied—and are often wary of unfamiliar males in a diversity of settings.

As in other crime-related areas, the popular media, special interest groups, and even the government have contributed to a certain degree of confusion about women's victimization. Very real concerns reflected in movies, television programs, and newspaper editorial pages have properly identified date rape, familial incest, spouse abuse, and the exploitation of women through social order offenses, such as prostitution and pornography, as major issues facing American society today. Testimony before Congress[56] has tagged domestic violence as the largest cause of injury to American women, and former Surgeon General Everett Koop identified violence against women by their partners as the number-one health problem facing women in America today. More recently, the 1995 murder trial of O. J. Simpson focused concerns on issues of spousal abuse and on the victimization of women by spouses and ex-husbands.

Theory Into Practice: Media Impact On the Public's Fear of Crime

Turn on nightly television in the United States on a typical day, and you will see killing after killing, frequent acts of gruesome violence, and murder and mayhem as typical prime-time fare. The same is true whether you choose to view one of the major networks, a pay-per-view channel, or a premium service such as Home Box Office, Cinemax, or Showtime. Only a few specialized forms of programming, such as the Home Shopping Network, the Disney Channel, and Public Broadcasting are relatively violence free.

Many argue that the networks and cable companies are simply giving viewers what they want. Violence (often tinged with sexuality or combined with explicit sexual behavior), because it is exciting, attracts audiences. And, of course, large audiences attract advertisers whose fees support the networks.

Not to be outdone by their highly visual counterparts, newspapers and newsmagazines depict real-life episodes of violent crime in every issue. For a year following the highly publicized murders of Nicole Brown Simpson and Ronald Goldman, for example, it was almost impossible to find a newspaper in the country that wasn't running a daily story about some aspect of the case, especially when O. J. Simpson, charged in the murders, went to trial. Even computer-based services, among them CompuServe and America Online, set up special O. J. Simpson sections to attract subscribers.

Unfortunately, what some have called the overemphasis on crime and violence now so characteristic of the media in this country, makes it extremely difficult to separate crime fiction from crime fact. If media emphasis is any guide, it would appear that the United States is awash in crime, especially violent personal crime. The impression given is that crime is likely to strike almost anyone when they least expect it—devastating their lives (should they survive) irreparably. In fact, though there are many victims of violent crime in this country, the media's preoccupation with crime and violence is much overdone. Worse still, such preoccupation had lead to an enormous fear of crime among the American public, which, for at least a substantial segment of the population, is probably misplaced.

As one social commentator points out: "Anxiety about crime grips the land but, looking at federal statistics, you have to wonder why. The FBI reports crime is merely crawling upward. Victim surveys show crime actually falling. Yet for many people, an evening stroll, an unlocked car or going alone to the mall hint at lunacy. After tucking in their children, many parents bolt the doors, check the alarms and pat the guns under their beds goodnight."[1] According to William Chambliss, past president of the American Society of Criminology, "[t]he best scientific evidence we have clearly shows there is no increase in crime or violent crime in the last 20 years....The fact is, even if the crime rate was going up, the victims who were the victims remain the victims."[2]

Realistically, crime—especially violent personal crime—though it may be on the rise, appears concentrated in certain poverty-stricken, population-dense regions of the nation. That is not to say that crime does not make an appearance in affluent neighborhoods and rural areas. It certainly does, but the nature and extent of criminal activity in such areas is a far cry from the inner-city areas where the daily threat of crime is a hard reality for most residents.

Yet, when surveys reporting the fear of crime are examined, Americans everywhere appear to be on guard. Fear of crime festers in people's minds like a specter haunting the land, and frightened residents routinely report taking self-protective steps. Statistics from the most recent *U.S. News/CNN* poll[3] on neighborhood crime, for example, show 37 percent of Americans own a gun for protection, and 45 percent think it's unsafe to let children play unsupervised where they live. Thirty-one percent of respondents also report that there are areas within a mile of their home in which they would be afraid to walk alone at night. Other surveys, however, have found that those most afraid of crime spend more time watching television than those who are less fearful[4]—lending support to the notion that media portrayals of criminal activity lead to a heightened fear of victimization.

Efforts are currently underway to reduce the degree of crime fear induced by the mass media.[5] A recent U.S. Senate hearing, for example, stressed the need for television producers and network executives to assume a socially responsible role by lowering the amount of violence in aired programming. Unfortunately, no one knows for sure whether television merely broadcasts what viewers most want to see or whether it presages and helps determine what we, as a nation, are becoming.

QUESTIONS FOR DISCUSSION

1. To what extent does television influence what people think about crime? What they do?
2. Does television help shape our culture, or does it merely reflect what we, as a nation, already are?
3. Would you support more socially responsible television programming? Why or why not? If so, how would you change the content of television shows?

1. Arlene Levinson, "America Behind Bars—Crime, Wanted: The True Crime Rate," the Associated Press online, northern edition, May 8, 1994.

2. Ibid.

3. CNN Online, the CompuServe Information Service, April 2, 1995.

4. Arthur Spiegelman, "America's Year in Crime—Enough to Scare Anyone," Reuters wire services, December 15, 1994.

5. For a good collection of articles detailing the role of the media in crime causation and social policy creation, see Ray Surette, *The Media and Criminal Justice Policy: Recent Research and Social Effects* (Springfield, Ill.: Charles C. Thomas, 1990).

When the data on women's victimization are examined closely, however, a slightly different pattern emerges. The Bureau of Justice Statistics,[57] in a detailed analysis of female victims of violent crime, found that about twice as many women who are victims of violent crimes are more likely to be victimized by strangers than by people whom they know. However, when women do fall victim to violent crime, they are far more likely to be victimized by individuals with whom they are (or have been) in intimate relationships than are men. When the perpetrators are known to them, women are most likely to be violently victimized by ex-spouses, boyfriends, and spouses (in descending order of incidence). The BJS study also found that separated or divorced women are six times more likely to be victims of violent crime than widows, four and a half times more likely than married women, and three times more likely than widowers and married men. Other findings indicated that (1) women living in central-city areas are considerably more likely to be victimized than women residing in the suburbs; (2) suburban women, in turn, are more likely to be victimized than women living in rural areas; (3) women from low-income families experience the highest amount of violent crime; (4) the victimization of women falls as family income rises; (5) unemployed women, female students, and those in the armed forces are the most likely of all women to experience violent victimization; (6) black women are victims of violent crimes more frequently than are women of any other race; (7) Hispanic women find themselves victimized more frequently than white women; and (8) women in the age range 20–24 are most at risk for violent victimization, and those aged 16–19 comprise the second most likely group of victims.

These findings show that greater emphasis needs to be placed on alleviating the social conditions that victimize women. Suggestions already under consideration call for expansion in the number of federal and state laws designed to control domestic violence, a broadening of the federal Family Violence Prevention and Services Act, federal help in setting up state advocacy offices for battered women, increased funding for battered women's shelters, and additional moneys for prosecutors and courts to develop spouse abuse units. The federal Violent Crime Control and Law Enforcement Act of 1994, whose initiatives face review by a Republican-controlled Congress, purports to meet many of these needs through a subsection entitled the "Violence Against Women Act" (VAWA). That act allocates $1.6 billion to fight violence against women. Included are funds to (1) educate police, prosecutors, and judges about the special needs of women victims; (2) encourage pro-arrest policies in cases of domestic abuse; (3) provide specialized services for female victims of crime; (4) fund battered women's shelters across the country; and (5) support rape education in a variety of settings nationwide. The law also provides for new civil rights remedies for victims of felonies motivated by gender bias and extends "rape shield law" protections to civil cases and to all criminal cases in order to bar irrelevant inquiries into a victim's sexual history.

In an insightful article built around issues in criminal justice education, Nanci Koser Wilson[58] suggests a multifaceted role for women who are interested in improving the position of women in the criminal justice system. Aspects of the role include:

1. *Women lobbying for change in the criminal justice system.* Wilson points to the success that has met women who have worked to change rape laws, police procedure in domestic violence cases, and the recognition of the plight of battered women in cases of spousal homicide.

2. *Women creating help for women outside the system.* The creation of rape crisis centers, centers for battered women, and the like all point to the possibility of women helping women through noncriminal justice channels.

3. *Women working in movements outside traditional crime areas.* Ecofeminism, peace work, and other social movements have done much to enhance the status of women in general and may work in the long run to reduce some of the factors that result in the criminal victimization of women.

4. *Women producing research from a woman's perspective.* Wilson points out that the tendency to dismiss the criminality of women because it is less frequent than that of males misses the opportunity to learn about crime in general via the model provided by women's criminality. Dismissing the criminality of women implies that the criminality of men is somehow "normal" and that other behavior patterns are less worthy of study. A gender-balanced approach to the study of crime should have something to teach us all.

5. *Women working within the traditional criminal justice system in woman-defined ways.* Women who choose police work, or who work within correctional environments, have something to contribute to both professions by virtue of the unique perspective they bring to their jobs. Because of potential benefits to the system and to themselves, women should not be expected to automatically accept traditional masculinized understandings of criminal justice roles.

Women Offenders

In 1992, Aileen Carol Wuornos, labeled by the FBI the "first textbook female serial killer,"[59] was sentenced to die in Florida's electric chair for one of seven Florida highway slayings of which she had been accused. Wuornos, 35, had been arrested a year earlier in Ocala, Florida, and charged with the murder of a man who had apparently offered her a ride as she hitchhiked through Florida. The would-be Samaritan was shot, stripped of his clothing, and dumped on a roadside, while Aileen and a female companion drove off in his car. Property belonging to all seven victims—most of whom were robbed, killed, and left naked—was found in a storage unit rented by Ms. Wuornos. One victim was a former police chief, another a security guard. All were white, middle-aged men with blue-collar jobs who were traveling alone. Each was killed with a small-caliber handgun.[60] If found guilty of all the charges that are pending, Ms. Wuornos would become the first *documented* female serial killer in decades.

In 1995, another woman, Susan Smith of Union, South Carolina, rose to prominence in the national media after she confessed to the drowning murders of her two young sons, Alex, 1, and Michael, 3. The boys died after their mother rolled their car off the end of a pier and into a lake, leaving her sons strapped in their safety seats. Smith's confession came after investigators found a letter from Smith's adulterous lover, suggesting that he felt unable to continue the relationship because of the children.

The crimes committed by Aileen Wuornos and Susan Smith, gruesome as they are, fall outside what we know of as the pattern for female criminality. Although the popular media has sometimes portrayed female criminals as similar to their male counterparts in motivation and behavior, that image is misleading. Similarly, the academic study of women's criminality has been fraught with misconceptions.

A bruised Nicole Brown Simpson after one of many alleged attacks by her husband, O. J. Simpson. According to sociologists, violence against women is perpetuated by social conditions that devalue females. Photo by Sigma.

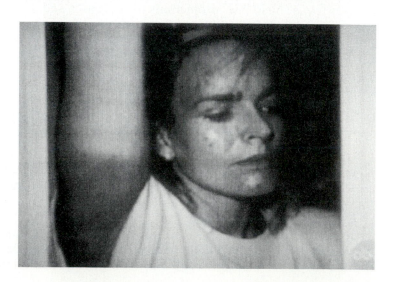

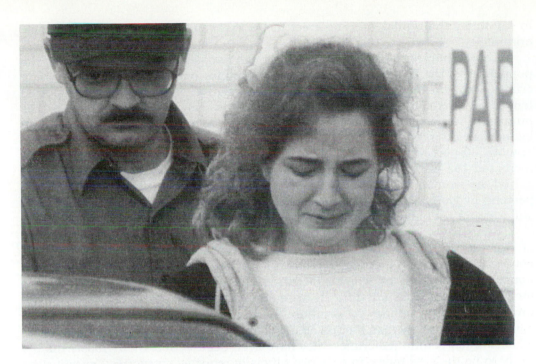

Female criminality has recently been the subject of much study. Shown above is Susan Smith, the Union, South Carolina, mother who confessed to the 1994 drowning deaths of her two sons, Alex, 1, and Michael, 3 (left photo). Smith was sentenced to life in prison although many felt that she should have received the death penalty, and others claimed that her "lenient" sentence revealed gender biases in the criminal justice system. Photos by Spartan Herald Journal/Sygma and American Fast Photo/SABA Press Photos, Inc.

One of the first writers to attempt a definitive explanation of the criminality of women was Otto Pollak. Pollak's book, *The Criminality of Women*,[61] written in 1950, suggested that women commit the same number of offenses as men—but that most of their criminality is hidden. Pollak claimed that women's roles (at the time, primarily those of homemaker and mother) served to disguise the criminal undertakings of women. He also proposed that chivalrous treatment by a male-dominated justice system acted to bias every stage of criminal justice processing in favor of women. Hence, according to Pollak, although women are just as criminal as men, they are rarely arrested, tried, or imprisoned. In fact, though the criminality of women may approach or exceed that of men in selected offense categories, it is safe to say today that Pollak was incorrect in his assessment of the degree of female criminality.

Contemporary statistics tell us that, though females compose 51 percent of the population of the United States, they are arrested for only 14 percent of all violent crimes and 27 percent of property crimes. The relatively small amount of reported female involvement in the FBI's eight major crimes can be seen in Table 2-6. The number of women committing crime appears to be increasing faster than the number of male offenders, however. Between 1970 and 1994, crimes committed by men grew by 80 percent, whereas crimes reported to have been committed by women increased 163 percent. Violent crimes by males increased 155 percent during the period; by women 282 percent.[62] Property crimes perpetrated by men grew by 60 percent; by women 150 percent. Nonetheless, as the table shows, female offenders still account for only a small proportion of all reported crimes.

Statistics on the FBI's Part II offenses tell a somewhat different story. Arrests of women for embezzlement, for example, increased by more than 160 percent between 1970 and 1994, arrests of females for drug abuse grew by 217 percent, and liquor law violations by women increased 222 percent (versus 104 percent for men).[63] Such statistics are difficult to interpret, however, since reports of female involvement in crime may reflect more the growing equality accorded women in contemporary society than they do actual increases in criminal activity. In the past, when women committed crimes, they have been dealt with less officiously than is likely to be the case today. In only two officially reported categories—prostitution and runaways—do women outnumber men in the volume of offenses committed.[64] Other crimes in which significant numbers of women (relative to men) are involved include larceny-theft (where 33 percent of reported crimes are committed by women), forgery and counterfeiting (36 percent), fraud (39 percent), and embezzlement (41 percent). These statistics dispel the myth that the female criminal in America has taken her place alongside male offenders—at least in terms of the absolute number of crimes committed.

The Economic Cost of Crime

Recently, Florida state officials came face to face with the economic consequences of criminal activity: three robbery-related killings of foreign visitors near Miami in the summer of 1993 caused many potential "Sunshine State" tourists to

---

TABLE 2-6

Male–Female Involvement in Crime: Offense Patterns Differ

Percentage of All Arrests

UCR INDEX CRIMES	MALES	FEMALES	GENDER DIFFERENCES
Murder and nonnegligent manslaughter	90.1%	9.9%	Men are more likely than women to be arrested for more serious crimes such as murder, rape, robbery, or burglary
Rape	98.9	1.1	
Robbery	90.8	9.2	
Aggravated assault	83.4	16.6	
Burglary	89.6	10.4	Arrest, jail, and prison data all suggest that a higher proportion of women than men who commit crimes are involved in property crimes such as larceny, forgery, fraud, and embezzlement, and in drug offenses
Larceny-theft	66.7	33.3	
Motor vehicle theft	87.6	12.4	
Arson	85.3	14.7	

SOURCE: Federal Bureau of Investigation, *Crime in the United States, 1994* (Washington, D.C.: U.S. Government Printing Office, 1995).

cancel their reservations and stay home. Tourism is Florida's number-one industry. In a typical year, more than 40 million tourists visit the state, including 7 million foreigners. All told, they spend more than $31 billion on their Florida vacations.

Following the highly publicized robbery-murder incidents, European tabloids labeled the "Sunshine State" the "State of Terror," and the British newspaper *Independent* called Florida "the main danger area" in the United States. Indicative of media sentiment across Europe, the London *Times* ran a cartoon picturing a revolver with a trigger shaped like the state of Florida, and Britain's largest newspaper, the *Sun*, ran a headline advising Florida tourists to "Get Your Butts Outta Here." The image portrayed by the media was one of a state and a nation where crime, and guns, are out of control. In response, Governor Chiles canceled foreign advertising, fearing that it would provoke only further cynicism. Although the tourism industry in Florida has begun to recover, the summer of 1993 showed state officials across the nation just how costly crime can be in terms of tourist dollars.

The national costs of crime are difficult to measure. The Bureau of Justice Statistics estimates the personal cost of crime (direct dollar losses to individuals, not including criminal justice system costs) at around $17.6 billion per year.[65] Robberies cost the nation about $680 million annually, burglaries nearly $4 billion, and larceny-thefts account for approximately $4.5 billion in losses per year. Not included in the Bureau's figures are the costs to crime victims of lost work, needed medical care, and the expense of new security measures they may implement. Lost work time was reported in 12 percent of aggravated assaults and 17 percent of rapes in 1992. A significant shortcoming of the BJS estimates is that they involve only dollar amounts and give no real picture of personal trauma, psychological disabilities resulting from victimization, and individual suffering caused by crime.

A more encompassing estimate is offered by the journal *Health Affairs*, which, in 1994, placed the economic cost of violent crime at $202 billion annually. This huge figure includes the costs of medical and psychological treatment services, as well as health costs associated with the lost quality of life suffered by crime victims.

The economic impact of crime is different for different groups. In 1991, for example, households reporting an annual family income of less than $7,500 suffered from twice the rate of burglary as did households reporting incomes over $50,000. In fact, as family income rose, the rate of reported burglaries steadily declined. The opposite was true of auto theft, where rates of auto vehicle theft rose in direct proportion to household income—and were three times greater for families in the highest income categories than for those in the lowest.[66]

The commercial costs of crime are substantial as well. Losses from commercial robberies (including bank robberies) and business burglaries have been put at $1.2 billion per year.[67] Frauds perpetrated against financial institutions in 1994 numbered 9,180 discovered cases with an associated dollar loss of nearly $3 billion.[68] The cost to businesses of white-collar crime are not known but are thought to be substantial. To guard against crimes by employees and members of the public, private businesses spend in excess of $21 billion per year for alarms, surveillance, and private security operations.[69]

Costs to the government for the apprehension, prosecution, and disposition of offenders, including crime prevention efforts by the police, far outstrip the known dollar losses to all criminal enterprises other than drugs. Federal criminal justice expenditures for fiscal year 1996 were in excess of $16.5 billion,[70] whereas federal, state, and local expenditures totaled more than $80 billion.[71] Nonetheless, government spending on criminal justice services amounts to only about 5 percent of all governmental expenditures. State and local governments absorb most of the costs of criminal justice–related activity.

Drugs and Crime

Drugs and crime are often found together. Drug law violations are themselves criminal, but more and more studies are linking drug abuse to other serious crimes. A study by the Rand Corporation found that most of the "violent predators" among prisoners had extensive histories of heroin abuse, often in combination with alcohol and other drugs.[72] Some cities report that a large percentage of their homicides are drug related.[73] Many property crimes are committed to sustain "habits," and the numbers of both violent and property crimes committed by drug users have been shown to be directly related to the level at which they use drugs.[74] Substance abuse may well be the most expensive of all illegal activity. The social cost of drug abuse has been estimated at nearly $60 billion per year, with half of that amount being in lost job productivity.[75] Drunk driving alone is thought to cost more than $13 billion in property losses and medical expenses yearly.[76] The link between crime and substance abuse appears strong and shows few signs of abating.

The Elderly and Crime

UCR statistics define "older offenders" as those over 55 years of age. Relative to other age groups, older offenders rarely appear in the crime statistics. Criminality seems to decline with age, suggesting that a burn-out factor applies to criminal behavior as it does to many other areas of life. In 1994, persons aged 65 and over accounted for less than 1 percent of all arrests.[77]

The types and number of crimes committed by older people, however, appear to be changing. According to the UCR, arrests of the elderly for serious crimes more than doubled between 1975 and 1994, whereas arrests in the same age category for minor crimes tended to remain about the same.[78] Overall, arrests of persons 65 and older declined by about 10 percent during the period, whereas fraud arrests jumped nearly 400 percent.[79] When elderly people are sent to prison, it is usually for violent crimes, whereas violent crimes account for far less than 50 percent of prison admissions among younger people. The population of prisoners aged 55 and over has steadily increased, having risen from 13,800 inmates nationally in mid-1988 to 25,000 by mid-1994, an increase of more than 50 percent.[80]

Some authors have interpreted these statistics to presage the growth of a "geriatric delinquent" population, freed by age and retirement from jobs and responsibilities. Such people, say these authors, may turn to crime as one way of averting boredom and adding a little spice to life.[81] Statistics on geriatric offenders, however, probably require a more cautious interpretation. They are based on relatively small numbers, and to say that "serious crime among the elderly doubled" does not mean that a geriatric crime wave is upon us. The apparent increase in criminal activity among the elderly may be because the older population in this country is growing substantially, with even greater increases expected over the next three decades. Advances in health care have increased life expectancy and have made the added years more productive than ever before. World War II "baby boomers" will be reaching their late middle years by the year 2000, and present trends in criminal involvement among the elderly can be expected to continue. Hence, it may not be that elderly individuals in this country are committing crimes more frequently than before, but rather that the greater number of elderly in the population make for a greater prevalence of crimes committed by the elderly in the official statistics.

The elderly are also victims of crime. Although persons aged 65 and older generally experience the lowest rate of victimization of any age group,[82] some aspects of serious crime against older people are worth noting. Elderly violent crime victims are more likely than younger victims to:

1. Face offenders armed with guns
2. Be victimized by total strangers
3. Be victimized in or near their homes
4. Report their victimization to the police

Older victims are also less likely to attempt to protect themselves than are younger ones. The older the victim, the greater the likelihood of physical injury.

Elderly people are victimized disproportionately if they fall into certain categories. Relative to their numbers in the elderly population, black men are overrepresented as victims. Similarly, separated or divorced persons and urban residents have higher rates of victimization than do other elderly persons. As observed earlier, older people live in greater fear of crime than do younger people even though their risk of victimization is considerably less. Elderly people, however, are less likely to take crime preventive measures than any other age group. Only 6 percent of households headed by persons over the age of 65 have a burglar alarm, and only 16 percent engrave their valuables (versus a 25 percent national average).

Hate Crimes

The American criminal justice system of the 21st century will be buffeted by the expanding power of politically oriented endemic groups with radical agendas. Domestic terrorism in the 1960s and early 1970s required the expenditure of considerable criminal justice resources. The Weathermen, Students for a Democratic Society, the Symbioneze Liberation Army, the Black Panthers, and other radical groups challenged the authority of federal and local governments. Bombings, kidnappings, and shootouts peppered the national scene.

A new era of domestic terrorism may have been ushered in with the terrorist bombing attack on the World Trade Centers in 1993, which left four dead and a 100-foot hole through four subfloors of concrete. The 1995 bombing of the Alfred P. Murrah Federal Building in Oklahoma City, Oklahoma, which killed 168 people and injured hundreds more, demonstrated just how vulnerable the United States is to such attacks. Overseas terrorists are making continued efforts to invade American population centers, and there are indicators that "sleeper agents" residing within the United States are poised to act on the command of distant authorities.

Worrisome to many enforcement agencies are underground survivalist groups with their own vision of a future America. Among them are the White Patriot Party; the Order; Aryan Nations; Posse Comitatus; the Covenant, the Sword, and the Arm of the Lord; the Ku Klux Klan; and umbrella organizations such as the Christian Conservative Church. Described variously as the radical right, neo-Nazis, skinheads, white supremacists, and racial hate groups, indications are that these groups are organized, well financed, and extremely well armed. John R. Harrell, leader of the Christian Conservative Church, preaches that the nation is on the eve of destruction. According to some authorities, Christian patriots are exhorted to stand ready to seize control of the nation before leadership can fall into the "wrong hands."[83] Such extremist groups adhere to "identity theology," a religion that claims that members of the white race are God's chosen people. Identity theology envisions an America ruled exclusively by white people under "God's law."[84]

Just as Hitler's biography *Mein Kampf* served as a call to arms for Nazis in Europe during the 1930s, a novel called *The Turner Diaries* is now used by extremist groups to map their rise to power.[85] *The Turner Diaries* describes an Aryan revolution set in the 1990s in which Jews, blacks, and other minorities are removed from positions of influence in government and society.

In 1993, eight men and women were arrested by the FBI and accused of plotting to start a race war in Los Angeles. The plot allegedly involved bombing the prominent 8,500-member First African Methodist Episcopal Church in South Central Los Angeles, spraying its members with machine-gun fire, and assassinating

Hate Crimes. Criminal offenses in which there is evidence of prejudice based on race, religion, sexual orientation, or ethnicity.

Rodney King. Other targets may have included the Reverend Al Sharpton in New York, Nation of Islam Minister Louis Farrakhan, officials of the NAACP, and members of the black rap group Public Enemy. News reports linked groups known as the Fourth Reich Skinheads, the Florida Church of the Creator, and the White Aryan Resistance.[86] In the same year, a confrontation between David Koresh's Branch Davidian followers and federal agents left 91 Davidians and 4 federal agents dead in Waco, Texas. Figure 2-5 shows the location of the various supremacist and survivalist groups in the United States.

The American justice system of today is ill-prepared to deal with the threat represented by supremacist and radical groups, although new federal antiterrorist legislation is on the horizon. Intelligence-gathering efforts focused on such groups have largely failed. Military-style organization and training are characteristic of the groups that are known, making them difficult to penetrate. The armaments at their disposal include weapons of mass destruction, which the firepower and tactical mobility of law enforcement agencies could not hope to match.

In any event, certain acrivities of supremacist groups may be constitutionally protected. Recent authors[87] suggest that statutes intended to control hate crimes may run afoul of constitutional considerations insofar as they (1) are vague, (2) criminalize thought, (3) attempt to control free speech, and (4) deny equal protection of the laws to those who wish to express their biases. In fact, in the 1992 case of *R.A.V.* v. *City of St. Paul*,[88] which involved a burning cross on the front lawn of a black family, the U.S. Supreme Court struck down a city ordinance designed to prevent the bias-motivated display of symbols or objects, such as Nazi swastikas or burning crosses. In the same year, in the case of *Forsyth County, Ga.* v. *Nationalist Movement*,[89] the Court held that a county requirement regulating parades was unconstitutional because it regulated freedom of speech —in this case, a plan by an affiliate of the Klu Klux Klan to parade in opposition to a Martin Luther King birthday celebration. In 1995, in the case of *Capitol Square Review and Advisory Board* v. *Pinette*, the Court reiterated its position, saying that KKK organizers in Ohio could legimately erect an unattended cross on the Statehouse Plaza in Columbus's Capitol

FIGURE 2-5
White supremacist groups in the United States. Source: Klanwatch Project, reprinted with permission.

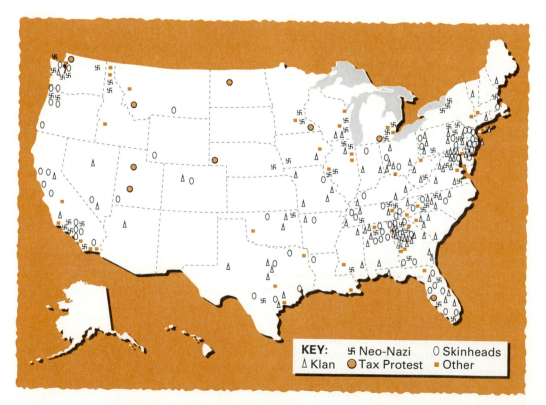

Square. However, in 1993, in the case of *Wisconsin* v. *Mitchell*,[90] the Court held that Mitchell, a black man whose severe beating of a white boy was racially motivated, could be punished with additional severity as permitted by Wisconsin law because he acted out of race hatred. The Court called the assault "conduct unprotected by the First Amendment" and upheld the Wisconsin statute saying, "[since] the statute has no 'chilling effect' on free speech, it is not unconstitutionally overbroad."

Organized Crime

Although hate groups are often internally well coordinated, criminal organizations have existed in America since before the turn of the 20th century. **Organized crime** has been defined by the Omnibus Crime Control Act of 1970 as "the unlawful activities of the members of a highly organized, disciplined association engaged in supplying illegal goods and services, including but not limited to gambling, prostitution, loansharking, narcotics, labor racketeering, and other unlawful activities of members of such organizations."[91] Contemporary organized crime groups are involved to some degree in just about every aspect of American life, but the manufacture, transportation, and sale of controlled substances has provided an especially lucrative form of illegal enterprise for many of them. A few such groups are thought to be among the largest businesslike enterprises in the world.

The Mafia, perhaps the best known criminal organization in the United States, rose to power in this country largely through its exploitation of the widespread demand for consumable alcohol during prohibition years. The Mafia, now called the Cosa Nostra, came into existence when a group of small-time hoods, largely of Italian descent, began selling "protection" and other services such as gambling and prostitution in turn-of-the-

Organized Crime. The unlawful activities of the members of a highly organized, disciplined association engaged in supplying illegal goods and services, including but not limited to gambling, prostitution, loansharking, narcotics, labor racketeering, and other unlawful activities of members of such organizations. Source: The Organized Crime Control Act of 1970.

Theory into Practice: Hate Crimes

In 1987, Glenn Miller, then-leader of the White Patriot Party in North Carolina, declared war on ZOG—the "Zionist Occupational Government"—a conspiratorial coalition that Miller and his followers believed held the true reins of power in the United States. What follows is a portion of that strongly worded original document—authentically reproduced here to include the misspellings and typographical errors found in the original. Not long after the declaration was issued, Miller was arrested and sent to prison for his part in various crimes against the government.

DECLARATION OF WAR

Dear White Patriots:

All 5,000 White Patriots are now honor bound and duty bound to pick up the sword and do battle against the forces of evil. In the name of our Aryan God, thru His beloved son, I Glenn Miller now this 6th day of April 1987 do hereby declare total war. I ask for no quarter. I will give none. I declare war against Niggers, Jews, Queers, assorted Mongrels, White Race traitors and despicable informants. We White Patriots will now begin the Race War and it will spread gloriously thru-out the nation. We will cleanse the land of

evil, corruption, and mongrels. And, we will build a glorious future and a nation in which all our People can scream proudly, and honestly, "This is our Land. This is our People. This is our God, and this we will defend." War is the only way now, brothers and sisters. ZOG has pointed the way for us. He has left us no other choice. And, so fellow Aryan Warriors strike now. Strike for your home land. Strike for your Southern honor. Strike for the little children. Strike for your wives and loved ones. Strike for sweet Mother Dixie. Strike for the 16 million innocent White babies murdered by Jew-legalized abortion and who cry out from their graves for vengeance. Strike for the millions of your People who have been raped, assaulted, and murdered by niggers and other mongrels. Strike in vengence against the Jews for all the millions of our Race slaughtered in Jew-Wars. Strike my brothers and sisters, strike, for all the outrages committed against our People...

For God, Race, Nation and Southern Honor

Glenn Miller, Leader White Patriot Party and Loyal member of "The Order"

"THE ORDER WILL LIVE SO LONG AS ONE OF US BREATHES"

century New York City. With the advent of prohibition, financial opportunities became enormous for those willing to circumvent the law, and organized gang activity spread. Soon Chicago, Detroit, Miami, San Francisco, and other major cities became gang havens. It was during this period that infamous gangsters such as Lucky Luciano and Al Capone were catapulted to the forefront of popular attention.

Today, the Cosa Nostra consists of 24 families based in various cities across the country. Their illegal take is estimated at around $60 billion per year.[92]

Families are involved in a variety of illegal activities, including drug trafficking, loan sharking, gambling, shakedowns of drug dealers, killings-for-hire, and the infiltration of various labor unions. Many run legitimate businesses as fronts for money laundering and other financial activities. Such businesses are often rife with "ghost workers," paid at high rates, but who actually do no work at all. Organized crime families will stop at little to increase their influence. Nicholas Caramandi, a former member of the Philadelphia mob led by Nicodemo Scarfo, responded to a question about how high the mob reaches into American society this way: "If politicians, doctors, lawyers, entertainment people all come to us for favors, there's got to be a reason. It's because we're the best. There are no favors we can't do."[93]

The Cosa Nostra requires new members to undergo an initiation ritual that has changed little since the days it was brought to American shores by Sicilian immigrants more than a hundred years ago. During a secretly recorded candle-lit Cosa Nostra induction ceremony recently held in Medford, Massachusetts, for example, new members were required to hold a burning picture of a Catholic saint in their cupped palms and made to swear to uphold the code of *omerta* (silence). "*Come si brucia questa santa, cosi si brucera la mia anima,*" the men repeated, which means "As burns this saint, so will burn my soul." Anyone violating the Cosa Nostra's code of silence recognizes that death is the penalty.

Crime families are hierarchically organized under a boss, and consist of a number of levels, each with varying authority. Bosses exercise their power through underbosses and lieutenants. Lieutenants pass orders along to soldiers.

CAREERS IN JUSTICE
Working as a U.S. Marshal

TYPICAL POSITIONS. U.S. marshals are involved in the following activities: (1) court security, (2) fugitive investigations, (3) personal and witness security, (4) asset seizure, (5) special operations, and (6) transportation and custody of federal prisoners.

EMPLOYMENT REQUIREMENTS: General employment requirements with the Marshals Service include (1) a comprehensive written exam, (2) a complete background investigation, (3) an oral interview, (4) excellent physical condition, and (5) a bachelor's degree or three years of "responsible experience." Applicants must be between 21 and 35 years of age and be U.S. citizens with a valid driver's license.

OTHER REQUIREMENTS: Successful applicants must complete 13 weeks of training.

SALARY: At midyear 1995, starting salary was $23,938 per year for individuals hired at GS-5 level, $29,644 per year for individuals hired at GS-7 level.

BENEFITS: Benefits include (1) 13 days of sick leave annually, (2) 2½ to 5 weeks of annual paid vacation and 10 paid federal holidays each year, (3) federal health and life insurance, and (4) a comprehensive retirement program.

DIRECT INQUIRIES TO: U.S. Marshals Service, 600 Army-Navy Drive, Arlington, Virginia 22202. Phone: (202) 307-9400.

Soldiers, the lowest level of mob operatives, are charged with directly carrying out the activities of their families. In doing so, they often make use of local community members, allowing organized crime to seamlessly integrate itself into almost any locale. Hierarchical organization has frequently allowed many Cosa Nostra higher-ups to avoid arrest and prosecution. Recently, however, federal agents armed with new statutes have been able to make inroads into many such operations. For example, John Gotti, leader of New York City's infamous Gambino crime family, was recently sent to federal prison, and 1,170 Cosa Nostra bosses, soldiers, and associates across the nation have been convicted and sentenced during the last few years.[94] Peter Milano, once boss of Los Angeles, is in prison. So, too, are leaders of Kansas City's Civella family, and a few years ago, 13 members of New England's Patriarca family were convicted of murdering one of their underbosses.

Even as the power of the Cosa Nostra wanes, other groups stand ready to take its place. There is historical precedent for such a transition. Italian-led gangs were preceded in New York City and other places by Jewish criminal organizations. One infamous Jewish gang, for example, was headed at the start of the century by Arnold Rothstein, who dreamed of becoming kingpin of all organized criminal activity in America. Ethnic succession has typified organized criminal activity. Today gangs of Hispanics, Chinese, Japanese, Vietnamese, Puerto Ricans, Mexicans, Colombians, and African Americans have usurped power traditionally held by the Cosa Nostra in many parts of the country. Similarly, evidence indicates that Russian-led and Arabic-speaking gangs have begun to move into New York and other cities.

Summary

Crime statistics provide a useful but conceptually limited approach to the social reality of crime. Statistics delineate the extent of crime according to the categories they are designed to measure, and they give a picture of victim characteristics through both self-reports and reports to the police. Today's comprehensive program of data gathering allows for a tabulation of the dollar costs of crime and permits a degree of predictability about trends in crime.

Lacking in most crime statistics, however, are any realistic appraisals of the human costs of crime. The trauma suffered by victims and survivors, the lowered sense of security experienced after victimization, and the loss of human productivity and quality of life caused by crime are difficult to gauge.

On the other side of the balance sheet, statistics fail to identify social costs suffered by offenders and their families. The social deprivation that may lead to crime, the fragmentation of private lives following conviction, and the loss of individuality that comes with confinement are all costs to society, just as they are the culturally imposed consequences of crime and failure. Except for numbers on crimes committed, arrests, and figures on persons incarcerated, today's data-gathering strategies fall far short of gauging the human suffering and wasted human potential that both causes and follows from crime.

Even where reports do provide quantitative measures, they may still fail to assess some of the objective costs of crime, including lowered property values in high-crime areas and inflated prices for consumer goods caused by the underground economy in stolen goods. White-collar crimes in particular are often well hidden and difficult to measure, yet many produce the largest direct dollar losses of any type of criminal activity.

Modern crime statistics are useful, but they do not provide the whole picture. Students of criminal justice need to be continually aware of aspects of the crime picture that fall outside official data.

Homework Due

Discussion Questions

1. What are the two major sources of crime statistics for the United States? How do they differ?
2. What can crime statistics tell us about the crime picture in America? How has that picture changed over time?
3. What are the potential sources of error in the major reports on crime? Can you depict some popular usage of those statistics that might be especially misleading?
4. Why are many crime statistics expressed as a *rate*? How does the use of crime rates improve the reporting of crime data (over a simple numerical tabulation)?
5. What is the Crime Index? Why is it difficult to add offenses to (or remove them from) the Index and still have it retain its value as a comparative tool?
6. What are the two major offense categories in Part I crimes? Are there some property crimes that might have a violent aspect? Are there any personal crimes that could be nonviolent?
7. What is the hierarchy rule in crime-reporting programs? What purpose does it serve? What do you think of the proposed modifications in the hierarchy rule?
8. What does it mean to say that a crime has been "cleared"? Can you imagine a better way of reporting clearances?

References

1. "Point of View," *The Chronicle of Higher Education*, June 10, 1992, p. A40.
2. Carol J. Castaneda, "In California, A Case of Murder and Money," *USA Today*, April 3, 1995, p. 3A.
3. As quoted in Frank Hagan, *Research Methods in Criminal Justice* (New York: Macmillan, 1982), from Eugene Webb et al., *Nonreactive Measures in the Social Sciences*, 2nd ed. (Boston: Houghton Mifflin, 1981), p. 89.
4. U.S. Bureau of Justice Statistics, *Criminal Victimization in the United States, 1985* (Washington, D.C.: U.S. Government Printing Office, 1987), p. 1.
5. Federal Bureau of Investigation, *Uniform Crime Reports for the United States, 1987* (Washington, D.C.: U.S. Government Printing Office, 1988), p. 1.
6. Hagan, *Research Methods in Criminal Justice and Criminology*.
7. Federal Bureau of Investigation, *Uniform Crime Reports for the United States, 1994* (Washington, D.C.: U.S. Government Printing Office, 1995), p. 16.
8. Federal Bureau of Investigation, *Uniform Crime Reports for the United States, 1975* (Washington, D.C.: U.S. Government Printing Office, 1976), p. 22.
9. All offense definitions in this chapter are derived from those used by the UCR reporting program and are taken from the *Uniform Crime Reports for the United States, 1994* or from *Criminal Justice Data Terminology*, 2nd ed. (Washington, D.C.: Bureau of Justice Statistics, 1981).
10. FBI, *Uniform Crime Reports, 1994*.
11. These and other statistics in this chapter are derived primarily from the *Uniform Crime Reports for the United States, 1994* (Washington, D.C.: U.S. Government Printing Office, 1995).
12. Bureau of Justice Statistics, *Report to the Nation on Crime and Justice*, 2nd ed. (Washington, D.C.: U.S. Government Printing Office, 1988), p. 4.
13. Ibid.
14. Ibid.
15. "Study: Rape Vastly Underreported," *The Fayetteville Observer-Times* (North Carolina), April 26, 1992, p. 16A.
16. Ronald Barri Flowers, *Women and Criminality: The Woman as Victim, Offender and Practitioner* (Westport, Conn.: Greenwood Press, 1987), pp. 33–36.
17. A. Nichols Groth, *Men Who Rape: The Psychology of the Offender* (New York: Plenum Press, 1979).
18. Flowers, *Women and Criminality*, p. 36.
19. "Swim Coach Guilty of Statutory Rape," *USA Today*, August 13, 1993, p. 3A.

20. *Report to the Nation on Crime and Justice*, 2nd ed., p. 5.

21. Ibid.

22. *Uniform Crime Reports, 1994*. For UCR reporting purposes, "minorities" are defined as blacks, American Indians, Asians, Pacific Islanders, and Alaskan Natives.

23. Sometimes called assault with a deadly weapon with intent to kill, or AWDWWIK.

24. *Report to the Nation on Crime and Justice*, 2nd ed., p. 6.

25. Ibid., p. 6.

26. Ibid.

27. "Yale Says Student Stole His Education," *USA Today*, April 12, 1995, p. 3A.

28. Gale Holland and Jonathan T. Lovitt, "Fertility Pioneer is Accused of Stealing Embryos," *USA Today*, May 25, 1995, p. 8A.

29. FBI, *Uniform Crime Reporting Handbook* (Washington, D.C.: U.S. Dept. of Justice, 1984), p. 28.

30. "Carjacking Case Goes to Trial," *USA Today*, April 13, 1993, p. 2A.

31. *Uniform Crime Reports, 1994*.

32. As indicated in the UCR definition of arson, *Uniform Crime Reports, 1994*.

33. *Uniform Crime Reports, 1994*.

34. Ibid., p. 5.

35. Although the old rule would have counted only one murder where a woman was raped and her husband murdered in the same criminal incident, the new rule would report both a murder and a rape.

36. "Anti-Defamation League Concerned About Incomplete 1994 FBI Hate Crime Figures," *ADL Press Release*, (Washington, D.C.: November 14, 1995).

37. For additional information, see: U.S. Department of Justice, Bureau of Justice Statistics, *Criminal Victimization in the United States, 1994* (Washington, D.C.: BJS, 1996).

38. Bureau of Justice Statistics, *Criminal Victimization in the United States, 1991* (Washington, D.C.: BJS, 1992).

39. Ibid.

40. *Report to the Nation on Crime and Justice*, 2nd ed., p. 26.

41. U.S. Department of Justice, "The Risk of Violent Crime," *BJS Special Report* (Washington, D.C.: Bureau of Justice Statistics, May 1985), p. 2.

42. Bureau of Justice Statistics, "National Crime Victimization Survey Redesign," October 30, 1994.

43. Ronet Bachman, "Violence and Theft in the Workplace," A BJS Crime Data Brief, July 1994.

44. Bureau of Justice Statistics, "Violence Between Intimates," November 1994.

45. *Report to the Nation on Crime and Justice*, 2nd ed., p. 27.

46. Georgette Bennett, *Crimewarps: The Future of Crime in America* (Garden City, N.Y.: Anchor/Doubleday, 1987).

47. Ibid.

48. Ibid., p. xiv.

49. *Report to the Nation on Crime and Justice*, 2nd ed., p. 24.

50. "Job Worries Persist, Poll Shows," *USA Today*, December 15, 1993, p. 4A, reporting on the 1994 *Battleground Survey* by the Tarrance Group and Mellman-Lazarus-Lake.

51. *Washington Post* wire services, December 20, 1993.

52. *Report to the Nation on Crime and Justice*, 2nd ed., p. 32.

53. The definition of rape employed by the UCR, however, automatically excludes crimes of homosexual rape such as might occur in prisons and jails. As a consequence, the rape of males is excluded from the official count for crimes of rape.

54. *Report to the Nation on Crime and Justice*, 2nd ed., p. 25.

55. See, for example, Elizabeth Stanko, "When Precaution Is Normal: A Feminist Critique of Crime Prevention," in Loraine Gelsthorpe and Allison Morris, *Feminist Perspectives in Criminology* (Philadelphia: Open University Press, 1990).

56. "Battered Women Tell Their Stories to the Senate," *The Charlotte Observer* (North Carolina), July 10, 1991, p. 3A.

57. Caroline Wolf Harlow, *Female Victims of Violent Crime* (Washington, D.C.: Bureau of Justice Statistics, 1991).

58. Nanci Koser Wilson, "Feminist Pedagogy in Criminology," *Journal of Criminal Justice Education*, Vol. 2, no. 2 (Spring 1991), pp. 81–93.

59. "Florida Woman Sentenced to Death," *USA Today*, February 1, 1992, p. 3A.

60. "Fla. Slayings: Men Beware," *USA Today*, December 17, 1990, p. 3A.

61. Otto Pollak, *The Criminality of Women* (Philadelphia: University of Pennsylvania Press, 1950).

62. *Uniform Crime Reports, 1970* and *1994*.

63. Ibid.

64. *Uniform Crime Reports, 1994*.

65. Patsy A. Klaus, "The Costs of Crime to Victims," A Bureau of Justice Statistics Crime Data Brief, 1994.

66. Bureau of Justice Statistics, *Criminal Victimization in the United States, 1991* (Washington, D.C.: BJS, 1992).

67. *Report to the Nation on Crime and Justice*, 2nd ed.

68. Kathleen Maguire, and Ann Pastore, eds. *Sourcebook of Criminal Justice Statistics, 1994* (Washington, D.C.: Bureau of Justice Statistics, 1995).

69. *Report to the Nation on Crime and Justice*, 2nd ed., p. 114.

70. "President Asks for 20% Growth in Justice Department Funding," *Criminal Justice Newsletter*, February 1, 1995, p. 1.

71. Ibid.

72. J. M. Chaiken and M. R. Chaiken, *Varieties of Criminal Behavior* (Santa Monica, Calif.: The Rand Corporation, 1982).

73. D. McBride, "Trends in Drugs and Death," paper presented at American Society of Criminology annual meeting, Denver, Colorado, 1983.

74. B. Johnson et al., *Taking Care of Business: The Economics of Crime by Heroin Abusers* (Lexington, Mass.: Lexington Books, 1985). See also Bernard A. Grooper, *Research in Brief: Probing the Links Between Drugs and Crime* (Washington, D.C.: National Institute of Justice, February 1985).

75. *Report to the Nation on Crime and Justice*, 2nd ed., p. 114.

76. Ibid.

77. *Uniform Crime Reports, 1994.*

78. *Uniform Crime Reports, 1975* and *1994.*

79. Ibid.

80. American Correctional Association, *1993 Directory of Juvenile and Adult Correctional Departments, Institutions, Agencies and Paroling Authorities* (Laurel, Md.: ACA, 1993).

81. Bennett, *Crimewarps*, p. 61.

82. Much of the data in this section comes from Bureau of Justice Statistics, "Elderly Crime Victims," March 1994. See also, Catherine J. Whitaker, *BJS Special Report: Elderly Victims* (Rockville, Md.: Bureau of Justice Statistics, November 1987).

83. Michael E. Wiggins, "Societal Changes and Right Wing Membership," paper presented at the Academy of Criminal Justice Sciences Annual Meeting, San Francisco, California, April 1988.

84. Richard Holden, "God's Law: Criminal Process and Right Wing Extremism in America," paper presented at the annual meeting of the Academy of Criminal Justice Sciences, San Francisco, California, April 1988.

85. Michael E. Wiggins, "Rationale and Justification for Right-Wing Terrorism: A Politico-Social Analysis of the Turner Diaries," paper presented at the annual meeting of the American Society of Criminology, Atlanta, GA, October 1986.

86. "8 Accused of Plotting Los Angles Race War," *The Austin American-Statesman*, July 16, 1993, p. A1, and "FBI: L.A. Race War Plot 'Despicable,'" *USA Today*, July 16–18, 1993, p. 1A.

87. John Kleinig, "Penalty Enhancements for Hate Crimes," *Criminal Justice Ethics* (Summer/Fall 1992), pp. 3–6.

88. *R.A.V.* v. *City of St. Paul, Minn.*, 112 S.Ct. 2538 (1992).

89. *Forsyth County, Ga.* v. *Nationalist Movement*, 112 S.Ct. 2395 (1992).

90. *Wisconsin* v. *Mitchell*, 113 S.Ct. 2194, 124 L.Ed. 2d 436 (1993).

91. The Omnibus Crime Control Act of 1970.

92. Bonnie Angelo, "Wanted: A New Godfather," *Time*, April 13, 1992, Vol. 139, no. 15, p. 30.

93. Richard Behar, "In the Grip of Treachery," *Playboy*, November 1991, Vol. 38, no. 11, p. 92.

94. William Sherman, "Kingpins of the Underworld," *Cosmopolitan*, March 1992, Vol. 212, no. 3, p. 158.

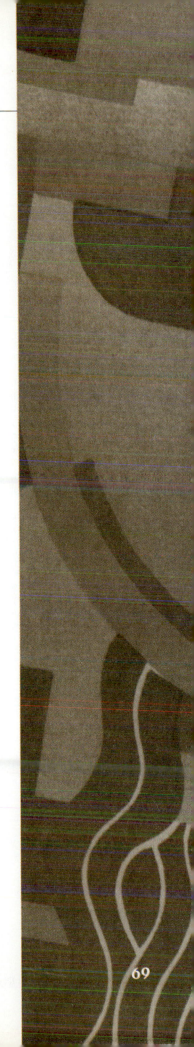

CHAPTER 3

Criminal Law

—*PHOTO BY BILL GALLERY/STOCK BOSTON*

*L*aw is the art of the good and the fair.
—ULPIAN, ROMAN JUDGE (CIRCA 200 A.D.)

*E*very law is an infraction of liberty.
—JEREMY BENTHAM (1784–1832)

*L*aw should be like death, which spares no one.
—MONTESQUIEU (1689–1755)

*N*o State shall make or enforce any law which shall abridge the privileges or immunities of citizens of the United States; nor shall any State deprive any person of life, liberty, or property, without due process of law; nor deny to any person within its jurisdiction the equal protection of the laws.
—FOURTEENTH AMENDMENT TO THE U.S. CONSTITUTION

KEY CONCEPTS

law	statutory law	case law
criminal law	penal code	precedent
civil law	tort	misdemeanor
felony	treason	espionage
inchoate offense	*mens rea*	defenses
insanity defense	self-defense	entrapment

Sources of Modern Criminal Law

Twenty years ago, as South American jungles were being cleared to make way for farmers and other settlers, a group of mercenaries brutally attacked and wiped out a small tribe of local Indians. About 20 native men, women, and children were shot or hacked to death with machetes. The Indians had refused to give up their land and would not move. At their arrest, the killers uttered something that, to our ears, sounds frightening: "How can you arrest us?" they said. "We didn't know it was illegal to kill Indians!"

These men killed many people. But they claimed they were ignorant of the fact that the law forbade such a thing. In this case, these killers didn't consider their victims "human." It may seem obvious to us that what they had done was commit murder, but to them it was something else. Nevertheless, their ignorance of the law was rejected as a defense at their trial, and they were convicted of murder. All received lengthy prison sentences.

The men in this story were hardly literate, with almost no formal education. They knew very little about the law and, apparently, even less about basic moral principles. We, on the other hand, living in a modern society with highly developed means of communications, much formal schooling, and a large workforce of professionals skilled in interpreting the law, usually know what the law *says*. But do we really know what the law *is*? The purpose of this chapter is to discuss the law both as a product of rule creation and as a guide for behavior. We will also examine criminal law in some detail, as well as discuss defenses commonly used by defendants charged with violations of the criminal law.

The Nature of Law

Practically speaking, **laws** regulate relationships between people and also between parties (such as agencies of government and individuals). Most of us would probably agree that the law is whatever legislators, through the exercise of their politically sanctioned wisdom, tell us it is. If we hold to that belief, we would expect to be able to find the law unambiguously specified in a set of books or codes. As we shall see, however, such is not always the case.

The laws of our nation, or of a state, are found in **statutory** provisions and constitutional enactments,[1] as well as in hundreds of years of rulings by courts at all levels.

Law. A rule of conduct, generally found enacted in the form of a statute, which proscribes or mandates certain forms of behavior. Statutory law is often the result of moral enterprise by interest groups which, through the exercise of political power, are successful in seeing their valuative perspectives enacted into law.

Statutory Law. Written or codified law. The "law on the books," as enacted by a governmental body or agency having the power to make laws.

John Salvi III, confers with counsel. Salvi was convicted in 1996 of the murders of two abortion clinic workers in the Boston area. His arrest and trial demonstrated that no one, regardless of his or her personal or moral convictions, is above the law. Photo courtesy of Sygma.

According to the authoritative *Black's Law Dictionary*, the word law "generally contemplates both statutory and case law."[2] If "the law" could be found entirely ensconced in written legal codes, it would be plain to nearly everyone, and we would need far fewer lawyers than we find practicing today. But some laws (in the sense of precedents established by courts) do not exist "on the books," and even those that do are open to interpretation.

Types of Law

"Criminal" and "civil" law are the best known types of modern law. However, scholars and philosophers have drawn numerous distinctions between categories of the law that rest on their source, intent, and application. Laws in modern societies can be usefully described in terms of the following groups:

- ✔ Criminal law
- ✔ Case law
- ✔ Procedural law
- ✔ Civil law
- ✔ Administrative law

This typology is helpful in understanding and thinking about the law, and we will now discuss each type of law in some detail.

Criminal Law

Fundamental to the concept of **criminal law** is the assumption that criminal acts injure not just individuals, but society as a whole. Social order, as reflected in the values supported by statute, is reduced to some degree whenever a criminal act occurs. In England (from which much of American legal tradition evolves), in olden times offenders were said to violate the "King's Peace" when they committed a crime. They offended not just their victims, but contravened the order established under the rule of the monarch. For this reason, in criminal cases, the state, as the injured party, begins the process of bringing the offender to justice. Even if the victim is dead and has no one to speak on his or her behalf, the agencies of justice will investigate the crime and file charges against the offender. Because crimes injure the fabric of society, the state becomes the plaintiff in criminal proceedings. Court cases reflect this fact by being cited as follows: *State of New York* v. *Smith* (where state law has been violated) or *U.S.* v. *Smith* (where the federal government is the injured party).

Violations of the criminal law result in the imposition of punishment. Punishment is philosophically justified by the fact that the criminal *intended* the

Criminal Law. That branch of modern law which concerns itself with offenses committed against society, members thereof, their property, and the social order.

Theory into Practice: What Does Law Do?

Laws Maintain Order in Society
Laws Regulate Human Interaction
Laws Enforce Moral Beliefs
Laws Define the Economic Environment
Laws Enhance Predictability
Laws Support the Powerful

Laws Promote Orderly Social Change
Laws Sustain Individual Rights
Laws Redress Wrongs
Laws Identify Evildoers
Laws Mandate Punishment and Retribution

harm and is responsible for it. Punishment serves a variety of purposes, which we will discuss later in Chapter 9, "Sentencing." When punishment is imposed in a criminal case, however, it is for one basic reason: to express society's fundamental displeasure with the offensive behavior.

Criminal law, which is built on constitutional principles and operates within an established set of procedures applicable to the criminal justice system, comprises both statutory and case law. Statutory law is the "law on the books." It is the result of legislative action and is often thought of as the "law of the land." Written laws exist in both criminal and civil areas, and are called codes. Once laws have been written down in organized fashion, they are called "codified." Federal statutes are compiled in the United States Code (U.S.C.). State codes and municipal ordinances are also readily available in written, or statutory, form. The written form of the criminal law is called the **penal code**.

*P*enal Code. The written, organized, and compiled form of the criminal laws of a jurisdiction.

Written criminal law in this country is of two types: substantive and procedural. Substantive law deals directly with specifying the nature of, and appropriate punishment for, particular offenses. For example, every state in our country has laws against murder, rape, robbery, and assault. Differences in the law among these various jurisdictions can be studied in detail because each offense and the punishments associated with it are available in the substantive law in written form. Procedural laws, on the other hand, specify acceptable methods for dealing with violations of substantive laws, especially within the context of a judicial setting.

Case Law

Case law (which comes from judicial decisions) is also referred to as the law of **precedent**. It represents the accumulated wisdom of trial and appellate courts (those that hear appeals) in criminal and civil cases over the years. Once a court decision is rendered, it is written down. At the appellate level, the reasoning behind the decision is recorded as well. Under the rule of precedent, this reasoning should then be taken into consideration by other courts in settling future cases.

*P*recedent. A legal principle which operates to ensure that previous judicial decisions are authoritatively considered and incorporated into future cases.

Appellate courts have considerable power to influence new court decisions at the trial level. The court with the greatest influence, of course, is the U.S. Supreme Court. The precedents it establishes are incorporated as guidelines into the process of legal reasoning by which lower courts reach conclusions.

The principle of recognizing previous decisions as precedents to guide future deliberations is called *stare decisis* and forms the basis for our modern "law of precedent." Lief H. Carter has pointed out how precedent operates along two dimensions.[3] He calls them the vertical and the horizontal. The vertical rule requires that decisions made by a higher court be taken into consideration by lower courts in their deliberations. Under this rule, state appellate courts, for example, should be expected to follow the spirit of decisions rendered by their state supreme courts.

The horizontal dimension means that courts on the same level should be consistent in their interpretation of the law. The U.S. Supreme Court, operating under the horizontal rule, for example, should not be expected to change its ruling in cases similar to those it has already decided.

Stare decisis makes for predictability in the law. Defendants walking into a modern courtroom will have the opportunity to be represented by lawyers who are trained in legal precedents as well as procedure. As a consequence, they will have a good idea of what to expect about the manner in which their trial will proceed.

Procedural Law

Procedural law is another kind of statutory law. It is a body of rules that regulates the processing of an offender by the criminal justice system. Procedural law, for example, specifies in most jurisdictions that the testimony of one party to certain "victimless crimes" cannot be used as the sole evidence against the other party. General rules of evidence, search and seizure, procedures to be followed in an arrest, and other specified processes by which the justice system operates are contained in procedural law.

As a great jurist once said, however, the law is like a living thing. It changes and evolves over time. Legislatures enact new statutory laws, and justices set new precedents, sometimes overruling established ones. Many jurisdictions today, for example, because of the changed role of women in society, are beginning to allow wives to bring charges of rape against their husbands. Similarly, wives may testify against their husbands in certain cases even though both actions are contrary to years of previously created precedents.

Civil Law

Civil law provides a formal means for regulating noncriminal relationships between persons, business and other organizations, and agencies of government. The body of civil law contains rules for contracts, divorce, child support and custody, the creation of wills, property transfers, negligence, libel, unfair practices in hiring, the manufacture and sale of consumer goods with hidden hazards for the user, and many other contractual and social obligations. When the civil law is violated, a civil suit may follow.

Civil suits seek not punishment, but compensation, usually in the form of property or monetary damages. They may also be filed in order to achieve an injunction or a kind of judicial cease-and-desist order. A violation of the civil law may be a **tort** (a breach of duty resulting in an injury to an individual), or a contract violation, but it is not a crime. Because a tort is a personal wrong, it is left to

Civil Law. That portion of the modern law which regulates contracts and other obligations involving primarily personal interests.

Tort. A private or civil wrong or injury. A breach of duty to an individual that results in harm to that person.

CAREERS IN JUSTICE
Working for the U.S. Park Police

TYPICAL POSITIONS: U.S. Park Police provide enforcement services in the nation's national parks. They also serve the nation's capitol and grounds, including federal areas within the District of Columbia. Branches include the Horse-Mounted Unit, the Criminal Investigations Branch, the Traffic Safety Unit, the Special Equipment and Tactics Team, the Motor Unit (which employs motorcycles), the Canine Unit, the Marine Unit, and the Aviation Unit.

EMPLOYMENT REQUIREMENTS: Applicant must (1) be at least 21 years of age and have not reached his or her 31st birthday by the time of appointment, (2) be a U.S. citizen, (3) possess a high school diploma or equivalent, (4) have 20/40 vision or better that is correctable to 20/20, (5) have had two years of progressively responsible experience.

OTHER REQUIREMENTS: Applicants must (1) successfully complete 18 weeks of intensive training at the Federal Law Enforcement Training Center (Glynco, Georgia) and (2) perform satisfactorily on periodic written tests.

SALARY: Starting salary in mid-1995 was $29,082.

BENEFITS: Benefits include (1) participation in the Federal Employee's Retirement System, (2) paid annual leave, (3) paid sick leave, (4) overtime that is compensated at the rate of time and one-half of regular pay, and (5) all uniforms and equipment, which are provided.

DIRECT INQUIRIES TO: U.S. Park Police, Personnel Office, 1100 Ohio Drive, S.W., Washington, D.C. 20242. Phone: (202) 619-7056.

the aggrieved individual to set the machinery of the court in motion—that is, to bring a suit.

Civil law is more concerned with assigning "blame" than it is with intent. Civil suits arising from automobile crashes, for example, do not allege that either driver intended to inflict bodily harm. Nor do they claim that it was the intent of the driver to damage either vehicle. However, when someone is injured, or property damage occurs, even in an accident, civil procedures make it possible to gauge responsibility and assign blame to one party or the other. The parties to a civil suit are referred to as the plaintiff (who seeks relief) and the defendant (against whom relief is sought).

In a tragic 1995 case, which provides a good example of civil liability, Willie King, a diabetic undergoing amputation of a leg, awoke after surgery to find that surgeons at University Community Hospital in Tampa, Florida, had removed the wrong limb. King later settled out of court, and the hospital suspended all elective surgery until it could review safety procedures.[4] In a similar case, which is ongoing at the time of this writing, and which may also result in a massive civil award, a Grand Rapids, Michigan, cancer patient had the wrong breast removed during a 1995 mastectomy.[5]

The largest civil liability action ever successfully undertaken resulted in a September 1, 1994, settlement, when a judge agreed to accept a financial agreement that had been reached between makers of silicon breast implants and members of a class action suit against the manufacturers. Under the terms of the agreement, Dow-Corning and other implant manufacturers agreed to pay members of the class of litigants more than $4.2 billion. Dow-Corning later reorganized its operations under bankruptcy protection.

Civil law pertains to injuries suffered by individuals that are unfair or unjust according to the standards operative in the social group. Breeches of contract, unfair practices in hiring, the manufacture and sale of consumer goods with hidden hazards for the user, and slanderous comments made about others have all been grounds for civil suits. Suits may, on occasion, arise as extensions of criminal action. Monetary compensation, for example, may be sought through our system of civil laws by a victim of a criminal assault after a criminal conviction has been obtained.

Willie King, shown here, agreed to settle a civil liability case out of court after doctors at University Community Hospital in Tampa, Florida, removed the wrong leg during surgery. Civil law allows individuals to pursue legal remedies when they believe they have been wronged, but not criminally victimized. Photo by Chris O'Meara, courtesy of AP/Wide World Photos.

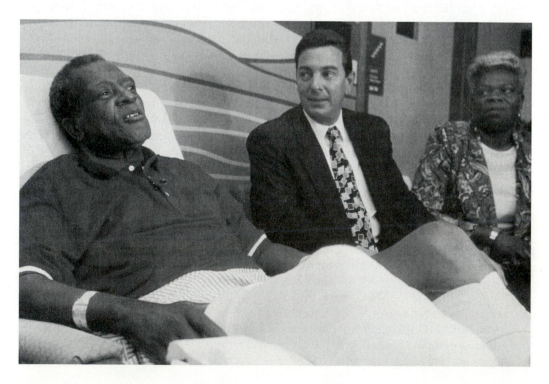

Following the murder a few years ago of Sandra Black, for example, her son and mother successfully sued *Soldier of Fortune* magazine, winning damages of $9.4 million.[6] *Soldier of Fortune* had printed a classified advertisement by a mercenary, who, as a result of the ad, eventually contracted with Mrs. Black's husband to commit the murder. In a quite different type of civil suit, Robert McLaughlin was awarded $1.9 million by a New York State Court of Claims in October 1989, after having spent six and one-half years in prison for a murder and robbery he did not commit.[7]

A 1993 civil case, which may hold considerable significance for the criminal justice system, found a Florida jury holding K-mart stores liable for selling a gun to a drunken man. The buyer, Thomas W. Knapp, later used the weapon to shoot his girlfriend, Deborah Kitchen, in the neck—leaving her permanently paralyzed. K-mart was ordered to pay Kitchen $11 million, sending a message to gun retailers across the nation. In 1995, in what may eventually involve a far more massive settlement and have wide-reaching implications, a San Francisco judge ruled that a lawsuit brought by a widow of a man slain by gunfire was based on solid legal principles and could proceed.[8] At issue was whether the handgun maker, Miami-based Navegar, Incorporated, could be sued under a legal theory that holds manufacturers liable for injuries caused by their products. In this case, Michelle Scully sued the gun manufacturer after her husband, John, was killed by an assailant who opened fire on workers in a California law office in 1993. As the shooting started, John Scully threw himself over his wife and shielded her with his body. Some criticized the judge's ruling, saying that it opened a Pandora's box of potential suits against manufacturers of all kinds of products—since lawsuits targeting products that are not defective and that function precisely as intended might result in suits against automobile manufacturers, makers of alcohol, tobacco, and high-cholesterol foods, and even against companies that make knives, gasoline, candles, and other flammable materials when irresponsible individuals choose to use those products to harm others.

Criminal action, not otherwise excusable, may even be grounds for a civil suit by the offender. In 1992, for example, a civil jury awarded $2.15 million to convicted murderer William Freeman and his family. Freeman, a former assistant chief of police from Fort Stockton, Texas, is serving a life term in prison for killing his friend, Donnie Hazelwood. A jury agreed with Freeman's claim that the sleeping pill Halcion altered his personality and caused him to kill Hazelwood.[9]

Some claim that civil suits have taken on the characteristics of a lottery—offering instant riches to those "lucky" enough to win them. In a typical year, 100 million lawsuits are filed in this country—approximately one for every two living Americans. Although most of these suits, involving divorces, wills, and bad debts, for example, are legitimate, some are simply shots in the dark, taken by lawsuit-happy citizens hoping to win at least some limited type of fame or fortune through the courts. It is becoming increasingly clear to critics of the current system that American civil courts can unwittingly serve the get-rich-quick schemes of the greedy and those who feign injury.

The largest civil suit ever filed, for example, was brought by Allen and Kathy Wilson in 1994.[10] The Wilsons filed suit in Carson City, Nevada, asking the state to pay them $657 trillion—the amount the couple say they are owed on a $1,000 state-issued bond purchased in 1865. The Wilsons bought the bond in 1992 from a widow who had inherited it from her husband. They calculated the amount they claim they are owed by compounding interest at an annual rate of 24% for 130 years. The state of Nevada maintains that time has run out for redeeming the bond.

Legislation now before the U.S. Congress would place punitive damage limits on civil suits brought in federal and state courts. Under the proposed Civil Justice Fairness Act of 1995, punitive damage awards (those intended to compensate for mental anguish, degradation, shame, or hurt feelings suffered by the plaintiff) would be held to a maximum of $250,000 or three times the plaintiff's economic damages from such things as lost income and medical expenses—whichever is greater—whereas compensatory damages would continue to be awarded only for the amount of damages the plaintiff could prove were actually incurred.[11] Under the proposed act, punitive damages could be awarded only if there was clear and convincing evidence that the defendant flagrantly disregarded the safety of others. Currently, many states award punitive damages when jurors determine that the chances were better than 50 percent that the defendant acted with gross negligence (where gross negligence is defined as "the intentional failure to perform a manifest duty in reckless disregard of the consequences as affecting the life or property of another"[12]). Opponents of the federal initiative argue that limits on punitive damages are inherently unfair and claim that federal restrictions on suits filed in state courts illegally preempt state authority over such matters.

Administrative Law

Administrative law refers to the body of *regulations* that have been created by governments to control the activities of industry, business, and individuals. Tax laws, health codes, restrictions on pollution and waste disposal, vehicle registration, building codes, and the like are examples of administrative law.

Other administrative laws cover practices in the areas of customs (imports/exports), immigration, agriculture, product safety, and most areas of manufacturing. Modern individualists claim that overregulation characterizes the American way of life although they are, in turn, criticized for failing to adequately recognize the complexity of modern society. Overregulation has also been used on occasion as a rallying cry for political hopefuls who believe that many Americans wish to return to an earlier and simpler form of free enterprise.

Although the criminal law is, for the most part, separate from administrative regulations, the two may overlap. For instance, the rise in organized criminal activity in the area of toxic waste disposal has led to criminal prosecutions in several states. Denial of civil rights is another area that may lead to criminal sanctions through the federal system of laws.

Administrative agencies will sometimes arrange settlements that fall short of court action but which are considered binding on individuals or groups who have not lived up to the intent of federal regulations. Education, environmental protection, and discriminatory hiring practices are all areas in which settlements have been employed.

eneral Categories of Crime

Violations of the criminal law can be of many different types and can vary in severity. In this section, we will discuss the following five categories of violation:

✔ Misdemeanors
✔ Felonies
✔ Offenses
✔ Treason
✔ Inchoate offenses

Misdemeanor. An offense punishable by incarceration, usually in a local confinement facility, for a period of which the upper limit is prescribed by statute in a given jurisdiction, typically limited to a year or less.

Misdemeanors

Violations of the criminal law can be more or less serious. **Misdemeanors** are relatively minor crimes, consisting of offenses such as petty theft (the theft of items of little worth), simple assault (in which the victim suffers no serious injury), breaking and entering, the possession of burglary tools, disorderly conduct, disturbing

CAREERS IN JUSTICE

Working for the U.S. Customs Service

TYPICAL POSITIONS: Criminal investigator, special agent, customs inspector, canine enforcement officer, and import specialist. Support positions include intelligence research specialist, computer operator, auditor, customs aide, investigative assistant, and clerk.

EMPLOYMENT REQUIREMENTS: Applicants must (1) be U.S. citizens, (2) pass an appropriate physical examination, (3) pass a personal background investigation, (4) submit to urinalysis for the presence of controlled substances, (5) have at least three years of work experience, and (6) be under 35 years of age. Appointment at the GS-7 level also requires (1) one year of specialized experience (that is, "responsible criminal investigative or comparable experience"), (2) a bachelor's degree with demonstration of superior academic achievement (a 3.0 grade point average in all courses completed at the time of application, or a 3.5 grade point average for all courses in the applicant's major field of study, or rank in the upper third of the applicant's undergraduate class, or membership in a national honorary scholastic society), or (3) one year of successful graduate study in a related field.

OTHER REQUIREMENTS: Applicants must be (1) willing to travel frequently, (2) able to work overtime, (3) capable of working under stressful conditions, and (4) willing to carry weapons and able to qualify regularly with firearms.

SALARY: Mid-1995, customs inspector: GS-5 $19,407, GS-7 $24,038; customs investigator: GS-5 $23,938, GS-7 $29,644.

BENEFITS: Benefits include (1) 13 days of sick leave annually, (2) 2½ to 5 weeks of annual paid vacation and 10 paid federal holidays each year, (3) federal health and life insurance, and (4) a comprehensive retirement program.

DIRECT INQUIRIES TO: Office of Human Resources, U.S. Customs Service, 1301 Constitution Ave., Room 220, Washington, D.C. 20229. Phone: (202) 634-2534.

---

the peace, filing a false crime report, and writing bad checks (though the amount for which the check is written may determine the classification of this offense).

In general, misdemeanors are thought of as any crime punishable by a year or less in prison. In fact, most misdemeanants receive suspended sentences involving a fine and supervised probation. If an "active sentence" is received for a misdemeanor violation of the law, it probably will involve time in a local jail, perhaps on weekends, rather than imprisonment in a long-term facility. Some misdemeanants have recently been sentenced to community service activities, requiring them to do such things as wash school buses, paint local government buildings, or clean parks and other public areas.

Normally, a police officer cannot arrest a person for a misdemeanor unless the crime was committed in the officer's presence. If the in-presence requirement is missing, the officer will need to seek an arrest warrant from a magistrate or other judicial officer. Once a warrant has been issued, the officer may proceed with the arrest.

Felonies

Felonies are serious crimes. The felony category includes crimes such as murder, rape, aggravated assault, robbery, burglary, and arson. Under common law, felons could be sentenced to death or have their property confiscated. Many felons receive prison sentences although the potential range of penalties can

Felony. A criminal offense punishable by death or by incarceration in a prison facility for at least a year.

include anything from probation and a fine to capital punishment in many jurisdictions. The federal government and many states have moved to a scheme of classifying felonies, from most to least serious, using a number or letter designation. The federal system,[13] for example, for purposes of criminal sentencing, assigns a score of 43 to first-degree murder, whereas the crime of theft is rated only a "base offense level" of 4. Attendant circumstances and the criminal history of the offender are also considered in sentencing decisions.

Because of differences between the states, a crime classified as a felony in one part of the country may be a misdemeanor in another. This is especially true of drug law violations and certain other social order crimes such as homosexuality, prostitution, and gambling.

People who have been convicted of felonies usually lose certain privileges. Some states make conviction of a felony and incarceration grounds for uncontested divorce. Others prohibit offenders from running for public office or owning a firearm, and exclude them from some professions such as medicine, law, and police work.

Offenses

A third category of crime is the offense. Offenses are minor violations of the law such as jaywalking, spitting on the sidewalk, littering, and certain traffic violations, including the failure to wear a seat belt. Another word used to describe offenses is "infraction." People committing infractions are typically ticketed and released, usually upon a promise to later appear in court. Court appearances may often be waived through payment of a small fine, which is often mailed in.

Treason

Felonies, misdemeanors, offenses, and the people who commit them constitute the daily work of the justice system. Special categories of crime, however, exist and should be recognized. They include treason and espionage.

Treason has been defined as "the act of a U.S. citizen's helping a foreign government to overthrow, make war against, or seriously injure the United States."[14] **Espionage**, an offense akin to treason, refers to the "gathering, transmitting or losing"[15] of information related to the national defense in such a manner that the information becomes available to enemies of the United States and may be used to their advantage. In 1994, in what may be the last widely publicized incident of espionage of the cold war period, CIA agent Aldrich Hazen Ames and his wife, Rosario, were arrested and charged with conspiracy to commit espionage in a plot to sell U.S. government secrets to the Russian KGB. The Ameses allegedly told their Russian handlers of CIA operatives within the former Soviet Union and revealed the extent of American knowledge of KGB plans. Their activities had apparently gone undetected for nearly a decade. Following arrest, the Ameses pleaded guilty to charges of espionage and tax fraud. Aldrich Ames was sentenced to life in prison; his wife received a five-year term.

Treason and espionage may be committed for personal gain (the Ames's received millions of dollars from the Russians for secrets they sold) or for ideological reasons, or both. They are crimes only under federal law and are often regarded as the most serious of felonies.

Inchoate Offenses

Another special category of crime is called inchoate. The word *inchoate* means incomplete or partial, and **inchoate offenses** are those that have not yet been fully carried out. Conspiracies are an example. When a person conspires to commit a crime, any action undertaken in furtherance of the conspiracy is generally regarded as a sufficient basis for arrest and prosecution. For instance, a woman who

Treason. "A U.S. citizen's actions to help a foreign government overthrow, make war against, or seriously injure the United States." Source: Daniel Oran, *Oran's Dictionary of the Law* (St. Paul, Minn.: West Publishing, 1983).

Espionage. The "gathering, transmitting, or losing" of information related to the national defense in such a manner that the information becomes available to enemies of the United States and may be used to their advantage. Source: Henry Campbell Black, Joseph R. Nolan, and Jacqueline M. Nolan-Haley, *Black's Law Dictionary*, 6th ed. (St. Paul, Minn.: West Publishing, 1990), p. 24.

Inchoate Offense. One not yet completed. Also, an offense which consists of an action or conduct which is a step toward the intended commission of another offense.

intends to kill her husband may make a phone call in order to find a "hit man" to carry out her plan. The call itself is evidence of her intent and can result in her imprisonment for conspiring to murder.

Not all conspiracy statutes require actions in furtherance of the "target crime" before an arrest can be made. Technically speaking, crimes of conspiracy can be seen as entirely distinct from the crimes that are contemplated by the conspiracy. So, for example, in 1994,[16] the U.S. Supreme Court upheld the drug-related conviction of Reshat Shabani when it ruled that in the case of certain antidrug laws[17] "it is presumed that Congress intended to adopt the common law definition of conspiracy, which does not make the doing of any act other than the act of conspiring a condition of liability...." Hence, according to the Court, "the criminal agreement itself," even in the absence of actions directed toward realizing the target crime, can be grounds for arrest and prosecution.

Another type of inchoate offense is the attempt. Sometimes an offender is not able to complete the crime. Homeowners may arrive just as a burglar is beginning to enter their residence. The burglar may drop his tools and run. Even so, in most jurisdictions, this frustrated burglar can be arrested and charged with attempted burglary.

General Features of Crime

From the perspective of Western jurisprudence, all crimes can be said to share certain features, and the notion of crime itself can be said to rest on such general principles. Taken together, these features, which are described next, comprise the legal essence of the concept of crime.

The Criminal Act

A necessary first feature of any crime is some act in violation of the law. Such an act is termed the *actus reus* of a crime. The term means a "guilty act." Generally, a person must commit some act before he or she is subject to criminal sanctions. Someone who admits (perhaps on a TV talk show) that he or she is a drug user, for example, cannot be arrested on that basis. To *be something* is not a crime—to *do something* is. In the case of the admitted drug user, police who heard the admission might begin gathering evidence to prove some specific law violation in that person's past, or perhaps they might watch that individual for future behavior in violation of the law. An arrest might then occur. If it did, it would be based on a specific action in violation of the law pertaining to controlled substances.

Vagrancy laws, popular in the early part of the 20th century, have generally been invalidated by the courts because they did not specify what act violated the law. In fact, the *less* a person did, the more vagrant they were.

An *omission to act*, however, may be criminal where the person in question is required by law to do something. Child-neglect laws, for example, focus on parents and child guardians who do not live up to their responsibilities for caring for their children.

Threatening to act can itself be a criminal offense. Telling someone, "I'm going to kill you," might result in an arrest based on the offense of "communicating threats." Threatening the President of the United States is taken seriously by the Secret Service, and individuals are regularly arrested for boasting about planned violence to be directed at the president.

Attempted criminal activity is also illegal. An attempt to murder or rape, for example, is a serious crime even though the planned act was not accomplished.

Conspiracy statutes were mentioned earlier in this chapter. When a conspiracy unfolds, the ultimate act that it aims to bring about does not have to occur for the parties to the conspiracy to be arrested. When people plan to bomb a public building, for example, they can be legally stopped before the bombing. As soon as they take steps to "further" their plan, they have met the requirement for an act. Buying explosives, telephoning one another, or drawing plans of the building may all be actions in "furtherance of the conspiracy."

Similar to conspiracy statutes are many newly enacted antistalking laws. Antistalking statutes are intended to prevent harassment and intimidation, even when no physical harm occurs. According to the U.S. Senate's Judiciary Committee, "there are 200,000 people in the United States who are currently 'stalking' someone...."[18] It is estimated that half of those being stalked are celebrities. Stalkers often strike after their victims have unsuccessfully complained to authorities about stalking-related activities such as harassing phone calls and letters. Antistalking statutes, however, still face a constitutional hurdle of attempting to prevent people not otherwise involved in criminal activity from walking and standing where they wish, and from speaking freely. Ultimately, the U.S. Supreme Court will probably have to decide the legitimacy of such statutes.

Mens Rea

Mens Rea. The state of mind which accompanies a criminal act. Also, guilty mind.

Mens rea is the second component of crime. It literally means "guilty mind" and recognizes a mental component to crime. The modern interpretation of *mens rea*, however, does not focus so much on whether a person feels guilty about his or her act—but rather looks to whether or not the act was intended. As the famous Supreme Court Justice Oliver Wendell Holmes once wrote, "even a dog distinguishes between being stumbled over and being kicked."[19]

The idea of *mens rea* has undergone a gradual evolution during recent centuries such that today the term can be generally described as signifying *blameworthiness*. The question asked, at least theoretically, in criminal prosecutions, is whether or not the person charged with an offense *should be blamed* and held accountable for his or her actions.

Mens rea is said to be present when a person *should have known better*, even if the person did not directly intend the consequences of his or her action. A person who acts recklessly, and thereby endangers others, may be found guilty of a crime when harm occurs even though no negative consequences were intended. For example, a mother who left her 15-month-old child alone in the tub can be later prosecuted for negligent homicide if the child drowns.

It should be recognized, however, that negligence in itself is not a crime. Negligent conduct can be evidence of crime only when it falls below some acceptable standard of care. That standard is today applied in courts through the fictional creation of a *reasonable person*. The question to be asked in a given case is whether or not a reasonable person, in the same situation, would have known better, and acted differently, than the defendant. The reasonable person criterion provides a yardstick for juries faced with thorny issues of guilt or innocence.

Concurrence

The concurrence of act and intent is the third component of crime. A person may intend to kill a rival, for example. As she drives to the intended victim's house, gun in hand, fantasizing about how she will commit the murder, the victim may be crossing the street on the way home from grocery shopping. If the two accidentally collide, and the intended victim dies, there has been no concurrence of act and intent.

Some scholars contend that the three features of crime that we have just outlined are sufficient to constitute the concept of crime. Other scholars, however, see modern Western law as more complex. They argue that four additional principles are necessary, including: (1) a harm, (2) a causal relationship between the act and the harm, (3) the principle of legality, and (4) the principle of punishment.

Harm

A harm occurs in any crime although not all harms are crimes. When a person is murdered or raped, harm can clearly be identified. Some crimes, however, have come to be called "victimless." Perpetrators maintain that they are not harming anyone in committing such crimes. Rather, they say, the crime is pleasurable. Prostitution, gambling, homosexuality, "crimes against nature" (sexual deviance), and drug use are but a few crimes classified as victimless. People involved in such crimes will argue that, if anyone is being hurt, it is only they. What these offenders fail to recognize, say legal theorists, is the social harm caused by their behavior. Areas afflicted with chronic prostitution, drug use, sexual deviance, and illegal gambling usually will find property values falling, family life disintegrating, and other, more traditional crimes increasing as money is sought to support the "victimless" activities and law-abiding citizens flee the area.

Causation

Causation refers to the fact that a clear link needs to be identifiable between the act and the harm occasioned by the crime. A classic example of this principle involves assault with a deadly weapon with intent to kill. If a person shoots another, but the victim is seriously injured and not killed, the victim might survive for a long time in a hospital. Death may occur, perhaps a year later, because pneumonia sets in, or because blood clots form in the injured person from lack of activity. In such cases, defense attorneys will likely argue that the defendant did not cause the death, but rather the death occurred because of disease. If a jury agrees with the defense's claim, the shooter may go free or be found guilty of a lesser charge, such as assault.

Legality

The principle of legality is concerned with the fact that a behavior cannot be criminal if no law exists that defines it as such. It is all right to drink beer, if you are of drinking age, because there is no statute "on the books" prohibiting it. During prohibition times, of course, the situation was quite different. (In fact, some parts of the United States are still "dry," and the purchase or public consumption of alcohol can be a law violation regardless of age.) The principle of legality also includes the notion that a law cannot be created tomorrow that will hold a person legally responsible for something he or she does today. These are called *ex post facto* laws. Laws are binding only from the date of their creation, or from some future date at which they are specified as taking effect.[20]

Punishment

Finally, the principle of punishment says that no crime can be said to occur where punishment has not been specified in the law. Larceny, for example, would not be a crime if the law simply said, "It is illegal to steal." Punishment needs to be specified so that, if a person is found guilty of violating the law, sanctions can be lawfully imposed.

lements of a Specific Criminal Offense

Although we can discuss the principles that constitute the general notion of crime, we can also examine individual statutes in order to see what specific elements comprise a given crime. Written laws specify exactly what conditions are necessary for a person to be charged in a given instance of crime, and they do so for every particular offense. The crime of first-degree murder, for example, in almost every jurisdiction in the United States involves four quite distinct elements:

1. An unlawful killing
2. Of a human being
3. Intentionally
4. With planning (or "malice aforethought")

The elements of any specific crime are the *statutory minimum* without which that crime cannot be said to have occurred. In any case that goes to trial, the task of the prosecution is to prove that all the elements were indeed present and that the accused was ultimately responsible for producing them.

The *Corpus Delicti* of a Crime

When all the needed elements are present, we say that the *corpus delicti* of a crime has been established. *Corpus delicti* is a Latin term that refers to the "body of the crime" and means the lawful body or substance, or legal foundation, of the offense itself. It does *not* mean the body of the victim, as is sometimes thought. For a criminal definition to be imposed upon a social situation (that is, in order to be able to say that a particular crime has occurred), it is necessary that the body of the crime be established. The specific statutory elements that constitute a particular type of crime must be shown to be present. *Black's Law Dictionary* puts it another way: "[t]he corpus delicti [of a crime] is the fact of its having been actually committed."[21]

The Example of First-Degree Murder

Every statutory element in a given instance of crime serves some purpose and is necessary. The crime of first-degree murder, as mentioned, includes "an unlawful killing." Even if all the other elements of first-degree murder are present, the act may still not be first-degree murder if the first element has not been met. In a wartime situation, for instance, killings of human beings occur. They are committed with planning and sometimes with malice. They are certainly intentional. Yet killing in war is not unlawful, so long as the belligerents wage war according to international conventions.

The second element of first-degree murder specifies that the killing must be of a "human being." People kill all the time. They kill animals for meat, they hunt, and they practice euthanasia on aged and injured pets. Even if the killing of an animal is planned and involves malice (perhaps a vendetta against a neighborhood dog that barks throughout the night), it does not constitute first-degree murder. Such a killing, however, may violate statutes pertaining to cruelty to animals.

The third element of first-degree murder, "intentionality," is the basis for the defense of accident. An unintentional killing is not first-degree murder although it may violate some other statute.

Finally, murder has not been committed unless "malice" is involved. There are different kinds of malice. Second-degree murder involves malice in the sense of hatred or spite. A more extreme form of malice is necessary for a finding of first-degree murder. Sometimes the phrase used to describe this type of feeling is "malice aforethought." This extreme kind of malice can be demonstrated by showing that planning was involved in the commission of the murder. Often, first-degree murder is described as "lying in wait," a practice that shows that thought and planning went into the illegal killing.

Whether any particular behavior meets the specific statutory minimums to qualify as a crime may be open to debate. A few years ago, for example, Adam Brown, 30, of Roseburg, Oregon, was charged with attempted first-degree murder for having knowingly exposed five children to the AIDS virus when he allegedly had unprotected sex with them. Mr. Brown, a lay minister, was informed that he had tested positive for the AIDS virus more than a year prior to the incidents. Brown was also charged with sodomy, rape, sexual penetration with a foreign object, and reckless endangerment.[22]

A charge of second-degree murder in most jurisdictions would necessitate proving that a voluntary (or intentional) killing of a human being took place—although such a "crime of passion" may have been committed without the degree of malice necessary for it to be classified as first degree. Third-degree murder, or manslaughter, can be defined simply as the unlawful killing of a human being. Not only is malice lacking in third-degree murder cases, but the killer may not have even intended that any harm come to the victim. Third-degree murder statutes, however, frequently necessitate some degree of negligence on the part of the killer, and charges such as negligent homicide may result from automobile accidents resulting in death in which the driver did not exercise due care. When legally defined "gross negligence" (involving a wanton disregard for human life) is present, however, some jurisdictions permit the offender to be charged with a more serious count of murder.

In 1995, for example, in the case of Karin Smith, a grand jury returned a homicide indictment against a laboratory doctor and technician for a fatal misdiagnosis.[23] The laboratory workers had misread a Pap smear performed on Smith, returning a clean bill of health to the doctor in charge of her care. Smith died on March 8, 1995, at age 29 from cervical cancer that had spread throughout her body. Experts testifying before a grand jury said that evidence of the presence of cancer was "unequivocal" in slides from Pap smears done on Smith in 1988 and 1989—but that the laboratory which received the sample tissue had misread the test results. The prosecutor in the case claimed that laboratory personnel had demonstrated a wanton disregard for human life when they "failed to install random controls to check the quality of the Pap smear analysis; [a]nd showed indifference toward professional standards and the need for continuing education."[24]

Although most people think that homicide charges are brought primarily against those who intend to kill, the recent trend in charging negligent medical personnel with murder is evidence that the machinery of the criminal justice system is being increasingly applied outside its traditional sphere. About the time of the Smith case, for example, Denver anesthesiologist, Dr. Joseph J. Verbrugge, Sr., was charged with manslaughter in the death of an 8-year-old boy undergoing ear surgery.[25] Police investigators said the doctor had fallen asleep during the surgery, allowing the boy to receive a lethal dose of anesthetic. Also in 1995, Dr. Gerald Einaugler of New York was ordered to spend 52 weekends in jail for causing the death of a nursing home patient when he mistook a dialysis tube for a feeding tube, and pumped food into the patient's kidneys;[26] and Dr. David Benjamin faced a possible life prison sentence after being convicted of murder in the death of a woman who went to him for an abortion. On his August 8, 1995, conviction, Dr. Benjamin became the first doctor in New York state to be found guilty of murder for the medical mistreatment of a patient.[27] The patient, Guadalupe Negron, bled to death following a bungled abortion in the doctor's storefront clinic.

Types of Defenses to a Criminal Charge

When a person is charged with a crime, he or she frequently offers some defense. Our legal system has generally recognized three broad categories of **defenses**: personal, situational, and procedural. A number of innovative defense strategies that have emerged in recent years can also be identified. Table 3-1 lists both traditional and innovative defenses. We will discuss each in the pages that follow.

Defenses. (To a criminal charge) include claims based on personal, special, and procedural considerations that defendants should not be held accountable for their actions even though they may have acted in violation of the criminal law.

Personal Defenses

Personal defenses are based on some characteristic of the individual who is charged with the crime. They include the following.

Age

Age can offer a good defense to a criminal charge, and the defense of "infancy"—as it is known in legal jargon—has its roots in the ancient belief that children cannot reason logically until around the age of 7. Early doctrine in the Christian church sanctioned that belief by declaring that rationality develops around the age of 7. As a consequence, only children past that age could be held responsible for their crimes.

The defense of infancy today has been expanded to include people well beyond the age of 7. Many states set the 16th birthday as the age at which a person becomes an adult for purposes of criminal prosecution. Others use the age of 14, and still others 18. When a person below the age required for adult prosecution commits a "crime," it is termed a *juvenile offense*. He or she is not guilty of a criminal violation of the law by virtue of youth.

In most jurisdictions, children below the age of 7 cannot be charged even with juvenile offenses, no matter how serious their actions may appear to others. However, in a rather amazing 1994 case, prosecutors in Cincinnati, Ohio, charged a 12-year-old girl with murder after she confessed to drowning her toddler cousin 10 years previously. The cousin, 13-month-old Lamar Howell, drowned in 1984 in a bucket of bleach mixed with water. Howell's drowning had been ruled an accidental

Age 18 is considered as an adult. Juvenile can be wave to adult from age 14-18 depending on the crime.

death until his cousin came forward. In discussing the charges with the media, Hamilton (Ohio) County prosecutor Joe Deters admitted that the girl could not be prosecuted. "Frankly," he said, "anything under 7 cannot be an age where you form criminal intent...."[28] The prosecution's goal, claimed one of Deters's associates, was simply to "make sure she gets the counseling she needs."

Insanity

Insanity is the second form of personal defense. It is important to realize that, for purposes of the criminal law, insanity is a legal definition and not a psychiatric one. Legal definitions of insanity often have very little to do with psychological or psychiatric understandings of mental illness. Legal insanity is a concept developed over time to meet the needs of the judicial system in assigning guilt or innocence to particular defendants. It is not primarily concerned with understanding the origins of mental pathology or with treatment, as is the idea of mental illness in psychiatry. As a consequence, medical conceptions of mental illness do not always fit well into the legal categories created by courts and legislators to deal with the phenomenon. The differences between psychiatric and legal conceptualizations of insanity often lead to disagreements among expert witnesses who, in criminal court, may appear to provide conflicting testimony on the sanity of a defendant.

THE MCNAUGHTEN RULE Prior to the 19th century, the insanity defense was nonexistent. Insane people who committed crimes were punished in the same way as other law violators. It was Daniel McNaughten (also spelled M'Naghten), a woodworker from Glasgow, Scotland, who, in 1844, became the first person to be found not guilty of a crime by reason of insanity. McNaughten had tried to assassinate Sir Robert Peel, the British prime minister. He mistook Edward Drummond, Peel's secretary, for Peel himself, and killed Drummond instead. At his trial, defense attorneys argued that McNaughten suffered from vague delusions centered on the idea that the Tories, a British political party, were persecuting him. Medical testimony at the trial agreed with the assertion of McNaughten's lawyers that he didn't know what he was doing at the time of the shooting. The judge accepted McNaughten's claim, and the insanity defense was born. The McNaughten rule, as it has come to be called, was defined later by the courts and still plays a major role in determining insanity in criminal prosecutions in 15 states today.[29]

The McNaughten rule holds that *people are not guilty of a crime if, at the time of the crime, they either didn't know what they were doing, or didn't know that what they were doing was wrong.* The inability to distinguish right from wrong must be the result of some mental defect or disability. The McNaughten case established a

---

TABLE 3-1

Types of Defenses

Personal	Situational	Procedural	Innovative
Age	Self-defense, including:	Double jeopardy	Black rage
Insanity	Defense of others	*Collateral estoppel*	Urban survival
Involuntary intoxication	Defense of home	Selective prosecution	syndrome
Unconsciousness	Duress	Denial of a speedy trial	Abuse
Premenstrual stress syndrome	Entrapment	Prosecutorial misconduct	Police fraud
Other biological defenses	Accident		
	Mistake		
	Necessity		
	Provocation		
	Consent		
	Alibi		

rule for the determination of insanity that is still followed in many U.S. jurisdictions today. However, in most states, the burden of proving insanity falls on the defendant. Just as defendants are assumed innocent, they are also assumed to be sane at the outset of any criminal trial.

IRRESISTIBLE IMPULSE The McNaughten rule worked well for a time. Eventually, however, some cases arose in which defendants clearly knew what they were doing, and they knew it was wrong. Even so, they argued in their defense, they couldn't help themselves. They couldn't stop doing that which was wrong. Such people are said to suffer from an irresistible impulse and may be found not guilty by reason of that particular brand of insanity in 18 of the United States. Some states that do not use the irresistible impulse test in determining insanity may still allow the successful demonstration of such an impulse to be considered in sentencing decisions.

In a spectacular 1994 Virginia trial, Lorena Bobbitt successfully employed the irresistible impulse defense against charges of malicious wounding stemming from an incident in which she cut off her husband's penis with a kitchen knife as he slept. The case, which made headlines around the world, found Bobbitt's defense attorney telling the jury, "what we have is Lorena Bobbitt's life juxtaposed against John Wayne Bobbitt's penis. The evidence will show that in her mind it was his penis from which she could not escape, that caused her the most pain, the most fear, the most humiliation."[30] The impulse to sever the organ, said the lawyer, became irresistible.

The irresistible impulse test has been criticized on a number of grounds. Primary among them is the belief that all of us suffer from compulsions. Most of us, however, learn to control them. Should we give in to a compulsion, the critique goes, then why not just say it was unavoidable so as to escape any legal consequences.

THE DURHAM RULE A third rule for gauging insanity is called the Durham rule. It was originally created in 1871 by a New Hampshire court and later adopted by Judge David Bazelon in 1954 as he decided the case of *Durham* v. *United States* for the Court of Appeals in the District of Columbia. The Durham rule states that *people are not criminally responsible for their behavior if their illegal actions were the result of some mental disease or defect*. Courts that follow the Durham rule will typically hear from an array of psychiatric specialists regarding the mental state of the defendant. Their testimony will inevitably be clouded by the need to address the question of cause. A successful defense under the Durham rule necessitates that jurors be able to see the criminal activity in question as the *product* of mental deficiencies harbored by the defendant. And, yet, many people who suffer from mental diseases or defects never commit crimes. In fact, low IQ, mental retardation, and lack of general mental capacity are not allowable as excuses for criminal behavior. Because the Durham rule is especially vague, it provides fertile grounds for conflicting claims.

THE SUBSTANTIAL CAPACITY TEST Nineteen states follow another guideline—the Substantial Capacity Test—as found in the Model Penal Code of the American Law Institute.[31] Also called the ALI rule or the MPC rule, it suggests that insanity should be defined as the lack of a substantial capacity to control one's behavior. This test requires a judgment to the effect that the defendant either had or lacked "the mental capacity needed to understand the wrongfulness of his act, or to conform his behavior to the requirements of the law."[32] The Substantial Capacity Test is a blending of the McNaughten rule with the irresistible impulse standard. "Substantial capacity" does not require total mental incompetence, nor does the rule require the behavior in question to live up to the criterion of total irresistibility. The problem, however, of establishing just what constitutes "substantial mental capacity" has plagued this rule from its conception.

THE BRAWNER RULE Judge Bazelon, apparently dissatisfied with the application of the Durham rule, created a new criterion for gauging insanity in the 1972 case of *U.S. v. Brawner*. The Brawner rule, as it has come to be called, places responsibility for deciding insanity squarely with the jury. Bazelon suggested that the jury should be concerned with whether or not the defendant could be *justly* held responsible for the criminal act in the face of any claims of insanity. Under this proposal, juries are left with few rules to guide them other than their own sense of fairness.

INSANITY AND SOCIAL REALITY The insanity defense originated as a means of recognizing the social reality of mental disease. Unfortunately, the history of this defense has been rife with change, contradiction, and uncertainty. Psychiatric testimony is expensive, sometimes costing thousands of dollars per day for one medical specialist. Still worse is the fact that each "expert" is commonly contradicted by another.

Public dissatisfaction with the jumble of rules defining legal insanity peaked in 1982, when John Hinckley was acquitted of trying to assassinate President Reagan. At his trial, Hinckley's lawyers claimed that a series of delusions brought about by a history of schizophrenia left him unable to control his behavior. Government prosecutors were unable to counter defense contentions of insanity. The resulting acquittal shocked the nation and resulted in calls for a review of the insanity defense.

One response has been to ban the insanity defense from use at trial. A ruling by the U.S. Supreme Court in support of a Montana law allows states to prohibit defendants from claiming that they were insane at the time they committed their crimes. In 1994, without comment, the high Court let stand a Montana Supreme Court ruling which held that eliminating the insanity defense does not violate the U.S. Constitution. Currently, only three states, Montana, Idaho, and Utah, bar use of the insanity defense.[33]

GUILTY BUT INSANE A new finding of "guilty but insane" (in a few states the finding is "guilty but mentally ill," or GBMI) is now possible in some jurisdictions. It is one form the response to public frustration with the insanity issue has taken. "Guilty but insane" means that a person can be held responsible for a specific criminal act even though a degree of mental incompetence may be present in his or her personality. On return of this verdict, a judge may impose any sentence possible under the law for the crime in question. However, mandated psychiatric treatment will generally be part of the commitment order. The offender, once cured, will usually be placed in the general prison population to serve any remaining sentence. In 1975, Michigan became the first state to pass a "guilty but mentally ill" statute, permitting a GBMI finding.[34] At the time of this writing, 11 other states have also passed legislation making a verdict of "guilty but insane" possible.

As some authors have observed, the legal possibility of a guilty but mentally ill finding has three purposes: "[F]irst, to protect society; second, to hold some offenders who were mentally ill accountable for their criminal acts; (and) third, to make treatment available to convicted offenders suffering from some form of mental illness."[35]

The guilty but insane plea represents a conservative direction in criminal prosecution. The Supreme Court case of *Ford v. Wainwright*,[36] however, recognized a problem of a different sort. The 1986 decision specified that prisoners who become insane while incarcerated cannot be executed. Hence, although insanity may not be a successful defense to criminal prosecution, it can later become a block to the ultimate punishment.

TEMPORARY INSANITY Temporary insanity is another possible defense against a criminal charge. Widely used in the 1940s and 1950s, temporary insanity meant that the offender claimed to be insane only at the time of the commission of the offense. If a jury agreed, the defendant virtually went free. The suspect was not guilty of the criminal action by virtue of having been insane and could not be ordered to undergo psychiatric counseling or treatment because the insanity was no longer present. This type of plea has become less popular as legislatures have regulated the circumstances under which it can be made.

THE INSANITY DEFENSE UNDER FEDERAL LAW In 1984, the U.S. Congress passed the federal Insanity Defense Reform Act. The act created major revisions in the federal insanity defense. Insanity under the law is now defined as a condition in which the defendant can be shown to have been suffering under a "severe mental disease or defect" and, as a result "was unable to appreciate the nature and quality or the wrongfulness of his acts."[37] This definition of insanity comes close to that set forth in the old McNaughten rule.

The act also places the burden of proving the insanity defense squarely on the defendant—a provision that has been challenged a number of times since the act was passed. Such a requirement was supported by the Supreme Court prior to the act's passage. In 1983, in the case of *Jones* v. *U.S.* (1983),[38] the Court ruled that defendants can be required to prove their insanity when it becomes an issue in their defense. Shortly after the act became law, the Court in *Ake* v. *Oklahoma* (1985),[39] held that the government must assure access to a competent psychiatrist whenever a defendant indicates that insanity will be an issue at trial.

CONSEQUENCES OF AN INSANITY RULING The insanity defense today is not an "easy way out" of criminal prosecution, as some have assumed. Once a verdict of "not guilty by reason of insanity" is returned, the judge may order the defendant to undergo psychiatric treatment until cured. Because psychiatrists are reluctant to declare any potential criminal "cured," such a sentence may result in more time spent in an institution than would have resulted from a prison sentence.

Involuntary Intoxication

Another personal defense is involuntary intoxication. Either drugs or alcohol may produce intoxication. Intoxication itself is rarely a defense to a criminal charge because it is usually a self-induced state. An altered mental condition that is voluntary cannot be used to exonerate guilty actions that follow from it.

If you take drugs on your own, you have no defense

Insanity Defense. A personal defense which claims that the person charged with a crime did not know what he or she was doing or did not know that what he or she was doing was wrong.

When does mental illness excuse criminal behavior? Attorneys for Francisco Martin Duran, shown here being subdued after shooting at the White House with a Chinese-made automatic weapon in 1994, claimed that their client, in a fit of paranoid schizophrenia, thought he had been chosen to kill an evil "mist" that was enveloping the White House. Duran was sentenced to 40 years in prison with no chance of parole on charges of attempting to assassinate President Clinton. Photo courtesy of AP/Wide World Photos.

Involuntary intoxication, however, is different. On occasion, a person may be tricked into consuming an intoxicating substance. Secretly "spiked" punch, popular aphrodisiacs, or LSD-laced desserts all might be ingested unknowingly. In 1995, for example, the Drug Enforcement Administration reported that a powerful sedative manufactured by Hoffmann-LaRoche Pharmaceuticals and sold under the brand name Rohypnol, was quickly becoming popular with college students and with "young men [who] put doses of Rohypnol in women's drinks without their consent in order to lower their inhibitions."[40] What other behavioral effects the pills (known variously as "roples," "roche," "ruffles," "roofies," and "rophies" on the street) might have, is unknown.

Because the effects and taste of alcohol are so widely known in our society, the defense of involuntary intoxication due to alcohol consumption can be difficult to demonstrate. A more unusual situation results from a disease caused by the yeast *Candida albicans*, occasionally found living in human intestines. A Japanese physician was the first to identify this disease, in which a person's digestive processes ferment the food they eat. Fermentation turns a portion of the food into alcohol, and people with this condition become intoxicated whenever they eat. First recognized about ten years ago, the disease has not yet been used successfully in this country to support the defense of involuntary intoxication.

Unconsciousness

A very rarely used form of personal defense is that of unconsciousness. An individual who is unconscious cannot be held responsible for anything he or she does. Because unconscious people rarely do anything at all, this defense is almost never seen. However, cases of sleepwalking, epileptic seizure, and neurological dysfunction may result in injurious, although unintentional, actions by people so afflicted. Under such circumstances, the defense of unconsciousness might be argued with success.

Premenstrual Stress Syndrome

The use of premenstrual stress syndrome (PMS) as a defense against criminal charges is very new and demonstrates how changing social conceptions and advancing technology may modify the way in which courts view illegal behavior. In 1980, British courts heard the case of Christine English, who killed her live-in lover when he threatened to leave her. An expert witness at the trial testified that English had been the victim of PMS for more than a decade. The witness, Dr. Katharina Dalton, advanced the claim that PMS had rendered Ms. English "irritable, aggressive,…and confused, with loss of self-control."[41] The jury, apparently accepting the claim, returned a verdict of "not guilty."

PMS is not an officially acceptable defense in American criminal courts. However, in 1991, a Fairfax, Virginia, judge dismissed drunk-driving charges against a woman who cited the role PMS played in her behavior.[42] The woman, an orthopedic surgeon named Dr. Geraldine Richter, admitted to drinking four glasses of wine and allegedly kicked and cursed a state trooper who stopped her car because it was weaving down the road. A Breathalyzer test showed a blood-alcohol level of 0.13 percent—higher than the 0.10 percent needed to meet the requirement for drunken driving under Virginia law. But a gynecologist who testified on Dr. Richter's behalf said that the behavior she exhibited is characteristic of PMS. "I guess this is a new trend," said the state's attorney in commenting on the judge's ruling.

Other Biological Considerations

Modern nutritional science appears to be on the verge of establishing a new category of personal defense related to "chemical imbalances" in the human body produced by eating habits. Vitamins, food allergies, the consumption of stimulants (including coffee and nicotine), and the excessive ingestion of sugar all will probably soon be advanced by attorneys in defense of their clients.

The case of Dan White provides an example of this new direction in the development of personal defenses.[43] In 1978, White, a former San Francisco policeman, walked into the office of Mayor Moscone and shot both the mayor and City Councilman Harvey Milk to death. It was established at the trial that White had spent the night before the murders drinking Coca-Cola and eating Twinkies, a packaged pastry. Expert witnesses testified that the huge amounts of sugar consumed by White prior to the crime substantially altered his judgment and ability to control his behavior. The jury, influenced by the expert testimony, convicted White of a lesser charge, and he served a short prison sentence.

The strategy used by White's lawyers has come to be known as the "Twinkie defense." It may well be characteristic of future defense strategies now being developed in cases across the nation.

Situational Defenses

A defense against criminal charges can be based on circumstances as well as personal attributes. Defenses based on circumstance take into consideration the situation surrounding a crime. They are typically built around a claim of external pressures, operating at the time the crime was committed, that might have lessened the responsibility or the resolve of the defendant in a way with which the rest of us can sympathize. There are nine situational defenses. We briefly discuss each of them in the following pages.

Self-Defense

Self-Defense. The protection of oneself or one's property from unlawful injury or the immediate risk of unlawful injury; the justification for an act which would otherwise constitute an offense, that the person who committed it reasonably believed that the act was necessary to protect self or property from immediate danger.

Self-defense is probably the best known of the situational defenses. This defense strategy makes the claim that harm was committed in order to ensure one's own safety in the face of certain injury. A person who harms an attacker can generally use this defense. However, the courts have held that where a "path of retreat" exists for a person being attacked, it should be taken. In other words, the safest use of self-defense is only when "cornered," with no path of escape.

The extent of the injury inflicted in self-defense must be reasonable with respect to the degree of the perceived threat. In other words, although it may be acceptable for a person to defensively kill someone who is shooting at them, it would be inappropriate to shoot and kill someone who is just verbally insulting. Deadly force generally cannot be used to repel nondeadly force.

Self-defense extends to defense of others and to the defense of one's home. A person whose loved ones are being attacked can claim self-defense if the person injures or kills the attacker. Similarly, a person can defend his or her home from invasion or forced entry, even to the point of using deadly force. However, the circumstances that surround the claim of self-defense are limited. The defense is useless where the person provoked an attack or where the attacker is justified. In cases of forcible arrest, for example, family members may not intervene to protect their relatives, providing the use of force by the police is legitimate.

Self-defense has been used recently in a spate of killings, by wives, of their abusive spouses. Killings that occur while the physical abuse is in process, especially where a history of such abuse can be shown, are likely to be excused by juries as self-defense. On the other hand, wives who suffer repeated abuse, but coldly plan the killing of their husbands, have not fared well in court.

Duress

Duress is another of the defenses that depend on an understanding of the situation. Duress has been defined as "any unlawful threat or coercion used by a person to induce another to act (or to refrain from acting) in a manner he or she otherwise would not (or would)."[44] A person may act under duress if, for example, he or she steals an employer's payroll in order to meet a ransom demand for kidnappers holding the person's children. Should the person later be arrested for larceny or embezzlement, the person can claim that he or she felt compelled to commit the crime to help ensure the safety of the children. The defense of duress is sometimes also called coercion. Duress is generally not a useful defense when the crime committed involves serious physical harm since the harm committed may outweigh the coercive influence in the minds of jurors and judges.

Entrapment *only done by an low enforcement agent*

Entrapment, which can be defined as an inducement to crime by agents of enforcement, is a defense that has become relatively popular in the news media and in the courts. It is also a defense that regulates the enthusiasm with which police officers may enforce the law. Entrapment defenses argue that enforcement agents effectively create a crime where there would otherwise have been none. For entrapment to have occurred, the idea for the criminal activity must have originated with official agents of the criminal justice system. Entrapment can also result when overzealous police officers, acting undercover, convince a defendant that the contemplated law-violating behavior is not a crime.

Entrapment was claimed in the famous case of automaker John DeLorean. DeLorean was arrested on October 19, 1982, by federal agents near the Los Angeles airport.[45] An FBI videotape, secretly made at the scene, showed him allegedly "dealing" with undercover agents and holding packets of cocaine, which he said were "better than gold." DeLorean was charged with narcotics smuggling violations involving a large amount of drugs.

At his 1984 trial, DeLorean claimed that he had been "set up" by the police to commit a crime that he would not have been involved in were it not for their urging. DeLorean's auto company had fallen on hard times, and he was facing heavy debts. Federal agents, acting undercover, proposed to DeLorean a plan whereby he could make a great deal of money through drugs. Because the idea originated with the police, not with DeLorean, and because DeLorean was able to demonstrate successfully that he was repeatedly threatened not to "pull out" of the deal by a police informant, the jury returned a "not guilty" verdict.

The concept of entrapment is well summarized in a statement made by DeLorean's defense attorney to *Time* before the trial: "This is a fictitious crime. Without the Government there would be no crime. This is one of the most insidious and misguided law-enforcement operations in history."[46]

Accident

The defense of accident claims that the action in question was not intended but the result of some happenstance. Hunting accidents, for example, rarely result in criminal prosecution because the circumstances surrounding them clearly show the unintentional nature of the shootings. What appear to be accidents, of course, may actually be disguised criminal behavior. A hunter in North Carolina, for example, was convicted of shooting at an airplane (in which a passenger was seriously injured) even though he claimed that his gun accidentally discharged into the air. His defense fell apart when his girlfriend told authorities that he had confided in her about what really happened.

Mistake

Mistake is a situational defense with two components. One is mistake of law, and the other is mistake of fact. Rarely is the defense of mistake of law acceptable. Most people realize that it is their responsibility to know the law as it applies to them. "Ignorance of the law is no excuse" is an old dictum still heard today. On

Entrapment. An inducement to crime by agents of enforcement.

occasion, however, humorous cases do arise in which such a defense is accepted by authorities—for example, the instance of the elderly woman who raised marijuana plants because they could be used to make a tea that relieved her arthritis. When her garden was discovered, she was not arrested but advised on how the law applied to her.

Mistake of fact is a much more useful form of the "mistake" defense. In 1987, Jerry Hall, fashion model and girlfriend of Mick Jagger, a well-known rock star, was arrested in Barbados as she attempted to leave a public airport baggage claim area after picking up a suitcase.[47] The bag contained 20 pounds of marijuana and was under surveillance by officials who were waiting for just such a pickup. Ms. Hall defended herself by arguing that she had mistaken the bag for her own, which looked similar. She was released after a night in jail.

Necessity

Necessity, or the claim that some illegal action was needed to prevent an even greater harm, is a useful defense in cases that do not involve serious bodily harm. One of the most famous uses of this defense occurred in *Crown* v. *Dudly & Stephens* in the late 1800s.[48] The case involved a shipwreck in which three sailors and a cabin boy were set adrift in a lifeboat. After a number of days at sea without rations, two of them decided to kill and eat the cabin boy. At their trial, they argued that it was necessary to do so, or none of them would have survived. The court, however, reasoned that the cabin boy was not a direct threat to the survival of the men and rejected this defense. Convicted of murder, they were sentenced to death although they were spared the gallows by royal intervention.

Although cannibalism is usually against the law, courts have sometimes recognized the necessity of consuming human flesh where survival was at issue. Those cases, however, involved only "victims" who had already died of natural causes.

Provocation

Provocation recognizes that a person can be emotionally enraged by another. Should that person then strike out at the tormentor, some courts have held, he or she may not be guilty of any criminality. The defense of provocation is commonly used in barroom brawls where a person's parentage may have been called into question although most states don't look favorably on verbal provocation alone. It has also been used in some recent spectacular cases where wives have killed their husbands, or children their fathers, citing years of verbal and physical abuse. In these latter instances, perhaps because the degree of physical harm inflicted appears to be out of proportion to the claimed provocation, the defense of provocation has not been as readily accepted by the courts. As a rule, the defense of provocation is generally more acceptable in minor offenses than in serious violations of the law.

Consent

The defense of consent claims that whatever harm was done occurred only after the injured person gave his or her permission for the behavior in question. A 1980s trial saw Robert Chambers plead guilty to first-degree manslaughter in the killing of 18-year-old Jennifer Levin. In what was dubbed "the Preppy Murder Case,"[49] Chambers had claimed Levin died as a result of "rough sex," during which she had tied his hands behind his back and injured his testicles. Other cases, some involving sexual asphyxia (partial suffocation designed to heighten erotic pleasures) and bondage, culminated in a headline in *Time* heralding the era of "The Rough-Sex Defense."[50] The article suggested that such a defense works best with a good-looking defendant who appears remorseful; "[a] hardened type of character…,"[51] said the story, could not effectively use the defense.

In the "condom rapist" case, Joel Valdez was found guilty of rape in 1993 after a jury in Austin, Texas, rejected his claim that the act became consensual once he complied with his victim's request to use a condom. Valdez, who was drunk and armed with a knife at the time of the offense, claimed that his victim's request was a consent to sex. After that, he said, "we were making love."[52]

Alibi

A current reference book for criminal trial lawyers says, "Alibi is different from all of the other defenses...because...it is based upon the premise that the defendant is truly innocent...."[53] All the other defenses we have discussed are accepted ways to alleviate criminal responsibility. Although they may produce findings of "not guilty," the defense of alibi, if believed, should support a ruling of "innocent."

Alibi is best supported by witnesses and documentation. A person charged with a crime can use the defense of alibi to show that he or she was not present at the scene when the crime was alleged to have occurred. Hotel receipts, eyewitness identification, and participation in social events have all been used to prove alibis.

Procedural Defenses

Chapter 5 describes the legal environment in which the police must operate. When police officers violate constitutional guarantees of due process through improper police procedure, they may create a situation in which guilty defendants can go free. Defenses based on procedure may also occur as a consequence of actions by prosecutors and judges, and are called procedural defenses. Included among procedural defenses are double jeopardy, collateral estoppel, selective prosecution, denial of a speedy trial, and prosecutorial misconduct.

Double Jeopardy

The Fifth Amendment to the U.S. Constitution makes it clear that no person may be tried twice for the same offense. People who have been acquitted or found innocent may not be again put in "jeopardy of life or limb" for the same crime. The same is true of those who have been convicted: They cannot be tried again for the same offense. Cases that are dismissed for a lack of evidence generally also come under the double jeopardy rule and cannot result in a new trial.

Double jeopardy does not apply in cases of trial error. Hence, convictions that are set aside because of some error in proceedings at a lower court level (for example, inappropriate instructions to the jury by the trial court judge) will permit a retrial on the same charges. Similarly, when a defendant's motion for a mistrial is successful, or members of the jury cannot agree on a verdict (resulting in a "hung jury"), a second trial may be held.

Defendants, however, may be tried in both federal and state courts without necessarily violating the principle of double jeopardy. For example, 33-year-old Rufina Canedo pleaded guilty to possession of 50 kilograms of cocaine in 1991 and received a six-year prison sentence in a California court.[54] Federal prosecutors, however, indicted her again—this time under a federal law—for the same offense. They offered her a deal—testify against her husband or face federal prosecution and the possibility of 20 years in a federal prison. Because state and federal statutes emanate from different jurisdictions, this kind of dual prosecution has been held constitutional by the U.S. Supreme Court. To prevent abuse, the U.S. Justice Department acted in 1960 to restrict federal prosecution in such cases to situations involving a "compelling federal interest"—such as civil rights violations. However, in recent years, in the face of soaring drug law violations, the restriction has been relaxed.

In 1992, in another drug case, the U.S. Supreme Court ruled that the double jeopardy clause of the U.S. Constitution "only prevents duplicative prosecution for the same offense," but that "a substantive offense and a conspiracy to commit that offense are not the same offense for double jeopardy purposes." In the case, *U.S. v. Felix* (1992),[55] a Missouri man was convicted in that state of manufacturing methamphetamine, and then convicted again in Oklahoma of the "separate crime" of conspiracy to manufacture a controlled substance—in part based on his activities in Missouri.

Collateral Estoppel

Collateral estoppel is similar to double jeopardy and applies to facts that have been determined by a "valid and final judgment."[56] Such facts cannot become the object of new litigation. Where a defendant, for example, has been acquitted of a multiple murder charge by virtue of an alibi, it would not be permissible to try that person again for the murder of a second person killed along with the first.

Selective Prosecution

The procedural defense of selective prosecution is based on the Fourteenth Amendment's guarantee of equal protection of the laws. The defense may be available where two or more individuals are suspected of criminal involvement, but not all are actively prosecuted. Selective prosecution based fairly on the strength of available evidence is not the object of this defense. But when prosecution proceeds unfairly on the basis of some arbitrary and discriminatory attribute, such as race, sex, friendship, age, or religious preference, protection may be feasible under it.

Denial of Speedy Trial

The Sixth Amendment to the Constitution guarantees a right to a speedy trial. The purpose of the guarantee is to prevent unconvicted and potentially innocent people from languishing in jail. The federal government[57] and most states have laws (generally referred to as "speedy trial acts") that define the time limit necessary for a trial to be "speedy" and generally set a reasonable period such as 90 or 120 days following arrest. Excluded from the counting procedure are delays that result from requests by the defense to prepare their case. If the limit set by law is exceeded, the defendant must be set free, and no trial can occur.

Some legal experts expect speedy trial claims to be raised by defense attorneys in the case of Byron De La Beckwith, the unrepentant 75-year-old white supremacist, who was recently convicted of the murder of black civil rights leader Medgar Evers in Mississippi in 1963. More than 30 years after the killing, Beckwith was sentenced to life in prison, but only after two previous trials ended in hung juries.

Prosecutorial Misconduct

A final procedural defense may be found in prosecutorial misconduct. Generally speaking, prosecutorial misconduct is a term used by legal scholars to describe actions undertaken by prosecutors that give the government an unfair advantage or that prejudice the rights of a defendant or witness. Prosecutors are expected to uphold the highest ethical standards in the performance of their roles. When they knowingly permit false testimony, when they hide information that would clearly help the defense, or when they make unduly biased statements to the jury in closing arguments, the defense of prosecutorial misconduct may be available to the defendant.

The most famous instance of prosecutorial misconduct in recent history may have occurred during a convoluted 17-year-long federal case against former Cleveland autoworker John Demjanjuk. Demjanjuk, who was accused of committing war crimes as the notorious Nazi guard "Ivan the Terrible," was extradited in 1986 by the federal government to Israel to face charges there. In late 1993, however, the 6th U.S. Circuit Court of Appeals in Cincinnati, Ohio, ruled that federal prosecutors, working under what the court called a "win-at-any-cost" attitude, had intentionally withheld evidence that might have exonerated Demjanjuk (who was stripped of his U.S. citizenship when extradited, but later returned to the United States after the Supreme Court of Israel overturned his sentence there).[58]

Innovative Defenses

In recent years, some innovative defensive strategies have been employed, with varying degrees of success, in criminal cases—and it is to these that we now turn our attention. Technically speaking, any defense that is not situational or procedural falls under the category of "personal defense." Hence, the defenses discussed in this section may be appropriately listed as personal defenses. However, the unique and emerging character of these novel defenses makes discussing them in a separate section worthwhile.

Black Rage

The defense of "black rage" originated with the multiple-murder trial of Colin Ferguson, who was charged with killing 6 passengers and wounding 19 others in what authorities described as "a racially motivated attack" on the Long Island Railroad in December of 1993. In preparation for trial, Ferguson's original attorneys, William Kunstler and Ronald Kuby, had planned to argue that Ferguson, who is black, was overcome by rage resulting from societywide mistreatment of blacks by whites. (All the victims in the shooting spree initiated by Ferguson were either white or Asian.)

Kunstler suggested that the "black rage" defense is fundamentally a claim of insanity. "We are mounting a traditional insanity defense, long recognized in our law, with 'black rage' triggering last December's massacre,"[59] Kunstler and Kuby wrote in a letter to *The New York Times*. "Without a psychiatric defense, Colin has no defense," Kunstler was quoted as saying.[60] "There was no doubt that he was there, that he fired the weapon, that he would have fired it more if he had not been wrestled to the ground. There is no doubt that Colin Ferguson, if sane, was guilty," said Kunstler.

Ferguson eventually rejected the recommendation of Kuby and Kunstler that he plead not guilty by reason of insanity caused by "black rage" at racial injustice. After conducting his own defense, in what some called a mockery of an accused's right to act as their own attorney, Ferguson was convicted of all the charges against him. Ferguson had maintained his innocence throughout the trial even though he was identified by more than a dozen eyewitnesses, including some he had shot.

Urban Survival Syndrome

A little over a year ago, in a Fort Worth, Texas, murder case, a mistrial was declared after jurors deadlocked over lawyers' claims that their client, 18-year-old Daimion Osby, had killed two men because he suffered from "urban survival syndrome." Although Osby admitted to shooting both unarmed men in the head in a downtown parking lot, his attorneys told jurors that he had simply staged a preemptive strike against vicious people who had been threatening him for a year.

Jurors in Osby's trial heard defense attorneys argue that urban survival syndrome is a predilection to engage in violence in order to prevent oneself from being victimized—a kind of "shoot first and ask questions later" response to the growing violence now so characteristic of many American inner cities. Lawyers described the syndrome as "a sort of mind fix that comes over a young black male living in an urban neighborhood when he's been threatened with deadly force by another black male."[61] "For young blacks to take into account what they see happening in their own neighborhoods is not being racist," said David Bays, one of Osby's lawyers. "It's being realistic." Osby, said his lawyers, had been scared into a

RACE AND JUSTICE: AMERICAN ATTITUDES IN THE WAKE OF THE O. J. SIMPSON TRIAL

 The 1995 double-murder trial of O. J. Simpson had been watched almost daily for a year by millions on television throughout the world. Countless others read about it in newspapers and magazines or heard about it over the radio. The Simpson trial was truly *the* megamedia event of the late 20th century. Its sudden and dramatic close, with "not guilty" verdicts on October 3, 1995, sent social and political reverberations throughout the United States that are still being felt. In the trial's immediate wake, however, it was easy to discern a huge gap between the attitudes of white Americans and African Americans toward the criminal justice system.

Many whites remained firmly convinced that Simpson was guilty and felt he should have been convicted. The "not-guilty" verdicts (one verdict for each person Simpson was charged with killing) and his subsequent release, some felt, were a travesty. This remark, which came across an online service shortly after the verdict was read, sums up what many whites felt at the time: "A sense of sadness overwhelms me. And I am not the only one. You can feel it all over the...building where I work....It just doesn't feel like justice." Some whites claimed that Simpson had been found "not guilty by reason of race."

A large proportion of the nation's blacks, on the other hand, celebrated Simpson's acquittal—seeing in the verdicts a triumph over racism and a vindication of the deep distrust many in the black community feel toward the justice system in this country. Reflecting on the Simpson trial, one black man put it this way: "Whether he's innocent or guilty, let him go—I think that's the way a lot of black people are feeling."[1]

Central to the controversy were strong feelings aroused in many black Americans by charges of racism leveled against key prosecution witness LAPD Detective Mark Fuhrman. Fuhrman, a white police investigator, had gathered much of the crucial evidence against Simpson—including a bloody glove collected from a walkway at Simpson's estate. In a well-planned strategy, defense attorneys were able to show that Fuhrman had lied on the stand about having repeatedly referred to black people as "niggers" during the course of his police career. Although many whites saw such a revelation as irrelevant to the facts of the case, it may have convinced the mostly black jury that a racist cop could not be trusted to testify truthfully about other matters. Once Fuhrman had been successfully portrayed as a racist, it became easy for black jurors to conclude that he might have planted evidence or lied about critical issues in a case involving a black man accused of murdering a white woman and a white man.

For many black people, once the specter of racial discrimination had been raised, the underlying issue in the Simpson trial became one of social justice rather than criminal justice. As one writer put it, "The Fuhrman factor evoked a powerful story in the African-American experience: of the black man fighting a system that's rigged against him. So when blacks applauded the verdict, many were cheering less for the literal event than its allegorical significance—for a different ending to the story."[2]

Some analysts suggested that the successful portrayal of Detective Mark Fuhrman as a racist by the Simpson defense team effectively decided the trial. It may have been all that was needed for a jury with 9

(of 12) black members to return a "not guilty" verdict—regardless of the apparent strength of the evidence. A public opinion poll taken just before the verdict, but after Fuhrman had been cast as a racist, showed that 77 percent of whites surveyed thought Simpson was guilty, but that 72 percent of black respondents said he was innocent.[3]

When the Simpson defense played "the race card" during the trial, it built upon a distrust of the police and of the criminal justice system among African Americans that runs deep. Recent surveys, for example, show that only 33 percent of black people in this country believe that police officers testify truthfully, and only 18 percent of blacks say they would believe a police officer over other witnesses in a criminal trial.[4] John Mack, the black president of the Los Angeles Urban League, explained that though many whites have "a user friendly relationship" with police, many black people—especially young ones—have come to distrust the police because law enforcement officers are prone to viewing them and their activities suspiciously.

Such distrust, it should be noted, can have a significant impact on the entire criminal justice process, wielding influence far beyond that of a single trial—even a highly publicized one. "Interestingly," observed a *Wall Street Journal* article[5] published shortly after the Simpson verdict, "jury watchers are concluding that...race plays a far more significant role in jury verdicts than many people involved in the justice system prefer to acknowledge... The willingness of many blacks...to side with African-American defendants against a mostly white-dominated justice system is a relatively new phenomenon with specific roots and ramifications," said the *Journal.*

(Continued on next page)

RACE AND JUSTICE: AMERICAN ATTITUDES IN THE WAKE OF THE O. J. SIMPSON TRIAL—*Continued*

The tenacity of those roots, some say, are founded in a realistic distrust of the justice system ingrained in the subculture of black Americans by years of experience with a system that was often biased against them. Others say that such verdicts merely reflect informal social understandings within the black community. Some jurors, for example, may simply feel that there are too many blacks in prison, whereas others may not believe that prison will do any good—even though they know a suspect is guilty.

Defense attorney Johnnie Cochran echoed such sentiments near the close of the Simpson trial, when he told reporters that African Americans shouldn't avoid jury summonses because their voices are needed to combat racism at all levels of the justice system.[6] "You go and you serve on jury duty," Cochran told a nearly all-black audience. "Nobody is going to save us but us."

Many black jurors seem to be taking Cochran's message to heart. In the Bronx, a New York City borough, for example, where juries are often composed mostly of African Americans, the acquittal rate for black defendants in felony cases is nearly three times greater than the national average.[7]

Unfortunately, the Simpson verdict and the black–white differences it revealed, may have fed a long-standing racial divide that many had thought was beginning to heal. Following the verdict, 53 percent of blacks and 77 percent of whites interviewed in a *USA Today* poll said that the Simpson trial had done more to hurt race relations than to help them. The consequences of the Simpson trial for the justice system, however, may ultimately transcend racial lines. A survey conducted after the trial found a large proportion of both blacks and whites reporting a heightened distrust of the justice system—and especially of police officers and defense attorneys. Echoing that feeling, a *Newsweek* article said that the problem in today's justice system is not differing attitudes among races, but the uniquely American "license that we give lawyers to engage in truth-defeating distortion and trickery at trial."[8]

What lasting changes the Simpson trial may have wrought are difficult to discern. However, as Georgetown University Law School professor Paul Rothstein put it, one thing is certain: "Whites have had an unrealistic view of how perfect things function. Minorities...have had an unrealistic view of how badly they function."[9] The Simpson trial has probably made attitudes on both sides of the racial divide more realistic—and if it has done that, it may serve us all well in the long run.

1. "Nation Seeing Simpson Case in Black and White," The Associated Press, October 1, 1995.

2. Mark Whitaker, "Whites v. Blacks," *Newsweek*, October 16, 1995, p. 34.

3. "Nation Seeing Simpson Case."

4. Maria Puente, "Poll: Blacks' Confidence in Police Plummets," *USA Today*, March 21, 1995, p. 3A.

5. Benjamin A. Holden, Laurie P. Cohen, and Eleena de Lisser, "'Color-Blinded' Race Seems to Play an Increasing Role in Many Jury Verdicts," *The Wall Street Journal*, October 4, 1995, p. 1A.

6. "Cochran," The Associated Press online, September 23, 1995.

7. Holden, "Color Blinded," p. 1A.

8. John H. Langhein, "Money Talks, Clients Walk," *Newsweek*, April 17, 1995, p. 32.

9. Joe Urschel, "74% Say O.J. Verdict Hurt Racial Ties," *USA Today*, October 9, 1995, p. 1A.

state of "hypervigilance," convinced that he had no alternative but to kill in order to ensure his own survival. Recently, however, Osby was tried again. This time jurors rejected urban survival syndrome as a defense. Osby was convicted and sentenced to life in prison.[62]

As one commentator on the new defense put it: "I certainly don't like the idea of using some syndrome to get someone off a murder beef. But I've met enough people who use bathtubs as bulletproof beds to know that urban survival syndrome is real. How long can people live in fear before they snap?"[63]

A similar defense, that of "urban fear syndrome," was used in the 1995 murder trial of Nathaniel Hurt. Hurt, 62, fired a .357 Magnum revolver at teenagers, killing a 13-year-old, after young people had repeatedly trashed his yard and thrown rocks at his car. His attorneys claimed that Hurt snapped under the strain of constant harassment from inner-city thugs and that his murderous reaction was excusable because he lived in constant fear. Hurt was convicted of lesser charges after the judge in the case limited application of the defense by ruling that the syndrome claimed by Hurt's lawyers was not "medically recognized."[64]

Abuse

Another innovative defense being offered today, especially in murder cases, is that of abuse. Actually, the abuse defense is not new, having evolved from domestic abuse cases in the 1970s that emphasized the inability of some battered women to escape from the demeaning situations surrounding them. "Battered women's syndrome," involving long-term abuse, was said to effectively prevent women from seeking divorce and, in some cases, to drive women temporarily insane—turning them into killers. Hence, early versions of the abuse defense depended on its link to the more traditional defenses of insanity and self-defense. As judges and juries increasingly accepted such defenses, however, "attorneys began to use similar arguments to defend not only wives, but also homosexual lovers, and then children, husbands and a slew of other accused criminals."[65]

The abuse defense attempts to turn the tables on criminal prosecutors by claiming that chronic abuse sufferers may have to defend themselves at times when their abusers are most vulnerable—such as when they are asleep or otherwise distracted. This kind of argument is more frequently offered where the "victim" is weaker than the abuser, as in the case of women and children said to be abused by men.

Aspects of the abuse defense could be seen in the trials of Lorena Bobbitt, discussed earlier in this chapter, who was acquitted on charges of malicious wounding after admitting she severed her husband's penis with a kitchen knife, and Lyle and Erik Menendez, brothers whose first trial on charges of murdering their parents ended in hung juries after their attorneys claimed the boys' actions were the results of a lifetime of sexual abuse at the hands of their father.[66]

Some observers of the American scene say that jurors in today's society are especially sympathetic to abuse victims who act out their frustrations through crime. New York attorney Ronald L. Kuby, a former associate of the now deceased famed trial lawyer William Kunstler, says, for example, "One of the salutary effects of the pop psychology boom of the 1970s is that people increasingly ask, 'How did I end up like this and what can I do about it.'"[67] Popular television talk shows have probably also played a part in sensitizing people to the role of personal and family tragedies in people's lives. As a consequence, people everywhere may be ready to excuse criminal culpability if they can be shown its roots in a given situation. Southwestern University Law School professor Robert Pugsley puts it this way: "We are entering the age of the empathetic or sympathetic jury that is willing to turn the courtroom into the Oprah [Winfrey] or Phil [Donahue] show."[68]

Not everyone is enamored with the willingness of juries to consider the abuse defense, however. Los Angeles Deputy District Attorney Kathleen Cady, for example, recently saw Moosa Hanoukai convicted of voluntary manslaughter rather than first-degree murder as Cady had hoped. Hanoukai had beaten his wife to death with a wrench, but attorneys claimed he killed her because she made him sleep on the floor, called him names, and paid him a small allowance for work he did around the house. Jurors were told that Hanoukai, whose Jewish background prevented divorce, had been psychologically emasculated by his overbearing wife.

But, as Cady puts it: "Every single murderer has a reason why they killed someone....I think it sends a very frightening message to the rest of society that all you have to do is come up with some kind of excuse when you commit a crime."[69] Even a history of abuse, others say, should not be a license to kill.

Even so, the long-term trend may favor those with an abuse defense available to them. James Blatt, the attorney who defended Hanoukai says, "I think the trend is, if you can show legitimate psychological abuse over a prolonged period of time, then be prepared for a jury's reaction to that....Whether a lot of people like it or not, it may become an inherent part of American jurisprudence."[70]

Police Fraud

During the 1995 double-murder trial of O. J. Simpson, defense attorneys suggested the possibility that evidence against Simpson may have been concocted and even planted by police officers with a personal dislike of the defendant. In particular, defense attorneys pointed the finger at Los Angeles police department detective Mark Fuhrman, suggesting that he may have planted a bloody glove at the Simpson estate and tampered with blood stain evidence taken from the infamous white Ford Bronco Simpson was known to drive. In order to support allegations that Fuhrman was motivated by racist leanings, defense attorneys subpoenaed tapes Fuhrman made over a ten-year period with a North Carolina screenwriter who had been documenting life within the LAPD.

As one observer put it, however, the defense of police fraud builds on extreme paranoia about the government and police agencies. This type of defense, said Francis Fukuyama, carries "to extremes a distrust of government and the belief that public authorities are in a vast conspiracy to violate the rights of individuals."[71] It can also be extremely unfair to innocent people, for a strategy of this sort subjects what may otherwise be well-meaning public servants to intense public scrutiny, effectively shifting attention away from criminal defendants and onto them—sometimes with disastrous personal results. Anthony Pellicano, a private investigator hired by Fuhrman's lawyers, put it this way: "His life right now is in the toilet. He has no job, no future. People think he's a racist. He can't do anything to help himself. He's been ordered not to talk. His family and friends, he's told them not to get involved...Mark Fuhrman's life is ruined. For what? Because he found a key piece of evidence."[72] The 43-year-old Fuhrman retired from police work before the Simpson trial concluded.

The Future of Innovative Defenses

Future years will no doubt hold many surprises for students of the criminal law as defense attorneys become ever more willing to experiment with innovative tactics. As David Rosenhan, a professor of law and psychology at Stanford University,

LAPD detective Mark Fuhrman, around whom allegations of police misconduct swirled during the double-murder trial of O. J. Simpson. Some innovative defenses now attempt to shift blame away from criminal suspects and onto investigating officers. Photo by AFP/Vince Bucci, courtesy of Bettmann.

explains it: "We're getting to see some very, very interesting things, and obviously some long shots....There are a terrific number of them."[73] To make his case, Rosenhan points to a number of situations where people who didn't file income taxes escaped IRS prosecution by arguing that traumatic life experiences gave them an aversion to forms—a condition their legal counselors termed "failure to file syndrome." Some defenses to even very serious charges seem to border on the ludicrous. In 1995, for example, the state of Texas executed John Fearance, Jr., 40, for stabbing a man 19 times during a burglary, killing him while the man's spouse watched. In his defense, Fearance had claimed that he was temporarily insane at the time of the burglary-murder, saying his "wife had baked a meat casserole" for dinner on the night of the crimes and he "likes his meat served separately."[74]

The number of innovative defenses being tried on juries and judges today is staggering. Some attribute the phenomenon to what they call "creative lawyering." Others, like Kent Scheidegger of the Criminal Justice Legal Foundation, call most such defenses "outrageous." They're the tactics of lawyers "who have nothing left to argue," Scheidegger says.[75] He includes defenses like those of 37-year-old Michael Ricksgers, a Pennsylvania man who argued that sleep apnea (a disorder that causes irregular breathing during sleep) led him to pick up a .357-caliber Magnum and kill his wife; and Edward Kelly who says he's not guilty of rape because the crime was committed by one of his 30 personalities, and not by him. Ricksgers was convicted of first-degree murder in 1995, whereas Kelly's case is still pending.

In an insightful article,[76] Stephen J. Morse, an expert in psychiatry and the law, says that American criminal justice is now caught in the grips of a "new syndrome excuse syndrome"—meaning that new excuses are being offered on an almost daily basis for criminal activity. Many of these "excuses" are documented in the psychiatric literature as "syndromes" or conditions, and include antisocial personality disorder, posttraumatic stress disorder, intermittent explosive disorder, kleptomania, pathological gambling, postconcussional disorder, caffeine withdrawal, and premenstrual dysphoric disorder (discussed earlier as premenstrual stress syndrome). All these conditions are listed in the American Psychiatric Association's authoritative *Diagnostic and Statistical Manual of Mental Disorders*.[77] Emerging defenses, says Morse, include battered women's syndrome, Vietnam syndrome, child sexual abuse syndrome, Holocaust survivor syndrome, urban survival syndrome, rotten social background syndrome, and adopted child syndrome. "Courts," says Morse, "are increasingly inundated with claims that syndromes old and new, validated and unvalidated, should be the basis for two types of legal change: (1) the creation of new defenses to a criminal charge and (2) the expansion of old defenses: for example, loosening objective standards for justifications such as self-defense." Morse says that the new syndromes tend to work as defenses because they describe personal abnormalities, and most people are willing to accept abnormalities as "excusing conditions that bear on the accused's responsibility." The mistake, says Morse, is to think "that if we identify a cause for conduct, including mental or physical disorders, then the conduct is necessarily excused." "Causation," he cautions, "is not an excuse, only an explanation for the behavior."

Even so, attempts to offer novel defenses that are intended to convince jurors that even admitted criminal offenders should not be held responsible for their actions are becoming increasingly characteristic of the American way of justice. Whether such strategies will ultimately provide effective defenses may depend more on finding juries sympathetic to them than it will on the inherent quality of the defenses themselves.

Summary

Law serves many purposes. Primary among them is the maintenance of social order. Laws reflect the values held by society. The emphasis placed by law on individual rights, personal property, and criminal reformation and punishment can tell us much about the cultural and philosophical basis of the society of which it is a part. Legal systems throughout the world reflect the experiences of the societies that created them. Islamic law, for example, which provides the basis for many Middle Eastern systems of criminal justice, has a strong religious component and requires judicial decisions in keeping with the Moslem Koran.

Western criminal law generally distinguishes between serious crimes (felonies) and those that are less grave (misdemeanors). Guilt can only be demonstrated if the *corpus delicti* of a crime can be proved in court.

Our judicial system has come to recognize a number of defenses to a criminal charge. Insanity and self-defense are two of the most important of the modern defenses. The insanity defense has met with considerable recent criticism, and efforts to reduce its blanket application are now underway in a number of states. Even as limits are being placed on some traditional defenses, however, innovative defenses continue to emerge.

iscussion Questions

1. What kinds of concerns have influenced the development of the criminal law? How are social values and power arrangements in society represented in laws today?

2. What is meant by the *corpus delicti* of a crime? Are there any elements of a particular crime that you might identify as unnecessary? If so, which crime, and what might they be?

3. Does the insanity defense serve a useful function today? If you could create your own rule for determining insanity in criminal trials, what would it be? How would it differ from existing rules?

4. Near the end of this chapter, Stephen J. Morse describes many emerging defenses, saying that an explanation for behavior is not the same thing as an excuse. What does he mean? Might an explanation be an excuse under some circumstances? If so, when?

eferences

1. Henry Campbell Black, Joseph R. Nolan, and Jacqueline M. Nolan-Haley, *Black's Law Dictionary*, 6th ed. (St. Paul, Minn.: West Publishing, 1990), p. 884.

2. Ibid.

3. Lief H. Carter, *Reason in Law*, 2nd ed. (Boston: Little, Brown, 1984).

4. Deborah Sharp, "Errors Renew the Call for Doctor Review," *USA Today*, March 27, 1995, p 1A.

5. Mary Smaragdis, "Cancer Drugs—Not Disease—Kill Illinois Man," *USA Today*, June 16, 1995, 3A.

6. *Facts on File, 1988* (New York: Facts on File, 1988), p. 175.

7. "Man Who Spent 6½ Years in Jail Is Awarded $1.9 Million by Judge," *The Fayetteville Times* (North Carolina), October 20, 1989, p. 7A.

8. Robert Davis and Tony Mauro, "Judge OKs Suit Against Gun Maker," *USA Today*, April 12, 1995, p. 3A.

9. "Jury Says Halcion Led to Murder, Awards $2.15 Million," *The Fayetteville Observer-Times* (North Carolina), November 13, 1992, p. 4A.

10. "Part-Time Carpenter Seeks $657 Trillion Payment," Reuters world wire services, June 13, 1994.

11. See, Liz Spayd, "America, the Plaintiff; In Seeking Perfect Equity, We've Made a Legal Lottery," *Washington Post* online, March 5, 1995.

12. *Black's Law Dictionary*, 6th ed.

13. United States Sentencing Commission, *Federal Sentencing Guidelines Manual* (St. Paul, MN: West Publishing, 1987).

14. Daniel Oran, *Oran's Dictionary of the Law* (St. Paul, Minn.: West Publishing, 1983).

15. *Black's Law Dictionary*, 6th ed., p. 24.

16. *United States* v. *Shabani*, 115 S.Ct. 382, 138 L. Ed. 2d (1994).

17. Specifically 21 U.S.C. 846.

18. "Senate Begins to Consider Anti-Stalking Legislation," *Criminal Justice Newsletter*, March 2, 1993, p. 2.

19. Oliver Wendell Holmes, *The Common Law*, Vol. 3 (1881).

20. The same is not true for procedures within the criminal justice system, which can be modified even after a person has been sentenced and, hence, become retroactive. See, for example, the U.S. Supreme Court case of *California Department of Corrections v. Morales* (1995), which approved of changes in the length of time between parole hearings even though those changes applied to offenders already sentenced.

21. Henry Campbell Black, Joseph R. Nolan, and Jacqueline M. Nolan-Haley, *Black's Law Dictionary*, 6th ed. (St. Paul, Minn.: West Publishing, 1990), p. 343.

22. "Murder Attempt Charged in AIDS Exposure Case," *The Fayetteville Observer-Times* (North Carolina), November 16, 1992, p. 11A.

23. James A. Carlson, "Cancer Inquest," The Associated Press online, April 10, 1995.

24. Ibid.

25. Ibid.

26. Ibid.

27. Lynette Holloway, "Doctor Found Guilty of Murder in Botched Abortion," *New York Times News Service*, August 8, 1995.

28. "Girl Charged," The Associated Press online, northern edition, February 28, 1994.

29. *American Jurisprudence*, 21/2 §§ 55–57.

30. "Mrs. Bobbitt's Defense 'Life Worth More Than Penis,'" Reuters world wire services, January 10, 1994.

31. American Law Institute, *Model Penal Code: Official Draft and Explanatory Notes* (Philadelphia: The Institute, 1985).

32. Ibid.

33. See Joan Biskupic, "Insanity Defense: Not a Right; In Montana Case, Justices Give States Option to Prohibit Claim," *The Washington Post* online, March 29, 1994.

34. John Klofas and Ralph Weischeit, "Guilty but Mentally Ill: Reform of the Insanity Defense in Illinois," *Justice Quarterly*, Vol. 4, No. 1 (March 1987), pp. 40–50.

35. Ibid.

36. *Ford* v. *Wainright*, 477 U.S. 106 S.Ct. 2595 (1986).

37. 18 United States Code, § 401.

38. *Jones* v. *U.S.*, U.S. Sup. Ct. (1983), 33 CrL 3233.

39. *Ake* v. *Oklahoma*, U.S. Sup. Ct. (1985), 35 CrL 3159.

40. "'Rophies' Reported Spreading Quickly Throughout the South," *Drug Enforcement Report*, June 23, 1995, pp. 1,5.

41. As reported in Arnold Binder, *Juvenile Delinquency: Historical, Cultural, Legal Perspectives* (New York: Macmillan, 1988), p. 494.

42. "Drunk Driving Charge Dismissed: PMS Cited," *The Fayetteville Observer-Times* (North Carolina), June 7, 1991, p. 3A.

43. *Facts on File, 1978* (New York: Facts on File, 1979).

44. *Black's Law Dictionary*, 6th ed., p. 504.

45. *Time*, March 19, 1984, p. 26.

46. Ibid.

47. *Facts on File, 1987* (New York: Facts on File, 1988).

48. *The Queen v. Dudly & Stephens*, 14 Q.B.D. 273, 286, 15 Cox C. C. 624, 636 (1884).

49. "The Rough-Sex Defense," *Time*, May 23, 1988, p. 55.

50. Ibid., p. 55.

51. "The Preppie Killer Cops a Plea," *Time*, April 4, 1988, p. 22.

52. "Jury Convicts Condom Rapist," *USA Today*, May 14, 1993, p. 3A.

53. Patrick L. McCloskey and Ronald L. Schoenberg, *Criminal Law Deskbook* (New York: Matthew Bender, 1988), Section 20.03[13].

54. "Dual Prosecution Can Give One Crime Two Punishments," *USA Today*, March 29, 1993, p. 10A.

55. *U.S.* v. *Felix*, 112 S.Ct. 1377 (1992).

56. McCloskey and Schoenberg, *Criminal Law Deskbook*, Section 20.02[4].

57. Speedy Trial Act, 18 U.S.C. § 3161. Significant cases involving the U.S. Speedy Trial Act are those of *U.S.* v. *Carter* (1986) and *Henderson* v. *U.S.* (1986).

58. See, for example, Jim McGee, "Judges Increasingly Question U.S. Prosecutors' Conduct," *The Washington Post* online, November 23, 1993.

59. Niko Price, "Abuse Defenses," The Associated Press online, May 29, 1994.

60. "Train Shooting," The Associated Press online, August 12, 1994.

61. Courtland Milloy, "Self-Defense Goes Insane In the City," *The Washington Post* online, May 18, 1994.

62. Robert Davis, "We Live in Age of Exotic Defenses," *USA Today*, November 22, 1994, p. 1A.

63. Ibid.

64. "Murder Acquittal in 'Urban Fear' Trial," *USA Today*, April 12, 1995, p. 3A.

65. Niko Price, "Abuse Defenses," The Associated Press online, May 29, 1994.

66. In 1996 the Menendez brothers were convicted of first degree murder charges in a new trial.

67. "Abuse Defenses," The Associated Press online, May 29, 1994.

68. "In S.C. Case, Reports of Abuse," *USA Today*, April 12, 1995, p. 3A.

69. "Abuse Defenses," May 29, 1994.

70. Ibid.

71. Francis Fukuyama, "Extreme Paranoia About Government Abounds," *USA Today*, August 24, 1995, p. 17A.

72. Lorraine Adams, "Simpson Trial Focus Shifts to Detective With Troubling Past," *The Washington Post* online, August 22, 1995.

73. Ibid.

74. "Nationline: Execution," *USA Today*, June 21, 1995, p. 3A.

75. Robert Davis, "We Live in Age of Exotic Defenses."

76. Stephen J. Morse, "The 'New Syndrome Excuse Syndrome,'" *Criminal Justice Ethics*, Winter-Spring, 1995, p. 3–15.

77. American Psychiatric Association, *Diagnostic and Statistical Manual of Mental Disorders*, 4th ed. (1994).

PART 2

Policing

INDIVIDUAL RIGHTS VERSUS SOCIAL CONCERNS

The Rights of the Accused under Investigation

Common law, constitutional, statutory,
and humanitarian rights of the accused:

A Right Against Unreasonable Searches
A Right Against Unreasonable Arrest
A Right Against Unreasonable Seizures of Property
A Right to Fair Questioning by Authorities
A Right to Protection from Personal Harm

The individual rights listed must be effectively balanced against
these community concerns:

The Efficient Apprehension of Offenders
The Prevention of Crimes

How does our system of justice work toward balance?

To protect and to serve.

*F*amed police administrator and former New York City police commissioner, Patrick V. Murphy, once said, "It is a privilege to be a police officer in a democratic society." While Murphy's words still ring true, many of today's law enforcement officers might hear in them only the echo of a long-dead ideal, unrealistic for today's times.

America's police officers form the front line in the unending battle against crime—a battle which seems to get more sinister and demanding with each passing day. It is the police who are called when a crime is in progress, or when one has been committed. The police are expected to objectively and impartially investigate law violations, gather evidence, solve crimes, and make arrests resulting in the successful prosecution of suspects—all while adhering to strict due process standards set forth in the Constitution and enforced by the courts. The chapters in this section of *Criminal Justice: A Brief Introduction* provide an overview of police management, police-community relations, and critical issues in policing. They also discuss the due process and legal environments surrounding police activity.

As you will see, while the police are ultimately charged with protecting the public, they often feel that members of the public do not accord them the respect they deserve, and the distance between the police and the public is not easily bridged. Recently, however, a new image of policing has emerged which holds the promise to heal that divide. This new viewpoint, known as "community policing" goes well beyond traditional conceptions of the police as mere law enforcers, and encompasses the idea that police agencies should take counsel from the communities they serve. Under this new model the police are expected to prevent crime as well as to solve it, and to help members of the community deal with other pressing social issues.

CHAPTER 4

Police Management

—PHOTO BY BETSY HERZOG/AP/WIDE WORLD PHOTOS

*T*here is more law at the end of the policeman's nightstick than in all the decisions of the Supreme Court.

—ALEXANDER "CLUBBER" WILLIAMS
TURN-OF-THE-CENTURY NYPD OFFICER

I liken the Los Angeles police to a business. We have 3½ million customers…[1]

—WILLIE WILLIAMS
LOS ANGELES CHIEF OF POLICE

*T*he single most striking fact about the attitudes of citizens, black and white, toward the police is that in general those attitudes are positive, not negative.[2]

—JAMES Q. WILSON

KEY CONCEPTS

police management	watchman style	legalistic style
service style	police-community relations	team policing
strategic policing	problem-solving policing	community policing
scientific police management	directed patrol	discretion

Contemporary Policing: The Administrative Perspective

In November 1992, a Stanislaus County police SWAT team wearing ski masks, and acting on a tip that an illegal methamphetamine lab was in operation, kicked down the doors of the Oakdale, California, home of Marian and William Hauselmann.[3] Once inside, they handcuffed Mrs. Hauselmann, put a pillowcase over her head, and wrestled her to the floor. Her 64-year-old husband, who suffers from a heart condition, was shouted into silence. His face was cut and officers stepped on his back after throwing him down. No illegal drugs were found. Police soon realized that they had been misled by their informant and apologized to the Hauselmanns. Then they borrowed a knife from the couple's kitchen to cut the plastic handcuffs from their wrists. The county sheriff offered to pay for the broken doors. Following the incident, the Hauselmanns reported being unable to sleep.

A few months prior to the Hauselmann's ordeal, multimillionaire rancher Donald Scott was fatally shot during a drug raid gone terribly wrong. His Malibu, California, property, the target of a police attack, yielded no drugs, and Scott appears to have been trying to protect himself from what he thought were intruders when he was shot.

Both these cases highlight the potentially disastrous consequences of improper police action. Effective police management, through which laws are enforced while the rights of suspects and of innocent people are protected, may be the most important emerging issue facing the criminal justice system in the 21st century. As Dorothy Ehrlich of northern California's ACLU says, efficient enforcement of the laws is necessary, "[b]ut terrorizing innocent people is a price no one should have to pay."[4]

Police Management

Police Management. The administrative activities of controlling, directing, and coordinating police personnel, resources, and activities in the service of crime prevention, the apprehension of criminals and the recovery of stolen property, and the performance of a variety of regulatory and helping services.

Police management refers to the administrative activities of controlling, directing, and coordinating police personnel, resources, and activities in the service of crime prevention, the apprehension of criminals, the recovery of stolen property, and the performance of a variety of regulatory and helping services.[5] Police managers include any "sworn" law enforcement personnel with administrative authority, from the rank of sergeant to captain, chief or sheriff—and civilian personnel such as police commissioners, attorneys general, state secretaries of crime control, public safety directors, and so on.

In a recent symposium, members of Harvard University's Kennedy School of Government divided the history of American policing into three different eras.[6] Each era was distinguished from the others by the apparent dominance of a particular administrative approach to police operations. The first period, the political era, was characterized by close ties between police and public officials. It began in the 1840s and ended around 1930. Throughout the period, American police agencies tended to serve the interests of powerful politicians and their cronies, while providing community order maintenance services almost as an afterthought. The second period, the reform era, began in the 1930s and lasted until the 1970s. The reform era was characterized by pride in professional crime fighting. Police departments during this period focused most of their resources on solving "traditional" crimes such as murder, rape, and burglary and on capturing offenders. The final era—one which is just beginning—is the era of community problem solving. The problem-solving approach to police work stresses the service role of police officers and envisions a partnership between police agencies and their communities.

The influence of each historical phase identified by the Harvard team survives today in what James Q. Wilson calls policing styles.[7] Simply put, a style of policing describes how a particular police agency sees its purpose, and the methods and techniques it undertakes to fulfill that purpose. Wilson's three types of policing—which he did not identify with a particular historical era—are (1) the watchman style (characteristic of the Harvard symposium's political era), (2) the legalistic style (professional crime fighting), and (3) the service style (which is becoming more commonplace today). These three styles, taken together, characterize nearly all municipal law enforcement agencies now operating in this country—although some departments are a mixture of two or more styles.

Management Styles

Police departments marked by the **watchman style** of policing are primarily concerned with achieving a goal that Wilson calls "order maintenance." They see their job as one of controlling illegal and disruptive behavior. The watchman style, however, as opposed to the legalistic, makes considerable use of discretion. Order in watchman-style communities may be arrived at through informal police intervention, including persuasion and threats, or even by "roughing up" a few disruptive people from time to time. Some authors have condemned this style of policing, suggesting that it is unfairly found in lower-class, or lower-middle-class, communities, especially where interpersonal relations may include a fair amount of violence or physical abuse.

The watchman style of policing appears to have been operative in Los Angeles, California, at the time of the well-known Rodney King beating. Following the riots that ensued, the Independent Commission on the Los Angeles Police Department (The Christopher Commission) determined that the Los Angeles "[p]olice placed greater emphasis on crime control over crime prevention, a policy that distanced cops from the people they serve."

Departments operating under the **legalistic style** are committed to enforcing the "letter of the law." Years ago, for example, when the speed limit on I-95 running north and south through North Carolina was 55 mph, a state highway patrol official was quoted by newspapers as saying that troopers would issue tickets at 56 mph. The law was the law, he said, and it would be enforced.

Conversely, legalistically oriented departments can be expected to routinely avoid involvement in community disputes arising from violations of social norms which do not break the law. Gary Sykes calls this enforcement style "laissez-faire policing," in recognition of its "hands-off" approach to behaviors which are simply bothersome or inconsiderate of community principles.

Departments which stress the goal of service reflect the felt needs of the community. In service-oriented departments, the police see themselves more as helpers than as embattled participants in a war against crime. Such departments work hand in hand with social service and other agencies to provide counseling for minor offenders and to assist community groups in preventing crimes and solving problems. Prosecutors may support the **service style** of policing by agreeing not to prosecute law violators who seek psychiatric help or who voluntarily participate in programs like Alcoholics Anonymous, family counseling, and drug treatment. The service style of policing is commonly found in wealthy neighborhoods, where the police are well paid and well educated. The service style is supported in part by citizen attitudes that strive to avoid the personal embarrassment which might result from a public airing of personal problems. Such attitudes reduce the number of criminal complaints filed, especially in minor disputes.

Evolving Styles of Policing

Historically, American police work has involved a fair amount of order maintenance activity. The United States a few decades ago consisted of a large number of immigrant communities, socially separated from one another by custom and language. Immigrant workers were often poorly educated, and some were prone

Discretionary

Watchman Style. A style of policing marked by a concern for order maintenance. This style of policing is characteristic of lower-class communities where informal police intervention into the lives of residents is employed in the service of keeping the peace.

Legalistic Style. A style of policing marked by a strict concern with enforcing the precise letter of the law. Legalistic departments, however, may take a "hands-off" approach to otherwise disruptive or problematic forms of behavior which are not violations of the criminal law.

Service Style. A style of policing which is marked by a concern with helping rather than strict enforcement. Service-oriented agencies are more likely to take advantage of community resources such as drug treatment programs, than are other types of departments.

to displays of "manhood," which challenged police authority in the cities. Reports of police in "pitched battles" with bar-hopping laborers out for Saturday night "good times" were not uncommon. Arrests were infrequent, but "street justice" was often imposed through the use of the "billy stick" and blackjack. In these historical settings, the watchman style of policing must have seemed especially appropriate to both the police and many members of the citizenry.

As times changed, so too have American communities. Even today, however, it is probably fair to say that the style of policing which characterizes a community tends to flow, at least to some degree, from the lifestyles of those who live there. Rough-and-tumble lifestyles encourage an oppressive form of policing; refined lifestyles produce a service emphasis with stress on working together.

Police–Community Relations

In the 1960s, the legalistic style of policing, so common in America until then, began to yield to the newer service-oriented style of policing. The decade of the 1960s was one of unrest, fraught with riots and student activism. The war in

Vietnam, civil rights concerns, and other burgeoning social movements produced large demonstrations and marches. The police, who were generally inexperienced in crowd control, all too often found themselves embroiled in tumultuous encounters with citizen groups. The police came to be seen by many as agents of "the establishment," and pitched battles between the police and the citizenry sometimes occurred.

As social disorganization increased, police departments across the nation sought ways to understand and deal better with the problems they faced. Significant outgrowths of this effort were the **police–community relations** (PCR) programs, which many departments created. Some authors have traced the development of the police–community relations concept to an annual conference begun in 1955.[8] Entitled, the "National Institute of Police and Community Relations," the meetings were sponsored jointly by the National Conference of Christians and Jews and the Michigan State University Department of Police Administration and Public Safety. The emphasis on police–community relations also benefited substantially from the 1967 report by the President's Commission on Law Enforcement and the Administration of Justice,[9] which found that police agencies were often socially isolated from the communities they served.

PCR represented a movement away from an exclusive police emphasis on the apprehension of law violators and meant increasing the level of positive police–citizen interaction. At the height of the PCR movement, city police departments across the country opened storefront centers where citizens could air complaints and easily interact with police representatives. As Egon Bittner recognized,[10] for PCR programs to be truly effective, they need to reach to "the grassroots of discontent," where citizen dissatisfaction with the police exists.

Many contemporary PCR programs involve public relations officers, appointed to provide an array of services to the community. "Neighborhood Watch" programs, drug awareness workshops, "Project ID"—which uses police equipment and expertise to mark valuables for identification in the event of theft—and police-sponsored victims' assistance programs are all examples of services embodying the spirit of PCR. Modern PCR programs, however, often fail to achieve their goal of increased community satisfaction with police services because they focus on providing services to groups that already are well satisfied with the police. On the other

Police–Community Relations. (PCR) An area of emerging police activity which stresses the need for the community and the police to work together effectively and emphasizes the notion that the police derive their legitimacy from the community they serve. PCR began to be of concern to many police agencies in the 1960s and 1970s.

The maintenance of social order is a police function closely akin to strict law enforcement. Here Austin, Texas, police officers remove protesters at an antiabortion sit-in. Photo by Bob Daemmrich, courtesy of Stock Boston.

hand, PCR initiatives which do reach disaffected community groups are difficult to manage and may even alienate participating officers. Thus, as Bittner says, "while the first approach fails because it leaves out those groups to which the program is primarily directed, the second fails because it leaves out the police department."[11]

Team Policing

During the 1960s and 1970s, a number of communities began to experiment with the concept of **team policing**. An idea thought to have originated in Aberdeen, Scotland,[12] team policing, which in its heyday was defined as the reorganization of conventional patrol strategies into "an integrated and versatile police team assigned to a fixed district,"[13] rapidly became an extension of the PCR movement. Some authors have called team policing a "technique to deliver total police services to a neighborhood."[14] Others, however, have dismissed it as "little more than an attempt to return to the style of policing that was prevalent in the United States over a century ago."[15]

Team policing assigned officers on a semipermanent basis to particular neighborhoods, where it was expected they would become familiar with the inhabitants and with their problems and concerns. Patrol officers were given considerable authority in processing complaints from receipt through to resolution. Crimes were investigated and solved at the local level, with specialists called in only if the needed resources to continue an investigation were not locally available.

Community Policing

In recent years, the police–community relations concept has undergone a substantial shift in emphasis. The old PCR model was built around the unfortunate self-image held by many police administrators as enforcers of the law who were isolated from, and often in opposition to, the communities they policed. Under such jaded administrators, PCR easily became a shallowly disguised and insecure effort to overcome public suspicion and community hostility.

In contrast, an increasing number of enlightened law enforcement administrators today are embracing the role of service provider. Modern police departments are frequently called on to help citizens resolve a vast array of personal problems—many of which involve no law-breaking activity. Such requests may involve help for a sick child or the need to calm a distraught person, open a car with the keys locked inside, organize a community crime prevention effort, investigate a domestic dispute, regulate traffic, or give a talk to a class of young people on the dangers of drug abuse. Calls for service today far exceed the number of calls received by the police which directly relate to law violations. As a consequence, the referral function of the police is crucial in producing effective law enforcement. Officers may make referrals, rather than arrests, for interpersonal problems to agencies as diverse as Alcoholics Anonymous, departments of social service, domestic violence centers, drug rehabilitation programs, and psychiatric clinics.

In contemporary America, according to Harvard University's Executive Session on Policing, police departments function a lot like business corporations. According to the Session, three generic kinds of "corporate strategies" guide American policing:[16] (1) strategic policing, (2) problem-solving policing, and (3) community policing.

The first, strategic policing, is something of a holdover from the reform era of the mid-1900s. **Strategic policing** "emphasizes an increased capacity to deal with crimes that are not well controlled by traditional methods."[17] Strategic policing retains the traditional police goal of professional crime fighting, but enlarges the enforcement target to include nontraditional kinds of criminals such as serial offenders, gangs and criminal associations, drug distribution networks, and sophisticated white-collar and computer criminals. To meet its goals,

Theory into Practice: Community Policing in Reno, Nevada

Reno, Nevada, is a city of 120,000 with a police department of 313 sworn officers. The department also serves the needs of as many as 60,000 visitors who frequent the city's gambling districts weekly. Community policing began in Reno following a 1987 survey of public opinion that revealed that the police department suffered from a serious image problem. Public opinion described policing in Reno as "uncaring and heavy handed." At the time of the survey, the Reno police department was run via a "management by objectives" (MBO) administrative philosophy that equated high arrest rates with successful policing. The first community policing efforts began under Chief R. V. Bradshaw, following the defeat of two public referendums to increase funding levels for the department.

In 1992, Richard Kirkland was appointed Reno's chief of police and immediately initiated a new program called "Community Oriented Policing and Problem Solving" (COPPS). COPPS was implemented as a department-wide philosophy under the motto "Your police, our community." A new 40-hour training program was required of every police employee, and administrative decentralization brought about a major change in the department's organizational structure. Neighborhood advisory groups (NAGs) were developed, and a Quality Assurance Bureau was created to conduct both internal and external surveys with an eye toward improving police–community relations. NAGs encouraged the sharing of ideas between police officials and community groups. Patrol officers were encouraged to identify community groups that could host NAG meetings, and NAG sessions began in earnest.

As a result of NAG meetings and community surveys, the Reno Police Department initiated a number of new police efforts. Among them were (1) an eviction program in the North/Stead area to remove drug traffickers from HUD-sponsored apartments; (2) an effort to take back control of Pat Baker Park from an army of drug dealers and users who had been using the park as a storefront for illicit transactions; (3) the use of a number of out-of-state undercover officers to eliminate "crack houses" in the Trainer Way portion of the city; (4) department-initiated towing of abandoned vehicles from Stead, an abandoned Air Force Base within the city limits; (5) establishment of a foodbeat program in the Patton Drive area, where drive-by shootings and gang-related activities had been identified as problems;

(6) development of the Comprehensive Mental Health Assessment Program (COMPAS) to deal effectively with the city's mentally ill and homeless populations; (7) changes in traffic enforcement procedures to use a greater number of warning tickets, and the department's acquisition of a radar trailer displaying the speed of oncoming vehicles; (8) initiation of foot, bicycle, and dirtbike patrols in downtown areas to meet the needs of Reno's many visitors; and (9) the establishment of a new communications network to better link downtown casino security operations to the police department.

Following these and other well-publicized efforts to improve the department's image, community surveys reported a considerable degree of success. Although the initial 1987 survey found only 31.6 percent of residents feeling good about the police department, a similar 1992 survey revealed 68.7 percent of the populace reporting such feelings. Similarly, the percentage of respondents reporting that officers "did not convey a feeling of concern" was cut by two-thirds between surveys. Eventually, renewed citizen satisfaction with the Reno Police Department resulted in the success of a local tax referendum that provided the department with 88 additional officers—a 39 percent increase in sworn personnel.

QUESTIONS FOR DISCUSSION

1. Why do you think more citizens reported "feeling good" about the Reno, Nevada, police department after it implemented a community policing program? Why didn't everyone report feeling that way?

2. How do community policing programs convey a feeling that the police are concerned about citizens? What other kinds of feelings might such programs convey?

Richard Kirkland, *Community Oriented Police and Problem Solving: COPPS* (Reno, NV.: Reno Police Department, 1992); Jim Weston, "Community Oriented Policing: An Approach to Traffic Management," *Law and Order*, May 1991; Robert V. Bradshaw, Ken Peak, and Ronald W. Glensor, "Community Policing Enhances Reno's Image," *The Police Chief*, October 1990; David M. Kennedy, "The Strategic Management of Police Resources," *Perspectives on Policing* (Washington, D.C.: National Institute of Justice, January 1993); and Ronald W. Glensor and Ken Peak, "Improving Perceptions of the Police with Community Policing: The Reno Experience," paper presented at the annual meeting of the Academy of Criminal Justice Sciences, March 1993.

strategic policing generally makes use of innovative enforcement techniques, including intelligence operations, undercover stings, electronic surveillance, and sophisticated forensic methods.

The other two strategies give greater cognizance to the service style described by Wilson. **Problem-solving policing** (or problem-oriented policing) takes the view that many crimes are caused by existing social conditions in the communities served by the police. To control crime, problem-solving police managers attempt to uncover and effectively address underlying social problems. Problem-solving policing makes thorough use of other community resources such as counseling centers, welfare programs, and job training facilities. It also attempts to involve citizens in the job of crime prevention through education, negotiation, and conflict management. Residents of poorly maintained housing areas, for example, might be asked to clean up litter, install better lighting, and provide security devices for their homes and apartments in the belief that clean, secure, and well-lighted areas are a deterrent to criminal activity.

The third, and newest, police strategy goes a step beyond the other two. **Community policing** can be defined as "a collaborative effort between the police and the community that identifies problems of crime and disorder and involves all elements of the community in the search for solutions to these problems."[18] It has also been described as "a philosophy based on forging a partnership between the police and the community, so that they can work together on solving problems of crime, [and] fear of crime and disorder, thereby enhancing the overall quality of life in their neighborhoods."[19]

Community policing is a concept which evolved out of the early work of Robert C. Trojanowicz and George L. Kelling, who conducted studies of foot-patrol programs in Newark, New Jersey,[20] and Flint, Michigan,[21] showing that "police could develop more positive attitudes toward community members and could promote positive attitudes toward police if they spent time on foot in their neighborhoods."[22] The definitive work in the area is said by many to be Trojanowicz's book *Community Policing*,[23] published in 1990.

Contemporary police work involves a lot more than enforcing the law. Photo courtesy of the New York City Police Department.

Community policing attempts to involve the community actively with the police in the task of crime control by creating an effective working partnership between the community and the police.[24] As a consequence, community policing permits members of the community to participate more fully than ever before in defining the police role. In the words of Jerome Skolnick, community policing is "grounded on the notion that, together, police and public are more effective and more humane coproducers of safety and public order than are the police alone."[25] According to Skolnick, community policing involves at least one of four elements: (1) community-based crime prevention, (2) the reorientation of patrol activities to emphasize the importance of nonemergency services, (3) increased police accountability to the public, and (4) a decentralization of command, including a greater use of civilians at all levels of police decision making.[26] As one writer explains it, "Community policing seeks to integrate what was traditionally seen as the different law enforcement, order maintenance, and social service roles of the police. Central to the integration of these roles is a working partnership with the community in determining what neighborhood problems are to be addressed, and how."[27] Table 4-1 highlights the differences between traditional and community policing.

Community policing is a two-way street. It not only requires the police to be aware of community needs, it also mandates both involvement and crime-fighting action by citizens themselves. As Detective Tracie Harrison of the Denver, Colorado, police department explains it: "When the neighborhood takes stock in their community and they're serious they don't want crime, then you start to see crime go down. They're basically fed up and know the police can't do it alone."[28]

Creative approaches to policing have produced a number of innovative programs in recent years. In the early 1980s, for example, Houston's DART Program (Directed Area Responsibility Teams) emphasized problem-oriented policing; the Baltimore County, Maryland, police department began project COPE (Citizen Oriented Police Enforcement) in 1982; and Denver, Colorado, initiated its Community Service Bureau—one of the first major community policing programs. By the late 1980s, Jerome H. Skolnick and David Bayley's study of six American cities, entitled *The New Blue Line: Police Innovation in Six American Cities*,[29] documented the growing strength of community–police cooperation throughout the nation, giving further credence to the continuing evolution of service-oriented styles of policing.

Police departments throughout the country continue to join the community policing bandwagon. In April 1993, the city of Chicago launched a comprehensive community policing program called CAPS (Chicago's Alternative Policing Strategy). The Chicago plan uses rapid response teams comprising roving officers to handle emergencies, and many other officers have been put on permanent beats where they are highly visible throughout the city, with the avowed goal of maintaining and heightening citizens' perceptions of a police presence in their neighborhoods. Central to the CAPS program are monthly "beat meetings" between patrol officers and members of local neighborhoods. District Neighborhood Relations Offices provide an additional channel for communications between the police department and members of the public. CAPS actively brings other city agencies into the process of community order maintenance, tearing down deserted buildings, towing away abandoned cars, erasing graffiti, improving street lighting, and removing pay phones frequented by drug dealers. "Most of all," says Chicago Mayor Richard M. Daley, "we've enlisted the active participation of the people of Chicago. We have formed citizen advisory councils to track court cases and address other community issues that contribute to crime...CAPS only works when people get involved."[30]

The CAPS program also makes innovative use of cutting-edge technology. At the start of the program, citywide cellular service providers Ameritech and Cellular One developed a plan to equip Chicago police officers and selected community

TABLE 4-1

Traditional versus Community Policing

Question	Traditional	Community Policing
Who are the police?	A government agency principally responsible for law enforcement	Police are the public, and the public are the police: The police officers are those who are paid to give full-time attention to the duties of every citizen
What is the relationship of the police force to other public service departments?	Priorities often conflict	The police are one department among many responsible for improving the quality of life
What is the role of the police?	Focusing on solving crimes	A broader problem-solving approach
How is police efficiency measured?	By detection and arrest rates	By the absence of crime and disorder
What are the highest priorities?	Crimes that are high value (for example, bank robberies) and those involving violence	Whatever problems disturb the community most
What, specifically, do police deal with?	Incidents	Citizens' problems and concerns
What determines the effectiveness of police?	Response times	Public cooperation
What view do police take of service calls?	Deal with them only if there is no real police work to do	Vital function and great opportunity
What is police professionalism?	Swift effective response to serious crime	Keeping close to the community
What kind of intelligence is most important?	Crime intelligence (study of particular crimes or series of crimes) or groups)	Criminal intelligence (information about the activities of individuals
What is the essential nature of police accountability?	Highly centralized; governed by rules, regulations, and policy directives; accountable to the law	Emphasis on local accountability to community needs
What is the role of headquarters?	To provide the necessary rules and policy directives	To preach organizational values
What is the role of the press liaison department?	To keep the "heat" off operational officers so that they can get on with the job	To coordinate an essential channel of communication with the community
How do the police regard prosecutions?	As an important goal	As one tool among many

SOURCE: Malcolm K. Sparrow, *Implementing Community Policing*, National Institute of Justice (Washington, D.C.: U.S. Department of Justice, 1988), pp. 8–9.

members with cellular phones and voice mail to facilitate communication, and Chicago's new high-tech Emergency Communications Center is improving the department's response to emergency calls for police service. As Matt L. Rodriguez, Superintendent of Police for the city of Chicago explains it, "when most people think of community policing, they tend to focus on the interpersonal aspects of this new strategy—beat officers working with individual residents to address neighborhood problems. This type of personal partnership is certainly critical to CAPS. In Chicago, however, we have also invested heavily in the technological aspects of community policing. We are using technology to strengthen the partnership between police and community, and to help us work together on identifying and solving crime problems in our neighborhoods."[31]

A 1995 evaluation of CAPS found that the program had "impr_____
residents in virtually every area."[32] Survey-based measures show__
problems declining after CAPS implementation. Residents reporte____
dealing, shootings, violence by gangs, and robbery victimization l___
the two years since CAPS had been implemented although it w_____
clude that the decline had been entirely due to CAPS. The study_____
sively, however, that city residents experienced a significant in____
about police services since CAPS began, especially in the area _____
ness to neighborhood concerns.

In another example of the continuing move toward co_____
1994, the Los Angeles Police Department began helping res_____
lems that provide a breeding ground for crime. Throughout _____
now help find jobs for teenagers, assist tenants in getting la_____
down rental property, and accompany citizen patrols in_____
department also developed a "Community Enhancemen_____
"enables an officer to request specific services from city age_____
tions that may result in crime or community decay."[33] Their efforts appea____
paying off. FBI crime statistics released a year after the program began show that
major crimes in Los Angeles fell by 12 percent.[34]

The emphasis on community policing continues to grow. Title I of the Violent
Crime Control and Law Enforcement Act of 1994, known as the Public Safety
Partnership and Community Policing Act of 1994, highlights the role of community
policing in combating crime nationwide and makes funding available for (among
other things) "increas(ing) the number of law enforcement officers involved in activities that are focused on interaction with members of the community on proactive
crime control and prevention by redeploying officers to such activities." The avowed
purposes of the Community Policing Act are to (1) substantially increase the number
of law enforcement officers interacting directly with members of the community
(through a funded program known as "cops on the beat"); (2) provide additional and
more effective training to law enforcement officers in order to enhance their problem-solving, service, and other skills needed in interacting with members of the community; (3) encourage the development and implementation of innovative programs
to permit members of the community to assist local law enforcement agencies in the

Police officers serve food
during an anti-crime
rally to encourage citizen
involvement in crime
fighting. Activities such
as this help foster the
community policing
ideal—through which
law enforcement officers
and members of the
public become partners
in controlling crime and
keeping communities
safe.

...on of crime in the community; and (4) encourage the development of new ...ologies to assist local law enforcement agencies in reorienting the emphasis of ...r activities from reacting to crime to preventing crime.

Also in 1994, the Community Policing Consortium, based in Washington, D.C., began operations. The Consortium, which is administered and funded by the U.S. Department of Justice's Bureau of Justice Assistance, provides a forum for training and information exchange in the area of community policing. Members of the Consortium include the International Association of Chiefs of Police, the National Sheriffs' Association, the Police Executive Research Forum, the Police Foundation, and the National Organization of Black Law Enforcement Executives.

Critique of Community Policing

Unfortunately, problems remain in the community policing area.[35] For one thing, there is evidence that not all police officers or police managers are ready to accept new images of police work. Many are loathe to take on new responsibilities as service providers whose role is increasingly defined by community needs and less by strict interpretation of the law. As one writer, a police sergeant with a Ph.D. in sociology, puts it: "It is an unrealistic leap of faith to presume that the police institution has the resources or capability to carry on all that its newly defined function will demand of it. There is no valid reason for the police to take on all of these responsibilities other than what appears to be a tacit argument that the agency of last resort is the only one that can be held strictly accountable to the public."[36] In this writer's view, the police, once their role is broadly defined by community needs, become a kind of catch-all agency, or "agency of last resort," required to deal with problems ranging from handling the homeless to "worrying about the small mountains of trash on the all-too-many empty lots that once housed people and businesses..."

A New York City police officer offers yet another criticism: "If we make the goals of community policing impossible to achieve we doom the undertaking to failure. If we overwhelm police administrators with the enormity and vagueness of their proposed function, they will resist all attempts at reform."[37] He adds, "The notion of allowing the 'community' to participate in defining the police role is ill-conceived, and the most potentially explosive idea associated with community policing. If we follow the proposal that the police function is now anything the community defines it to be, it will become virtually impossible for police departments to accomplish any goals."[38]

Some authors have warned that the police subculture is so committed to a traditional view of police work, which is focused almost exclusively on crime fighting, that efforts to promote community policing can demoralize an entire department, rendering it ineffective at its basic tasks.[39] As the Independent Commission on the Los Angeles Police Department (The Christopher Commission) found following the "Rodney King riots," "[t]oo many...patrol officers view citizens with resentment and hostility; too many treat the public with rudeness and disrespect."[40] Some analysts warn that only when the formal values espoused by today's innovative police administrators begin to match those of rank-and-file officers can any police organization begin to be high performing in terms of the goals espoused by community police reformers.[41]

Nor are all public officials ready to accept community policing. In 1994, for example, New York City mayor Rudolph W. Giuliani criticized the NYPD Community Police Officer Program (CPOP), saying that it "has resulted in officers doing too much social work and making too few arrests."[42] Similarly, many citizens are not ready to accept a greater involvement of the police in their personal lives. Although the turbulent protest-prone years of the 1960s and early 1970s are but a memory, some groups remain suspicious of the police. No matter how inclusive community policing programs become, it is doubtful that the gap between the police and the public will ever be entirely bridged. The police role of restraining behavior which violates the law will always produce friction between police departments and some segments of the community.

cientific Police Management

The 1960s and 1970s were a time of cultural reflection in America which forever altered the legal and valuative environment in which the police must work. During that period, in conjunction with a burgeoning civil rights movement, the U.S. Supreme Court frequently enumerated constitutionally based personal rights for those facing arrest, investigation, and criminal prosecution within the American system of criminal justice. Although a "chipping away" at those rights, which some say is continuing today, may have begun in the 1980s, the earlier emphasis placed on the rights of defendants undergoing criminal investigation and prosecution will have a substantial impact on law enforcement activities for many years to come.

The 1960s and 1970s were also a period which saw intense examination of police operations, from day-to-day enforcement decisions to administrative organization and police community relations. In 1967, the President's Commission on Law Enforcement and the Administration of Justice issued its report, *The Challenge of Crime in a Free Society*,[43] which found that the police were often interpersonally isolated from the communities they served. In 1969, the Law Enforcement Assistance Administration (LEAA) was formed to assist police forces across the nation in acquiring the latest in technology and enforcement methods. In 1973, the National Advisory Commission on Criminal Justice Standards and Goals[44] issued a comprehensive report detailing strategies for attacking and preventing crime, and for increasing the quality of law enforcement efforts at all levels. Included in the report was a call for greater participation in police work by women and ethnic minorities, and the recommendation that a college degree should become a basic prerequisite for police employment by the 1980s.

In 1969, with passage of the Omnibus Crime Control and Safe Streets Act, the U.S. Congress created the Law Enforcement Assistance Administration. LEAA was charged with combating crime via the expenditure of huge amounts of money in support of crime prevention and crime reduction programs. Some have compared the philosophy establishing LEAA to that which supported the American space program's goal of landing people on the moon: "Put enough money into whatever problem there is, and it will be solved!" Unfortunately, the crime problem was more difficult to address than the challenge of a moon landing; even after the expenditure of nearly $8 billion, LEAA had not come close to its goal. In 1982, LEAA expired when Congress refused it further funding.

The legacy of LEAA is an important one for police managers, however. The research-rich years of 1969–1982, supported largely through LEAA funding, have left a plethora of scientific findings of relevance to police administration and, more important, have established a tradition of program evaluation within police management circles. This tradition, known as **scientific police management**, is a natural outgrowth of LEAA's insistence that any funded program had to contain a plan for its evaluation. Scientific police management means the application of social scientific techniques to the study of police administration for the purpose of increasing effectiveness, reducing the frequency of citizen complaints, and enhancing the efficient use of available resources. The heyday of scientific police management occurred in the 1970s, when federal monies were far more readily available to support such studies than they are today.

LEAA was not alone in funding police research during the 1970s. On July 1, 1970, the Ford Foundation announced the start of a Police Development Fund totaling $30

Scientific Police Management. The application of social scientific techniques to the study of police administration for the purpose of increasing effectiveness, reducing the frequency of citizen complaints, and enhancing the efficient use of available resources.

million, to be spent over the next five years on police departments to support major crime-fighting strategies. This funding led to the establishment of the Police Foundation, which continues to exist today with the mission of "foster(ing) improvement and innovation in American policing."[45] Police Foundation–sponsored studies over the past 20 years have added to the growing body of scientific knowledge which concerns itself with policing.

Federal support for criminal justice research and evaluation continues today under the National Institute of Justice (NIJ) and the Bureau of Justice Statistics (BJS), both a part of the Office of Justice Assistance, Research, and Statistics (OJARS). OJARS was created by Congress in 1980 and functions primarily as a clearinghouse for criminal justice statistics and information. The National Criminal Justice Reference Service (NCJRS), a part of NIJ, is available to assist researchers nationwide in locating information applicable to their research projects. "Custom searches" of the NCJRS computer database can be arranged at a small charge and yield voluminous information in most criminal justice subject areas. NIJ also publishes, each month, a series of informative reports (*NIJ Reports*), which serve to keep criminal justice practitioners and researchers informed about recent findings.

Exemplary Projects

Beginning in 1973, LEAA established the Exemplary Projects Program designed to recognize outstanding innovative efforts to combat crime and provide assistance to crime victims so that such initiatives might serve as models for the nation. One project which won exemplary status early in the program was the Street Crimes Unit of the New York City Police Department. The SCU used officers disguised as potential mugging victims and put them in areas where they were most likely to be attacked. In its first year, the SCU made nearly 4,000 arrests and averaged a successful conviction rate of around 80 percent. Perhaps the most telling statistic was the "average officer days per arrest." The SCU invested only 8.2 days in each arrest, whereas the department average for all uniformed officers was 167 days.[46]

Many other programs were supported and evaluated. The Hidden Cameras Project in Seattle, Washington, was one of those. The project used cameras hidden in convenience stores which were triggered when a "trip" bill located in the cash register drawer was removed. Clearance rates for robberies of businesses with hidden cameras were twice that of other similar businesses. Conviction rates for photographed robbers were shown to be more than twice those of suspects arrested for robbing noncamera-equipped stores. Commercial robbery in Seattle decreased by 38 percent in the year following the start of the project.

The Kansas City Experiment

By far the most famous application of social research principles to police management was the Kansas City Preventive Patrol Experiment.[47] Sponsored by The Police Foundation, the results of this year-long study were published in 1974. The study divided the southern part of Kansas City into 15 areas. Five of these "beats" were patrolled in the usual fashion. Another five beats experienced a doubling of patrol activities and had twice the normal number of patrol officers assigned to them. The final third of the beats received a novel "treatment" indeed—no patrols were assigned to them, and no uniformed officers entered that part of the city unless they were called. The program was kept something of a secret, and citizens were unaware of the difference between the patrolled and "unpatrolled" parts of the city.

The results of the Kansas City experiment were surprising. Records of "preventable crimes," those toward which the activities of patrol were oriented—like burglary, robbery, auto theft, larceny, and vandalism—showed no significant differences in rate of occurrence among the three experimental beats. Similarly, citizens didn't seem to notice the change in patrol patterns in the two areas where patrol frequency was changed. Surveys conducted at the conclusion of the experiment showed no difference among citizens in the three areas in their fear of crime before and after the study.

The 1974 study can be summed up in the words of the author of the final report: "...the whole idea of riding around in cars to create a feeling of omnipresence just hasn't worked....Good people with good intentions tried something that logically should have worked, but didn't."[48]

A second Kansas City study focused on "response time."[49] It found that even consistently fast police response to citizen reports of crime had little effect either on citizen satisfaction with the police or on the arrest of suspects. The study uncovered the fact that most reports made to the police came only after a considerable amount of time had passed. Hence, the police were initially handicapped by the timing of the report, and even the fastest police response was not especially effective.

The Kansas City study has been credited with beginning the now established tradition of scientific police evaluation. Patrick Murphy, former police commissioner in New York City and past president of the Police Foundation, said the Kansas City study "ranks among the very few *major* social experiments ever to be completed."[50] It, and other scientific studies of special significance to law enforcement, are summarized in Table 4-2.

TABLE 4-2

Scientific Studies in Law Enforcement

Year	Study Name	Focus
1994	The Kansas City Gun Experiment	Supplemental police patrol to reduce gun crime
1992	The New York City Police Department's Cadet Corps Study	Level of education among officers and hiring of minority officers
1992	Metro–Dade Spouse Abuse Experiment Replication	Replication of the 1984 Minneapolis study (but conducted in Florida)
1991	Quality Policing in Madison, Wisconsin	Community policing and participatory police management
1990	Minneapolis "Hot Spot" Patrolling	Intensive patrol of problem areas
1987	Newport News (Virginia) Problem-Oriented Policing	Police solutions to community crime problems
1986	Crime Stoppers: A National Evaluation	Media crime reduction programs
1986	Reducing Fear of Crime in Houston and Newark	Strategies for fear reduction among urban populations
1984	Minneapolis Domestic Violence Experiment	Effective police action in domestic violence situations
1981	Newark Foot Patrol Experiment	Costs versus benefits of foot patrol
1977	Cincinnati Team Policing Experiment	Team versus traditional policing
1977	Patrol Staffing in San Diego	One- versus two-officer units
1976	Police Response Time (Kansas City)	Citizen satisfaction with police response
1976	The Police and Interpersonal Conflict	Police intervention in domestic and other disputes
1976	Managing Investigations teams	Detective and patrol officer
1976	Kansas City Peer Review Panel	Improving police behavior
1974	Kansas City Patrol Study	Effectiveness of police patrol

Effects of the Kansas City Study on Patrol

The Kansas City studies greatly affected managerial assumptions about the role of preventive patrol and traditional strategies for responding to citizen calls for assistance. As Joseph Lewis, then director of evaluation at the Police Foundation said, "I think that now almost everyone would agree that almost anything you do is better than random patrol...."[51]

Although some basic assumptions about patrol were called into question by the Kansas City studies, patrol remains the backbone of police work. New patrol strategies for the effective utilization of human resources have led to various kinds of **directed patrol** activities. One form of directed patrol varies the number of officers involved in patrolling according to time of day or on the basis of frequency of reported crimes within areas. The idea is to put the most officers where and when crime is most prevalent.

Other cities have prioritized calls for service,[52] ordering a quick police response only when crimes are in progress or where serious crimes have occurred. Less significant offenses, such as minor larcenies or certain citizen complaints, are handled through the mail or by having citizens come to the police station to make a report. Wilmington, Delaware, was one of the first cities to make use of split-force patrol, in which only a part of the patrol force performed routine patrol.[53] The remainder were assigned the duty of responding to calls for service, taking reports, and conducting investigations.

*D*irected Patrol. A police management strategy designed to increase the productivity of patrol officers through the application of scientific analysis and evaluation to patrol techniques.

Recent Studies

Recent studies of the police have been designed to identify and probe some of the basic, and often "taken for granted," assumptions which have guided police work throughout this century. The initial response to many of these studies was, "Why should we study that? Everybody knows the answer already!" The value of applying evaluative techniques to police work, however, can be seen in the following examples:

- The 1994 Kansas City "gun experiment" was designed to "learn whether vigorous enforcement of existing gun laws could reduce gun crime." The Kansas City police department's "weed and seed" program targeted areas designated as "hot spots" within the cities. These were locations identified by computer analysis as having the most gun-related crimes within the metropolitan area. A special gun detection unit was assigned to the area, and guns were removed from citizens following searches incident to arrest for other (non-gun-related) crimes, traffic-stops, and as the result of other legal stop-and-frisk activities. While the program was in operation, gun crimes declined by 49 percent in the target area, whereas they increased slightly in a comparison area. Drive-by shootings, which dropped from seven (in the six months prior to the program) to only one (following implementation of the program), were particularly affected.[54]

- The 1984 Minneapolis domestic violence experiment was the first scientifically engineered social experiment to test the impact of the use of arrest (versus alternative forms of disposition) upon crime.[55] In this case, the crime in focus was violence in the home environment. Investigators found that offenders who were arrested were less likely to commit repeat offenses than those who were handled in some other fashion. A Police Foundation–sponsored 1992 study of domestic violence in the Metro–Dade (Florida) area reinforced the Minneapolis findings, but found that the positive effect of arrest applied almost solely to those who were employed.

- A third example of modern scientific police management comes from Newport News, Virginia.[56] In the late 1980s, the police in Newport News decided to test traditional incident-driven policing against a new approach called problem-oriented policing. Incident-driven policing mobilizes police forces to respond to citizen complaints and offenses reported by citizens. It is what the Newport News police called "the standard method for delivering police services." Problem-oriented policing, on the other hand, was developed in Newport News to identify critical crime problems in the community and to address effectively the underlying causes of crime. For example, one identified problem involved thefts from vehicles parked in the Newport News shipbuilding yard. As many as 36,000 cars were parked in those lots during the day. Applying the principles of problem-oriented policing, Newport News officers sought to explore the dimensions of the problem. After identifying theft-prone lots and a small group of frequent offenders, officers arrested one suspect in the act of breaking into a vehicle. That suspect provided the information police were seeking: It turned out that drugs were the real target of the car thieves. "Muscle cars," rock music bumper stickers, and other indicators were used by the thieves as clues to which cars had the highest potential for yielding drugs. The police learned that what seemed to be a simple problem of thefts from automobiles was really a search for drugs by a small group of "hard-core" offenders. Strategies to address the problem were developed, including wider efforts to reduce illicit drug use throughout the city.

These and other studies have established a new basis for the use of scientific evaluation in police work today. The accumulated wisdom of police management studies can be summed up in the words of Patrick Murphy who, near retirement as director of the Police Foundation, stated five tenets for guiding American policing into the next century:[57]

1. Neighborhood policing programs of all kinds need to be developed, improved, and expanded.
2. More police officers need college and graduate-level education.
3. There should be more "civilianization" of police departments. Civilian specialists can add to department operations and release sworn officers for police duties.
4. Departments must continue to become more representative of the communities they serve by recruiting more women and minorities.
5. Restraint in the use of force, especially deadly force, must be increased.

ontemporary Policing: The Individual Officer

Regardless of the "official" policing style espoused by a department, individual officers retain considerable **discretion** in what they do. Police discretion refers to the exercise of choice by law enforcement officers in the decision to investigate or apprehend, the disposition of suspects, the carrying out of official duties, and the application of sanctions. As one author has observed, "police authority can be, at once, highly specific and exceedingly vague."[58] The determination to stop and question suspects, the choice to arrest, and many other police practices are undertaken solely by individual officers acting in a decision-making capacity. Kenneth Culp Davis says, "The police make policy about what law to enforce, how much to enforce it, against whom, and on what occasions."[59] The discretionary authority exercised by individual law enforcement officers is of potentially greater significance to the individual who has contact with the police than are all department manuals and official policy statements combined.

Patrolling officers will often decide against a strict enforcement of the law, preferring instead to handle situations informally. Minor law violations, crimes committed out of the officer's presence where the victim refuses to file a complaint, and certain violations of the criminal law where the officer suspects sufficient evidence to guarantee a conviction is lacking may all lead to discretionary action short of arrest. Although the widest exercise of discretion is more likely in routine situations involving relatively less serious violations of the law, serious and clear-cut criminal behavior may occasionally result in discretionary decisions to avoid an

Discretion. The exercise of choice, by law enforcement agents, in the disposition of suspects, in the carrying out of official duties, and in the application of sanctions.

arrest. Drunk driving, possession of controlled substances, and assault are but a few examples of crimes in which on-the-scene officers may decide warnings or referrals are more appropriate than arrest.

Discretionary Decision Making

A summation of various studies of police discretion tells us that a number of factors influence the discretionary decisions of individual officers. Some of these factors are:

■ *Background of the officer.* Law enforcement officers bring to their job all of life's previous experiences. Values shaped through early socialization in family environments, as well as attitudes acquired from ongoing socialization, affect the decisions an officer will make. If the officer has learned prejudice against certain ethnic groups, it is likely that such prejudices will manifest themselves in enforcement decisions. Officers who place a high value on the nuclear family may handle spouse abuse, child abuse, and other forms of domestic disputes in predetermined ways.

■ *Characteristics of the suspect.* Some officers may treat men and women differently. A police friend of the author's has voiced the belief that women "are not generally bad…but when they do go bad, they go *very* bad." His official treatment of women has been tempered by this belief. Very rarely will this officer arrest a woman, but when he does, he spares no effort to see her incarcerated. Other characteristics of the suspect which may influence police decisions include demeanor, style of dress, and grooming. Belligerent suspects are often seen as "asking for it" and as challenging police authority. Well-dressed suspects are likely to be treated with deference, but poorly groomed suspects can expect less exacting treatment. Suspects sporting personal styles with a "message"—biker's attire, unkempt beards, outlandish haircuts, and other nonconformist styles—are more likely to be arrested than are others.

■ *Department policy.* Discretion, though not entirely subject to control by official policy, can be influenced by it. If a department has targeted certain kinds of offenses, or if especially close control of dispatches and communications is held by supervisors who adhere to strict enforcement guidelines, discretionary release of suspects will be quite rare.

■ *Community interest.* Public attitudes toward certain crimes will increase the likelihood of arrest for suspected offenders. Contemporary attitudes toward crimes involving children, including child sex abuse, the sale of drugs to minors, domestic violence involving children, and child pornography, have all led to increased and strict enforcement of laws governing such offenses across the nation. Communities may identify particular problems affecting them and ask law enforcement to respond. Fayetteville, North Carolina, adjacent to a major military base, was plagued a few years ago by a downtown area notorious for prostitution and "massage" parlors. Once the community voiced its concern over the problem, and clarified the economic impact on the city, the police responded with a series of highly effective arrests which eliminated massage parlors within the city limits. Departments which require officers to live in the areas they police are operating in recognition of the fact that community interests affect citizens and officers alike.

■ *Pressures from victims.* Victims who refuse to file a complaint are commonly associated with certain crimes such as spouse abuse, the "robbery" of drug merchants, and assaults on customers of prostitutes. When victims refuse to cooperate with the police, there is often little that can be done. On the other hand, some victims are very vocal in insisting that their victimization be recognized and dealt with. Modern victims' assistance groups, including People Assisting Victims, the Victims' Assistance Network, and others, have sought to keep pressure on police departments and individual investigators to ensure the arrest and prosecution of suspects.

■ *Disagreement with the law.* Some laws lack a popular consensus. Among them are many "victimless" offenses such as homosexuality, lesbianism, drug use, gambling, pornography, and some crimes involving alcohol. Not all these behaviors are even crimes in certain jurisdictions. Gambling is legal, for instance, in Atlantic City,

New Jersey, on board cruise ships, and in Nevada. Many states have now legalized homosexuality and lesbianism and most forms of sexual behavior between consenting adults. Prostitution is officially sanctioned in portions of Nevada, and some drug offenses have been "decriminalized," with offenders being ticketed rather than arrested. Unpopular laws are not likely to bring much attention from law enforcement officers. Sometimes such crimes are regarded as just "part of the landscape" or as the consequence of laws which have not kept pace with a changing society. When arrests do occur, it may be because individuals investigated for more serious offenses were caught in the act of violating an unpopular statute. Drug offenders, for example, arrested in the middle of the night, may be "caught in the act" of an illegal sexual performance when the police break in. Charges may then include "crime against nature," as well as possession or sale of drugs.

CAREERS IN JUSTICE

Working for the U.S. Secret Service

TYPICAL POSITIONS: Special agent, Uniformed Division police officers, and special officer. Clerical and administrative positions are also available.

EMPLOYMENT REQUIREMENTS: Requirements for appointment at GS-5 level include (1) successful completion of the Treasury Enforcement Agent examination; (2) a bachelor's degree from an accredited college or university; (3) excellent physical condition, including at least 20/40 vision in each eye, correctable to 20/20; and (4) successful completion of a thorough background investigation. Appointment at the GS-7 level also requires (1) one additional year of specialized experience, (2) a bachelor's degree with superior academic achievement, or (3) one year of graduate study in a related field (police science, police administration, criminology, law, law enforcement, business administration, accounting, economics, finance, or other directly related fields).

Superior academic achievement is defined as meeting one or more of the following criteria: (1) a B average (3.0 on a 4.0 scale) for all courses completed at time of application or for all courses during the last two years of the undergraduate curriculum, (2) a B+ average (3.5 on a 4.0 scale) for all courses in the major field of study or all courses in the major during the last two years of the undergraduate curriculum, (3) rank in the upper third of the undergraduate class or major subdivision (for example, school of liberal arts), and (4) membership in an honorary scholastic society which meets the requirements of the Association of College Honor Societies.

Specialized experience is defined as responsible criminal investigative or comparable experience which require (1) the exercise of tact, resourcefulness, and judgment in collecting, assembling, and developing facts, evidence and other pertinent data through investigative techniques which include personal interviews; (2) the ability to make oral and written reports and presentations of personally conducted or personally directed investigations; and (3) the ability to analyze and evaluate evidence and arrive at sound conclusions.

OTHER REQUIREMENTS: Valid driver's license, urinalysis test for the presence of illegal drugs prior to appointment, and the ability to qualify for top-secret security clearance.

SALARY: Special Agent: GS-5 $23,938, GS-7 $29,644; Uniformed Division Police: $31,283; Special Officer: GS-5 $24,585, as of mid-1995. A high-cost area supplement ranging from 4 to 16 percent is paid in specified geographic areas.

BENEFITS: Benefits include (1) 13 days of sick leave annually, (2) 2½ to 5 weeks of annual paid vacation and 10 paid federal holidays each year, (3) federal health and life insurance, and (4) a comprehensive retirement program.

DIRECT INQUIRIES TO: Chief of Staffing, U.S. Secret Service, 1800 G. Street, N.W., Room 912, Washington, D.C. 20223. Phone: (202) 435-5800. Applications are not accepted earlier than nine months prior to graduation.

On the other hand, certain behaviors which are not law violations, and which may even be protected by guarantees of free speech, may be annoying, offensive, or disruptive according to the normative standards of a community or the personal standards of an officer. Where the law has been violated, and the guilty party is known to the officer, the evidence necessary for a conviction in court may be "tainted" or in other ways not usable. Sykes, in recognizing these possibilities, says, "One of the major ambiguities of the police task is that officers are caught between two profoundly compelling moral systems: justice as due process...and conversely, justice as righting a wrong as part of defining and maintaining community norms."[60] In such cases, discretionary police activity may take the form of "street justice" and approach vigilantism.

- *Available alternatives.* Police discretion can be affected by the officer's awareness of alternatives to arrest. Community treatment programs, including outpatient drug and alcohol counseling, psychiatric or psychological services, domestic dispute resolution centers, and other options, may all be kept in mind by officers looking for a "way out" of official action.

- *Personal practices of the officer.* Some officers, because of actions undertaken in their personal lives, view potential law violations more or less seriously than other officers. The police officer who has an occasional marijuana cigarette with friends at a party may be inclined to deal less harshly with minor drug offenders than nonuser officers. The officer who routinely exceeds speed limits while driving the family car may be prone to lenient action toward speeders encountered while on duty.

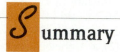 ummary

Contemporary police management has become increasingly scientific, applying the principles and techniques of the social sciences to police organization and administration. At the same time, a strong emphasis on service has led American law enforcement agencies at the local level toward a greater sensitivity to community needs and expectations. Community policing, a concept which has emerged over the past two decades, and which is now a primary model for police agencies everywhere, stresses the need for an integration of law enforcement activities and local priorities. Community policing is built on the principle that police departments and the communities they serve can work together effectively as partners in the fight against crime.

Not to be forgotten in the idealism surrounding community policing, however, is the huge amount of discretion allowable to individual officers engaged in the daily work of law enforcement. Such discretion can easily circumvent the best intentions of police administrators and community leaders, or it can embody and uphold the highest principles of both.

 iscussion Questions

1. What is community policing? Do you think that community policing offers an important opportunity to improve policing services in the United States? Why or why not?
2. Do you think police officers exercise too much discretion in the performance of their duties? Why or why not? If it is desirable to limit discretion, how would you do it?
3. Describe scientific police management. What scientific studies of the police would you like to see undertaken? Why?

References

1. "L.A. Police Chief: Treat People Like Customers," *USA Today*, March 29, 1993, p. 13A.

2. James Q. Wilson, *Thinking About Crime* (New York: Basic Books, 1975), p. 99.

3. "Bust 180 Degrees Wrong," *USA Today*, December 1, 1992, p. 3A.

4. Ibid.

5. The elements of this definition draw on the now classic work: O.W. Wilson, *Police Administration* (New York: McGraw-Hill, Inc., 1950), pp. 2–3.

6. Francis X. Hartmann, "Debating the Evolution of American Policing," *Perspectives on Policing*, No. 5 (Washington, D.C.: National Institute of Justice, November 1988).

7. James Q. Wilson, *Varieties of Police Behavior: The Management of Law and Order in Eight Communities* (Cambridge, Mass.: Harvard University Press, 1968).

8. Louis A. Radelet, *The Police and the Community* (Encino, Calif.: Glencoe, 1980).

9. President's Commission on Law Enforcement and Administration of Justice, *The Challenge of Crime in a Free Society* (Washington, D.C.: U.S. Government Printing Office, 1967).

10. Egon Bittner, "Community Relations," in Alvin W. Cohn and Emilio C. Viano, eds., *Police Community Relations: Images, Roles, Realities* (Philadelphia: J. B. Lippincott, 1976), pp. 77–82.

11. Ibid.

12. Charles Hale, *Police Patrol: Operations and Management* (New York: John Wiley, 1981), p. 112.

13. Sam Souryal, *Police Administration and Management* (St. Paul, Minn.: West, 1977), p. 261.

14. Paul B. Weston, *Police Organization and Management* (Pacific Palisades, Calif.: Goodyear, 1976), p. 159.

15. Hale, *Police Patrol*.

16. Mark H. Moore and Robert C. Trojanowicz, "Corporate Strategies for Policing," *Perspectives on Policing*, No. 6 (Washington, D.C.: National Institute of Justice, November 1988).

17. Ibid., p. 6.

18. The Community Policing Consortium, "What Is Community Policing" (1995).

19. The Community Policing Consortium, "Community Policing Is Alive and Well," (1995), p. 1.

20. George L. Kelling, *The Newark Foot Patrol Experiment* (Washington, D.C.: Police Foundation, 1981).

21. Robert C. Trojanowicz, "An Evaluation of a Neighborhood Foot Patrol Program," *Journal of Police Science and Administration* 11 (1983).

22. Bureau of Justice Assistance, *Understanding Community Policing: A Framework for Action* (Washington, D.C.: BJS, 1994), p. 10.

23. Robert C. Trojanowicz and Bonnie Bucqueroux, *Community Policing* (Cincinnati, Ohio: Anderson Publishing Co., 1990).

24. *Perspectives on Policing*, p. 8.

25. See Jerome H. Skolnick and David H. Bayley, *Community Policing: Issues and Practices Around the World* (Washington, D.C.: National Institute of Justice, 1988), and Jerome H. Skolnick and David H. Bayley, "Theme and Variation in Community Policing," in Norval Morris and Michael Tonry, eds., *Crime and Justice: An Annual Review of Research*, Vol. 10 (Chicago: University of Chicago Press, 1988), pp. 1–37.

26. Ibid.

27. William L. Goodbody, "What Do We Expect New-Age Cops to Do?" *Law Enforcement News*, April 30, 1995, pp. 14, 18.

28. Sam Vincent Meddis and Desda Moss, "Many 'Fed-Up' Communities Cornering Crime," *USA Today*, May 22, 1995, p. 8A.

29. Jerome H. Skolnick and David H. Bayley, *The New Blue Line: Police Innovation in Six American Cities* (New York: The Free Press, 1986).

30. Richard M. Daley, "A Message from the Mayor," The Chicago Police Department's World Wide Web home page, June 9, 1995.

31. Matt L. Rodriguez, "A Message from the Superintendent of Police," The Chicago Police Department's World Wide Web home page, June 9, 1995.

32. The Chicago Community Policing Evaluation Consortium, *Community Policing in Chicago, Year Two: An Interim Report* (Chicago: Illinois Criminal Justice Information Authority, June 1995).

33. Edwin Meese III, "Community Policing and the Police Officer," *Perspectives on Policing* (Washington, D.C.: National Institute of Justice, January 1993), p. 8.

34. Meddis and Moss, "Many 'Fed-Up' Communities Cornering Crime."

35. For a good critique of community policing, and of the current state of American policing in general, see Malcolm K. Sparrow, Mark H. Moore, and David M. Kennedy, *Beyond 911: A New Era for Policing* (New York: Basic Books, 1990).

36. William L. Goodbody, "What Do We Expect New-Age Cops to Do?"

37. Ibid.

38. Ibid.

39. Malcolm K. Sparrow, "Implementing Community Policing," *Perspectives on Policing*, No. 9 (Washington, D.C.: National Institute of Justice, 1988).

40. "L.A. Police Chief: Treat People Like Customers," *USA Today*, March 29, 1993, p. 13A.

41. Robert Wasserman and Mark H. Moore, "Values in Policing," *Perspectives in Policing*, No. 8 (Washington, D.C.: National Institute of Justice, November 1988), p. 7.

42. "New York City Mayor Sparks Debate on Community Policing," *Criminal Justice Newsletter*, Vol. 25, No. 2 (January 18, 1994), p. 1.

43. President's Commission on Law Enforcement and Administration of Justice, *The Challenge of Crime in a Free Society* (Washington, D.C.: U.S. Government Printing Office, 1967).

44. The National Advisory Commission on Criminal Justice Standards and Goals, *A National Strategy to Reduce Crime* (Washington, D.C.: U.S. Government Printing Office, 1973).

45. Thomas J. Deaken, "The Police Foundation: A Special Report," *FBI Law Enforcement Bulletin* (November 1986), p. 2.

46. National Institute of Justice, *The Exemplary Projects Program* (Washington, D.C.: U.S. Government Printing Office, 1982), p. 11.

47. George L. Kelling et al., *The Kansas City Patrol Experiment* (Washington, D.C.: The Police Foundation, 1974).

48. Kevin Krajick, "Does Patrol Prevent Crime?" *Police Magazine* (September 1978), quoting Dr. George Kelling.

49. William Bieck and David Kessler, *Response Time Analysis* (Kansas City, Mo.: Board of Police Commissioners, 1977). See also, J. Thomas McEwen et al., *Evaluation of the Differential Police Response Field Test: Executive Summary* (Alexandria, Va.: Research Management Associates, 1984), and Lawrence Sherman, "Policing Communities: What Works?" in Michael Tonry and Norval Morris, eds., *Crime and Justice: An Annual Review of Research*, Vol. 8 (Chicago: University of Chicago Press, 1986).

50. Ibid., p. 8.

51. "Does Patrol Prevent Crime?"

52. Ibid.

53. Ibid.

54. Lawrence W. Sherman, Dennis P. Rogan, and James W. Shaw, "The Kansas City Gun Experiment—NIJ Update," *Research in Brief*, November 1994.

55. Lawrence W. Sherman and Richard A. Berk, *Minneapolis Domestic Violence Experiment*, Police Foundation Report #1 (Washington, D.C.: Police Foundation, April 1984).

56. National Institute of Justice, *Newport News Tests Problem-Oriented Policing*, National Institute of Justice Reports (Washington, D.C.: U.S. Government Printing Office, January–February 1987).

57. Adapted from Deakin, "The Police Foundation."

58. Howard Cohen, "Overstepping Police Authority," *Criminal Justice Ethics* (Summer–Fall 1987), pp. 52–60.

59. Kenneth Culp Davis, *Police Discretion* (St. Paul, Minn.: West Publishing, 1975).

60. Sykes, "Street Justice," p. 505.

CHAPTER 5

—*Photo by Venegez/SIPA Press*

Policing: Legal Aspects

"Yeah," the detective mumbled. "Fifteen guys. You might want to think about that. Only two of us."…"On the other hand."…He shook his head. "Sneaking a bunch of cops into a neighborhood like this is going to be like trying to sneak the sun past a rooster."…As he started up the stairs, Angelo reached not for his gun but for his wallet. He took out a Chase Manhattan calendar printed on a supple but firm slip of plastic. He flicked the card at Rand. "I'll open the door with this. You step in and freeze them."

"Jesus Christ, Angelo," the agent almost gasped. "We can't do that. We haven't got a warrant."

"Don't worry about it, kid," Angelo said, drawing up to the second door on the right on the second floor. "It ain't a perfect world."[1]

—LARRY COLLINS AND DOMINIQUE LAPIERRE
THE FIFTH HORSEMAN

The right of the people to be secure in their persons, houses, papers, and effects, against unreasonable searches and seizures, shall not be violated, and no warrants shall issue but upon probable cause, supported by oath or affirmation, and particularly describing the place to be searched, and the persons or things to be seized.

—FOURTH AMENDMENT TO THE U. S. CONSTITUTION

KEY CONCEPTS

Bill of Rights	landmark cases	*Miranda* warnings
due process	Warren Court	Burger Court
search and seizure	exclusionary rule	good faith
probable cause	plain view	Rehnquist Court
illegally seized evidence	writ of *certiorari*	fruit of the poisoned tree doctrine
emergency searches	suspicionless searches	arrest
compelling interest	interrogation	inherent coercion
psychological manipulation	*Miranda* triggers	ECPA

The Abuse of Police Power

In the spring of 1991, Rodney King, an unemployed 25-year-old black man, was stopped by Los Angeles police for an alleged violation of motor vehicle laws. Police said King had been speeding and refused to stop for a pursuing patrol car. Officers claimed to have clocked King's 1988 Hyundai at 115 mph on suburban Los Angeles's Foothill Freeway—even though the car's manufacturer later said the vehicle was not capable of speeds over 100 mph and recordings of police radio communications surrounding the incident never mentioned excessive speed.

Eventually, King did stop, but then officers of the Los Angeles Police Department attacked him—shocking him twice with electronic stun guns and striking him with nightsticks and fists. Kicked in the stomach, face, and back, he was left with 11 skull fractures, missing teeth, a crushed cheekbone, and a broken ankle. A witness told reporters she heard King begging officers to stop the beating, but that they "were all laughing, like they just had a party."[2] King eventually underwent surgery for brain injuries.

Twenty-five police officers—21 from the LAPD, 2 California Highway Patrol officers, and 2 school district officers—were involved in the incident. Four of them, who were later indicted, beat King, as the other 21 watched. Los Angeles County District Attorney Ira Reiner called the behavior of the officers who watched, "irresponsible and offensive," but not criminal.[3]

There are two important differences between this incident and the other crime stories related in this textbook: (1) this time the criminals wore police uniforms, and (2) the entire incident was captured on videotape by an amateur photographer from a nearby balcony, who was trying out his new night-sensitive video camera. The two-minute videotape was repeatedly broadcast over national television and picked up by hundreds of local stations. The furor that erupted over the tape led to the ouster of LAPD Chief Daryl Gates and initiated a Justice Department review of law enforcement practices across the country.[4] Some defended the police, citing the "war zone" mentality of today's inner-city crime fighters as fostering a violent mindset. Officers involved in the beating claimed that King, at 6 feet 3 inches and 225 pounds, appeared strung out on PCP and that he and his two companions made officers feel threatened.[5]

In 1992, a jury found the four police defendants not guilty—a verdict that resulted in days of rioting across Los Angeles. A year later, however, in the spring of 1993, two of the officers, Sergeant Stacey Koon and Officer Laurence Powell, were found guilty by a jury in federal court of denying King his constitutional right "not to be deprived of liberty without due process of law, including the right to be...free from the intentional use of unreasonable force."[6] Later that year, both were sentenced to 2½ years in prison, far less than might have been expected under federal sentencing guidelines. Officers Theodore Briseno and Timothy Wind were found not guilty of the same charge.

In 1994, King settled a civil suit against the city of Los Angeles for a reported $3.8 million. Although King himself may not have been a model citizen (he was on parole at the time of the beating, after having served time for robbery, came under investigation for another robbery after the beating, and was arrested again three months after his release from the hospital—for allegedly picking up a male prostitute dressed as a woman and for trying to run over police who confronted him)[7] investigative reporters began to highlight a history of police abuse in Los Angeles. The month before the videotaped beating took place, Baseball Hall of Famer Joe Morgan won $540,000 in damages against the city of Los Angeles for mistreatment at the hands of the police who mistook him for a drug runner,[8] and the Southern California branch of the American Civil Liberties Union reported receiving 55 complaints each week about police brutality from black and Hispanic citizens. Even today, years after it occurred, the King incident continues to serve as a rallying point for individual rights activists concerned with ensuring that citizens remain protected from the abuse of police power in an increasingly conservative society.

This chapter shows how the police, like everyone else, are not above the law. It describes the legal environment surrounding police activities—from search and seizure through arrest and the interrogation of suspects. As we shall see throughout, it is democratically inspired legal restraints on the police which help ensure individual freedoms in our society and which prevent the development of a "police state" in America. Like anything else, however, the rules by which the police are expected to operate are in constant flux, and their continuing development forms the meat of this chapter.

 Changing Legal Climate

The Constitution of the United States is designed—especially in the Bill of Rights—to protect citizens against abuses of police power (see Table 5-1). However, the legal environment surrounding the police in modern America is much more complex

The beating of Rodney King by Los Angeles police officers, captured here by a man trying out a new video camera. The 1991 incident raised many questions about police integrity while highlighting the power of new technology to uncover police abuses. Photo by Rob Crandall/Picture Group, courtesy of Sygma.

than it was just 30 years ago. Until that time, the Bill of Rights was largely given only lip service in criminal justice proceedings around the country. In practice, law enforcement, especially on the state and local level, revolved around tried and true methods of search, arrest, and interrogation, which sometimes left little room for recognition of individual rights. Police operations during that period were often far more informal than they are today, and investigating officers frequently assumed that they could come and go as they pleased, even to the extent of invading someone's personal space without the need for a search warrant. Interrogations could quickly turn violent, and the infamous "rubber hose," which was reputed to leave few marks on the body, was probably more widely used during the questioning of suspects than many would like to believe. Similarly, "doing things by the book" could mean the use of thick telephone books for beating suspects since the books spread out the force of blows and left few visible bruises. Although such abuses were not necessarily day-to-day practices in all police agencies, and though they probably did not characterize more than a relatively small proportion of all officers, such conduct pointed to the need for greater control over police activities so that even the potential for abuse might be curtailed.

It was during the 1960s that the U.S. Supreme Court, under the direction of Chief Justice Earl Warren, accelerated the process of guaranteeing individual rights in the face of criminal prosecution. **Warren Court** rulings bound the police to strict procedural requirements in the areas of investigation, arrest, and interrogation. Later rulings scrutinized trial court procedure and enforced humanitarian standards in sentencing and punishment. The Warren Court also seized on the Fourteenth Amendment and made it a basis for judicial mandates requiring that both state and federal criminal justice agencies adhere to the Court's interpretation of the Constitution. The apex of the individual rights emphasis in Supreme Court decisions was reached in the 1965 case of *Miranda* v. *Arizona*, which established the famous requirement of a police "rights advisement" of suspects. In wielding its brand of idealism, the Warren Court (which held sway from 1953 until 1969) accepted the fact that a few guilty people would go free in order that the rights of the majority of Americans, as it understood them, would be protected.

Supreme Court decisions of the last few years, however, the product of a new and still emerging conservative Court philosophy, have begun what some call a "reversal" of Warren-era advances in the area of individual rights. By creating exceptions to some of the Warren Court's rules and restraints, and in allowing for the emergency questioning of suspects before they are read their rights, a changing Supreme Court has recognized the realities attending day-to-day police work and

TABLE 5-1

Constitutional Amendments of Special Significance to the American System of Justice, from the Bill of Rights

This Right Is Guaranteed	By This Amendment
The Right Against Unreasonable Searches and Seizures	Fourth
No Arrest Without Probable Cause	Fourth
The Right Against Self-Incrimination	Fifth
The Right Against "Double Jeopardy"	Fifth
The Right to Due Process of Law	Fifth, Fourteenth
The Right to a Speedy Trial	Sixth
The Right to a Jury Trial	Sixth
The Right to Know the Charges	Sixth
The Right to Cross-Examine Witnesses	Sixth
The Right to a Lawyer	Sixth
The Right to Compel Witnesses on One's Behalf	Sixth
The Right to Reasonable Bail	Eighth
The Right Against Excessive Fines	Eighth
The Right Against Cruel and Unusual Punishments	Eighth
The Applicability of Constitutional Rights to All Citizens, Regardless of State Law or Procedure (not part of the Bill of Rights)	Fourteenth

Theory into Practice: The "Rodney King" Trials

Until the summer of 1992, most Americans would probably have agreed that the justice system, though flawed in numerous individual instances, was the most equitable mechanism available for the apprehension of wrongdoers, for determinations of guilt or innocence, and for the imposition of punishment upon criminal offenders in an otherwise imperfect world. At the same time, most probably felt, at least intuitively, that the exercise of criminal justice occurred within a framework that was basically fair and impartial and that embodied our highest cultural ideals of social justice. In short, the symbolism of "blind justice" as equitable justice, was, for many Americans, an article of faith.

This is not to say that the system was without its detractors. On the contrary, the voices of the poor, the disenfranchised, the unempowered—in particular ethnic minorities and what sociologists have come to call "underrepresented groups"—have long appealed to the conscience of the American people, chanting a litany of claimed injustices for more than 200 years. The system, they said, understood only one type of justice: justice for the rich and for the powerful, justice for those who make the laws and for those who stand to benefit from them. From time to time, academicians and liberal politicians joined the fray on the side of the disenfranchised, claiming that law enforcement is fundamentally a tool of power, exercised exclusively in the service of the wealthy and the well connected. They, along with a variety of social commentators, portrayed criminal justice as one more aspect of a much broader issue—social *injustice*.

Then came an event that grabbed our nation's attention. In 1991, the videotaped police beating of a black Los Angeles motorist, Rodney King, burst on the national scene and transfixed the American national conscience via television. And the images wouldn't fade. In 1992, a Simi Valley, California, jury, with but one minority member, found the police officers who had been arrested for assaulting King innocent of the charges brought against them. The nation was aghast—unable to reconcile what it had perceived clearly in the media with the workings of American criminal justice. In an instant, Rodney King became, to many, the symbol of justice denied. Within hours, Los Angeles was embroiled in social protests, rioting, and looting. Racial tensions increased dramatically. In the spring of 1993, two of the officers, Sergeant Stacey Koon and Officer Laurence Powell, were found guilty by a jury in federal court of depriving King of his constitutional right "not to be deprived of liberty without due process of law, including the right to be...free from the intentional use of unreasonable force."[1] Officers Theodore Briseno and Timothy Wind were found not guilty of the same charge. Commenting on the differences between the two trials, *Newsweek* magazine said, "A...cynical explanation for the convictions this time is that the 12 jurors knew all too well what a full acquittal could mean." "The difference between this case and last year's were the riots," says Harland Braun, Briseno's lawyer. "The Simi Valley trial surely taught the perils of a criminal justice system that's perceived to be racist. But a system that's perceived as political— one that responds to public pressure as much as evidence—isn't much better."[2] As controversy over the case continued, the American Civil Liberties Union, in heated debate, voted to protest the convictions, claiming that "repeat prosecution by different jurisdictions for the same act amounted to double jeopardy."[3]

The Rodney King "incident" was a transfiguring event in the history of American criminal justice. It brought us to realize that the strokes which paint the canvas of intergroup relations in the United States are broader than the particulars of any one case. There is little denying that minorities are overrepresented at all stages of criminal justice processing. Similarly, there is little denying that minority youth violate laws with considerably greater frequency than do other youths and that the violations they commit are often found to be especially socially reprehensible—typified by crimes of violence, drug dealing, and the like. And yet whose laws are these people violating? By whose standards are they being held accountable? Because crime is a social construct arising out of a nexus of legislative action, social conditions, and individual choice, it becomes possible to ask: "Whose crime is it, after all?" From the perspective of those involved in it, drug dealing may seem like a reasonable way out from poverty, and violence a day-to-day necessity rooted in the will to survive. From the perspective of official agents of justice, these same behaviors confer criminal responsibility, and those who engage in them are condemned—arrested and sentenced to be removed from society until they are adjudged fit to return. And therein lies the rub. Return to what? To the social order understood by the law makers? Or a society inherently different and populated by less forgiving foes than criminal justice policy makers and enforcers of official law?

Ultimately we have to ask: "Is there one form of justice for the poor and another for the rich?" "Is there a separate system of justice that embodies the values of the powerful while condemning the strivings of the underclass?" "Are the felt needs of certain people being denied by the contemporary American criminal justice system?" "Can the scales of justice be balanced?" "In a more fundamental sense, can justice be truly equitable in a society built on the free pursuit of individual wealth and the often unbridled drive toward personal power?"

(Continued on next page)

Some have suggested creating two systems of criminal justice: one for the rich and one for the poor, one for the socially downtrodden and another for the well connected. After all, they say, isn't it necessary for enforcement agents, judges, juries, and probation or parole officers to understand the backgrounds and values of the criminal justice clients with whom they must deal? Shouldn't the system recognize the harsh realities of life in the inner city, and the desperation of the indigent and the disenfranchised? But if we lose faith in our existing system's ability to deliver justice, what is left? How do we remake a system that for more than 200 years has formed the bedrock of a tenuous social order and which has held in check the excesses of the criminally compelled?

QUESTIONS FOR DISCUSSION

1. What, in your opinion, has been the significance of the

Rodney King beating and subsequent trials for our nation's criminal justice system? Have those events affected the practice of criminal justice in this country? If so, how?

2. This box asks, "Is there one form of justice for the poor and another for the rich? Is there a separate system of justice which embodies the values of the powerful while condemning the strivings of the underclass? Are the felt needs of certain people being denied by the contemporary American criminal justice system? Can the scales of justice be balanced? In a more fundamental sense, can justice be truly equitable in a society built on the free pursuit of individual wealth and the often unbridled drive toward personal power?" What do you think?

1. "Cries of Relief," *Time*, April 26, 1993, p. 18.
2. "King II: What Made the Difference?" *Newsweek*, April 26, 1993, p. 26.
3. "A.C.L.U.—Not All That Civil," *Time*, April 26, 1993, p. 31.

the need to ensure public safety. This practical approach to justice, which came into vogue during the Reagan–Bush political era and is still with us, is all the more interesting for the fact that it must struggle to emerge from the confines of earlier Supreme Court decisions.

Individual rights

The Constitution of the United States provides for a system of checks and balances among the legislative, judicial, and executive (presidential) branches of government. By this we mean that one branch of government is always held accountable to other branches. The system is designed to ensure that no *one* individual or agency can become powerful enough to usurp the rights and freedoms guaranteed under the Constitution. Without accountability, it is possible to imagine a police state in which the power of law enforcement is absolute and related to political considerations and personal vendettas more than to any objective considerations of guilt or innocence.

Under our system of government, courts become the arena for dispute resolution, not just between individuals, but between citizens and the agencies of government itself. After handling by the justice system, people who feel they have not received the respect and dignity due them under law can appeal to the courts for redress. Such appeals are usually based on procedural issues and are independent of more narrow considerations of guilt or innocence.

In this chapter, we spend a great deal of time on cases that are important because they are famous for having clarified constitutional guarantees concerning individual liberties within the criminal justice arena. They involve issues which have come to be called "rights" by most of us. It is common to hear arrestees today say: "You can't do that! I know my rights!" Rights are concerned with procedure, that is, with how police and other actors in the criminal justice system handle each part of the process of dealing with suspects. Rights violations have often become the basis for the dismissal of charges, acquittal of defendants, or the release of convicted offenders after an appeal to a higher court.

Due Process Requirements

As you may recall from Chapter 1, **due process** is a requirement of the Fifth, Sixth, and Fourteenth Amendments to the U.S. Constitution, which mandates that justice system officials respect the rights of accused individuals throughout the criminal justice process. Most due process requirements of relevance to the police pertain to three major areas: (1) evidence and investigation (often called search and seizure), (2) arrest, and (3) interrogation. Each of these areas has been addressed by a plethora of landmark U.S. Supreme Court decisions. **Landmark cases** are recognizable by the fact that they produce substantial changes in both the understanding of the requirements of due process and in the practical day-to-day operations of the justice system. Another way to think of landmark decisions is that they help significantly in clarifying the "rules of the game"—the procedural guidelines by which the police and the rest of the justice system must abide.

The three areas we are about to discuss have been well defined by decades of court precedent. Keep in mind, however, that judicial interpretations of the constitutional requirement of due process are constantly evolving. As new decisions are rendered, and as the composition of the Court itself changes, additional refinements (and even major changes) may occur.

earch and Seizure

The U.S. Constitution declares that people must be secure in their homes and in their persons against unreasonable searches and seizures. This right is asserted by the Fourth Amendment, which reads: "The right of the people to be secure in their persons, houses, papers, and effects, against unreasonable searches and seizures shall not be violated, and no warrants shall issue but upon probable cause, supported by oath or affirmation, and particularly describing the place to be searched, and the persons or things to be seized." This amendment, a part of the Bill of Rights, was adopted by Congress and became effective on December 15, 1791.

The language of the Fourth Amendment is familiar to all of us. "Warrants," "probable cause," and other phrases from the amendment are frequently cited in editorials, TV news shows, and daily conversation. It is the interpretation of these phrases over time by the U.S. Supreme Court, however, which has given them the impact they have on the justice system today.

The Exclusionary Rule

The first landmark case concerning **search and seizure** was that of *Weeks* v. *U.S.* (1914).[9] Freemont Weeks was suspected of using the U.S. mail to sell lottery tickets, a federal crime. Weeks was arrested, and federal agents went to his home to conduct a search. They had no search warrant since at the time investigators did not routinely use warrants. They confiscated many incriminating items of evidence, as well as personal possessions of the defendant, including clothes, papers, books, and even candy.

Prior to trial, Weeks's attorney asked that the personal items be returned, claiming that they had been illegally seized under Fourth Amendment guarantees. A judge agreed and ordered the materials returned. On the basis of the evidence which was retained, however, Weeks was convicted in federal court and sentenced

Landmark Cases. High court cases that result in substantial and lasting changes in due process requirements, or in the day-to-day operation of the justice system.

Illegally Seized Evidence. Evidence seized in opposition to the principles of due process as described by the Bill of Rights. Most illegally seized evidence is the result of police searches conducted without a proper warrant or of improperly conducted interrogations.

to prison. He appealed his conviction through other courts and eventually reached the U.S. Supreme Court. There his lawyer reasoned that if some of his client's belongings had been illegally seized, then the remainder of them were also taken improperly. The Supreme Court agreed and overturned Weeks's earlier conviction.

The *Weeks* case forms the basis of what is now called the exclusionary rule. The **exclusionary rule** means that evidence illegally seized by the police cannot be used in a trial. The rule acts as a control over police behavior and specifically focuses on the failure of officers to obtain warrants authorizing them to either conduct searches or effect arrests (especially where arrest may lead to the acquisition of incriminating statements or to the seizure of physical evidence).

It is important to note, incidentally, that Freemont Weeks could have been retried on the original charges following the Supreme Court decision in his case. He would not have faced double jeopardy because he was in fact not *finally convicted* on the earlier charges. His conviction was nullified on appeal, resulting in neither a conviction nor an acquittal. Double jeopardy becomes an issue only when a defendant faces retrial on the same charges following acquittal at his or her original trial or when the defendant is retried after having been convicted.

It is also important to recognize that the decision of the Supreme Court in the *Weeks* case was binding, at the time, only on federal officers because it was federal agents who were involved in the illegal seizure.

Problems with Precedent

The *Weeks* case demonstrates the power of the Supreme Court in *enforcing* what we have called the "rules of the game." It also lays bare the much more significant role that the Court plays in rule creation. Until the *Weeks* case was decided, federal law enforcement officers had little reason to think they were acting in violation of due process. Common practice had not required that they obtain a warrant before conducting searches. The rule which resulted from *Weeks* was new, and it would forever alter the enforcement activities of federal officers. Yet the *Weeks* case was also retroactive in that it was applied to Weeks himself.

There is a problem in the way in which our system generates and applies principles of due process that may be obvious from our discussion of the *Weeks* case. The problem is that the present appeals system, focusing as it does on the "rules of the game," presents a ready-made channel for the guilty to go free. There can be little doubt that Freemont Weeks had violated federal law. A jury had convicted him. Yet he escaped punishment because of the illegal behavior of the police—behavior which, until the Court ruled, had not been regarded as anything but legitimate.

Even if the police knowingly violate the principles of due process, which they sometimes do, our sense of justice is compromised when the guilty go free. Famed Supreme Court Justice Benjamin Cardozo (1870–1938) once complained, "The criminal is to go free because the constable has blundered." Students of criminal justice have long considered three possible solutions to this problem. The first solution suggests that rules of due process, especially when newly articulated by the courts, should be applied only to future cases, but not to the initial case in which they are stated. The justices in the *Weeks* case, for example, might have said, "We are creating the 'exclusionary rule,' based upon our realization in this case. Law enforcement officers are obligated to use it as a guide in all future searches. However, insofar as the guilt of Mr. Weeks was decided by a jury under rules of evidence existing at the time, we will let that decision stand."

A second solution would punish police officers or other actors in the criminal justice system who act illegally, but would not allow the guilty defendant to escape punishment. This solution would be useful in applying established precedent where officers and officials had the benefit of clearly articulated rules and should have known better. Under this arrangement, any officer today who intentionally violates due process guarantees might be suspended, reduced in rank, lose pay, or be fired.

Exclusionary Rule. The understanding, based on Supreme Court precedent, that incriminating information must be seized according to Constitutional specifications of due process, or it will not be allowed as evidence in criminal trials.

Some authors have suggested that "decertification" might serve as "an alternative to traditional remedies for police misconduct."[10] Departments which employed the decertification process would punish violators by removing their certification as police officers. Because officers in every state except Hawaii must meet the certification requirements of state boards (usually called Training and Standards Commissions or Peace Officer Standards and Training Boards) in order to hold employment, some authors[11] argue that decertification would have a much more personal (and therefore more effective) impact on individual officers than the exclusionary rule ever could.

A third possibility would allow the Supreme Court to address theoretical questions involving issues of due process. Concerned supervisors and officials could ask how the Court would rule "if…." As things now work, the Court can address only real cases and does so on a **writ of certiorari**, in which the Court orders the record of a lower court case to be prepared for review.

The obvious difficulty with these solutions, however, is that they would substantially reduce the potential benefits available to defendants through the appeals process and, hence, would effectively eliminate the process itself.

The Fruit of the Poisoned Tree Doctrine

The Court further built on the rules concerning evidence with its ruling in *Silverthorne Lumber Co.* v. *U.S.* In 1918, Frederick Silverthorne and his sons operated a lumber company and were accused of avoiding payment of federal taxes. When asked to turn over the company's books to federal investigators, the Silverthornes refused, citing their Fifth Amendment privilege against self-incrimination.

Shortly thereafter, federal agents, without a search warrant, descended on the lumber company and seized the wanted books. The Silverthornes's lawyer appeared in court and asked that the materials be returned, citing the need for a search warrant as had been established in the *Weeks* case. The prosecutor agreed, and the books were returned to the Silverthornes.

The Silverthornes came to trial thinking they would be acquitted because the evidence against them was no longer in the hands of prosecutors. In a surprise move, however, the prosecution introduced photocopies of incriminating evidence which they had made from the returned books. The Silverthornes were convicted in federal court. Their appeal eventually reached the Supreme Court of the United States. The Court ruled that just as **illegally seized evidence** cannot be used in a trial, neither can evidence be used which *derives* from an illegal seizure.[12] The conviction of the Silverthornes was overturned, and they were set free.

The *Silverthorne* case articulated a new principle of due process which we today call the **fruit of the poisoned tree doctrine**. This doctrine is potentially far reaching. Complex cases developed after years of police investigative effort may be ruined if defense attorneys are able to demonstrate that the prosecution's case, however complex, was originally based on a search or seizure which violated due process. In such cases, it is likely that all evidence will be declared "tainted" and become useless.

Still, prior to the Warren Court era, most U.S. Supreme Court decisions were regarded as applicable only to federal law enforcement agencies.

The Warren Court Era (1953–1969)

Before the 1960s, the U.S. Supreme Court intruded only infrequently on the overall operation of the criminal justice system at the state and local level. As some authors have observed, however, the 1960s provided a time of youthful idealism, and "without the distraction of a depression or world war, individual liberties were examined at all levels of society."[13] Hence, although the exclusionary rule became an overriding consideration in federal law enforcement from the time that it was first defined by the Supreme Court in the *Weeks* case in 1914, it was not until 1961

Writ of Certiorari. An order, by an appellate court, specifying whether or not that court will review the judgment of a lower court.

Fruit of the Poisoned Tree Doctrine. A legal principle which excludes from introduction at trial any evidence later developed as a result of an originally illegal search or seizure.

Illegally Seized Evidence. Evidence seized in violation of law and legal precedent.

that the Warren Court, under Chief Justice Earl Warren, decided a case that was to change the face of American law enforcement forever. That case, *Mapp* v. *Ohio* (1961),[14] made the exclusionary rule applicable to criminal prosecutions at the state level.[15] Beginning with the now famous *Mapp* case, the Warren Court set out to chart a course which would guarantee nationwide recognition of individual rights, as it understood them, by agencies at all levels of the criminal justice system.

The Warren Court Applies the Exclusionary Rule to the States

The *Mapp* case began like many others during the protest-prone 1960s. Dolree Mapp was suspected of harboring a fugitive wanted in a bombing. When Ohio police officers arrived at her house, she refused to admit them. Eventually, they forced their way in. During the search which ensued, pornographic materials, including photographs, were uncovered. Mapp was arrested, and eventually convicted, under a state law which made possession of such materials illegal.

Prior decisions by the U.S. Supreme Court, including *Wolf* v. *Colorado*,[16] had led officers to expect that the exclusionary rule did not apply to agents of state and local law enforcement. Nonetheless, in a wide-reaching and precedent-setting decision, Mapp's conviction was overturned upon appeal by a majority of Warren Court justices who decided that the U.S. Constitution, under the Fourteenth Amendment's due process guarantee, mandates that state and local law enforcement officers must be held to the same standards of accountability as federal officers. There could be little doubt, said the justices, that the evidence against Mapp had been illegally obtained and therefore could not be used against her in any court of law in the United States. The precedent established in *Mapp* v. *Ohio* firmly applied the principles developed in *Weeks* and *Silverthorne* to trials in state courts, making police officers at all levels accountable to the rule of law, which, as embodied in the words of the Fourteenth Amendment, reads: "nor shall any State deprive any person of life, liberty, or property, without due process of law; nor deny to any person within its jurisdiction the equal protection of the laws."

Another important Warren-era case, that of *Chimel* v. *California* (1969)[17] involved both arrest and search activities by local law enforcement officers. Ted Chimel was convicted of the burglary of a coin shop, based on evidence gathered at the scene of his arrest—his home. Officers, armed with an arrest warrant but not a search warrant, had taken Chimel into custody when they arrived at his residence and proceeded with a search of his entire three-bedroom house, including the attic, a small workshop, and the garage. Although officers realized that the search might be challenged in court, they justified it by claiming that it was conducted not so much to uncover evidence, but as part of the arrest process. Searches which are conducted incidental to arrest, they argued, are necessary for the officers' protection and should not require a search warrant. Coins taken from the burglarized coin shop were found at various places in Chimel's residence, including the garage, and provided the evidence used against him at trial.

Chimel's appeal eventually reached the U.S. Supreme Court, which ruled that the search of Chimel's residence, though incidental to arrest, became invalid when it went beyond the person arrested and the area subject to that person's "immediate control." The thrust of the Court's decision was that searches during arrest can be made to protect arresting officers but that without a search warrant, their scope must be strongly circumscribed. Legal implications of *Chimel* v. *California* are summarized in Table 5-2.

The decision in the case of Ted Chimel was predicated on earlier reasoning by the Court in the case of *U.S.* v. *Rabinowitz* (1950).[18] Rabinowitz, a stamp collector, had been arrested and charged by federal agents with selling altered postage stamps in order to defraud other collectors. Employing a valid arrest warrant, officers arrested Rabinowitz at his place of employment and then proceeded to search his desk, file cabinets, and safe. They did not have a search warrant, but his office was small—only one room—and the officers conducted the search with a specific object in mind, the illegal stamps. Eventually, 573 altered postage stamps were seized in the search, and Rabinowitz was convicted in federal court of charges related to selling altered stamps.

Rabinowitz's appeal to the U.S. Supreme Court, based on the claim that the warrantless search of his business was illegal, was denied. The Court ruled that the Fourth Amendment provides protection against *unreasonable* searches, but that the search, in this case, followed legally from the arrest of the suspect. In the language used by the Court, "It is not disputed that there may be reasonable searches, incident to arrest, without a search warrant. Upon acceptance of this established rule that some authority to search follows from lawfully taking the person into custody, it becomes apparent that such searches turn upon the reasonableness under all the circumstances and not upon the practicability of procuring a search warrant, for the warrant is not required."

Since the early days of the exclusionary rule, other court decisions have highlighted the fact that "the Fourth Amendment protects people, not places."[19] In other words, although the commonly heard claim that "a person's home is his or her castle" has a great deal of validity within the context of constitutional law, persons can have a reasonable expectation to privacy in "homes" of many descriptions. Apartments, duplex dwellings, motel rooms—even the cardboard boxes or makeshift tents of the "homeless"—can all become protected places under the Fourth Amendment. In *Minnesota* v. *Olson*[20] (1990), for example, the U.S. Supreme Court extended the protection against warrantless searches to overnight guests residing in the home of another. The capacity to claim the protection of the Fourth Amendment, said the Court, depends on whether the *person* who makes that claim has a legitimate expectation of privacy in the place searched.

The Burger (1969–1986) and Rehnquist (1986–Present) Courts

The swing toward conservatism which our country experienced during the 1980s and early 1990s gave rise to "yuppies," "generation X," designer clothes, and a renewed concern with protecting the financial and other interests of those who live within the law. The Reagan–Bush years, and the popularity of two presidents in whom many saw the embodiment of "old-fashioned" values, reflected the tenor of a nation seeking a return to simpler times.

A California police officer spot-checks a seized substance suspected of being cocaine. The exclusionary rule means that illegally gathered evidence cannot be used later in court, requiring that police officers pay close attention to the way in which they gather and handle evidence. Photo by Mark Richards.

TABLE 5-2

Implications of Chimel v. California

What Arresting Officers May Search
✔ The defendant
✔ The physical area within easy reach of the defendant

Valid Reasons for Conducting a Search
✔ To protect the arresting officers
✔ To prevent evidence from being destroyed
✔ To keep the defendant from escaping

When a Search Becomes Illegal
✔ When it goes beyond the defendant and the area within the defendant's immediate control
✔ When it is conducted for other than a valid reason

Throughout the late 1980s, the U.S. Supreme Court mirrored the nation's conservative tenor by distancing itself from certain earlier decisions of the Warren Court. The underlying theme of the new Court, the **Burger Court** (which held sway from 1969 until 1986), was its adherence to the principle that criminal defendants, in claiming violations of their due process rights, need to bear the bulk of responsibility in showing that police went beyond the law in the performance of their duties. That trend continues into the present day under the **Rehnquist Court** (1986–present), led by Chief Justice William H. Rehnquist.

Good Faith Exceptions to the Exclusionary Rule

The Burger Court, led by Chief Justice Warren E. Burger, began what some have called a "chipping away" at the strict application of the exclusionary rule originally set forth in the *Weeks* and *Silverthorne* cases. In the case of *Illinois* v. *Gates* (1983),[21] the Court was asked to modify the exclusionary rule to permit the use of evidence in court which had been seized in "reasonable **good faith**" by officers even though the search was later ruled illegal. The Court, however, chose not to address the issue at that time.

But only a year later, in the 1984 case of *U.S.* v. *Leon*,[22] the Court recognized what has now come to be called the "good faith exception to the exclusionary rule." The *Leon* case involved the Burbank, California, Police Department and its investigation of a drug trafficking suspect. The suspect, Leon, was placed under surveillance following a tip from a confidential informant. Investigators applied for a search warrant based on information gleaned through the surveillance. They believed that they were in compliance with the Fourth Amendment requirement that "no warrants shall issue but upon probable cause." **Probable cause**, a tricky but important concept, can be defined as "a legal criterion residing in a set of facts and circumstances which would cause a reasonable person to believe that a particular other person has committed a specific crime." Probable cause must be satisfactorily demonstrated by police officers in a written affidavit to a magistrate before a search warrant can be issued. Magistrates[23] are low-level judges and, under our system of checks and balances, act to ensure that the police have established the probable cause needed for warrants to be obtained.

In *U.S.* v. *Leon*, the affidavit submitted by police to a magistrate requesting a search warrant was reviewed by numerous deputy district attorneys, and the magistrate decided to issue the warrant. A search of Leon's three residences yielded a large amount of drugs and other evidence. Although Leon was convicted of drug trafficking, a later ruling in a federal district court resulted in the suppression of evidence against him on the basis that the original affidavit prepared by the police had not, in the opinion of the court, been sufficient to establish probable cause.

Good Faith. A possible legal basis for an exception to the exclusionary rule. Law enforcement officers who conduct a search, or seize evidence, on the basis of good faith (that is, where they believe they are operating according to the dictates of the law) and who later discover that a mistake was made (perhaps in the format of the application for a search warrant) may still use, in court, evidence seized as the result of such activities.

Probable Cause. (Also discussed in Chapter 1) Refers to that necessary level of belief which would allow for police seizures (arrests) of individuals and searches of dwellings, vehicles, and possession. Probable cause can generally be found in a set of facts and circumstances which would cause a reasonable person to believe that a particular individual has committed a specific crime. Upon a demonstration of probable cause, magistrates will issue warrants authorizing law enforcement officers to effect arrests and conduct searches.

The government petitioned the U.S. Supreme Court to consider whether evidence gathered by officers acting in good faith as to the validity of a warrant should fairly be excluded at trial. The impending modification of the exclusionary rule was intoned in the first sentence of that Court's written decision:

"This case presents the question whether the Fourth Amendment exclusionary rule should be modified so as not to bar the use in the prosecution's case-in-chief of evidence obtained by officers acting in reasonable reliance on a search warrant issued by a detached and neutral magistrate but ultimately found to be unsupported by probable cause." The Court continued: "When law enforcement officers have acted in objective good faith or their transgressions have been minor, the magnitude of the benefit conferred on such guilty defendants offends basic concepts of the criminal justice system." Reflecting the renewed conservatism of the Burger Court, the justices found for the government and reinstated the conviction of Leon.

In that same year, the Supreme Court case of *Massachusetts* v. *Sheppard*[24] (1984) further reinforced the concept of "good faith." In the *Sheppard* case, officers executed a search warrant which failed to describe accurately the property to be seized. Although they were aware of the error, they had been assured by a magistrate that the warrant was valid. After the seizure was complete and a conviction had been obtained, the Massachusetts Supreme Judicial Court reversed the finding of the trial court. Upon appeal, the U.S. Supreme Court reiterated the good faith exception and let the original conviction stand.

Although the cases of *Leon* and *Sheppard* represented a clear reversal of Warren Court philosophy, the trend continued with the 1987 case of *Illinois* v. *Krull*.[25] In *Krull*, the Court, now under the leadership of Chief Justice William H. Rehnquist, held that the good faith exception applied to a warrantless search supported by state law even where the state statute was later found to violate the Fourth Amendment. Similarly, another 1987 Supreme Court case, *Maryland* v. *Garrison*,[26] supported the use of evidence obtained with a search warrant which was inaccurate in its specifics. In *Garrison*, officers had procured a warrant to search an apartment believing it was the only dwelling on a building's third floor. After searching the entire floor, they discovered that it housed more than one apartment. Even so, evidence acquired in the search was held to be admissible based on the reasonable mistake of the officers.

The 1990 case of *Illinois* v. *Rodriguez*[27] further diminished the scope of the exclusionary rule. In *Rodriguez*, a badly beaten woman named Gail Fischer complained to police that she had been assaulted in a Chicago apartment. Fischer led police to the apartment—which she indicated she shared with the defendant—produced a key, and opened the door to the dwelling. Inside, investigators found the defendant, Edward Rodriguez, asleep on a bed, with drug paraphernalia and cocaine spread around him. Rodriguez was arrested and charged with assault and possession of a controlled substance.

Upon appeal, Rodriguez demonstrated that Fischer had not lived with him for at least a month—and argued that she could no longer be said to have legal control over the apartment. Hence, the defense claimed, Fischer had no authority to provide investigators with access to the dwelling. According to arguments made by the defense, the evidence, which had been obtained without a warrant, had not been properly seized. The Supreme Court disagreed, ruling that "even if Fischer did not possess common authority over the premises, there was no Fourth Amendment violation if the police *reasonably believed* at the time of their entry that Fischer possessed the authority to consent."

Legal scholars have suggested that the exclusionary rule may undergo even further modification in the near future. One analyst of the contemporary scene points to the fact that "the [Rehnquist] Court's majority is [now] clearly committed to the idea that the exclusionary rule is not directly part of the Fourth Amendment (and Fourteenth Amendment due process), but instead is an evidentiary device

TABLE 5-3

Established Exceptions to the Exclusionary Rule

Police Powers	Supported by
Stop and frisk	*Terry v. Ohio* (1968)
Warrantless searches incident to a lawful arrest	*U.S. v. Rabinowitz* (1950)
Seizure of evidence in "good faith," even in the face of some exclusionary rule violations	*U.S. v. Leon* (1984) *Illinois v. Krull* (1987)
Warrantless vehicle searches where probable cause exists to believe that the vehicle contains contraband and/or the occupants have been lawfully arrested	*Carroll v. U.S.* (1925) *New York v. Belton* (1981) *U.S. v. Ross* (1982) *California v. Carney* (1985) *California v. Acevedo* (1991)
Gathering of incriminating evidence during interrogation in noncustodial circumstances	*Beckwith v. United States* (1976)
Authority to search incidental to arrest and/or to conduct a protective sweep in conjunction with an in-home arrest	*Chimel v. California* (1969) *U.S. v. Edwards* (1974) *Maryland v. Buie* (1990)
Authority to enter or search an "open field" without a warrant	*Hester v. U.S.* (1924) *Oliver v. U.S.* (1984) *U.S. v. Dunn* (1987)
Permissibility of warrantless naked-eye aerial observation of open areas and/or greenhouses	*California v. Ciraolo* (1986) *Florida v. Riley* (1989)
Warrantless seizure of abandoned materials and refuse	*California v. Greenwood* (1988)
Prompt action in the face of threats to public safety	*Warden v. Hayden* (1967) *Borchardt v. U.S.* (1987) *New York v. Quarles* (1984)
Evidence in "plain view" may be seized	*Harris v. New York* (1968) *Coolidge v. New Hampshire* (1971) *Horton v. California* (1990)
Use of police informants in jail cells	*Kuhlman v. Wilson* (1986) *Illinois v. Perkins* (1990) *Arizona v. Fulminante* (1991)
Lawfulness of arrests based on computer errors made by clerks	*Arizona v. Evans* (1995)

instituted by the Court to effectuate it."[28] In other words, if the Court should be persuaded that the rule is no longer effective, or that some other strategy could better achieve the aim of protecting individual rights, the rule could be abandoned entirely. A general listing of established exceptions to the exclusionary rule is provided in Table 5-3, including three which we will now discuss.

The Plain View Doctrine

Plain View. A legal term describing the ready visibility of objects which might be seized as evidence during a search by police in the absence of a search warrant specifying the seizure of those objects. In order for evidence in plain view to be lawfully seized, officers must have a legal right to be in the viewing area and must have cause to believe that the evidence is somehow associated with criminal activity.

Police officers have the opportunity to begin investigations or confiscate evidence, without the need for a warrant, based on what they find in plain view and open to public inspection. The **plain view** doctrine was first stated in the Supreme Court case of *Harris* v. *U.S.*[29] (1968) in which a police officer inventorying an impounded vehicle discovered evidence of a robbery. In the *Harris* case, the Court ruled that "objects falling in the plain view of an officer who has a right to be in the position to have that view are subject to seizure and may be introduced in evidence."[30]

Common situations in which the plain view doctrine is applicable include emergencies such as crimes in progress, fires, and accidents. A police officer responding to a call for assistance, for example, might enter a residence intending to provide aid to an injured person and find drugs or other contraband in plain view. If so, he or she would be within his or her legitimate authority to confiscate the materials and effect an arrest if the owner of the substance could be identified.

The plain view doctrine applies only to sightings by the police under legal circumstances—that is, in places where the police have a legitimate right to be, and typically only if the sighting was coincidental. Similarly, the incriminating nature of the evidence seized must have been "immediately apparent" to the officers making the seizure.[31] If officers conspired to avoid the necessity for a search warrant by helping to create a plain view situation through surveillance, duplicity, or other means, the doctrine likely would not apply.

The plain view doctrine, however, has been restricted by more recent federal court decisions. In the 1982 case of *U.S.* v. *Irizarry,*[32] the First Circuit Court of Appeals held that officers could not move objects to gain a view of evidence otherwise hidden from view. Agents had arrested a number of men in a motel room in Isla Verde, Puerto Rico. A valid arrest warrant formed the legal basis for the arrest, and some quantities of plainly visible drugs were seized from the room. An agent, looking through a window into the room prior to the arrest, had seen one of the defendants with a gun. After the arrest was complete, and no gun had been found on the suspects, another officer noticed a bathroom ceiling panel out of place. The logical conclusion was that a weapon had been secreted there. On inspection, a substantial quantity of cocaine and various firearms were found hidden in the ceiling. The Court, however, refused to allow these weapons and drugs to be used as evidence because, it said, "the items of evidence found above the ceiling panel were not plainly visible to the agents standing in the room."[33]

In the Supreme Court case of *Arizona* v. *Hicks* (1987),[34] the requirement that evidence be in plain view, without the need for officers to move or dislodge evidence, was reiterated. In the *Hicks* case, officers responded to a shooting in an apartment. A bullet had been fired in a second floor apartment and had gone through the floor, injuring a man in the apartment below. The quarters of James Hicks were found to be in considerable disarray when entered by investigating officers. As officers looked for the person who might have fired the weapon, they discovered and confiscated a number of guns and a stocking mask such as might be used in robberies. In one corner, however, officers noticed two expensive stereo sets. One of the officers, suspecting that the sets were stolen, went over to the equipment and was able to read the serial numbers of one of the components from where it rested. Some of the serial numbers, however, were not clearly visible, and the investigating officer moved some of the components in order to read the numbers. When he called the numbers into headquarters, he was told that the equipment indeed had been stolen. The stereo components were seized, and James Hicks was arrested. Hicks was eventually convicted on a charge of armed robbery, based on the evidence seized.

Upon appeal, the *Hicks* case reached the U.S. Supreme Court, which ruled that the officer's behavior had become illegal when he moved the stereo equipment to record serial numbers. The Court held that persons have a "reasonable expectation to privacy,"[35] which means that officers, lacking a search warrant, even when invited into a residence, must act more like guests than inquisitors.

Most evidence seized under the plain view doctrine is discovered "inadvertently," that is, by accident.[36] However, in 1990, the U.S. Supreme Court, in the case of *Horton* v. *California*, ruled that "even though inadvertence *is* a characteristic of most legitimate 'plain view' seizures, it *is not* a necessary condition."[37] In the *Horton* case, a warrant was issued authorizing the search of a defendant's home for stolen jewelry. The affidavit, completed by the officer who requested the warrant, alluded to an Uzi submachine gun and a stun gun—weapons purportedly used in the jewel robbery. It did not request that those weapons be listed on the search warrant. Officers searched the defendant's home but did not find the stolen jewelry. They did, however, seize a number of weapons—among them the Uzi, two stun guns, and a .38-caliber revolver. Horton was convicted of robbery in a trial where the seized weapons were introduced into evidence. He appealed his conviction, claiming that officers had reason to believe that the weapons were in his home at the time of the search, and were, therefore, not seized inadvertently. His appeal was rejected by the Court. As a result of the *Horton* case, "inadvertence" is no longer considered a condition necessary to ensure the legitimacy of a seizure that results when evidence other than that listed in a search warrant is discovered.

Emergency Searches of Property

Certain emergencies may justify a police officer in searching the premises, even without a warrant. Recent decisions by U.S. Appeals Courts have resulted in such activities being termed exigent circumstances searches. According to the Legal Counsel Division of the FBI, three threats "provide justification for emergency warrantless action."[38] They are clear dangers (1) to life, (2) of escape, and (3) of the removal or destruction of evidence. Any one of these situations may create an exception to the Fourth Amendment's requirement of a search warrant. Where emergencies necessitate a quick search of premises, however, law enforcement officers are responsible for demonstrating that a dire situation existed which justified their actions. Failure to do so successfully in court, will, of course, taint any seized evidence and make it unusable.

Emergency Searches.
Those searches conducted by the police without a warrant, which are justified on the basis of some immediate and overriding need—such as public safety, the likely escape of a dangerous suspect, or the removal or destruction of evidence.

The need for **emergency searches** was first recognized by the U.S. Supreme Court in 1967 in the case of *Warden* v. *Hayden*.[39] There, the Court approved the search of a residence which was conducted without a warrant, but which followed reports that an armed robber had fled into the building. In *Mincey* v. *Arizona* (1978),[40] the Supreme Court held that "the Fourth Amendment does not require police officers to delay in the course of an investigation if to do so would gravely endanger their lives or the lives of others."[41]

A 1990 decision, rendered in the case of *Maryland* v. *Buie*,[42] extended the authority of police to search locations in a house where a potentially dangerous person could hide while an arrest warrant is being served. The *Buie* decision was meant primarily to protect investigators from potential danger and can apply when officers lack a warrant, probable cause, or even reasonable suspicion.

In 1995, in the case of *Wilson* v. *Arkansas*,[43] the U.S. Supreme Court ruled that police officers generally must knock and announce their identity before entering a dwelling or other premises with a search warrant. Under certain emergency circumstances, however, officers armed with a warrant need not knock or identify themselves. In *Wilson*, the Court added that Fourth Amendment requirements that searches be reasonable "should not be read to mandate a rigid rule of announcement that ignores countervailing law enforcement interests." Hence, officers need not announce themselves, the Court said, when suspects may be in the process of destroying evidence, when officers are pursuing a recently escaped arrestee, or where officers' lives may be endangered by such an announcement.

The Computer Errors Exception

In 1995, in the case of *Arizona* v. *Evans*,[44] the Court created a "computer errors exception" to the exclusionary rule by holding that a traffic stop which led to the seizure of marijuana was legal even though officers conducted the stop based on an arrest warrant improperly stored in their computer. The case began in 1991 when Isaac Evans was stopped in Phoenix, Arizona, for driving the wrong way on a one-way street in front of a police station. A routine computer check reported an outstanding arrest warrant for Evans, and he was taken into custody. Police found marijuana in the car Evans had been driving, and he was eventually convicted on charges of possessing a controlled substance. After his arrest, however, police learned that the arrest warrant reported to them by their computer had actually been quashed a few weeks earlier, but through the clerical oversight of a court employee, had never been removed from the computer.

In upholding Evans's conviction, the high Court reasoned that officers could not be held responsible for a clerical error make by a court worker and concluded that the arresting officers were acting in good faith based on the information available to them at the time of the arrest. In addition, the majority opinion said that "the rule excluding evidence obtained without a warrant was intended to deter police misconduct, not mistakes by court employees."

In what may have been a warning to police administrators not to depend on the excuse of computer error, however, Justice Sandra Day O'Connor, in a concurring opinion, wrote, "The police, of course, are entitled to enjoy the substantial advantages this [computer] technology confers....They may not, however, rely on it blindly. With the benefits of more efficient law enforcement mechanisms comes the burden of corresponding constitutional responsibilities."

Arrest

Officers seize not only property, but persons as well—a process we refer to as arrest. Most people think of arrest in terms of what they see on popular television crime shows. The suspect is chased, subdued, and "cuffed" after committing some loathsome act in view of the camera. Some arrests do occur that way. In reality, however, most instances of arrest are far more mundane.

In technical terms, an **arrest** occurs whenever a law enforcement officer restricts a person's freedom to leave. There may be no yelling *"You're under arrest!"* no *Miranda* **warnings** may be offered, and, in fact, the suspect may not even consider himself or herself to be in custody. Such arrests, and the decision to enforce them, evolve as the situation between the officer and suspect develops. They usually begin with polite conversation and a request by the officer for information. Only when the suspect tries to leave, and tests the limits of the police response, may the suspect discover that he or she is really in custody. In the 1980 case of *U.S.* v. *Mendenhall*,[45] Justice Stewart set forth the "free to leave" test for determining whether a person has been arrested. Stewart wrote: "a person has been 'seized' within the meaning of the Fourth Amendment only if in view of all the circumstances surrounding the incident, a reasonable person would have believed that he was not free to leave." The "free to leave" test "has been repeatedly adopted by the Court as the test for a seizure."[46] In 1994, in the case of *Stansbury* v. *California*,[47] the Court once again used such a test in determining the point at which an arrest had been made. In *Stansbury*, where the focus was on the interrogation of a suspected child molester and murderer, the Court ruled, "In determining whether an individual was in custody, a court must examine all of the circumstances surrounding the interrogation, but the ultimate inquiry is simply whether there [was] a formal arrest or restraint on freedom of movement of the degree associated with a formal arrest."

Arrests which follow the questioning of a suspect are probably the most common type. When the decision to arrest is reached, the officer has come to the conclusion that a crime has been committed and that the suspect is probably the one who committed it. The presence of these mental elements constitutes the probable cause needed for an arrest. Probable cause is the minimum necessary for an arrest under any circumstances.

Arrests may also occur when the officer arrives while a crime is in progress. Such situations often require apprehension of the offender to ensure the safety of the public. Most arrests made during crimes in progress, however, are for misdemeanors rather than felonies. In fact, many states do not allow arrest for a misdemeanor unless it is committed in the presence of an officer. In any event, crimes in progress clearly provide the probable cause necessary for an arrest.

Most jurisdictions allow arrest for a felony without a warrant when a crime is not in progress, as long as probable cause can be established.[48] Some, however, require a warrant. In the case of *Payton* v. *New York* (1980), the U.S. Supreme Court ruled that, unless the suspect gives consent or an emergency exists, an arrest warrant is necessary if an arrest requires entry into a suspect's private residence.[49] Arrest warrants are issued by magistrates when police officers can demonstrate probable cause. Magistrates will usually require that the officers seeking an arrest warrant submit a written affidavit outlining their reason for the arrest.

Arrest. Taking an adult or juvenile into physical custody by authority of law, for the purpose of charging the person with a criminal offense or a delinquent act or status offense, terminating with the recording of a specific offense. Technically, an arrest occurs whenever a person's freedom to leave is curtailed by a law enforcement officer.

Searches Incident to an Arrest. Those warrantless searches of arrested individuals that are conducted in order to ensure the safety of the arresting officer(s). Because individuals placed under arrest may be in the possession of weapons, courts have recognized the need for arresting officers to protect themselves by conducting an immediate and warrantless search of arrested individuals without the need for a warrant.

The U.S. Supreme Court has established a clear rule that police officers have the right to conduct a search of a person being arrested, and to search the area under the immediate control of that person to protect themselves from attack. This is true even if the officer and the arrestee are of different sexes.

This "rule of the game" was created in the *Rabinowitz* and *Chimel* cases cited earlier. It became firmly established in other cases involving personal searches, such as the 1973 case of *Robinson* v. *U.S.*[50] Robinson was stopped for a traffic violation, when it was learned that his driver's license was expired. He was arrested for operating a vehicle without a valid license. Officers subsequently searched the defendant to be sure he wasn't carrying a weapon and discovered a substance which later proved to be heroin. Convicted of drug possession, he appealed. When Robinson's appeal reached the U.S. Supreme Court, the Court upheld the officer's right to conduct a search without a warrant for purposes of personal protection, and to use the fruits of such a search when it turns up other contraband. In the words of the Court, "A custodial arrest of a suspect based upon probable cause is a reasonable intrusion under the Fourth Amendment; that intrusion being lawful, a search incident to the arrest requires no additional jurisdiction."[51]

The Court's decision in *Robinson* reinforced an earlier ruling involving a seasoned officer who conducted a "pat-down" search of two men who he suspected were "casing" a store, about to commit a robbery.[52] The officer in the case was a 39-year veteran of police work, who testified that the men "did not look right." When he approached them, he suspected they might be armed. Fearing for his life, he quickly spun the men around, put them up against a wall, patted down their clothing, and found a gun on one of the men. The man, Terry, was later convicted in Ohio courts of carrying a concealed weapon.

Terry's appeal was based on the argument that the suspicious officer had no probable cause to arrest him and, therefore, no cause to search him. The search, he argued, was illegal, and the evidence obtained should not have been used against

The courts have generally held that, in order to protect themselves and the public, officers have the authority to search persons being arrested. Here arresting officers "pat down" a drug suspect. Photo by Craig/Filipacchi, courtesy of Gamma-Liaison, Inc.

him. The Supreme Court disagreed, saying, "In view of these facts, we cannot blind ourselves to the need for law enforcement officers to protect themselves and other prospective victims of violence in situations where they may lack probable cause for an arrest."[53]

The *Terry* case has become the basis for a type of on-the-street interrogation that we today refer to as "field interrogation," also called "stop and frisk." Police also refer to it as a "Terry-type stop." The *Terry* case, for all the authority it conferred on officers, also made it clear that officers must have reasonable grounds for any stop or frisk that they conduct.

In 1989, the Supreme Court, in the case of *U.S.* v. *Sokolow*,[54] clarified the basis on which law enforcement officers, lacking probable cause to believe that a crime has occurred, may stop and briefly detain a person for investigative purposes. In *Sokolow*, the Court ruled that the legitimacy of such a stop must be evaluated according to a "totality of circumstances" criteria—in which all aspects of the defendant's behavior, taken in concert, may provide the basis for a legitimate stop. In this case, the defendant, Sokolow, appeared suspicious to police because, while traveling under an alias from Honolulu, he had paid $2,100 in $20 bills (from a large roll of money) for two airplane tickets after spending a surprisingly small amount of time in Miami. In addition, the defendant was obviously nervous and checked no luggage. A warrantless airport investigation by DEA agents uncovered more than 1,000 grams of cocaine in the defendant's belongings. The Court, in upholding Sokolow's conviction, ruled that, although no single activity was proof of illegal activity, taken together they created circumstances under which suspicion of illegal activity was justified.

In 1993, however, in the case of *Minnesota* v. *Dickerson*,[55] the U.S. Supreme Court placed new limits on an officer's ability to seize evidence discovered during a pat-down search conducted for protective reasons when the search itself was based merely on suspicion and failed to immediately reveal the presence of a weapon. In this case, Timothy Dickerson, who was observed leaving a building known for cocaine trafficking, was stopped by Minneapolis police officers after they noticed him acting suspiciously. The officers decided to investigate further and ordered Dickerson to submit to a pat-down search. The search revealed no weapons, but the officer conducting it testified that he felt a small lump in Dickerson's jacket pocket, believed it to be a lump of crack cocaine on examining it with his fingers, and then reached into Dickerson's pocket and retrieved a small bag of cocaine. Dickerson was arrested, tried, and convicted of possession of a controlled substance. His appeal, which claimed that the pat-down search had been illegal, eventually made its way to the U.S. Supreme Court. The high Court ruled that "if an officer lawfully pats down a suspect's outer clothing and feels an object whose contour or mass makes its identity immediately apparent, there has been no invasion of the suspect's privacy beyond that already authorized by the officer's search for weapons." However, in *Dickerson*, the justices ruled, "the officer never thought that the lump was a weapon, but did not immediatley recognize it as cocaine." The lump was determined to be cocaine only after the officer "squeezed, slid, and otherwise manipulated the pocket's contents." Hence, the Court held, the officer's actions in this case did not qualify under what might be called a "plain feel" exception. In any case, said the Court, the search in *Dickerson* went far beyond what is permissible under *Terry*—where officer safety was the crucial issue. The Court summed up its ruling in *Dickerson* this way: "While *Terry* entitled [the officer] to place his hands on respondent's jacket and to feel the lump in the pocket, his continued exploration of the pocket after he concluded that it contained no weapon was unrelated to the sole justification for the search under Terry" and was therefore illegal.

Just as arrest must be based on probable cause, officers may not stop and question an unwilling citizen whom they have no reason to suspect of a crime. In the case of *Brown* v. *Texas*[56] (1979), two Texas law enforcement officers stopped the defendant and asked for identification. Brown, they later testified, had not been acting suspiciously, nor did they think he might have a weapon. The stop was made simply because officers wanted to know who he was. Brown was arrested under a Texas statute which required a person to identify himself properly and accurately when requested to do so by peace officers. Eventually, his appeal reached the U.S. Supreme Court, which ruled that, under circumstances found in the *Brown* case, a person "may not be punished for refusing to identify himself."

In *Smith* v. *Ohio* (1990),[57] the Court held that an individual has the right to protect his or her belongings from unwarranted police inspection. In *Smith*, the defendant was approached by two officers in plain clothes who observed that he was carrying a brown paper bag. The officers asked him to "come here a minute" and, when he kept walking, identified themselves as police officers. The defendant threw the bag onto the hood of his car and attempted to protect it from the officers' intrusion. Marijuana was found inside the bag, and the defendant was arrested. Since there was little reason to stop the suspect in this case, and because control over the bag was not thought necessary for the officer's protection, the Court found that the Fourth Amendment protects both "the traveler who carries a toothbrush and a few articles of clothing in a paper bag" and "the sophisticated executive with the locked attaché case."[58]

The following year, however, in what some Court observers saw as a turnabout, the U.S. Supreme Court ruled in *California* v. *Hodari D.* (1991)[59] that suspects who flee from the police and throw away evidence as they retreat may later be arrested based on the incriminating nature of the abandoned evidence. The case, which began in Oakland, California, centered on the behavior of a group of juveniles who had been standing around a parked car. Two city police officers, driving an unmarked car, but with the word "Police" emblazoned in large letters on their jackets, approached the youths. As they came close, the juveniles apparently panicked and fled. One of them tossed away a "rock" of crack cocaine, which was retrieved by the officers. The juvenile was later arrested and convicted of the possession of a controlled substance, but the California Court of Appeals reversed his conviction, reasoning that the officers did not have sufficient reasonable suspicion to make a "Terry-type stop." The Supreme Court, in reversing the finding of the California court, found that reasonable suspicion was not needed since no "stop" was made. The suspects had not been "seized" by the police, the Court ruled. Therefore, the evidence taken was not the result of an illegal seizure within the meaning of the Fourth Amendment. The significance of *Hodari* for future police action was highlighted by California prosecutors who pointed out that cases like *Hodari* occur "almost every day in this nation's urban areas."[60]

In a sharply worded dissenting opinion, Justices John Paul Stevens and Thurgood Marshall wrote "It is too early to know the consequences of the court's holding. If carried to its logical conclusion, it will encourage unlawful displays of force that will frighten countless innocent citizens into surrendering whatever privacy rights they may still have."[61]

Emergency Searches of Persons

It is possible to imagine emergency situations in which officers may have to search people based on quick decisions: a person who matches the description of an armed robber, a woman who is found lying unconscious, a man who has what appears to be blood on his shoes. Such searches can save lives by disarming fleeing felons or by uncovering a medical reason for an emergency situation. They may also prevent criminals from escaping or destroying evidence.

Emergency searches of persons, like those of premises, fall under the exigent circumstances exception to the warrant requirement of the Fourth Amendment. The Supreme Court, in the 1979 case of *Arkansas* v. *Sanders*,[62] recognized the need for such searches "where the societal costs of obtaining a warrant, such as danger to law officers or the risk of loss or destruction of evidence, outweigh the reasons for prior recourse to a neutral magistrate."[63]

Theory into Practice: Plain View Requirements

Following the opinion of the U.S. Supreme Court in the case of *Horton* v. *California* (1990), items seized under the plain view doctrine may be admissible as evidence in a court of law if the officer who seized the evidence:

1. was lawfully in the viewing area and
2. had probable cause to believe the evidence was somehow associated with criminal activity.

The 1987 case of *Borchardt* v. *U.S.*,[64] decided by the Fifth Circuit Court of Appeal, held that Borchardt could be prosecuted for heroin uncovered during medical treatment even though the defendant had objected to the treatment. Borchardt was a federal inmate at the time he was discovered unconscious in his cell. He was taken to a hospital where tests revealed heroin in his blood. His heart stopped, and he was revived using CPR. Borchardt was given three doses of Narcan, a drug used to counteract the effects of heroin, and he improved, regaining consciousness. The patient refused requests to pump his stomach but began to become lethargic, indicating the need for additional Narcan. Eventually, he vomited nine plastic bags full of heroin, along with two bags which had burst. The heroin was turned over to federal officers, and Borchardt was later convicted of heroin possession. Attempts to exclude the heroin from evidence were unsuccessful, and the appeals court ruled that the necessity of the emergency situation overruled the defendant's objections to search his person.

The Legal Counsel Division of the FBI provides the following guidelines in conducting emergency warrantless searches of individuals, where the possible destruction of evidence is at issue (keep in mind that there may be no probable cause to *arrest* the individual being searched). All four conditions must apply:[65]

1. There was probable cause to believe at the time of the search that there was evidence concealed on the person searched.
2. There was probable cause to believe an emergency threat of destruction of evidence existed at the time of the search.
3. The officer had no prior opportunity to obtain a warrant authorizing the search.
4. The action was no greater than necessary to eliminate the threat of destruction of evidence.

Vehicle Searches

Vehicles present a special law enforcement problem. They are highly movable, and when an arrest of a driver or an occupant occurs, the need to search them may be immediate.

The first significant Supreme Court case involving an automobile was that of *Carroll* v. *U.S.*[66] in 1925. In the *Carroll* case, a divided Court ruled that a warrantless search of an automobile or other vehicle is valid if it is based on a reasonable belief that contraband is present. In 1964, however, in the case of *Preston* v. *U.S.*,[67] the limits of warrantless vehicle searches were defined. Preston was arrested for vagrancy and taken to jail. His vehicle was impounded, towed to the police garage, and later searched. Two revolvers were uncovered in the glove compartment, and more incriminating evidence was found in the trunk. Preston was convicted on weapons possession and other charges and eventually appealed to the U.S. Supreme Court. The Court held that the warrantless search of Preston's vehicle had occurred while the automobile was in secure custody and had been, therefore, illegal. Time and circumstances would have permitted, the Court reasoned, acquisition of a warrant to conduct the search.

When the search of a vehicle occurs after it has been impounded, however, that search may be legitimate if it is undertaken for routine and reasonable purposes. In the case of *South Dakota* v. *Opperman* (1976),[68] for example, the Court held that a warrantless search undertaken for purposes of the inventorying and safekeeping of personal possessions of the car's owner was not illegal even though it turned up marijuana. The intent of the search had not been to discover contraband, but to secure the owner's belongings from possible theft. Again, in *Colorado* v. *Bertine* (1987), the Court reinforced the idea that officers may open closed containers found in a vehicle while conducting a routine search for inventorying purposes. In the words of the Court, such searches are "now a well-defined exception in the warrant requirement...."[69] In 1990, however, in the precedent-setting case of *Florida* v. *Wells*,[70] the Court agreed with a lower court's suppression of marijuana discovered in a locked suitcase in the trunk of a defendant's impounded vehicle. In *Wells*, the Court held that standardized criteria authorizing the search of a vehicle for inventorying purposes were necessary before such a discovery could be legitimate. Standardized criteria, said the Court, might take the form of department policies, written general orders, or established routines.

Warrantless vehicle searches may extend to any area of the vehicle and may include sealed containers, the trunk area, and the glove compartment if officers have probable cause to conduct a purposeful search or if officers have been given permission to search the vehicle. In the 1991 case of *Florida* v. *Jimeno*,[71] arresting officers stopped a motorist who gave them permission to search his car. The defendant was later convicted on a drug charge, when a bag on the floor of the car was found to contain cocaine. Upon appeal to the Supreme Court, however, he argued that the permission given to search his car did not extend to bags and other items within the car. In a decision which may have implications beyond vehicle searches, the Court held that "[a] criminal suspect's Fourth Amendment right to be free from unreasonable searches is not violated when, after he gives police permission to search his car, they open a closed container found within the car that might reasonably hold the object of the search. The Amendment is satisfied when, under the circumstances, it is objectively reasonable for the police to believe that the scope of the suspect's consent permitted them to open the particular container."[72]

In *United States* v. *Ross* (1982),[73] the Court found that officers had not exceeded their authority in opening a bag in the trunk which was found to contain heroin. The search was held to be justifiable on the basis of information developed from a search of the passenger compartment. The Court said, "if probable cause justifies the search of a lawfully stopped vehicle, it justifies the search of every part of the vehicle and its contents that may conceal the object of the search."[74]

The 1983 case of *U.S.* v. *Villamonte-Marquez*[75] widened the *Carroll* decision (discussed earlier in this chapter) to include water craft. The case involved an anchored sailboat occupied by Villamonte-Marquez which was searched by a U.S. Customs officer after one of the crew members appeared unresponsive to being hailed. The officer thought he smelled burning marijuana after boarding the vessel and saw burlap bales through an open hatch which he suspected might be contraband. A search proved him correct, and the ship's occupants were arrested. Their conviction was overturned upon appeal, but the U.S. Supreme Court reversed the appeals court. The Court reasoned that a vehicle on the water can easily leave the jurisdiction of enforcement officials, just as a car or truck can.

In *California* v. *Carney* (1985),[76] the Court extended police authority to conduct warrantless searches of vehicles to include motor homes. Earlier arguments had been advanced that a motor home, because it is more like a permanent residence, should not be considered a vehicle in the same sense of an automobile for purposes of search and seizure. The Court, in a 6-to-3 decision, rejected those arguments, reasoning that a vehicle's appointments and size do not alter its basic function of providing transportation.

Houseboats were brought under the automobile exception to the Fourth Amendment warrant requirement in the 1988 Tenth Circuit Court case of *U.S.* v. *Hill*.[77] In the *Hill* case, DEA agents developed evidence which led them to believe that methamphetamine was being manufactured on board a houseboat traversing Lake Texoma in Oklahoma. Because a storm warning had been issued for the area, agents decided to board and search the boat prior to obtaining a warrant. During the search, an operating amphetamine laboratory was discovered, and the boat was seized. In an appeal, the defendants argued that the houseboat search had been illegal because agents lacked a warrant to search their home. The appellate court, however, in rejecting the claims of the defendants, ruled that a houseboat, because it is readily mobile, may be searched without a warrant where probable cause exists to believe that a crime has been or is being committed.

Suspicionless Searches

The 1991 Supreme Court case of *Florida* v. *Bostick*,[78] which permitted warrantless "sweeps" of intercity buses, moved the Court deeply into conservative territory. The *Bostick* case came to the attention of the Court as a result of the Broward County (Florida) Sheriff Department's routine practice of boarding buses at scheduled stops and asking passengers for permission to search their bags. Terrance Bostick, a passenger on one of the buses, gave police permission to search his luggage, which was found to contain cocaine. Bostick was arrested and eventually pleaded guilty to charges of drug trafficking. The Florida Supreme Court, however, found merit in Bostick's appeal, which was based on a Fourth Amendment claim that the search of his luggage had been unreasonable. The Florida court held that "a reasonable passenger in [Bostick's] situation would not have felt free to leave the bus to avoid questioning by the police" and overturned the conviction.

The state appealed to the U.S. Supreme Court, which held that the Florida Supreme Court erred in interpreting Bostick's *feelings* that he was not free to leave the bus. In the words of the Court, "Bostick was a passenger on a bus that was scheduled to depart. He would not have felt free to leave the bus even if the police had not been present. Bostick's movements were 'confined' in a sense, but this was the natural result of his decision to take the bus." In other words, Bostick was constrained not so much by police action as by his own feelings that he might miss the bus were he to get off. Following this line of reasoning, the Court concluded that police warrantless, suspicionless "sweeps" of buses, "trains, planes, and city streets" are permissible so long as officers (1) ask individual passengers for permission before searching their possessions, (2) do not coerce passengers to consent to a search, and (3) do not convey the message that citizen compliance with the search request is mandatory. Passenger compliance with police searches must be voluntary for the searches to be legal.

In contrast to the tone of Court decisions more than two decades earlier, the justices did not require officers to inform passengers that they were free to leave, nor that they had the right to deny officers the opportunity to search (although Bostick himself was so advised by Florida officers). Any reasonable person, the Court ruled, should feel free to deny the police request. In the words of the Court, "[t]he appropriate test is whether, taking into account all of the circumstances surrounding the encounter, a reasonable passenger would feel free to decline the officers' requests or otherwise terminate the encounter." The Court continued: "[r]ejected, however, is Bostick's argument that he must have been seized because no reasonable person would freely consent to a search of luggage containing drugs, since the 'reasonable person' test presumes an innocent person."

Critics of the decision saw it as creating new "Gestapo-like" police powers in the face of which citizens on public transportation will feel compelled to comply with police requests for search authority. Dissenting Justices Blackmun, Stevens, and Marshall held that "the bus sweep at issue in this case violates the core values

Suspicionless Searches. Those searches conducted by law enforcement personnel without a warrant and without suspicion. Suspicionless searches are permissible only if based on an overriding concern for public safety.

of the Fourth Amendment." However, in words which may presage a significant change of direction for other Fourth Amendment issues, the Court's majority defended its ruling by intoning: "[t]he Fourth Amendment proscribes unreasonable searches and seizures; it does not proscribe voluntary cooperation."

he Intelligence Function

The police role includes the need to gather information through the questioning of both suspects and informants. Even more often, the need for information leads police investigators to question potentially knowledgeable citizens who may have been witnesses or victims. Data gathering is a crucial form of intelligence, without which enforcement agencies would be virtually powerless to plan and effect arrests.

The importance of gathering information in police work cannot be overstressed. Studies have found that the one factor most likely to lead to arrest in serious crimes is the presence of a witness who can provide information to the police. Undercover operations, neighborhood watch programs, "crime stopper" groups, and organized detective work all contribute information to the police.

Informants

Information gathering is a complex process, and many ethical questions have been raised about the techniques police use to gather information. Police use of paid informants, for example, is an area of concern to ethicists who believe that informants are often paid to get away with crimes. The police practice (endorsed by some prosecutors) of agreeing not to charge one offender out of a group if he or she will "talk," and testify against others, is another concern of students of justice ethics.

As we have seen, probable cause is an important aspect of both police searches and legal arrests. The Fourth Amendment specifies, "No warrants shall issue, but upon probable cause." As a consequence, the successful use of informants in supporting requests for a warrant depends on the demonstrable reliability of their information. The case of *Aguilar* v. *Texas* (1964)[79] clarified the use of informants and

Warrantless vehicle searches such as this one, where the driver is suspected of a crime, have generally been justified by the fact that vehicles are highly mobile and can quickly leave police jurisdiction. Photo by Curtis Ackerman, courtesy of The Boston Herald.

established a two-pronged test to the effect that informant information could establish probable cause if *both* of the following criteria are met:

- ✔ The source of the informant's information is made clear.
- ✔ The police officer has a reasonable belief that the informant is reliable.

The two-pronged test of *Aguilar* v. *Texas* was intended to prevent the issuance of warrants on the basis of false or fabricated information. Two later cases provided exceptions to the two-pronged test. *Harris* v. *United States* (1971)[80] recognized the fact that when an informant provided information that was damaging to him or her, it was probably true. In *Harris*, an informant told police that he had purchased nontax-paid whiskey from another person. Since the information also implicated the informant in a crime, it was held to be accurate even though it could not meet the second prong of the *Aguilar* test. The 1969 Supreme Court case of *Spinelli* v. *United States*[81] created an exception to the requirements of the first prong. In *Spinelli*, the Court held that some information can be so highly specific that it must be accurate, even if its source is not revealed. In 1983, in the case of *Illinois* v. *Gates*,[82] the Court adopted a totality of circumstances approach, which held that sufficient probable cause for issuing a warrant exists where an informer can be reasonably believed on the basis of everything that is known by the police. The *Gates* case involved an anonymous informant who provided incriminating information about another person through a letter to the police. Although the source of the information was not stated, and the police were unable to say whether or not the informant was reliable, the overall *sense* of things, given what was already known to police, was that the information supplied was probably valid.

In the 1990 case of *Alabama* v. *White*,[83] the Supreme Court ruled that an anonymous tip, even in the absence of other, corroborating information about a suspect, could form the basis for an investigatory stop where the informant accurately predicts the *future* behavior of the suspect. The ability to predict a suspect's behavior demonstrates, the Court reasoned, a significant degree of familiarity with the suspect's affairs. In the words of the Court, "Because only a small number of people are generally privy to an individual's itinerary, it is reasonable for the police to believe that a person with access to such information is likely to also have access to reliable information about that individual's illegal activities."[84]

The identity of informants may be kept secret if sources have been explicitly assured of confidentiality by investigating officers or if a reasonably implied assurance of confidentiality has been made. In *U.S. Department of Justice* v. *Landano* (1993),[85] the U.S. Supreme Court required that an informant's identity be revealed through a request made under the federal Freedom of Information Act. In that case, the FBI had not specifically assured an informant of confidentiality, and the Court ruled that "the government is not entitled to a presumption that all sources supplying information to the FBI in the course of a criminal investigation are confidential sources…"

Police Interrogation

Interrogation has been defined by the U.S. Supreme Court as any behaviors by the police "that the police should know are reasonably likely to elicit an incriminating response from the suspect." Hence, interrogation may involve activities which go well beyond mere verbal questioning, and the Court has held that interrogation may include "staged lineups, reverse lineups, positing guilt, minimizing the moral seriousness of crime, and casting blame on the victim or society." It is noteworthy that the Court has also held that "police words or actions normally attendant to arrest and custody do not constitute interrogation"[86] unless they involve pointed or directed questions. Hence, an arresting officer may instruct a suspect on what to do and may chit-chat with the offender without engaging in interrogation within the meaning of the law. Once police officers make inquiries intended to elicit information about the

Interrogation. The information-gathering activities of police officers which involve the direct questioning of suspects. The actions of officers during suspect interrogation are constrained by a number of Supreme Court decisions, the first of which was *Brown* v. *Mississippi* (1936).

Theory into Practice: Public Interest and the Right to Privacy—Suspicionless Searches

The right to privacy is a fundamental guarantee of the U.S. Constitution.[1] Most of us would probably agree that privacy is also a basic human need. Our legal system, on the other hand, has long recognized that the right to privacy must be limited in cases where individuals are reasonably suspected of having committed crimes. Arrest warrants, search warrants, and orders permitting electronic surveillance may be issued by courts upon a showing of probable cause by law enforcement officers that a crime has been committed. In two 1989 decisions, however, the U.S. Supreme Court ruled for the first time in its history that there may be instances when the need to ensure public safety provides a "**compelling interest**" which negates the rights of any individual to privacy, permitting searches even when a person is not suspected of a crime.

In the case of *National Treasury Employees Union* v. *Von Raab*[2] (1989), the Court, by a 5-to-4 vote, upheld a program of the U.S. Customs Service which required mandatory drug testing for all workers seeking promotions or job transfers involving drug interdiction and the carrying of firearms. The Court's majority opinion read: "We think the government's need to conduct the suspicionless searches required by the Customs program outweighs the privacy interest of employees engaged directly in drug interdiction, and of those who otherwise are required to carry firearms."

The second case, *Skinner* v. *Railway Labor Executives' Association*[3] (1989), was decided on the same day. In *Skinner*, the justices voted 7 to 2 to permit the mandatory testing of railway crews for the presence of drugs or alcohol following serious train accidents. The *Skinner* case involved evidence of drugs in a 1987 train wreck outside Baltimore, Maryland, in which 16 people were killed and hundreds injured.

Both decisions were decried by civil libertarians as indicating a dangerous change in high court direction. The Court's new willingness to permit "**suspicionless searches**" was condemned as infringing on the rights of innocent citizens. Justices William J. Brennan, Jr., and Thurgood Marshall summed up the concerns of many when they warned in a dissenting opinion in *Skinner* that, "the first, and worst, casualty of the war on drugs will be the precious liberties of our citizens."

QUESTIONS FOR DISCUSSION

1. Can you think of any instances, other than those mentioned here, where a "compelling interest" might justify the search of persons not considered suspects in a crime? If so, what might they be?

2. Do you agree with the assertion that "the first, and worst, casualty of the war on drugs will be the precious liberties of our citizens"? Why or why not?

1. The word used in the Fourth Amendment of the U.S. Constitution is "secure," not "private." Courts have generally equated the two terms.

2. *National Treasury Employees Union* v. *Von Raab*, 489 U.S. 656 (1989).

3. *Skinner* v. *Railway Labor Executives' Association*, 489 U.S. 602 (1989).

SOURCES: *All Things Considered*, National Public Radio, March 21, 1989; *Criminal Justice Newsletter*, April 3, 1989, p. 4; *Drug Enforcement Report*, March 23, 1989, p. 4; and "The High Court Weighs Drug Tests," *Newsweek*, April 3, 1989, p. 8.

Compelling Interest. A legal concept which provides a basis for suspicionless searches (urinalysis tests of train engineers, for example) when public safety is at issue. It is the concept on which the Supreme Court cases of *Skinner* v. *Railway Labor Executives' Association* (1989) and *National Treasury Employees Union* v. *Von Rabb* (1989) turned. In those cases, the Court held that public safety may provide a sufficiently compelling interest such that an individual's right to privacy can be limited under certain circumstances.

crime in question, however, interrogation has begun. The interrogation of suspects, like other areas of police activity, is subject to constitutional limits as interpreted by the courts, and a series of landmark decisions by the U.S. Supreme Court have clearly focused on issues of police interrogation.

Physical Abuse

The first in a series of significant cases was that of *Brown* v. *Mississippi*,[87] decided in 1936. The *Brown* case began with the robbery of a white store owner in Mississippi in 1934. During the robbery, the victim was killed. A posse formed spontaneously and went to the home of a local black man rumored to have been one of the perpetrators. They dragged the suspect from his home, put a rope around his neck, and hoisted him into a tree. They repeated this process a number of times, hoping to get a confession from the man, but failing. The posse was joined by a deputy sheriff who led them to the home of other suspects, where they repeated their "interrogation" technique. Finally, they were able to get a confession from one of the men. The remaining defendants were laid over chairs in the jail and whipped with belts and buckles until they also "confessed." These confessions were used in the trial which followed, and the three defendants were convicted of murder. Their convictions were upheld by the Mississippi Supreme Court.

One of the defendants, named Brown, made further appeals. In 1936, his case was reviewed by the U.S. Supreme Court, which overturned Brown's conviction, saying that it was difficult to imagine techniques of interrogation more "revolting" to the sense of justice than those used in this case.

Inherent Coercion

Interrogation need not involve physical abuse for it to be contrary to constitutional principles. In the case of *Ashcraft* v. *Tennessee*,[88] the Court found that **inherent coercion** during interrogation was not acceptable. Ashcraft had been charged with the murder of his brother-in-law. He was arrested on a Friday night and interrogated by relays of skilled interrogators until Monday morning, when he finally confessed to the murder. During questioning, he had been faced by a blinding light but not physically mistreated. Investigators later testified that when the suspect requested cigarettes, food, or water, they "kindly" provided them. The Supreme Court's ruling in this case made it plain that the Fifth Amendment guarantee against self-incrimination excludes *any* form of official coercion or pressure during interrogation.

A similar case, involving four black defendants, occurred in Florida in 1940.[89] The four men, including one whose name was Chambers, were arrested without warrants as suspects in a robbery and murder of an aged white man. After several days of questioning in a hostile atmosphere, the men confessed to the murder. The confessions were used as the primary evidence against them at a trial which ensued, and all four were sentenced to die. Upon appeal to the Supreme Court, the Court held that "the very circumstances surrounding their confinement and their questioning without any formal charges having been brought, were such as to fill petitioners with terror and frightful misgivings."[90]

Inherent Coercion. Those tactics used by police interviewers which fall short of physical abuse, but which, nonetheless, pressure suspects to divulge information.

Psychological Manipulation

Interrogation must not only be free of coercion and hostility, but it also cannot involve sophisticated trickery designed to ferret out a confession. Although interrogators do not necessarily have to be scrupulously honest in confronting suspects, and though the expert opinions of medical and psychiatric practitioners may be sought in investigations, the use of professionals skilled in **psychological manipulation** to gain confessions was banned by the Court in the case of *Leyra* v. *Denno*[91] in 1954.

The early 1950s were the "heyday" of psychiatric perspectives on criminal behavior. In the *Leyra* case, detectives employed a psychiatrist to question Leyra, who had been charged with the hammer slayings of his parents. Leyra had been led to believe that the medical doctor to whom he was introduced in an interrogation room had actually been sent to help him with a sinus problem. Following a period of questioning, including subtle suggestions by the psychiatrist that he would feel better if he confessed to the murders, Leyra did indeed confess.

The Supreme Court, on appeal, ruled that the defendant had been effectively, and improperly, duped by the police. In the words of the Court, "Instead of giving petitioner the medical advice and treatment he expected, the psychiatrist by subtle and suggestive questions simply continued the police effort of the past days and nights to induce petitioner to admit his guilt. For an hour and a half or more, the techniques of a highly trained psychiatrist were used to break petitioner's will in order to get him to say he had murdered his parents."[92] After a series of three trials, each with less and less evidence permitted into the courtroom by appeals courts, and following convictions in each, Leyra was finally set free by a state appeals court which found insufficient evidence for the final conviction.

Psychological Manipulation. Manipulative actions by police interviewers, designed to pressure suspects to divulge information, which are based on subtle forms of intimidation and control.

*T*heory into Practice: Individual Rights versus Group Interests—
The Fourth Amendment and Sobriety Checkpoints

The Fourth and Fourteenth Amendments to the U.S. Constitution guarantee liberty and personal security to all persons residing within the United States. Lacking probable cause to believe that a crime has been committed, the courts have generally held that police officers have no legitimate authority to detain or arrest people who are going about their business in a peaceful manner. The U.S. Supreme Court has, however, in a number of cases, decided that community interests may necessitate a temporary suspension of personal liberty, even where probable cause is lacking. One such case is that of *Michigan Department of State Police* v. *Sitz* (1990),[1] which involved the legality of highway sobriety checkpoints—even those at which nonsuspicious drivers are subjected to scrutiny.

The Court had previously established that traffic stops, including those at checkpoints along a highway, are "seizures" within the meaning of the Fourth Amendment.[2] In *Michigan Department of State Police* v. *Sitz*, however, an increasingly conservative Court ruled that such seizures are reasonable insofar as they are essential to the welfare of the community as a whole. That the Court reached its conclusion based on pragmatic social interests is clear from the words used by Chief Justice Rehnquist:

No one can seriously dispute the magnitude of the drunken driving problem or the States' interest in eradicating it. Media reports of alcohol-related death and mutilation on the Nation's roads are legion. Drunk drivers cause an annual death toll of over 25,000 and in the same time span cause nearly one million personal injuries and more than five billion dollars in property damage...[t]he balance of the States' interest in preventing drunken driving, the extent to which this

system can reasonably be said to advance that interest, and the degree of intrusion upon individual motorists who are briefly stopped, weighs in favor of the state program.

But, critics say, how far should the Court go in allowing officers to act without probable cause? Figures on domestic violence (child and spouse abuse, murder, incest, and other forms of victimization in the home), if compared to traffic statistics, are probably far more shocking. Using the same kind of reasoning as in *Michigan Department of State Police* v. *Sitz*, one could imagine the chief justice writing, "the balance of the State's interest in preventing domestic violence, the extent to which preventive programs briefly inconvenience individual citizens, and the relatively small degree of intrusion upon law-abiding citizens which such a program represents, weighs in favor of random home incursions by well-intentioned police officers."

QUESTIONS FOR DISCUSSION

1. Do you agree with the assertion that "community interests may necessitate a temporary suspension of personal liberty, even where probable cause is lacking?" Why or why not? If so, under what circumstances might liberties be suspended?

2. Would you, as this box suggests, be willing to "take intrusion upon law-abiding citizens" further? If so, what areas would you consider?

1. *Michigan Department of State Police* v. *Sitz*, 110 S.Ct. 2481 (1990).

2. *U.S.* v. *Martinea-Fuerte*, 428 U.S. 543, 96 S.Ct. 3074 (1976), and *Brower* v. *County of Inyo*, 109 S.Ct. 1378 (1989).

In 1991, the Supreme Court, in the case of *Arizona* v. *Fulminante*[93] threw an even more dampening blanket of uncertainty over the use of sophisticated techniques to gain a confession. Oreste Fulminante was an inmate in a federal prison when he was approached secretly by a fellow inmate who was an FBI informant. The informant told Fulminante that other inmates were plotting to kill him because of a rumor that he had killed a child. He offered to protect Fulminante if he was told the details of the crime. Fulminante then described his role in the murder of his 11-year-old step-daughter. Fulminante was arrested for that murder, tried, and convicted. Upon appeal to the U.S. Supreme Court, his lawyers argued that Fulminante's confession had been coerced because of the threat of violence communicated by the informant. The Court agreed that the confession had been coerced and ordered a new trial at which the confession could not be admitted into evidence. Simultaneously, however, the Court found that the admission of a coerced confession should be considered a harmless "trial error" which need not necessarily result in reversal of a conviction if other evidence still proves guilt. The decision was especially significant because it partially reversed the Court's earlier ruling, in *Chapman* v. *California*,[94] where it was held that forced confessions were such a basic form of constitutional error that they could never be used and automatically invalidated any conviction to which they related.

The Right to a Lawyer at Interrogation

In 1964, in the case of *Escobedo* v. *Illinois*,[95] the right to have legal counsel present during police interrogation was recognized. Danny Escobedo was arrested without a warrant for the murder of his brother-in-law, made no statement during his interrogation, and was released the same day. A few weeks later, another person identified Escobedo as the killer. Escobedo was rearrested and taken back to the police station. During the interrogation which followed, officers told him that they "had him cold" and that he should confess. Escobedo asked to see his lawyer, but was told that an interrogation was in progress, and that he couldn't just go out and see his lawyer. Soon the lawyer arrived and asked to see Escobedo. Police told him that his client was being questioned and could be seen after questioning concluded. Escobedo later claimed that while he repeatedly asked for his lawyer, he was told, "Your lawyer doesn't want to see you."

Eventually, Escobedo confessed and was convicted at trial on the basis of his confession. Upon appeal to the U.S. Supreme Court, the Court overturned Escobedo's conviction, ruling that counsel is necessary at police interrogations to protect the rights of the defendant and should be provided when the defendant desires.

In 1981, the case of *Edwards* v. *Arizona*[96] established a "bright-line rule" for investigators to use in interpreting a suspect's right to counsel. In *Edwards*, the Supreme Court reiterated its *Miranda* concern that once a suspect, who is in custody and who is being questioned, has requested the assistance of counsel, all questioning must cease until an attorney is present. In 1990, the Court refined the rule in *Minnick* v. *Mississippi*, when it held that interrogation may *not* resume after the suspect has had an opportunity to consult his or her lawyer when the lawyer is no longer present. Similarly, according to *Arizona* v. *Roberson* (1988),[97] the police may not avoid the defendant's request for a lawyer by beginning a new line of questioning, even if it is about an unrelated offense. In 1994, however, the Court, in the case of *Davis* v. *United States*,[98] "put the burden on custodial suspects to make unequivocal invocations of the right to counsel." In the Davis case, a man being interrogated in the death of a sailor waived his *Miranda* rights, but later said, "Maybe I should talk to a lawyer." Investigators asked the defendant clarifying questions, and he responded, "No, I don't want a lawyer." Upon conviction he appealed, claiming that interrogation should have ceased when he mentioned a lawyer. The Court, in affirming the conviction, stated that "it will often be good police practice for the interviewing officers to clarify whether or not (the defendant) actually wants an attorney."

Suspect Rights: The Miranda Decision

In the area of suspect rights, no case is as famous as that of *Miranda* v. *Arizona*,[99] which was decided in 1966. Many people regard *Miranda* as the centerpiece of Warren court due process rulings.

The case involved Ernesto Miranda, who was arrested in Phoenix, Arizona, and accused of having kidnapped and raped a young woman. At police headquarters, he was identified by the victim. After being interrogated for two hours, Miranda signed a confession which formed the basis of his later conviction on the charges.

Upon eventual appeal to the U.S. Supreme Court, the Court rendered what some regard as the most far-reaching opinion to have affected criminal justice in the last few decades. The Court ruled that Miranda's conviction was unconstitutional

Miranda Warnings. The advisement of rights due criminal suspects by the police prior to the beginning of questioning. *Miranda* warnings were first set forth by the Court in the 1966 case of *Miranda* v. *Arizona*.

because "The entire aura and atmosphere of police interrogation without notification of rights and an offer of assistance of counsel tends to subjugate the individual to the will of his examiner."

The Court continued, saying that the defendant:

> must be warned prior to any questioning that he has the right to remain silent, that anything he says can be used against him in a court of law, that he has the right to the presence of an attorney, and that if he cannot afford an attorney one will be appointed for him prior to any questioning if he so desires. Opportunity to exercise these rights must be afforded to him throughout the interrogation. After such warnings have been given, and such opportunity afforded him, the individual may knowingly and intelligently waive these rights and agree to answer the questions or make a statement. But unless and until such warnings and waiver are demonstrated by the prosecution at the trial, no evidence obtained as a result of interrogation can be used against him.[100]

To ensure that proper advice is given to suspects at the time of their arrest, the now famous *Miranda* rights are read before any questioning begins. These rights, as they appear on a *Miranda* warning card commonly used by police agencies, appear in the box on page 159.

Once suspects have been advised of their *Miranda* rights, they are commonly asked to sign a paper which lists each right, in order to confirm that they were advised of their rights, and that they understand each right. Questioning may then begin, but only if suspects waive their rights not to talk or to have a lawyer present during interrogation.

When the *Miranda* decision was made, some hailed it as one which ensured the protection of individual rights guaranteed under the Constitution. To guarantee those rights, they suggested, what better agency is available than the police themselves since the police are present at the initial stages of the criminal justice process. Critics of *Miranda*, however, have argued that the decision puts police agencies in the uncomfortable and contradictory position of not only enforcing the law, but also having to offer defendants advice on how potentially to circumvent conviction and punishment. Under *Miranda*, the police partially assume the role of legal advisor to the accused. During the last years of the Reagan administration, Attorney General Edwin Meese focused on the *Miranda* decision as the antithesis of "law and order." He pledged the resources of his office to an assault on the *Miranda* rules to eliminate what he saw as the frequent release of guilty parties on the basis of "technicalities." Nonetheless, the *Miranda* decision survives into the present day virtually unscathed.

Waiver of Miranda Rights by Suspects

Suspects in police custody may legally waive their *Miranda* rights through a voluntary "knowing and intelligent" waiver. A *knowing waiver* can only be made if a suspect has been advised of his or her rights, and was in a condition to understand the advisement. A rights advisement made in English, for example, to a Spanish-speaking defendant, cannot produce a knowing waiver. Likewise, an *intelligent waiver* of rights requires that the defendant be able to understand the consequences of not invoking the *Miranda* rights. In the case of *Moran* v. *Burbine* (1986),[101] the Supreme Court defined an intelligent and knowing waiver as one "made with a full awareness both of the nature of the right being abandoned and the consequences of the decision to abandon it."[102] Similarly, in *Colorado* v. *Spring* (1987),[103] the court held that an intelligent and knowing waiver can be made even though a suspect has not been informed of all the alleged offenses about which he or she is about to be questioned.

In 1992, *Miranda* rights were effectively extended to illegal immigrants living in the United States. In a settlement of a class-action lawsuit reached in Los Angeles with the Immigration and Naturalization Service, U.S. District Court Judge William Byrne, Jr., approved the printing of millions of notices in several languages to be

Theory into Practice: Adult Rights Warning

Persons 18 years old or older who are in custody must be given this advice of rights before any questioning.

1. You have the right to remain silent.
2. Anything you say can be used against you in a court of law.
3. You have the right to talk to a lawyer and to have a lawyer present while you are being questioned.
4. If you want a lawyer before or during questioning but cannot afford to hire a lawyer, one will be appointed to represent you at no cost before any questioning.
5. If you answer questions now without a lawyer here, you still have the right to stop answering questions at any time.

WAIVER OF RIGHTS

After reading and explaining the rights of a person in custody, an officer must also ask for a waiver of those rights before any questioning. The following waiver questions must be answered affirmatively, either by express answer or by clear implication.

Silence alone is not a waiver.

1. Do you understand each of these rights I have explained to you? (Answer must be YES.)
2. Having these rights in mind, do you now wish to answer questions? (Answer must be YES.)
3. Do you now wish to answer questions without a lawyer present? (Answer must be YES.)

For juveniles age 14, 15, 16, and 17, the following question must be asked:

4. Do you now wish to answer questions without your parents, guardians, or custodians present? (Answer must be YES.)

QUESTIONS FOR DISCUSSION

1. Are there any other "rights" that you would add to those listed here? If so, which ones?

2. Are there any "rights" that you would remove from those listed here? If so, which ones?

SOURCE: N.C. Justice Academy. Reprinted with permission.

---

given to those arrested. The approximately 1.5 million illegal aliens arrested each year must be told they may (1) talk with a lawyer, (2) make a phone call, (3) request a list of available legal services, (4) seek a hearing before an immigration judge, (5) possibly obtain release on bond, and (6) contact a diplomatic officer representing their country. This kind of thing was "long overdue," said Roberto Martinez of the American Friends Service Committee's Mexico–U.S. border program. "Up to now, we've had total mistreatment of civil rights of undocumented people."[104]

Inevitable Discovery Exception to Miranda

A good example of the change in Supreme Court philosophy, alluded to earlier in this chapter as a movement away from an individual rights and toward a social order perspective, can be had in the case of *Nix* v. *Williams* (1984).[105] The *Nix* case epitomizes what some have called a "nibbling away" at the advances in defendant rights which reached their apex in *Miranda*. The case had its beginnings in 1969, at the close of the Warren Court era, when Robert Anthony Williams was convicted of murdering a 10-year-old girl, Pamela Powers, around Christmas time. Although Williams had been advised of his rights, detectives searching for the girl's body were riding in a car with the defendant, when one of them made what has since come to be known as the "Christian burial speech." The detective told Williams that, since Christmas was almost upon them, it would be "the Christian thing to do" to see to it that Pamela could have a decent burial rather than having to lie in a field somewhere. Williams relented and led detectives to the body. However, because Williams had not been reminded of his right to have a lawyer present during his conversation with the detective, the Supreme Court overturned Williams's conviction, saying that the detective's remarks were "a deliberate eliciting of incriminating evidence from an accused in the absence of his lawyer."[106]

In 1977, Williams was retried for the murder, but his remarks in leading detectives to the body were not entered into evidence. The discovery of the body was itself used, however, prompting another appeal to the Supreme Court based on the argument that the body should not have been used as evidence since it was discovered because of the illegally gathered statements. This time the Supreme Court affirmed Williams's conviction, holding that the body would have been found anyway since detectives were searching in the direction where it lay when Williams revealed its location. That ruling came in 1984, during the heyday of the Burger Court, and clearly demonstrates a tilt by the Court away from suspect's rights, and an accommodation with the imperfect world of police procedure. The *Nix* case, as it was finally resolved, is said to have created the "inevitable discovery exception" to the *Miranda* requirements.

Public Safety Exceptions to Miranda

In 1984, the U.S. Supreme Court also established what has come to be known as the public safety exception to the *Miranda* rule. The case, *New York* v. *Quarles*,[107] centered on an alleged rape in which the victim told police her assailant had fled, with a gun, into a nearby A&P supermarket. Two police officers entered the store and apprehended the suspect. One officer immediately noticed that the man was wearing an empty shoulder holster and, apparently fearing that a child might find the discarded weapon, quickly asked, "Where's the gun?"

Quarles was convicted of rape, but appealed his conviction, requesting that the weapon be suppressed as evidence because officers had not advised him of his *Miranda* rights before asking him about it. The Supreme Court disagreed, stating that considerations of public safety were overriding and negated the need for rights advisement prior to limited questioning which focused on the need to prevent further harm.

Where the police have not been coercive, and have issued *Miranda* warnings, the Supreme Court has held that even a later demonstration that a person may have been suffering from mental problems will not necessarily negate a confession. *Colorado* v. *Connelly* (1986)[108] involved a man who approached a Denver police officer and said he wanted to confess to the murder of a young girl. The officer immediately informed him of his *Miranda* rights, but the man waived them and continued to talk. When a detective arrived, the man was again advised of his rights, and he again waived them. After being taken to the local jail, the man began to hear "voices" and later claimed that it was these voices which had made him confess. At the trial, the defense moved to have the earlier confession negated on the basis that it was not voluntarily or freely given because of the defendant's mental condition. Upon appeal, the Supreme Court disagreed, saying that "no coercive government conduct occurred in this case."[109] Hence, "self-coercion," be it through the agency of a guilty conscience or faulty thought processes, does not appear to bar prosecution based on information revealed willingly by the defendant.

In a further refinement of *Miranda*, the lawful ability of a police informant, placed in a jail cell along with a defendant to gather information for later use at trial, was upheld in the 1986 case of *Kuhlmann* v. *Wilson*.[110] The passive gathering of information was judged to be acceptable, provided that the informant did not make attempts to elicit information.

In the case of *Illinois* v. *Perkins* (1990), the Court expanded its position to say that, under appropriate circumstances, even the active questioning of a suspect by an undercover officer posing as a fellow inmate does not require *Miranda* warnings. In *Perkins*, the Court found that, lacking other forms of coercion, the fact that the suspect was not aware of the questioner's identity as a law enforcement officer ensured that his statements were freely given. In the words of the Court, "[t]he essential ingredients of a 'police-dominated atmosphere' and compulsion are not present when an incarcerated person speaks freely to someone that he believes to be a fellow inmate."[111]

Miranda and the Meaning of Interrogation

Modern interpretations of the applicability of "*Miranda* warnings" turn upon an understanding of *interrogation*. The *Miranda* decision, as originally rendered, specifically recognized the necessity for police investigators to make inquiries at crime scenes in order to determine facts or establish identities. So long as the individual questioned is not yet in custody, and so long as probable cause is lacking in the investigator's mind, such questioning can proceed without the need for *Miranda* warnings. In such cases, interrogation, within the meaning of *Miranda*, has not yet begun.

The case of *Rock* v. *Zimmerman* (1982)[112] provides a different sort of example—one in which a suspect willingly made statements to the police before interrogation began. The suspect had burned his own house and shot and killed a neighbor. When the fire department arrived, he began shooting again and killed the fire chief. Cornered later in a field, the defendant, gun in hand, spontaneously shouted at police, "How many people did I kill, how many people are dead?"[113] This spontaneous statement was held to be admissible evidence at the suspect's trial.

It is also important to recognize that the Supreme Court in the *Miranda* decision required that officers provide warnings only in those situations involving *both* arrest and custodial interrogation. In other words, it is generally permissible for officers to take a suspect into custody, and listen, without asking questions, while he or she tells a story. Similarly, they may ask questions without providing a *Miranda* warning, even within the confines of a police station house, as long as the person questioned is not a suspect and is not under arrest.[114] Warnings are required only when officers begin actively to solicit responses from the defendant. Recognizing this fact, the FBI, in some of its training literature, has referred to interrogation as the **Miranda trigger**.

Officers were found to have acted properly in the case of *South Dakota* v. *Neville*, (1983)[115] in informing a DWI suspect, without reading him his rights, that he would stand to lose his driver's license if he did not submit to a breathalyzer test. When the driver responded, "I'm too drunk. I won't pass the test," his answer became evidence of his condition and was permitted at trial.

A third-party conversation recorded by the police after a suspect has invoked the *Miranda* right to remain silent may be used as evidence, according to a 1987 ruling in *Arizona* v. *Mauro*.[116] In *Mauro*, a man who willingly conversed with his wife in the presence of a police tape recorder, even after invoking his right to keep silent, was held to have effectively abandoned that right.

When a waiver is not made, however, in-court references to a defendant's silence following the issuing of *Miranda* warnings are unconstitutional. In 1976 (*Doyle* v. *Ohio*),[117] the U.S. Supreme Court definitively ruled that "a suspect's [post-*Miranda*] silence will not be used against him." Even so, according to the Court in *Brecht* v. *Abrahamson* (1993),[118] prosecution efforts to use such silence against

Miranda Triggers. The dual principles of custody and interrogation, both of which are necessary before an advisement of rights is required.

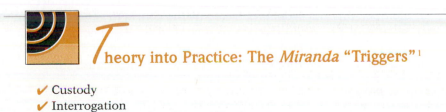

*T*heory into Practice: The *Miranda* "Triggers"[1]

✔ Custody
✔ Interrogation

1. Custodial interrogation triggers the need for *Miranda* warnings.

A suspect being read his Miranda rights immediately after arrest. Officers often read Miranda rights from a card to prelcude the possiblility of mistake. Photo by Bob Daemmrich, courtesy of Stock Boston.

a defendant may not invalidate a finding of guilt by a jury unless such "error had substantial and injurious effect or influence in determining the jury's verdict."[119]

Gathering Special Kinds of Nontestimonial Evidence

The police environment is complicated by the fact that suspects are often privy to special evidence of a nontestimonial sort. Nontestimonial evidence is generally physical evidence, and most physical evidence is subject to normal procedures of search and seizure. A special category of nontestimonial evidence, however, includes very personal items which may be within or part of a person's body, such as ingested drugs, blood cells, foreign objects, medical implants, and human DNA. Also included in this category might be fingerprints and other kinds of biological residue. The gathering of such special kinds of nontestimonial evidence is a complex area rich in precedent. The Fourth Amendment guarantee that persons be secure in their homes and in their persons has been interpreted by the courts to generally mean that the improper seizure of physical evidence of any kind is illegal and will result in exclusion of that evidence at trial. When very personal kinds of nontestimonial evidence are considered, however, the issue becomes more complicated still.

The Right to Privacy

Two cases, *Hayes* v. *Florida*[120] and *Winston* v. *Lee*,[121] are examples of limits the courts have placed on the seizure of very personal forms of nontestimonial evidence. The *Hayes* case established the right of suspects to refuse to be fingerprinted when probable cause necessary to effect an arrest does not exist. *Winston* demonstrated the inviolability of the body against surgical and other substantially invasive techniques which might be ordered by authorities against a suspect's will.

In the *Winston* case, Rudolph Lee, Jr., was found a few blocks from a store robbery with a gunshot wound in his chest. The robbery had involved an exchange of gunshots by the store owner and the robber, with the owner noting that the robber had apparently been hit by a bullet. At the hospital, the store owner identified Lee as the robber. The prosecution sought to have Lee submit to surgery to remove the bullet in his chest, arguing that the bullet would provide physical evidence linking him to the crime. Lee refused the surgery, and the Supreme Court in *Winston* v. *Lee* (1985) ruled that Lee could not be ordered to undergo surgery because such a magnitude of intrusion into his body was unacceptable under the right to privacy guaranteed by the Fourth Amendment. The *Winston* case was based on a precedent established in *Schmerber* v. *California* (1966).[122] The *Schmerber* case turned upon the extraction of a blood sample to be measured for alcohol content against the defendant's will. In *Schmerber*, the Court ruled that warrants must be obtained for bodily intrusions unless fast action is necessary to prevent the destruction of evidence by natural physiological processes.

Body Cavity Searches

Body cavity searches are among the most problematic for police today. "Strip" searches of convicts in prisons, including the search of body cavities, have generally been held permissible. The 1985 Supreme Court case of *U.S.* v. *Montoya de Hernandez*[123] focused on the issue of "alimentary canal smuggling," in which the suspect typically swallows condoms filled with cocaine or heroin and waits for nature to take its course to recover the substance.

In the *Montoya* case, a woman known to be a "balloon swallower" arrived in the United States on a flight from Colombia. She was detained by customs officials and given a pat-down search by a female agent. The agent reported that the woman's abdomen was firm and suggested that X rays be taken. The suspect refused and was given the choice of submitting to further tests or taking the next flight back to Colombia. No flight was immediately available, however, and the suspect was placed in a room for 16 hours, where she refused all food and drink. Finally, a court order for an X ray was obtained. The procedure revealed "balloons," and the woman was detained another four days, during which time she passed numerous cocaine-filled plastic condoms. The Court ruled that the woman's confinement was not unreasonable, based as it was on the supportable suspicion that she was "body-packing" cocaine. Any discomfort she experienced, the court ruled, "resulted solely from the method that she chose to smuggle illicit drugs."[124]

Electronic Eavesdropping

Modern technology makes possible increasingly complex forms of communication. From fiber optic phone lines, microwave and cellular transmissions, and fax machines to computer communications involving modems and databases, today's global village is a close-knit weave of flowing information.

One of the first and best known of the Supreme Court decisions in the area of electronic communications was the 1928 case of *Olmstead* v. *U.S.*[125] In *Olmstead*, bootleggers used their personal telephones to discuss and transact business. Agents had tapped the lines and based their investigation and ensuing arrests on conversations they had overheard. The defendants were convicted and eventually appealed to the High Court, arguing that the agents had in effect seized information illegally without a search warrant in violation of their Fourth Amendment right to be secure in their homes. The Court ruled, however, that telephone lines were not an extension of the defendant's homes and, therefore, were not protected by the constitutional guarantee of security.

Subsequent federal statutes (discussed shortly) have substantially modified the significance of *Olmstead*.

Recording devices carried on the body of an undercover agent or an informant were ruled to produce admissible evidence in *On Lee v. U.S.* (1952)[126] and *Lopez v. U.S.* (1963).[127] The 1967 case of *Berger v. New York*[128] permitted wiretaps and "bugs" in instances where state law provided for the use of such devices and where officers obtained a warrant based on probable cause.

The Court appeared to undertake a significant change of direction in the area of electronic eavesdropping when, in 1967, it decided the case of *Katz v. U.S.*[129] Federal agents had monitored a number of Katz's telephone calls from a public phone using a device separate from the phone lines and attached to the glass of the phone booth. The Court, in this case, stated that what a person makes an effort to keep private, even in a public place, requires a judicial decision, in the form of a warrant issued on probable cause, to unveil. In the words of the Court, "The government's activities in electronically listening to and recording the petitioner's words violated the privacy upon which he justifiably relied while using the telephone booth and thus constituted a 'search and seizure' within the meaning of the Fourth Amendment."

In 1968, with the case of *Lee v. Florida*,[130] the Court applied the Federal Communications Act[131] to telephone conversations which may be the object of police investigation and held that evidence obtained without a warrant could not be used in state proceedings if it resulted from a wiretap. The only person who has the authority to permit eavesdropping, according to that act, is the sender of the message.

The Federal Communications Act was originally passed in 1934 but did not specifically mention the potential interest of law enforcement agencies in monitoring communications. Title III of the Omnibus Crime Control and Safe Streets Act of 1968, however, mostly prohibits wiretaps but does allow officers to listen to electronic communications where (1) the officer is one of the parties involved in the communication, or (2) one of the parties is not the officer, but willingly decides to share the communication with the officer, or (3) officers obtain a warrant based on probable cause. In the 1971 case of *U.S. v. White*,[132] the Court held that law enforcement officers may intercept electronic information when one of the parties involved in the communication gives his or her consent, even without a warrant.

In 1984, the Supreme Court decided the case of *U.S. v. Karo*,[133] in which DEA agents had arrested James Karo for cocaine importation. Officers had placed a radio transmitter inside a 50-gallon drum of ether purchased by Karo for use in processing the cocaine. The transmitter was placed inside the drum with the consent of the seller of the ether, but without a search warrant. The shipment of ether was followed to the Karo house, and Karo was arrested and convicted of cocaine-trafficking charges. Karo appealed to the Supreme Court, claiming that the radio beeper had violated his reasonable expectation of privacy inside his premises and that, without a warrant, the evidence it produced was tainted. The Court agreed and overturned his conviction.

Minimization Requirements in Electronic Surveillance

The Supreme Court established a minimization requirement pertinent to electronic surveillance in the 1978 case of *United States v. Scott*.[134] Minimization means that officers must make every reasonable effort to monitor only those conversations, through the use of phone taps, body bugs, and the like, which are specifically related to criminal activity under investigation. As soon as it becomes obvious that a conversation is innocent, the monitoring personnel are required to cease their invasion of privacy. Problems arise if the conversation occurs in a foreign language, if it is "coded," or if it is ambiguous. It has been suggested that investigators involved in electronic surveillance maintain log books of their activities which specifically show monitored conversations, as well as efforts made at "minimization."[135]

The Electronic Communications Privacy Act

Passed by Congress in 1986, the Electronic Communications Privacy Act (**ECPA**)[136] has brought major changes in the requirements law enforcement officers must meet when using wiretaps. The ECPA deals specifically with three areas of communication: (1) wiretaps and bugs, (2) pen registers (which record the numbers dialed from a telephone), and (3) tracing devices which determine the number from which a call emanates. The act also addresses the procedures to be followed by officers in obtaining records relating to communications services, and it establishes requirements for gaining access to stored electronic communications and records of those communications.

The ECPA basically requires that investigating officers must obtain wiretap-type court orders to eavesdrop on *ongoing communications*. The use of pen registers and recording devices, however, are specifically excluded by the law from court order requirements. *Stored communications*, such as computer files made from telephonic sources, fax reproductions, digitally stored information, electronic bulletin boards, and other physical and electronic records of communications which have already occurred are categorized by the act according to the length of time they have been stored. Messages stored fewer than 180 days are protected in the same manner as the contents of U.S. mail, and a search warrant issued on probable cause is required to access them.[137] Information which has been on file more than 180 days, however, can be accessed with a court order based on a simple showing that the information sought is relevant to an ongoing criminal investigation. Such a "showing" is less demanding than a demonstration of probable cause, which includes the claim that the information in question will provide evidence of a law violation.

ECPA. An acronym for the Electronic Communications Privacy Act.

Some provisions of the ECPA require that "service providers" give notification to users that stored information belonging to them has become the subject of a police request. Subjects so notified might be tempted to remove or erase the stored information, and investigating officers should, under such circumstances, immediately request that backup copies of any important information be made.

Summary

The principles of individual liberty and social justice are the cornerstones on which the American way of life rests. Ideally, the work of the criminal justice system is to ensure justice while guarding liberty. The liberty–justice issue is the dual thread which weaves the tapestry of the justice system together—from the simplest daily activities of police on the beat to the often complex and lengthy renderings of the U.S. Supreme Court.

For the criminal justice system, the question becomes "How can individual liberties be maintained in the face of the need for official action, including arrest, interrogation, incarceration, and the like?" The answer is far from simple, but it begins with a recognition of the fact that "liberty" is a double-edged sword, entailing obligations as well as rights. For police action to be "just," it must recognize the rights of individuals while holding them accountable to the social obligations defined by law.

Discussion Questions

1. Which Supreme Court decisions discussed in this chapter do you see as most important? Why?
2. Are there any Supreme Court decisions discussed in this chapter with which you disagree? If so, which ones? Why do you disagree?
3. Do you agree with the theme of this chapter's summary, that "for police action to be just, it must recognize the rights of individuals while holding them accountable to the social obligations defined by law"? What is the basis for your agreement or disagreement?
4. In your opinion, should the Supreme Court have created exceptions to the exclusionary rule? To *Miranda*? Why or why not?
5. What does the due process environment mean to you? How do you think we should try to ensure due process in our legal system?
6. Justice Benjamin Cardozo once complained, "The criminal is to go free because the constable has blundered." Can we afford to let some guilty people go free in order to ensure that the rights of the rest of us are protected? Is there some other (better) way to achieve the same goal?

References

1. Larry Collins and Dominique Lapierre, *The Fifth Horseman* (New York: Simon & Schuster, 1980).
2. "Police Brutality!" *Time*, March 25, 1991, p. 18.
3. "L.A. Officers Not Indicted," *The Fayetteville Observer-Times* (North Carolina), May 11, 1991, p. 10C.
4. "Police Brutality!" pp. 16–19.
5. "Police Charged in Beating Case Say They Feared for Their Lives," *The Boston Globe*, May 22, 1991, p. 22.
6. "Cries of Relief," *Time*, April 26, 1993, p. 18.
7. "Rodney King's Run-ins," *USA Today*, May 30, 1991, 2A.
8. "Morgan awarded $540,000 by Jurors," *Los Angeles Times*, February 15, 1991, p. B1.
9. *Weeks* v. *U.S.*, 232 U.S. 383 (1914).

10. Roger Goldman and Steven Puro, "Decertification of Police: An Alternative to Traditional Remedies for Police Misconduct," *Hastings Constitutional Law Quarterly,* Vol. 15 (1988), pp. 45–80.

11. Ibid.

12. *Silverthorne Lumber Co.* v. *U.S.,* 251 U.S. 385 (1920).

13. Clemmens Bartollas, *American Criminal Justice* (New York: Macmillan, 1988), p. 186.

14. *Mapp* v. *Ohio,* 367 U.S. 643 (1961).

15. *Mapp* v. *Ohio.*

16. *Wolf* v. *Colorado,* 338 U.S. 25 (1949).

17. *Chimel* v. *California,* 395 U.S. 752 (1969).

18. *U.S.* v. *Rabinowitz,* 339 U.S. 56 (1950).

19. *Katz* v. *U.S.,* 389 U.S. 347, 88 S.Ct. 507 (1967).

20. *Minnesota* v. *Olson,* 110 S.Ct. 1684 (1990).

21. *Illinois* v. *Gates,* 426 U.S. 318 (1982).

22. *U.S.* v. *Leon,* 468 U.S. (1984), 104 S.Ct. 3405.

23. Judicial titles vary between jurisdictions. Many lower-level state judicial officers are referred to as "magistrates." Federal magistrates, however, are generally regarded as functioning at a significantly higher level of judicial authority.

24. *Massachusetts* v. *Sheppard,* 104 S.Ct. 3424 (1984).

25. *Illinois* v. *Krull,* 107 S.Ct. 1160 (1987).

26. *Maryland* v. *Garrison,* 107 S.Ct. 1013 (1987).

27. *Illinois* v. *Rodriguez,* 110 S.Ct. 2793 (1990).

28. William H. Erickson, William D. Neighbors, and B. J. George, Jr., *United States Supreme Court Cases and Comments* (New York: Matthew Bender, 1987), Section 1.13 [7].

29. *Harris* v. *U.S.,* 390 U.S. 234 (1968).

30. As cited in Kimberly A. Kingston, "Look But Don't Touch: The Plain View Doctrine," *FBI Law Enforcement Bulletin* (December 1987), p. 18.

31. *Horton* v. *California,* 110 S.Ct. 2301, 47 CrL. 2135 (1990).

32. *U.S.* v. *Irizarry* (1982).

33. *FBI Law Enforcement Bulletin* (December 1987), p. 20.

34. *Arizona* v. *Hicks,* 107 S.Ct. 1149 (1987).

35. See *Criminal Justice Today,* North Carolina Justice Academy (Fall 1987), p. 24.

36. "Inadvertency" as a requirement of legitimate plain view seizures was first cited in the U.S. Supreme Court case of *Coolidge* v. *New Hampshire,* 403 U.S. 443, 91 S.Ct. 2022 (1971).

37. *Horton* v. *California.*

38. John Gales Sauls, "Emergency Searches of Premises," Part 1, *FBI Law Enforcement Bulletin* (March 1987), p. 23.

39. *Warden* v. *Hayden,* 387 U.S. 294 (1967).

40. *Mincey* v. *Arizona,* 437 U.S. 385, 392 (1978).

41. Sauls, "Emergency Searches of Premises," p. 25.

42. *Maryland* v. *Buie,* 110 S.Ct. 1093 (1990).

43. *Wilson* v. *Arkansas,* Docket Number 94-5707. Decided May 22, 1995.

44. *Arizona* v. *Isaac Evans,* No. 93-1660 (1995).

45. *U.S.* v. *Mendenhall,* 446 U.S. 544 (1980).

46. A. Louis DiPietro, "Voluntary Encounters or Fourth Amendment Seizures," *FBI Law Enforcement Bulletin,* January 1992, pp. 28–32 at note 6.

47. *Stansbury* v. *California,* No. 93-5770 (1994).

48. In 1976, in the case of *Watson* v. *U.S.* (432 U.S. 411) the U.S. Supreme Court refused to impose a warrant requirement for felony arrests that occur in public places.

49. In 1981, in the case of *U.S.* v. *Steagald* (451 U.S. 204), the Court ruled that a *search* warrant is also necessary when the planned arrest involves entry into a third party's premises.

50. *Robinson* v. *U.S.,* 414 U.S. 218 (1973).

51. Ibid.

52. *Terry* v. *Ohio,* 392 U.S. 1 (1968).

53. Ibid.

54. *U.S.* v. *Sokolow,* 109 S.Ct. 1581 (1989).

55. *Minnesota* v. *Dickerson,* 113 S.Ct. 2130, 124 L.Ed. 2d 334 (1993).

56. *Brown* v. *Texas,* 443 U.S. 47 (1979).

57. *Smith* v. *Ohio,* 110 S.Ct. 1288 (1990).

58. Ibid., at 1289.

59. *California* v. *Hodari D.,* 111 S.Ct. 1547 (1991).

60. *Criminal Justice Newsletter,* May 1, 1991, p. 2.

61. Dissenting opinion in *California* v. *Hodari D.*

62. *Arkansas* v. *Sanders,* 442 U.S. 753 (1979).

63. Ibid.

64. *Borchardt* v. *U.S.,* 809 F.2d 1115 (5th Cir. 1987).

65. *FBI Law Enforcement Bulletin,* January 1988, p. 28.

66. *Carroll* v. *U.S.,* 267 U.S. 132 (1925).

67. *Preston* v. *U.S.,* 376 U.S. 364 (1964).

68. *South Dakota* v. *Opperman,* 428 U.S. 364 (1976).

69. *Colorado* v. *Bertine,* 479 U.S. 367, 107 S.Ct. 741 (1987).

70. *Florida* v. *Wells,* 110 S.Ct. 1632 (1990).

71. *Florida* v. *Jimeno,* 111 S.Ct. 1801 (1991).

72. *Jimeno,* online syllabus.

73. *United States* v. *Ross,* 456 U.S. 798 (1982).

74. Ibid.

75. *U.S.* v. *Vilamonte-Marquez,* 462 U.S. 579 (1983).

76. *California* v. *Carney,* 471 U.S. (1985).

77. *U.S.* v. *Hill* 855 F.2d 664 (10th Cir. 1988).

78. *Florida* v. *Bostick,* 111 S.Ct. 2382 (1991).

79. *Aguilar* v. *Texas,* 378 U.S. 108 (1964).

80. *Harris* v. *United States,* 403 U.S. 573 (1971).

81. *Spinelli* v. *United States,* 393 U.S. 410 (1969).

82. *Illinois* v. *Gates,* 426 U.S. 318 (1982).

83. *Alabama* v. *White*, 110 S.Ct. 2412 (1990).

84. Ibid., at 2417.

85. *U.S. Department of Justice* v. *Landano*, 133 S.Ct. 2014, 214 L. Ed. 2d 84 (1993).

86. *South Dakota* v. *Neville*, 103 S.Ct. 916 (1983).

87. *Brown* v. *Mississippi*, 297 U.S. 278 (1936).

88. *Ashcraft* v. *Tennessee*, 322 U.S. 143 (1944).

89. *Chambers* v. *Florida*, 309 U.S. 227 (1940).

90. Ibid.

91. *Leyra* v. *Denno*, 347 U.S. 556 (1954).

92. Ibid.

93. *Arizona* v. *Fulminante*, 111 S.Ct. 1246 (1991).

94. *Chapman* v. *California*, 386 U.S. 18 (1967).

95. *Escobedo* v. *Illinois*, 378 U.S. 478 (1964).

96. *Edwards* v. *Arizona*, U.S. 477, 101 S.Ct. 1880 (1981).

97. *Arizona* v. *Roberson*, 486 U.S. 675, 108 S.Ct. 2093 (1988).

98. *Davis* v. *United States*, 114 S.Ct. 2350 (1994).

99. *Miranda* v. *Arizona*, 384 U.S. 436 (1966).

100. Ibid.

101. *Moran* v. *Burbine*, 475 U.S., 106 S.Ct. 1135 (1986).

102. Ibid.

103. *Colorado* v. *Spring*, 479 U.S. 564, 107 S.Ct. 851 (1987).

104. "Immigrants Get Civil Rights," *USA Today*, June 11, 1992, p. 1A.

105. *Nix* v. *Williams*, 104 S.Ct. 2501 (1984).

106. Ibid.

107. *New York* v. *Quarles*, 104 S.Ct. 2626, 81 L.Ed. 2d 550 (1984).

108. *Colorado* v. *Connelly*, 107 S.Ct. 515, 93 L.Ed. 2d 473 (1986).

109. Ibid.

110. *Kuhlmann* v. *Wilson*, 477 U.S., 106 S.Ct. 2616 (1986).

111. *Illinois* v. *Perkins*, 495 U.S. 292 (1990).

112. *Rock* v. *Zimmerman*, 543 F.Supp. 179 (M.D. Penna. 1982).

113. Ibid.

114. See *Oregon* v. *Mathiason*, 429 U.S. 492, 97 S.Ct. 711 (1977).

115. *South Dakota* v. *Neville*, 103 S.Ct. 916 (1983).

116. *Arizona* v. *Mauro*, 107 S.Ct. 1931, 95 L.Ed. 2d 458 (1987).

117. *Doyle* v. *Ohio*, 426 U.S. 610 (1976).

118. *Brecht* v. *Abrahamson*, 113 S.Ct. 1710, 123 L. Ed. 2d 353 (1993).

119. Citing *Kotteakos* v. *United States*, 328 U.S. 750 (1946).

120. *Hayes* v. *Florida*, 470 U.S., 105 S.Ct. 1643 (1985).

121. *Winston* v. *Lee*, 470 U.S., 105 S.Ct. 1611 (1985).

122. *Schmerber* v. *California*, 384 U.S. 757 (1966).

123. *U.S.* v. *Montoya de Hernandez*, 473 U.S., 105 S.Ct. 3304 (1985).

124. Ibid.

125. *Olmstead* v. *U.S.*, 277 U.S. 438 (1928).

126. *On Lee* v. *U.S.*, 343 U.S. 747 (1952).

127. *Lopez* v. *U.S.*, 373 U.S. 427 (1963).

128. *Berger* v. *New York*, 388 U.S. 41 (1967).

129. *Katz* v. *U.S.*, 389 U.S. 347 (1967).

130. *Lee* v. *Florida*, 392 U.S. 378 (1968).

131. Federal Communications Act, 1934.

132. *U.S.* v. *White*, 401 U.S. 745 (1971).

133. *U.S.* v. *Karo*, 104 S.Ct. 3296, 3301 (1984).

134. *United States* v. *Scott*, 436 U.S. 128 (1978).

135. For more information, see *FBI Law Enforcement Bulletin* (June 1987), p. 25.

136. The Electronic Communications Privacy Act, 1986.

137. For more information on the ECPA, see Robert A. Fiatal, "The Electronic Communications Privacy Act: Addressing Today's Technology," *FBI Law Enforcement Bulletin* (April 1988), pp. 24–30.

CHAPTER 6

Issues In Policing

—*Photo by Peter Marlow/Magnum Photos, Inc.*

The police in the United States are not separate from the people. They draw their authority from the will and consent of the people, and they recruit their officers from them. The police are the instrument of the people to achieve and maintain order; their efforts are founded on principles of public service and ultimate responsibility to the public.

—The National Advisory Commission
on Criminal Justice Standards and Goals

The ability of the police to fulfill their sacred trust will improve as a lucid sense of ethical standards is developed.

—Patrick V. Murphy
Former commissioner of the NYC Police Department

Effective police work in the emerging society will depend less on the holster and more on the head.

—Alvin Toffler

KEY CONCEPTS		
police culture	police working personality	POST standards
corruption	police ethics	internal affairs
police professionalism	Bivens suit	1983 lawsuits
private security		

Contemporary Policing: Issues and Challenges

A number of issues hold special interest for today's police administrators and officers. Some concerns, such as police stress, danger, and the use of deadly force, derive from the very nature of police work. Others have arisen over the years because of commonplace practice, characteristic police values, and public expectations surrounding the enforcement of laws. Included here are such negatives as the potential for corruption, as well as positive efforts which focus on ethics and recruitment strategies to increase professionalism.

Police Personality and Culture

A few years ago, Jerome Skolnick described what he called the "working personality" of police officers.[1] Skolnick's description was consistent with William Westley's classic study[2] of the Gary, Indiana, police department, in which he found a **police culture** with its own "customs, laws, and morality," and with Niederhoffer's observation that cynicism was pervasive among officers in New York City.[3] More recent authors[4] have claimed that the "big curtain of secrecy" surrounding much of police work shields knowledge of the nature of the police personality from outsiders.

Skolnick found that a process of informal socialization, through which officers learn what is appropriate police behavior, occurs when new officers begin to work with seasoned veterans. Such informal socialization is often far more important than formal police academy training in determining how rookies will see police work. In everyday life, formal socialization occurs through schooling, church activities, job training, and so on. Informal socialization is acquired primarily from one's peers in less institutionalized settings and provides an introduction to value-laden subcultures. The information that passes between officers in the locker room, in a squad car, over a cup of coffee, or in many other relatively private moments produces a shared view of the world that can be best described as "streetwise." The streetwise cop may know what official department policy is, but he or she also knows the most efficient way to get a job done. By the time they become streetwise, rookie officers will know just how acceptable various informal means of accomplishing the job will be to other officers. The police subculture creates few real "mavericks," but it also produces few officers who view their job exclusively in terms of public mandates and official dictums.

Skolnick says that the **police working personality** has at least six recognizable characteristics. Additional writers[5] have identified others. Taken in concert, they create the picture of the police personality shown in Table 6-1.

Some components of the police working personality are essential for survival and effectiveness. Officers are exposed daily to situations which are charged with emotions and potentially threatening. The need to gain control quickly over belligerent people leads to the development of authoritarian strategies for handling people. Eventually, such strategies become "second nature," and the cornerstone of the police personality is firmly set. Cynicism evolves from a constant flow of experiences which demonstrate that people and events are not always what they seem to be. The natural tendency of most suspects, even when they are clearly guilty in the eyes of the police, is denial. Repeated attempts to mislead the police in the performance of their duty creates an air of suspicion and cynicism in the minds of most officers.

The police personality has at least two sources. On the one hand, some aspects of the world view that composes that personality can be attributed to the socialization which occurs when rookie officers are inducted into police ranks. On the other, it may be that some of the components of the police personality already exist in some individuals and lead them into police work.[6] Supporting the latter view are

Police Culture. (Also called Police Subculture) A particular set of values, beliefs, and acceptable forms of behavior characteristic of American police, with which the police profession strives to imbue new recruits. Socialization into the police subculture commences with recruit training and is ongoing thereafter.

Police Working Personality. All aspects of the traditional values and patterns of behavior evidenced by police officers who have been effectively socialized into the police subculture. Characteristics of the police personality often extend to the personal lives of law enforcement personnel.

TABLE 6-1

The Police Personality

Authoritarian	Insecure
Cynical	Loyal
Conservative	Efficient
Suspicious	Honorable
Hostile	Secret
Individualistic	Prejudiced

studies which indicate that police officers who come from conservative backgrounds continue to view themselves as defenders of middle-class morality.[7]

Police methods and the police culture are not static, however. Lawrence Sherman, for example, has reported on the modification of police tactics surrounding the use of weapons that characterized the period from 1970 to the 1980s.[8] Firearms, Sherman tells us, were routinely brought into play 25 years ago. Although not often fired, they would be frequently drawn and pointed at suspects. Few departmental restrictions were placed on the use of weapons, and officers employed them almost as they would their badge in the performance of duties. Today, the situation has changed. It is a rare officer who will unholster a weapon during police work, and those who do know that only the gravest of situations can justify the public display of firearms.

Some authors attribute this shift in thinking about firearms to increased training and the growth of restrictive policies.[9] Changes in training, however, are probably more a response to a revolution in social understandings about the kind of respect due citizens. For example, the widespread change in social consciousness regarding the worth of individuals, which has taken place over the past few decades, appears to have had considerable impact on police subculture itself.

Corruption

The police role carries considerable authority, and officers are expected to exercise a well-informed discretion in all of their activities. The combination of authority and discretion, however, produces great potential for abuse.

Police deviance has been a problem in American society since the early days of policing. It is probably an ancient and natural tendency of human beings to attempt to placate or "win over" those in positions of authority over them. This tendency is complicated in today's materialistic society by greed and by the personal and financial benefits to be derived from evading the law. Hence, the temptations toward illegality offered to police range all the way from a free cup of coffee given by a small restaurant owner in the thought that one day it may be necessary to call on the goodwill of the officer, perhaps for something as simple as a traffic ticket, to huge monetary bribes arranged by drug dealers to guarantee the police will look the other way as an important shipment of contraband arrives.

Exactly what constitutes **corruption** is not always clear. In recognition of what some have called corruption's "slippery slope,"[10] even the acceptance of minor gratuities is now explicitly prohibited by most police departments. The slippery slope perspective holds that even small "thank you's" which are accepted from members of the public can lead to a more ready acceptance of larger bribes. An officer who begins to accept, and then expect, gratuities may soon find that his or her practice of policing becomes influenced by such gifts, and that larger ones soon follow. At that point, the officer may easily slide to the bottom of the moral slope, one made slippery by previous small concessions.

Ethicists say that police corruption ranges from minor "offenses" to those that are themselves serious violations of the law. Another useful distinction is made by

Corruption. Behavioral deviation from an accepted ethical standard.

Barker and Carter, who distinguish between *occupational deviance* and *abuse of authority*.[11] Occupational deviance, they say, is motivated by the desire for personal benefit. Abuse of authority, however, occurs most often in order to further the organizational goals of law enforcement—including arrest, ticketing, and the successful conviction of suspects.

Examples of police deviance, ranked in what this author judges to be an increasing level of severity, are shown in Table 6-2. Not everyone, however, would agree with this ranking. A 1995 survey[12] of 6,982 New York City Police officers found that 65 percent did not classify excessive force as corrupt behavior. Likewise, 71.4 percent of responding officers said that accepting a free meal is not a corrupt practice. Another 15 percent said that the use of illegal drugs should not be considered corruption.

Years ago, Frank Serpico made headlines as he testified before the Knapp Commission on police corruption in New York City.[13] Serpico, an undercover operative within the police department, revealed a complex web of corruption in which money and services routinely changed hands in "protection rackets" created by unethical officers. The Knapp Commission report distinguished between two types of corrupt officers, which they termed "grass eaters" and "meat eaters."[14] "Grass eating," the most common form of police deviance, was described as illegitimate activity which occurs from time to time in the normal course of police work. It involves mostly small bribes or relatively minor services offered by citizens seeking to avoid arrest and prosecution. "Meat eating" is a much more serious form of corruption, involving as it does the active seeking of illicit money-making opportunities by officers. Meat eaters solicit bribes through threat or intimidation, whereas grass eaters make the simpler mistake of not refusing those which are offered.

Popular books often tell the story of police misbehavior. A few years ago, Robert Daley's best-seller *Prince of the City*[15] detailed the adventures of New York City detective Robert Leuci who walked among corrupt cops with a tape recorder hidden on his body. The more recent best-seller *Buddy Boys*,[16] by Mike McAlary, is subtitled *When Good Cops Turn Bad*. McAlary, an investigative reporter with *New York Newsday*, began his efforts to uncover police corruption with a list of 13 names of officers who had been suspended in New York's 77th precinct. His book describes organized criminal activity among police in the "Big Apple," involving holdups of drug dealers, organized burglaries, fencing operations, and numerous other illegal activities conducted from behind the shield. McAlary says New York's criminal officers saw themselves as a kind of "elite" within the department and applied the name "Buddy Boys" to their gang.[17]

TABLE 6-2

Types of Police Deviance by Category and Example

High-Level Corruption

Violent crimes: The physical abuse of suspects, including torture and nonjustifiable homicide
Denying civil rights: Routinized schemes to circumvent constitutional guarantees
Criminal enterprise: The resale of confiscated drugs, stolen property, etc.
Property crimes: Burglary, theft, etc., committed by police
Major bribes: Accepting $1,000 to "overlook" contraband shipments, and other law violations
Role malfeasance: Destroying evidence, offering biased testimony, and protecting "crooked" cops
Being "above" inconvenient laws: Speeding, smoking marijuana
Minor bribes: Twenty dollars to "look the other way" on a ticket
Playing favorites: Not ticketing friends, etc.
Gratuities: Accepting free coffee, meals, etc.

Low-Level Corruption

In 1993, during 11 days of corruption hearings reminiscent of the Knapp Commission era, a parade of crooked New York police officers testified before the Mollen Commission, headed by former judge and deputy mayor Milton Mollen. Among the many revelations, officers spoke of dealing drugs, stealing confiscated drug funds, stifling investigations, and beating innocent people. Officer Michael Dowd, for example, told the commission that he had run a cocaine ring out of his station house in Brooklyn and bought three homes on Long Island and a Corvette with the money he made. Most shocking of all, however, were allegations that high-level police officials attempted to hide embarrassing incidents in a "phantom file" and that many such officials may have condoned unprofessional and even criminal practices by law enforcement officers under their command. Honest officers, including internal affairs investigators, reported on how their efforts to end corruption among their fellows had been defused and resisted by higher authorities.

Spectacular as they were, however, many doubt that the Mollen hearings will have much long-term impact on policing in New York City. "The Knapp Commission exposed a form of corruption that was systemic and pervasive," said Daniel Guido, a professor at John Jay College of Criminal Justice in New York. "It involved not only the working levels of the force and plainclothes men but their supervisors. It was part of the culture of the force....What we're seeing [with the Mollen Hearings] is not systemic, and it involves only police officers in the main. It's all been sensational and revolting, but it's important not to overgeneralize the extent to which this is going on."

Some experts say that the New York Police Department actually has corruption under better control than most other large-city departments and that the few cases of corruption identified by the Mollen Commission were trivial relative to the size of the department. Even so, the hearings do seem to show that corruption is nearly impossible to completely stamp out and that it reemerges with each new generation of officers.

Corruption, of course, is not unique to New York. In 1992, Detroit Police Chief William Hart was sentenced to a maximum of ten years in federal prison for embezzling $2.6 million from a secret police department fund and for tax evasion.[18] The fund, which was to be used for undercover drug buys and to pay informants, had secretly paid out nearly $10 million since its creation in 1980. Hart, who was 68 years old at the time of sentencing, had been police chief in Detroit since 1976. He resigned from office the day after his conviction, following a pension board ruling that entitled him to receive a $53,000 annual pension despite the conviction. Hart's arrest had come on the heels of other problems for Detroit police. Two years earlier, a city police officer was arrested for allegedly committing five robberies in one evening, and eight other officers were arrested for breaking and entering and assault. *The Detroit News*, a major newspaper in the city, conducted a study in which it found that Detroit police are "accused of committing crimes more often than officers in any other major U.S. city."[19]

Even small cities are not immune to corruption. In 1992, former Rochester, New York, chief of police Gordon F. Urlacher was sentenced to four years in federal prison and fined $150,000 for embezzling about $300,000 from the city. Urlacher denied guilt, claiming that he was simply a bad accountant.

Money—The Root of Police Evil?

The police personality provides fertile ground for the growth of corrupt practices. Police "cynicism" develops out of continued association with criminals and problem-laden people. The cop who is "streetwise" is also ripe for corrupt influences to take root. Years ago, the famous criminologist Edwin Sutherland applied the concept of differential association to deviant behavior.[20] Sutherland suggested that continued association with one type of person, more frequently than with any other, would make the associates similar. In short, said Sutherland, people become like the people they "hang out" with.

Sutherland was talking about criminals, not police officers. Consider, however, the dilemma of the average officer: a typical day is spent running down petty thieves, issuing traffic citations to citizens who try to talk their way out of the situation, dealing with prostitutes who feel "hassled" by the police presence, and arresting drug users who think it should be their right to do what they want as long as it "doesn't hurt anyone." The officer encounters personal hostility and experiences a constant, and often quite vocal, rejection of society's formalized norms. Bring into this environment low pay and the resulting sense that police work is not really valued, and it is easy to understand how an officer might develop a jaded attitude about the double standards of the civilization he or she is sworn to protect.

In fact, low pay may be a critical ingredient of the corruption mix. Salaries paid to police officers in this country have been notoriously low compared to other professions involving personal dedication, extensive training, high stress, and the risk of bodily harm. As police professionalism increases, many police administrators hope that salaries will rise. No matter how much police pay grows, however, it will never be able to compete with the staggering amounts of money to be made though dealing in contraband. In *The Underground Empire: Where Crime and Governments Embrace*, James Mills[21] tells the story of a man he calls a "young American entrepreneur," who, he writes, has "criminal operations on four continents and a daily income greater than U.S. Steel's."[22] Mills's book is about "Centac," a semisecret arm of the Drug Enforcement Administration, which coordinates the operations of various agencies in the ongoing battle against illicit drugs. Although international drug trafficking is the focus of *The Underground Empire*, the book contains details of international police corruption fostered via the vast resources available to the trade.

Working hand in hand with monetary pressures toward corruption are the moral dilemmas produced by unenforceable laws which provide the basis for criminal profit. The Wickersham Commission warned during the Prohibition Era of the potential for official corruption inherent in the legislative taboos on alcohol. The demand for drink, immense as it was, called into question the wisdom of the law, while providing vast resources designed to circumvent the law. Today's drug scene bears some similarities to the Prohibition Era. As long as substantial segments of the population are willing to make large financial and other sacrifices to feed the drug trade, the pressures on the police to embrace corruption will remain substantial.

Combating Corruption

High moral standards, embedded into the principles of the police profession, and effectively communicated to individual officers through formal training and peer group socialization, are undoubtedly the most effective way to combat corruption in police work. There are, of course, many officers of great personal integrity who hold to the highest of professional ideals, and there is evidence that law enforcement training programs are becoming increasingly concerned with instruction designed to reinforce the high ideals many recruits bring to police work. As a 1995 FBI article puts it, "ethics training must become an integral part of academy and in-service training for new and experienced officers alike."[23]

Besides training in ethics, most large law enforcement agencies have their own **internal affairs** divisions which are empowered to investigate charges of wrongdoing made against officers. Where necessary, state police agencies may be called on to examine reported incidents. Federal agencies, including the FBI and the DEA, involve themselves when corruption goes far enough to violate federal statutes. The U.S. Department of Justice, through various investigative offices, has the authority to examine possible violations of civil rights which may result from the misuse of police authority and is often supported by the American Civil Liberties Union, the NAACP, and other "watchdog" groups in such endeavors.

A little over a decade ago, a U.S. Department of Justice–sponsored report studied scandals involving police corruption in New York City; Oakland, California; Newburgh, New York; and an anonymous area termed "Central City" (somewhere in the Midwest).[24] A new police chief had been appointed in each city, and each arrived armed with a mandate to reform their departments. Three major strategies for controlling corruption evolved in the reorganized departments. The first of these, termed "managerial strategies" by the report, involved a four-pronged attack on corruption: (1) New officers were hired, and personnel were "turned over" on the theory that corruption cannot survive where the people perpetrating it are removed. (Personnel turnover can also be accomplished by simply shifting agents from one division to another or from one geographic area to another.) (2) "Accountability" was clearly expected of supervisors. Those who wouldn't accept responsibility for combating corruption were asked to retire early or were removed from their command positions. (3) Closer supervision was required of commanders, especially sergeants, and other "first-line" supervisors. Sergeants were expected to spend more time with their officers and to create procedures for making any work performed more visible within the context of the department. (4) "Corrupting practices" were ended. Quotas for vice arrests and reimbursements for out-of-pocket, job-related expenses (such as lunches and office supplies) were eliminated. Drug arrests through "buys" were well financed, ending the pressure to hold back money from other drug arrests to effect new ones.

A second strategy for reducing corruption was termed "changing the task environment." City officials made public pleas asking that citizens refrain from offering "gifts" to law enforcement officers. The chief of the Newburgh force asked for the repeal of a local ordinance allowing officers to accept gifts of under $25.00 in value. Special teams of officers concentrated on making highly visible arrests of citizens who attempted to bribe the police.

The last strategy identified in the report was called "changing the political environment." One police chief clearly communicated a new policy of enforcing "all the laws against all the people, including City Council Members." The Newburgh, New York, police executive tried to organize a federal investigation of political officials in the county. Corrupt politicians were either forced out of office or encouraged to retire.

A final technique to combat corruption, which was used by all the departments in the study, relied on "internal policing strategies." Each department either created an Internal Affairs Division (IAD) or increased the numbers of officers participating in internal investigations. The New York City Police Department, for example, originally had only one officer assigned to internal affairs for every 533 officers. Following reorganization, internal affairs increased in size almost ten times. One officer was assigned to IAD for every 64 enforcement officers. Each department also encouraged the IAD to become more active in seeking out information about corruption. Complaints were taken from numerous sources, including citizens who wished to remain anonymous, and former "reactive" strategies were turned into "proactive" efforts to gather information on corruption. The report revealed that Internal Affairs Divisions found especially useful wiretaps of known offenders (which sometimes implicated police "on the take"), "corruption patrolling" (in which IAD agents patrolled areas where the potential for police corruption was high), and "integrity tests" (which provided officers with an easy opportunity to commit criminal or corrupt acts).

Drug Testing of Police Employees

The widespread potential for corruption created by illicit drugs has led to focused efforts to combat drug use by officers. Drug testing programs at the department level are an example of such efforts. When concern was at its highest, the National Institute of Justice (NIJ) conducted a telephone survey of 33 large police departments across the nation to determine what measures were being taken to identify officers and civilian employees who were using drugs.[25] NIJ learned that almost all departments had written procedures to test employees who were reasonably suspected of drug abuse. Applicants for police positions were being tested by 73 percent of the departments surveyed, and 21 percent of the departments were actively considering testing all officers. In what some people found a surprisingly low figure, 21 percent reported that they might offer treatment to identified violators rather than dismiss them, depending on their personal circumstances.

The International Association of Chiefs of Police has made available to today's police managers a "Model Drug Testing Policy." It is directed toward the needs of local departments and suggests:[26]

✔ Testing all applicants and recruits for drug or narcotics use
✔ Testing current employees when performance difficulties or documentation indicate a potential drug problem
✔ Testing current employees when they are involved in the use of excessive force or suffer or cause on-duty injury
✔ Routine testing of all employees assigned to special "high-risk" areas such as narcotics and vice

Drug testing based on a reasonable suspicion that drug abuse has been or is occurring has been supported by the courts (*Maurice Turner* v. *Fraternal Order of Police*, 1985)[27] although random testing of officers was banned by the New York State Supreme Court in the case of *Philip Caruso, President of P.B.A.* v. *Benjamin Ward, Police Commissioner* (1986).[28] Citing overriding public interests, a 1989 decision by the U.S. Supreme Court upheld the testing of U.S. Customs personnel applying for transfer into positions involving drug law enforcement or carrying a firearm.[29] Many legal issues surrounding employee drug testing, however, remain to be resolved in court.

Complicating the situation is the fact that drug and alcohol addiction are "handicaps" protected by the Federal Rehabilitation Act of 1973. As such, federal law enforcement employees, as well as those working for agencies with federal contracts, are entitled to counseling and treatment before action toward termination can be taken.

The issue of employee drug testing in police departments, as in many other agencies, is a sensitive one. Some claim that existing tests for drug use are inaccurate, yielding a significant number of "false positives." Repeated testing and high "threshold" levels for narcotic substances in the blood may eliminate many of these concerns. Less easy to address, however, is the belief that drug testing intrudes on the personal rights and professional dignity of individual employees.

The Dangers of Police Work

On October 15, 1991, the National Law Enforcement Memorial was unveiled in Washington, D.C. Initially, the memorial contained the names of 12,561 law enforcement officers killed in the line of duty. Other names have since been added.

Police work is, by its very nature, dangerous. Although it is true that most officers throughout their careers never draw their weapons in the line of duty, it is also plain that some officers meet death while performing their jobs. On-the-job police deaths occur from stress, training accidents, and auto crashes. However, it is violent death at the hands of criminal offenders that police officers and their families fear most.

Violence in the Line of Duty

At 3:25 on a Friday morning in March 1988, New York City Police Officer Edward Byrne was gunned down while he sat in his patrol car protecting the home of a witness in a major narcotics case. Officer Byrne, who was 22-years-old, had decided to make policing his career. The cold-blooded killing motivated then-Mayor Ed Koch to place a large advertisement in *The New York Times* condemning the world of drug peddling and American policies which support countries where drugs are produced.[30] The ad, accompanied by a large picture of Officer Byrne in uniform, called for New Yorkers to exert political pressures to end economic and other forms of U.S. aid to countries from which drugs are smuggled.

Execution-style killings like those of Officer Byrne are rare. More common are line-of-duty deaths in battles with fleeing felons, in domestic disturbances, and while apprehending criminal suspects. Deputy Sheriff Douglas Hartman, for example, was killed when he attempted to serve a warrant on Larry Parker in Allentown, Pennsylvania, in July 1992. Hartman, who was not wearing his bulletproof vest, was shot once, with the bullet severing his aorta and spinal cord. Unknown to Hartman, the unemployed Parker, with a record of arrests for petty theft, had told friends that he intended to use his new .45-caliber handgun to "kill a police officer."[31]

In 1994, 157 American law enforcement officers were killed in the line of duty. Figure 6-1 shows the percentage of officers killed by circumstances and type of assignment. A recent study by the FBI found that slain officers appeared to be good-natured and conservative in the use of physical force, "as compared to other law enforcement officers in similar situations. They were also perceived as being well-liked by the community and the department, friendly to everyone, laid back, and easy going."[32] Finally, the study also found, officers who were killed failed to wear protective vests.

For statistics on police killings to have meaning beyond the personal tragedy they entail, however, it is necessary to place them within a larger framework. There are approximately 800,000 state and local police employees in this country, and another 70,000 federal agents nationwide. Such numbers demonstrate that the rate of violent death among law enforcement officers in the line of duty is small indeed.

Risk of Disease and Infected Evidence

Not all the dangers facing law enforcement officers are as direct as outright violence and assault. The increasing incidence of serious diseases capable of being transmitted by blood and other bodily fluids, combined with the fact that crime and accident scenes are inherently dangerous, has made "caution" a necessary byword among investigators and "first on the scene" officers. Potential for minor cuts and abrasions abounds in the broken glass and torn metal of a wrecked car, in the sharp edges of weapons remaining at the scene of an assault or murder, and in drug implements such as razor blades and hypodermic needles secreted in vehicles, apartments, and in pockets. Such minor injuries, previously shrugged off by many police personnel, have become a focal point for warnings about the dangers of AIDS (Acquired Immune Deficiency Syndrome), hepatitis B, tuberculosis, and other diseases spread through contact with infected blood.

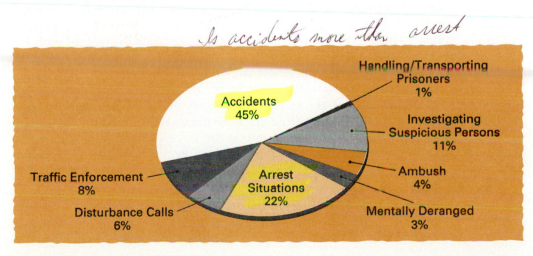

Is accidents more than arrest

U.S. law enforcement officers killed in the line of duty—by type of incident, 1994. Source: *Federal Bureau of Investigation*, Uniform Crime Reports 1994 *(Washington, D.C.: U.S. Government Printing Office, 1995).*

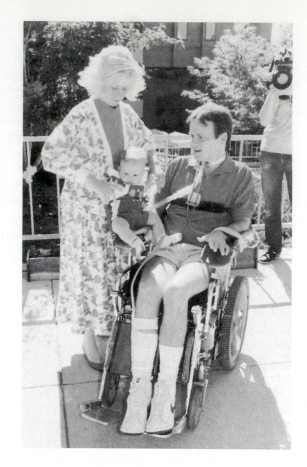

Police work can be dangerous. Steven McDonald, paralyzed and wheelchair bound after being shot in the neck while working as a New York City police officer, is shown here with his wife and young son. Photo by J. David Ake/UPI, courtesy of Bettmann.

In 1988, Sonoma County, California, Sheriff Dick Michaelson became the first law enforcement supervisor to announce a clear-cut case of AIDS infection in an officer caused by interaction with a suspect. A deputy in Michaelson's department apparently contracted AIDS a few years earlier when he was pricked by a hypodermic needle during a "pat down" search.[33]

In 1992, a 46-year-old San Francisco police officer won $50,547 in disability pay and AIDS medical treatment expenses[34] and a possible $25,000-per-year permanent retirement benefit. Inspector Thomas Cady became infected with the HIV virus after being bitten and splashed with blood during an arrest a few years earlier.

Understandably, there is much concern among officers over how to deal with the threat of AIDS and other bloodborne diseases. However, as a manual of the New York City Police Department reminds its officers, "Police officers have a professional responsibility to render assistance to those who are in need of our services. We cannot refuse to help. Persons with infectious diseases must be treated with the care and dignity we show all citizens."[35]

The FBI has also become concerned with the use of breath alcohol instruments on infected persons, the handling of evidence of all types, seemingly innocuous implements such as staples, the emergency delivery of babies in squad cars, and the risk of attack (especially bites) by infected individuals who are being questioned or who are in custody. The following are among the 16 recommendations made by the FBI as "defenses against exposure" to infectious substances (others are listed in Table 6-3):[36]

1. The first line of defense against infection at the crime scene is protecting the hands and keeping them away from the eyes, mouth, and nose.
2. Any person with a cut, abrasion, or any other break in the skin on the hands should never handle blood or other body fluids without protection.

3. Use gloves, and replace them whenever you leave the crime scene. Wash hands thoroughly.

4. No one at the crime scene should be allowed to smoke, eat, drink, or apply makeup.

5. Use the utmost care when handling knives, razors, broken glass, nails, and the like to prevent a puncture of the skin.

6. If a puncture of the skin does occur, cleanse it thoroughly with rubbing alcohol and wash with soap and water. Then seek immediate medical assistance.

7. When possible, use disposable items at the crime scene, such as pencils, gloves, and throw-away masks. These items should be incinerated after use.

8. Nondisposable items such as cameras, notebooks, and so on, should be decontaminated using bleach mixed with water.

The National Institute of Justice adds to this list the recommendations that suspects should be asked to empty their own pockets, where possible, and that puncture wounds should be "milked" as in the case of snakebites in order to help flush infectious agents from the wound.[37]

In order to better combat the threat of infectious diseases among health care professionals and public safety employees, the recently enacted federal Bloodborne Pathogens Act requires that police officers receive proper training in how to prevent contamination by bloodborne infectious agents. The Act also requires that police officers undergo an annual refresher course on the topic.

Police departments will face an increasing number of legal challenges in the years to come in cases involving infectious diseases such as AIDS. Some predictable areas of concern will involve (1) the need to educate officers and other police

---

TABLE 6-3

Responses to AIDS-Related Law Enforcement Concerns

Issue/Concern	Educational and Action Messages
Human bites	Person who bites usually receives the victim's blood; viral transmission through saliva is highly unlikely. If bitten by anyone, milk wound to make it bleed; wash the area thoroughly, and seek medical attention.
Spitting	Viral transmission through saliva is highly unlikely.
Urine/feces	Virus isolated in only very low concentrations in urine; not at all in feces; no cases of AIDS or AIDS virus infection associated with either urine or feces.
Cuts/puncture wounds	Use caution in handling sharp objects and searching areas hidden from view; needle-stick studies show risk of infection is very low.
CPR/first aid	To eliminate the already minimal risk associated with CPR, use masks and airways; avoid blood-to-blood contact by keeping open wounds covered and wearing gloves when in contact with bleeding wounds.
Body removal	Observe crime scene rules: do not touch anything. Those who must come into contact with blood or other bodily fluids should wear gloves.
Casual contact	No cases of AIDS or AIDS virus infection attributed to casual contact.
Any contact with blood or body fluids	Wear gloves if contact with blood or body fluids is considered likely. If contact occurs, wash thoroughly with soap and water; clean up spills with one part water to nine parts household bleach.
Contact with dried blood	No cases of infection have been traced to exposure to dried blood. The drying process itself appears to inactivate the virus. Despite low risk, however, caution dictates wearing gloves, a mask, and protective shoe coverings if exposure to dried blood particles is likely (e.g., crime scene investigation).

SOURCE: National Institute of Justice, Report No. 206 (November–December 1987), p. 6.

employees relative to AIDS and other serious infectious diseases, (2) the responsibility of police departments to prevent the spread of AIDS in police lockups, and (3) the necessity of effective and nondiscriminatory enforcement activities and life-saving measures by police officers in AIDS environments. With regard to nondiscriminatory activities, the National Institute of Justice has suggested that legal claims in support of an officer's refusal to render assistance to people with AIDS would probably not be effective in court.[38] The reason is twofold: The officer has a basic duty to render assistance to individuals in need of it, and the possibility of AIDS transmission by casual contact has been scientifically established as extremely remote. A final issue of growing concern involves activities by police officers infected with the AIDS virus. A recent issue of *Law Enforcement News* reports, "Faced with one of the nation's largest populations of AIDS sufferers—and perhaps one of the largest cadres of AIDS-infected officers—the New York City Police Department has debuted its own AIDS awareness effort."[39] Few statistics are currently available on the number of officers with AIDS, but public reaction to those officers may be a developing problem area which police managers will soon need to address.

Stress amoung Police Officers

Perhaps the most insidious and least visible of all threats facing law enforcement personnel today is debilitating stress. Although some degree of stress can be a positive motivator, serious stress, over long periods, is generally regarded as destructive, even life threatening. Police detectives, for example, who worked around the clock in 1994 searching for two missing South Carolina boys whose mother first reported them as kidnapped but later confessed to drowning them, found the case especially stressful since it brought to mind many emotions. "I feel like I aged 10 years in 10 days,"[40] said Union County Sheriff Howard Wells, after Susan Smith confessed to her son's murders.

Stress is a natural component of police work. The American Institute of Stress, based in Yonkers, New York, ranks policing among the top ten stress-producing jobs in the country.[41] Danger, frustration, paperwork, the daily demands of the job, and a lack of understanding from family members and friends contribute to the negative stresses officers experience.

Joseph Victor has identified four sources of police stress:[42] (1) external stress, which results from "real dangers," such as responding to calls involving armed suspects; (2) organizational stress, generated by the demands of police organizations themselves, such as scheduling, paperwork, and training requirements; (3) personal stress, produced by interpersonal relationships among officers themselves; and (4) operational stress, which Victor defines as "the total effect of the need to combat daily the tragedies of urban life."

Some of the stressors in police work are particularly destructive. One is frustration brought on by the inability to be effective, regardless of the amount of personal effort expended. From the point of view of the individual officer, the police mandate is to bring about some change in society for the better. The crux of police work involves making arrests based on thorough investigations which lead to convictions and the removal of individuals who are damaging to the social fabric of the community—all under the umbrella of the criminal law. Unfortunately, reality is often far from the ideal. Arrests may not lead to convictions. Evidence which is available to the officer may not be allowed in court. Sentences which are imposed may seem too "light" to the arresting officer. The feelings of powerlessness and frustration which come from seeing repeat offenders back on the streets, and from experiencing numerous injustices worked upon seemingly innocent victims, may greatly stress police officers and cause them to question the purpose of their professional lives.

Another source of stress—that of living with constant danger—is incomprehensible to most of us, even to the family members of many officers. As one officer says, "I kick in a door and I've gotta talk some guy into putting a gun down....And

I go home, and my wife's upset because the lawn isn't cut and the kids have been bad. Now, to her that's a real problem."[43]

Stress is not unique to the police profession, but because of the "macho" attitude that has traditionally been associated with police work, denial of the stress experience may be found more often among police officers than in other occupational groups. Certain types of individuals are probably more susceptible to the negative effects of stress than are others. The Type A personality was popularized some years ago as the category of person more likely to perceive life in terms of pressure and performance. Type B personalities were said to be more "laid back" and less likely to suffer from the negative effects of stress. Police ranks, drawn as they are from the general population, are filled with both stress-sensitive and stress-resistant personalities.

Stress Reduction

It is natural to try to reduce and control stress. Humor helps, even if it's somewhat cynical. Health care professionals, for example, have long been noted for their ability to joke around patients who may be seriously ill or even dying. Police officers may similarly use humor to defuse their reactions to dark or threatening situations. Keeping an emotional distance from stressful events is another way of coping with them although such distance is not always easy to maintain. Police officers who have had to deal with serious cases of physical child abuse have often reported on the emotional turmoil they experienced as a consequence of what they saw.

The support of family and friends can be crucial in developing other strategies to handle stress. Exercise, meditation, abdominal breathing, biofeedback, self-hypnosis, guided imaging, induced relaxation, subliminal conditioning, music, prayer, and diet have all been cited as techniques which can be useful in stress reduction. Devices to measure stress levels are available in the form of hand-held heart rate monitors, blood pressure devices, "biodots" (which change color according to the amount of blood flow in the extremities), and psychological inventories.

Police Civil Liability

An area of growing concern among police managers today is that of civil liability for official misconduct. Police officers may become involved in a variety of situations which create the potential for civil suits against the officers, their superiors, and their departments. Table 6-4 lists major sources of police civil liability. Swanson says that the most common source of lawsuits against the police involve "assault, battery, false imprisonment, and malicious prosecution."[44]

Civil suits brought against law enforcement personnel are of two types: state or federal. Suits brought into state courts have generally been the most common form of civil litigation involving police officers. In recent years, however, an increasing number of suits are being brought into federal courts on the basis of the legal rationale that the civil rights of the plaintiff, as guaranteed by federal law, have been denied.

Common Sources of Civil Suits

Of all complaints brought against the police, assault charges are the best known, being, as they are, subject to high media visibility. Less visible, but not uncommon, are civil suits charging the police with false arrest or false imprisonment. In the 1986 case of *Malley* v. *Briggs*,[45] the U.S. Supreme Court held that a police officer who effects an arrest or conducts a search on the basis of an improperly issued warrant may be liable for monetary damages when a reasonably well-trained officer, under the same circumstances, "would have known that his affidavit failed to establish probable cause and that he should not have applied for the warrant." Significantly, the Court, in *Malley*, also ruled that an officer "cannot excuse his own default by pointing to the greater incompetence of the magistrate."[46] That is, the officer, rather than the judge who issued the warrant, is ultimately responsible for establishing the basis for pursuing the arrest or search.

When an officer makes an arrest without just cause, or simply impedes an individual's right to leave the scene without good reason, he or she may also be liable for the charge of false arrest. Officers who enjoy "throwing their weight around" are especially subject to this type of suit, grounded as it is on the abuse of police authority. Because employers may generally be sued for the negligent or malicious actions of their employees, many police departments are finding themselves named as codefendants in lawsuits today.

Negligent actions by officers may also provide the basis for suits. High-speed chases are especially dangerous because of the potential they entail for injury to innocent bystanders. Flashing blue or red lights (the color of police vehicle lights varies by state) legally only request the right-of-way on a highway, they do not demand it. Officers who drive in such a way as to place others in danger may find themselves the subject of suits. In the case of *Biscoe* v. *Arlington* (1984),[47] for example, Alvin Biscoe was awarded $5 million after he lost both legs as a consequence of a high-speed chase while he was waiting to cross the street. Biscoe was an innocent bystander and was struck by a police car which had gone out of control. The fact that the police department in *Biscoe* had sanctioned high-speed chases as a part of official policy made the department especially liable. Departments may protect themselves to some degree through regulations limiting the authority of their personnel. In a 1985 case, for example, a Louisiana police department was exonerated in an accident which occurred during a high-speed chase because of its policy limiting emergency driving to no more than 20 miles over the posted speed limit. The officer, however, who drove 75 mph in a 40-mph zone was found to be negligent and held liable for damages.[48]

Law enforcement supervisors may find themselves the object of lawsuits by virtue of the fact that they are responsible for the actions of their officers. Where it can be shown that supervisors were negligent in hiring (as when someone with a history of alcoholism, mental problems, sexual deviance, or drug abuse is employed), or if supervisors failed in their responsibility to properly train officers before they armed and deployed them, they may be found liable for damages.

In the 1989 case of the City of Canton, *Ohio* v. *Harris*,[49] the U.S. Supreme Court ruled that a "failure to train" can become the basis for legal liability on the part of a municipality where the "failure to train amounts to deliberate indifference to the rights of persons with whom the police come in contact."[50] In that case, Geraldine Harris was arrested and taken to the Canton, Ohio, police station. While at the station, she slumped to the floor several times. Officers finally decided to leave her on the floor and never called for qualified medical assistance. Upon release, Ms. Harris was taken by family members to a local hospital. She was hospitalized for a week and received follow-up outpatient treatment for the next year. The Court ruled that

TABLE 6-4

Major Sources of Police Civil Liability

Failure to protect property in police custody
Negligence in the care of persons in police custody
Failure to render proper emergency medical assistance
Failure to prevent a foreseeable crime
Failure to aid private citizens
Lack of due regard for the safety of others
False arrest
False imprisonment
Inappropriate use of deadly force
Unnecessary assault or battery
Malicious prosecution
Violations of constitutional rights

Theory into Practice: An Example of Police Civil Liability—The Case of Bernard McCummings

A 1993 U.S. Supreme Court decision in a civil suit which drew wide outrage saw convicted subway mugger Bernard McCummings awarded $4.3 million in a suit he had brought against the city of New York. McCummings was shot twice in the back in 1984 by Transit Authority officer Manuel Rodriguez as he attempted to flee a subway platform after beating and robbing a 71-year-old man. At the time of the crime, McCummings had just gotten out of prison for robbery. Since the shooting, McCummings, who was 23-years-old when he was injured, has remained paralyzed from the chest down. After pleading guilty to the mugging, he was sentenced to prison, where he served two years. When McCummings brought suit against the city, however, a jury and appeals court found that officers had used excessive force. Before paying the award, the city appealed to the Supreme Court. In upholding the cash award to McCummings, the Supreme Court reiterated earlier rulings that police officers cannot use deadly force against unarmed fleeing suspects who pose no apparent threat to officers or to the public.

McCummings's victim, Jerome Sandusky, who was carrying less than $30 at the time he was attacked, decried the ruling, saying "[i]t's justice turned upside down...and it sends a terrible message...that crime *does* pay....Ordinarily I would be sorry for anyone that was made a cripple. But he was made a cripple because of his own action." Gerald Arenberg of the National Association of Chiefs of Police sided with Sandusky. "The criminal is very well protected by the Supreme Court," Arenberg said in a national interview. Lawyers for the city were disappointed. "The message is," said one, when faced with a fleeing suspect, "it's probably wiser for a police officer to do nothing, in terms of civil liability."

Opinions on the case were, however, varied. "It was the right decision," said David Breibart, McCummings's lawyer. "It gives me great faith in the system." A *Washington Post* editorial, on the other hand, suggested that police should not be bound by the rules of fairplay when criminals are not. "What if felons knew that cops could shoot them if they fled?" the editorial asked. " "More of them would likely freeze and put up their hands....[C]riminal behavior should not be treated as if it were some sort of quasi-legitimate enterprise, governed by the laws of negligence." "McCummings" said the writer, "was as much a victim of his own criminality as he was of a violation of the rules regarding the use of deadly force. Once he chose to break the law he wasn't entitled to be compensated by it." McCummings's victim agreed. Recently, Sandusky filed suit against McCummings seeking to get the $4.3 million award. Sandusky brought suit under New York's modified "Son of Sam" law, which is intended to prevent criminals from profiting from their crimes.

QUESTIONS FOR DISCUSSION

1. Do you feel McCummings should have been compensated for his injuries? Why or why not?

2. Do you agree with the assertion, in this box, that "cops should not be bound by the rules of fairplay when criminals are not"? Why or why not?

SOURCES: "Mugger Shot by Cop to Keep $4.3 million," *USA Today*, November 30, 1993, 1A. "Mugging Lawsuit," Associated Press wire services, December 15, 1993. "Compensation for a Criminal." *Washington Post* wire services, December 2, 1993. "Scotus-Excessive Force," Associated Press wire services, November 30, 1993.

---

although municipalities could not justifiably be held liable for limited instances of unsatisfactory training, they could be held accountable where the failure to train results from a deliberate or conscious choice.

Federal Lawsuits

Federal suits are often called **1983 lawsuits** because they are based on Section 1983 of Title 42 of the United States Code—an act passed by Congress in 1871 to ensure the civil rights of men and women of all races. That act requires due process of law before any person can be deprived of life, liberty, or property and specifically provides redress for the denial of these constitutional rights by officials acting under color of *state* law. For example, a 1983 suit may be brought against officers who shoot suspects under questionable circumstances—thereby denying them of their

1983 Lawsuits. Civil suits, brought under Title 42, Section 1983 of the United States Code, against anyone denying others of their constitutional rights to life, liberty, or property without due process of law.

right to life without due process. The 1981 case of *Prior* v. *Woods*[51] resulted in a $5.7 million judgment against the Detroit Police Department after David Prior—who was mistaken for a burglar—was shot and killed in front of his home.

Another type of liability action, this one directed specifically at federal officials or enforcement agents, is called a **Bivens suit**. The case of *Bivens* v. *Six Unknown Federal Agents* (1971)[52] established a path for legal action against agents enforcing federal laws which is similar to that found in a 1983 suit. Bivens actions may be addressed against individuals, but not the United States or its agencies.[53] Federal officers have generally been granted a court-created qualified immunity and have been protected from suits where they were found to have acted in the belief that their action was consistent with federal law.[54]

In times past, the doctrine of sovereign immunity barred legal actions against state and local governments. Sovereign immunity was a legal theory which held that a governing body could not be sued because it made the law and therefore could not be bound by it. Immunity is a much more complex issue today. Some states have officially abandoned any pretext of immunity through legislative action. New York State, for example, has declared that public agencies are as liable as private agencies for violations of constitutional rights. Other states, like California, have enacted statutory provisions which define and place limits on governmental liability.[55] A number of state immunity statutes have been struck down by court decision. In general, states are moving in the direction of setting dollar limits on liability and adopting federal immunity principles to protect individual officers, including "good faith" and "reasonable belief" rules.

At the federal level, the concept of sovereign immunity is embodied in the Federal Tort Claims Act (FTCA),[56] which grants broad immunity to federal government agencies engaged in discretionary activities. When a federal employee is sued for a wrongful or negligent act, the Federal Employees Liability Reform and Tort Compensation Act of 1988, commonly known as the Westfall Act, empowers the Attorney General to certify that the employee was acting within the scope of his or her office or employment at the time of the incident out of which the claim arose. On certification, the employee is dismissed from the action, and the United States is substituted as defendant. The case then falls under the governance of the FTCA.

In 1995, in a case involving the FTCA, a Miami federal judge ordered the federal government to pay out more than $1 million to five crew members and a passenger on board an airplane from Belize (a small Latin American country), which was scheduled to stop in Miami after taking on additional passengers in Honduras. Testimony revealed that DEA agents had planted cocaine on the plane at its point of origin and had planned to arrest Miami dealers when they retrieved the drugs. Unfortunately, the agents had failed to notify Honduran authorities of the planted drugs, and when the plane landed in Honduras, it was searched. Honduran police then arrested the six men—beating them with rubber hoses and kicking them

*B*ivens Action. The name given to civil suits, based on the case of *Bivens* v. *Six Unknown Federal Agents*, brought against federal government officials for denial of the constitutional rights of others.

---

*T*heory into Practice: Title 42, United States Code, Section 1983

Every person who, under color of any statute, ordinance, regulation, custom, or usage, of any State or Territory, subjects, or causes to be subjected, any citizen of the United States or other person within the jurisdiction thereof to the deprivation of any rights, privileges, or immunities secured by the Constitution and laws, shall be liable to the party injured in an action at law, suit in equity, or other proper proceeding for redress.

downstairs in an effort to get confessions.[57] The judge hearing the suit against the government ruled that although the FTCA gives broad immunity to government agencies whose officials exercise discretion in everyday activities, it was not the intent of Congress to extend immunity to government agencies when the actions of their officials fail to comply with established regulations. In effect, said the judge, the failure by DEA agents to notify Honduran police of the "sting" in progress constituted a failure to perform an official duty.

For its part, the U.S. Supreme Court has supported a type of "qualified immunity" for individual officers (as opposed to the agencies for which they work) which "shields law enforcement officers from constitutional lawsuits if reasonable officers believe their actions to be lawful in light of clearly established law and the information the officers possess." The Supreme Court has also described qualified immunity as a defense "which shields public officials from actions for damages unless their conduct was unreasonable in light of clearly established law."[58] According to the Court, "the qualified immunity doctrine's central objective is to protect public officials from undue interference with their duties and from potentially disabling threats of liability...."[59] In the context of a warrantless arrest, the Court said, in *Hunter* v. *Bryant* (1991),[60] "even law enforcement officials who reasonably but mistakenly conclude that probable cause is present are entitled to immunity."[61]

Most departments carry liability insurance to protect them against the severe financial damage which can result from the loss of a large suit. Some officers make it a point to acquire private policies which provide coverage in the event they are named as individuals in such suits. Both types of insurance policies generally provide for a certain amount of legal fees to be paid by the police for defense against the suit, regardless of the outcome of the case. Police departments who face civil prosecution because of the actions of an officer, however, may find that legal and financial liability extend to supervisors, city managers, and the community itself. Where insurance coverage does not exist, or is inadequate, city coffers may be nearly drained to meet the damages awarded.[62]

In a recent five-year period, for example, the city of Los Angeles, California, paid out $23 million to people who brought suits against the LAPD for civil rights violations.[63] Former Los Angeles Chief of Police Daryl Gates, in commenting on the prevalence of lawsuits against police officers today, has observed that although California cities are allowed to pay damage awards for individual officers, they do not have to. Gates continued: "Think about the chilling factor in that. [It says] 'Hey, Chief, you're on your own. We're not gonna pay anything.' Think what that does. It says, 'Hey Chief, don't open your mouth—Don't tell the public anything. Don't let them know what the real facts are in this case. Don't tell the truth.' And what does it tell the police officers? 'Don't do your work, because you're liable to wind up in court, being sued.' That, to me, is probably the most frightening thing that's happening in the United States today."[64]

Police Use of Deadly Force

The use of deadly force by police officers is one area of potential civil liability which has received considerable attention in recent years. Historically, the fleeing felon rule applied to most U.S. jurisdictions. It held that officers could use deadly force to prevent the escape of a suspected felon, even when that person represented no immediate threat to the officer or to the public. The fleeing felon rule probably stemmed from early common law punishments which specified death for a large number of crimes. Today, however, the death penalty is far less frequent in application, and the fleeing felon rule has been called into question in a number of courts.

The 1985 Supreme Court case of *Tennessee* v. *Garner*[65] specified the conditions under which deadly force could be used in the apprehension of suspected felons.

Edward Garner, a 15-year-old suspected burglar, was shot to death by Memphis police after he refused their order to halt and attempted to climb over a chain-link fence. In an action initiated by Garner's father, who claimed that his son's constitutional rights had been violated, the Court held that the use of deadly force by the police to prevent the escape of a fleeing felon could be justified only where the suspect could reasonably be thought to represent a significant threat of serious injury or death to the public or to the officer, and where deadly force is necessary to effect the arrest. In reaching its decision, the Court declared that "The use of deadly force to prevent the escape of *all* felony suspects, whatever the circumstances, is constitutionally unreasonable."[66]

In 1989, the Court, in the case of *Graham* v. *Connor,*[67] established the standard of "objective reasonableness" under which an officer's use of deadly force could be assessed in terms of "reasonableness at the moment." In other words, whether deadly force has been used appropriately or not should be judged, the Court said, from the perspective of a reasonable officer on the scene, and not with the benefit of "20/20 hindsight." "The calculus of reasonableness," wrote the Justices, "must embody allowance for the fact that police officers are often forced to make split-second judgments—in circumstances that are tense, uncertain, and rapidly evolving—about the amount of force that is necessary in a particular situation."[68]

Studies of killings by the police have often focused on claims of discrimination, that is, that black and minority suspects are more likely to be shot than whites. Research in the area, however, has not provided solid support for such claims. Although individuals shot by police are more likely to be minorities, James Fyfe[69] found that police officers will generally respond with deadly force when mortally threatened and that minorities are considerably more likely to use weapons in assaults on officers than are whites. Complicating the picture further were Fyfe's data showing that minority officers are involved in the shooting of suspects more often than other officers, a finding that may be due to the assignment of such officers to inner-city and ghetto areas. However, a more recent study by Fyfe,[70] which analyzed police shootings in Memphis, Tennessee, found that black property offenders were twice as likely as whites to be shot by police.

Although relatively few police officers will ever feel the need to draw their weapons during the course of their careers, those who do may find themselves embroiled in a web of social, legal, and personal complications. It is estimated that an average year sees 600 suspects killed by gunfire from public police in America, while another 1,200 are shot and wounded, and 1,800 individuals are shot at and missed.[71]

The personal side of police shootings is well summarized in the title of an article which appeared in *Police Magazine*. The article, "I've Killed That Man Ten Thousand Times,"[72] demonstrated how police officers who have to use their weapon may be haunted by years of depression and despair. Not long ago, according to Anne Cohen, author of the article, all departments did to help officers who had shot someone was to "give him enough bullets to reload his gun." The stress and trauma which result from shootings by officers in defense of themselves or others is only now beginning to be realized, and most departments have yet to develop mechanisms for adequately dealing with it.[73]

In 1993, the National Institute of Justice reported on efforts begun in 1987 to develop "less than lethal weapons" for use by law enforcement officers.[74] Questions to be answered include (1) "Can an officer stop a fleeing felon without use of deadly force?" (2) "Are there devices and substances that would rapidly subdue assailants before they could open fire or otherwise harm their hostages?" (3) "Can technology provide devices to incapacitate assailants without also harming nearby innocent hostages and bystanders?" Chemical agents, knockout gases, stunning explosives, tranquilizing darts, and remote-delivery electronic shocks are all being studied by the agency. NIJ says it is "moving forward with research development, and evaluation of devices for use by line patrol officers under a wide variety of circumstances….[T]he goal is to give line officers effective and safe alternatives to lethal force."[75]

Professionalism and Ethics

Police administrators have responded in a variety of ways to issues of danger, liability, and the potential for corruption. Among the most significant responses have been calls for increased ==police professionalism== at all levels. A profession is characterized by a body of specialized knowledge, acquired through extensive education,[76] and by a well-considered set of internal standards and ethical guidelines which hold members of the profession accountable to one another and to society. Associations of like-minded practitioners generally serve to create and disseminate standards for the profession as a whole.

Contemporary policing evidences many of the attributes of a profession. Specialized knowledge in policing includes a close familiarity with criminal law, laws of procedure, constitutional guarantees and relevant Supreme Court decisions, a working knowledge of weapons and hand-to-hand tactics, driving skills and vehicle maintenance, a knowledge of radio communications, report-writing abilities, interviewing techniques, and media and human relations skills. Other specialized knowledge may include breathalyzer operation, special weapons firing, polygraph operation, conflict resolution, and hostage negotiation skills. Supervisory personnel require an even wider range of skills, including administrative knowledge, management techniques, personnel administration, and department strategies for optimum utilization of officers and physical resources.

Basic law enforcement training requirements were begun in the 1950s by the state of New York and through a voluntary system of Peace Officer Standards and Training (POST) in California. Today, such requirements are mandated by law in every state in the nation although they vary considerably from region to region. Modern police education involves, at a minimum, more than 100 classroom contact hours (Missouri), and in some places nearly 1,000 hours of intensive training (Hawaii),[77] in subject areas which include human relations, firearms and weapons, communications, legal aspects of policing, patrol, criminal investigations, administration, report writing, and criminal justice systems. Contemporary California **POST standards** are shown in a Theory into Practice box on page 189.

Federal law enforcement agents receive schooling at the Federal Law Enforcement Training Center (FLETC) at Glynco, Georgia. The Center provides training for about 60 federal law enforcement agencies (excluding the FBI, which has its own training center at Quantico, Virginia) and has begun offering advanced training to state and local police organizations (through the National Center for State and Local Law Enforcement Training, located on the FLETC campus), where such training is not available under other auspices. Specialized schools, such as Northwestern University's Traffic Institute, have also been credited with raising the level of police practice from purely operational concerns to a more professional level.[78]

Police work is guided by an ethical code originated in 1956 by the Peace Officer's Research Association of California (PORAC), in conjunction with Dr. Douglas M. Kelley of Berkeley's School of Criminology.[79] *The Law Enforcement Code of Ethics* is reproduced in a box in this chapter. Training in **police ethics** is still not well integrated into most basic law enforcement training programs, but a movement in that direction has begun, and calls for expanded training in ethics are on the increase.

Professional associations abound in police work. The Fraternal Order of Police (FOP) is one of the best known organizations of public service workers in the United States. The International Association of Chiefs of Police (IACP) has done much to raise professional standards in policing and continually strives for improvements in law enforcement nationwide.

Accreditation provides another channel toward police professionalism. The Commission on Accreditation for Law Enforcement Agencies was formed in 1979.

Police Professionalism. The increasing formalization of police work and the rise in public acceptance of the police which accompanies it. Any profession is characterized by a specialized body of knowledge and a set of internal guidelines which hold members of the profession accountable for their actions. A well-focused code of ethics, equitable recruitment and selection practices, and informed promotional strategies among many agencies contribute to a growing level of professionalism among American police agencies today.

Police Ethics. The special responsibility for adherence to moral duty and obligation inherent in police work.

Police departments wishing to apply for accreditation through the Commission must meet hundreds of standards relating to areas as diverse as day-to-day operations, administration, review of incidents involving the use of a weapon by officers, and evaluation and promotion of personnel. To date, relatively few police agencies are accredited although a number have applied to begin the process. Those agencies are now conducting self-evaluations as part of the application process. Although accreditation makes possible the identification of high-quality police departments, it is often undervalued because it carries few incentives. Accreditation is still only "icing on the cake" and does not guarantee a department any rewards beyond the recognition of peers.

Educational Requirements

As the concern for quality policing builds, increasing emphasis is being placed on the education of police officers. As early as 1931, the National Commission on Law Observance and Enforcement (the Wickersham Commission) highlighted the importance of a well-educated police force by calling for "educationally sound" officers.[80] In 1967, the President's Commission on Law Enforcement and the Administration of Justice voiced the belief that "(t)he ultimate aim of all police departments should be that all personnel with general enforcement powers have baccalaureate degrees." At the time, the average educational level of police officers in the United States was 12.4 years—slightly beyond a high school degree. In 1973, the National Advisory Commission on Criminal Justice Standards and Goals made the following rather specific recommendation:[81] "Every police agency should, no later than 1982, require as a condition of initial employment the completion of at least 4 years of education...at an accredited college or university."[82]

Recommendations, of course, do not always translate into practice. A 1988 survey of 699 police departments by PERF found that the average level of educational achievement among both black and white officers was 14 years of schooling, nearly the equivalent of an associate's degree from a "2-year" or community college.[83] Female officers (with an average level of educational achievement of 14.6 years) tend to be better educated than their male counterparts (who report an average attainment level of 13.6 years). Only 3.3 percent of male officers hold graduate degrees, whereas almost one-third (30.2 percent) of women officers hold such degrees. On the down side, 34.8 percent of male officers have no college experience, and 24.1 percent of female officers have none. The PERF report explained the difference between male and female educational achievement by saying that "[w]omen tend to rely on higher education more than men as a springboard for a law enforcement career...[and] [p]olice departments may utilize higher standards—consciously or unconsciously—for selecting women officers."[84]

The report also stressed the need for educated police officers, citing the following benefits which accrue to police agencies from the hiring of educated officers:[85] (1) better written reports, (2) enhanced communications with the public, (3) more effective job performance, (4) fewer citizens' complaints, (5) greater initiative, (6) a wiser use of discretion, (7) a heightened sensitivity to racial and ethnic issues, and (8) fewer disciplinary problems. On the other hand, a greater likelihood that educated officers will leave police work, and their tendency to question orders and request reassignment with relative frequency, are some education-related drawbacks.

To meet the growing needs of police officers for college-level training, the International Association of Police Professors (IAPP) was formed in 1963. The IAPP later changed its name to the Academy of Criminal Justice Sciences (ACJS) and widened its focus to include criminal justice education.

A number of agencies now require the completion of at least some college-level work for officers seeking promotion. The San Diego Police Department, for example, requires two years of college work for promotion to the rank of sergeant.[86]

*T*heory into Practice: Police Training—California's POST Standards

The California Peace Officer Standards and Training program was one of this country's first selection and training standards-setting programs for law enforcement officers. Today, an updated POST program serves as a model for other similar programs in many parts of the United States. Shown here are the latest POST Regular Basic Course subject areas and required minimum hours, which took effect on July 15, 1995.

BASIC POST TRAINING (664 MINIMUM REQUIRED HOURS)

History, Professionalism, and Ethics	8 hours	Hazardous Materials	4 hours
Criminal Justice System	4 hours	Vehicle Pullovers	14 hours
Community Relations	12 hours	Crimes in Progress	16 hours
Victimology/Crisis Interventions	6 hours	Handling Disputes/Crowd Control	12 hours
Introduction to Criminal Law	6 hours	Domestic Violence	8 hours
Crimes Against Property	10 hours	Unusual Occurrences	4 hours
Crimes Against Persons	10 hours	Missing Persons	4 hours
General Criminal Statutes	4 hours	Traffic Enforcement	22 hours
Crimes Against Children	6 hours	Traffic Accident Invest.	12 hours
Sex Crimes	6 hours	Preliminary Investigation	42 hours
Juvenile Law and Procedure	6 hours	Custody	4 hours
Controlled Substances	12 hours	Physical Fitness/Officer Stress	40 hours
ABC Law	4 hours	Person Searches, Baton, etc.	60 hours
Laws of Arrest	12 hours	Search and Seizure	12 hours
Presentation of Evidence	8 hours	First Aid and CPR	21 hours
Investigative Report Writing	40 hours	Firearms/Chemical Agents	72 hours
Vehicle Operations	24 hours	Information Systems	4 hours
Use of Force	12 hours	Persons with Disabilities	6 hours
Patrol Techniques	12 hours	Crimes Against the Justice System	4 hours
Gang Awareness	8 hours	Cultural Diversity/Discrimination	24 hours
Weapons Violations	4 hours		

Minimum Instructional Hours   **599**

The minimum number of hours allocated to testing in the Regular Basic Course are shown here:

TEST TYPE	HOURS
Scenario Tests	40 hours
POST-Constructed Knowledge Tests	25 hours

Total Minimum Hours   **664**

Successful curriculum completion also requires that "the Law Enforcement Code of Ethics shall be administered to peace officer trainees during the basic course."

QUESTIONS FOR DISCUSSION

1. What classes or subject areas would you like to see added to (or deleted from) POST training? Why?

2. Do you believe that police training, such as POST, results in better officers? Why or why not? If so, in what way are they "better"?

Note: Every peace officer below the first middle-management level must satisfactorily complete the advanced officer course of 24 or more hours at least once every 2 years after completion of the basic course. This requirement may also be met by satisfactory completion of an accumulation of certified technical courses totaling 24 or more hours, or satisfactory completion of an alternative method of compliance as determined by the Commission. Supervisors may also satisfy the requirement by completing supervisory or management training courses.

SOURCE: State of California, Commission on Peace Officer Standards and Training, Commission Regulation, 1005, *POST Administrative Manual* (Sacramento, Calif.: POST, 1995).

In 1988, the Sacramento, California, Police Department set completion of a four-year college degree as a requirement for promotion to lieutenant, and, in the same year, the New York City Police Department announced a requirement of at least 64 college credits for promotion to supervisory ranks. At the state level, a variety of plans exist for integrating college work into police careers. Minnesota now requires a college degree for new candidates taking the state's Peace Office Standards and Training Board's licensing examination. Successful completion of all POST requirements permits employment as a fully certified law enforcement officer in the state of Minnesota. Beginning in 1991, the state of New York set 60 semester hours of college-level work as a mandated minimum for hiring into the New York State Police. Finally, as the boxes on careers found throughout this book show, many federal agencies require college degrees for entry-level positions. Among them are the FBI, DEA, ATF, Secret Service, the U.S. Customs Service, and the Immigration and Naturalization Service.

Recruitment and Selection

Any profession needs informed, dedicated, and competent personnel. When the National Advisory Commission on Criminal Justice Standards and Goals issued its 1973 report on the police, it bemoaned the fact that "many college students are unaware of the varied, interesting, and challenging assignments and career opportunities that exist within the police service."[87] In the intervening years, the efforts made by police departments to correct such misconceptions have had a considerable effect. Today, police organizations actively recruit new officers from college campuses, professional organizations, and two-year junior colleges and technical institutes. Education is an important criterion in selecting today's police recruits.[88] Some departments require a minimum number of college credits for entry-level work. A policy of the Dallas, Texas, Police Department requiring a minimum of 45 semester hours of successful college-level study for new recruits was upheld in 1986 by the U.S. Supreme Court in the case of *Davis v. Dallas*.[89]

Theory into Practice: The Law Enforcement Code of Ethics

As a Law Enforcement Officer, my fundamental duty is to serve mankind; to safeguard lives and property; to protect the innocent against deception, the weak against oppression or intimidation, and the peaceful against violence or disorder; and to respect the Constitutional rights of all men to liberty, equality, and justice.

I will keep my private life unsullied as an example to all; maintain courageous calm in the face of danger, scorn, or ridicule; develop self-restraint; and be constantly mindful of the welfare of others. Honest in thought and deed in both my personal and official life, I will be exemplary in obeying the laws of the land and the regulations of my department. Whatever I see or hear of a confidential nature or that is confided to me in my official capacity will be kept secret unless revelation is necessary in the performance of my duty.

I will never act officiously or permit personal feelings, prejudices, animosities or friendships to influence my decisions. With no compromise for crime and with relentless prosecution of criminals, I will enforce the law courteously and appropriately without fear or favor, malice or ill will, never employing unnecessary force or violence and never accepting gratuities.

I recognize the badge of my office as a symbol of public faith, and I accept it as a public trust to be held so long as I am true to the ethics of the police service. I will constantly strive to achieve these objectives and ideals, dedicating myself before God to my chosen profession...law enforcement.

Source: International Association of Chiefs of Police. Reprinted with permission.

The National Commission report stressed the setting of high standards for police recruits and recommended a strong emphasis on minority recruitment, an elimination of residence requirements (which required officers to live in the area they were hired to serve) for new officers, a decentralized application and testing procedure, and various recruiting incentives. The Commission also suggested that a four-year college degree should soon become a reasonable expectation for police recruits. The survey also found that 62 percent of responding agencies had at least one formal policy in support of officers pursuing higher education.[90]

Effective policing, however, may depend more on personal qualities than it does on educational attainment. O. W. Wilson once enumerated some of the "desirable personal qualities of patrol officers."[91] They include (1) initiative; (2) the capacity for responsibility; (3) the ability to deal alone with emergencies; (4) the capacity to communicate effectively with persons of diverse social, cultural, and ethnic backgrounds; (5) the ability to learn a variety of tasks quickly; (6) the attitude and ability necessary to adapt to technological changes; (7) the desire to help people in need; (8) an understanding of others; (9) emotional maturity; and (10) sufficient physical strength and endurance.

Standard procedures employed by modern departments in selecting trainees usually include basic skill tests, physical agility measurements, interviews, physical examinations, eye tests, psychological evaluations, and background investigations into the personal character of applicants. After training, successful applicants are typically placed on a period of probation approximately one year in length. The probationary period in police work has been called the "first true job-related test…in the selection procedure,"[92] providing as it does the opportunity for supervisors to gauge the new officer's response to real-life situations.

Ethnic and Racial Minorities and Women

In 1967, the National Advisory Commission on Civil Disorders conducted a survey of supervisory personnel in police departments.[93] They found a marked disparity between the number of black and white officers in leadership positions. One of every 26 black police officers had been promoted to the rank of sergeant, whereas the ratio among whites was 1 of 12. Only 1 of every 114 black officers had become a lieutenant, whereas among whites the ratio was 1 of 26. At the level of captain, the disparity was even greater—1 of every 235 black officers had achieved the rank of captain, whereas 1 of every 53 whites had climbed to that rank.

Since then, the emphasis placed on minority recruitment by task forces, civil rights groups, courts, and society in general, has done much to rectify the situation. In 1979, for example, one of the first affirmative action disputes involving a police department was settled out of court. The settlement required the San Francisco Police Department to ensure that over the next ten years minorities would receive 50 percent of all promotions and that 20 percent of all new officers hired would be women.[94]

Today, the situation is changing. Many departments, through dedicated recruitment efforts, have dramatically increased their complement of officers from underrepresented groups. The Metropolitan Detroit Police Department, for example, now has a force that is more than 30 percent black.

Although ethnic minorities have moved into policing in substantial numbers (see Figure 6-2), females are still significantly underrepresented. A recent study by the Police Foundation[95] found that women accounted for nearly 9 percent of all officers in municipal departments serving populations of 50,000 or more but that they composed only 3 percent of all supervisors in city agencies, and 1% of supervisors in state police agencies. Female officers made up 10.1 percent of the total number of officers in departments which were functioning under court order to increase their proportion of women officers, whereas women constituted 8.3 percent of officers in agencies with voluntary affirmative action programs, and only 6.1 percent of officers in departments without such programs.

A recent report[96] on women police officers in Massachusetts found that female officers (1) are "extremely devoted to their work," (2) "see themselves as women first, and then police officers," and (3) were more satisfied when working in nonuniformed capacities. Two groups of women officers were identified: (1) those who felt themselves to be well integrated into their departments and were confident in their jobs and (2) those who experienced strain and on-the-job isolation. The officers' children were cited as a significant influence on their self-perceptions and on the way in which they viewed their jobs. The demands which attend child rearing in contemporary society were found to be major factors contributing to the resignation of female officers. The study also found that the longer women officers stayed on the job, the greater the stress and frustration they tended to experience—primarily as a consequence of the noncooperative attitudes of male officers. Some of the female officers interviewed identified networking as a potential solution to the stresses encountered by female officers, but also said that when women get together to solve problems they are seen as "crybabies" rather than professionals. Said one of the women in the study, "[w]e've lost a lot of good women who never should have left the job. If we had helped each other maybe they wouldn't have left."[97]

Networking is a concept which is quickly taking root among the nation's women police officers, as attested to by the growth of organizations like the International Association of Women Police, based in New York City. Mentoring, another method for introducing women to police work, has been suggested by some authors.[98] Mentoring would create semiformal relationships between experienced women officers and rookies entering the profession. Through such relationships, problems could be addressed as they arose, and the experienced officer could serve to guide her junior partner through the maze of formal and informal expectations which surround the job of policing.

Other studies, like those already discussed, have found that female officers are often underutilized and that many departments are hesitant to assign women to patrol and other potentially dangerous field activities. As a consequence, some women in

FIGURE 6-2
Ethnic minorities as a proportion of sworn state law enforcement officers and as a proportion of the U.S. population. Source: Adapted from Kathleen Maquire and Ann L. Pastore, Sourcebook of Criminal Justice Statistics 1993 *(Washington, D.C.: Bureau of Justice Statistics, 1994). Part I of Figure 6-2, Ethnic minorities in law enforcement. Part 2 of Figure 6-2, Minorities as a proportion of the U.S. population.*

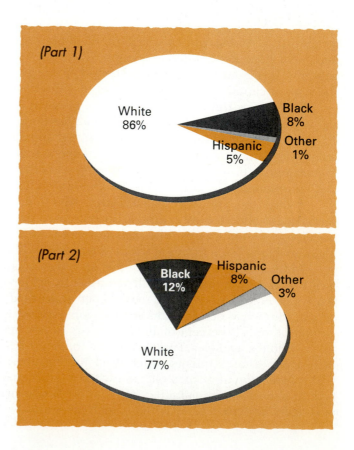

police work experience frustrations and a lack of satisfaction with their jobs.[99] Other women are hesitant to consider a police career, and a few departments complain that it is difficult to find significant numbers of well-qualified minority recruits interested in police work. Further, harassment on the job continues to be a reality for some minority officers. For example, in the late 1980s, a black FBI agent complained to his superiors and to the Justice Department's Office of Professional Responsibility about death threats, obscene mail, and threats against his family, apparently generated by fellow agents because he is black. An Equal Employment Opportunity Commission decision in the case concluded that the agent had indeed been the victim of a series of discriminatory activities, and the officer filed suit against the FBI alleging violation of his civil rights.[100] In 1993, settlement of a racial discrimination suit brought against the FBI by black agents required the FBI to provide increased training for blacks and placed supervision of the FBI's employment practices in the hands of a federal judge for a period of five years.[101] Only about 5 percent of the Bureau's agents are black.

Barriers continue to fall. In 1979, for example, San Francisco became the first city in the world to actively recruit homosexuals for its police force. That action resulted in a reduced fear of reporting crimes among many city homosexuals, who for years had been victims of organized assaults by bikers and street gangs. Recently, Attorney General Janet Reno ordered all Justice Department agencies to end hiring discrimination based on sexual orientation. Other barriers are falling as women begin to enter the ranks of police administration. For example, the International Association of Women Police estimates that in 1994 there were nearly 100 female chiefs of police throughout the country.[102]

In a continuing effort to increase the representation of women and ethnic minorities in police work, the Police Foundation recommends (1) involving underrepresented groups in affirmative action and long-term planning programs which are undertaken by police departments, (2) encouraging the development of an open system of promotions whereby women can feel free to apply for promotion and in which qualified individuals of any race or gender will face equity in the promotion process, and (3) using periodic audits to ensure that women officers are not being underutilized by being ineffectively tracked into clerical and support positions.[103]

Private Protective Services

Private police constitute an increasingly important type of enforcement activity in the United States today. **Private security** has been defined as "those self-employed individuals and privately funded business entities and organizations

Private Protective Services. Independent or proprietary commercial organizations which provide protective services to employers on a contractual basis. Private security agencies, which already employ about half again as many people as public law enforcement, are expected to experience substantial growth over the next few decades.

Women in uniform have become a common sight throughout our nation's cities and towns. Here a female officer lectures a man who ran a red light. Photo by Sepp Seitz, courtesy of Woodfin Camp & Associates.

Ethnic minorities, though still underrepresented in the criminal justice system, have many opportunities for employment throughout the system. Here Boston police officer Michael Watson carries a child rescued from a burning building to a waiting ambulance. Photo by Jon Hill, courtesy of The Boston Herald.

providing security-related services to specific clientele for a fee, for the individual or entity that retains or employs them, or for themselves, in order to protect their persons, private property, or interests from various hazards."[104] Public police are employed by the government and enforce public laws. Private security personnel work for corporate employers and secure private interests.

According to the *Hallcrest Report II*,[105] a major government-sponsored analysis of the private security industry, nearly 1.5 million people are employed in private security today—more than in all local, state, and federal police agencies combined. Employment in the field of private security is anticipated to expand by around 4 percent per year through the end of the century (see Figure 6-3), while public police agencies are expected to grow by only 2.8 percent per year during the same period. By the year 2000, 1.9 million people will be working in private security if projections hold, while only 700,000 persons will be engaged in public law enforcement. Still faster growth is predicted in private security industry revenues—anticipated to increase at around 7 percent per year through the year 2000, a growth rate almost three times greater than that projected for the nation's GNP. Table 6-5 lists the largest private security agencies in business today. It also lists some of the types of services they offer.

Private agencies provide tailored policing funded by the guarded organization rather than through the expenditure of public monies. Experts estimate that private security services cost American industries an astounding $52 billion in 1990, while monies spent on public policing totaled only $30 billion.[106] Contributing to this vast expenditure is the federal government, which is itself a major employer of private security personnel, contracting for services which range from guards to highly specialized electronic snooping and countermeasures at military installations and embassies throughout the world.

Major reasons for the quick growth of the American proprietary security sector include "(1) an increase in crimes in the workplace, (2) an increase in fear (real or perceived) of crime, (3) the fiscal crises of the states, [which] has limited public protection, and (4) an increased public and business awareness and use of...more cost-effective private security products and services."[107] In 1990, the influential yearly "Forecast Survey"[108] of private security operations identified substance abuse as the number one worry of security managers throughout American industry—the first time in the survey's 25-year history that property crime was replaced as the industry's front-running concern.

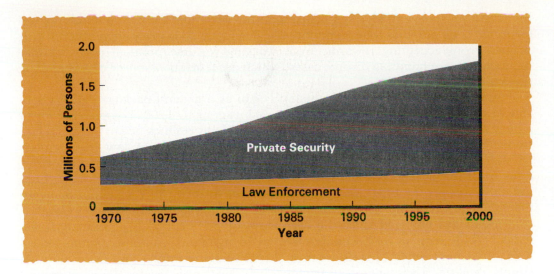

FIGURE 6-3
Private security and law enforcement; projected growth to 2000 A.D. Source: William C. Cunningham, John J. Struchs, and Clifford W. Van Meter, "Private Security: Patterns and Trends," A National Institute of Justice Research in Brief (Washington, D.C.: U.S. Department of Justice, 1991).

The Development of Private Policing

Private policing in America has a long and rich history. The first security firms began operation in the mid-1800s, hired mostly by the railroad companies which were laying tracks to support the burgeoning westward expansion of our nation. Company shipments of supplies, guns, and money, as well as engineers and company officials, all needed protection from Indians, outlaws, and assorted desperadoes.

Allan Pinkerton opened his Pinkerton National Detective Agency in 1851 with the motto "We Never Sleep."[109] Pinkerton's agency specialized in railroad security and would protect shipments as well as hunt down thieves who had made a get-away. The Pinkerton service emblazoned an open eye, to signify constant vigilance, on its office doors and stationery. The term "private eye" is thought to have developed out of the use of this logo. Henry Wells and William Fargo built their still famous Wells Fargo Company in 1852 and supplied detective and protective services to areas west of Missouri. Anyone willing to pay their fee could have a force of private guards and investigators working for them.

The early days of private security services led quickly to abuses by untrained and poorly disciplined agents. No licensing standards applied to the private security field, and security personnel sometimes became private "goons," catering only to

TABLE 6-5

Private Police Agencies

The Largest Private Security Agencies in the United States[1]

Security Bureau, Inc.	Globe Security	Pinkerton's, Inc.
The Wackenhut Corp.	Wells Fargo Guard Services	Stanley Smith Security, Inc.
Allied Security, Inc.	Guardsmark, Inc.	Advance Security, Inc.
Burns International Security Services	American Protective Services	

Private Security Services

Company guards	Store/mall security	Automated Teller Machine services
Airport security	School security	Railroad detectives
Bank guards	Nuclear facility security	Loss prevention specialists
Executive protection agencies	Hospital security	Computer/information security

1. From *The Hallcrest Report II* (McLean, Va.: Hallcrest Systems, 1990).

the wishes of their employers. To cope with the situation, Pinkerton developed an elaborate code of ethics for his employees. Pinkerton's code prohibited his men and women from accepting rewards, from working for one political party against another, or from handling divorce cases (which are a primary source of revenue for private detectives today).

Another firm, the Brink's Company, began as a general package delivery service in 1859 and grew to a fleet of 85 armored wagons by 1900. The year 1859 was a busy one for private security, for in that year Edwin Holmes began the first electronic burglar alarm firm in Boston, Massachusetts. Former law enforcement administrators began to get into the private security field in 1909 when a former director of the Bureau of Investigation formed the William J. Burns International Detective Agency. In 1954, George R. Wackenhut formed the Wackenhut Security Corporation, which has become one of the largest private security firms today.

Much has changed since the early days of private policing. Security firms today provide services for hospitals, manufacturing plants, communications industries, retirement homes, hotels, casinos, exclusive communities and clubs, nuclear storage facilities and reactors, and many other types of businesses. Physical security, loss prevention, information security, and the protection of personnel are all service areas for private security organizations.

Private security agencies have been praised for their ability to adapt to new situations and technology. Although most security personnel are poorly paid and perform typical "watchmen" roles, the security industry is able to contract with experts in almost any area. Specially assembled teams, hired on a subcontractual basis, have allowed some firms to move successfully into information and technology security. As financial opportunities continue to build in high-tech security, the industry is seeing the creation of a well-educated and highly specialized cadre of workers able to meet the most exacting needs of today's large and multinational corporations. The ability of private agents to work across state lines, and even international boundaries, is an added benefit of private security to many employers.

Security personnel sometimes work undercover, blending with company employees to learn who is pilfering inventories or selling business secrets to competitors. According to the Society of Competitor Intelligence Professionals, more than 80 percent of the *Fortune* 1000 companies have regular in-house "snoops" on the payroll.[110] Interestingly, a corporate backlash is now occurring which has led to the hiring of even more security specialists by private industry—companies everywhere are becoming concerned with "spookproofing" their files and corporate secrets.[111]

Bodyguards, another area of private security activity, are commonplace among wealthy business executives, media stars, and successful musicians. One of the most respected executive protection programs in the world is offered by Executive Security International (ESI) in Aspen, Colorado. ESI was incorporated in 1981, and its founder, Bob Duggan, built terrorist simulation exercises into most course sequences.[112] A few years ago, another firm, the Richard W. Kobetz Company, began an executive protection training program at its North Mountain Pines Training Center in Berryville, Virginia.[113] Training at Kobetz includes "offensive and escort driving techniques," threat assessment education, searches, alarms, weapons, communications, protocol, legal issues, and firearms and defensive techniques. Activities focus on "low-profile" protection using limited personnel and resources, in contrast to the use of very expensive "high-profile" security as a deterrent technique which agencies like the Secret Service are able to use.[114] The Kobetz company offers "certification" as a personal protection specialist (PPS) following successful completion of its training.

The Private System of Justice

Security agencies work for paying clients, whereas law enforcement agencies are government entities. Differences between the role of private and public agencies were recently revealed in a National Institute of Justice-sponsored survey,[115] which showed that security executives order their managerial priorities as follows: (1) the protection of lives and property, (2) crime prevention, (3) loss prevention, (4) fire prevention, and (5) access control. In contrast, public law enforcement officials list a somewhat different set of priorities: (1) the protection of lives and property, (2) the arrest and prosecution of suspects, (3) the investigation of criminal incidents, (4) the maintenance of public order, and (5) crime prevention.

This difference in priorities, combined with the fact that hired security operatives serve the interest of corporate employers rather than the public, has led to charges that a private justice system operates next to the official government-sponsored system of criminal justice in America. The private system may see behavior, which public police agencies would interpret as a violation of the criminal law, as merely misguided employee activity. Within the private justice system, conflict resolution, economic sanctions, and retraining can supplant criminal prosecution as the most efficacious system for dealing with offending parties. According to a survey[116] published by the National Institute of Justice, "security managers in all sectors...report that the most frequently investigated crime is employee theft, and nearly half of them resolve such incidents within their own organizations."

One reason white-collar and business crimes may be substantially underreported in official crime statistics is that unofficial resolutions, based on investigations by proprietary security forces, may be the most frequent method of handling such offenses. As some writers have observed, the public justice system may find itself increasingly bypassed by proprietary security operations who generally find in the courts "an unsympathetic attitude...concerning business losses due to crime."[117] The *Hallcrest* report points out that not only has a "fundamental shift in protection resources...occurred from public policing to the private sector," but "this shift has also been accompanied by a shift in the character of social control."[118] According to the report, "private security defines deviance in instrumental rather than moral terms: protecting corporate interests becomes more important than fighting crime, and sanctions are applied more often against those who create opportunities for loss rather than those who *capitalize* on the opportunity—the traditional offenders."[119]

Hallcrest II identifies the growth of the private justice system as a major source of friction between private security and public law enforcement. According to the report, "(l)aw enforcement agencies have enjoyed a dominant position in providing protective services to their communities but now foresee an erosion of their 'turf' to private security."[120] Other sources of friction between the two include (1) "moonlighting" for private agencies by public officers, (2) the fact that "(c)ases brought by private security are usually well developed, putting the law enforcement agency in the thankless position of being an information processor for the prosecutor's office,"[121] and (3) the fact that many cases developed by private security agencies are disposed of through "plea bargaining, which police officers may not understand or support, but which may suit the purposes of a company interested in (deterrence)."[122] Moonlighting by public officers is a source of conflict because, under such circumstances, (1) police authority may be seen as used for personal gain, (2) officers who moonlight long hours may not be seen as fit for their official duties due to exhaustion, and (3) public police departments may be legally liable for the actions of their uniformed officers even though they are temporarily working for private employers.

The Professionalization of Private Security

An issue facing law makers across the country today is the extent of authority and the degree of force that can be legitimately used by security guards. Courts have generally held that private security personnel derive their legitimacy from the same basic authority that an employer would have in protecting his or her own property. In other words, if I have the legal right to use force to protect my home or business, then so do guards whom I have hired to act in my place. According to some courts, private security personnel, because their authority is simply an extension of private rights, are not directly bound by the legal strictures which govern the use of force, the gathering of evidence, and so on by sworn police officers.

Other courts, however, have ruled that private security personnel should be bound by the same procedural rules as sworn officers because they are perceived by the public as wielding the authority of public law enforcement officers.[123] The situation is complicated by the fact that, as previously discussed, many police officers "moonlight" as private guards when they are off duty.

In order to ensure at least a minimal degree of competence among private security personnel, a number of states have moved to a licensing process for officers although a few still require little other than an application and a small fee.[124] Twenty-three states mandate training if the security officers are to be armed, but only 14 require any training for unarmed guards.[125] Most training which does occur is relatively simplistic. Topics typically covered include (1) fire prevention, (2) first aid, (3) building safety, (4) equipment use, (5) report writing, and (6) the legal powers of private security personnel.[126] Reflecting on training and licensing requirements, one specialist has warned, "We have a vast private police force largely untrained, with few restraints, with the power to use force to take liberty and life."[127]

Most private security firms today depend on their own training programs to prevent actionable mistakes by employees. Training in private security operations is also available from a number of schools and agencies. One is the International Foundation for Protection Officers, with offices in Cochrane, Alberta (Canada), and Midvale, Utah. Following a home study course, successful students are accorded the status of certified protection officer (CPO). In an effort to increase the professional status of the private security industry, the 20,000-member American Society for Industrial Security (ASIS), established in 1955, administers a comprehensive examination periodically in various locations across the country. Applicants who pass the examination win the coveted title of certified protection professional (CPP). CPP examinations are thorough and usually require a combination of experience and study to earn a passing grade. Examination subject areas include[128] (1) security management, (2) physical security, (3) loss prevention, (4) investigations, (5) internal and external relations, (6) protection of sensitive information, (7) personnel security, (8) emergency planning, (9) legal aspects of security, and (10) substance abuse. In addition, candidates are allowed to select from a group of specialized topic areas (such as nuclear power security, public utility security, retail security, and computer security) that pertain to the fields in which they plan to work.

ASIS also functions as a professional association, with yearly meetings held to address the latest in security techniques and equipment. ASISNET, an online computer bulletin board system sponsored by ASIS, provides subscribers with daily security news, up-to-date international travel briefings, and a searchable security news database. In its efforts to heighten professionalism throughout the industry, ASIS has developed a private security code of ethics for its members, which is reproduced in a Theory into Practice box in this chapter.

An additional sign of the increasing professionalization of private security is the ever-growing number of publications offered in the area. The *Journal of Security Administration*, published in Miami, Florida, ASIS's *Security Management* magazine, and *Security Management* newsletter published semimonthly by the National Foremen's Institute in Waterford, Connecticut, along with the older journal *Security World*, serve the field as major sources of up-to-date information.

Integrating Public and Private Security

As the private security field grows, its relationship to public law enforcement continues to evolve. Although competition among the sectors remains, many experts now recognize that each can help the other. A government-sponsored report[129] makes the following policy recommendations designed to maximize the cooperative crime-fighting potential of existing private and public security resources:

---

*T*heory into Practice: Ethics In Private Security

AMERICAN SOCIETY FOR INDUSTRIAL SECURITY CODE OF ETHICS

I. A member shall perform professional duties in accordance with the law and the highest moral principles.

II. A member shall observe the precepts of truthfulness, honesty, and integrity.

III. A member shall be faithful and diligent in discharging professional responsibilities.

IV. A member shall be competent in discharging professional responsibilities.

V. A member shall safeguard confidential information and exercise due care to prevent its improper disclosure.

VI. A member shall not maliciously injure the professional reputation or practice of colleagues, clients, or employers.

Source: Courtesy of the American Society for Industrial Security.

1. The resources of proprietary and contract security should be brought to bear in cooperative, community-based crime prevention and security awareness programs.
2. An assessment should be made of (a) the basic police services the public is willing to support financially, (b) the types of police services most acceptable to police administrators and the public for transfer to the private sector, and (c) which services might be performed for a lower unit cost by the private sector with the same level of community satisfaction.
3. With special-police powers, security personnel could resolve many or most minor criminal incidents prior to police involvement. State statutes providing such powers could also provide for standardized training and certification requirements, thus assuring uniformity and precluding abuses....Ideally, licensing and regulatory requirements would be the same for all states, with reciprocity for firms licensed elsewhere.
4. Law enforcement agencies should be included in the crisis-management planning of private organizations....Similarly, private security should be consulted when law enforcement agencies are developing SWAT and hostage-negotiation teams. The federal government should provide channels of communication with private security with respect to terrorist activities and threats.
5. States should enact legislation permitting private security firms access to criminal history records in order to improve the selection process for security personnel and also to enable businesses to assess the integrity of key employees.
6. Research should...attempt to delineate the characteristics of the private justice system; identify the crimes most frequently resolved; assess the types and amount of unreported crime in organizations; quantify the redirection of [the] public criminal justice workload...and examine [the]...relationships between private security and...components of the criminal justice system.
7. A federal tax credit for security expenditures, similar to the energy tax credit, might be a cost-effective way to reduce police workloads.

he Future of Policing

At the close of this chapter, it seems appropriate to ask: "What does the future hold for policing in America?" In a "Delphi" exercise[130] held some years ago at the FBI Academy in Quantico, Virginia, a panel of leading law enforcement management experts, scholars, and executives constructed the scenario in Table 6-6, describing what they anticipated would be future developments of specific relevance to the police in the United States over the next half-century. If the accuracy of their early predictions is any guide, American law enforcement agencies will face some serious challenges during the coming century.

ummary

Police work today is characterized by the opportunity for individual officers to exercise considerable discretion, by a powerful subculture which communicates select values in support of a "police personality," and by the very real possibility of corruption and deviance. Opposed to the illegitimate use of police authority, however, are increased calls for police professionalism and demands for adherence to strict ethical principles.

Given the tendencies existing today, we can expect that police departments of the next century, though they will continue to fill many of today's law enforcement roles, will be highly professional organizations which emphasize ethical enforcement of the criminal law and limit the discretionary activities of their members. Similarly, as American police forces continue to evolve, the role of underrepresented groups in police work—including women and ethnic and racial minorities—will face continued examination.

TABLE 6-6

Possible Future Developments for Policing In America, 1995–2050

Year	Occurrence
1995	Community involvement and self-help (e.g., community-oriented policing) in local policing will become common practice in more than 70% of the nation.
	University and professionally conducted research will have a direct and positive influence on the development of crime reduction strategies.
	Acts of political terrorism in the United States will increase in number more than 50% over the 1984 rate.
1997	State-of-the-art high technology will be routinely used in crime reduction.
1999	Urban unrest and civil disorder (of the 1960–1970s variety) will take place throughout America.
2000	Computer-based instruction will become the standard for training in more than 70% of police agencies.
	More than 70% of all "invasion of privacy" lawsuits will successfully demonstrate inadequacies of, and inaccuracies in, police computerized files.
	Crime committed using high technology will become so complex that the police will be unable to do more than take initial reports.
2005	Disparity between the "haves" and the "have-nots" will be identified as the major causative factors for traditional crime.
2025	Formal education will become the standard for entry and advancement in more than 70% of police agencies.
	More than 70% of police executives will adopt a nontraditional (proactive/goal-oriented) leadership style.
2035	Private security agencies will assume more than 50% of all law enforcement responsibilities.
2050	Law enforcement will achieve professional status.
	More than 50% of police agencies will have personnel competent to conduct rigorous empirical research.
	Medical (biochemical, genetic, nutritional, and brain) research will discover the means of identifying and treating violence.

SOURCE: William L. Tafoya, "The Future of Law Enforcement: A Chronology of Events," *Criminal Justice International* (May–June 1991), p. 4.

Discussion Questions

1. What are the central features of the police "working personality?" How does the police working personality develop? What programs might be initiated to "shape" the police personality in a more desirable way?

2. What shared themes run through the findings of the Knapp Commission and the Wickersham Commission? What innovative steps might police departments take to reduce or eliminate corruption among their officers?

3. Is police work a profession? Why do you think it is, or why do you think it is not? What advantages are there to viewing policing as a profession? How do you think most police officers today see their work—as a "profession," or as "just a job"?

4. Reread the Law Enforcement Code of Ethics found in this chapter. Do you think most police officers make conscious efforts to apply the code in the performance of their duty? How might ethics training in police departments be improved?

References

1. Jerome H. Skolnick, *Justice Without Trial: Law Enforcement in a Democratic Society* (New York: John Wiley, 1966).

2. William A. Westley, *Violence and the Police: A Sociological Study of Law, Custom, and Morality* (Cambridge, Mass.: MIT Press, 1970), and William A. Westley "Violence and the Police," *American Journal of Sociology*, Vol. 49 (1953), pp. 34–41.

3. Arthur Niederhoffer, *Behind the Shield: The Police in Urban Society* (Garden City, N.Y.: Anchor Press, 1967).

4. Thomas Barker and David L. Carter, *Police Deviance* (Cincinnati: Anderson, 1986).

5. See, for example, Michael Brown, *Working the Street: Police Discretion and the Dilemmas of Reform* (New York: Russell Sage Foundation, 1981).

6. Richard Bennett and Theodore Greenstein, "The Police Personality: A Test of the Predispositional Model," *Journal of Police Science and Administration*, Vol 3. (1975), pp. 439–445.

7. James Teevan and Bernard Dolnick, "The Values of the Police: A Reconsideration and Interpretation," *Journal of Police Science and Administration* (1973), pp. 366–369.

8. Lawrence Sherman and Robert Langworthy, "Measuring Homicide by Police Officers," *Journal of Criminal Law and Criminology*, Vol. 4 (1979), pp. 546–560, and Lawrence W. Sherman et al., *Citizens Killed by Big City Police, 1970–1984* (Washington, D.C.: Crime Control Institute, 1986).

9. Joel Samaha, *Criminal Justice* (St. Paul, Minn.: West, 1988), p. 235.

10. Tim Prenzler and Peta Mackay, "Police Gratuities: What the Public Thinks," *Criminal Justice Ethics*, Winter–Spring 1995, pp. 15–25.

11. Barker and Carter, *Police Deviance*.

12. "Nationline: NYC Cops—Excess Force Not Corruption," *USA Today*, June 16, 1995, p. 3A.

13. *Knapp Commission Report on Police Corruption* (New York: George Braziller, 1973).

14. Ibid.

15. Robert Daley, *Prince of the City: The Story of a Cop Who Knew Too Much* (Boston: Houghton Mifflin, 1978).

16. Mike McAlary, Buddy Boys: *When Good Cops Turn Bad* (New York: G. P. Putnam's Sons, 1987).

17. Ibid.

18. "Ex-Detroit Police Chief Sentenced," *Fayetteville Observer-Times* (North Carolina), August 28, 1992, p. 6A.

19. Ibid., p. 5A.

20. Edwin H. Sutherland and Donald Cressey, *Principles of Criminology*, 8th ed. (Philadelphia: J. B. Lippincott, 1970).

21. James Mills, *The Underground Empire: Where Crime and Governments Embrace* (New York: Dell, 1986), p. 15.

22. Ibid.

23. Tim R. Jones, Compton Owens, and Melissa A. Smith, "Police Ethics Training: A Three-Tiered Approach," *FBI Law Enforcement Bulletin*, June, 1995, p. 22–26.

24. National Institute of Law Enforcement and Criminal Justice, *Controlling Police Corruption: The Effects of Reform Policies, Summary Report* (Washington, D.C.: U.S. Department of Justice, 1978).

25. See National Institute of Justice, "Employee Drug Testing Policies in Police Departments," National Institute of Justice Research in Brief (Washington, D.C.: U.S. Department of Justice, 1986).

26. Ibid.

27. *Maurice Turner* v. *Fraternal Order of Police*, No. 83-1213, D.C. Court of Appeals, November 13, 1985.

28. *Philip Caruso, President of P.B.A.* v. *Benjamin Ward, Police Commissioner*, New York State Supreme Court, Pat. 37, Index no. 12632-86, 1986.

29. *National Treasury Employees Union* v. *Von Raab*, 44 CRL 3192 (1989).

30. *The New York Times*, February 29, 1988, p. B7.

31. "Suspect Had Wanted to Kill Officer," *The Morning Call*, July 9, 1992, p. A1.

32. Anthony J. Pinizzotto and Edward F. Davis, "Cop Killers and Their Victims," *FBI Law Enforcement Bulletin*, December 1992, p. 10.

33. As reported by "The Headline News Network," April 26, 1988.

34. "Homosexual Officer Wins AIDS Ruling," *Fayetteville Observer-Times* (North Carolina), June 8, 1992, p. 5A.

35. New York City Police Department pamphlet, "AIDS and Our Workplace" (November 1987).

36. "Collecting and Handling Evidence Infected with Human Disease-Causing Organisms," *FBI Law Enforcement Bulletin* (July 1987).

37. Theodore M. Hammett, "Precautionary Measures and Protective Equipment: Developing a Reasonable Response," National Institute of Justice Bulletin (Washington, D.C.: U.S. Government Printing Office, 1988).

38. *National Institute of Justice Reports*, No. 206 (November–December 1987).

39. "Taking Aim at a Virus: NYPD Tackles AIDS on the Job and in the Ranks," *Law Enforcement News*, March 15, 1988, p. 1.

40. "Drowned Boys Case Takes Toll on Officers, Clergy," *The Florida Times-Union* (Jacksonville), November 10, 1994, p. A6.

41. "Stress on the Job," *Newsweek*, April 25, 1988, p. 43.

42. Joseph Victor, "Police Stress: Is Anybody Out There Listening?" *New York Law Enforcement Journal* (June 1986), pp. 19–20.

43. Ibid.

44. Charles R. Swanson, Leonard Territo, and Robert W. Taylor, *Police Administration: Structures, Processes, and Behavior*, 2nd ed. (New York: Macmillan, 1988).

45. *Malley* v. *Briggs*, 475 U.S. 335, 106 S.Ct. 1092 (1986).

46. Ibid., *Malley* at 4246.

47. *Biscoe* v. *Arlington* (1984). See *National Law Journal*, May 13, 1985.

48. *Kaplan* v. *Lloyd's Insurance Co.*, 479 So. 2d 961 (La. App. 1985).

49. *City of Canton, Ohio* v. *Harris*, U.S. 109 S.Ct. 1197 (1989).

50. Ibid., at 1204.

51. *Prior* v. *Woods* (1981), *National Law Journal*, November 2, 1981.

52. *Bivens* v. *Six Unknown Federal Agents*, 403 U.S. 388 (1971).

53. See *FDIC* v. *Meyer* (1994), in which the U.S. Supreme Court reiterated its ruling under *Bivens*, stating that only government employees and not agencies can be sued.

54. *Wyler* v. *U.S.*, 725 F. 2d 157 (2d Cir. 1983).

55. California Government Code, §818.

56. Federal Tort Claims Act, 28 U. S. C. 1346(b), 2671-2680.

57. "Victims of Failed DEA Sting Win More Than $1 Million Judgment," *Drug Enforcement Report*, March 23, 1995, pp. 1–2.

58. *Elder* v. *Holloway*, 114 S.Ct. 1019, 127 L. Ed. 2d 344 (1994).

59. Ibid.

60. *Hunter* v. *Bryant*, 112 S.Ct. 534 (1991).

61. William U. McCormack, "Supreme Court Cases: 1991–1992 Term," *FBI Law Enforcement Bulletin*, November, 1992, p. 30.

62. For more information on police liability, see Daniel L. Schofield, "Legal Issues of Pursuit Driving," *FBI Law Enforcement Bulletin* (May 1988), pp. 23–29.

63. "Playboy Interview: Daryl Gates," *Playboy*, August 1991, p. 60.

64. Ibid., p. 63.

65. *Tennessee* v. *Garner*, 471 U.S. 1 (1985).

66. Ibid.

67. *Graham* v. *Connor*, 490 U.S. 386, 396–397 (1989).

68. Ibid.

69. James Fyfe, *Shots Fired: An Examination of New York City Police Firearms Discharges* (Ann Arbor, Mich.: University Microfilms, 1978).

70. James Fyfe, "Blind Justice? Police Shootings in Memphis," paper presented at the annual meeting of the Academy of Criminal Justice Sciences, Philadelphia, March 1981.

71. It is estimated that American police shoot at approximately 3,600 people every year. See William Geller, "Deadly Force" study guide Crime File Series (Washington, D.C.: National Institute of Justice, no date).

72. Anne Cohen: "I've Killed That Man Ten Thousand Times," *Police Magazine* (July 1980).

73. For more information, see Joe Auten, "When Police Shoot," *North Carolina Criminal Justice Today*, Vol. 4, no. 4 (Summer 1986), pp. 9–14.

74. David W. Hayeslip and Alan Preszler, "NIJ Initiative on Less-than-Lethal Weapons," *NIJ Research in Brief* (Washington, D.C.: National Institute of Justice, 1993).

75. Ibid.

76. As quoted by Michael Siegfried, "Notes on the Professionalization of Private Security," *The Justice Professional* (Spring 1989).

77. Timothy J. Flanagan and Kathleen Maguire, *Sourcebook of Criminal Justice Statistics— 1989* (Washington, D.C.: U.S. Government Printing Office, 1990), p. 16.

78. See Edward A. Farris, "Five Decades of American Policing, 1932–1982: The Path to Professionalism," *The Police Chief* (November 1982), p. 31.

79. Ibid., p. 34.

80. National Commission on Law Observance and Enforcement, *Report on Police* (Washington, D.C.: U.S. Government Printing Office, 1931).

81. National Advisory Commission on Criminal Justice Standards and Goals, *Report on the Police* (Washington, D.C.: U.S. Government Printing Office, 1973).

82. Ibid.

83. David L. Carter, Allen D. Sapp, and Darrel W. Stephens, *The State of Police Education: Policy Direction for the 21st Century* (Washington, D.C.: Police Executive Research Forum 1989).

84. Ibid., p. xiv.

85. Ibid., pp. xxii–xxiii.

86. Carter, Sapp, and Stephens, *The State of Police Education*, p. 84.

87. National Advisory Commission on Criminal Justice Standards and Goals, *Police* (Washington, D.C.: U.S. Government Printing Office, 1973), p. 238.

88. "Dallas PD College Rule Gets Final OK," *Law Enforcement News*, July 7, 1986, pp. 1, 13.

89. *Davis* v. *Dallas*, 1986.

90. David L. Carter and Allen Sapp, *The State of Police Education: Critical Findings* (Washington, D.C.: Police Executive Research Forum, no date).

91. O. W. Wilson and Roy Clinton McLaren,

Police Administration, 4th ed. (New York: McGraw-Hill, 1977), p. 259.

92. Ibid., p. 270.

93. Report of the National Advisory Commission on Civil Disorders, p. 332.

94. As reported in Charles Swanson and Leonard Territo, *Police Administration: Structures, Processes, and Behavior* (New York: Macmillan, 1983), p. 203, from *Affirmative Action Monthly* (February 1979), p. 22.

95. The Police Foundation, *On the Move: The Status of Women in Policing* (Washington, D.C.: The Foundation, 1990).

96. C. Lee Bennett, *Interviews with Female Police Officers in Western Massachusetts*, paper presented at the annual meeting of the Academy of Criminal Justice Sciences, Nashville, Tennessee, March 1991.

97. Ibid., p. 9.

98. See, for example, Pearl Jacobs, "Suggestions for the Greater Integration of Women into Policing," paper presented at the annual meeting of the Academy of Criminal Justice Sciences, Nashville, Tenn., March 1991, and Cynthia Fuchs Epstein, *Deceptive Distinctions: Sex, Gender, and the Social Order* (New Haven, Conn.: Yale University Press, 1988).

99. Carole G. Garrison, Nancy K. Grant, and Kenneth L. J. McCormick, "Utilization of Police Women," unpublished manuscript.

100. "Foot-Dragging Charged in FBI Racism Probe," *Fayetteville Times* (North Carolina), March 27, 1988.

101. "FBI Settles Bias Suit: Judge to Oversee Efforts," *USA Today*, January 27, 1993, p. 1A.

102. Dorothy Moses Schulz, "California Dreaming: Leading the Way to Gender-Free Police Management?" *Criminal Justice: The Americas*, Vol. 7, no. 3 (June–July 1994), pp. 1, 8–10.

103. The Police Foundation, *On the Move*.

104. *Private Security: Report of the Task Force on Private Security* (Washington, D.C.: U.S. Government Printing Office, 1976), p. 4.

105. William C. Cunningham, John J. Strauchs, and Clifford W. Van Meter, *The Hallcrest Report II: Private Security Trends 1970–2000* (McLean, Va.:Hallcrest Systems, 1990).

106. Ibid., p. 229.

107. Ibid., p. 236.

108. "Forecast Survey: Executive Summary," *Security*, January 1990.

109. Dae H. Chang and James A. Fagin, eds., *Introduction to Criminal Justice: Theory and Application*, 2nd ed. (Geneva, Ill.: Paladin House, 1985), pp. 275–277.

110. "George Smiley Joins the Firm," *Newsweek*, May 2, 1988, pp. 46–47.

111. Ibid.

112. For more information on ESI, see E. Duane Davis, "Executive Protection: An Emerging Trend in Criminal Justice Education and Training," *The Justice Professional*, Vol. 3, no. 2 (Fall 1988).

113. "More than a Bodyguard," *Security Management*, February 10, 1986.

114. "A School for Guards of Rich, Powerful," *The Akron Beacon Journal* (Ohio), April 21, 1986.

115. National Institute of Justice, *Crime and Protection in America: A Study of Private Security and Law Enforcement Resources and Relationships*, Executive Summary (Washington, D.C.: U.S. Department of Justice, 1985), p. 42.

116. Ibid., p. 60.

117. Cunninghum, Strauch, and Van Meter, *Hallcrest II*, p. 299.

118. Ibid., p. 301.

119. Ibid. (italics added).

120. Ibid., p. 117.

121. National Institute of Justice, *Crime and Protection in America*, p. 12.

122. Ibid., p. 12.

123. *People v. Zelinski*, 594 P.2d 1000 (1979).

124. For additional information, see Jospeh G. Deegan, "Mandated Training for Private Security," *FBI Law Enforcement Bulletin*, March 1987, pp. 6–8.

125. Cunninghum, Strauchs, and Van Meter, *Hallcrest II*, p. 147.

126. National Institute of Justice, *Crime and Protection in America*, p. 37.

127. Richter Moore, "Private Police: The Use of Force and State Regulation," unpublished manuscript.

128. "The Mark of Professionalism," Security Management, 35th Anniversary Supplement, 1990, pp. 97–104.

129. National Institute of Justice, *Crime and Protection in America*, pp. 59–72.

130. William L. Tafoya, "The Future of Law Enforcement? A Chronology of Events," *Criminal Justice International* (May–June 1991), p. 4.

PART 3

Adjudication

INDIVIDUAL RIGHTS VERSUS SOCIAL CONCERNS

The Rights of the Accused before the Court

Common law, constitutional, and humanitarian rights of the accused:

The Right to a Speedy Trial
The Right to Legal Counsel
The Right Against Self-Incrimination
The Right Not to Be Tried Twice for the Same Offense
The Right to Know the Charges
The Right to Cross-Examine Witnesses
The Right to Speak and Present Witnesses
The Right Against Excessive Bail

The individual rights listed must be effectively balanced against these community concerns:

Conviction of the Guilty
Exoneration of the Innocent
The Imposition of Appropriate Punishment
Protection of Society
Efficient and Cost-Effective Procedures
Seeing Justice Done

How does our system of justice work toward balance?

Equal justice under law.

*T*he well-known British philosopher and statesman, Benjamin Disraeli (1804–1881), once defined justice as "truth in action." The study of criminal case processing by courts at all levels provides perhaps the best opportunity available to us from within the criminal justice system to observe what should ideally be "truth in action." The courtroom search for truth, which is characteristic of criminal trials, pits the resources of the accused against those of the state. The ultimate outcome of such procedures, say advocates of our adversarial-based system of trial practice, should be both truth and justice.

Others are not so sure. British novelist, William McIlvanney (1936–) once wrote: "Who thinks the law has anything to do with justice? It's what we have because we can't have justice." Indeed, many critics of the present system claim that courts at all levels have become so concerned with procedure and with sets of formalized rules that they have lost sight of truth.

The chapters which compose this section of *Criminal Justice: A Brief Introduction* provide an overview of American courts, including their history and present structure, and examine the multifaceted roles played by both professional and lay courtroom participants. Sentencing, the practice whereby juries recommend and judges impose sanctions on convicted offenders, is covered in the concluding chapter of this section. Whether American courts routinely uncover truth and therefore dispense justice, or whether they are merely locked into a pattern of hollow procedure which does little other than mock the justice ideal will be for you to decide.

CHAPTER 7

The Courts

—*Photo by Alex Webb/Magnum Photos, Inc.*

*T*here is no such thing as justice—in or out of court.

—Clarence Darrow (1857–1938)

*N*o person shall be held to answer for a capital or otherwise infamous crime, unless on a presentment or indictment of a grand jury...nor shall any person be subject for the same offense to be twice put in jeopardy of life or limb; nor shall be compelled in any criminal case to be a witness against himself, nor be deprived of life, liberty, or property, without due process of law....

—Fifth Amendment to the U.S. Constitution

*A*fter years of twisting the Constitution into a pretzel, handcuffing cops and drooling over the rights of killers and rapists, America's federal judges have suddenly discovered violent crime, and they're fretting that it might come to their neighborhood soon.

—*Washington Times* editorial

KEY CONCEPTS

federal court system	state court systems	appeal
trial *do novo*	state court administrator	plea
dispute resolution center	original jurisdiction	judicial review
first appearance	bail bond	release on recognizance
property bond	deposit bail	conditional release
third-party custody	unsecured bond	signature bond
danger laws	appellate jurisdiction	plea bargaining
no contest (*nolo contendere*)		

KEY CASES

U.S. v. *Montalvo-Murillo*	*County of Riverside (CA)*	*Herrera* v. *Collins*
Keeney v. *Tamayo-Reyes*	v. *McLaughlin*	*United States* v.
Minnick v. *Mississippi*		*Alvarez-Machain*

Introduction

Between the often enthralling police quest for suspects and the sometimes hopeless incarceration of offenders stands the **federal court system** and the **state court systems**. Courts at all levels dispense justice on a daily basis and work to ensure that all official actors in the justice system carry out their duties in recognition of the rule of law.

At many points in this volume, and in three specific chapters (Chapter 5, "Policing—Legal Aspects"; Chapter 10, "Probation, Parole, and Community Corrections"; and Chapter 11, "Prisons and Jails"), we take a close look at court precedents which have defined the legality of enforcement efforts and correctional action. In Chapter 3 ("Criminal Law") we explored the lawmaking function of courts. This chapter, in order to provide readers with a picture of how courts work, will describe the American court system at both the state and federal levels. Then in Chapter 8, we will look at the roles of courtroom actors—from attorneys to victims, and from jurors to judges—and examine each of the steps in a criminal trial.

American Court History

Two criminal court systems coexist in America today: (1) state courts and (2) federal courts. Figure 7-1 outlines the structure of today's federal court system, whereas Figure 7-2 diagrams a typical state court system. This dual court system is the result of general agreement among the nation's founders about the need for individual states to retain significant legislative authority and judicial autonomy separate from federal control. Under this concept, the United States developed as a relatively loose federation of semi-independent provinces. New states joining the union were assured of limited federal intervention into local affairs. Under this arrangement, state legislatures were free to create laws, and state court systems were needed to hear cases in which violations of those laws occurred. The last 200 years have seen a slow ebbing of states' rights relative to the power of the federal government. Even today, however, state courts do not hear cases involving alleged violations of federal law, nor do federal courts involve themselves in deciding issues of state law unless there is a conflict between local or state statutes and federal constitutional guarantees. When that happens, however, claimed violations of federal due process guarantees, especially those found in the Bill of Rights, can provide the basis for appeals made to federal courts by offenders convicted in state court systems.

This chapter describes both federal and state court systems in terms of their historical development and current structure. Because it is within state courts that the large majority of criminal cases originate, we turn our attention first to them.

State Court Development

Each of the original American colonies had its own court system for resolving disputes, both civil and criminal. As early as 1629, the Massachusetts Bay Colony had created a "General Court," composed of the governor, his deputy, 18 assistants, and 118 elected officials. The General Court was a combined legislature/court, which made laws, held trials, and imposed sentences.[1] By 1639, as the colony grew, county courts were created, and the General Court took on as its primary job the hearing of appeals, retaining original jurisdiction only in cases involving "tryalls of life, limm, or banishment..." (and divorce).[2]

Pennsylvania began its colonial existence with the belief that "every man could serve as his own lawyer."[3] The Pennsylvania system utilized "common

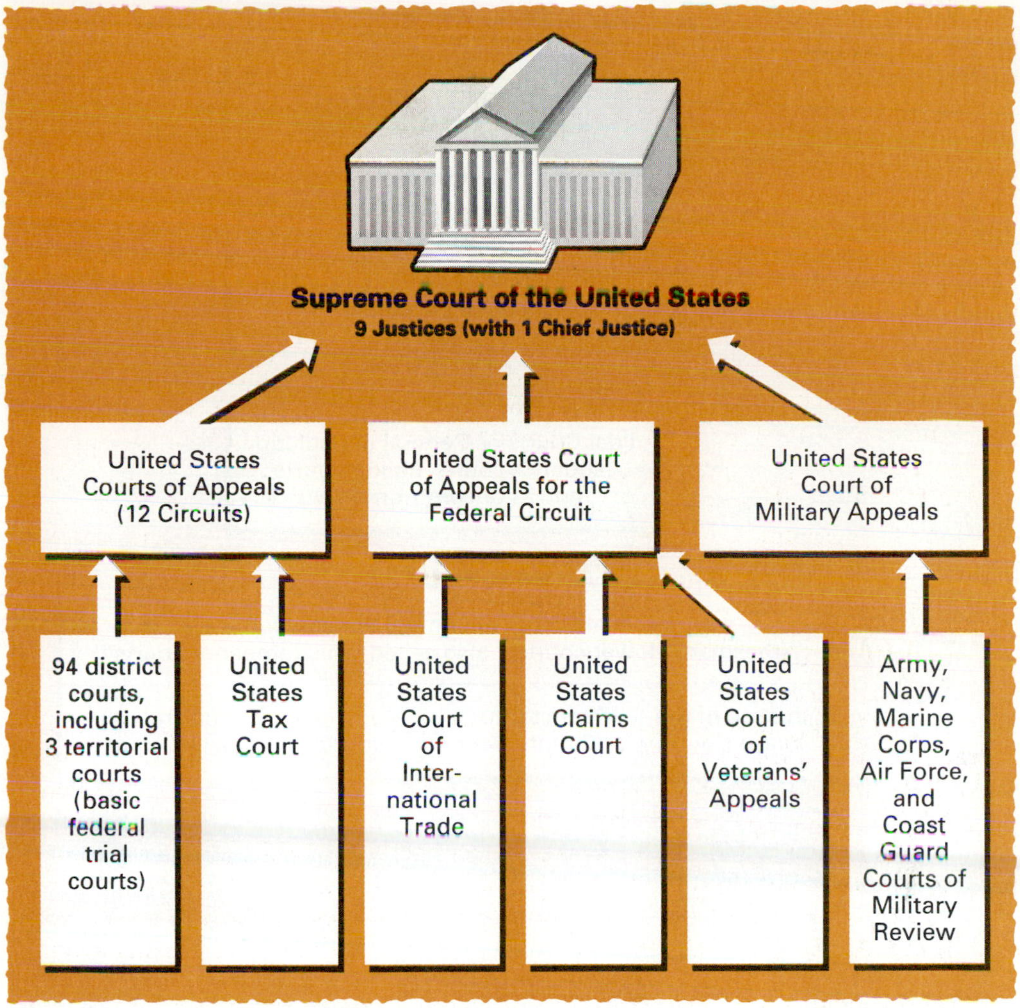

FIGURE 7-1
The structure of federal courts.

Supreme Court of the United States
9 Justices (with 1 Chief Justice)

United States Courts of Appeals (12 Circuits)	United States Court of Appeals for the Federal Circuit	United States Court of Military Appeals

94 district courts, including 3 territorial courts (basic federal trial courts)	United States Tax Court	United States Court of International Trade	United States Claims Court	United States Court of Veterans' Appeals	Army, Navy, Marine Corps, Air Force, and Coast Guard Courts of Military Review

peacemakers" who served as referees in disputes. Parties to a dispute, including criminal suspects, could plead their case before a common peacemaker they had chosen. The decision of the peacemaker was binding upon the parties. Although the Pennsylvania referee system ended in 1766, lower-level judges, called magistrates in many other jurisdictions, are still referred to as "justices of the peace" in Pennsylvania and a few other states.

Prior to 1776, all American colonies had established fully functioning court systems. The practice of law, however, was substantially inhibited by a lack of trained lawyers. A number of the early colonies even displayed a strong reluctance to recognize the practice of law as a profession. A Virginia statute, for example, enacted in 1645, provided for the removal of "mercenary attorneys" from office and prohibited the practice of law for a fee. Most other colonies retained strict control over the number of authorized barristers (another name for lawyers) by requiring formal training in English law schools and appointment by the governor. New York, which provided for the appointment of "counselors at law," permitted a total of only 41 lawyers to practice law between 1695 and 1769[4]—in large part due to the distrust of formally trained attorneys which was then widespread.

The tenuous status of lawyers in the colonies was highlighted by the 1735 New York trial of John Zenger. Zenger was editor of the *New York Journal*, a newspaper, and was accused of slandering governor Cosby. When Cosby threatened to disbar any lawyer who defended Zenger, he hired Pennsylvania lawyer Andrew Hamilton, who was immune to the governor's threats because he was from out of state.[5]

FIGURE 7-2
A typical state court system.

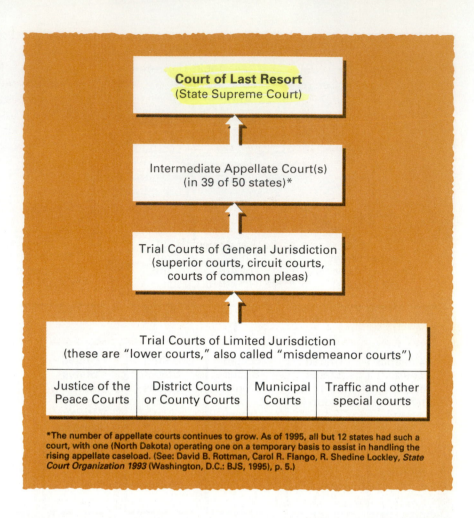

Following the American Revolution, colonial courts provided the organizational basis for the growth of fledgling state court systems. Since there had been considerable diversity in the structure of colonial courts, state courts were anything but uniform. Initially, most states made no distinction between **original jurisdiction** (the lawful authority of a court to hear cases which arise within a specified geographic area or which involve particular kinds of law violations) and **appellate jurisdiction** (the lawful authority of a court to review a decision made by a lower court). Many, in fact, had no provisions for appeal. Delaware, for example, did not allow for appeals in criminal cases until 1897. States which did permit appeals often lacked any established appellate courts and sometimes used state legislatures for that purpose.

By the late 1800s, a dramatic increase in population, growing urbanization, the settlement of the West, and other far-reaching changes in the American way of life led to a tremendous increase in civil litigation and criminal arrests. Legislatures tried to keep pace with the rising tide of suits. They created a multiplicity of courts at the trial, appellate, and supreme court levels, calling them by a diversity of names and assigning them functions which sometimes bore little resemblance to like-sounding courts in neighboring states. City courts, which were limited in their jurisdiction by community boundaries, arose to handle the special problems of urban life such as disorderly conduct, property disputes, and the enforcement of restrictive and regulatory ordinances. Other tribunals, such as juvenile courts, developed to handle special kinds of problems or special clients. Some, like magistrates' or small claims courts, handled only petty disputes and minor law violations. Still others, like traffic courts, were very narrow in focus. The result was a patchwork of hearing bodies, some only vaguely resembling modern notions of a trial court.

Jurisdiction. The territory, subject matter, or persons over which lawful authority may be exercised by a court or other justice agency, as determined by statute or constitution.

Original Jurisdiction. The authority of a given court over a specific geographic area or over particular types of cases. We say that a case falls "within the jurisdiction" of the court.

State court systems did, however, have several models to follow during their development. One was the New York State Field Code of 1848, which was eventually copied by most other states. The Field Code clarified jurisdictional claims and specified matters of court procedure, but was later amended so extensively that its usefulness as a model dissolved. Another court systems model was provided by the federal Judiciary Act of 1789 and the later federal Reorganization Act of 1801. States which followed the federal model developed a three-tiered structure of (1) trial courts of limited jurisdiction, (2) trial courts of general jurisdiction, and (3) appellate courts.

State Court Systems Today

The three-tiered federal model was far from a panacea, however. Within the structure it provided, many local and specialized courts proliferated. Traffic courts, magistrates' courts, municipal courts, recorders' courts, probate courts, and courts held by justices of the peace were but a few which functioned at the lower levels. A movement toward simplification of state court structures, led primarily by the American Bar Association and the American Judicature Society, began in the early 1900s. Proponents of state court reform sought to unify redundant courts which held overlapping jurisdiction. Most reform-minded thinkers suggested a uniform model for states everywhere which would build on (1) a centralized court structure composed of a clear hierarchy of trial and appellate courts, (2) the consolidation of numerous lower-level courts holding overlapping jurisdiction, and (3) a centralized state court authority which would be responsible for budgeting, financing, and management of all courts within a state.

The court reform movement is still ongoing today. Although it has made a substantial number of inroads in many states, there are still many differences between and among state court systems. Reform states, which early on embraced the reform movement, are now characterized by streamlined judicial systems consisting of precisely conceived trial courts of limited and general jurisdiction, supplemented by one or two appellate court levels. Nonreform, or traditional, states retain judicial systems which are a conglomeration of multilevel and sometimes redundant courts with poorly defined jurisdiction. Even in nonreform states, however, most criminal courts can be classified within the three-story structure of two trial court echelons and an appellate tier.

State Trial Courts

Trial courts are where criminal cases begin. The trial court conducts arraignments, sets bail, takes pleas, and conducts trials. (We will discuss each of these separate functions in more depth later.) If the defendant is found guilty (or pleads guilty), the trial court imposes sentence. Trial courts of limited or special jurisdiction are also called lower courts. Lower courts are authorized to hear only less serious criminal cases, usually involving misdemeanors, or to hear special types of cases such as traffic violations, family disputes, and small claims. Courts of limited jurisdiction, which are depicted in television shows like *Night Court* and *Family Court*, rarely hold jury trials, depending instead on the hearing judge to make determinations of both fact and law. At the lower court level, a detailed record of the proceedings is not maintained. Case files will include only information on the charge, the plea, the finding of the court, and the sentence. All but six of the United States make use of trial courts of limited jurisdiction.[6]

Lower courts are much less formal than are courts of general jurisdiction. In an intriguing analysis of court characteristics, Thomas Henderson[7] found that misdemeanor courts process cases according to what he called a "decisional model." The decisional model, said Henderson, is informal, personal, and decisive. It depends on the quick resolution of relatively uncomplicated issues of law and fact.

Trial courts of general jurisdiction, called variously, high courts, circuit courts, or superior courts, are authorized to hear any criminal case. In many states, they also provide the first appellate level for courts of limited jurisdiction. In most cases, superior courts offer defendants whose cases originated in lower courts the chance for a new trial instead of a review of the record of the earlier hearing. When a new trial is held, it is referred to as **trial *de novo***.

Henderson[8] describes courts of general jurisdiction according to a procedural model. Such courts, he says, make full use of juries, prosecutors, defense attorneys, witnesses, and all the other actors we usually associate with American courtrooms. The procedural model, which is far more formal than the decisional model, is fraught with numerous court appearances to ensure that all a defendant's due process rights are protected. The procedural model makes for a long, expensive, relatively impersonal, and highly formal series of legal maneuvers involving many professional participants—a fact clearly seen in the widely televised 1995 double-murder trial of famed athlete and television personality O. J. Simpson.

Trial courts of general jurisdiction operate within a fact-finding framework called the adversarial process. That process pits the interests of the state, represented by prosecutors, against the professional skills and abilities of defense attorneys. The adversarial process is not a free-for-all, but is, rather, constrained by procedural rules specified in law and sustained through tradition.

State Appellate Courts

Most states today have an appellate division, consisting of an intermediate appellate court (often called the Court of Appeals) and a high-level appellate court (generally termed the state supreme court). High-level appellate courts are referred to as courts of last resort so as to indicate that no other appellate route remains to a defendant within the state court system once the high court rules on a case. All states have supreme courts although only 39 have intermediate appellate courts.[9]

An **appeal** by a convicted defendant asks that a higher court review the actions of a lower one. Courts within the appellate division, once they accept an appeal, do not conduct a new trial. Instead they provide a review of the case on the record. In other words, appellate courts examine the written transcript of lower court hearings to ensure that those proceedings were carried out fairly and in accordance with proper procedure and state law. They may also allow brief oral arguments to be made by attorneys for both sides and will generally consider other briefs or information filed by the appellant (the party initiating the appeal) or appellee (the side opposed to the appeal). State statutes generally require that sentences of death or life imprisonment be automatically reviewed by the state supreme court.

Most convictions are affirmed upon appeal. Occasionally, however, an appellate court will determine that the trial court erred in allowing certain kinds of evidence to be heard or that it failed to interpret properly the significance of a relevant statute. When that happens, the verdict of the trial court will be reversed, and the case may be remanded, or sent back for a new trial. Where a conviction is overturned by an appellate court because of constitutional issues, or where a statute is determined to be invalid, the state usually has recourse to the state supreme court, or the U.S. Supreme Court (when an issue of federal law is involved, as when a state court has ruled a federal law unconstitutional).

Defendants who are not satisfied with the resolution of their case within a state court system may attempt an appeal to the U.S. Supreme Court. For such an appeal to have any chance of being heard, it must be based on claimed violations of the defendant's rights as guaranteed under federal law or the U.S. Constitution. Under certain circumstances, federal district courts may also provide a path of relief for state defendants who can show that their federal constitutional rights have been violated. However, in the 1992 case of *Keeney* v. *Tamayo-Reyes*,[10] the U.S.

Trial de Novo. Literally, a new trial. The term is applied to cases which are retried on appeal, as opposed to those which are simply reviewed on the record.

Appeal. Generally, the request that a court with appellate jurisdiction review the judgment, decision, or order of a lower court and set it aside (reverse it) or modify it.

Supreme Court ruled that a "respondent is entitled to a federal evidentiary hearing [only] if he can show cause for his failure to develop the facts in the state-court proceedings and actual prejudice resulting from that failure, or if he can show that a fundamental miscarriage of justice would result from failure to hold such a hearing." Justice Byron White, writing for the Court, said "[i]t is hardly a good use of scarce judicial resources to duplicate fact-finding in federal court merely because a petitioner has negligently failed to take advantage of opportunities in state court proceedings." Likewise, in *Herrera* v. *Collins* (1993),[11] the Court ruled that new evidence of innocence is no reason for a federal court to order a new state trial if constitutional grounds are lacking. In *Herrera*, where the defendant was under a Texas death sentence for the murder of two police officers, the Court said:

> [w]here a defendant has been afforded a fair trial and convicted of the offense for which he was charged, the constitutional presumption of innocence disappears....Thus, claims of actual innocence based on newly discovered evidence have never been held [to be] grounds for relief absent an independent constitutional violation occurring in the course of the underlying state criminal proceedings. To allow a federal court to grant relief...would in effect require a new trial 10 years after the first trial, not because of any constitutional violation at the first trial, but simply because of a belief that in light of his new found evidence a jury might find him not guilty at a second trial.

The *Keeney* and *Herrera* decisions have had the effect of severely limiting routine access by state defendants to federal courts.

The Florida Court System: An Example

Florida provides an example of a reform state which has streamlined the structure of its courts. Prior to a 1973 reorganization, Florida had more different kinds of trial courts than any state except New York.[12] Today, the Florida system, which is diagrammed in Figure 7-3, consists of one state supreme court, five district courts of appeal, trial courts of general jurisdiction called "circuit courts," and county courts of limited jurisdiction which hear cases involving petty offenses and civil disputes involving $15,000 or less. County courts are often called "people's courts" in Florida.

Courts have often been called "the fulcrum of the criminal justice system." Photo courtesy of Michal Heron.

Florida's surpeme court, headquartered in the Supreme Court Building in Tallahassee, comprises seven justices, at least four of whom must agree on a decision in each case. By a majority vote of the justices, one of them is elected to serve as chief justice (an office which is rotated every two years). The supreme court must review final orders imposing death sentences, district court decisions declaring a state statute or provisions of the state constitution invalid, and actions of statewide agencies relating to public utilities. At its discretion, the court may also review any decision of a district court of appeal that declares invalid a state statute, interprets a provision of the state or federal constitution, affects a class of state officers, or directly conflicts with a decision of another district court or of the state supreme court on a question of law.

The bulk of trial court decisions which are appealed are never heard by the supreme court. Rather, they are reviewed by three-judge panels of the district courts of appeal. Florida's constitution provides that the legislature shall divide the state into appellate court districts and that there shall be a district court of appeal (DCA) serving each district. There are five such districts, which are headquartered in Tallahassee, Lakeland, Miami, West Palm Beach, and Daytona Beach. As of January 1995, 15 judges served in the first DCA, 14 in the second, 11 in the third, 12 in the fourth, and 9 in the fifth. Like supreme court justices, district court judges serve terms of six years and are eligible for successive terms under a merit retention vote of the electors in their districts. In each district court, a chief judge, who is selected by other district court judges, is responsible for the administrative duties of the court.

The jurisdiction of the district courts of appeal extends to appeals from judgments or orders of trial courts, and to the review of certain nonfinal orders. By law, district courts in Florida have been granted the power to review most actions taken by state agencies. As a general rule, decisions of the district courts of appeal represent the final appellate review of litigated cases. A person who is displeased with a district court's express decision may ask for review in the Florida supreme court or in the United States Supreme Court, but neither tribunal is required to accept the case for further hearing.

The majority of jury trials in Florida take place before one judge sitting as judge of a circuit court. The circuit courts are sometimes referred to as courts of general jurisdiction, in recognition of the fact that most criminal and civil cases originate at this level. Florida's constitution provides that a circuit court shall be established to serve each judicial circuit established by the legislature, of which there are 20. Within each circuit, there may be any number of judges, depending on the population and caseload of the particular area. At present, the most judges sit in the Eleventh Judicial Circuit, and the fewest judges sit in the Sixteenth Judicial Circuit. To be eligible for the office of circuit judge, a person must be a resident elector of Florida and must have been admitted to the practice of law in the state for the preceding five years. Circuit court judges are elected by the voters of the various circuits. Circuit court judges serve six-year terms and are subject to the same disciplinary standards and procedures as Supreme Court justices and district court judges. A chief judge is chosen from among the circuit judges in each judicial circuit to carry out administrative responsibilities for all trial courts (both circuit and county courts) within the circuit.

Circuit courts have general trial jurisdiction over matters not assigned by statute to the county courts and also hear appeals from county court cases. Thus, circuit courts are simultaneously the highest trial courts and the lowest appellate courts in Florida's judicial system. The trial jurisdiction of circuit courts includes, among other matters, original jurisdiction over civil disputes involving more than $15,000; controversies involving the estates of decedents, minors, and persons adjudicated to be incompetent; cases relating to juveniles; criminal prosecutions for all felonies; tax disputes; and actions to determine the title and boundaries of real property.

County courts represent the lowest trial court level in Florida. State constitution establishes a county court in each of Florida's 67 counties. The number of judges in each county court varies with the population and caseload of the county. To be eligible for the office of county judge, a person must be a resident of the county and must have been a member of the Florida Bar for five years; in counties with a population of 40,000 or fewer, a person must only be a member of the Florida Bar.

County judges serve four-year terms, and they are subject to the same disciplinary standards, as all other judicial officers. The trial jurisdiction of county courts is established by statute. The jurisdiction of county courts extends to civil disputes involving $15,000 or less. The majority of nonjury trials in Florida take place before one judge sitting as a judge of the county court. The county courts are sometimes referred to as "the people's courts," probably because a large part of the court's work involves high-volume citizen disputes, such as traffic offenses, less serious criminal matters (misdemeanors), and relatively small monetary disputes.

Other, special-purpose, courts do exist in the state. In 1989, for example, the Florida legislature authorized the establishment of a Civil Traffic Infraction Hearing Officer Program to free up county judges for other county court work and for circuit court assignments. Initially, participation in the program was limited to those counties with a civil traffic infraction caseload of 20,000 hearings, but the threshold was subsequently lowered to 15,000. The 1990–1991 legislature expanded the magistrate's jurisdiction to include accidents resulting in property damage (not bodily injury). At the end of the year-long pilot project, the Florida supreme court recommended, and the legislature approved, the program for continuation on a local option basis.

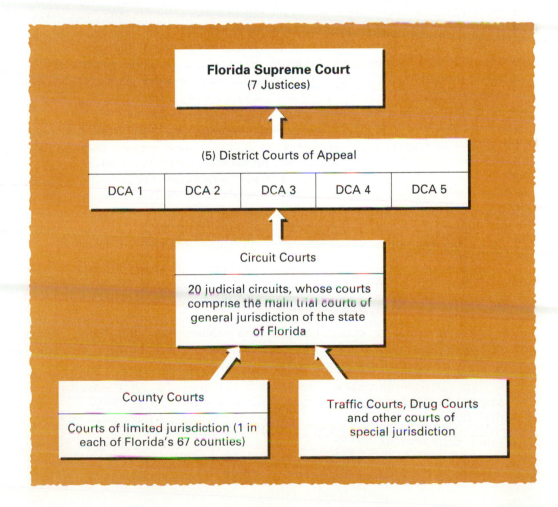

FIGURE 7-3
The court system of the state of Florida.

State Court Administration

State Court Administrators. Coordinating personnel who assist with case flow management, budgeting of operating funds, and court docket administration.

To function efficiently, courts require uninterrupted funding, adequate staffing, trained support personnel, a well-managed case flow, and coordination between levels and among jurisdictions. To oversee these and other aspects of judicial management, every state today has its own mechanism for court administration. Most make use of **state court administrators** who manage these operational functions.

The first state court administrator was appointed in New Jersey in 1948.[13] Although other states were initially slow to follow the New Jersey lead, increased federal funding for criminal justice administration during the 1970s, and a growing realization that some form of coordinated management was necessary for effective court operation, eventually led most states to create similar administrative offices.

Florida, discussed earlier, created its Office of the State Courts Administrator (OSCA) on July 1, 1972. Florida's OSCA is divided into three sections with a deputy state courts administrator heading each one. The Information Systems and Program Support section includes Research, Planning and Court Services, Alternative Dispute Resolution, and Information Systems Services. The Administrative Services section includes Finance and Accounting, Budget, Personnel Services, and General Services. The Legal Affairs and Education section includes Legal Affairs, Judiciary Education Services, and various commissions and committees authorized by the legislature and the court. As in many others states, the state courts administrator in Florida serves as the liaison between the court system and the legislative branch, the executive branch, the auxiliary agencies of the court, and national court research and planning agencies.

The following tasks are typical of state court administrators across the country today:[14]

1. The preparation, presentation, and monitoring of a budget for the state court system
2. The analysis of case flows and backlogs to determine where additional resources such as judges, prosecutors, and other court personnel are needed
3. The collection and publication of statistics describing the operation of state courts
4. Efforts to streamline the flow of cases through individual courts and the system as a whole
5. Service as a liaison between state legislatures and the court system
6. The development or coordination of requests for federal and other outside funding
7. The management of state court personnel, including promotions for support staff and the handling of retirement and other benefits packages for court employees
8. The creation and the coordination of plans for the training of judges and other court personnel (in conjunction with local chief judges and supreme court justices)
9. The assignment of judges to judicial districts (especially in states that use rotating judgeships)
10. The administrative review of payments to legal counsel for indigent defendants

At the federal level, the federal court system is administered by the Administrative Office of the United State Courts (AO), located in Washington, D.C. The AO was created by Congress in 1939 and prepares the budget and legislative agenda for federal courts. It also performs audits of court accounts, manages funds for the operation of federal courts, compiles and publishes statistics on the volume and type of business conducted by the courts, and recommends plans and strategies to efficiently manage court business.

Dispute Resolution Centers

Dispute Resolution Centers. Informal hearing infrastructures designed to mediate interpersonal disputes without need for the more formal arrangements of criminal trial courts.

Some communities have begun to recognize that it is possible to resolve at least minor disputes without the need for formal court hearings. **Dispute resolution centers,** which function to hear victims' claims of minor wrongs, such as passing bad checks, trespassing, shoplifting, and petty theft, function today in more than 200 locations throughout the country.[15] Frequently staffed by volunteer mediators, such programs work to resolve disagreements (in which minor criminal offenses might otherwise be charged) without the need to assign blame. Dispute resolution programs began in the early 1970s, with the earliest being the Community Assistance Project in Chester, Pennsylvania; the Columbus, Ohio, Night Prosecutor Program; and the Arbitration as an Alternative Program in Rochester, New York. Following the lead of these programs, the U.S. Department of Justice helped promote the development of three experimental "Neighborhood Justice Centers" in Los Angeles, Kansas City, and Atlanta. Each center accepted both minor civil and criminal cases.

Mediation centers are often closely integrated with the formal criminal justice process and may substantially reduce the caseload of lower-level courts. Some centers are, in fact, run by the courts and work only with court-ordered referrals. Others are semiautonomous, but may depend on courts for endorsement of their decisions, whereas others function with complete autonomy. Rarely, however, do dispute resolution programs entirely supplant the formal criminal justice mechanism, and defendants who appear before a community mediator may also later be charged with a crime.

Mediation centers have been criticized for the fact that they typically work only with minor offenses, thereby denying the opportunity for mediation to victims and offenders in more serious cases, and for the fact that they may be seen by defendants as just another form of criminal sanction rather than a true alternative to criminal justice system processing.[16] Other critiques claim that community dispute resolution centers do little other than provide a forum for shouting matches between the parties involved.

The Rise of the Federal Courts

As we have seen, state courts had their origins in early colonial arrangements. Federal courts, however, were created by the U.S. Constitution. Section 1 of Article III of the Constitution provides for the establishment of "one supreme Court, and...such inferior Courts as the Congress may from time to time ordain and establish." Article III, Section 2, specifies that such courts are to have jurisdiction over cases arising under the Constitution, federal laws, and treaties. Federal courts are also to settle disputes between states and to have jurisdiction in cases where one of the parties is a state.

Today's federal court system represents the culmination of a series of congressional mandates which have expanded the federal judicial infrastructure so that it can continue to carry out the duties envisioned by the Constitution. Notable federal statutes which have contributed to the present structure of the federal court system include the Judiciary Act of 1789, the Judiciary Act of 1925, and the Magistrate's Act of 1968.

As a result of constitutional mandates, congressional action, and other historical developments, today's federal judiciary consists of three levels: (1) U.S. district courts, (2) U.S. courts of appeals, and (3) the U.S. Supreme Court. Each is described in turn in the following sections.

Federal District Courts

The lowest level of the federal court system consists of 94 district courts located in the 50 states (except for the District of Wyoming, which includes the Montana and Idaho portions of Yellowstone National Park), Puerto Rico, the District of Columbia, and the U.S. territories of Guam, the Virgin Islands, and the Northern Mariana Islands. District courts are the trial courts of the federal judicial system. They have original jurisdiction over all cases involving alleged violations of federal statutes. Each state has at least one U.S. district court, and some, like New York and

Federal Court System. The three-tiered structure of federal courts, involving U.S. District Courts, U.S. Courts of Appeal, and the U.S. Supreme Court.

California, have as many as four. A district may itself be divided into divisions and may have several places where the court hears cases. As we discussed, district courts were first authorized by Congress through the 1789 Judiciary Act, which allocated one federal court to each state. Because of population increases over the years, new courts have been added in a number of states.

Nearly 650 district court judges staff federal district courts. District court judges are appointed by the president, confirmed by the Senate, and serve for life. An additional 369 full-time and 110 part-time magistrate judges (referred to as "U.S. magistrates" prior to 1990) serve the district court system and assist federal judges. Magistrate judges have the power to conduct arraignments and may set bail, issue warrants, and try minor offenders.[17]

U.S. district courts handle thousands of criminal cases per year. In 1994, for example, 45,473 criminal cases and 236,391 civil cases were filed in U.S. district courts.[18] Because some courts are much busier than others, the number of district court judges varies from a low of 2 in some jurisdictions to a high of 27 in others. During the past 20 years, the number of cases handled by the entire federal district court system has grown exponentially. The hiring of new judges has not kept pace with the increase in caseload, and questions persist about the quality of justice that can be delivered by overworked judges.

One of the most pressing issues facing district court judges is the fact that their pay, which at $133,600 in mid-1993[19] placed them in the top 1 percent of incoming-earning Americans, is small compared to what most could earn in private practice. Many federal judges, however, made substantial amounts of money from private practice before assuming the bench, whereas others had income from investments or held family fortunes.

U.S. Courts of Appeals

The intermediate appellate courts in the federal judicial system are the courts of appeals.[20] Twelve of these courts have jurisdiction over cases from certain geographic areas. The Court of Appeals for the Federal Circuit has national jurisdiction over specific types of cases.

The U.S. Court of Appeals for the Federal Circuit and the 12 regional courts of appeals are often referred to as circuit courts. That is because early in the nation's history, the judges of the first courts of appeals visited each of the courts in one region in a particular sequence, traveling by horseback and riding "circuit." These courts of appeals review matters from the district courts of their geographic regions, the U.S. Tax Court, and from certain federal administrative agencies. A disappointed party in a district court usually has the right to have the case reviewed in the court of appeals for the circuit. Appeals court judges are appointed for life by the president with the advice and consent of the Senate. The First through Eleventh Circuits each include three or more states, as illustrated by Figure 7-4.

Each court of appeals consists of six or more judges, depending on the caseload of the courts. The judge who has served on the court the longest and who is under 65 years of age is designated the chief judge and performs administrative duties in addition to hearing cases. The chief judge serves for a maximum term of seven years. Each court of appeals judge is appointed for life. There are 167 judges on the 12 regional courts of appeals.

The U.S. Court of Appeals for the District of Columbia, which is called the twelfth circuit, hears cases arising in the District of Columbia and has appellate jurisdiction assigned by Congress in legislation concerning many departments of the federal government. The U.S. Court of Appeals for the Federal Circuit (in effect, the thirteenth circuit) was created in 1982 by the merging of the U.S. Court of Claims and the U.S. Court of Customs and Patent Appeals. The court hears appeals in cases from the U.S. Court of Federal Claims, the U.S. Court of International

Trade, the U.S. Court of Veterans Appeals, the International Trade Commission, the Board of Contract Appeals, the Patent and Trademark Office, and the Merit Systems Protection Board. The Federal Circuit also hears appeals from certain decisions of the secretaries of the Department of Agriculture and the Department of Commerce, and cases from district courts involving patents and minor claims against the federal government.

Federal appellate courts have mandatory jurisdiction over the decisions of district courts within their circuits. Mandatory jurisdiction means that U.S. courts of appeals are required to hear the cases brought to them. Criminal appeals from federal district courts are usually heard by panels of three judges sitting on a court of appeals rather than by all the judges of each circuit.

Federal appellate courts operate under the *Federal Rules of Appellate Procedure*, although each has also created its own separate Local Rules. Local Rules may mean that one circuit, such as the Second, will depend heavily on oral arguments, whereas others may substitute written summary depositions in their place. Appeals generally fall into one of three categories:[21] (1) frivolous appeals, which have little substance, raise no significant new issues, and are generally quickly disposed of; (2) ritualistic appeals, which are brought primarily because of the demands of litigants even though the probability of reversal is negligible; and (3) nonconsensual appeals, which entail major questions of law and policy, and on which there is considerable professional disagreement among the courts and within the legal profession. The probability of reversal is, of course, highest in the case of nonconsensual appeals.

Because the Constitution guarantees a right to an appeal, federal circuit courts have found themselves facing an ever-increasing workload. Almost all appeals from federal district courts go to the court of appeals serving the circuit in which the case was first heard. A defendant's right to appeal, however, has been interpreted to mean the right to one appeal. Hence, the U.S. Supreme Court need not hear the appeals of defendants who are dissatisfied with the decision of a federal appeals court.

Appellate Jurisdiction. The lawful authority of a court to review a decision made by a lower court.

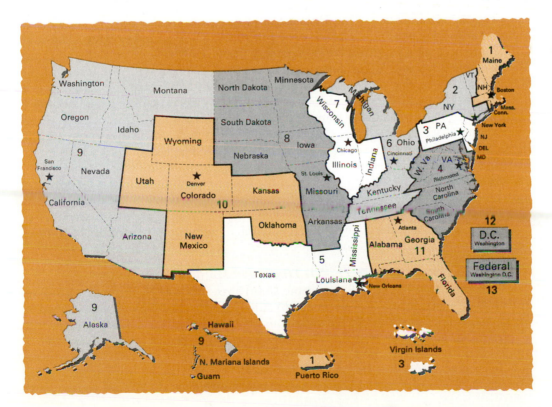

FIGURE 7-4
The 13 federal judicial circuits.

TABLE 7-1

Justices of the U.S. Supreme Court

Justice	Entered Duty	Views
CHIEF JUSTICE		
William H. Rehnquist[1]	January 1972	Very conservative
ASSOCIATE JUSTICES		
John Paul Stevens	December 1975	Moderate to liberal
Sandra Day O'Connor	September 1981	Moderate to conservative
Antonin Scalia	September 1986	Very conservative
Anthony M. Kennedy	February 1988	Conservative
David H. Souter	October 1990	Conservative
Clarence Thomas	October 1991	Conservative
Ruth Bader Ginsburg	August 1993	Moderate
Stephen Breyer	August 1994	Moderate

1. Appointed Chief Justice September 1986.

The Supreme Court of the United States

At the apex of the federal court system stands the U.S. Supreme Court. The Supreme Court is located in Washington, D.C., across the street from the U.S. Capitol Building. The Court consists of nine justices, eight of whom are referred to as associate justices. The ninth presides over the Court as the chief justice of the United States (see Table 7-1). Supreme Court justices are nominated by the president, confirmed by the Senate, and serve for life. Lengthy terms of service are a tradition among justices. One of the earliest chief justices, John Marshall, served the Court for 34 years, from 1801 to 1835. The same was true of Justice Stephen J. Field who sat on the bench for 34 years, between 1863 and 1897. Justice Hugo Black passed the 34-year milestone, serving an additional month, before he retired in 1971. Justice William O. Douglas set a record for longevity on the bench, retiring in 1975, after 36 years and 6 months of service.

Judicial Review. The power of a court to review actions and decisions made by other agencies of government.

The Supreme Court of the United States wields immense power. The Court's greatest authority lies in its capacity for **judicial review** of lower court decisions and state and federal statute. By exercising its power of judicial review, the Court decides what laws and lower court decisions are in keeping with the intent of the U.S. Constitution. The power of judicial review is not explicit in the Constitution, but was anticipated by its framers. In the *Federalist Papers*, which urged adoption of the Constitution, Alexander Hamilton wrote that, through the practice of judicial review, the Court would ensure that "the will of the whole people," as grounded in the Constitution, would be supreme over the "will of the legislature...," which might be subject to temporary whims.[22]

It was not until 1803, however, that the Court forcefully asserted its power of judicial review. In an opinion written for the case of *Marbury* v. *Madison* (1803),[23] Chief Justice John Marshall established the Court's authority as final interpreter of the U.S. Constitution, declaring that "It is emphatically the province of the judicial department to say what the law is...."

INCREASING COMPLEXITY AND THE SUPREME COURT

The evolution of the U.S. Supreme Court provides one of the most dramatic examples of institutional development in American history. Sparsely described in the Constitution, the Court has grown from a handful of circuit riding justices into a modern organization that wields tremendous legal power over all aspects of American life. Much of the Court's growth has been due to its increasing willingness to mediate fundamental issues of law and to act as a resort from arbitrary and capricious processing by the justice systems of the states and national government.

The *Marbury* decision, described earlier, established the Court as a mighty force in federal government by virtue of the power of judicial review. As we have discussed at length earlier in this book, the Court began to apply that power during the 1960s to issues of crime and justice at the state and local levels. You may recall that the Court signaled its change in orientation in 1961 with the case of *Mapp* v. *Ohio*,[24] which extended the exclusionary rule to the states. Such extension, combined with the near simultaneous end of the hands-off doctrine which had previously exempted state prison systems from Court scrutiny, placed the authority of the Court squarely over the activities of state criminal justice systems. From that time forward, the Court's workload became increasingly heavy and even today shows few signs of abatement.

THE SUPREME COURT TODAY

The Supreme Court has limited original jurisdiction and does not conduct trials, except in disputes between states and some cases of attorney disbarment. The Court, rather, reviews the decisions of lower courts and may accept cases from both U.S. courts of appeals and state supreme courts. For a case to be heard, at least four justices must vote in favor of a hearing. When the Court agrees to hear a case, it will issue a writ of *certiorari* to a lower court, ordering it to send the records of the case forward for review. Once having granted *certiorari*, the justices can revoke the decision. In such cases, a writ is dismissed by ruling it improvidently granted.

The U.S. Supreme Court may review any decision appealed to it which it decides is worthy of review. In fact, however, the Court elects to review only cases which involve a substantial federal question. Of approximately 5,000 requests for review received by the Court yearly, only about 200 are actually heard.

A term of the Supreme Court begins, by statute, on the first Monday in October and lasts until early July. The term is divided between sittings, when cases will be heard, and time for the writing and delivering of opinions. Between 22 and 24 cases will be heard at each sitting, with each side alloted 30 minutes for arguments before the justices. Intervening recesses allow justices time to study arguments and supporting documentation and to work on their opinions.

Decisions rendered by the Supreme Court are rarely unanimous. Instead, opinions that a majority of the Court's justices agree upon become the judgment of the Court. Justices who agree with the Court's judgment, but for a different reason, or because they feel that they have some new light to shed on a particular legal issue involved in the case, write concurring opinions. Justices who do not agree with the decision of the Court write dissenting opinions. Those dissenting opinions may offer new possibilities for successful appeals made at a later date.

IDEAS FOR CHANGE

Increasing caseloads at the federal appellate court level, combined with the many requests for Supreme Court review, have led to proposals to restructure the federal appellate court system. In 1973, a study group appointed by Chief Justice Burger suggested the creation of a National Court of Appeals, which would serve as a kind of "mini–Supreme Court."[25] Under the proposal, the National Court of Appeals would be staffed on a rotating basis by judges who now serve the various circuit courts of appeal. The purpose of the new court was suggested to include a review of cases awaiting hearings before the Supreme Court, so that that Court's workload might be reduced.

A similar National Court of Appeals was proposed in 1975 by the Congressional Commission on Revision of the Federal Court Appellate System. The National Court proposed by the Commission would have heard cases sent to it via transfer jurisdiction, from lower appellate courts, and through reference jurisdiction—when the Supreme Court decided to forward cases to it. The most recent version of a mini–Supreme Court was proposed by the Senate Judiciary Committee in 1986, when it called for the creation of an Intercircuit Tribunal of the U.S. courts of appeals. To date, however, no legislation to establish such a court has passed both houses of Congress.

Interior of Supreme Court Building. Photo by Doug Mills, courtesy of AP/Wide World Photos.

Pretrial Activities

In the next chapter, we will discuss typical stages in a criminal trial, as well as the many roles assumed by courtroom participants like judges, prosecutors, defense attorneys, victims, and suspects. A number of court-related pretrial activities, however, routinely take place before trial can begin. These activities are described in the following pages.

First Appearance

First Appearance. (Also called Initial Appearance) An appearance before a magistrate which entails the process whereby the legality of a defendant's arrest is initially assessed, and he or she is informed of the charges on which he or she is being held. At this stage in the criminal justice process, bail may be set or pretrial release arranged.

Most defendants do not come into contact with an officer of the court until their **first appearance** before a magistrate.[26] Following arrest (especially one made without an arrest warrant), most states require a magistrate's review in order to determine whether or not there is just cause to detain the suspect. The magistrate's review of the arrest proceeds in a relatively informal fashion, with the judge seeking to decide whether, at the time of apprehension, the arresting officer had reason to believe both (1) that a crime had been or was being committed and (2) that the defendant was the person who committed it. Most of the evidence presented to the magistrate comes from either the arresting officer or the victim. At this stage in the criminal justice process, the suspect generally is not given an opportunity to present evidence. The U.S. Supreme Court has held that defendants are entitled to representation by counsel at their first appearance.[27] Indigent defendants may have counsel appointed to represent them, and proceedings may be adjourned until counsel can be obtained.

In cases where the suspect is unruly, intoxicated, or uncooperative, the magistrate's review may occur in their absence. Some states waive a magistrate's review and proceed directly to arraignment (discussed later), especially when the defendant has been arrested on a warrant. In states which move directly to arraignment,

Theory into Practice: The U.S. Supreme Court—A Shift to the Right

The U.S. Supreme Court is the final interpreter of the U.S. Constitution and of laws passed by Congress. It is supposed to be above politics. Given the power of the Court, however, a number of observers have called it a "second legislature"—one which, with increasing frequency, steps into the middle of social issues and makes its own laws through the powerful process of judicial decree. Even the justices themselves are occasionally surprised by the Court's unchallenged ability to impose its unique interpretations upon the law. In 1990, for example, Justices Scalia and Rehnquist bemoaned what they saw as the Court's virtual and misguided independence from constitutional principles. In all too many instances, the Court, they claimed, has freely used its wide power to create ideologically driven and self-serving rules which bear little relationship to the Constitution. In a dissenting opinion in the 1990 case of *Minnick* v. *Mississippi*,[1] Scalia and Rehnquist wrote: "Today's [ruling] is the latest stage of [prohibition] built upon [prohibition], producing a veritable fairyland castle of imagined constitutional restriction upon law enforcement." This newest tower, according to the Court, is needed to avoid "inconsistency with [a previous] rule,...which was needed to protect Miranda's...right to have counsel present, which was needed to protect the right against compelled self-incrimination found—at last—in the Constitution."

If the Court does have an agenda, what kind of law is it making? During the 1970s and for part of the 1980s, the Court appeared to lean heavily in favor of the rights of criminal defendants and jealously guarded the concept of due process. By 1996, under the leadership of Chief Justice William Rehnquist, however, it had become clear that the Court has moved toward a much more conservative position. Some now charge that—with the death of Thurgood Marshall and the retirements of liberal Justices William Brennan and Harry Blackmun—a conservative juggernaut is running the Court. Many suspect that a new emphasis on victim's rights and community interests will soon replace the Court's historical concern with the rights of defendants. The sentiments of many individual rights advocates were captured in a *USA Today* editorial, which intoned, "The trend is worrisome. An innocent person is now far more vulnerable to harassment by police."[2]

Victim's rights advocates, however, are applauding the change. "Victims of crime and their families have a right to a fair and speedy trial, too," says the Criminal Justice Legal Foundation's Kent Scheidegger. "The Supreme Court recognizes that. It is high time."[3] Still, more is to come. As one commentator said at the close of the Court's 1995 term, "If people think what [the Court] has done this term is bold, fasten your seat belts!"[4]

QUESTIONS FOR DISCUSSION

1. Do you agree with the assertion that the U.S. Supreme Court has begun a "swing to the right?" Why or why not?

2. Do you believe that the Supreme Court can be affected by politics or by the political leanings of the justices who serve it? If so, how?

3. Do you believe that it is possible to have a Supreme Court which is value free and totally objective? If so, how?

---

1. *Minnick* v. *Mississippi*, 111 S.Ct. 486 (1990).
2. "Debate," *USA Today*, June 28, 1991, p. 14A.
3. Kent S. Scheidegger, "Stop All the Fretting; Our Liberties Are Safe," *USA Today*, June 28, 1991, p. 14A.
4. Tony Mauro, "Court's Move to the Right Confirmed," *USA Today*, June 27, 1995, p. 1A.

---

the procedures undertaken to obtain a warrant are regarded as sufficient to demonstrate a basis for detention prior to arraignment.

According to the procedural rules of all jurisdictions, defendants who have been taken into custody must be offered an in-court appearance before a magistrate "without unnecessary delay." The 1943 Supreme Court case of *McNabb* v. *U.S.*[28] established that any unreasonable delay in an initial court appearance would make confessions inadmissible if interrogating officers obtained them during the delay. Based on the *McNabb* decision, 48 hours following arrest became the rule of thumb for reckoning the maximum time by which a first appearance should have been held.

The 48-hour rule was formalized by the U.S. Supreme Court in a 1991 class action suit, entitled the *County of Riverside (California)* v. *McLaughlin*.[29] In *McLaughlin*, the Court held that "a jurisdiction that provides judicial determinations of probable cause within 48 hours of arrest will, as a general matter, comply with the promptness requirement...." The Court specified, however, that weekends and holidays could not be excluded from the 48-hour requirement (as they had been in Riverside County) and that, depending on the specifics of the case, delays of less than two days may still be unreasonable. In a dissenting opinion, Justice Thurgood Marshall spurned the idea that an appropriate time limit of any kind could be usefully specified. He wrote, a "probable cause hearing is sufficiently 'prompt'...only when provided immediately upon completion of the 'administrative steps incident to arrest'...."[30]

Bail

Bail Bond. An agreement guaranteeing the required appearance of a defendant in court, which records a pledge of money or property to be paid to the court if he or she does not appear, and which is signed by the person to be released and any other persons acting in his or her behalf.

A highly significant aspect of the first appearance hearing is consideration of bail or pretrial release. Defendants charged with very serious crimes, or those thought likely to escape or injure others, will usually be held in jail until trial. Such a practice is called pretrial detention.

The majority of defendants, however, will be afforded the opportunity for release. However, since it is important to make sure that a released defendant will return for further court processing, he or she is asked to "post bail." Bail serves two purposes: (1) it helps ensure reappearance of the accused, and (2) it prevents unconvicted persons from suffering imprisonment unnecessarily.

Bail involves the posting of a bond as a pledge that the accused will return for further hearings. **Bail bonds** are usually cash deposits, but may consist of property or other valuables. A fully secured bond requires the defendant to post the full amount of bail set by the court. The usual practice, however, is for a defendant to seek privately secured bail through the services of a professional bail bondsman. The bondsman will assess a percentage (usually 15 percent) of the required bond as a fee which the defendant will have to pay up front. Those who "skip bail" by hiding or fleeing will sometimes find their bond ordered forfeit by the court. Forfeiture hearings must be held before a bond can be taken, and most courts will not order bail forfeit unless it appears that the defendant intends permanently to avoid prosecution. Bail forfeiture will often be reversed where the defendant later willingly appears to stand trial.

In many states, bondsmen are empowered to hunt down and bring back defendants who have fled. In some jurisdictions, bondsmen hold virtually unlimited powers and have been permitted by courts to pursue, arrest, and forcibly extradite their charges from foreign jurisdiction without concern for the due process considerations or statutory limitations which apply to law enforcement officers.[31] Recently, however, a number of states have enacted laws which eliminate for-profit bail bond businesses, replacing them instead with state-operated pretrial service agencies.

Alternatives to Bail

Release on Recognizance. (ROR) Refers to the pretrial release of a criminal defendant on his or her written promise to appear. No cash or property bond is required.

The Eighth Amendment to the U.S. Constitution, though it does not guarantee the opportunity for bail, does state that "Excessive bail shall not be required...." Some studies, however, have found that many defendants who are offered the opportunity for bail are unable to raise the needed money. Years ago, a report by the National Advisory Commission on Criminal Justice Standards and Goals found that as many as 93 percent of felony defendants in some jurisdictions were unable to make bail.[32]

To extend the opportunity for pretrial release to a greater proportion of non-dangerous arrestees, a number of states and the federal government now make available various alternatives to the cash bond system. Alternatives include (1) release on recognizance, (2) property bond, (3) deposit bail, (4) conditional release, (5) third-party custody, and (6) unsecured or signature bond.

Release on recognizance (ROR) involves no cash bond, requiring as a guarantee only that the defendant agree in writing to return for further hearings as specified by the court. As an alternative to cash bond, release on recognizance was

U.S. Supreme Court Justices. From front left, Antonin Scalia, John Paul Stevens, Chief Justice William H. Rehnquist, Sandra Day O'Connor, and Anthony Kennedy. Rear, from left, Ruth Bader Ginsburg, David Souter, Clarence Thomas, and Stephen Breyer. Photo by Markel, courtesy of Gamma-Liaison, Inc.

tested during the 1960s in a social experiment called the Manhattan Bail Project.[33] In the experiment, not all defendants were eligible for release on their own recognizance. Those arrested for serious crimes, including murder, rape, and robbery, and defendants with extensive prior criminal records, were excluded from participating in the project. The rest of the defendants were scored and categorized according to a number of "ideal" criteria used as indicators of both dangerousness and the likelihood of pretrial flight. Criteria included (1) no previous convictions, (2) residential stability, and (3) a good employment record. Those likely to flee were not released.

Studies of the bail project revealed that it released four times as many defendants prior to trial as had been freed under the traditional cash bond system.[34] Even more surprising was the finding that only 1 percent of those released fled from prosecution—a figure which was the same as for those set free on cash bond.[35] Later studies, however, were unclear about the effectiveness of release on recognizance, with some finding a no-show rate as high as 12 percent.[36]

Property bonds substitute other items of value in place of cash. Land, houses, automobiles, stocks, and so on may be consigned to the court as collateral against pretrial flight.

An alternative form of cash bond available in some jurisdictions is **deposit bail**. Deposit bail places the court in the role of the bondsman, allowing the defendant to post a percentage of the full bail with the court. Unlike private bail bondsmen, court-run deposit bail programs usually return the amount of the deposit except for a small (perhaps 1 percent) administrative fee. If the defendant fails to appear for court, the entire amount of court-ordered bail is forfeit.

Conditional release imposes a set of requirements on the defendant. Requirements might include attendance at drug treatment programs, staying away from specified others such as potential witnesses, and regular job attendance. Release under supervision is similar to conditional release, but adds the stipulation that defendants report to an officer of the court or a police officer at designated times.

Third-party custody is a bail bond alternative that assigns custody of the defendant to an individual or agency which promises to assure his or her later appearance in court.[37] Some pretrial release programs allow attorneys to assume responsibility for their clients in this fashion. If clients fail to appear, however, the attorney's privilege to participate in the program may be ended.[38]

Property Bond. The setting of bail in the form of land, houses, stocks, or other tangible property. In the event the defendant absconds prior to trial, the bond becomes the property of the court.

An **unsecured bond** is based on a court-determined dollar amount of bail. Like a credit contract, it requires no monetary deposit with the court. The defendant agrees in writing that failure to appear will result in forfeiture of the entire amount of the bond, which might then be taken in seizures of land, personal property, bank accounts, and so on.

A **signature bond** allows release based on the defendant's written promise to appear. Signature bonds involve no particular assessment of the defendant's dangerousness or likelihood of later appearance in court. They are used only in cases of minor offenses such as traffic law violations and some petty drug law violations. Signature bonds may be issued by the arresting officer acting on behalf of the court.

Pretrial release is common practice. Approximately 85 percent of all state-level criminal defendants[39] and 82 percent of all federal criminal defendants[40] are released prior to trial. Sixty-three percent of all state-level *felony* defendants,[41] and 62 percent of federal felony defendants[42] are similarly released (see Figure 7-5). A growing movement, however, stresses the fact that defendants released prior to trial may be dangerous to themselves or others and seeks to reduce the number of defendants released under any conditions. This conservative policy has been promoted by an increasing concern for public safety in the face of a number of studies documenting crimes committed by defendants released on bond. One such study found that 16 percent of defendants released before trial were rearrested, and, of those, 30 percent were arrested more than once.[43] Another determined that as many as 41 percent of those released prior to trial for serious crimes, such as rape and robbery, were rearrested before their trial date.[44] Not surprisingly, such studies generally find that the longer the time spent on bail prior to trial, the greater the likelihood of misconduct.

In the margin:

*D*anger Laws. Those intended to prevent the pretrial release of criminal defendants judged to represent a danger to others in the community.

In response to claims like these, some states have enacted **danger laws**, which limit the right to bail for certain kinds of offenders.[45] Others, including Arizona, California, Colorado, Florida, and Illinois, have approved constitutional amendments restricting the use of bail.[46] Most such provisions exclude persons charged with certain crimes from being eligible for bail and demand that other defendants being considered for bail meet stringent conditions. Some states combine these strictures with tough release conditions designed to keep close control over defendants prior to trial.

The 1984 federal Bail Reform Act allows federal judges to assess the danger represented by an accused to the community and to deny bail to persons who are thought dangerous. In the words of the act, a suspect held in pretrial custody on federal criminal charges is required to be detained if "after a hearing...he is found to pose a risk of flight and a danger to others or the community and if no condition of release can give reasonable assurances against these contingencies."[47] Defendants seeking bail are faced with the necessity of demonstrating a high likelihood of later court appearance. The act also requires that a defendant is entitled to a speedy first appearance and, if he or she is to be detained, that a detention hearing must be held together with the initial appearance.

In the 1990 case of *U.S.* v. *Montalvo-Murillo*,[48] however, a defendant who was not provided with a detention hearing at the time of his first appearance and was subsequently released by an appeals court, was found to have no "right" to freedom because of this "minor" statutory violation. The Supreme Court held that "unless it has a substantial influence on the outcome of the proceedings...failure to comply with the Act's prompt hearing provision does not require release of a person who should otherwise be detained" because "[a]utomatic release contravenes the statutory purpose of providing fair bail procedures while protecting the public's safety and assuring a defendant's appearance at trial."[49]

Court challenges to the constitutionality of pretrial detention legislation have not met with much success. The U.S. Supreme Court case of *U.S.* v. *Hazzard*[50] (1984), decided only a few months after enactment of federal bail reform, held that Congress was justified in providing for denial of bail to offenders who represent a danger to the community. Later cases have supported the presumption of flight which federal law presupposes for certain types of defendants.[51]

Bail bond office. Photo courtesy of Mark Richards.

The Preliminary Hearing

Although the preliminary hearing is not nearly as elaborate as a criminal trial, it has many of the same characteristics. The defendant is taken before a lower court judge who will summarize the charges and review the rights to which all criminal defendants are entitled. The prosecution may present witnesses and will offer evidence in support of the complaint. The defendant will be afforded the right to testify and may also call witnesses. The purpose of the preliminary hearing is to afford the defendant an opportunity to challenge the legal basis for his or her detention. The hearing will turn on a determination of whether there is probable cause to believe that a crime has been committed and that the defendant committed it.

At this stage of the criminal justice process, the defendant's guilt need not be proved beyond a reasonable doubt. All that is required for the wheels of justice to grind forward is a demonstration "sufficient to justify a prudent man's belief that the suspect has committed or was committing an offense."[52] If the magistrate finds enough evidence to justify a trial, the defendant is bound over to the grand jury— or sent directly to the trial court in those states which do not require grand jury

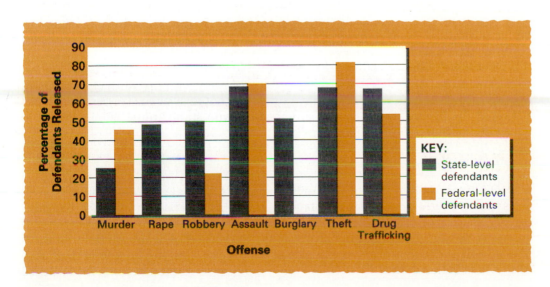

FIGURE 7-5

Proportion of state and federal felony defendants released prior to trial. Source: Brian A. Reaves and Jacob Perez, "Pretrial Release of Felony Defendants, 1992," (Washington, D.C.: Bureau of Justice Statistics, November 1994), and Brian A. Reaves, "Pretrial Release of Federal Felony Defendants," (Washington, D.C.: Bureau of Justice Statistics, February 1994). Note: Federal pretrial release statistics are not available for the crimes of rape and burglary.

review. If the complaint against the defendant cannot be substantiated, the defendant is released. A release is not a bar to further prosecution, and the defendant may be rearrested if further evidence comes to light.

The Grand Jury

The federal government and about half of the states use grand juries as part of the pretrial process. Grand juries are composed of private citizens (often 23 in number) who hear evidence presented by the prosecution. Grand juries serve primarily as filters to eliminate from further processing cases for which there is not sufficient evidence.

In early times, grand juries served a far different purpose. The grand jury system was begun in England in 1166 as a way of identifying law violators. Lacking a law enforcement agency with investigative authority, the government looked to the grand jury as a source of information on criminal activity in the community. Even today, grand juries in most jurisdictions may initiate prosecution independently of the prosecutor although they rarely do.

Grand jury hearings are held in secret, and the defendant is not afforded the opportunity to appear before the grand jury.[53] Similarly, the opportunity to cross-examine prosecution witnesses is absent. Grand juries have the power to subpoena witnesses and to mandate a review of books, records, and other documents crucial to their investigations.

After hearing the evidence, the grand jury votes on the indictment presented to it by the prosecution. The indictment is a formal listing of proposed charges. If the majority of grand jury constituents agree to forward the indictment to the trial court, it becomes a "true bill" on which further prosecution will turn. Jurisdictions which do not make use of the grand jury system depend instead on a piece of information, or complaint, filed by the prosecutor with the trial court.

Arraignment and the Plea

Once an indictment has been returned, or information filed, the accused will be formally arraigned before the trial court. The arraignment is generally a brief process with two purposes: (1) to inform the defendant of the specific charges against him or her, and (2) to allow the defendant to enter a **plea**. The Federal Rules of Criminal Procedure allow for one of three types of pleas to be entered: guilty, not guilty, and *nolo contendere* (no contest). A **no contest** (*nolo contendere*) plea is much the same as a plea of guilty. A defendant who pleads no contest is immediately convicted and may be sentenced just as though he or she had entered a plea of guilty. A no contest plea, however, is no admission of guilt and provides one major advantage to defendants: It may not be used as a later basis for civil proceedings which seek monetary or other damages against the defendant.

Some defendants refuse to enter any plea and are said to "stand mute." Standing mute is a defense strategy that is rarely employed by an accused. Defendants who choose this alternative simply do not answer the request for a plea. However, for procedural purposes, a defendant who stands mute is considered to have entered a plea of not guilty.

Plea Bargaining

Guilty pleas often are not as straightforward as they might seem and are typically arrived at only after complex negotiations known as plea bargaining. **Plea bargaining** is a process of negotiation which usually involves the defendant, prosecutor, and defense counsel. It is founded upon the mutual interests of all involved. Defense attorneys and their clients will agree to a plea of guilty when they are unsure of their ability to win acquittal at trial. Prosecutors may be willing to bargain because the evidence

Plea. In criminal proceedings, a defendant's formal answer in court to the charge contained in a complaint, information, or indictment that he or she is guilty or not guilty of the offense charged or does not contest the charge.

Nolo Contendere. A plea of "no contest." A no contest plea may be used where the defendant does not wish to contest conviction. Because the plea does not admit guilt, however, it cannot provide the basis for later civil suits which might follow on the heels of a criminal conviction.

Plea Bargaining. The negotiated agreement between defendant, prosecutor, and the court concerning what an appropriate plea and associated sentence should be in a given case. Plea bargaining circumvents the trial process and dramatically reduces the time required for the resolution of a criminal case.

they have against the defendant is weaker than they would like it to be. From the prosecutorial perspective, plea bargaining results in a quick conviction, without the need to commit the time and resources necessary for trial. Benefits to the accused include the possibility of reduced or combined charges, lessened defense costs, and a lower sentence than might have otherwise been anticipated.

The U.S. Supreme Court has held that a guilty plea constitutes conviction.[54] In order to validate the conviction, negotiated pleas require judicial consent. Judges are often likely to accept pleas which are the result of a bargaining process because such pleas reduce the workload of the court. Although few judges are willing to guarantee a sentence before a plea is entered, most prosecutors and criminal trial lawyers know what sentences to expect from typical pleas.

In the past, plea bargaining, though apparently common, had often been veiled in secrecy. Judicial thinking held that, for pleas to be valid, they had to be freely given. Pleas struck as the result of bargains seemed to depend on the state's coercive power to encourage the defendant's cooperation. The 1973 National Advisory Commission on Criminal Justice Standards and Goals recommended abolishing the practice of plea negotiation.[55] That recommendation came amid a national debate over the virtues of trading pleas for reductions in sentences. However, in 1970, even before the Commission's recommendation, the U.S. Supreme Court had given its consent to the informal decision-making processes of bargained pleas. In the case of *Brady* v. *U.S.*,[56] the court reasoned that such pleas were voluntarily and knowingly made. A year later, in *Santobello* v. *New York* (1971),[57] the High Court forcefully ruled that plea bargaining is an important and necessary component of the American system of justice. In the words of the Court, "The disposition of criminal charges by agreement between the prosecutor and the accused, sometimes loosely called 'plea bargaining' is an essential component of the administration of justice. Properly administered, it is to be encouraged. If every criminal charge were subjected to a full-scale trial, the States and the Federal Government would need to multiply by many times the number of judges and court facilities."[58]

Today, bargained pleas are commonplace. Some surveys have found that 90 percent of all criminal cases prepared for trial are eventually resolved through a negotiated plea.[59] In a study of 37 big-city prosecutors,[60] the Bureau of Justice Statistics found that for every 100 adults arrested on a felony charge, half were eventually convicted of either a felony or a misdemeanor. Of all convictions, fully 94 percent were the result of a plea. Only 6 percent of convictions were the result of a criminal trial.

After a guilty plea has been entered, it may be withdrawn with the consent of the court. In the case of *Henderson* v. *Morgan* (1976),[61] for example, the U.S. Supreme Court permitted a defendant to withdraw a plea of guilty nine years after it had been given. In *Henderson*, the defendant had originally entered a plea of guilty to second-degree murder, but attempted to withdraw it before trial. Reasons for wanting to withdraw the plea included the defendant's belief that he had not been completely advised about the nature of the charge or the sentence he might receive as a result of the plea.

Recent Supreme Court decisions, however, have enhanced the prosecutor's authority in the bargaining process by declaring that negotiated pleas cannot be capriciously withdrawn by defendants.[62] Other rulings have supported discretionary actions by prosecutors in which sentencing recommendations were retracted even after bargains had been struck.[63] Some lower court cases have upheld the government's authority to withdraw from a negotiated plea where the defendant fails to live up to certain conditions.[64] Conditions may include requiring the defendant to provide information on other criminal involvement, criminal cartels, the activities of smugglers, and so on.

Because it is a process of negotiation involving many interests, plea bargaining may have unintended consequences. For example, although it is generally agreed that bargained pleas should relate in some way to the original charge, actual practice may not adhere to such expectations. Many plea negotiations turn on the acceptability of the anticipated sentence rather than on a close relationship between the charge and the plea. Entered pleas may be chosen for the punishments likely to be associated with them rather than for their accuracy in describing the criminal offense in which the defendant was involved.[65] This is especially true where the defendant is concerned with minimizing the socially stigmatizing impact of the offense. A charge of "indecent liberties," for example, in which the defendant is accused of sexual misconduct, may be pled out as assault. Such a plea, which takes advantage of the fact that indecent liberties can be thought of as a form of sexual assault, would effectively disguise the true nature of the offense.

Even though plea bargaining has been endorsed by the Supreme Court, the public continues to view it suspiciously. "Law and order" advocates, who generally favor harsh punishments and long jail terms, claim that plea bargaining results in unjustifiably light sentences. As a consequence, prosecutors who regularly engage in the practice rarely advertise it. Often unrealized is the fact that plea bargaining can be a powerful prosecutorial tool.

Power carries with it, however, the potential for misuse. Plea bargains, because they circumvent the trial process, hold the possibility of abuse by prosecutors and defense attorneys who are more interested in a speedy resolution of cases than they are in seeing justice done. Carried to the extreme, plea bargaining may result in defendants being convicted of crimes they did not commit. Although it probably happens only rarely, it is conceivable that innocent defendants (especially those with prior criminal records) who—for whatever reason—think a jury will convict them, may plead guilty to lessened charges in order to avoid a trial. In an effort to protect defendants against hastily arranged pleas, the *Federal Rules of Criminal Procedure* require judges to (1) inform the defendant of the various rights he or she is surrendering by pleading guilty, (2) determine that the plea is voluntary, (3) require disclosure of any plea agreements, and (4) make sufficient inquiry to ensure there is a factual basis for the plea.[66]

Bargained pleas can take many forms and be quite inventive. The case of Steven Allen Butler illustrates an unusual bargained plea. In 1992, Butler, a 28-year-old Houston man, voluntarily agreed to surgical castration and a 10-year probationary sentence for repeatedly raping a 13-year-old girl while already on probation for molesting a 7-year-old. His alternative was to stand trial, facing a potential life sentence. However, after considerable public outcry over the arranged sentence, Judge Michael McSpadden withdrew the offer, saying no physician could be found to perform the surgery.[67]

Summary

Within the United States, there are two judicial systems. One system consists of state and local courts established under the authority of state governments. The other is the federal court system, created by Congress under the authority of the Constitution of the United States.

State courts have virtually unlimited power to decide nearly every type of case, subject only to the limitations of the U.S. Constitution, their own state constitutions, and state law. State and local courts are located in almost every town and county across the nation, and are the courts with which citizens usually have contact. These courts handle most criminal matters and the great bulk of legal business concerning wills and inheritance, estates, marital disputes, real estate and land dealings, commercial and personal contracts, and other day-to-day matters.

State criminal courts present an intriguing contrast. On the one hand, they exude an aura of highly formalized judicial procedure, whereas on the other, they demonstrate a surprising lack of organizational uniformity. Courts in one jurisdiction may bear little resemblance to those in another state. Court reform, because it has not equally affected all areas of the country, has in some instances exacerbated the differences between court systems.

Federal courts have power to decide only those cases over which the Constitution gives them authority. These courts are located principally in the larger cities. Only carefully selected types of cases may be heard in federal courts. The highest federal court, the U.S. Supreme Court, is located in Washington, D.C., and hears cases only on appeal from lower courts.

This chapter also described pretrial practices in preparation for a detailed consideration of trial-related activities which are described in the next chapter. Prior to trial, courts often act to shield the accused from the punitive power of the state through the use of pretrial release. In doing so, they must balance the rights of the unconvicted defendant against the potential for future harm which that person may represent. A significant issue facing pretrial decision makers is how to ensure that all defendants, rich and poor, are afforded the same degree of protection.

Discussion Questions

1. What is the "dual court system"? Why do we have a dual court system in America? Could the drive toward court unification eventually lead to a monolithic court system? Would such a system be effective?
2. This chapter says that 90 percent of all criminal cases carried beyond the initial stages are finally resolved through bargained pleas. What are some of the problems associated with plea bargaining? Given those problems, do you believe that plea bargaining is an acceptable practice in today's criminal justice system? Give reasons for your answer.
3. People who are accused of crimes are often granted pretrial release. Do you think all defendants accused of crimes should be so released? If not, what types of defendants might you keep in jail? Why?
4. What inequities exist in today's system of pretrial release? How might the system be improved?

References

1. Law Enforcement Assistance Administration, *Two Hundred Years of American Criminal Justice* (Washington, D.C.: U.S. Government Printing Office, 1976), p. 31.

2. Ibid., p. 31.

3. Ibid.

4. Ibid., p. 32.

5. Ibid.

6. David B. Rottman, Carol R. Flango, R. Shedine Lockley, *State Court Organization 1993* (Washington, D.C.: BJS, 1995), p. 11.

7. Thomas A. Henderson, Cornelium M. Kerwin, Randall Guynes, Carl Baar, Neal Miller, Hildy Saizow, and Robert Grieser, *The Significance of Judicial Structure: The Effects of Unification on Trial Court Operations* (Washington, D.C.: National Institute of Justice, 1984).

8. Ibid.

9. As recently as 1957, only 13 states had permanent intermediate appellate courts. Now, all but 12 states have such a court, one of them (North Dakota) is operating one on a temporary basis to assist in handling their rising appellate caseload. See: David B. Rottman, Carol R. Flango, R, Shedine Lockley, *State Court Organization 1993* (Washington, D.C.: BJS, 1995), p. 5.

10. *Keeney, Superintendent, Oregon State Penitentiary v. Tamayo-Reyes*, 113 S.Ct. 853, 122 L. Ed. 2d 203 (1993).

11. *Herrera v. Collins*, 113 S.Ct. 853, 122 L.Ed. 2d 203 (1993).

12. Some of the wording in this section is taken from "Overview of the Florida State Courts System," on *Joshua*, the Florida court's World Wide Web page on the Internet, July 25, 1995.

13. H. Ted Rubin, *The Courts: Fulcrum of the*

Justice System (Pacific Palisades, Calif.: Goodyear, 1976), p. 200.

14. Ibid., p. 198.

15. Martin Wright, *Justice for Victims and Offenders* (Bristol, Pa.: Open University Press, 1991), p. 56.

16. Ibid., pp. 104 and 106.

17. Administrative Office of the U.S. Courts, *The United States Courts: A Pictoral Summary for the Twelve Month Period Ended June 30, 1985* (Washington, D.C.: U.S. Government Printing Office, 1985), p. 16.

18. Administrative Office of the United States Courts, World Wide Web site, July 22, 1995.

19. Telephone conversation, Administrative Office of the United States Courts, May 20, 1993.

20. Some of the material in this section is adapted from the Administrative Office of the United States Courts, "Courts of Appeals," and "U.S. Court of Appeals for the Federal Circuit," Administrative Office of the United States Courts, World Wide Web site, July 27, 1995.

21. Stephen L. Wasby, *The Supreme Court in the Federal Judicial System*, 3rd ed. (Chicago: Nelson-Hall, 1988), p. 58.

22. *The Supreme Court of the United States* (Washington, D.C.: U.S. Government Printing Office, no date), p. 4.

23. 1 Cranch 137 (1803).

24. *Mapp* v. *Ohio*, 367 U.S. 643 (1961).

25. Wasby, *The Supreme Court*, pp. 58–59.

26. "Arraignment" is also a term used to describe an initial appearance although we will reserve use of that word to describe a later court appearance following the defendant's indictment by a grand jury or the filing of information by the prosecutor.

27. *White* v. *Maryland*, 373 U.S. 59 (1963).

28. *McNabb* v. *United States*, 318 U.S. 332 (1943).

29. *County of Riverside* v. *McLaughlin*, 111 S.Ct. 1661 (1991).

30. *McLaughlin*, dissenting opinion.

31. *Taylor* v. *Taintor*, 83 U.S. 66 (1873).

32. National Advisory Commission on Criminal Justice Standards and Goals, *The Courts* (Washington, D.C.: U.S. Government Printing Office, 1973), p. 37.

33. C. Ares, A. Rankin, and H. Sturz, "The Manhattan Bail Project: An Interim Report on the Use of Pre-Trial Parole," *New York University Law Review*, Vol. 38 (January 1963), pp. 68–95.

34. H. Zeisel, "Bail Revisited," *American Bar Foundation Research Journal*, Vol. 4 (1979), pp. 769–789.

35. Ibid.

36. "12% of Those Freed on Low Bail Fail to Appear," *The New York Times*, December 2, 1983, p. 1.

37. Bureau of Justice Statistics, *Report to the Nation on Crime and Justice*, 2nd ed., p. 76.

38. Joseph B. Vaughn and Victor E. Kappeler, "The Denial of Bail: Pre-Trial Preventive Detention," *Criminal Justice Research Bulletin*, Vol. 3, no. 6 (Huntsville, Tex.: Sam Houston State University, 1987), p. 1.

39. M. A. Toborg, *Pretrial Release: A National Evaluation of Practice and Outcomes* (McLean, Va.: Lazar Institute, 1981).

40. Bureau of Justice Statistics, *Report to the Nation on Crime and Justice*, 2nd ed., p. 77.

41. Brian A. Reaves and Jacob Perez, "Pretrial Release of Felony Defendants, 1992," (Washington, D.C.: Bureau of Justice Statistics, November 1994).

42. Brian A. Reaves, "Pretrial Release of Federal Felony Defendants," (Washington, D.C.: Bureau of Justice Statistics, February 1994).

43. Donald E. Pryor and Walter F. Smith, "Significant Research Findings Concerning Pretrial Release," *Pretrial Issues*, Vol. 4, no. 1 (Washington, D.C.: Pretrial Services Resource Center, February 1982).

44. Bureau of Justice Statistics, *Report to the Nation on Crime and Justice*, 2nd ed., p. 77.

45. According to Vaughn and Kappeler, "The Denial of Bail," the first such legislation was the 1970 District of Columbia Court Reform and Criminal Procedure Act.

46. Ibid.

47. Bail Reform Act of 1984, 18 U.S.C. 3142(e).

48. *U.S.* v. *Montalvo-Murillo*, 495 U.S. 711 (1990).

49. *U.S.* v. *Montalvo-Murillo* (1990), online syllabus.

50. *U.S.* v. *Hazzard*, 35 CrL 2217 (1984).

51. See, for example, *U.S.* v. *Motamedi*, 37 CrL 2394, CA 9 (1985).

52. Federal Rules of Criminal Procedure 5.1(a).

53. A few states now have laws that permit the defendant to appear before the grand jury.

54. *Kercheval* v. *U.S.*, 274 U.S. 220, 223, 47 S.Ct. 582, 583 (1927); *Boykin* v. *Alabama*, 395 U.S. 238 (1969); and *Dickerson* v. *New Banner Institute, Inc.*, 460 U.S. 103 (1983).

55. The National Advisory Commission on Criminal Justice Standards and Goals, *Courts* (Washington, D.C.: U.S. Government Printing Office, 1973), p. 46.

56. *Brady* v. *United States*, 397 U.S. 742 (1970).

57. *Santobello* v. *New York*, 404 U.S. 257 (1971).

58. Ibid.

59. U.S. Department of Justice, Bureau of Justice Statistics, *The Prosecution of Felony Arrests* (Washington, D.C.: U.S. Government Printing Office, 1983).

60. Barbara Borland, Wayne Logan, Ronald Sones, and William Martin, *The Prosecution of Felony Arrests*, 1982 (Washington, D.C.: U.S. Government Printing Office, May 1988).

61. *Henderson* v. *Morgan*, 426 U.S. 637 (1976).

62. *Santobello* v. *New York*.

63. *Mabry* v. *Johnson*, 467 U.S. 504 (1984).

64. *U.S.* v. *Baldacchino*, 762 F.2d 170 (1st Cir. 1985); *U.S.* v. *Reardon*, 787 F.2d 512 (10th Cir. 1986); and *U.S.* v. *Donahey*, 529 F.2d 831 (11th Cir. 1976).

65. For a now classic discussion of such considerations, see David Sudnow, "Normal Crimes: Sociological Features of the Penal Code in a Public Defender Office," *Social Problems*, Vol. 12 (1965), p. 255.

66. *Federal Rules of Criminal Procedure*, No. 11.

67. "Nationline," *USA Today*, March 17, 1992, p. 3A, and "Man Volunteers Castration over Prison for Raping Child," *Fayetteville Observer-Times* (North Carolina), March 7, 1992, p. 1A.

—Photo by John Youngbear, courtesy of AP/Wide World Photos

CHAPTER 8

The Courtroom Work Group *and the* Criminal Trial

*T*o hear patiently, to weigh deliberately and dispassionately, and to decide impartially; these are the chief duties of a judge.

—ALBERT PIKE (1809–1891)

*I*n civil jurisprudence it too often happens that there is so much law, there is no room for justice, and the claimant expires of wrong, in the midst of right, as mariners die of thirst in the midst of water.

—CHARLES CALEB COLTON (1780–1832)

*I*n all criminal prosecutions the accused shall enjoy the right to a speedy and public trial, by an impartial jury...and to be informed of the nature and cause of the accusation; to be confronted with the witnesses against him; to have compulsory process for obtaining witnesses in his favor; and to have the assistance of counsel for his defense.

—SIXTH AMENDMENT TO THE U.S. CONSTITUTION

KEY CONCEPTS

courtroom work group	prosecuting attorney	verdict
prosecutorial discretion	defense counsel	public defender
adversarial system	bailiff	expert witness
lay witness	subpoena	victim assistance program
juror	rules of evidence	Speedy Trial Act
change of venue	jury selection	peremptory challenge
opening statement	sequestered jury	evidence
direct evidence	circumstantial evidence	perjured testimony
testimony	hearsay	hearsay rule
closing argument	judge	

KEY CASES

Edmonson v. *Leesville Concrete Co., Inc.*	*Michigan* v. *Lucas*	*Idaho* v. *Wright*
Burns v. *Reed*	*Ohio* v. *Powers*	*Coy* v. *Iowa*
Mu'Min v. *Virginia*	*Demarest* v. *Manspeaker*	*Imbler* v. *Pachtman*
Crosby v. *U.S.*	*Maryland* v. *Craig*	*White* v. *Illinois*
Doggett v. *U.S.*	*Zafiro* v. *U.S.*	*Fex* v. *Michigan*
	Georgia v. *McCollum*	

Introduction

"Every day, as he ambles through the cobwebbed halls of the New Orleans criminal court building, public defender Richard Teisser feels he violates his clients' constitutional rights"[1] to legal counsel. Teisser, an attorney who is paid just $18,500 per year by the state of Louisiana, has so many clients and so few resources he believes that he can't possibly do them all justice. To bring his plight before the public, Teisser, in the spring of 1993, filed suit against his own office. A local judge agreed, finding Louisiana's system of indigent defense unconstitutional. Louisiana Governor Edwin Edwards, commenting on the ruling, said that underfunding of public defenders is not limited to New Orleans, but is "a state problem and a national problem."[2]

Were it not for people like Richard Teisser, few would be aware of the problems facing our nation's courts. To the public eye, criminal trials generally appear to be well managed and even dramatic events. Like plays on a stage, they involve many participants playing many different roles. Parties to the event can be divided into two categories: professionals and outsiders. The professional category includes official courtroom actors, well versed in criminal trial practice, who set the stage for and conduct the business of the court. Judges, prosecuting attorneys, defense attorneys, public defenders, and others who earn a living serving the court fall into this category. Professional courtroom actors are also called the **courtroom work group**. Some writers have pointed out that, aside from statutory requirements and ethical considerations, courtroom interaction between professionals involves an implicit recognition of informal rules of civility, cooperation, and shared goals. Hence, even within the adversarial framework of a criminal trial, the courtroom work group is dedicated to bringing the procedure to a successful close.[3]

In contrast, outsiders are generally unfamiliar with courtroom organization and trial procedure. Most outsiders visit the court temporarily to provide information or to serve as members of the jury. Similarly, because of their temporary involvement with the court, defendant and victim are also outsiders, even though they may have more of a personal investment in the outcome of the trial than anyone else.

This chapter continues to examine trial court activities, building on the pretrial process described in the last chapter. In order to place the trial process within its human context, however, we first discuss the various roles of the many participants in a criminal trial.

The Courtroom Work Group: Professional Courtroom Actors

The Judge

Role of the Judge

The trial judge is probably the figure most closely associated with a criminal trial. The **judge** has the primary duty of ensuring justice. In the courtroom, the judge holds ultimate authority, ruling on matters of law, weighing objections from either side, deciding on the admissibility of evidence, and disciplining anyone who challenges the order of the court. In most jurisdictions, judges also sentence offenders after a verdict has been returned, and in some states, judges serve to decide guilt or innocence for defendants who waive a jury trial.

Courtroom Work Group. Professional courtroom actors, including judges, prosecuting attorneys, defense attorneys, public defenders, and others who earn a living serving the court.

Judge. An elected or appointed public official who presides over a court of law and who is authorized to hear and sometimes to decide cases and to conduct trials.

Each state jurisdiction normally has a chief judge who, besides serving on the bench as a trial judge, must manage the court system. Management includes hiring staff, scheduling sessions of court, ensuring the adequate training of subordinate judges, and coordinating activities with other courtroom actors. Chief judges usually assume their positions by virtue of seniority and rarely have any formal training in management. Hence, the managerial effectiveness of a chief judge is often a matter of personality and dedication more than anything else.

Judicial Selection

As we discussed in Chapter 7, at the federal level, judges are nominated by the president of the United States and take their place on the bench only after confirmation by the Senate. At the state level, things work somewhat differently. Depending on the jurisdiction, state judgeships are won either through popular election or political (usually gubernatorial) appointment. The processes involved in judicial selection at the state level are set by law.

Both judicial election and appointment have been criticized for the fact that each system allows politics to enter the judicial arena—although in somewhat different ways. Under the appointment system, judicial hopefuls must be in favor with incumbent politicians in order to receive appointments. Under the elective system, judicial candidates must receive the endorsement of their parties, generate contributions, and manage an effective campaign. Because partisan politics plays a role in both systems, critics have claimed that sitting judges can rarely be as neutral as they should be. They carry to the bench with them campaign promises, personal indebtedness, and possible political agendas.

To counter some of these problems, a number of states have adopted what has come to be called the Missouri Plan[4] (or the Missouri Bar Plan) for judicial selection. The Missouri Plan combines elements of both election and appointment. It requires candidates for judicial vacancies to undergo screening by a nonpartisan state judicial nominating committee. Candidates selected by the committee are reviewed by an arm of the governor's office which selects a final list of names for appointment. Incumbent judges must face the electorate after a specified term in office. They then run unopposed, in nonpartisan elections, in which only their records may be considered. Voters have the choice of allowing a judge to continue in office or asking that another be appointed to take his or her place. Because the Missouri Plan provides for periodic public review of judicial performance, it is also called the merit plan of judicial selection.

 ## Theory into Practice: The Functions of the Trial Judge

The American Bar Association Standards for Criminal Justice set forth the following duties of the trial judge:

6-1.1 (a) General responsibility of the trial judge.

(a) The trial judge has the responsibility for safeguarding both the rights of the accused and the interests of the public in the administration of criminal justice. The adversary nature of the proceedings does not relieve the trial judge of the obligations of raising on his or her initiative, at all appropriate times and in an appropriate manner, matters which may significantly promote a just determination of the trial. The only purpose of a criminal trial is to determine whether the prosecution has established the guilt of the accused as required by law, and the trial judge should not allow the proceedings to be used for any other purpose.

SOURCE: *ABA Standards for Criminal Justice*, 2nd. ed. (1980). Reprinted with permission. Copies of this publication are available from the American Bar Association, 750 North Lake Shore Drive, Chicago, IL 60611.

Qualifications of Judges

Only two decades ago, many states did not require any special training, education, or other qualifications for judges. Anyone (even someone without a law degree) who won election or was appointed could assume a judgeship. Today, however, almost all states require that judges in appellate and general jurisdiction courts hold a law degree, be licensed attorneys, and be members of their state bar associations. Many states also require newly elected judges to attend state-sponsored training sessions dealing with subjects such as courtroom procedure, evidence, dispute resolution, judicial writing, administrative record keeping, and ethics.

Whereas most states provide instruction to meet the needs of trial judges, other organizations also provide specialized training. The National Judicial College, located on the campus of the University of Nevada at Reno, is one such institution. The National Judicial College was established in 1963 by the Joint Committee for the Effective Administration of Justice chaired by Justice Tom C. Clark of the U.S. Supreme Court.[5] Courses offered by the college attract more than 1,500 judges every year.

Lower court judges such as justices of the peace, local magistrates, and "district" court judges in some parts of the United States may still be elected without educational and other professional requirements. Today, in 43 states, some 1,300 nonlawyer judges are serving in mostly rural courts of limited jurisdiction.[6] In New York, for example, lay judges hear around 3 million cases each year and collect $45 million in fines.[7] The majority of cases which come before New York lay judges involve alleged traffic violations although they may also include misdemeanors, small claims actions, and some civil cases (of up to $3,000). Some authors have defended lay judges as being closer to the citizenry in their understanding of justice.[8] Even so, in most areas, there is a tendency to eliminate lay judges. States which continue to use lay judges in lower courts do require that candidates for judgeships not have criminal records and that most attend special training sessions if elected.

Judicial Misconduct

Occasionally, judges overstep the limits of their authority or commit social transgressions. Poor judgment may result from bad taste or archaic attitudes, as in the case of a lower court judge who kept telling a woman defense counselor that she was too pretty to be a lawyer and should be at home having children. Other sexist comments

Judge Lance Ito presiding over the O. J. Simpson double-murder case. Ito proved to be an insightful and no-nonsense judge who also became the focus of many discussions about the judicial role and our expectations about what makes an effective judge. Photo by Nick Ut, Pool; courtesy of AP/Wide World Photos.

resulted in calls for that judge's dismissal. Many states have judicial conduct commissions to investigate allegations of impropriety against judges. In 1995, for example, Pennsylvania district justice Bradford C. Timbers was suspended by the state's Judicial Conduct Board after being charged with "trying to fix a friend's speeding ticket, slapping a female co-worker's buttocks, and drinking alcohol on the job."[9] The 36-year-old judge was also charged with failing to perform his duties properly.

Federal law provides a mechanism for administratively dealing with complaints about judicial conduct. The Judicial Councils Reform and Judicial Conduct and Disability Act, passed by Congress in 1980, specifies the precise mechanisms which can be employed to register complaints against federal judges and, in serious cases, to begin the process of impeachment—or forced removal from the bench.

In 1987, for example, Walter L. Nixon, Jr., a chief judge of the U.S. District Court for the Southern District of Mississippi, was convicted by a jury of two counts of making false statements before a federal grand jury and sentenced to prison.[10] In 1993, his appeal to the U.S. Supreme Court was denied.[11]

The Prosecuting Attorney

The **prosecuting attorney**, called variously the solicitor, district attorney, state's attorney, chief prosecutor, and so on, is responsible for presenting the state's case against the defendant. Technically speaking, the prosecuting attorney is the primary representative of the people by virtue of the belief that violations of the criminal law are an affront to the public. Except for federal prosecutors (called U.S. attorneys) and solicitors in five states, prosecutors are elected and generally serve four-year terms with the possibility of continuing by reelection.[12] Widespread criminal conspiracies, whether they involve government officials or private citizens, may require the services of a special prosecutor whose office can spend the time and resources needed for efficient prosecution.[13]

In many jurisdictions, because the job of prosecutor entails too many duties for one person to handle, most prosecutors supervise a staff of assistant district attorneys who do most in-court work. Assistants are trained attorneys, usually hired directly by the chief prosecutor, and licensed to practice law in the states where they work. Approximately 2,300 chief prosecutors, assisted by 20,000 deputy attorneys, serve the nation's counties and independent cities.[14]

Another prosecutorial role has traditionally been that of quasi-legal advisor to local police departments. Because prosecutors are sensitive to the kinds of information needed for conviction, they may help guide police investigations and will exhort detectives to identify usable witnesses, uncover additional evidence, and the like. This role is limited, however. Police departments are independent of the administrative authority of the prosecutor, and cooperation between them, although based on the common goal of conviction, is purely voluntary.[15]

Once trial begins, the job of the prosecutor is to vigorously present the state's case against the defendant. Prosecutors introduce evidence against the accused, steer the testimony of witnesses "for the people," and argue in favor of conviction. Since defendants are presumed innocent until proven guilty, the burden of demonstrating guilt beyond a reasonable doubt rests with the prosecutor.

Prosecutorial Discretion

Prosecutors occupy a unique position in the nation's criminal justice system by virtue of the considerable **prosecutorial discretion** they exercise. As Justice Robert H. Jackson noted in 1940, "the prosecutor has more control over life, liberty, and reputation than any other person in America."[16] Before a case comes to trial, prosecutors may decide to accept a plea bargain, divert suspects to a public or private social service agency, or dismiss the case entirely for lack of evidence or for a variety for other reasons. Various studies have found that from one-third to one-half of all felony cases

Prosecutor. (Also called District Attorney or State's Attorney) An elected or appointed public official, licensed to practice law, whose job it is to conduct criminal proceedings on behalf of the state or the people against an accused person.

Prosecutorial Discretion. The decision-making power of prosecutors based on the wide range of choices available to them in the handling of criminal defendants, the scheduling of cases for trial, the acceptance of bargained pleas, and so on. The most important form of prosecutorial discretion lies in the power to charge, or not to charge, a person with an offense.

are dismissed by the prosecution prior to trial or before a plea bargain is made.[17] Prosecutors also play a significant role before grand juries. States which use the grand jury system depend on prosecutors to bring evidence before the grand jury and to be effective in seeing indictments returned against suspects.

In preparation for trial, the prosecutor decides what charges are to be brought against the defendant, examines the strength of incriminating evidence, and decides what witnesses to call. Two important Supreme Court decisions have held that, in effect, it is the duty of prosecutors to assist the defense in building its case, by making available any evidence in their possession. The first case, that of *Brady* v. *Maryland*,[18] was decided in 1963. In *Brady*, the Court held that the prosecution is required to disclose to the defense exculpatory evidence that directly relates to claims of either guilt or innocence. A second, and more recent, case is that of *U.S.* v. *Bagley*,[19] decided in 1985. In *Bagley*, the Court ruled that the prosecution must disclose any evidence that the defense requests. The Court reasoned that to withhold evidence, even when it does not relate directly to issues of guilt or innocence, may mislead the defense into thinking that such evidence does not exist.

One special decision the prosecutor makes concerns the filing of separate or multiple charges. The decision to try a defendant simultaneously on multiple charges can allow for the presentation of a considerable amount of evidence and permit an in-court demonstration of a complete sequence of criminal events. Such a strategy has a practical side as well; it saves time and money by substituting one trial for what might otherwise be any number of trials if each charge were to be brought separately before the court. From the prosecutor's point of view, however, trying the charges one at a time carries the advantage of allowing for another trial on a new charge if a "not guilty" verdict is returned the first time.

The activities of the prosecutor do not end with a finding of guilt or innocence. Following conviction, prosecutors usually are allowed to make sentencing recommendations to the judge. They can be expected to argue that aggravating factors (which we will discuss in Chapter 9), prior criminal record, or especially heinous qualities of the offense in question call for strict punishment. When convicted defendants appeal, prosecutors may need to defend their own actions, and to argue, in briefs filed with appellate courts, that convictions were properly obtained. Most jurisdictions also allow prosecutors to make recommendations when defendants they have convicted are being considered for parole or early release from prison.

Until recently, it has generally been held that prosecutors enjoyed much the same kind of immunity against liability in the exercise of their official duties that judges do. The 1976 Supreme Court case of *Imbler* v. *Pachtman*[20] provided the basis for such thinking with its ruling that "state prosecutors are absolutely immune from liability...for their conduct in initiating a prosecution and in presenting the State's case." However, the Court, in the 1991 case of *Burns* v. *Reed*,[21] held that "[a] state prosecuting attorney is absolutely immune from liability for damages...for participating in a probable cause hearing, but not for giving legal advice to the police." The *Burns* case involved Cathy Burns of Muncie, Indiana, who allegedly shot her sleeping sons while laboring under a multiple personality disorder. In order to explore the possibility of multiple personality further, the police asked the prosecuting attorney if it would be appropriate for them to hypnotize the defendant. The prosecutor agreed that hypnosis would be a permissible avenue for investigation, and the suspect confessed to the murders while hypnotized. She later alleged in her complaint to the Supreme Court "that [the prosecuting attorney] knew or should have known that hypnotically induced testimony was inadmissible"[22] at trial.

The Abuse of Discretion

Because of the large amount of discretion prosecutors wield, there is considerable potential for them to abuse it. Discretionary decisions not to prosecute friends or political cronies, or to accept guilty pleas to drastically reduced charges for personal considerations, are always inappropriate and potentially dangerous possibilities. On the other hand, overzealous prosecution by district attorneys seeking heightened visibility in order to support grand political ambitions can be another source of abuse. Administrative decisions, such as case scheduling, which can wreak havoc with the personal lives of defendants and the professional lives of defense attorneys, can also be used by prosecutors to harass defendants into pleading guilty. Some forms of abuse may be unconscious. At least one study suggests that some prosecutors may tend toward leniency for female defendants but tend to discriminate against minorities in deciding whether or not to prosecute.[23]

Although the electorate are the final authority to which prosecutors must answer, gross misconduct by prosecutors may be addressed by the state supreme court or by the state attorney general's office. Short of criminal misconduct, however, most of the options available to either the court or the attorney general are limited.

The Prosecutor's Professional Responsibility

As members of the legal profession, prosecutors are subject to the American Bar Association's (ABA) Code of Professional Responsibility. Serious violations of the code may result in a prosecutor being disbarred from the practice of law. The ABA Standard for Criminal Justice 3-1.1 describes the prosecutor's duty this way: "The duty of the prosecutor is to seek justice, not merely to convict." Hence, a prosecutor is barred by the standards of the legal profession from advocating any fact or position which he or she knows is untrue.

Defense Counsel

Role of the Defense Attorney

The **defense counsel** is a trained lawyer who may specialize in the practice of criminal law. The task of the defense attorney is to represent the accused as soon as possible after arrest and to ensure that the civil rights of the defendant are not violated through processing by the criminal justice system. Other duties of the defense counsel include testing the strength of the prosecution's case, being involved in plea negotiations, and preparing an adequate defense to be used at trial. In the preparation of a defense, criminal lawyers may enlist private detectives, experts, witnesses to the crime, and character witnesses. Some will perform aspects of the role of private detective or of investigator themselves. They will also review relevant court precedents in order to determine what the best defense strategy might be.

Defense preparation may involve intense communications between lawyer and defendant. Such discussions are recognized as privileged communications which are protected under the umbrella of lawyer-client confidentiality. In other words, lawyers cannot be compelled to reveal information which their client has confided in them.

If their client is found guilty, defense attorneys will be involved in arguments at sentencing, may be asked to file an appeal, and will probably counsel the defendant and the defendant's family on what civil matters (payment of debts, release from contractual obligations, and so on) may need to be arranged after sentence is imposed. Hence, the role of defense attorney encompasses many aspects, including attorney, negotiator, confidant, family and personal counselor, social worker, investigator, and, as we shall see, bill collector.

The Criminal Lawyer

Three major categories of defense attorneys assist defendants in the United States: (1) private attorneys, usually referred to as "criminal lawyers," (2) court-appointed counsel, and (3) public defenders.

Defense Counsel. (Also called Defense Attorney) A licensed trial lawyer, hired or appointed to conduct the legal defense of an individual accused of a crime and to represent him or her before a court of law.

Private attorneys (also called retained counsel) either have their own legal practices or work for law firms in which they may be partners or employees. As those who have had to hire defense attorneys know, the fees of private attorneys can be high. Most privately retained criminal lawyers charge in the range of $100 to $200 per hour. Included in their bill is the time it takes to prepare for a case as well as time spent in the courtroom. High-powered criminal defense attorneys who have established a regional or national reputation for successfully defending their clients can be far more expensive still. A few such attorneys, such as Alan Dershowitz, Robert Shapiro, F. Lee Bailey, Johnnie Cochran (who was catapulted to fame during the O. J. Simpson trial), and Stephen Jones (who defended Timothy McVeigh), have become household names by virtue of their association with famous defendants and well-publicized trials.

Although the job of a criminal lawyer may appear glamorous, few law students actually choose to specialize in criminal law. Monetary incentives attract most to contract law or civil law, where the litigation of major suits can result in healthy financial rewards. Some criminal defense attorneys begin their careers immediately following law school, whereas others seek to gain experience working as assistant district attorneys or assistant public defenders for a number of years before going into private practice. As one can imagine, the collection of fees can be a significant source of difficulty for criminal lawyers. Many defendants are poor. Those who aren't are often reluctant to pay what may seem to them to be an exorbitant fee, and woe be it to the defense attorney whose client is convicted before the fee has been paid!

CRIMINAL DEFENSE OF THE POOR

In 1990, state and local governments spent $1.3 billion to provide legal representation for criminal defendants unable to afford their own—and more than 80 percent of all defendants in felony cases depend on court-appointed attorneys or **public defenders** to represent them.[24] A series of U.S. Supreme Court decisions have

A heated exchange between prosecutor Marcia Clark and defense attorney F. Lee Bailey during the O. J. Simpson trial. "I do not appreciate being called a liar in any court!" Bailey told the judge. The Simpson trial gave the public a bird's-eye view of the adversarial nature of our criminal justice system. Photo by AFP, courtesy of Bettmann.

guaranteed that defendants unable to pay for private criminal defense attorneys will receive adequate representation at all stages of criminal justice processing.

In *Powell* v. *Alabama* (1932),[25] the Court held that the Fourteenth Amendment required state courts to appoint counsel for defendants in capital cases who were unable to afford their own. In 1938, in *Johnson* v. *Zerbst*,[26] the Court established the right of indigent defendants to receive the assistance of appointed counsel in all criminal proceedings in federal courts. The 1963 case of *Gideon* v. *Wainwright*[27] extended the right to appointed counsel in state courts to all indigent defendants charged with a felony. *Argersinger* v. *Hamlin* (1972)[28] saw the Court require adequate legal representation for anyone facing a potential sentence of imprisonment. Juveniles charged with delinquent acts were granted the right to appointed counsel in the case of *In re Gault* (1967).[29]

States have responded to the federal mandate for indigent defense in a number of ways. Most now use one of three systems to deliver legal services to criminal defendants who are unable to afford their own: (1) court-assigned counsel, (2) public defenders, and (3) contractual arrangements. Most such systems are administered at the county level, although funding arrangements may involve state, county, and municipal monies.

Court-appointed defense attorneys, whose fees are paid at a rate set by the state or local government, compose the most widely used system of indigent defense. Such defenders, also called assigned counsel, are usually drawn from a roster of all practicing criminal attorneys within the jurisdiction of the trial court.

One problem with assigned counsel concerns degree of effort. Although most attorneys assigned by the court to indigent defense probably take their jobs seriously, some feel only a loose commitment to their clients. Paying clients, in their eyes, deserve better service and are apt to get it. The nationwide average cost per case for indigent defense in a recent year was $223 although the figure varied from a low of $63 in Arkansas to a high of $540 in New Jersey.[30]

The second type of indigent defense, the public defender program (such as the one described in the opening paragraph of this chapter), depends on full-time salaried staff. Staff members include defense attorneys, defense investigators, and office personnel. Defense investigators gather information in support of the defense effort. They may interview friends, family members, and employers of the accused, with an eye toward effective defense. Public defender programs have shown some increase in popularity in recent years, with approximately 37 percent of counties nationwide now funding them. Critics charge that public defenders, because they are government employees, are not sufficiently independent from prosecutors and judges. For the same reason, clients may be suspicious of public defenders, viewing them as state functionaries. Finally, the huge caseloads typical of public defender's offices create pressures toward an excessive use of plea bargaining.

A third type of indigent defense, contract attorney programs, arrange with local criminal lawyers to provide for indigent defense on a contractual basis. Individual attorneys, local bar associations, and multipartner law firms may all be used to provide for such arranged services. Contract defense programs are the least widely used form of indigent defense at present though their numbers are growing.

Critics of the current system of indigent defense point out that the system is woefully underfunded. "In 1990," for example, "states spent $1.3 billion to prosecute individuals, but only $548 million on indigent defense; local governments spent $2.7 billion versus only $788 million; and the federal government $1.6 billion versus $408 million."[31] Overall, only 2.3 percent of monies spent on criminal justice activities goes to pay for indigent defense—an amount many consider too small.[32] As a consequence of such limited funding, many public defender's offices employ what critics call a "plead-'em-and-speed-'em through" strategy, often involving a heavy use of plea bargaining and initial meetings with clients in courtrooms as trials are about to begin. Mary Broderick of the National Legal Aid and Defender Association says, "We aren't being given the

Public Defender. An attorney employed by a government agency or subagency, or by a private organization under contract to a unit of government, for the purpose of providing defense services to indigents.

same weapons....It's like trying to deal with smart bombs when all you've got is a couple of cap pistols."[33]

Of course, defendants need not accept any assigned counsel. Defendants who elect to do so may waive their right to an attorney and undertake their own defense—a right held to be inherent in the Sixth Amendment to the U.S. Constitution by the U.S. Supreme Court in the 1975 case of *Faretta v. California*.[34] The most famous instance of self-representation in recent years was probably the 1995 trial of Long Island Railroad commuter train shooter, Colin Ferguson, which we discuss later in this chapter.

Defendants who are not pleased with the lawyer appointed to defend them are in a somewhat different situation. They may request, through the court, that a new lawyer be assigned to them. However, unless there is clear reason for reassignment, such as an obvious personality conflict between defendant and attorney, few judges are likely to honor a request of this sort. Short of obvious difficulties, most judges will trust in the professionalism of appointed counselors.

The Ethics of Defense

As we have discussed, at trial the job of defense counsel is to prepare and offer a vigorous defense on behalf of the accused. A proper defense often involves the presentation of evidence and the examination of witnesses, all of which require careful thought and planning. Good attorneys, like quality craftspeople everywhere, may find themselves emotionally committed to the outcome of trials in which they are involved. Beyond the immediacy of a given trial, attorneys also realize that their reputations can be influenced by lay perceptions of their performance and that their careers and personal financial success depend on consistently "winning" in the courtroom.

The nature of the adversarial process, fed by the emotions of the participants, conspires with the often privileged and extensive knowledge that defense attorneys have about a case, to tempt the professional ethics of some counselors. Because the defense counsel may often know more about the guilt or innocence of the

---

Theory into Practice: *Gideon* v. *Wainwright* and Indigent Defense

In the 1963 case of *Gideon v. Wainwright*, the U.S. Supreme Court extended the right to legal counsel to indigent defendants charged with a criminal offense. The reasoning of the Court is well summarized in this excerpt from the majority opinion written by Justice Hugo Black:

> ...Governments, both state and federal, quite properly spend vast sums of money to establish machinery to try defendants accused of crime. Lawyers to prosecute are everywhere deemed essential to protect the public's interest in an orderly society. Similarly, there are few defendants charged with crime, few indeed, who fail to hire the best lawyers they can get to prepare and present their defenses. That government hires lawyers to prosecute and defendants who have the money hire lawyers to defend are the strongest indications of the widespread belief that lawyers in criminal courts are necessities, not luxuries. The right of one

charged with crime to counsel may not be deemed fundamental and essential to fair trials in some countries, but it is in ours. From the very beginning, our state and national constitutions and laws have laid great emphasis on procedural and substantive safeguards designed to assure fair trials before impartial tribunals in which every defendant stands equal before the law. This noble ideal cannot be realized if the poor man charged with crime has to face his accusers without a lawyer to assist him.

QUESTIONS FOR DISCUSSION

1. Do you agree with the Court that all indigent defendants should have the opportunity to have counsel appointed to represent them? Why or why not?

2. What would our system of criminal justice be like if court-appointed attorneys were not available to poor defendants?

---

defendant than anyone else prior to trial, the defense role is one which is carefully prescribed by ethical and procedural considerations. Attorneys violate both law and the standards of their own profession if they knowingly misrepresent themselves or their clients.

To help attorneys know what is expected of them, ethical standards abound. Four main groups of standards, each drafted by the American Bar Association, are especially applicable to defense attorneys:

Canons of Professional Ethics
Model Code of Professional Responsibility
Model Rules of Professional Conduct
Standards for Criminal Justice

Each set of standards is revised periodically. The ABA Standard for Criminal Justice, Number 4-1.1, reads in part:

…(c) The defense lawyer, in common with all members of the bar, is subject to standards of conduct stated in statutes, rules, decisions of courts, and codes, canons, or other standards of professional conduct. The defense lawyer has no duty to execute any directive of the accused which does not comport with law or such standards. The defense lawyer is the professional representative of the accused, not the accused's alter ego…

…(d) It is unprofessional conduct for a lawyer intentionally to misrepresent matters of fact or law to the court…

…(e) It is the duty of every lawyer to know the standards of professional conduct as defined in codes and canons of the legal profession and in this chapter. The functions and duties of defense counsel are governed by such standards whether defense counsel is assigned or privately retained…

Even with these directives, however, defense attorneys are under no obligation to reveal information obtained from a client without the client's permission. Sometimes, however, they may go too far. In 1992, Minneapolis multimillionaire Russell Lund, Jr., was arrested and charged with the murder of his estranged wife and her boyfriend—a former Iowa state senator. Following the murder, attention shifted to the activities of Lund's attorneys who, police claim, waited until the day after the killings before reporting the shooting, hired a private detective who may have destroyed some evidence, and checked Mr. Lund into a private psychiatric facility under a different name without telling police where he was—all activities which may have been both unethical and illegal.[35]

In 1986, the Supreme Court case of *Nix* v. *Whiteside*[36] clarified the duty of lawyers to reveal known instances of client perjury. The *Nix* case came to the Court upon the complaint of the defendant, Whiteside, who claimed that he was deprived of the assistance of effective counsel during a murder trial because his lawyer would not allow him to testify untruthfully. Whiteside wanted to testify that he had seen a gun or something metallic in his victim's hand before killing him. Before trial, however, Whiteside admitted to his lawyer that he had actually seen no weapon, but he believed that to testify to the truth would result in his conviction. The lawyer told Whiteside that, as a professional counselor, he would be forced to challenge Whiteside's false testimony, if it occurred, and to explain to the court the facts as he knew them. On the stand, Whiteside said only that he thought the victim was reaching for a gun, but did not claim to have seen one. He was found guilty of second-degree murder and appealed to the Supreme Court, on the claim of inadequate representation.

The Court, recounting the development of ethical codes in the legal profession, held that a lawyer's duty to a client "is limited to legitimate, lawful conduct compatible with the very nature of a trial as a search for truth.…counsel is precluded from taking steps or in any way assisting the client in presenting false evidence or otherwise violating the law."[37]

Theory into Practice: Court-Appointed Counsel and the Oklahoma City Bombing

When terrorist bombers struck the Alfred P. Murrah Federal Building in Oklahoma City in the spring of 1995, they killed 168 people (19 of them children in a day-care center on the building's first floor) and highlighted two important issues facing court-appointed criminal defense counsel: whether or not attorneys can be required to defend unpopular suspects, and whether unpopular and widely despised clients can get a fair trial even if they do defend them.

Timothy McVeigh, the first defendant arrested in the Oklahoma City case, and a former army munitions expert, seemed guilty well before trial. For one thing, McVeigh had rented the truck used to deliver the bomb to the explosion site, even using his own name and driver's license when filling out the rental forms. Immediately after the bombing, McVeigh was arrested fleeing the scene in an old car with a missing license plate. McVeigh quickly became despised and hated in the public eye—a living symbol of a cowardly attack which killed many innocent people. As one writer observed, soon after McVeigh's arrest: "Across the ideological spectrum, Americans are united in hatred of him."[1]

The first two lawyers appointed to represent McVeigh were assigned 24-hour armed guards after one of them received death threats. John W. Coyle III, McVeigh's first court-appointed counsel, and Susan Otto, a public defender assigned to defend McVeigh, asked to be removed from the case because they had friends among those killed in the bombing. In addition, said Coyle, "It's too much to ask any grand juror or trial juror to be fair in a trial like this."[2] Local residents, those most likely to be called to jury duty, knew many of the victims or had friends who knew them.

Finding a lawyer elsewhere was equally difficult. Miami attorney Roy Black, who successfully defended William Kennedy Smith against rape charges, turned down the case, saying he didn't think he could mount an effective defense because of his personal feelings about the crime. "Our system would not operate unless lawyers are willing to undertake the representation of the most hated and despised person," Black said.[3] "But," he added, "I just think of that fireman carrying out that baby," referring to a widely published photograph which came to symbolize the horrors of the case.

The Sixth Amendment guarantees every criminal defendant the right to counsel, but not the right to any particular lawyer. Lawyers can and do turn down cases but may do so legally only if they can prove that there would be a genuine conflict of interest if they were to accept the case.

Finally, after a nationwide poll of candidates who might have defended McVeigh, attorney Stephen Jones was appointed by the court and took the job.[4] "I recognize that I am not the most popular person in Oklahoma," Jones said, but added: "We honor the memory of the victims by granting the accused effective assistance of counsel, due process, a vigorous defense and trial by jury, not hysteria."[5]

Comparing the McVeigh case with that of O. J. Simpson, one writer observed: "The test of our [criminal justice] system is not whether a rich celebrity can get justice in America, but whether a hated fanatic can."[6] Susan Estrich, a University of Southern California professor, explains it this way: "The adversary system of justice is frustrating and inefficient. But it is still the best way to get to the truth, particularly when we think we already know it. Only if the state's case is subjected to painstaking scrutiny can we be certain enough of guilt to take a man's life." Estrich adds: "The job of defending a hated man should win the respect of the community, not its contempt. Not everyone can do it. But there is no more honorable task for an attorney."[7]

Some were more pragmatic in their assessment of the situation. "McVeigh's problem is not that he's despicable; it's that he's despicable and broke," said New York lawyer Ronald Kuby.[8] "If he had money," Kuby claimed, "lawyers would be lined up outside his jail cell...thumping their chests about how he deserves representation...for their usual rate of X-hundred dollars an hour."

Even if McVeigh and other defendants can get helpful and unbiased counsel to represent them, the question still remains of whether they can get a fair trial. Given the impact the bombing has had on the American psyche and continuing media coverage of the incident, some critics charge that Timothy McVeigh will inevitably be found guilty. "The challenge to the legal system becomes monumental in an age of mass communications,"[9] says Ron Carlson, a professor at the University of Georgia. "The media leave no stone unturned and already they have told us things about McVeigh that would never be admitted into evidence at the trial," he adds.

Legal experts have suggested McVeigh might get both a fair trial and an adequate defense if (1) his trial can be delayed (difficult to do under the federal Speedy Trial Act); (2) a change of venue (perhaps to another state within the 10th federal circuit, although rarely done in federal court), can be arranged; (3) federal

(Continued on next page)

Theory into Practice: Court-Appointed Counsel and the Oklahoma City Bombing—*Continued*

judges order a news ban and restrict the ability of federal prosecutors, police, and defense attorneys to publicly discuss the case, and; (4) members of the jury are carefully and individually selected for their ability to be objective when hearing the evidence.

Even if all that could be arranged, said famed criminal defense attorney William Kunstler, "The law can't cope with this one." Added Kunstler: "If Christ and all the angels testified [McVeigh] was innocent, he would still be found guilty."[10]

QUESTIONS FOR DISCUSSION

1. If you were an attorney, might you have found it difficult to defend Timothy McVeigh? Why or why not?

2. Do you agree with professor Estrich that "The job of defending a hated man should win the respect of the community, not its contempt"? Explain your answer.

1. Susan Estrich, "Fair Trial for McVeigh?" USA Today, April 27, 1995, p. 13A.
2. Tony Mauro, "'The Law Can't Cope' With This Challenge," *USA Today,* April 27, 1995, p. 4A.
Kevin Johnson, "McVeigh's Ex-Lawyer: Suspect Far from 'Cool,'" *USA Today,* May 15, 1995, p. 3A.
3. Saundra Torry, "Lawyers: Finding Counsel for McVeigh a True Test of Legal System," *The Washington Post* online, May 8, 1995.
4. Laurie Asseo, "The Few & the Hated," the Associated Press online, May 12, 1995.
5. Ibid.
6. Estrich, "Fair Trial for McVeigh?"
7. Ibid.
8. Torry, "Lawyers."
9. Tony Mauro, "The Law Can't Cope."
10. Ibid.

Theory into Practice: American Bar Association
Model Code of Professional Responsibility

The intense effort of defense advocacy results, for most criminal trial lawyers, in an emotional and personal investment in the outcome of a case. To strike a balance between zealous and effective advocacy, on the one hand, and just professional conduct within the bounds of the law on the other, the American Bar Association has developed a *Model Code of Professional Responsibility*, which reads in part:

In his representation of a client, a lawyer shall not:

File a suit, assert a position, conduct a defense, delay a trial, or take other action on behalf of his client when he knows or when it is obvious that such action would serve merely to harass or maliciously injure another.

Knowingly advance a claim or defense that is unwarranted under existing law.

Conceal or knowingly fail to disclose that which he is required by law to reveal.

Knowingly use perjured testimony or false evidence.

Knowingly make a false statement of law or fact.

Participate in the creation or preservation of evidence when he knows or it is obvious that the evidence is false.

Counsel or assist his client in conduct that the lawyer knows to be illegal or fraudulent.

SOURCE: Excerpted from American Bar Association, *Model Code of Professional Responsibility*, Disciplinary Rule 7-102. All rights reserved. Copies of this publication are available from Service Center, American Bar Association, 750 North Lake Shore Drive, Chicago, IL 60611.

Bailiff. The court officer whose duties are to keep order in the courtroom and to maintain physical custody of the jury.

The Bailiff   *sheriff officer*

Also called a court officer, the **bailiff**, another member of the professional courtroom work group, is usually an armed law enforcement officer. The job of the bailiff is to ensure order in the courtroom, announce the judge's entry into the

Timothy McVeigh, the first suspect to be arrested in the 1995 Oklahoma City bombing incident. After McVeigh's arrest, a number of court-appointed lawyers refused to defend him, and critics charged that McVeigh could not get a fair trial. Source: Robert Hanashiro, USA Today. Photo by Bob Daemmrich, courtesy of Sygma.

courtroom, call witnesses, and prevent the escape of the accused (if the accused has not been released on bond). The bailiff also supervises the jury when it is sequestered and controls public and media access to the jury. Bailiffs in federal courtrooms are deputy U.S. marshals.

Courtrooms can be dangerous places. In 1993, George Lott was sentenced to die for a courtroom shooting in Tarrant County, Texas, which left two lawyers dead and three other people injured.[38] Lott said he had been frustrated by the court's handling of his divorce and by child molesting charges filed against him by his ex-wife. In a similar case, on May 5, 1992, a man opened fire with two pistols in a St. Louis courtroom during divorce proceedings, killing his wife and wounding her two lawyers and a security officer. The same day, a presiding judge in Grand Forks, North Dakota, was shot to death by a man accused of failing to pay child support.[39]

Local Court Administrators

Many states now employ trial court administrators whose job it is to facilitate the smooth functioning of courts in particular judicial districts or areas. A major impetus toward the hiring of local court administrators came from the 1967 President's Commission on Law Enforcement and Administration of Justice. Examining state courts, the report found a "system that treats defendants who are charged with minor offenses with less dignity and consideration than it treats those who are charged with serious crimes."[40] A few years later, the National Advisory Commission on Criminal Justice Standards and Goals recommended that all courts with five or more judges should create the position of trial court administrator.[41]

Court administrators provide uniform court management, assuming many of the duties previously performed by chief judges, prosecutors, and court clerks. Where court administrators operate, the ultimate authority for running the court still rests with the chief judge. Administrators, however, are able to relieve the judge of many routine and repetitive tasks such as record keeping, scheduling, case flow analysis, personnel administration, space utilization, facilities planning, and budget management. They may also serve to take minutes at meetings of judges and their committees.

Juror management is another area in which trial court administrators are becoming increasingly involved. Juror utilization studies can identify such problems as the overselection of citizens for the jury pool and the reasons for what may be excessive requests to be excluded from jury service. They can also reduce the amount of wasted time jurors spend waiting to be called or empaneled.

Effective court administrators are able to track lengthy cases and identify bottlenecks in court processing. They then suggest strategies to make the administration of justice increasingly efficient for courtroom professionals and more humane for lay participants.

The Court Recorder

Also called the court stenographer or court reporter, the role of the court recorder is to create a record of all that occurs during trial. Accurate records are very important in criminal trial courts because appeals may be based entirely on what went on in the courtroom. Especially significant are all verbal comments made in the courtroom, including testimony, objections, the rulings of the judge, the judge's instructions to the jury, arguments made by attorneys, and the results of conferences between the attorneys and the judge. Occasionally, the judge will rule that a statement should be "stricken from the record" because it is inappropriate or unfounded. The official trial record, often taken on a stenotype machine or audio recorder, may later be transcribed in manuscript form and will become the basis for any appellate review of the trial. Today's court stenographers often employ computer-aided transcription (CAT) software, which translates typed stenographic shorthand into complete and readable transcripts. Court reporters may be members of the National Court Reporters Association, the United States Court Reporters Association, and the Association of Legal Administrators—all of which support the activities of these professionals.

Clerk of Court

The duties of the clerk of court (also known as the county clerk) extend beyond the courtroom. The clerk maintains all records of criminal cases, including all pleas and motions made both before and after the actual trial. The clerk also prepares a jury pool and issues jury summonses and subpoenas witnesses for both the prosecution and defense. During the trial, the clerk (or an assistant) marks physical evidence for identification as instructed by the judge and maintains custody of such evidence. The clerk also swears in witnesses and performs other functions as the judge directs.

Some states allow the clerk limited judicial duties such as the power to issue warrants and to serve as judge of probate—overseeing wills and the administration of estates and handling certain matters relating to persons declared mentally incompetent.[42]

The Expert Witness

Most of the "insiders" we've talked about so far are either employees of the state or have ongoing professional relationships with the court (as in the case of defense counsel). Expert witnesses, however, may or may not have that kind of status although some do. **Expert witnesses** are recognized for specialized skills and knowledge in an established profession or technical area. They must demonstrate their expertise through education, work experience, publications, and awards. By testifying at a trial, they provide an effective way of introducing scientific evidence in such areas as medicine, psychology, ballistics, crime scene analysis, photography, and many other disciplines. An expert witness, like the other courtroom "actors" described in this chapter, is generally a paid professional. And, like all other witnesses, they are subject to cross-examination. Unlike other ("lay") witnesses, they are allowed to express opinions and draw conclusions, but only within their particular area of expertise. Expert witnesses may be veterans of many trials. Some well-known expert witnesses traverse the country and earn very high fees by testifying at one trial after another.

Expert witnesses have played significant roles in many well-known cases. The trial of O. J. Simpson, for example, became a stage for a battle between experts in the analysis of human DNA, and expert testimony in the trial of John Hinckley resulted in a finding of "not guilty by reason of insanity" for the man accused of shooting President Reagan. Similarly, the highly publicized trial of Susan Smith, the South Carolina mother who confessed to the murder by drowning of her two young children, relied heavily on the testimony of psychiatric experts and social workers.

One of the difficulties with expert testimony is that it can be confusing to the jury. Sometimes the trouble is due to the nature of the subject matter, and sometimes to disagreements between the experts themselves. Often, however, it arises from the strict interpretation given to expert testimony by procedural requirements. The difference between medical and legal definitions of insanity, for example, points to a divergence in both history and purpose between the law and science. Courts that attempt to apply criteria such as the McNaughten rule (discussed earlier) in deciding claims of "insanity" often find themselves faced with the testimony of psychiatric experts who refuse even to recognize the word. Such experts may prefer, instead, to speak in terms of psychosis and neurosis—words which have no place in judicial jargon. Legal requirements, because of the uncertainties they create, may pit experts against one another and confuse the jury.

Even so, most authorities agree that expert testimony is usually interpreted by jurors as more trustworthy than other forms of evidence. In a study of scientific evidence, one prosecutor commented that if he had to choose between presenting a fingerprint or an eyewitness at trial, he would always go with the fingerprint.[43] As a consequence of the effectiveness of scientific evidence, the National Institute of Justice recommends that "prosecutors consider the potential utility of such information in all cases where such evidence is available."[44] Some authors have called attention to the difficulties surrounding expert testimony. Procedural limitations often severely curtail the kinds of information which experts can provide.

Expert witnesses can earn substantial fees. DNA specialist John Gerdes, for example, was paid $100 per hour for his work in support of the defense in the O. J. Simpson trial; and New York forensic pathologist Michael Baden charged $1,500 per day for time spent working for Simpson in Los Angeles. Baden billed Simpson

Expert Witness. A person who has special knowledge and skills recognized by the court as relevant to the determination of guilt or innocence. Expert witnesses may express opinions or draw conclusions in their testimony—unlike lay witnesses.

more than $100,000, and the laboratory for which Gerdes works received more than $30,000 from Simpson's defense attorneys.[45]

Outsiders: Nonprofessional Courtroom Participants

A number of people find themselves either unwilling or unwitting participants in criminal trials. Into this category fall defendants, victims, and most witnesses. Although they are "outsiders" who lack the status of paid professional participants, these are precisely the people who provide the "grist" for the judicial mill. Without them, trials could not occur, and the professional roles described earlier would be rendered meaningless.

Lay Witnesses

Lay Witness. An eyewitness, character witness, or any other person called on to testify who is not considered an expert. Lay witnesses must testify to facts alone and may not draw conclusions or express opinions.

Subpoena. An order issued by a court of law requiring an individual to appear in court and to give testimony. Some subpoenas mandate that books, papers, and other items be surrendered to the court.

Nonexpert witnesses, otherwise known as **lay witnesses**, may be called by either the prosecution or defense. Lay witnesses may be eyewitnesses who saw the crime being committed or who came upon the crime scene shortly after the crime had occurred. Another type of lay witness is the character witness, who provides information about the personality, family life, business acumen, and so on of the defendant in an effort to show that this is not the kind of person who would commit the crime he or she is charged with. Of course, the victim may also be a witness, providing detailed and sometimes lengthy testimony about the defendant and the event in question.

Witnesses are officially notified that they are to appear in court to testify by a written document called a **subpoena**. Subpoenas are generally "served" by an officer of the court or by a police officer although they are sometimes mailed. Both sides in a criminal case may subpoena witnesses and might ask that persons called to testify bring with them books, papers, photographs, videotapes, or other forms of physical evidence. Witnesses who fail to appear when summoned may face contempt of court charges.

The job of a witness is to provide accurate testimony concerning only those things of which he or she has direct knowledge. Normally, witnesses will not be allowed to repeat things told to them by others unless it is necessary to do so in order to account for certain actions of their own. Since few witnesses are familiar with courtroom procedure, the task of testifying is fraught with uncertainty and can be traumatizing.

Anyone who testifies in a criminal trial must do so under oath, in which some reference to God is made, or after affirmation,[46] where a pledge to tell the truth is used by those who find either "swearing" or a reference to God objectionable. All witnesses are subject to cross-examination, a process that we will discuss in detail later in this chapter. Lay witnesses may be surprised to find that cross-examination can force them to defend their personal and moral integrity. A cross-examiner may question a witness about past vicious, criminal, or immoral acts, even where such matters have never been the subject of a criminal proceeding.[47] As long as the intent of such questions is to demonstrate to the jury that the witness may not be a person who is worthy of belief, they will normally be permitted by the judge.

Witnesses have traditionally been shortchanged by the judicial process. Subpoenaed to attend court, they have often suffered from frequent and unannounced changes in trial dates. A witness who promptly responds to a summons to appear may find that legal maneuvering has resulted in unanticipated delays. Strategic changes by either side may make the testimony of some witnesses entirely unnecessary, and people who have prepared themselves for the psychological rigors of testifying often experience an emotional letdown.

In order to compensate witnesses for their time, and to make up for lost income, many states pay witnesses for each day that they spend in court. Payments range from $5 to $30 per day[48] although some states pay nothing at all. In the case of *Demarest* v. *Manspeaker* (1991),[49] the U.S. Supreme Court held that federal prisoners, subpoenaed to testify, are entitled to witness fees just as nonincarcerated witnesses would be.

In another move to make the job of witnesses less onerous, 39 states and the federal government have laws or guidelines requiring that witnesses be notified of scheduling changes and cancellations in criminal proceedings.[50] In 1982, Congress passed the Victim and Witness Protection Act, which required the U.S. attorney general to develop guidelines to assist victims and witnesses in meeting the demands placed on them by the justice system. A number of **victim assistance programs** (also called victim/witness assistance programs), described shortly, have taken up a call for the rights of witnesses and are working to make the courtroom experience more manageable.

Jurors

Article III of the U.S. Constitution requires that "[t]he trial of all crimes…shall be by jury…." States have the authority to determine the size of criminal trial juries. Most states use juries comprising 12 persons and 1 or 2 alternates designated to fill in for **jurors** who are unable to continue because of accident, illness, or personal emergency. Some states allow for juries smaller than 12, and juries with as few as 6 members have survived Supreme Court scrutiny.[51]

Jury duty is regarded as a responsibility of citizenship. Other than juveniles and certain job occupants such as police personnel, physicians, members of the armed services on active duty, and emergency services workers, persons called for jury duty must serve unless they can convince a judge that they should be excused for overriding reasons. Aliens, those convicted of a felony, and citizens who have served on a jury within the past two years are excluded from jury service in most jurisdictions.

The names of prospective jurors are often gathered from the tax register, DMV records, or voter registration rolls of a county or municipality. Minimum qualifications for jury service include adulthood, a basic command of spoken English, citizenship, "ordinary intelligence," and local residency. Jurors are also expected to possess their "natural faculties," meaning that they should be able to hear, speak, see, move, and so forth. Some jurisdictions have recently allowed handicapped persons to serve as jurors although the nature of the evidence to be presented in a case may preclude persons with certain kinds of handicaps from serving.

Ideally, the jury is to be a microcosm of society, reflecting the values, rationality, and common sense of the average person. The U.S. Supreme Court has held that criminal defendants have a right to have their cases heard before a jury of their peers.[52] Ideally, peer juries are those comprising a representative cross section of the community in which the alleged crime has occurred and where the trial is to be held. The idea of a peer jury stems from the Magna Carta's original guarantee of jury trials for "freemen." Freemen in England during the 13th century, however, were more likely to be of similar mind than is a cross section of Americans today. Hence, although the duty of the jury is to deliberate on the evidence and, ultimately, determine guilt or innocence, social dynamics may play just as great a role in jury verdicts as do the facts of a case.

In a 1945 case, *Thiel* v. *Southern Pacific Company*,[53] the Supreme Court clarified the concept of a "jury of one's peers" by noting that although it is not necessary for every jury to contain representatives of every conceivable racial, ethnic, religious, gender, and economic group in the community, court officials may not systematically and intentionally exclude any juror solely because of his or her social characteristics.

Victim Assistance Program. An organized program which offers services to victims of crime in the areas of crisis intervention and follow-up counseling and which helps victims secure their rights under the law.

Juror. A member of a jury, selected for jury duty, and required to serve as an arbiter of the facts in a court of law. Jurors are expected to render verdicts of guilt or innocence on the charges brought against an accused although they may sometimes fail to do so (as in the case of a hung jury).

Jurors
14 capital case

6 civil case

*T*heory into Practice: The O. J. Simpson Trial—
The Jurors' Role

The jury is the crucial decision-making body in any criminal trial. Accordingly, the first few paragraphs of the opening statements of both the prosecution and the defense in the O. J. Simpson double-murder trial were directed at members of the jury. Here's what Los Angeles County prosecutor Christopher Darden told the jury:

I think it's fair to say that I have the toughest job in town today except for the job that you have. Your job may just be a little bit tougher. It's your job—like my job, we both have a central focus, a single objective, and that objective is justice obviously.

It's going to be a long trial and I want you to know how much we appreciate your being on the panel. We appreciate the personal sacrifices you're making by being sequestered. We understand that can be difficult.

And I would like to thank you in advance for keeping the promises you made to us when you were selected for the jury initially. You promised to be fair and you promised to be open-minded and you promised to hear and see and carefully consider all the evidence in the case and you promised to...come to a verdict in this case solely on the basis of the evidence and the law given to you by judge Ito.

And you promised to do that based on the law, based on the facts and the evidence and nothing else. You promised us that you had no hidden agenda, that you only wanted to see justice done and you promised us that you would do everything you could under the law to see that justice was done.

And so I thank you for that and I thank you in advance for the verdict you will at some point render in this case...

This is how defense attorney Johnnie Cochran, Jr., began the opening statement for the defense:

We started this process of trial back on September 26, 1994, on the first day we all met, when we came down [from] the jury room up on the 11th floor. And here we are now, several months later, in this search for justice. You've heard a lot about this talk of justice. I guess Dr. Martin Luther King said it best when he said that "Injustice anywhere is a threat to justice everywhere." So we are now embarked upon a search for justice, this search for truth, this search for the facts.

Each of you made a number of promises in the course of the *voir dire* examination, which is basically

unprecedented and due mainly to the largess of Judge Ito in understanding the possibility of media taint associated with this case. So we know a lot about you at this point and we, of course—all sides are very, very pleased with the fact you agreed to serve as jurors, to give us your time, to leave your lives, to be sequestered, as it were. That's a remarkable sacrifice. Abraham Lincoln said it best when he said that, "The highest act of citizenship is jury service." And you embarked on that jury service.

And it doesn't stop with just coming down and taking notes. It doesn't stop with the inconvenience of being away from your families. It stops when you can render a verdict in this case, and whether or not that verdict reflects the evidence in this case. A verdict void of sympathy for or passion against Mr. Simpson or any side in this case. You made these promises on both sides and we know you're going to keep those promises. Cicero said that "He who violates his oath profanes the faith of divinity itself." And, of course, we know that you will live up to your promises, and be fair, and keep an open mind and decide this case not on speculation, not on conjecture, not on surmise, but based upon the facts.

You, as jurors, are the conscience of this community. Your verdicts set the standards of what we should have and what should happen in this community. You have this rare opportunity, it seems to me, to be participants in this search for justice and for truth. In the final analysis, hopefully by April of this year—I'm optimistic still—you'll be able to render perhaps the most important decision of your lives. So we want to keep your minds open and fresh so you can render that decision impartially on both sides, so that people all across the world can say, "This system works. This was a fair trial. These were fair people." So thank you in advance for your service, for the verdict you're likely to render and for all the things you're doing here for us...

QUESTIONS FOR DISCUSSION

1. Do you believe that a criminal trial jury is truly the conscience of a community? If so, should a jury be able to render a verdict not in keeping with the facts of a case if it so chooses?

2. Given the length of the Simpson trial, and the many inconveniences brought about by sequestering, it must have taken special kinds of people to serve on the Simpson jury. What social characteristics might these jurors have had? How might such characteristics have affected the outcome of the trial?

The Role of the Victim in a Criminal Trial

Not all crimes have clearly identifiable victims. Some, like murder, do not have victims who survive. Where there is an identifiable surviving victim, however, he or she is often one of the most forgotten people in the courtroom. Although the victim may have been profoundly affected by the crime itself, and is often emotionally committed to the proceedings and trial outcome, he or she may not even be permitted to participate directly in the trial process. Although a powerful movement to recognize the interests of victims has begun (and is discussed in detail in the next chapter), it is still not unusual for crime victims to be totally unaware of the final outcome of a case which intimately concerns them.[54]

Hundreds of years ago, the situation surrounding victims was far different. During the early Middle Ages in much of Europe, victims, or their survivors, routinely played a central role in trial proceedings and in sentencing decisions. They testified, examined witnesses, challenged defense contentions, and pleaded with the judge or jury for justice, honor, and often revenge. Sometimes they were even expected to carry out the sentence of the court, by flogging the offender or by releasing the trapdoor used for hangings. This "golden age" of the victim ended with the consolidation of power into the hands of monarchs who declared that vengeance was theirs alone.

Today, victims, like witnesses, experience many hardships as they participate in the criminal court process. Some of the rigors they endure are as follows:

1. Uncertainties about their role in the criminal justice process
2. A general lack of knowledge about the criminal justice system, courtroom procedure, and legal issues
3. Trial delays which result in frequent travel, missed work, and wasted time
4. Fear of the defendant or of retaliation from the defendant's associates
5. The trauma of testifying and of cross-examination

The trial process itself can make for a bitter experience. If victims take the stand, defense attorneys may test their memory, challenge their veracity, or even suggest that they were somehow responsible for their own victimization. After enduring cross-examination, some victims report feeling as though they, and not the offender, have been portrayed as the criminal to the jury. The difficulties encountered by victims have been compared to a second victimization at the hands of the criminal justice system. In the next chapter, we provide additional information on victims and victims' issues, including victims' assistance programs.

The Role of the Defendant in a Criminal Trial

Generally, defendants must be present at their trials. Similar to state rules, federal rules of criminal procedure require that a defendant "must be present at every stage of a trial... [except that a defendant who] is initially present may...be voluntarily absent after the trial has commenced." In *Crosby* v. *U.S.* (1993),[55] the U.S. Supreme Court held that a defendant may not be tried in absentia even if he or she was present at the beginning of a trial where his or her absence is due to escape or failure to appear. In a related issue, *Zafiro* v. *U.S.* (1993)[56] held that, at least in federal courts, defendants charged with similar or related offenses may be tried together—even when their defenses differ substantially.

The majority of criminal defendants are poor, uneducated, and often alienated from the philosophy which undergirds the American justice system. A common view of the defendant in a criminal trial is that of a relatively powerless person at the mercy of judicial mechanisms. Many defendants are just that. However, such an image is often far from the truth. Defendants, especially those who seek an active role in their own defense, choreograph many courtroom activities. Experienced defendants, notably those who are career offenders, may be well versed in courtroom demeanor.

Defendants in criminal trials have a right to represent themselves and need not retain counsel or accept the assistance of court-appointed attorneys. Such a choice, however, may not be in their best interests. The most famous instance of self-representation in recent years was probably the 1995 trial of Long Island Railroad commuter train shooter, Colin Ferguson. Ferguson, who rejected both legal advice and in-court assistance from defense attorneys, and chose to represent himself during trial, was convicted of killing 6 passengers and wounding 19 others during a racially motivated shooting rampage in December 1993. Some observers said that Ferguson's performance as defendant turned defense attorney, "distressed his court-appointed lawyer-advisers, exacerbated the pain of the victims' family members and turned the courtroom of Nassau County Judge Donald E. Belfi into a theater of the bizarre."[57] Others called it a "sham," and a "circus," but astute observers noted that it set up the possibility for a successful appeal. Following conviction, Ferguson reportedly[58] asked famed defense attorney William M. Kunstler, one of his original lawyers, to file an appeal, focusing on whether Ferguson was mentally fit to represent himself and whether the judge erred in allowing him to do so.

Even without self-representation, every defendant who chooses to do so can substantially influence events in the courtroom. Defendants exercise choice in (1) deciding whether or not to testify personally, (2) selecting and retaining counsel, (3) planning a defense strategy in coordination with their attorney, (4) deciding what information to provide to (or withhold from) the defense team, (5) deciding what plea to enter, and (6) determining whether or not to file an appeal if convicted.

Nevertheless, even the most active defendants suffer from a number of disadvantages. One is the tendency of others to assume that anyone on trial must be guilty. Although a person is "innocent until proven guilty," the very fact that he or she is accused of an offense casts a shadow of suspicion that may foster biases in the minds of jurors and other courtroom actors. Another disadvantage lies in the often substantial social and cultural differences which separate the offender from the professional courtroom staff. Whereas lawyers and judges tend to identify with upper-middle-class values and lifestyles, few offenders do. The consequences of such a gap between defendant and courtroom staff may be insidious and far reaching.

The Press in the Courtroom

Often overlooked, because they do not have an "official" role in courtroom proceedings, are spectators and the press. At any given trial, both spectators and media representatives may be present in large numbers. Spectators include members of the families of both victim and defendant, friends of either side, and curious onlookers—some of whom are avocational court watchers.

Newswriters, television reporters, and other members of the press are apt to be present at "spectacular" trials (those involving some especially gruesome aspect or famous personality) and at those in which there is a great deal of community interest. The right of reporters and spectators to be present at a criminal trial is supported by the Sixth Amendment's insistence on a public trial.

Press reports at all stages of a criminal investigation and trial often create problems for the justice system. Significant pretrial publicity about a case may make it difficult to find jurors who have not already formed an opinion about the guilt or innocence of the defendant. News reports from the courtroom may influence nonsequestered jurors who hear them, especially when they contain information brought to the bench, but not heard by the jury.

In the 1976 case of *Nebraska Press Association v. Stuart*,[59] the U.S. Supreme Court ruled that trial court judges could not legitimately issue gag orders, preventing the pretrial publication of information about a criminal case, as long as the defendant's right to a fair trial and an impartial jury could be ensured by traditional means.[60] These means include (1) a **change of venue**, whereby the trial is moved to another jurisdiction less likely to have been exposed to the publicity; (2) trial postponement, which would allow for memories to fade and emotions to cool; and (3) jury selection and screening to eliminate biased persons from the jury pool. In 1986, the Court extended press access to preliminary hearings, which, it said, are

Change of Venue. The movement of a suit or trial from one jurisdiction to another or from one location to another within the same jurisdiction. A change of venue may be made in a criminal case to assure the defendant a fair trial.

"sufficiently like a trial to require public access."[61] In 1993, in the case of *Caribbean International News Corporation* v. *Puerto Rico*,[62] the Court effectively applied that requirement to territories under U.S. control.

Today, members of the press as well as video, television, and still cameras are allowed into most state courtrooms. Forty-seven states now allow courtroom cameras,[63] and organizations like Court TV have capitalized on the opportunity for live courtroom broadcasts. Court TVs broadcast of the 1995 O.J. Simpson murder trial, however, has led many states to reconsider televised trials.

The U.S. Supreme Court has been less favorably disposed to television coverage than have state courts. In 1981, a Florida defendant appealed his burglary conviction to the Supreme Court,[64] arguing that the presence of TV cameras at his trial had turned the court into a circus for attorneys and made the proceedings more a sideshow than a trial. The Supreme Court, recognizing that television cameras have an untoward effect on many people, agreed. In the words of the Court, "Trial courts must be especially vigilant to guard against any impairment of the defendant's right to a verdict based solely upon the evidence and the relevant law."[65]

The Judicial Conference of the United States, the primary policy-making arm of the federal courts, seems to agree with the High Court. A three-year pilot project which allowed television cameras into six U.S. District Courts and two appeals courts on an experimental basis closed on December 31, 1994, when the Conference voted to end the project. The Conference terminated the experiment, ruling that neither still nor video cameras would be allowed into federal courtrooms in the future. Conference members expressed concerns that cameras were a distracting influence and were having a "negative impact on jurors [and] witnesses"[66] by exposing them to possible harm by revealing their identities.

The Criminal Trial

From arrest through sentencing, the criminal justice process is carefully choreographed. Arresting officers must follow proper procedure in the gathering of evidence and in the arrest and questioning of suspects. Magistrates, prosecutors, jailers, and prison officials are all subject to similar strictures. Nowhere, however, is the criminal justice process more closely circumscribed than at the stage of the criminal trial.

Procedures in a modern courtroom are highly formalized. **Rules of evidence**, which govern the admissibility of evidence, and other procedural guidelines determine the course of a criminal hearing and trial. Rules of evidence are partially based on tradition. All U.S. jurisdictions, however, have formalized rules of evidence in written form. Criminal trials at the federal level generally adhere to the requirements of *Federal Rules of Evidence*.

Rules of Evidence. Rules of court which govern the admissibility of evidence at a criminal hearing and trial.

Trials are also circumscribed by informal rules and professional expectations. An important component of law school education is the teaching of rules which structure and define appropriate courtroom demeanor. In addition to statutory rules, law students are thoroughly exposed to the ethical standards of their profession as found in American Bar Association standards and other writings.

In the next few pages, we will describe the chronology of a criminal trial and comment on some of the widely accepted rules of criminal procedure. Before we begin the description, however, it is good to keep two points in mind. One is that the primary purpose of any criminal trial is the determination of the defendant's guilt or innocence. In this regard, it is important to recognize the crucial distinction that scholars make between legal guilt and factual guilt. Factual guilt deals with the issue of whether or not the defendant is actually responsible for the crime of which he or she stands accused. If the defendant "did it," then he or she is, in fact, guilty. Legal guilt is not so clear. Legal guilt is established only when the prosecutor presents evidence which is sufficient to convince the judge (where the judge determines the verdict) or jury that the defendant is guilty as charged. The distinction between legal guilt and factual guilt is crucial because it points to the fact that the burden of proof rests with the prosecution, and it indicates the possibility that guilty defendants may, nonetheless, be found "not guilty."

The second point to remember is that criminal trials under our system of justice are built around an adversary system and that central to such a system is the advocacy model. Participating in the adversary system are advocates for the state (the prosecution or district attorney) and for the defendant (defense counsel, public defender, and others). The philosophy behind the adversary system holds that the greatest number of just resolutions in all foreseeable criminal trials will occur when both sides are allowed to argue their cases effectively and vociferously before a fair and impartial jury. The system requires that advocates for both sides do their utmost, within the boundaries set by law and professional ethics, to protect and advance the interests of their clients (that is, the defendant and the state). The advocacy model makes clear that it is not the job of the defense attorney or the prosecution to judge the guilt of any defendant. Hence, even defense attorneys who are convinced that their client is guilty are still exhorted to offer the best possible defense and to counsel their client as effectively as possible.

The **adversarial system** has been criticized by some thinkers who point to fundamental differences between law and science in the way the search for truth is conducted.[67] Although proponents of traditional legal procedure accept the belief that truth can best be uncovered through an adversarial process, scientists adhere to a painstaking process of research and replication to acquire knowledge. Most of us would agree that scientific advances in recent years may have made factual issues less difficult to ascertain. For example, some of the new scientific techniques in evidence gathering, such as DNA fingerprinting, are now able to unequivocally link suspects to criminal activity. Whether scientific findings should continue to serve a subservient role to the adversarial process itself is a question now being raised. The ultimate answer will probably be couched in terms of the results either process is able to produce. If the adversarial model results in the acquittal of too many demonstrably guilty people because of legal "technicalities," or the scientific approach inaccurately identifies too many suspects, either could be restricted.

We turn now to a discussion of the steps in a criminal trial. As Figure 8-1 shows, trial chronology consists of eight stages:

trial initiation

jury selection

opening statements

presentation of evidence

closing arguments

the judge's charge to the jury

jury deliberations

the verdict

For purposes of brevity, jury deliberations and the verdict will be discussed jointly. If the defendant is found guilty, a sentence will be imposed by the judge at the conclusion of the trial. Sentencing is discussed in the next chapter.

Trial Initiation: The Speedy Trial Act

As we mentioned in Chapter 7, the Sixth Amendment to the U.S. Constitution guarantees that "In all criminal prosecutions, the accused shall enjoy the right to a speedy and public trial." Clogged court calendars, limited judicial resources, and general inefficiency, however, often combine to produce what appears to many to be unreasonable delays in trial initiation. The attention of the Supreme Court was

Adversarial System. The two-sided structure under which American criminal trial courts operate, and which pits the prosecution against the defense. In theory, justice is done when the most effective adversary is able to convince the judge or jury that his or her perspective on the case is the correct one.

Speedy Trial Act. A 1974 federal law requiring that proceedings in a criminal case against a defendant begin before passage of a specified period, such as 70 working days after indictment. Some states also have speedy trial requirements.

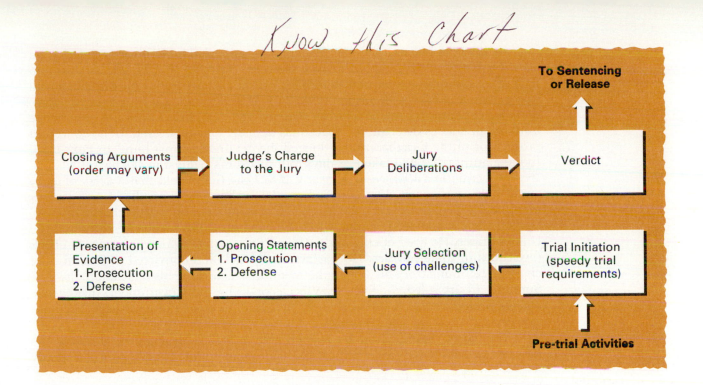

FIGURE 8-1
Stages in a criminal trial.

brought to bear on trial delays in three precedent-setting cases: *Klopfer* v. *North Carolina* (1967),[68] *Baker* v. *Wingo* (1972),[69] and *Strunk* v. *United States* (1973).[70] The *Klopfer* case involved a Duke University professor and focused on civil disobedience in a protest against segregated facilities. In Klopfer's long-delayed trial, the Court asserted that the right to a speedy trial is a fundamental guarantee of the Constitution. In the *Baker* case, the Court held that Sixth Amendment guarantees to a quick trial could be illegally violated even in cases where the accused did not explicitly object to delays. In *Strunk*, it found that denial of a speedy trial should result in a dismissal of all charges.

In 1974, against the advice of the Justice Department, the U.S. Congress passed the federal **Speedy Trial Act**.[71] The act, which was phased in gradually, and became fully effective in 1980, allows for the dismissal of federal criminal charges in cases where the prosecution does not seek an indictment or information within 30 days of arrest (a 30-day extension is granted when the grand jury is not in session) or where a trial does not begin within 70 working days after indictment for defendants who plead not guilty. If a defendant is not available for trial, or witnesses cannot be called within the 70-day limit, the period may be extended to 180 days. Delays brought about by the defendant, through requests for a continuance, or because of escape, are not counted in the specified periods. The Speedy Trial Act has been condemned by some as shortsighted. One federal trial court judge, for example, wrote: "The ability of the criminal justice system to operate effectively and efficiently has been severely impeded by the Speedy Trial Act. Resources are misdirected, unnecessary severances required, cases proceed to trial inadequately prepared, and in some indeterminate number of cases, indictments against guilty persons are dismissed."[72]

In an important 1988 decision, *U.S.* v. *Taylor*,[73] the U.S. Supreme Court applied the requirements of the Speedy Trial Act to the case of a drug defendant who had escaped following arrest. The Court made it clear that trial delays, when they derive from the willful actions of the defendant, do not apply to the 70-day period. The Court also held that trial delays, even when they result from government action, do not necessarily provide grounds for dismissal if they occur "without prejudice." Delays without prejudice are those which are due to circumstances beyond the control of criminal justice agencies.

In 1993, an Indiana prisoner, William Fex, appealed a Michigan conviction on armed robbery and attempted murder charges, claiming that he had to wait 196 days after submitting a request to Indiana prison authorities for his Michigan trial to commence. In *Fex* v. *Michigan* (1993),[74] the U.S. Supreme Court ruled that "common-sense compel[s] the conclusion that the 180-day period does not commence until the prisoner's disposition request has actually been delivered to the court and prosecutor of the jurisdiction that lodged the detainer against him." In Fex's case, Indiana authorities had taken 22 days to forward his request to Michigan.

However, in a 1992 case, *Doggett* v. *U.S.*,[75] the Court held that a delay of eight and a half years violated speedy trial provisions because it resulted from government negligence. In Doggett, the defendant was indicted on a drug charge in 1980, but left the country for Panama, where he lived until 1982 when he reentered the United States. He lived openly in the United States until 1988 when a credit check revealed him to authorities. He was arrested, tried, and convicted of federal drug charges stemming from his 1980 indictment. In overturning his conviction, the U.S. Supreme Court ruled: "...even delay occasioned by the Government's negligence creates prejudice that compounds over time, and at some point, as here, becomes intolerable."[76]

The federal Speedy Trial Act is applicable only to federal courts. However, the *Klopfer* case (discussed earlier) effectively made constitutional guarantees of a speedy

*T*heory into Practice: Pre- and Post-trial Motions

A motion is defined by the *Dictionary of Criminal Justice Data Terminology*[1] as "[a]n oral or written request made to a court at any time before, during, or after court proceedings, asking the court to make a specified finding, decision, or order." Written motions are called petitions. This box lists the typical kinds of motions that may be made by both sides in a criminal case before and after trial.

MOTION FOR DISCOVERY

A motion for discovery, filed by the defense, asks the court to allow the defendant's lawyers to view the evidence which the prosecution intends to present at trial. Physical evidence, lists of witnesses, documents, photographs, and so on, which the prosecution plans to introduce in court, will usually be made available to the defense as a result of such a motion.

MOTION TO SUPPRESS EVIDENCE

In the preliminary hearing, or through pretrial discovery, the defense may learn of evidence which the prosecution intends to introduce at the trial. If some of that evidence has been, in the opinion of the defense counsel, unlawfully acquired, a motion to suppress the evidence may be filed.

MOTION TO DISMISS CHARGES

A variety of circumstances may result in the filing of a motion to dismiss. They include (1) an opinion, by defense counsel, that the indictment or information is not sound; (2) violations of speedy trial legislation; (3) a plea bargain with the defendant (which may require testimony against codefendants); (4) the death of an important witness or the destruction or disappearance of necessary evidence; (5) the confession, by a supposed victim, that the facts in the case have been fabricated; and (6) the success of a motion to suppress evidence which effectively eliminates the prosecution's case.

MOTION FOR CONTINUANCE

This motion seeks a delay in the start of the trial. Defense motions for continuance are often based on the inability to locate important witnesses, the illness of the defendant, or a change in defense counsel immediately prior to trial.

MOTION FOR CHANGE OF VENUE

In well-known cases, pretrial publicity may lessen the opportunity for a case to be tried before an unbiased jury. A motion for a change in venue asks that the trial be moved to some other area where prejudice against the defendant is less likely to exist.

MOTION FOR SEVERANCE OF OFFENSES

Defendants charged with a number of crimes may ask to be tried separately on all or some of the charges. Although consolidating charges for trial saves time trial applicable to state courts. In keeping with the trend toward reduced delays, many states have since enacted their own speedy trial legislation. Typical state legislation sets limits of 120 or 90 days as a reasonable period for a trial to commence.

Jury Selection

As we mentioned in our discussion of the role of the jury in a criminal trial, the Sixth Amendment also guarantees the right to an impartial jury. An impartial jury is not necessarily an ignorant one. In other words, jurors will not always be excused from service on a jury if they have some knowledge of the case before them.[77] Jurors, however, who have already formed an opinion about the guilt or innocence of a defendant are likely to be excused.

Anyone who has ever been called as a juror knows that some prospective jurors try to get excused and others who would like to serve are excused because they are not judged to be suitable. Prosecution and defense attorneys use challenges to ensure the impartiality of the jury which is being empaneled. Three types of challenges are recognized in criminal courts: (1) challenges to the array, (2) challenges for cause, and (3) **peremptory challenges.**

Challenges to the array signify the belief, generally by the defense attorney, that the pool from which potential jurors are to be selected is not representative of

Jury Selection. The process whereby, according to law and precedent, members of a particular trial jury are chosen.

Peremptory Challenge. A means of removing unwanted potential jurors without the need to show cause for their removal. Prosecutors and defense attorneys routinely use peremptory challenges in order to eliminate from juries individuals who, although they express no obvious bias, may be thought to hold the potential to sway the jury in an undesirable direction.

---

*T*heory into Practice: Pre- and Post-trial Motions—*Continued*

and money, some defendants may think that it is more likely to make them appear guilty.

MOTION FOR SEVERANCE OF DEFENDANTS

Similar to the preceding motion, this request asks the court to try the accused separately from any co-defendants. Motions for severance are likely to be filed where the defendant believes that the jury may be prejudiced against him or her by evidence applicable only to other defendants.

MOTION TO DETERMINE PRESENT SANITY

"Present sanity," even though it may be no defense against the criminal charge, can delay trial. A person cannot be tried, sentenced, or punished while insane. If a defendant is insane at the time a trial is to begin, this motion may halt the proceedings until treatment can be arranged.

MOTION FOR A BILL OF PARTICULARS

This motion asks the court to order the prosecutor to provide detailed information about the charges which the defendant will be facing in court. Defendants charged with a number of offenses, or with a number of counts of the same offense, may make such a motion. They may, for example, seek to learn which alleged instances of an offense will become the basis for prosecution, or which specific items of contraband allegedly found in their possession are held to violate the law.

MOTION FOR A MISTRIAL

A mistrial may be declared at any time, and a motion for mistrial may be made by either side. Mistrials are likely to be declared where highly prejudicial comments are made by either attorney. Defense motions for a mistrial do not provide grounds for a later claim of double jeopardy.

MOTION FOR ARREST OF JUDGMENT

After the verdict of the jury has been announced, but before sentencing, the defendant may make a motion for arrest of judgment. Such a motion means the defendant believes that some legally acceptable reason exists as to why sentencing should not occur. Defendants who are seriously ill, hospitalized, or who have gone insane prior to judgment being imposed may file such a motion.

MOTION FOR A NEW TRIAL

After a jury has returned a guilty verdict, a defense motion for a new trial may be entertained by the court. Acceptance of such a motion is most often based on the discovery of new evidence which is of significant benefit to the defense and will set aside the conviction.

1. U.S. Department of Justice, *Dictionary of Criminal Justice Data Terminology,* 2nd ed. (Washington, D.C.: U.S. Government Printing Office, 1982).

---

the community or is biased in some significant way. A challenge to the array is argued before the hearing judge before jury selection begins.

During the **jury selection** process, both prosecution and defense attorneys question potential jurors in a process known as *voir dire* examination. Jurors are expected to be unbiased and free of preconceived notions of guilt or innocence. Challenges for cause, which may arise during *voir dire* examination, make the claim that an individual juror cannot be fair or impartial. One special issue of juror objectivity has concerned the Supreme Court. It is whether jurors with philosophical opposition to the death penalty should be excluded from juries whose decisions might result in the imposition of capital punishment. In the case of *Witherspoon* v. *Illinois* (1968),[78] the Court ruled that a juror opposed to the death penalty could be excluded from such juries if it were shown that (1) the juror would automatically vote against conviction without regard to the evidence or (2) the juror's philosophical orientation would prevent an objective consideration of the evidence. The *Witherspoon* case has left unresolved a number of issues, among them the concern that it is difficult to demonstrate how a juror would automatically vote, a fact which may not even be known to the juror before trial begins.

Another area of concern, which has been addressed by the Supreme Court, involves the potential that jurors may be biased because of being exposed to stories about a case in the news media that appear before the start of trial. Such concerns provided an especially tricky issue for Judge Lance Ito during the double-murder trial of O. J. Simpson, as Ito supervised the process of jury selection. A similar, but far less well-known, case which has been reviewed by the Court is that of *Mu'Min* v. *Virginia* (1991).[79] Mu'Min was a Virginia inmate who was serving time for first-degree murder. While accompanying a work detail outside the institution, he committed another murder. At the ensuing trial, 8 of the 12 jurors who were seated admitted that they had heard or read something about the case although none indicated that he or she had formed an opinion in advance concerning Mu'Min's guilt or innocence. Following his conviction, Mu'Min appealed to the Supreme Court, claiming that his right to a fair trial had been denied because of pretrial publicity. The Court disagreed, and upheld his conviction, citing the admittedly unbiased nature of the jurors.

The third kind of challenge, the peremptory challenge, effectively removes potential jurors without the need to give a reason. Peremptory challenges, used by both the prosecution and defense, are limited in number. Federal courts allow each side up to 20 peremptory challenges in capital cases and as few as 3 in minor criminal cases.[80] States vary in the number of peremptory challenges they permit.

A developing field, which seeks to take advantage of peremptory challenges, is scientific jury selection. Scientific jury selection uses correlational techniques from the social sciences to gauge the likelihood that potential jurors will vote for conviction or acquittal. It makes predictions based on the economic, ethnic, and other personal and social characteristics of each member of the juror pool. Intentional jury selection techniques appeared to play a significant role in the outcome of the trial of Larry Davis. Davis, who is black, was charged with the 1986 shooting of seven white New York City police officers as they attempted to arrest the heavily armed defendant for the alleged murder of four drug dealers.[81] None of the officers died, and Davis was later apprehended. At the trial, defense attorney William Kunstler assembled a jury of ten blacks and two Hispanics. On two occasions, Judge Bernard Fried had dismissed previous juries before the trial could begin, saying that Kunstler was packing the panel with blacks.[82] Although many of the wounded officers testified against Davis, and no one seriously disputed the contention that Davis was the triggerman in the shooting of the officers, the jury found him innocent. The finding prompted one of the injured policemen to claim, "It was a racist verdict."[83] Explaining the jury's decision another way, a spokesperson for the NAACP Legal Defense Fund said after the trial, "The experience of blacks in the criminal justice system may make them less prone to accept the word of a police officer."[84]

Criticisms of jury selection techniques have focused on the end result of the process. Such techniques generally remove potential jurors who have any knowledge or opinions about the case to be tried. Also removed are persons trained in the law or in criminal justice. Anyone working for a criminal justice agency, or anyone who has a family member working for such an agency, or for a defense attorney, will likely be dismissed through peremptory challenges on the chance that they may be biased in favor of one side or the other. Scientific jury selection techniques may result in the additional dismissal of educated or professionally successful individuals so as to eliminate the possibility of such individuals exercising undue control over jury deliberations. The end result of the jury selection process may be to produce a jury comprising people who are uneducated, uninformed, and generally inexperienced at making any type of well-considered decision. Some of the jurors may not understand the charges against the defendant or comprehend what is required for a finding of guilt or innocence. Likewise, some selected jurors may not even possess the span of attention needed to hear all the testimony that will be offered in a case. As a consequence, decisions rendered by such a jury may be based more on emotion than on findings of fact.

Jury Selection and Race

Juries intentionally selected so that they are racially imbalanced may soon be a thing of the past. As long ago as 1880, the U.S. Supreme Court held that "a statute barring blacks from service on grand or petit juries denied equal protection of the laws to a black man convicted of murder by an all-white jury."[85] Even so, peremptory challenges continued to tend to lead to racial imbalance. In 1965, for example, a black defendant in Alabama was convicted of rape by an all-white jury. The local prosecutor had used his peremptory challenges to exclude blacks from the jury. The case eventually reached the Supreme Court, where the conviction was upheld.[86] At that time, the Court refused to limit the practice of peremptory challenges, reasoning that to do so would place them under the same judicial scrutiny as challenges for cause.

However, in 1986, following what many claimed were widespread abuses of peremptory challenges by prosecution and defense alike, the Supreme Court was forced to overrule its earlier decision. It did so in the case of *Batson* v. *Kentucky*.[87] Batson, a black man, had been convicted of second-degree burglary and other offenses by an all-white jury. The prosecutor had used his peremptory challenges to remove all blacks from jury service at the trial. The Court agreed that the use of peremptory challenges for apparently purposeful discrimination constitutes a violation of the defendant's right to an impartial jury.

The *Batson* decision laid out the requirements which defendants seeking to establish the discriminatory use of peremptory challenges must prove. They include the need to prove that the defendant is a member of a recognized racial group which has been intentionally excluded from the jury and the need to raise a reasonable suspicion that the prosecutor used peremptory challenges in a discriminatory manner. Justice Thurgood Marshall, writing a concurring opinion in *Batson*, presaged what was to come: "The inherent potential of peremptory challenges to destroy the jury process," he wrote, "by permitting the exclusion of jurors on racial grounds should ideally lead the Court to ban them entirely from the criminal justice system."

A few years later, in *Ford* v. *Georgia* (1991),[88] the Court moved much closer to Justice Marshall's position when it remanded a case for a new trial, based on the fact that the prosecutor had used peremptory challenges to remove potential minority jurors. Nine of the ten peremptory challenges available to the prosecutor under Georgia law had been used to eliminate prospective black jurors. Following his conviction, on charges of kidnapping, raping, and murdering a white woman, the black defendant, James Ford, argued that the prosecutor had demonstrated a systematic and historical racial bias in other cases as well as his own. Specifically, Ford argued that his Sixth Amendment right to an impartial jury had been violated by the prosecutor's racially based method of jury selection. His defense attorney's written appeal to the Supreme Court made the claim that "The exclusion of members of the black race in the jury when a black accused is being tried is done in order that the accused will receive excessive punishment if found guilty, or to inject racial prejudice into the fact-finding process of the jury."[89] Although the Court did not find a basis for such a Sixth Amendment claim, it did determine that the civil rights of the jurors themselves were violated under the Fourteenth Amendment because of a pattern of discrimination based on race.

In another 1991 case, *Powers* v. *Ohio*[90] (see Theory into Practice, "Peremptory Challenges and Race"), the Court found in favor of a white defendant who claimed that his constitutional rights were violated by the intentional exclusion of blacks from his jury through the use of peremptory challenges. In *Powers*, the Court held that "[a]lthough an individual juror does not have the right to sit on any particular petit jury, he or she does possess the right not to be excluded from one on account of race." In a civil case with significance for the criminal justice system, the Court held in *Edmonson* v. *Leesville Concrete Co., Inc.* (1991),[91] that peremptory challenges in *civil* suits were not acceptable if based on race: "The importance of (*Edmonson*) lies in the Court's significant expansion of the scope of state action—the traditionally held doctrine that private attorneys are immune to constitutional requirements because they do not represent the government." Justice Anthony Kennedy, writing for the majority, said that race-based juror exclusions are forbidden in civil lawsuits because jury selection is a "unique governmental function delegated to private litigants" in a public courtroom.

Finally, in the 1992 case of *Georgia* v. *McCollum*,[92] the Court barred defendants and their attorneys from using peremptory challenges to exclude potential jurors on the basis of race. In *McCollum*, Justice Harry Blackman, writing for the majority, said, "Be it at the hands of the state or defense, if a court allows jurors to be excluded because of group bias, it is a willing participant in a scheme that could only undermine the very foundation of our system of justice—our citizens' confidence in it." Soon thereafter, peremptory challenges based on gender were similarly restricted (*J.E.B.* v. *Alabama*, 1994) although, at the time of this writing, the Court has refused to ban peremptory challenges which exclude jurors because of religious or sexual orientation.[93]

After wrangling over jury selection has run its course, the jury is sworn in, and alternates are selected. At this point, the judge will decide whether the jury is to be sequestered during the trial. Members of **sequestered juries**, like those in the O. J. Simpson trial, are not permitted to have contact with the public and are often housed in a motel or hotel until completion of the trial. Anyone who attempts to contact a sequestered jury or to influence members of a nonsequestered juror may be held accountable for jury tampering. Following jury selection, the stage is set for opening arguments[94] to begin.

Sequestered Jury. One which is isolated from the public during the course of a trial and throughout the deliberation process.

Opening Statements

The presentation of information to the jury begins with **opening statements** made by the prosecution and defense. (Excerpts from the opening statements in the O. J. Simpson double-murder trial are included in a Theory into Practice box earlier in this chapter.) The purpose of opening statements is to advise the jury of what the attorneys intend to prove and to describe how such proof will be offered. Evidence itself is not offered during opening statements. Eventually, however, the jury will have to weigh the evidence presented during trial and decide between the effectiveness of the arguments made by both sides. When a defendant has little evidence to present, the main job of the defense

Opening Statement. The initial statement of an attorney (or of a defendant representing himself or herself) made in a court of law to a judge, or to a judge and jury, describing the facts that he or she intends to present during trial in order to prove his or her case.

This pen and ink drawing (circa 1867) depicts one of the first jury trials on which both blacks and whites served. Courtesy of the Library of Congress.

attorney will be to dispute the veracity of the prosecution's version of the facts. Under such circumstances, defense attorneys may choose not to present any evidence or testimony at all, focusing instead on the burden of proof requirement facing the prosecution. Such plans will generally be made clear during opening statements. Further, during opening arguments, the defense attorney is likely to stress the human qualities of the defendant and to remind jurors of the awesome significance of their task.

Lawyers for both sides are bound by a "good faith" ethical requirement in their opening statements. That requirement limits the content of such statements to mentioning only that evidence which the attorneys actually believe can and will be presented as the trial progresses. Allusions to evidence which an attorney has no intention of offering are regarded as unprofessional and have been defined as "professional misconduct" by the Supreme Court.[95] When material alluded to in an opening statement cannot, for whatever reason, later be presented in court, it may offer opposing counsel an opportunity to discredit the other side.

The Presentation of Evidence

The crux of the criminal trial is the presentation of evidence. The state is first given the opportunity to present evidence intended to prove the defendant's guilt. After prosecutors have rested their case, the defense is afforded the opportunity to provide evidence favorable to the defendant.

Evidence is of two types: direct and circumstantial. **Direct evidence** is that which, if believed by the judge or jury, proves a fact without needing to draw inferences. Direct evidence may consist, for example, of the information contained on a photograph or videotape. It might also consist of testimonial evidence provided by a witness on the stand. A straightforward statement by a witness, such as "I saw him do it!" is a form of direct evidence.

Circumstantial evidence is indirect. It requires the judge or jury to make inferences and draw conclusions. At a murder trial, for example, a person who heard gunshots, and moments later saw someone run by with a smoking gun in hand, might testify to those facts. Even though there may have been no eyewitness to the actual homicide, the jury might later conclude that the person seen with the gun was the one who pulled the trigger and committed homicide. Contrary to popular belief, circumstantial evidence is sufficient to produce a verdict and conviction in a criminal trial. In fact, some prosecuting attorneys claim to prefer working entirely with circumstantial evidence, weaving a tapestry of the criminal act in their arguments to the jury.

Evidence. Anything useful to a judge or jury in deciding the facts of a case. Evidence may take the form of witness testimony, written documents, videotapes, magnetic media, photographs, physical objects, and so on.

Direct Evidence. Evidence which, if believed, directly proves a fact. Eyewitness testimony (and, more recently, videotaped documentation) account for the majority of all direct evidence heard in the criminal courtroom.

Circumstantial Evidence. Evidence which requires interpretation or which requires a judge or jury to reach a conclusion based on what the evidence indicates. From the proximity of a smoking gun to the defendant, for example, the jury might conclude that he or she pulled the trigger.

Theory into Practice: Peremptory Challenges and Race

"[A] peremptory challenge to a juror means that one side in a trial has been given the right to throw out a certain number of possible jurors before the trial without giving any reasons."[1]

Historically, as the definition—borrowed from a legal dictionary—indicates, attorneys had been able to remove unwanted potential jurors from a criminal case during jury selection procedures through the use of a limited number of peremptory challenges without having to provide any reason whatsoever for the choices they made. (Challenges for cause, on the other hand, although not limited in number, require an acceptable rationale for juror removal.) The understanding of peremptory challenges was changed forever by the 1991 landmark U.S. Supreme Court case of *Powers* v. *Ohio*.[2] The *Powers* case dealt with a white defendant's desire to ensure a racially balanced jury. In *Powers*, the Supreme Court identified three reasons why peremptory challenges may not be issued if based on race. The Court provided the following rationale for its decision:[3]

> First, the discriminatory use of peremptory challenges causes the defendant cognizable injury, and he or she has a concrete interest in challenging the practice, because racial discrimination in jury selection casts doubt on the integrity of the judicial process and places the fairness of the criminal proceeding in doubt.

> Second, the relationship between the defendant and the excluded jurors is such that...both have a common interest in eliminating racial discrimination from the courtroom....

> Third, it is unlikely that a juror dismissed because of race will possess sufficient incentive to set in motion the arduous process needed to vindicate his or her own rights.

The Court continued:

> The very fact that [members of a particular race] are singled out and expressly denied...all right to participate in the administration of the law, as jurors, because of their color, though they are citizens, and may be in other respects fully qualified, is practically a brand upon them, affixed by the law, an assertion of their inferiority, and a stimulant to that race prejudice which is an impediment to securing to individuals of that race equal justice which the law aims to secure to all others.

In a move that surprised many court watchers, the Supreme Court, near the end of its 1991 term, extended its ban on racially motivated peremptory challenges to civil cases. In *Edmonson* v. *Leesville Concrete Co., Inc.*,[4] the Court ruled: "The harms we recognized in *Powers* are not limited to the criminal sphere. A civil proceeding often implicates significant rights and interests. Civil juries, no less than their criminal counterparts, must follow the law and act as impartial fact-finders. And, as we have observed, their verdicts, no less than those of their criminal counterparts, become binding judgments of the court. Racial discrimination has no place in the courtroom, whether the proceeding is civil or criminal."

Following *Powers* and *Edmonson* v. *Leesville Concrete Co., Inc.*, it is clear that neither prosecuting nor civil attorneys in the future will be able to exclude minority potential jurors consistently unless they are able to articulate clearly credible race-neutral rationales for their actions.

Even so, recent dissenting opinions indicate that considerable sentiment may exist among the justices which could lead to the return of a broader use of peremptory challenges. In a dissenting opinion in *J.E.B.* v. *Alabama* (1994)[5], Justices Scalia, Rehnquist, and Thomas wrote: "the core of the Court's reasoning [banning peremptory challenges based on gender] is that peremptory challenges on the basis of any group characteristic subject to heightened scrutiny are inconsistent with the guarantee of the Equal Protection Clause...Since all groups are subject to the peremptory challenge...it is hard to see how any group is denied equal protection."

QUESTIONS FOR DISCUSSION

1. Do you agree with the Court's reasoning in *Powers* that peremptory challenges based on race should not be permitted in the selection of criminal trial juries? Why or why not?

2. Review the Bill of Rights in the Appendix. What support do you find there for the *Powers* ruling? Be as specific as possible.

1. Daniel Oran, *Oran's Dictionary of the Law* (St. Paul, Minn.: West Publishing, 1983), p. 312.
2. *Powers* v. *Ohio*, 499 U.S. 400 (1991).
3. Ibid., online syllabus of the majority opinion.
4. *Edmonson* v. *Leesville Concrete Co., Inc.*, 500 U.S. ___(1991).
5. *J.E.B.* v. *Alabama ex rel. T.B.*, 114 S.Ct. 1419, 128 L. Ed. 2d 89 (1994).

Real evidence consists of physical material or traces of physical activity. Weapons, tire tracks, ransom notes, and fingerprints all fall into the category of physical evidence. Real or physical evidence is introduced into the trial process by means of exhibits. Exhibits are objects or displays which, once formally accepted as evidence by the judge, may be shown to members of the jury. Documentary evidence is another type of real evidence that includes writings such as business records, journals, written confessions, and letters. Documentary evidence can extend beyond paper and ink to include magnetic and optical storage devices used in computer operations and video and voice recordings.

One of the most significant decisions a trial court judge makes is deciding what evidence can be presented to the jury. In making that decision, judges will examine the relevance of the information in question to the case at hand. Relevant evidence is that which has a bearing on the facts at issue. For example, a decade or two ago, it was not unusual for a woman's sexual history to be brought out in rape trials. Under "rape shield statutes," most states today will not allow such a practice, recognizing that these details often have no bearing on the case. Rape shield statutes have been strengthened by recent U.S. Supreme Court decisions, including the 1991 case of *Michigan* v. *Lucas*.[96] In this case, the defendant, Lucas, had been charged with criminal sexual conduct involving his ex-girlfriend. Lucas had forced the woman into his apartment at knifepoint, beat her, and forced her to engage in several nonconsensual sex acts. At his trial, Lucas asked to have evidence introduced demonstrating that a prior sexual relationship had existed between the two. At the time, however, Michigan law required that a written motion to use such information had to be made within ten days following arraignment—a condition Lucas failed to meet. Lucas was convicted and sentenced to a term of from 44 to 180 months in prison, but appealed his conviction, claiming that the Sixth Amendment to the U.S. Constitution guaranteed him the right to confront witnesses against him. The U.S. Supreme Court disagreed, however, and ruled that the Sixth Amendment guarantee does not necessarily extend to evidence of a prior sexual relationship between a rape victim and a criminal defendant.

In evaluating evidence, judges must also weigh the probative value of an item of evidence against its potential inflammatory or prejudicial qualities. Evidence has probative value when it is useful and relevant. Even useful evidence, however, may unduly bias a jury if it is exceptionally gruesome or presented in such a way as to imply guilt. For example, gory photographs, especially in full color, may be withheld from the jury's eyes. In one recent case, a new trial was ordered when 35 mm slides of the crime scene were projected on a wall over the head of the defendant as he sat in the courtroom, and were found by an appellate court to have prejudiced the jury.

On occasion, some evidence will be found to have only limited admissibility. Limited admissibility means that the evidence can be used for a specific purpose, but that it might not be accurate in other details. Photographs, for example, may be admitted as evidence for the narrow purpose of showing spatial relationships between objects under discussion even though the photographs themselves may have been taken under conditions that did not exist (such as daylight) when the offense was committed.

When judges err in allowing the use of evidence that may have been illegally or unconstitutionally gathered, grounds may be created for a later appeal if the trial concludes with a "guilty" verdict. Even when evidence is improperly introduced at trial, however, a number of Supreme Court decisions[97] have held that there may be no grounds for an effective appeal unless such introduction "had substantial and injurious effect or influence in determining the jury's verdict."[98] Called the "harmless error" rule, this standard does place the burden on the prosecution to show that the jury's decision would most likely have been the same even in the absence of such inappropriate evidence. The rule is not applicable when a defendant's constitutional guarantees are violated by "structural defects in the constitution of the trial mechanism"[99] itself—as when a judge gives constitutionally improper instructions to a jury. (We discuss those instructions later in this chapter.)

The Testimony of Witnesses

Testimony. Oral evidence offered by a sworn witness on the witness stand during a criminal trial.

Witness **testimony** is generally the chief means by which evidence is introduced at trial. Witnesses may include victims, police officers, the defendant, specialists in recognized fields, and others with useful information to provide. Some of these witnesses may have been present during the commission of the alleged offense, but most will have had only a later opportunity to investigate the situation or to analyze evidence.

Before a witness will be allowed to testify to any fact, the questioning attorney must establish the person's competence. Competency to testify requires that witnesses have personal knowledge of the information they will discuss and that they understand their duty to tell the truth.

One of the defense attorney's most critical decisions is whether or not to put the defendant on the stand. Defendants have a Fifth Amendment right to remain silent and to refuse to testify. In the precedent-setting case of *Griffin* v. *California* (1965),[100] the U.S. Supreme Court declared that if a defendant refuses to testify, prosecutors and judges are enjoined from even commenting on the fact, other than to instruct the jury that such a failure cannot be held to indicate guilt. Griffin was originally arrested for the beating death of a woman whose body was found in an alley. Charged with first-degree murder, he refused to take the stand when his case came to trial. At the time of the trial, Article I, Section 13, of the California Constitution provided in part: "...in any criminal case, whether the defendant testifies or not, his failure to explain or to deny by his testimony any evidence or facts in the case against him may be commented upon by the court and by counsel, and may be considered by the court or the jury." The prosecutor, remarking on the evidence in closing arguments to the jury, declared: "These things he has not seen fit to take the stand and deny or explain....Essie Mae is dead, she can't tell you her side of the story. The defendant won't." The judge then instructed the jury that they might infer from the defendant's silence his inability to deny the evidence which had been presented against him. Griffin was convicted of first-degree murder, and his appeal reached the Supreme Court. The Court ruled that the Fifth Amendment, which the Fourteenth Amendment made applicable to the states, protected the defendant from any inferences of guilt based upon a failure to testify. The verdict of the trial court was voided.

Direct examination of a witness takes place when a witness is first called to the stand. If the prosecutor calls the witness, the witness is referred to as a witness for the prosecution. Where the direct examiner is a defense attorney, witnesses are called witnesses for the defense.

The direct examiner may ask questions which require a yes or no answer but can also employ narrative questions which allow the witness to tell a story in his or her own words. During direct examination, courts generally prohibit the use of leading questions, or those which suggest answers to the witness.[101] Many courts also consider questions which call for yes or no answers to be inappropriate since they are inherently suggestive.

Cross-examination refers to the examination of a witness by anyone other than the direct examiner. Anyone who offers testimony in a criminal court has the duty to submit to cross-examination.[102] The purpose of cross-examination is to test the credibility and memory of a witness.

Most states and the federal government restrict the scope of cross-examination to material covered during direct examination. Questions about other matters, even though they may relate to the case before the court, are not allowed. A small number of states allow the cross-examiner to raise any issue as long as it is deemed relevant by the court. Leading questions, generally disallowed in direct examination, are regarded as the mainstay of cross-examination. Such questions allow for a concise restatement of testimony which has already been offered and serve to focus efficiently on potential problems that the cross-examiner seeks to address.

Some witnesses offer **perjured testimony**, or statements which they know to be untrue. Reasons for perjured testimony vary, but most witnesses who lie on the stand probably do so in an effort to help friends accused of crimes. Witnesses who perjure themselves are subject to impeachment, in which either the defense counsel or prosecution demonstrates that they have intentionally offered false testimony. Such a demonstration may occur through the use of prior inconsistent statements, whereby previous statements made by the witness are shown to be at odds with more recent declarations. Perjury is a serious offense in its own right, and dishonest witnesses may face fines or jail time. When it can be demonstrated that a witness has offered inaccurate or false testimony, the witness has been effectively impeached.

At the conclusion of the cross-examination, the direct examiner may again question the witness. This procedure is called redirect examination and may be followed by a recross-examination and so on, until both sides are satisfied that they have exhausted fruitful lines of questioning.

Children as Witnesses

An area of special concern involves the use of children as witnesses in a criminal trial, especially where the children may have been victims. Currently, in an effort to avoid what may be traumatizing direct confrontations between child witnesses and the accused, 37 states allow the use of videotaped testimony in their criminal courtrooms, and 32 permit the use of closed-circuit television—which allows the child to testify out of the presence of the defendant. In 1988, however, the U.S. Supreme Court, in the case of *Coy* v. *Iowa*,[103] ruled that a courtroom screen, used to shield child witnesses from visual confrontation with a defendant in a child sex abuse case, had violated the confrontation clause of the Constitution.

On the other hand, in the 1990 case of *Maryland* v. *Craig*,[104] the Court upheld the use of closed-circuit television to shield children who testify in criminal courts. The Court's decision was partially based on the realization that "...a significant majority of States have enacted statutes to protect child witnesses from the trauma of giving testimony in child-abuse cases...[which]...attests to the widespread belief in the importance of such a policy."

The case involved Sandra Craig, a former preschool owner and administrator in Clarksville, Maryland, who had been found guilty by a trial court of 53 counts of child abuse, assault, and perverted sexual practices which she had allegedly performed on

Perjury. The intentional making of a false statement as part of the testimony by a sworn witness in a judicial proceeding on a matter relevant to the case at hand.

Theory into Practice: "Pleading the Fifth"

The Fifth Amendment to the U.S. Constitution is one of the best known entries in the Bill of Rights. Television shows and crime novels have popularized phrases such as "pleading the Fifth," or "taking the Fifth." As these media recognize, the Fifth Amendment is a powerful ally of any criminal defendant. When the accused, generally on the advice of counsel, decides to invoke the Fifth Amendment right against self-incrimination, the state cannot require the defendant to testify. In the past, defendants who refused to take the stand were often denigrated by comments the prosecution made to the jury. In 1965, the U.S. Supreme

Court, in the case of *Griffin* v. *California*,[1] ruled that the defendant's unwillingness to testify could not be interpreted as a sign of guilt. The Court reasoned that such interpretations forced the defendant to testify and effectively negated Fifth Amendment guarantees. Defendants who choose to testify, however, but who fail to adequately answer the questions put to them, may lawfully find themselves the target of a prosecutorial attack.

1. *Griffin* v. *California*, 380 U.S. 609 (1965).

the children under her care. During the trial, four young children, none past the age of 6, had testified against Craig while separated from her in the judge's chambers. Questioned by the district attorney, the children related stories of torture, burying alive, and sexual assault with a screwdriver.[105] Sandra Craig watched the children reply over a television monitor which displayed the process to the jury seated in the courtroom. Following the trial, Craig appealed, arguing that her ability to communicate with her lawyer (who had been in the judge's chambers and not the courtroom during questioning of the children) had been impeded and that her right to a fair trial under the Sixth Amendment to the U.S. Constitution had been denied since she was not given the opportunity to be "confronted with the witnesses" against her. In finding against Craig, Justice Sandra Day O'Connor, writing for the Court's majority, stated, "...if the State makes an adequate showing of necessity, the State interest in protecting child witnesses from the trauma of testifying in a child-abuse case is sufficiently important to justify the use of a special procedure that permits a child witness in such cases to testify...in the absence of face-to-face confrontation with the defendant."[106]

Although a face-to-face confrontation with a child victim may not be necessary in the courtroom, until 1992 the Supreme Court had been reluctant to allow into evidence descriptions of abuse and other statements made by children, even to child-care professionals, when those statements are made outside the courtroom. The Court, in *Idaho* v. *Wright* (1990),[107] reasoned that such "statements [are] fraught with the dangers of unreliability which the Confrontation Clause is designed to highlight and obviate."

However, in *White* v. *Illinois* (1992),[108] the Court seemed to reverse its stance, ruling that in-court testimony provided by a medical provider and the child's baby-sitter, which repeated what the child had said to them concerning White's sexually abusive behavior, was permissible. The Court rejected White's claim that out-of-court statements should be admissible only when the witness is unavailable to testify at trial, saying instead: "a finding of unavailability of an out-of-court declarant is necessary only if the out-of-court statement was made at a prior judicial proceeding." Placing *White* within the context of generally established exceptions, the court intoned:

> A statement that has been offered in a moment of excitement—without the opportunity to reflect on the consequences of one's exclamation—may justifiably carry more weight with a trier of fact than a similar statement offered in the relative calm of the courtroom. Similarly, a statement made in the course of procuring medical services, where the declarant knows that a false statement may cause misdiagnosis or mistreatment, carries special guarantees of credibility that a trier of fact may not think replicated by courtroom testimony.[109]

The Hearsay Rule

One aspect of witness testimony bears special mention. **Hearsay** is anything not based on the personal knowledge of a witness. A witness may say, for example, "John told me that Fred did it!" Such a witness becomes a hearsay declarant, and, following a likely objection by counsel, the trial judge will have to decide whether the witness's statement will be allowed to stand as evidence. In most cases, the judge will instruct the jury to disregard such comments from the witness, thereby enforcing the **hearsay rule,** which does not permit the use of "secondhand evidence."

There are some exceptions to the hearsay rule, however, that have been established by both precedent and tradition. One is the dying declaration. Dying declarations are statements made by a person who is about to die. When heard by a second party, they may usually be repeated in court, providing that certain conditions have been met. Dying declarations are generally valid exceptions to the hearsay rule when they are made by someone who knows that he or she is about to die, and when the statements made relate to the cause and circumstances of the impending death.

Hearsay. Something which is not based on the personal knowledge of a witness. Witnesses who testify, for example, about something they have heard, are offering hearsay by repeating information about a matter of which they have no direct knowledge.

Hearsay Rule. The long-standing American courtroom precedent that hearsay cannot be used in court. Rather than accepting testimony based on hearsay, the American trial process asks that the person who was the original source of the hearsay information be brought into court to be questioned and cross-examined. Exceptions to the hearsay rule may occur when the person with direct knowledge is dead or otherwise unable to testify.

Spontaneous statements provide another exception to the hearsay rule. Statements are considered spontaneous when they are made in the heat of excitement before the person has time to make them up. For example, a defendant who is just regaining consciousness following a crime may make an utterance which could later be repeated in court by those who heard it.

Out-of-court statements made by a witness, especially when they have been recorded in writing or by some other means, may also become exceptions to the hearsay rule. The use of such statements usually requires the witness to testify that the statements were accurate at the time they were made. This "past recollection recorded" exception to the hearsay rule is especially useful in drawn-out court proceedings which occur long after the crime. Under such circumstances, witnesses may no longer remember the details of an event. Their earlier statements to authorities, however, can be introduced into evidence as past recollection recorded.

Closing Arguments

At the conclusion of a criminal trial, both sides have the opportunity for a final narrative presentation to the jury in the form of **closing arguments**. This summation provides a review and analysis of the evidence. Its purpose is to persuade the jury to draw a conclusion favorable to the presenter. Testimony can be quoted, exhibits referred to, and attention drawn to inconsistencies in the evidence which has been presented by the other side.

Closing Argument. An oral summation of a case presented to a judge, or to a judge and jury, by the prosecution or by the defense in a criminal trial.

States vary in the order of closing arguments. Nearly all allow the defense attorney to speak to the jury before the prosecution makes its final points. A few permit the prosecutor the first opportunity for summation. Some jurisdictions and the *Federal Rules of Criminal Procedure*[110] authorize a defense rebuttal. Rebuttals are responses to the closing arguments of the other side.

Some specific issues may need to be addressed during summation. If, for example, the defendant has not taken the stand during the trial, the defense attorney's closing argument will inevitably stress that this failure to testify cannot be regarded as indicating guilt. Where the prosecution's case rests entirely on circumstantial evidence, the defense can be expected to stress the lack of any direct proof, whereas the prosecutor is likely to argue that circumstantial evidence can be stronger than direct evidence since it is not as easily affected by human error or false testimony.

The Judge's Charge to the Jury

After closing arguments, the judge will charge the jury to "retire and select one of your number as a foreman...and deliberate upon the evidence which has been presented until you have reached a verdict." The words of the charge will vary somewhat between jurisdictions and among judges, but all judges will remind members of the jury of their duty to consider objectively only the evidence which has been presented, and of the need for impartiality. Most judges will also remind jury members of the statutory elements of the alleged offense, of the burden of proof which rests upon the prosecution, and of the need for the prosecution to have proven guilt beyond a reasonable doubt before a guilty verdict can be returned.

In their charge, many judges will also provide a summary of the evidence presented, usually from notes they have taken during the trial, as a means of refreshing the juror's memories of events. About half of all the states allow judges the freedom to express their own views on the credibility of witnesses and the significance of evidence. Other states only permit judges to summarize the evidence in an objective and impartial manner.

Following the charge, the jury will be removed from the courtroom and permitted to begin its deliberations. In the absence of the jury, defense attorneys may choose to challenge portions of the judge's charge. If they feel that some oversight has occurred in the original charge, they may also request that the judge provide the jury with additional instructions or information. Such objections, if denied by the judge, often become the basis for appeals when a conviction is returned.

Jury Deliberations and the Verdict

In cases where the evidence is either very clear or very weak, jury deliberations may be brief, lasting only a matter of hours or even minutes. Some juries, however, deliberate days or sometimes weeks, carefully weighing all the nuances of the evidence they have seen and heard. Many jurisdictions require that juries reach a unanimous **verdict** although the U.S. Supreme Court has ruled that unanimous verdicts are not required in noncapital cases.[111] Even so, some juries are unable to agree on any verdict. When a jury is deadlocked, it is said to be a hung jury. Where a unanimous decision is required, juries may be deadlocked by the strong opposition of only one member to a verdict agreed on by all the others.

In some states, judges are allowed to add a boost to nearly hung juries by recharging them under a set of instructions agreed on by the Supreme Court in the 1896 case of *Allen* v. *United States*.[112] The Allen Charge, as it is known in those jurisdictions, urges the jury to vigorous deliberations and suggests to obstinate jurors that their objections may be ill founded if they make no impression on the minds of other jurors.

Problems with the Jury System

The jury system has received much criticism as an inefficient and outmoded method for determining guilt or innocence.[113] Jurors cannot be expected to understand modern legal complexities and to appreciate all the nuances of trial court practice. Many instructions to the jury are probably poorly understood and rarely observed by even the best-meaning jurors.[114] Emotions are difficult to separate from fact. During deliberations, many juries are probably dominated by one or two forceful personalities. Jurors may also become confused over legal technicalities, suffer from inattention, or be unable to understand fully the testimony of expert witnesses or the significance of technical evidence.

Lyle and Erik Menendez. Their first trial on charges of killing their parents after an alleged lifetime of sexual abuse resulted in hung juries. They were convicted of the murders in a second trial in 1996 and sentenced to life in prison. Photo by Nick Ut, courtesy of AP/Wide World Photos.

Many such problems became evident in the trial of Raymond Buckey and his mother, Peggy McMartin Buckey, who were tried in Los Angeles for allegedly molesting dozens of children at their family-run preschool.[115] The trial, which involved 65 counts of child sexual molestation and conspiracy, and 61 witnesses, ran for more than three years. Many jurors were stressed to the breaking point by the length of time involved. Family relationships suffered as the trial droned on, and jurors were unable to accompany their spouses and children on vacation. Small-business owners, who were expected to continue paying salaries to employees serving as jurors, faced financial ruin and threatened their absent employees with termination. Careers were put on hold, and at least one juror had to be dismissed for becoming inattentive to testimony. The trial cost taxpayers more than $12 million, but was nearly negated as jury membership and the number of alternate jurors declined due to sickness and personal problems. Ultimately, the defendants were acquitted.

Another trial in which the defendants were similarly acquitted of the majority of charges against them involved state-level prosecution of the officers accused in the now-infamous Rodney King beating. Following the riots in Los Angeles and elsewhere which came on the heels of their verdict, jurors in the "Rodney King trial" reported being afraid for their lives. Some slept with weapons by their side, and others sent their children away to safe locales.[116] Because of the potential for harm jurors faced in the 1993 federal trial of the same officers, U.S. District Judge John G. Davies ruled that the names of jurors be forever kept secret. The secrecy order was called "an unprecedented infringement of the public's right of access to the justice system"[117] by members of the press. Similarly, in the 1993 trial of three black men charged with the beating of white truck driver Reginald Denny during the Los Angeles riots, Los Angeles Superior Court Judge John Ouderkirk ordered that the identities of jurors not be released.

Opponents of the jury system have argued that it should be replaced by a panel of judges who would both render a verdict and impose sentence. Regardless of how well considered such a suggestion may be, however, such a change could not occur without modification of the Constitution's Sixth Amendment right to trial by jury.

An alternative suggestion for improving the process of trial by jury has been the call for professional jurors. Professional jurors would be paid by the government, as are judges, prosecutors, and public defenders. Their job would be to sit on any jury, and they would be expected to have the expertise to do so. Professional jurors would be trained to listen objectively and would be schooled with the kinds of decision-making skills necessary to function effectively within an adversarial context. They could be expected to hear one case after another, perhaps moving between jurisdictions in cases of highly publicized crimes.

The advantages a professional jury system offers are:

1. *Dependability*. Professional jurors could be expected to report to the courtroom in a timely fashion and to be good listeners since both would be required by the nature of the job.
2. *Knowledge*. Professional jurors would be trained in the law, would understand what a finding of guilt requires, and would know what to expect from other actors in the courtroom.
3. *Equity*. Professional jurors would understand the requirements of due process and would be less likely to be swayed by the emotional content of a case, having been schooled in the need to separate matters of fact from personal feelings.

A professional jury system would not be without difficulties. Jurors under such a system might become jaded, deciding cases out of hand as routines lead to boredom and suspects are categorized according to whether they "fit the type" for guilt or innocence developed on the basis of previous experiences. Job requirements for professional jurors would be difficult to establish without infringing on the jurors' freedom to decide cases as they understand them. For the same reason, any evaluation of the job performance of professional jurors would be a difficult call. Finally, professional jurors might not truly be peer jurors since their social characteristics might be skewed by education, residence, and politics.

Improving the Adjudication Process

Courts today are coming under increasing scrutiny, and media-rich trials such as that of O. J. Simpson, Susan Smith, and the Menendez brothers, have heightened awareness of problems with the American court system. One of today's most important issues involves reducing the number of jurisdictions by unifying courts. The current multiplicity of jurisdictions frequently leads to what many believe are avoidable conflicts and overlaps in the handling of criminal defendants. Problems

---

Theory into Practice: What Will Courtrooms of the 21st Century Be Like?

Recently, the College of William and Mary, in conjunction with the National Center for State Courts (NCSC), unveiled Courtroom 21, the most technologically advanced courtroom in the United States. Courtroom 21, located in the McGlothlin Courtroom of the College of William and Mary, offers anyone concerned with the future of trial practice and with courtroom technology a glimpse at what American courtrooms may be like in the 21st century.

Courtroom 21 includes the following integrated capabilities:

1. Automatic video recording of proceedings using ceiling-mounted cameras with voice-initiated switching. A sophisticated voice-activation system directs cameras to tape the person speaking, to record what is said, and to tape evidence as it is being presented.

2. Recorded televised evidence display with optical disk storage. Documentary or real evidence may be presented to the judge and jury via television through the use of a video "presenter" which also makes a video record of the evidence as it is being presented for later use.

3. A remote, two-way television arraignment which allows video and audio signals to be sent from the judge's bench to areas throughout the courtroom, including the jury box.

4. Text-, graphics-, and TV-capable jury computers. Courtroom 21's jury box contains computers for information display and animation so that jury members can easily view documents, live or pre-

recorded video, and other graphics such as charts, diagrams, and pictures. TV-capable jury computers also allow for the remote appearance of witnesses—that is, for questioning witnesses who may be unable or unwilling to physically appear in the courtroom, and for the display of crime-scene reenactments via computer animation.

5. Access for judge and for counsel on both sides to online legal research databases. Available databases contain an extensive variety of state and federal statutes, case law, and other precedent which allow judges and attorneys to find answers to unanticipated legal questions that might arise during trial.

6. Built-in video playback facilities for out-of-court testimony. Because an increasing number of depositions are being video recorded by attorneys in preparation for trial, Courtroom 21 has capabilities for video deposition playback. To present expert witness testimony or to impeach a witness, video depositions can be played on court monitors.

7. Information storage with software search capabilities. Integrated software programs provide text-searching capabilities to courtroom participants. Previously transcribed testimony, as well as precedent-setting cases from other courts, can be searched and reviewed.

8. Concurrent (real-time) court reporter transcription, including the ability for each lawyer to mark an individual computerized copy for later use. A court reporter uses a self-contained computerized

(Continued on next page)

are exacerbated by the lack of any centralized judicial authority in some states which might resolve jurisdictional and procedural disputes.[118] Proponents of unification suggest the elimination of overlapping jurisdictions, the creation of special-purpose courts, and the formulation of administrative offices in order to achieve economies of scale.[119]

Court-watch citizens groups are also rapidly growing in number. Such organizations focus on the trial court level, but they are part of a general trend toward seeking greater openness in government decision making at all levels.[120] Court-watch groups regularly monitor court proceedings and attempt to document and often publicize inadequacies. They frequently focus on the handling of indigents, fairness in the scheduling of cases for trial, unnecessary court delays, the reduction of waiting time, the treatment of witnesses and jurors, and adequacy of rights advisements for defendants throughout judicial proceedings.

The statistical measurement of court performance is another area which is receiving increased attention. Research has looked at the efficiency with which prosecutors schedule cases for trial; the speed with which judges resolve issues; the amount of time judges spend on the bench; and the economic and other costs to

---

Theory into Practice: What Will Courtrooms of the 21st Century Be Like?—*Continued*

writing machine for real-time capture of testimony in the courtroom. When the reporter writes, the computer translates strokes into English transcripts which are immediately distributed to the judge and counsel via their personal computers. Using this technology, the judge and attorneys can take a copy of the day's testimony with them on their laptop computer or on a floppy diskette for evening review and trial preparation.

The technology now being demonstrated in Courtroom 21 suggests many possibilities. For one thing, court video equipment could be used by attorneys for filing remote motions and other types of hearings. As one of Courtroom 21's designers puts it: "Imagine the productivity gains if lawyers no longer need to travel across a city or county for a ten-minute appearance."

Courtroom 21 designers also suggest that the innovative use of audio and video technology can preserve far more evidence and trial detail than written records, making a comprehensive review of cases easier for appellate judges. One study, which has already been conducted by the NCSC, showed that when video records are available, appellate courts are less likely to reverse the original determinations of the trial court. Video court records, analysts say, "might also improve the performance of attorneys and judges. By preserving matters not now apparent on a written record, such as facial expressions, voice inflections, body gestures, and the like, video records may cause trial participants to be more circumspect in their behavior than at present."

High technology can also be expected to have considerable impact on the trial itself. The technology built into Courtroom 21 readily facilitates computer animations and crime-scene reenactments. As one of the designers of Courtroom 21 says, "*Jurassic Park* quality computer reenactment may have enormous psychological impact" (on jurors).

Courtroom 21 shows what a typical courtroom of the near future may be like, but it also raises questions about the appropriate use of innovative courtroom technologies. As Fred Lederer, one of Courtroom 21's designers, points out: "Modern technology holds enormous promise for our courts. We must recognize, however, that technology's utility often depends upon how people will use it. Although we must continue to improve our courts via technology, we must be sensitive to technology's impact and work to recognize and minimize any negative consequences it might have on our system of justice."

QUESTIONS FOR DISCUSSION

1. How might technologies such as those discussed in this box affect the outcome of criminal trials, if at all?

2. Can you imagine criminal trials in which the use of high-technology courtrooms might not be appropriate? If so, what might they be?

SOURCES: *Court Technology Bulletin* January–February 1994 (Volume 6, Number 1); *Court Technology Bulletin* March–April 1994 (Volume 6, Number 2); and the National Center for State Courts World Wide Web site on the Internet, from which some of the material in this box is taken.

defendants, witnesses, and communities involved in the judicial process.[121] Statistical studies of this type often attempt to measure elements of court performance as diverse as sentence variation, charging accuracy, fairness in plea bargaining, even-handedness, delays, and attitudes toward the court by lay participants.[122]

In 1994, the Federal Judicial Center, which is the research, education, and planning agency of the federal judicial system, conducted a nationwide survey intended to gather information for the federal Judicial Conference Committee on Long Range Planning. The Center's survey reached nearly all federal judges and covered a wide range of issues. Results of the survey[123] showed that federal judges: (1) were convinced that the most serious problem facing federal courts was the huge volume of criminal cases waiting to be processed; (2) believed that criminal case processing needs gravely affected the ability of federal courts to effectively handle civil cases; (3) hoped that the concerns of federal court judges and administrators would be considered before any new federal criminal legislation was passed; and (4) wanted more discretion in sentencing and fewer rules requiring mandatory minimum sentences for criminal defendants.

Summary

The criminal trial, which owes its legacy to the evolution of democratic principles, stands as a centerpiece of American criminal justice. It has long been seen as a peer-based fact-finding process intended to protect the rights of the accused while sifting out disputed issues of guilt or innocence. The adversarial environment, which has served American courts for more than 200 years, however, is now itself being questioned. A plethora of far-reaching social and technological changes, many of them unanticipated by the framers of our judicial system, have recently occurred. In many cases, new technologies, such as DNA fingerprinting, may soon unequivocally link suspects to criminal activity. Newspapers and the electronic media can rapidly and widely disseminate findings. This combination, of investigative technologies and readily available information, may eventually make courtroom debates about guilt or innocence obsolete. Whether the current adversarial system can continue to serve the interests of justice in an information-rich and technologically advanced society will be a central question for the future.

Discussion Questions

1. We described participants in a criminal trial as working together to bring about a successful close to courtroom proceedings. What do you think a "successful close" might mean to a judge? To a defense attorney? To a prosecutor? To the jury? To the defendant?
2. What is a dying declaration? Under what circumstances might it be a valid exception to the hearsay rule? Why do most courts seem to believe that a person who is about to die is likely to tell the truth?
3. Do you think the present jury system is outmoded? Might "professional jurors" be more effective than the present system of "peer jurors"? On what do you base your opinion?
4. What is an expert witness? A lay witness? What different kinds of testimony may both provide? What are some of the difficulties in expert testimony?
5. What are the three forms of indigent defense used throughout various regions of the United States? Why might defendants prefer private attorneys to public counsel?

References

1. Jill Smolowe, "The Trials of the Public Defender," *Time*, February 8, 1993, p. 46.

2. "Louisiana's Public Defender System Found Unconstitutional," *Criminal Justice Newsletter*, Vol. 23, no. 5, March 3, 1992, p. 1.

3. See, for example, Edward J. Clynch and David W. Neubauer, "Trial Courts as Organizations," *Law and Policy Quarterly*, Vol. 3 (1981), pp. 69–94.

4. In 1940, Missouri became the first state to adopt a plan for the "merit selection" of judges based on periodic public review.

5. The National Judicial College, *1988 Course Catalog* (Reno: University of Nevada Press, 1987), p. 3.

6. Doris Marie Provine, *Judging Credentials: Nonlawyer Judges and the Politics of Professionalism* (Chicago: University of Chicago Press, 1986).

7. Ibid.

8. Ibid.

9. Aminah Franklin, "District Justice Charged with Misconduct," *The Morning Call*, July 6, 1995, p. 1A.

10. *U.S.* v. *Nixon*, 816 F.2d 1022 (1987).

11. *Nixon* v. *U.S.*, 113, S.Ct. 732, 122 L. Ed. 2d 1 (1993).

12. Bureau of Justice Statistics, *Report to the Nation on Crime and Justice: The Data* (Washington, D.C.: U.S. Department of Justice, 1983).

13. For a discussion of the resource limitations of district attorneys in combating corporate crime, see Michael L. Benson, William J. Maakestad, Francis T. Cullen, and Gilbert Geis, "District Attorneys and Corporate Crime: Surveying the Prosecutorial Gatekeepers," *Criminology*, Vol. 26, no. 3 (August 1988), pp. 505–517.

14. John M. Dawson, *Prosecutors in State Courts, 1990* (Washington, D.C.: Bureau of Justice Statistics, 1992).

15. Many large police departments have their own legal counselors who provide advice on civil liability and who may also assist in weighing the quality of evidence which has been assembled.

16. Kenneth Culp Davis, *Discretionary Justice* (Baton Rouge: Louisiana State University Press, 1969), p. 190.

17. Barbara Borland, *The Prosecution of Felony Arrests* (Washington, D.C.: Bureau of Justice Statistics, 1983).

18. *Brady* v. *Maryland*, 373 U.S. 83 (1963).

19. *U.S.* v. *Bagley*, 473 U.S. 667 (1985).

20. *Imbler* v. *Pachtman*, 424 U.S. 409 (1976).

21. *Burns* v. *Reed*, 500 U.S. 478 (1991).

22. Ibid., complaint, p. 29.

23. Cassia Spohn, John Gruhl, and Susan Welch, "The Impact of the Ethnicity and Gender of Defendants on the Decision to Reject or Dismiss Felony Charges," *Criminology*, Vol. 25, no. 1 (1987), pp. 175–191.

24. "Pay the Costs of Justice," *USA Today*, March 30, 1993, p. 8A.

25. *Powell* v. *Alabama*, 287 U.S. 45 (1932).

26. *Johnson* v. *Zerbst*, 304 U.S. 458 (1938).

27. *Gideon* v. *Wainwright*, 372 U.S. 335 (1963).

28. *Argersinger* v. *Hamlin*, 407 U.S. 25 (1972).

29. *In re Gault*, 387 U.S. 1 (1967).

30. Bureau of Justice Statistics, *Criminal Defense for the Poor, 1986*.

31. "Pay the Costs of Justice," *USA Today*, March 30, 1993, p. 8A.

32. Smolowe, "The Trials of the Public Defender," p. 46.

33. Ibid.

34. *Faretta* v. *California*, 422 U.S. 806 (1975).

35. "Killings Spotlight Lawyers' Ethics," *The Fayetteville Observer-Times* (North Carolina), September 13, 1992, p. 11A.

36. *Nix* v. *Whiteside*, 475 U.S. 157 (1986).

37. Ibid.

38. "Courtroom Killings Verdict," *USA Today*, February 15, 1993, p. 3A.

39. "How Crucial Is Courtroom Security?" *Security Management* (August 1992), p. 78.

40. President's Commission on Law Enforcement and Administration of Justice, *The Challenge of Crime in a Free Society* (Washington, D.C.: U.S. Government Printing Office, 1967), p. 129.

41. National Advisory Commission on Criminal Justice Standards and Goals, *Courts* (Washington, D.C.: U.S. Government Printing Office, 1973), Standard 9.3.

42. See, for example, Joan G. Brannon, *The Judicial System in North Carolina* (Raleigh, NC: The Administrative Office of the Courts, 1984), p. 14.

43. Joseph L. Peterson, "Use of Forensic Evidence by the Police and Courts," a National Institute of Justice, *Research in Brief* (Washington, D.C.: NIJ, 1987), p. 3.

44. Ibid., p. 6.

45. Jennifer Bowles, "Simpson-Paid Experts," The Associated Press online, August 12, 1995.

46. *California* v. *Green*, 399 U.S. 149 (1970).

47. Patrick L. McCloskey and Ronald L. Schoenberg, *Criminal Law Deskbook* (New York: Matthew Bender, 1988), Section 17, p. 123.

48. Bureau of Justice Statistics, *Report to the Nation on Crime and Justice*, 2nd ed., p. 82.

49. *Demarest* v. *Manspeaker et al.*, No. 89-5916 (1991).

50. Ibid., p. 82.

51. *Williams* v. *Florida*, 399 U.S. 78, 90 S.Ct. 1893, 26 L.Ed. 2d 446 (1970).

52. *Smith* v. *Texas*, 311 U.S. 128 (1940).

53. *Thiel* v. *Southern Pacific Co.*, 328 U.S. 217 (1945).

54. Speaking from a personal experience, the author was himself the victim of a felony some years ago. My car was stolen in Columbus, Ohio, and recovered a year later in Cleveland. I was informed that the person who had taken it was in custody, but I never heard what happened to him, nor could I learn where or whether a trial was to be held.

55. *Crosby* v. *U.S.*, 113 S.Ct. 748,122 L. Ed. 2d 25 (1993).

56. *Zafiro* v. *U.S.*, 133 S.Ct. 933, 122 L. Ed. 2d 317 (1993).

57. Dale Russakoff, "N.Y. Defendant Keeps His Own Counsel; Alleged Killer of Six Commuter Train Passengers Shuns His Lawyers' Advice," *The Washington Post* online, January 27, 1995.

58. Larry Mcshane, "Ferguson-Why?" The Associated Press online, February 18, 1995.

59. *Nebraska Press Association* v. *Stuart*, 427 U.S. 539 (1976).

60. However, it is generally accepted that trial judges may issue limited gag orders aimed at trial participants.

61. *Press Enterprise Company* v. *Superior Court of California, Riverside County*, 478 U.S. 1 (1986).

62. *Caribbean International News Corporation* v. *Puerto Rico*, No. 92-949, May 17, 1993.

63. Dennis Cauchon, "Federal Courts Camera-Less," *USA Today*, March 10, 1993, p. 2A.

64. *Chandler* v. *Florida*, 499 U.S. 560 (1981).

65. Ibid.

66. Harry F. Rosenthal, "Courts-TV," Associated Press online, September 21, 1994. See also, "Judicial Conference Rejects Cameras in Federal Courts," *Criminal Justice Newsletter*, September 15, 1994, p. 6.

67. Marc G. Gertz and Edmond J. True, "Social Scientists in the Courtroom: The Frustrations of Two Expert Witnesses," in Susette M. Talarico, ed., *Courts and Criminal Justice: Emerging Issues* (Beverly Hills, Calif.: Sage Publications, 1985), pp. 81–91.

68. *Klopfer* v. *North Carolina*, 386 U.S. 213 (1967).

69. *Barker* v. *Wingo*, 407 U.S. 514 (1972).

70. *Strunk* v. *U.S.*, 412 U.S. 434 (1973).

71. The Federal Speedy Trial Act, 18 U.S.C., Section 3161 (1974).

72. *U.S.* v. *Brainer*, 515 F. Supp. 627 (D.Md.1981).

73. *U.S.* v. *Taylor*, U.S. 108, S.Ct. 2413 (1988).

74. *Fex* v. *Michigan*, 113 S.Ct. 1085, 122 L. Ed. 2d 406 (1993).

75. *Doggett* v. *U.S.*, 112 S.Ct. 2686 (1992).

76. William U. McCormack, "Supreme Court Cases: 1991–1992 Term," *FBI Law Enforcement Bulletin*, November, 1992, pp. 28–29.

77. See, for example, the U.S. Supreme Court's decision in the case of *Murphy* v. *Florida*, 410 U.S. 525 (1973).

78. *Witherspoon* v. *Illinois*, 391 U.S. 510 (1968).

79. *Mu'Min* v. *Virginia*, 500 U.S. 415 (1991).

80. Rule 24(6) of the *Federal Rules of Criminal Procedure*.

81. "Are Juries Colorblind?" *Newsweek*, December 5, 1988, p. 94.

82. Ibid.

83. Ibid.

84. Ibid.

85. Supreme Court majority opinion in *Powers* v. *Ohio*, 499 U.S. 400 (1991), citing *Strauder* v. *West Virginia*, 100 U.S. 303 (1880).

86. *Swain* v. *Alabama*, 380 U.S. 202 (1965).

87. *Batson* v. *Kentucky*, 476 U.S. 79, 106 S.Ct. 1712 (1986).

88. *Ford* v. *Georgia*, 498 U.S. 411 (1991), footnote 2.

89. Ibid.

90. *Powers* v. *Ohio*.

91. *Edmonson* v. *Leesville Concrete Co., Inc.*, 500 U.S. ____ (1991).

92. *Georgia* v. *McCollum*, 505 U.S. 42 (1992).

93. See, for example, *Davis* v. *Minnesota*, No. 93-6577 (1994).

94. Although the words *argument* and *statement* are sometimes used interchangeably in alluding to opening remarks, defense attorneys are enjoined from drawing conclusions or "arguing" to the jury at this stage in the trial. Their task, as described in the section which follows, is simply to provide information to the jury about how the defense will be conducted.

95. *U.S.* v. *Dinitz*, 424 U.S. 600, 612 (1976).

96. *Michigan* v. *Lucas*, 500 U.S. 145 (1991).

97. *Kotteakos* v. *United States*, 328 U.S. 750 (1946); *Becht* v. *Abrahamson*, 113 S.Ct. 1710, 123 L. Ed. 2d 353 (1993); and *Arizona* v. *Fulminante*, 111 S.Ct. 1246 (1991).

98. The Court, citing *Kotteakos* v. *United States*, 328 U.S. 750 (1946) in *Brecht* v. *Abrahamson*, No. 91-7358. Decided April 21, 1993.

99. *Sullivan* v. *Louisiana*, 113 S.Ct. 2078, 124 L. Ed. 2d 182 (1993).

100. *Griffin* v. *California*, 380 U.S. 609 (1965).

101. Leading questions may, in fact, be permitted for certain purposes, including refreshing a witness's memory, impeaching a hostile witness, introducing nondisputed material, and helping a witness with impaired faculties.

102. *In re Oliver*, 333 U.S. 257 (1948).

103. *Coy v. Iowa*, 487 U.S. 1012, 108 S.Ct. 2798 (1988).

104. *Maryland v. Craig*, 497, U.S. 836, 845-847 (1990).

105. "The Right to Confront Your Accuser," *The Boston Globe* magazine, April 7, 1991, pp. 19, 51.

106. *Maryland v. Craig*.

107. *Idaho v. Wright*, 497 U.S. 805 (1990).

108. *White v. Illinois*, 112 S.Ct. 736 (1992).

109. *White v. Illinois*, Project Hermes online decision.

110. Rule 29.1 of the *Federal Rules of Criminal Procedure*.

111. See *Johnson v. Louisiana*, 406 U.S. 356 (1972), and *Apodaca v. Oregon*, 406 U.S. 404 (1972).

112. *Allen v. U.S.*, 164 U.S. 492 (1896).

113. See, for example, John Baldwin and Michael McConville, "Criminal Juries," in Norval Morris and Michael Tonry, eds., *Crime and Justice*, Vol. 2 (Chicago: University of Chicago Press, 1980).

114. Amiram Elwork, Bruce D. Sales, and James Alfini, *Making Jury Instructions Understandable* (Charlottesville, Va.: Michie, 1982).

115. "Juror Hardship Becomes Critical as McMartin Trial Enters Year 3," *Criminal Justice Newsletter*, Vol. 20 (May 15, 1989), pp. 6–7.

116. "King Jury Lives in Fear from Unpopular Verdict," *Fayetteville Observer-Times* (North Carolina), May 10, 1992, p. 7A.

117. "Los Angeles Trials Spark Debate over Anonymous Juries," *Criminal Justice Newsletter*, February 16, 1993, pp. 3–4.

118. Some states have centralized offices called "Administrative Offices of the Courts" or something similar. Such offices, however, are often primarily data-gathering agencies which have little or no authority over the day-to-day functioning of state or local courts.

119. See, for example, Larry Berkson and Susan Carbon, *Court Unification: Its History, Politics, and Implementation* (Washington, D.C.: U.S. Government Printing Office, 1978), and Thomas Henderson et al., *The Significance of Judicial Structure: The Effect of Unification on Trial Court Operators* (Alexandria, Va.: Institute for Economic and Policy Studies, 1984).

120. See, for example, Kenneth Carlson, et al., *Citizen Court Watching: The Consumer's Perspectives* (Cambridge, Mass.: Abt Associates, 1977).

121. See, for example, Thomas J. Cook and Ronald W. Johnson, et al., *Basic Issues in Court Performance* (Washington, D.C.: National Institute of Justice, 1982).

122. See, for example, Sorrel Wildhorn et al., *Indicators of Justice:* Measuring the Performance of Prosecutors, Defense, and Court Agencies Involved in Felony Proceedings (Lexington, Mass.: Lexington Books, 1977).

123. Federal Judicial Center, *Planning for the Future: Results of a 1992 Federal Judicial Center Survey of United States Judges* (1994).

CHAPTER 9

Sentencing

—Photo by Bettmann

*W*e will not punish a man because he hath offended, but that he may offend no more; nor does punishment ever look to the past, but to the future; for it is not the result of passion, but that the same thing be guarded against in time to come.

—SENECA (B.C. 3–65 A.D.)

*I*f you want a small prison population, make punishment certain.
If you want a large prison population, make punishment uncertain.

—NEWT GINGRICH

*P*unishment, that is justice for the unjust.

—SAINT AUGUSTINE (345–430 A.D.)

*T*o make punishments efficacious, two things are necessary. They must never be disproportioned to the offense, and they must be certain.

—WILLIAM SIMS (1806–1870)

KEY CONCEPTS

sentencing	retribution	incapacitation
deterrence	specific deterrence	just deserts
rehabilitation	restoration	restorative justice
good time	determinate sentencing	indeterminate sentencing
aggravating circumstances	mitigating circumstances	presentence report
victim impact statement	victim compensation	capital punishment
general deterrence	truth in sentencing	

KEY CASES

Wilkerson v. *Utah*	*Coker* v. *Georgia*	*Deal* v. *U.S.*
Furman v. *Georgia*	*Woodson* v. *North Carolina*	*Stinson* v. *U.S.*
Mistretta v. *U.S.*	*Gregg* v. *Georgia*	*McCleskey* v. *Zandt*
In re Kemmler	*Booth* v. *Maryland*	*Coleman* v. *Thompson*
Smith v. *U.S.*	*Payne* v. *Tennessee*	

Crime and Punishment: Introduction

A few years ago, John Angus Smith and a friend went from Tennessee to Florida to buy cocaine. They hoped to resell it at a profit. While in Florida, they met an acquaintance of Smith's, Deborah Hoag. Hoag purchased cocaine for Smith and then accompanied him and his friend to her motel room, where they were joined by a drug dealer. While Hoag listened, Smith and the dealer discussed Smith's MAC-10 firearm, which had been modified to operate as an automatic. The MAC-10, small, compact, and lightweight, can be equipped with a silencer and is a favorite among criminals. A fully automatic MAC-10 can be devastating. It can fire more than 1,000 rounds per minute. The dealer expressed his interest in becoming the owner of a MAC-10, and Smith promised that he would discuss selling the gun if his arrangement with another potential buyer fell through.

Unfortunately for Smith, Hoag had contacts not only with narcotics traffickers but also with law enforcement officials. She was a confidential informant, and she informed the Broward County Sheriff's Office of Smith's activities. The sheriff's office responded quickly, sending an undercover officer to Hoag's motel room. Several other officers were assigned to keep the motel under surveillance. On arriving at Hoag's room, the undercover officer presented himself to Smith as a pawnshop dealer. Smith, in turn, presented the officer with a proposition: He had an automatic MAC-10 and silencer with which he might be willing to part if a good price could be arranged. Smith then pulled the MAC-10 out of a black canvas bag and showed it to the officer. The officer examined the gun and asked Smith what he wanted for it. Rather than asking for money, however, Smith asked for drugs. He was willing to trade his MAC-10, he said, for two ounces of cocaine. The officer told Smith that he was just a pawnshop dealer and did not distribute narcotics. Nonetheless, he indicated that he wanted the MAC-10 and would try to get the cocaine.

The undercover officer then left, promising to return within an hour, and went to the sheriff's office to arrange for Smith's arrest. But Smith did not wait. The officers who were conducting surveillance saw him leave the motel room carrying a gun bag; he then climbed into his van and drove away. The officers reported Smith's departure and began following him. When law enforcement authorities tried to stop Smith, he led them on a high-speed chase, which ended in his apprehension. Smith, it turns out, was well armed. A search of his van revealed the MAC-10, a silencer, ammunition, and a "fast-feed" mechanism. In addition, police found a MAC-11 machine gun, a loaded .45-caliber pistol, and a .22-caliber pistol with a scope and homemade silencer. Smith also had a loaded 9-millimeter handgun in his waistband.

A grand jury for the Southern District of Florida returned an indictment charging Smith with, among other offenses, two drug trafficking crimes—conspiracy to possess cocaine with intent to distribute, and attempt to possess cocaine with intent to distribute. More important, the indictment alleged that Smith knowingly used the MAC-10 and its silencer during and in relation to a drug trafficking crime. Under federal law, a defendant who so uses a firearm must be sentenced to five years' incarceration. And where, as here, the firearm is a "machine gun" or is fitted with a silencer, the sentence is 30 years. The jury convicted Smith on all counts.

This story is taken directly from the majority opinion in the 1993 U.S. Supreme Court case of *Smith* v. *U.S.*,[1] which held that "[a] criminal who trades his firearm for drugs 'uses' it within the meaning" of federal sentencing guidelines. The plain language of the statute, the Court explained, imposes no requirement that the firearm be used as a weapon. Smith's appeal of his 30-year sentence was denied.

Sentencing is the imposition of a penalty on a person convicted of a crime. Most sentencing decisions are made by judges although in some cases, especially where a death sentence is possible, juries may be involved in a special sentencing phase of courtroom proceedings. The sentencing decision is one of the most difficult

Sentencing. The imposition of a criminal sanction by a judicial authority.

made by any judge or jury. Not only does it involve the future, and perhaps the very life, of the defendant, but society looks to sentencing to achieve a diversity of goals—some of which may not be fully compatible.

This chapter examines sentencing in terms of both philosophy and practice. We will describe the goals of sentencing as well as the historical development of various sentencing models in the United States. We will also discuss the role of victims in contemporary sentencing practices, and this chapter contains a detailed overview of victimization and victim's rights in general—especially as they relate to courtroom procedure and to sentencing practice. Finally, we will describe federal sentencing guidelines and the significance of presentence investigations.

The Philosophy of Criminal Sentencing

Traditional sentencing options have included imprisonment, fines, probation, and—for very serious offenses—death. Limits on the range of options available to sentencing authorities are generally specified in law. Historically, those limits have shifted as understandings of crime and the goals of sentencing have changed. Sentencing philosophies, or the justifications on which various sentencing strategies are based, are manifestly intertwined with issues of religion, morals, values, and emotions.[2] Philosophies which gained ascendancy at a particular point in history were likely to be reflections of more deeply held social values. The mentality of centuries ago, for example, held that crime was due to sin, and suffering was the culprit's due. Judges were expected to be harsh. Capital punishment, torture, and painful physical penalties served this view of criminal behavior.

An emphasis on rehabilitation became more prevalent around the time of the American and French revolutions, brought about, in part, by Enlightenment philosophies. Offenders came to be seen as highly rational beings who, more often than not, intentionally and somewhat carefully chose their course of action. Sentencing philosophies of the period stressed the need for sanctions which outweighed the benefits to be derived from making criminal choices. Severity of punishment became less important than quick and certain penalties.

Recent thinking has emphasized the need to limit offenders' potential for future harm by separating them from society. We still also believe that offenders deserve to be punished, and we have not entirely abandoned hope for their rehabilitation. Modern sentencing practices are influenced by five goals which weave their way through widely disseminated professional and legal models, continuing public calls for sentencing reform, and everyday sentencing practice. Each goal represents a quasi-independent sentencing philosophy since each makes distinctive assumptions about human nature and holds implications for sentencing practice. The five goals of contemporary sentencing are:

1. Retribution
2. Incapacitation
3. Deterrence
4. Rehabilitation
5. Restoration

Retribution

Retribution. The act of taking revenge on a criminal perpetrator.

Retribution is a call for punishment predicated upon a felt need for vengeance. Retribution is the earliest known rationale for punishment. Most early societies punished offenders whenever they could catch them. Early punishments were swift and immediate—often without the benefit of a hearing—and they were often extreme, with little thought given to whether the punishment "fit" the crime. Death and exile, for example, were commonly imposed even on relatively minor

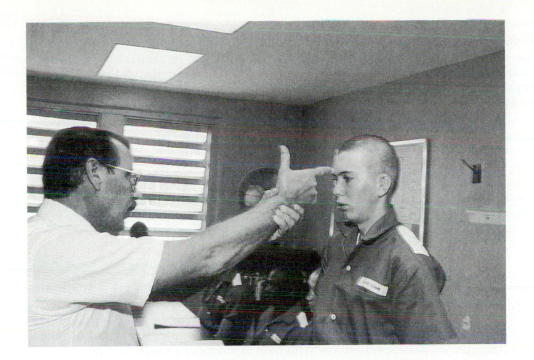

Modern-day retribution in practice: A counselor in a prison "boot camp" program shows a robber what it feels like to have a gun pointed at his head. Photo by Steve Starr, courtesy of Stock Boston.

offenders. In contrast, the Old Testament dictum of "An eye for an eye, a tooth for a tooth"—often cited as an ancient justification for retribution—was actually intended to reduce the severity of punishment for relatively minor crimes.

In its modern guise, retribution corresponds to the just deserts model of sentencing. The **just deserts** philosophy holds that offenders are responsible for their crimes. When they are convicted and punished, they are said to have gotten their "just deserts." Retribution sees punishment as deserved, justified—and even required[3]—by the offender's behavior. The primary sentencing tool of today's just deserts model is imprisonment, but in extreme cases, capital punishment (that is, death) may become the ultimate retribution.

Although it may be an age-old goal of criminal sentencing, retribution is very much in the forefront of public thinking and political policy-making today. Within the last few years, as the social order perspective with its emphasis on individual responsibility has gained ascendancy, public demands for retribution-based criminal punishments have been loud and clear. In 1994, for example, the Mississippi legislature, encouraged by Governor Kirk Fordice, voted to ban prison air conditioning, remove privately owned television sets from prison cells and dormitories, and prohibit weight lifting by inmates. Governor Fordice sent a "get tough" proposal to the legislature, which was quickly dubbed the "Clint Eastwood Hang 'em High Bill,"[4] and required inmates to wear striped uniforms with the word *CONVICT* stamped on the back. State Representative Mac McInnis explained the state's new retribution-inspired fervor this way: "We want a prisoner to look like a prisoner, to smell like a prisoner."[5]

With public anticrime sentiment at what may be an all-time high, says Jonathan Turley, director of the Prison Law Project, "It's difficult to imagine a measure draconian enough to satisfy the public desire for retribution."[6] As critics say, however, the fact that none of these measures will likely deter crime is beside the point. The goal of retribution, after all, is not deterrence, but satisfaction.[7]

Incapacitation

Incapacitation, the second goal of criminal sentencing, seeks to protect innocent members of society from offenders who might do them harm if they were not prevented in some way. In ancient times, mutilation and amputation of the extremities were sometimes used to prevent offenders from repeating their crimes.

Just Deserts. As a model of criminal sentencing, one which holds that criminal offenders deserve the punishment they receive at the hands of the law and that punishments should be appropriate to the type and severity of the crime committed.

Incapacitation. The use of imprisonment or other means to reduce the likelihood that an offender will be capable of committing future offenses.

Modern incapacitation strategies separate offenders from the community in order to reduce opportunities for further criminality. Incapacitation is sometimes called the "lock 'em up approach" and forms the basis for the movement toward prison "warehousing" discussed in Chapter 11.

Both incapacitation and retribution are used as justifications for imprisonment. A significant difference between the two perspectives, however, lies in the fact that incapacitation requires only restraint—and not punishment. Hence advocates of the incapacitation philosophy of sentencing are sometimes also active prison reformers, seeking to humanize correctional institutions. At the forefront of technology, confinement innovations are now offering ways to achieve the goal of incapacitation without the need for imprisonment. Electronic confinement (discussed shortly) and biomedical intervention (such as "chemical castration") may be able to achieve the goals of incapacitation without the need for imprisonment.

Deterrence

Deterrence uses punishment as an example to convince people that criminal activity is not worthwhile. Its overall goal is crime prevention. **Specific deterrence** seeks to reduce the likelihood of recidivism (repeat offenses) by convicted offenders, whereas **general deterrence** strives to influence the future behavior of people who have not yet been arrested and who may be tempted to turn to crime.

Deterrence is one of the more "rational" goals of sentencing. It is rational because it is an easily articulated goal and because it is possible to investigate objectively the amount of punishment required to deter. Jeremy Bentham's hedonistic calculus, discussed earlier in this text, laid the groundwork for many later calculations of just how harsh punishments need to be in order to deter effectively. It is generally agreed today that harsh punishments can virtually eliminate many minor forms of criminality.[8] Few traffic tickets would have to be written, for example, if minor driving offenses were punishable by death. A free society such as our own, of course, is not willing to impose extreme punishments on petty offenders, and even harsh punishments are not demonstrably effective in reducing the incidence of serious crimes such as murder and drug running.

Deterrence is compatible with the goal of incapacitation since at least specific deterrence can be achieved through incapacitating offenders. Hugo Bedau,[9] however, points to significant differences between retribution and deterrence. Retribution is oriented toward the past, says Bedau. It seeks to redress wrongs already committed. Deterrence, in contrast, is a strategy for the future. It aims to prevent new crimes. But as H. L. A. Hart has observed,[10] retribution can be the means through which deterrence is achieved. By serving as an example of what might happen to others, punishment may have an inhibiting effect.

Rehabilitation

Rehabilitation seeks to bring about fundamental changes in offenders and their behavior. As in the case of deterrence, the ultimate goal of rehabilitation is a reduction in the number of criminal offenses. Whereas deterrence depends on a "fear of the law" and the consequences of violating it, rehabilitation generally works through education and psychological treatment to reduce the likelihood of future criminality.

The term *rehabilitation*, however, may actually be a misnomer for the kinds of changes that its supporters seek. Rehabilitation literally means to return a person (or thing) to their previous condition. Hence, medical rehabilitation programs seek to restore functioning to atrophied limbs, rejuvenate injured organs, and mend shattered minds. In the case of criminal offenders, however, it is unlikely that restoring many to their previous state will result in anything other than a more youthful type of criminality.

In the past, rehabilitation as a sentencing strategy, if it existed at all, was primarily applied to youths. One of the first serious efforts to reform adult offenders was begun by the Pennsylvania Quakers, who initiated the development of the late–18th-century penitentiary. The penitentiary, which attempted to combine enforced penance with religious instruction, proved, however, to be something of an aberration. Within a few decades, it had been firmly supplanted by a retributive approach to corrections.

It was not until the 1930s that rehabilitation achieved a primary role in the sentencing of adult offenders in the United States. At the time, the psychological world view of therapists such as Sigmund Freud was entering popular culture. Psychology held out, as never before, the possibility of a structured approach to rehabilitation through therapeutic intervention. The rehabilitative approach of the mid-1900s became known as the medical model of corrections since it was built around a prescriptive approach to the treatment of offenders which provided at least the appearance of clinical predictability.

The primacy of the rehabilitative goal in sentencing fell victim to a "nothing works" philosophy in the late 1970s. The nothing works doctrine was based on studies of recidivism rates which consistently showed that rehabilitation was more an ideal than a reality. With as many as 90 percent of former convicted offenders returning to lives of crime following release from prison-based treatment programs, public sentiments in favor of incapacitation grew. Although the rehabilitation ideal has clearly suffered in the public arena, some emerging evidence has begun to suggest that effective treatment programs do exist and may even be growing in number.[11]

Restoration

Victims of crime or their survivors are frequently traumatized by their experiences. Some are killed and others receive lasting physical injuries. For many the world is never the same. The victimized may live in constant fear, reduced in personal vigor, and unable to form trusting relationships. **Restoration** is a sentencing goal that seeks to address this damage by making the victim and the community "whole again."

Restoration. A goal of criminal sentencing which attempts to make the victim "whole again."

A recent report by the U.S. Department of Justice explains restoration this way:

> "crime was once defined as a 'violation of the State.' This remains the case today, but we now recognize that crime is far more. It is—among other things—a violation of one person by another. While retributive justice may address the first type of violation adequately, restorative justice is required to effectively address the later...Thus (through restorative justice) we seek to attain a balance between the legitimate needs of the community, the...offender, and the victim."[12]

The "healing" of victims involves many aspects, ranging from victim assistance initiatives to legislation supporting victim compensation. Sentencing options which seek to restore the victim have focused primarily on restitution payments which offenders are ordered to make, either to their victims or to a general fund, which may then go to reimburse victims for suffering, lost wages, and medical expenses. In support of these goals, the 1984 Federal Comprehensive Crime Control Act specifically requires: "If sentenced to probation, the defendant must also be ordered to pay a fine, make restitution, and/or work in community service."[13]

Texas provides one example of a statewide strategy to utilize restitution as an alternative to prison.[14] The Texas Residential Restitution Program operates community-based centers which house selected nonviolent felony offenders. Residents work at regular jobs in the community, pay for support of their families, make restitution to their victims, and pay for room and board. During nonworking hours, they are required to perform community service work.

Vermont, which in 1995 began a new Sentencing Options Program built around the concept of reparative probation, provides a second example. According to state officials, the Vermont reparative options program, which "requires the offender to make reparations to the victim and to the community, marks the first time in the United States that the Restorative Justice model has been embraced by a state department of corrections and implemented on a statewide scale."[15] Vermont's reparative program builds on "community reparative boards" consisting of five or six citizens from the community where the crime was committed, and requires face-to-face public meetings between the offender and board representatives. Keeping in mind the program's avowed goals of "making the victim(s) whole again," and having the offender "make amends to the community," board members determine the specifics of the offender's sentence. Options include restitution, community work service, victim–offender mediation, victim empathy programs, driver improvement courses, and the like.

Some advocates of the restoration philosophy of sentencing point out that restitution payments and work programs which benefit the victim can also have the added benefit of rehabilitating the offender. The hope is that such sentences may teach offenders personal responsibility through structured financial obligations, job requirements, regularly scheduled payments, and so on.

Indeterminate Sentencing

Indeterminate Sentencing. A model of criminal punishment which encourages rehabilitation via the use of general and relatively unspecific sentences (such as a term of imprisonment of "from one to ten years").

Although the *philosophy* of criminal sentencing is reflected in the goals of sentencing we have just discussed, different sentencing *practices* have been linked to each goal. During most of the 20th century, for example, the rehabilitative goal has been influential. Since rehabilitation required that individual offenders' personal characteristics be closely considered in defining effective treatment strategies, judges were generally permitted wide discretion in choosing from among sentencing options. Incapacitation is increasingly becoming the sentencing strategy of choice, but many state criminal codes still allow judges to impose fines, probation, or widely varying prison terms, all for the same offense. These sentencing practices, characterized primarily by vast judicial choice, constitute an **indeterminate sentencing** model.

Indeterminate sentencing has both a historical and a philosophical basis in the belief that convicted offenders are more likely to participate in their own rehabilitation if they can reduce the amount of time they have to spend in prison. Inmates on good behavior will be released early, whereas recalcitrant inmates will remain in prison until the end of their terms. For that reason, parole generally plays a significant role in states which employ the indeterminate sentencing model.

Indeterminate sentencing relies heavily on judges' discretion to choose among types of sanctions and set upper and lower limits on the length of prison stays. Indeterminate sentences are typically imposed with wording such as "The defendant shall serve not less than five, not more than twenty-five years in the state's prison, under the supervision of the state department of correction...." Judicial discretion under the indeterminate model also extends to the imposition of concurrent or consecutive sentences, where the offender is convicted on more than one charge. Consecutive sentences are served one after the other, whereas concurrent sentences expire simultaneously.

The indeterminate model was also created to take into consideration detailed differences in degrees of guilt. Under the model, judges could weigh minute differences between cases, situations, and offenders. All the following could be considered before sentence was passed: (1) whether the offender committed the crime out of a need for money, for the thrill it afforded, out of a desire for revenge, or for the "hell of it"; (2) how much harm the offender intended; (3) how much the victim contributed to his or her own victimization; (4) the extent of the damages inflicted;

(5) the mental state of the offender; (6) the likelihood of successful rehabilitation; (7) the degree of the offender's cooperation with authorities; and (8) a near infinity of other individual factors.

Under the indeterminate sentencing model, the inmate's behavior (while incarcerated) is the primary determinant of the amount of time served. State parole boards wield great discretion under the model, acting as the final arbiters of the actual sentence served.

A few states employ a partially indeterminate sentencing model. Partially indeterminate sentencing systems allow judges to specify only the maximum amount of time to be served. Some minimum is generally implied by law but is not under the control of the sentencing authority. General practice is to set one year as a minimum for all felonies, but a few jurisdictions assume no minimum time at all—making persons sentenced to imprisonment eligible for immediate parole.

Problems with the Indeterminate Model

Indeterminate sentencing is still the rule in many jurisdictions, including New York, Texas, Ohio, South Carolina, Georgia, Alabama, Oklahoma, Missouri, Nevada, Massachusetts, Connecticut, Vermont, Hawaii, Alaska, and North and South Dakota.[16] The model, however, has come under increasing fire in recent years for contributing to inequality in sentencing. Critics claim that the indeterminate model allows divergent judicial personalities, and the often too-personal philosophies of judges, to produce a wide range of sentencing practices from very lenient to very strict. The "hanging judge," who still presides in some jurisdictions, is one who tends to impose the maximum sentence allowable under law on anyone who comes before the bench, regardless of circumstances. Worse still, the indeterminate model allows for the possibility that offenders might be sentenced, at least by some judges, more on the basis of social characteristics, such as race, gender, and social class, rather than culpability.

Because of the all-too personal nature of judicial decisions under the indeterminate model, offenders often depend on the counsel and ploys of their attorneys to appear before a judge who is thought to be a good sentencing risk. Requests for delays became a commonly used defense strategy in attempts to manipulate the selection of judicial personalities involved in sentencing decisions.

Another charge leveled against indeterminate sentencing is that it tends to produce dishonesty in sentencing. Because of sentence cutbacks for good behavior, and other reductions available to inmates through involvement in work and study programs, punishments rarely mean what they say. A sentence of five to ten years, for example, might actually see an inmate released in a matter of months after all **good time** and other special allowances have been calculated. (Some of the same charges can be leveled against determinant sentencing schemes under which correctional officials can administratively reduce the time served by an inmate.) In order to ensure long prison terms within indeterminate jurisdictions, some court officials have been led to extremes. In 1994, for example, a judge in Oklahoma, an indeterminate sentencing state, followed a jury's recommendation and sentenced convicted child molester Charles Scott Robinson, 30, to 30,000 years in prison.[17] Judge Dan Owens, complying with the jury's efforts to ensure that Robinson would spend the rest of his life behind bars, sentenced him to serve six consecutive 5,000-year sentences. Robinson had 14 previous felony convictions.

Due largely to indeterminate sentencing practices, time served in prison is generally far less than sentences would seem to indicate. A 1995 survey[18] by the Bureau of Justice Statistics found that even violent offenders, the most serious of all, who were released from state prisons during the study period, served, on average, only 48 percent of the sentences they originally received. Table 9-1 shows recent estimates of time to be served in prison versus actual sentences of felons convicted under state jurisdiction. Figure 9-1 provides a graphical representation of that data.

Good Time. The amount of time deducted from time to be served in prison on a given sentence(s) or under correctional agency jurisdiction, at some point after a prisoner's admission to prison, contingent on good behavior or awarded automatically by application of a statute or regulation.

TABLE 9-1

Estimated Time to Be Served in State Prison versus Mean Prison Sentence

Offense	Mean Prison Sentence	Estimated Time to Be Served in Prison
Murder	243 months	102 months
Rape	160	74
Robbery	115	49
Aggravated assault	78	35
Burglary	80	27
Larceny	49	18
Motor vehicle theft	60	21
Drug trafficking	74	26
Other felonies	44	17
AVERAGE FOR ALL FELONIES	**75 MONTHS**	**29 MONTHS**

SOURCE: Patrick A. Langan and Helen A. Graziadei, "Felony Sentences in State Courts, 1992" (Washington, D.C.: Bureau of Justice Statistics, January 1995), and Lawrence A. Greenfeld, "Prison Sentences and Time Served for Violence" (Washington, D.C.: Bureau of Justice Statistics, April 1995).

Determinate Sentencing. (Also called Presumptive or Fixed Sentencing) A model for criminal punishment which sets one particular punishment, or length of sentence, for each specific type of crime. Under the model, for example, all offenders convicted of the same degree of burglary would be sentenced to the same length of time behind bars.

The Rise of Determinate Sentencing

Until the 1970s, all 50 states used some form of indeterminate (or partially indeterminate) sentencing. Soon, however, calls for equity and proportionality in sentencing, heightened by claims of racial disparity in the sentencing practices[19] of some judges, led many states to move toward closer control over their sentencing systems.

Critics of the indeterminate model called for the recognition of three fundamental sentencing principles: proportionality, equity, and social debt. Proportionality refers to the belief that the severity of sanctions should bear a direct relationship to the seriousness of the crime committed. Equity is based on a concern with social equality and means that similar crimes should be punished with the same degree of severity, regardless of the general social or personal characteristics of offenders. According to the principle of equity, for example, two bank robbers in

FIGURE 9-1

Time served in state prisons versus court sentence for selected offenses. Source: Patrick A. Langan and Helen A. Graziadei, "Felony Sentences in State Courts, 1992," (Washington, D.C.: Bureau of Justice Statistics, January 1995), and Lawrence A. Greenfeld, "Prison Sentences and Time Served for Violence" (Washington, D.C.: Bureau of Justice Statistics, April 1995).

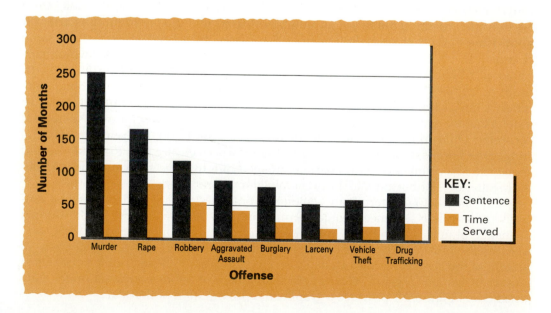

different parts of the country, who use the same techniques and weapons, with the same degree of implied threat, even though they are tried under separate circumstances, should receive roughly the same kind of sentence. The equity principle needs to be balanced, however, against the notion of social debt. In the case of the bank robbers, the offender who has a prior criminal record can be said to have a higher level of social debt than the one-time robber, where all else is equal. Greater social debt, of course, would suggest a heightened severity of punishment or a greater need for treatment, and so on.

Because of these three concerns in sentencing, a number of states moved to develop a different model of sentencing known as **determinate sentencing**. Determinate sentencing depends on a well-defined hierarchy of penalties that is codified in law, whereby specified terms of imprisonment are associated with each criminal offense category. Sentencing statutes may, for example, require that anyone who assaults a police officer be punished by six months in prison. In 1976, Maine became the first state to eliminate old sentencing practices and adopt determinate sentencing. It was quickly followed by many other states, and by mid-1995, Arizona, California, Delaware, Florida, Illinois, Indiana, Kansas, Minnesota, North Carolina, Oregon, Virginia, and Washington (along with Maine) had entirely eliminated discretionary parole release decisions.[20] Colorado, though opting for determinate sentencing in 1979, returned to the use of an indeterminate model in 1985.

Determinate sentencing states observe a pattern of abolishing traditional forms of discretionary parole, eliminating parole boards, and establishing sentencing commissions with the authority to develop and modify sentencing guidelines. Some determinate sentencing states, however, still use a period of postrelease supervision which many continue to call "parole." Delaware, Kansas, Minnesota, Oregon, and Washington, for example, require offenders to serve a set term, but still mandate a fixed period of postrelease supervision—a practice some call "reentry parole."

A 1995 survey[21] by the Bureau of Justice Statistics found that the movement toward determinate sentencing is expanding. In 1977, only 38 percent of convicts released from prison had served determinate sentences, but by 1992, the number had risen to 60 percent. Today, as many as 70 percent of state prisoners are serving determinate sentences.

Determinate sentencing is also called presumptive or fixed sentencing since it presumes a direct relationship between the offense and the sentence and sets sentences which are fixed by law. Even presumptive sentences, however, often allow judges a certain leeway in the actual sentences they impose. Presumptive sentencing guidelines in some jurisdictions specify only a range of sentences from which a judge is expected to choose. In California, for example, the presumptive term for a number of crimes is three years, but a judge may select a sentence anywhere between two and four years and still fall within statutory guidelines.

Even states which use a single presumptive sentence for a given offense generally allow for "aggravating" or "mitigating" factors, indicating greater or lesser degrees of culpability, which judges can take into consideration in imposing a sentence somewhat at variance from the presumptive term. **Aggravating circumstances** are those which appear to call for a tougher sentence and may include especially heinous behavior, cruelty, injury to more than one person, and so on. In death penalty cases, however, the U.S. Supreme Court has held that aggravating factors must "provide specific and detailed guidance and make rationally reviewable the death sentencing process....In order to decide whether a particular aggravating circumstance meets these requirements, a federal court must determine whether the statutory language defining the circumstance is itself too vague to guide the sentencer...."[22]

Mitigating circumstances, or those which indicate that a lesser sentence is called for, are generally similar to legal defenses although in this case they only reduce criminal responsibility, not eliminate it. Mitigating factors include such things as cooperation with the investigating authority, surrender, good character,

*A*ggravating Circumstances. Those elements of an offense or of an offender's background which could result in a harsher sentence under the determinate model than would otherwise be called for by sentencing guidelines.

*M*itigating Circumstances. Those elements of an offense or of an offender's background which could result in a lesser sentence under the determinate model than would otherwise be called for by sentencing guidelines.

and so on. Common aggravating and mitigating factors are listed in an accompanying Theory into Practice box.

Critiques of the Determinate Model

Determinate sentencing models, which have sought to address the shortcomings of indeterminate sentencing by curtailing judicial discretion in sentencing, are not without their critics. Detractors charge that determinate sentencing is oversimplistic, based on a primitive concept of culpability, and incapable of offering hope for rehabilitation and change. For one thing, they say, determinate sentencing has built-in limitations which render it far less able to judge the blameworthiness of individual offenders. Legislatures simply cannot anticipate all the differences that individual cases can present. Aggravating and mitigating factors, although intended to cover most circumstances, will inevitably shortchange some defendants who don't neatly fall into the categories they provide.

A second critique of determinate sentencing is that though it may reduce judicial discretion substantially, it may do nothing to hamper the huge discretionary decision-making power of prosecutors.[23] In fact, federal sentencing reformers, who have adopted the determinate sentencing model, have specifically decided not to modify the discretionary power of prosecutors, citing the large number of cases which are resolved through plea bargaining. Such a shift in discretionary authority, away from judges and into the hands of prosecutors, may be misplaced.

Another criticism of determinate sentencing questions its fundamental purpose. Advocates of determinate sentencing inevitably cite greater equity in sentencing as the

---

 *T*heory into Practice: Aggravating and Mitigating Factors

Listed here are some typical aggravating and mitigating factors which judges may take into consideration in arriving at sentencing decisions in determinate sentencing states.

AGGRAVATING FACTORS

- The defendant induced others to participate in the commission of the offense.
- The offense was especially heinous, atrocious, or cruel.
- The defendant was armed with or used a deadly weapon at the time of the crime.
- The offense was committed for the purpose of avoiding or preventing a lawful arrest or effecting an escape from custody.
- The offense was committed for hire.
- The offense was committed against a present or former law enforcement officer, or correctional officer, while engaged in the performance of official duties or because of the past exercise of official duties.
- The defendant took advantage of a position of trust or confidence to commit the offense.

MITIGATING FACTORS

- The defendant has no record of criminal convictions punishable by more than 60 days of imprisonment.

- The defendant has made substantial or full restitution.
- The defendant has been a person of good character or has had a good reputation in the community.
- The defendant aided in the apprehension of another felon or testified truthfully on behalf of the prosecution.
- The defendant acted under strong provocation, or the victim was a voluntary participant in the criminal activity, or otherwise consented to it.
- The offense was committed under duress, coercion, threat, or compulsion which was insufficient to constitute a defense but significantly reduced the defendant's culpability.
- The defendant was suffering from a mental or physical condition that was insufficient to constitute a defense but significantly reduced culpability for the offense.

QUESTIONS FOR DISCUSSION

1. What aggravating factors, if any, might you add to the list in this box? Why?

2. What mitigating factors, if any, might you add to the list in this box? Why?

---

primary benefit of such a model. Reduced to its essence, this means that "those who commit the same crime get the same time." Sentencing reformers have thus couched the drive toward determinate sentencing in progressive terms. Others, however, have pointed out that the philosophical underpinnings of the movement may be quite different. Albert Alschuler,[24] for example, suggests that determinate sentencing is a regressive social policy which derives from American weariness with considering offenders as individuals. Describing this kind of thinking, Alschuler writes: "Don't tell us that a robber was retarded. We don't care about his problems. We don't know what to *do* about his problems, and we are no longer interested in listening to a criminal's sob stories. The most important thing about this robber is simply that he *is* a robber."[25]

A different line of thought is proposed by Christopher Link and Neal Shover,[26] who found in a study of state-level economic, political, and demographic data that determinate sentencing may ultimately be the result of declining economic conditions and increasing fiscal strain on state governments rather than any particular set of ideals.

A fifth critique of determinate sentencing centers on its alleged inability to promote effective rehabilitation. Under indeterminate sentencing schemes, offenders have the opportunity to act responsibly and thus to participate in their own rehabilitation.[27] Lack of responsible behavior results in denial of parole and extension of the sentence. Determinate sentencing schemes, by virtue of dramatic reductions in good-time allowances and parole opportunities, leave little incentive for offenders to participate in educational programs, to take advantage of opportunities for work inside correctional institutions, to seek treatment, or to contribute in any positive way to their own change.

Although these critiques may be valid, they will probably do little to stem the tide of determinate sentencing. The rise of determinate sentencing represents the ascendancy of the just deserts perspective over other sentencing goals. In a growing number of jurisdictions, punishment, deterrence, and incapacitation have replaced rehabilitation and restitution as the goals which society seeks to achieve through sentencing practices.

Truth in Sentencing. A close correspondence between the sentence imposed upon those sent to prison and the time actually served prior to prison release.

ruth in Sentencing

Truth in Sentencing

In 1984, with passage of the Comprehensive Crime Control Act, the federal government adopted determinate sentencing for nearly all federal offenders.[28] The act also addressed the issue of honesty in sentencing. Under the old federal system, a sentence of ten years in prison might actually have meant only a few years spent behind bars before the offender was released. On average, good-time credits and parole reduced time served to about one-third of actual sentences.[29] At the time, sentencing practices of most states reflected the federal model. Although sentence reductions may have benefited offenders, they often outraged victims who felt betrayed by the sentencing process. The 1984 act nearly eliminated good-time credits,[30] and targeted 1992 (which was later extended to 1997) as the date for phasing out federal parole and eliminating the U.S. Parole Commission. The emphasis on honesty in sentencing, created, in effect, a sentencing environment of "what you get is what you serve."

More recently, the movement toward "truth in sentencing" has accelerated. **Truth in sentencing**, which has been described as "a close correspondence between the sentence imposed upon those sent to prison and the time actually served prior to prison release,"[31] has become an important policy focus of many state legislatures and the federal Congress. The Violent Crime Control and Law Enforcement Act of 1994 set aside $4 billion in federal prison construction funds (called "Truth in Sentencing Incentive Funds") for states which adopt truth in sentencing laws and which are able to guarantee that certain violent offenders will serve 85 percent of their sentences. By mid-1995, two states—Arizona and California—had legislatively embraced the 85 percent requirement. A recent report by the Bureau of Justice Statistics[32] found that, although many other states are moving toward practices which support truth in sentencing, most will need to greatly accelerate that trend if they are to be eligible for available federal monies. The report found, for example, that in 1992 violent offenders in state prisons served an average of 48 percent of their felony sentences prior to release. Meeting federal requirements, the study's authors found, would increase the time actually spent in prison by the average prison-bound offender by almost 50 percent.

Some states have chosen to approach truth in sentencing another way. In 1994, for example, the New Jersey Supreme Court imposed a truth in sentencing rule on New Jersey judges which, although it doesn't require lengthened sentences, mandates that judges publicly disclose how much time a convicted defendant is likely to spend behind bars. The New Jersey court held that lower criminal court judges must "inform the public of the actual period of time" a defendant is likely to spend imprisoned. Judges must also state when a defendant can get out of prison on good behavior. "Under the truth-in-sentencing policy, the public will not be left with the mistaken impression that the sentence imposed is what the defendant will actually serve," the state's high court said. Robert Egles, executive director of the New Jersey State Parole Board called the court's decision a good one. "This is a good decision, especially for victims and crime victims' families," Egles said. "The issue didn't seem to be how long the sentences were, but about the honesty of the system. If it's a 10-year sentence, but the defendant can get out in two years, it should be said," concluded Egles.[33]

ederal Sentencing Guidelines

Title II of the Comprehensive Crime Control Act, called the Sentencing Reform Act of 1984,[34] established the nine-member U.S. Sentencing Commission. The Commission comprises presidential appointees, including three federal judges. First to head the Sentencing Commission was William W. Wilkins, Jr., U.S. circuit judge for the Fourth Circuit.

The Sentencing Reform Act established mandatory minimum sentences for certain federal crimes, including drug offenses, and limited the discretion of federal judges by mandating the creation of federal sentencing guidelines which federal judges are required to follow. The newly formed Sentencing Commission was given the task of developing determinate sentencing guidelines in order to reduce disparity in sentencing, promote consistency and uniformity in sentencing, and increase sentencing fairness and equity. To guide the Commission, Congress specified the purposes of sentencing to include (1) deterring criminals, (2) incapacitating or rehabilitating offenders, and (3) providing just deserts in punishing criminals. Congress also charged the Commission with eliminating sentencing disparities and reducing confusion, and asked for a system which would permit flexibility in the face of mitigating or aggravating elements.

While developing federal sentencing guidelines, the Commission analyzed thousands of past cases and enacted a scale of punishments considered typical for given types of offenses.[35] It came up with a series of federal guidelines intended to make for predictability in sentencing, but which also allow individual judges to deviate from the guidelines when specific aggravating or mitigating factors are present. The Commission also considered relevant federal law, parole guidelines, and the anticipated impact of changes on federal prison populations. One boundary was set by statute: In creating the Sentencing Commission, Congress had also specified that the degree of discretion available in any one sentencing category could not exceed 25 percent of the basic penalty for that category or six months, whichever might be greater.

Now that the biggest part of its job is done, the Sentencing Commission continues to meet a least once each year in order to review the effectiveness of the guidelines it has created. As this book goes to press, the Commission is recommending parity between sentences for crack and powdered cocaine. Guidelines previously established by the Commission have had the effect of penalizing crack cocaine users and traffickers more harshly than those who use or traffic in powdered cocaine, and criticism has arisen over apparent racial disparities in sentencing practices due to the prevalence of crack cocaine in black neighborhoods (powdered cocaine seems to be a drug of choice among white drug abusers). Although changes recommended by the Commission become effective unless vetoed by Congress within 180 days, the U.S. Justice Department is disputing the Commission's recommended changes in cocaine sentencing practices. The Justice Department has strenuously objected to the proposed change because of what it sees as the "harsh and terrible impact of crack on communities across America."[36]

Federal Guideline Provisions

Guidelines established by the Sentencing Commission took effect in November 1987. They immediately became embroiled in appellate battles, many of which focused on the constitutionality of the membership of the Sentencing Commission.[37] The U.S. Supreme Court considered the constitutionality question in 1989. By the time it did, 158 federal district courts had ruled the guidelines unconstitutional, whereas 116 others had upheld them.[38] The Ninth U.S. Circuit Court of Appeals had struck the guidelines down, whereas the Third Circuit Court had found them acceptable. On January 18, 1989, in the case of *Mistretta* v. *U.S.*,[39] the Supreme Court, by a vote of 8 to 1, held that Congress had acted appropriately and that the guidelines developed by the Commission could be applied in federal cases nationwide.

The federal guidelines specify a sentencing range for each criminal offense, from which judges must choose. If a particular case has "atypical features," judges are allowed to depart from the guidelines. Departures are generally expected to be made only in the presence of mitigating or aggravating factors—a number of which are specified in the guidelines. Aggravating circumstances may include the possession of a weapon during the Commission of a crime, the degree of criminal involvement (whether the defendant was a leader or a follower in the criminal activity), and extreme psychological injury to the victim. Punishments also increase where a defendant violates a position of public or private trust, uses special skills to commit or conceal offenses, or has a criminal history. Defendants who express remorse, cooperate with authorities, or willingly make restitution may have their sentences reduced under the guidelines. Any departure from the guidelines may, however, become the basis for appellate review concerning the reasonableness of the sentence imposed, and judges who deviate from the guidelines must provide written reasons for doing so.

Federal sentencing guidelines are built around a table containing 43 rows, each corresponding to one offense level. Penalties associated with each level overlap those of levels above or below in order to discourage unnecessary litigation. A person charged with a crime involving $11,000, for example, upon conviction is unlikely to receive a penalty substantially greater than if the amount involved had been somewhat less than $10,000—a sharp contrast to the old system. A change of six levels roughly doubles the sentence imposed under the guidelines, regardless of the level at which one starts. Because of their matrixlike quality, federal sentencing provisions have also been referred to as "structured sentencing." The federal sentencing table is reproduced in Table 9-2.

The sentencing table also contains six rows, corresponding to the criminal history category into which an offender falls. Criminal history categories are determined on a point basis. Offenders earn points through previous convictions. Each prior sentence of imprisonment for more than one year and one month counts as three points. Two points are assigned for each prior prison sentence over six months, or if the defendant committed the offense while on probation, parole, or work release. The system also assigns points for other types of previous convictions and for offenses committed less than two years after release from imprisonment. Points are added to determine the criminal history category into which an offender falls. Thirteen points or more are required for the highest category. At each offense level, sentences in the highest criminal history category are generally two to three times as severe as for the lowest category.

Defendants may also move into the highest criminal history category (number VI) by virtue of being designated career offenders. Under the sentencing guidelines, a defendant is a career offender if "(1) the defendant was at least 18 years old at the time of the...offense, (2) the...offense is a crime of violence or trafficking in a controlled substance, and (3) the defendant has at least two prior felony convictions of either a crime of violence or a controlled substance offense."[40]

According to the U.S. Supreme Court, an offender may be adjudged a career offender in a single hearing—even when previous convictions are lacking. In *Deal* v. *U.S.* (1993),[41] the defendant, Thomas Lee Deal, was convicted in a single proceeding of six counts of carrying and using a firearm during a series of bank robberies which occurred in the Houston, Texas, area. A federal district court sentenced him to 105 years in prison as a career offender—5 years for the first count and 20 years each on the five other counts, with sentences to run consecutively. In the words of the Court, "[w]e see no reason why [the defendant should not receive such a sentence], simply because he managed to evade detection, prosecution, and conviction for the first five offenses and was ultimately tried on all six in a single proceeding."

Plea Bargaining under the Guidelines

Plea bargaining plays a major role in the federal judicial system. Approximately 90 percent of all federal sentences are the result of guilty pleas,[42] and the large majority of those are the result of plea negotiations. In the words of Commission Chairman Wilkins, "With respect to plea bargaining, the Commission has proceeded cautiously...the Commission did not believe it wise to stand the federal criminal justice system on its head by making too drastic and too sudden a change in these practices."[43]

Although the Commission allowed plea bargaining to continue, it did require that the agreement (1) be fully disclosed in the record of the court (unless there is an overriding and demonstrable reason why it should not) and (2) detail the actual conduct of the offense. Under these requirements, defendants will no longer be able to "hide" the actual nature of their offense behind a substitute plea.

The thrust of the federal rules concerning plea bargaining is to reduce the veil of secrecy that had previously surrounded the process. Information on the decision-making process itself is available to victims, the media, and the public.

The Sentencing Environment

A number of studies have attempted to investigate the decision-making process that leads to imposition of a particular sentence. Early studies[44] found a strong relationship between the informal influence of members of the courtroom work group and the severity, or lack thereof, of sentences imposed. A number suggested that minorities ran a much greater risk of imprisonment.[45] Other studies have found that sentencing variations are responsive to extralegal conditions[46] and that public opinion can play a role in the type of sentence handed down.[47] If these findings about public opinion are true, they might explain some of the increase in prison populations. A public opinion study conducted by Bowling Green State

TABLE 9-2

The Federal Sentencing Table (months)

Criminal History Category

OFFENSE Level	I 0 or 1	II 2 or 3	III 4, 5, 6	IV 7, 8, 9	V 10, 11, 12	VI 13 or more
1	0–1	0–2	0–3	0–4	0–5	0–6
2	0–2	0–3	0–4	0–5	0–6	0–7
3	0–3	0–4	0–5	0–6	2–8	3–9
4	0–4	0–5	0–6	2–8	4–10	6–12
5	0–5	0–6	1–7	4–10	6–12	9–15
6	0–6	1–7	2–8	6–12	9–15	12–18
7	1–7	2–8	4–10	8–14	12–18	15–21
8	2–8	4–10	6–12	10–16	15–21	18–24
9	4–10	6–12	8–14	12–18	18–24	21–27
10	6–12	8–14	10–16	15–21	21–27	24–30
11	8–14	10–16	12–18	18–24	24–30	27–33
12	10–16	12–18	15–21	21–27	27–33	30–37
13	12–18	15–21	18–24	24–30	30–37	33–41
14	15–21	18–24	21–27	27–33	33–41	37–46
15	18–24	21–27	24–30	30–37	37–46	41–51
16	21–27	24–30	27–33	33–41	41–51	46–57
17	24–30	27–33	30–37	37–46	46–57	51–63
18	27–33	30–37	33–41	41–51	51–63	57–71
19	30–37	33–41	37–46	46–57	57–71	63–78
20	33–41	37–46	41–51	51–63	63–78	70–87
21	37–46	41–51	46–57	57–71	70–87	77–96
22	41–51	46–57	51–63	63–78	77–96	84–105
23	46–57	51–63	57–71	70–87	84–105	92–115
24	51–63	57–71	63–78	77–96	92–115	100–125
25	57–71	63–78	70–87	84–105	100–125	110–137
26	63–78	70–87	78–97	92–115	110–137	120–150
27	70–87	78–97	87–108	100–125	120–150	130–162
28	78–97	87–108	97–121	110–137	130–162	140–175
29	87–108	97–121	108–135	121–151	140–175	151–188
30	97–121	108–135	121–151	135–168	151–188	168–210
31	108–135	121–151	135–168	151–188	168–210	188–235
32	121–151	135–168	151–188	168–210	188–235	210–262
33	135–168	151–188	168–210	188–235	210–262	235–293
34	151–188	168–210	188–235	210–262	235–293	262–327
35	168–210	188–235	210–262	235–293	262–327	292–365
36	188–235	210–262	235–293	262–327	292–365	324–405
37	210–262	235–293	262–327	292–365	324–405	360–life
38	235–293	262–327	292–365	324–405	360–life	360–life
39	262–327	292–365	324–405	360–life	360–life	360–life
40	292–365	324–405	360–life	360–life	360–life	360–life
41	324–405	360–life	360–life	360–life	360–life	360–life
42	360–life	360–life	360–life	360–life	360–life	360–life
43	life	life	life	life	life	life

SOURCE: U.S. Sentencing Commission, *Federal Sentencing Guideline Manual* (Washington, D.C.: U.S. Government Printing Office, 1987), p. 210.

University, for example, found that 71 percent of respondents identified incarceration as the preferred punishment for serious offenses.[48]

More recent analyses, especially in determinate sentencing jurisdictions, however, have begun to show that sentences in a number of jurisdictions are becoming more objective and, hence, predictable. A California study[49] of racial equity in sentencing, for example, found that the likelihood of going to prison was increased by:

✔ Having multiple current conviction counts, prior prison terms, and juvenile incarcerations.

✔ Being on adult and/or juvenile probation or parole at the time of the offense.

✔ Having been released from prison within 12 months of the current offense.

✔ Having a history of drug or alcohol abuse.

✔ Being over 21 years of age.
✔ Going to trial.
✔ Not being released prior to trial.
✔ Not being represented by a private attorney.

The same study found that, perhaps partly because of the 1977 California Determinate Sentencing Act, "California courts are making racially equitable sentencing decisions."[50] Findings applied only to the crimes of assault, robbery, burglary, theft, forgery, and drug abuse, but held for sentences involving both prison and probation. Similarly, no disparities were noted in the lengths of sentences imposed.[51] Other recent studies have found that female felons are not treated substantially differently by sentencing authorities than are their male counterparts.[52]

One of the most comprehensive studies of sentencing to date was published in 1987 by Martha Myers and Susette Talarico.[53] Myers and Talarico studied sentencing practices in Georgia and found an "absence of system-wide bias or discrimination"[54] and a reliance by judges on the seriousness of offenses and statutory guidelines in arriving at sentencing decisions. Myers and Talarico also reported that the social background of judges had little direct influence on sentencing outcomes. However, older judges, and those who were Baptists and religious fundamentalists, were found to be generally stricter than were younger judges. One interesting result of the study was the finding that Baptist and fundamentalist judges, though they did not appear to discriminate against minority defendants, seemed to hold white defendants to a higher standard of behavior.[55]

*P*resentence Investigation. The examination of a convicted offender's background prior to sentencing. Presentence examinations are generally conducted by probation/parole officers and submitted to sentencing authorities.

*T*he Presentence Investigation Report

Before imposing sentence, a judge may request information on the background of a convicted defendant. This is especially true in indeterminate sentencing jurisdictions, where judges retain considerable discretion in selecting sanctions.

Traditional wisdom has held that certain factors increase the likelihood of rehabilitation and reduce the need for lengthy prison terms. These factors include a good job record, satisfactory educational attainment, strong family ties, church attendance, an arrest history of only nonviolent offenses, and psychological stability.

Information about a defendant's background often comes to the judge in the form of a **presentence report**. The task of preparing presentence reports usually falls to the probation or parole office. Presentence reports take one of three forms: (1) a detailed written report on the defendant's personal and criminal history, including an assessment of present conditions in the defendant's life (often called the "long form"); (2) an abbreviated written report summarizing the type of information most likely to be useful in a sentencing decision (the "short form"); and (3) a verbal report to the court made by the investigating officer based on field notes, but structured according to categories established for the purpose. A presentence report is much like a resume or *vitae* except that it focuses on what might be regarded as negative as well as positive life experiences.

The length of the completed form is subject to great variation. One survey[56] found that Texas used one of the shortest forms of all—a one-page summary supplemented by other materials which the report writer thought might provide meaningful additional details. Orange County, California, provides an example of the opposite kind and may use the most detailed form of any jurisdiction in the

THREE STRIKES AND YOU'RE OUT—THE TOUGH NEW MOVEMENT IN CRIMINAL SENTENCING

 In the spring of 1994, California legislators passed the state's now-famous "three strikes and you're out" bill. Amid much fanfare, Governor Pete Wilson signed the "three-strikes" measure into law, calling it "the toughest and most sweeping crime bill in California history."

California's law, which is retroactive (in that it counts offenses committed before the date the legislation was signed), requires a 25-year-to-life sentence for three-time felons with convictions for two or more serious or violent prior offenses. Criminal offenders facing a "second strike" can receive up to double the normal sentence for their most recent offense. Parole consideration is not available until at least 80 percent of the sentence has been served.

By mid-1995, 14 states—California, Colorado, Connecticut, Georgia, Indiana, Kansas, Louisiana, Maryland, New Mexico, North Carolina, Tennessee, Virginia, Washington, and Wisconsin—had passed three-strikes legislation, and many other states were considering it. Further, the federal Violent Crime Control and Law Enforcement Act of 1994 contains a three-strikes provision, which mandates life imprisonment for federal criminals convicted of three violent felonies or drug offenses.

Questions remain, however, about the effectiveness of three-strikes legislation, and many are concerned about its impact on the justice system. One year after it was signed into law, the California three-strikes initiative was evaluated by the RAND Corporation. RAND researchers found that, in the first year, more than 5,000 defendants were convicted and sentenced under the law's provisions. The large majority of those sentenced, however, had committed nonviolent crimes such as petty theft and drug possession, causing critics of the law to argue that the

law is too broad. Eighty-four percent of two-strike cases, and nearly 77 percent of three-strike convictions resulted from nonviolent, drug, or property crimes. Supporters of the law, however, argued that those convicted under three strikes were career criminals being denied the opportunity to commit more violent crimes. "The real story here is the girl somewhere that did not get raped," said Mike Reynolds, a Fresno, California, photographer whose 18-year-old daughter was killed by a paroled felon. "The real story is the robbery that did not happen," he added.

Recent statistics from the California Department of Justice show that crime in California fell by 6.7 percent during the first nine months of 1994, with homicide dropping a dramatic 13 percent. Although some of the decline may be attributable to three-strikes legislation, it is difficult to tell. Crime also decreased in California in 1993 although by not so great a percentage.

(Continued on next page)

THREE STRIKES AND YOU'RE OUT—THE TOUGH NEW MOVEMENT IN CRIMINAL SENTENCING—*Continued*

Practically speaking, California's three-strikes law has had a dramatic impact on the state's criminal justice system. According to the California Youth and Adult Correctional Agency, the law has created a huge backlog of court cases, as defendants facing their third conviction opt for jury trials in the hopes of hearing an innocent verdict returned, rather than plead guilty and face certain and lengthy confinement. "'Three strikes and you're out' sounds great to a lot of people," says Alan Schuman, president of the American Probation and Parole Association. "But no one will cop a plea when it gets to the third time around. We will have more trials, and this whole country works on plea bargaining and pleading guilty, not jury trials," Schuman said at the association's 1995 meeting. Some California district attorneys have responded by choosing to prosecute fewer misdemeanants in order to concentrate on the more serious three-strikes defendants.

Critics also point to the law's costs. State correctional officials say they will need to build 15 new prisons by the year 2000, when the state's prison population is expected to climb to 210,000, to accommodate three-strikes convicts. Currently, California's prisons, the most populous in the nation, hold around 120,000 inmates. Full enforcement of the law, says RAND, could cost as much as $5.5 billion annually—or $300 per California taxpayer.

Researchers at RAND conclude that although California's sweeping three-strikes legislation holds the potential to cut serious adult crime by as much as one-third throughout the state, the high cost of enforcing the law may keep it from ever being fully implemented. In the meantime, as this book goes to press, proposals to amend California's law are before the state's legislature. Some who want to modify the law suggest that three-strikes sentences should be imposed only on offenders who commit violent crimes such as murder, rape, armed robbery, and certain types of arson.

QUESTIONS FOR DISCUSSION

1. Do you think three-strikes laws serve a useful purpose? If so, what is that purpose? Might other sentencing arrangements meet that same purpose? If so, what arrangements might those be?

2. How will three-strikes laws affect state and federal spending on the criminal justice system? Do you think that such shifts in spending can be justified? If so, how?

SOURCES: Bruce Smith, "Crime Solutions," The Associated Press online, January 11, 1995; Michael Miller, "California Gets 'Three Strikes' Anti-Crime Bill," Reuter's wire services, March 7, 1994; Dion Nissenbaum, "'Three-strikes' first year debated," United Press online northern edition, March 6, 1995.

---

country. The instructions for completing the form consist of a dozen single-spaced pages.[57]

A typical "long form" is divided into ten major informational sections as follows: (1) personal information and identifying data describing the defendant, (2) a chronology of the current offense and circumstances surrounding it, (3) a record of the defendant's previous convictions, if any, (4) home life and family data, (5) educational background, (6) health history and current state of health, (7) military service, (8) religious preference, (9) financial condition, and (10) sentencing recommendations made by the probation or parole officer completing the report.

The data on which a presentence report is based come from a variety of sources. Since the 1960s, modern computer-based criminal information clearinghouses, such as the FBI's National Crime Information Center (NCIC), have simplified at least a part of the data-gathering process. The NCIC began in 1967 and contains information on people wanted for criminal offenses throughout the United States. Individual jurisdictions also maintain criminal records repositories which are able to provide comprehensive files on the criminal history of persons processed by the justice system. In the late 1970s, the federal government encouraged states to develop criminal records repositories using computer technology.[58] The years that followed have been described as "the focus of a data gathering effort more massive and more coordinated than any other in criminal justice."[59]

In a presentence report, almost any third-party data are subject to ethical and legal considerations. The official records of almost any agency or organization, though they may prove to be an ideal source of information, are often protected by state and federal privacy requirements. In particular, the Federal Privacy Act of 1974[60] may limit records access. Investigators should first check on the legal availability of all records before requesting them and should receive in writing the defendant's permission to access records. Other public laws, among them the federal Freedom of Information Act,[61] may make the presentence report itself available to the defendant, although courts and court officers have generally been held to be exempt from the provision of such statutes.

Sometimes the defendant is a significant source of much of the information which appears in the presentence report. When such is the case, efforts should be made to corroborate the information provided by the defendant. Unconfirmed data will generally be marked on the report as "defendant supplied data" or simply "unconfirmed."

The final section of a presentence report is usually devoted to the investigating officer's recommendations. A recommendation may be made in favor of probation, split sentencing, a term of imprisonment, or any other sentencing options available in the jurisdiction. Participation in community service programs may be recommended for probationers, and drug or substance abuse programs may be suggested as well. Some analysts have observed that a "judge accepts an officer's recommendation in an extremely high percentage of cases."[62] Most judges are willing to accept the report writer's recommendation because they recognize the professionalism of presentence investigators and because they know that the investigator may well be the supervising officer assigned to the defendant should a community alternative be the sentencing decision.

Jurisdictions vary in their use of presentence reports and in the form they take. Federal law mandates presentence reports in federal criminal courts and specifies 15 topical areas which each report is to contain. The 1984 federal Determinate Sentencing Act directs report writers to include information on the classification of the offense and of the defendant under the offense level and criminal history categories established by the statute.

Some states require presentence reports only in felony cases, and others in cases where defendants face the possibility of incarceration for six months. Still others may have no requirement for presentence reports beyond those ordered by a judge. Even so, report writing, rarely anyone's favorite, may seriously tax the limited resources of probation agencies. According to Andrew Klein,[63] during a recent year, New York state probation officers wrote 108,408 presentence investigation reports. Most (63,902) were for misdemeanors, but 44,506 reports described the backgrounds of newly convicted felons. In the same year in New York City alone, more than 37,000 presentence investigation reports were completed, averaging 25 reports per probation officer per month.

Presentence reports may be useful sentencing tools. Many officers who prepare them take their responsibility seriously. A recent study,[64] however, shows a tendency among presentence investigators to satisfy judicial expectations about defendants by tailoring reports to fit the image the defendant projects. Prior criminal record and present offense may influence the interpretation of all the other data gathered.[65]

The Victim—Forgotten No Longer

Thanks to a grass-roots resurgence of concern for the plight of victims, which began in this country in the early 1970s and continues to grow, the sentencing environment frequently now includes consideration of the needs of victims and their survivors. Unfortunately, in times past, the concerns of victims were often forgotten.

Although victims might testify at trial, other aspects of the victimization experience were often downplayed by the criminal justice system—including the psychological trauma engendered by the victimization process itself. That changed in 1982, when the President's Task Force on Victims of Crime[66] gave focus to a burgeoning victim's rights movement and urged the widespread expansion of victim's assistance programs during what was then their formative period. Victim assistance programs today tend to offer services in the areas of crisis intervention and follow-up counseling, and help victims secure their rights under the law.[67] Following successful prosecution, some victim assistance programs also advise victims in the filing of civil suits in order to recoup financial losses directly from the offender.

The Alameda County (California) Victim/Witness Assistance Program is characteristic of others like it. A few years ago, the Alameda program discovered that victims were having difficulty learning the outcome of their cases and additional difficulties in recovering property used as evidence. The program promptly set up property return and information services as a way of helping victims.[68]

Victim advocates argue that a federal victim's bill of rights is needed to provide the same kind of fairness to victims that is routinely accorded to defendants. In 1982, two significant steps were taken toward the development of a comprehensive victim's rights bill. In that year, the President's Task Force on Victims of Crime[69] recommended 68 programmatic and legislative incentives for states and concerned citizens to pursue on behalf of victims. Also in 1982, voters in California approved "Proposition 8," a resolution which called for changes in the state's constitution to reflect concern for crime victims.

A continuing thrust of victim advocacy groups is in the direction of an amendment to the U.S. Constitution. The Victim's Constitutional Amendment Network (Victim's CAN), affiliated with the National Organization for Victim Assistance, Mothers Against Drunk Driving, Parents of Murdered Children, Justice for Crime Victims, and other groups, is seeking to add the phrase "likewise, the victim, in every criminal prosecution, shall have the right to be present and to be heard at all critical stages of judicial proceedings" to the Sixth Amendment. Recently, the National Policy Forum's Panel on Crime Policy[70] recommended that individual states adopt victims' bills of rights, which would include guarantees to a speedy trial for victims and mandate that victims be informed of their rights at the scene of a crime.

Although an amendment to the federal constitution specifying victim's rights may be a long way off, 26 states had passed victims' rights amendments as of mid-1995,[71] and significant federal legislation has already been adopted. The 1982 Victim and Witness Protection Act,[72] for example, requires victim impact statements to be considered at federal sentencing hearings and places responsibility for their creation on federal probation officers. In 1984, the federal Victims of Crime Act (VOCA) was enacted with substantial bipartisan support. VOCA authorized federal funding to help states establish victim assistance and victim compensation programs. Under VOCA, the U.S. Department of Justice's Office for Victims of Crime provides a significant source of both funding and information for victim assistance programs. For fiscal years 1991–1994, Congress authorized the office to provide $150 million annually to states to aid victims of state and federal criminal offenses.[73] Funds come from bond forfeitures, penalties, and fines imposed in federal criminal court cases.

The rights of victims were further increased under the Violent Crime Control and Law Enforcement Act of 1994, which created a federal right of allocution for victims of violent and sex crimes, permitting them to speak at the sentencing of their assailants. The 1994 law also requires sex offenders and child molesters to pay restitution to their victims, and prohibits the diversion of victims' funds to other federal programs. Still more provisions of the 1994 law provide civil rights remedies for victims of felonies which were motivated by gender bias, and extend "rape shield law" protections to civil cases and to all criminal cases to bar irrelevant inquiries into a victim's sexual history.

Much of the philosophical basis of today's victim's movement can be found in the restorative justice model. **Restorative justice**, which was discussed briefly earlier in this chapter, emphasizes offender accountability and victim reparation. Restorative justice (see Table 9-3 for a comparison of restorative justice with retributive justice) also provides the basis for **victim compensation** programs—which are another means still of recognizing the needs of crime victims. Today, all 50 states have passed legislation providing for monetary payments to victims of crime. Such payments are primarily designed to compensate victims for medical expenses and lost wages. All existing programs require that applicants meet certain eligibility criteria, and most set limits on the maximum amount of compensation that can be received. Generally disallowed are claims from victims who are significantly responsible for their own victimization.

Not everyone agrees that the contemporary victims' movement is as valuable as it might be. Robert Elias, whose book *Victims Still: The Political Manipulation of Crime Victims* provides one opposing view, argues that the movement "has supported progressively conservative legislation that attacks constitutional rights, and has adopted a retributive philosophy against offenders who themselves are victims of a repressive system."[74] Elias cites, for example, what he calls "the war on drug victims" (drug users), as symptomatic of the unfortunate policies inherent in conservative approaches to crime control.

Victim Impact Statements

Another consequence of the national victim–witness rights movement has been a call for the use of victim impact statements prior to sentencing. A **victim impact statement** generally takes the form of a written document which describes the losses, suffering, and trauma experienced by the crime victim or the victim's survivors. Judges are expected to consider such statements in arriving at an appropriate sanction for the offender.

Restorative Justice. A sentencing model which builds on restitution and community participation in an attempt to make the victim "whole again."

TABLE 9-3

Differences Between Restorative and Retributive Justice

Retributive Justice	Restorative Justice
Crime is an act against the state, a violation of a law, an abstract idea.	Crime is an act against another person or the community.
The criminal justice system controls crime.	Crime control lies primarily in the community.
Offender accountability is defined as taking punishment.	Accountability is defined as assuming responsibility and taking action to repair harm.
Crime is an individual act with individual responsibility.	Crime has both individual and social dimensions of responsibility.
Victims are peripheral to the process.	Victims are central to the process of resolving a crime.
The offender is defined by deficits.	The offender is defined by the capacity to make reparation.
Emphasis on adversarial relationship.	Emphasis on dialog and negotiation.
Imposition of pain to punish and deter or prevent.	Restitution as a means of restoring both parties; goal of reconciliation and restoration.
Community on sidelines, represented abstractly by state.	Community as facilitator in restorative process.
Response focused on offender's past behavior.	Response focused on harmful consequences of offender's behavior; emphasis on the future and on reparation.
Dependence on proxy professionals.	Direct involvement by both the offender and the victim.

SOURCE: Adapted from Gordon Bazemore and Mark S. Umbreit, *Balanced and Restorative Justice: Program Summary* (Washington, D.C.: Office of Juvenile Justice and Delinquency Prevention, October 1994), p. 7.

The drive to mandate inclusion of victim impact statements in sentencing decisions, already mandated in federal courts by the 1982 Victim and Witness Protection Act, was substantially enhanced by the "right of allocution" provision of the Violent Crime Control and Law Enforcement Act of 1994 (mentioned earlier). Some states, however, have gone the federal government one better. In 1984, the state of California, for example, passed legislation[75] giving victims a right to attend and participate in sentencing and parole hearings. Approximately 20 states now have laws mandating citizen involvement in sentencing, and all 50 states and the District of Columbia "allow for some form of submission of a victim impact statement either at the time of sentencing or to be contained in the presentence investigation reports" made by court officers.[76] Where written victim impact statements are not available, courts may invite the victim to testify directly at sentencing.

The case of actress Theresa Saldana is representative of the many victims who feel they need more say in sentencing and parole decisions. Saldana, featured in such movies as *Raging Bull* and *I Want to Hold Your Hand*, was attacked outside her apartment by a crazed drifter in 1982. She was stabbed ten times, and may have been saved only by the fact that the knife her attacker was wielding bent from the force of the blows. Although seriously injured, she recovered. The man who attacked her, Arthur Jackson, had a long history of psychiatric problems and claimed to be on a divine mission to unite with Ms. Saldana in heaven. Although imprisoned for the attack, Jackson continued to write his victim, promising that when he got out he would finish the job. California prison authorities claimed they were powerless to stop his letters.

In 1984, under the newly passed California victim's right statute, Ms. Saldana testified before a resentencing body considering Jackson's case. "I will never forget the searing, ghastly pain, the grotesque and devastating experience of this person nearly butchering me to death, or the bone-chilling sight of my own blood splattered everywhere,"[77] she told the examiners. Her testimony resulted in Jackson's release being delayed until June 1989. As Jackson's release date arrived, Ms. Saldana told reporters: "It is just unbelievable that he is getting out. I feel like I am in a nightmare. I really feel my rights are being overlooked. Why is it life, liberty and the pursuit of happiness (are) being taken from me?"[78]

There is little information to date on what changes, if any, the appearance of victims at sentencing is having on the criminal justice system. At least one study, however, found that very few victims are taking advantage of their newfound opportunities. Less than 3 percent of California victims chose to appear or testify at sentencing hearings after that state's victim's rights law was enacted.[79]

Tennis superstar Monica Seles grimaces in pain after being stabbed in the back during a 1993 German tennis tournament by a knife-wielding man. German courts refused to sentence her attacker to time behind bars even though Seles complained that the attack shattered her career and left her unable to compete on the professional tennis circuit for years. Photo courtesy of AP/Wide World Photos.

Hearing from victims, however, does not guarantee that a sentencing court will be sympathetic. On April 3, 1995, for example, a court in Berlin, Germany, refused to imprison Guenter Parche—the unemployed German machinist who stabbed 19-year-old tennis superstar Monica Seles in the back with a kitchen knife at the 1993 Hamburg Open. Even though Seles told the court that Parche "ruined my life" and ended my career "as the world's best tennis player,"[80] the judge ruled that a suspended sentence was appropriate because the man apparently had not intended to kill Seles—only disable her so that German star Steffi Graf could regain the number-one world ranking in women's tennis. At the hearing, Seles's American psychologist had testified that Seles "felt like a bird trapped in a cage and was terrified that Parche would strike again."[81] Seles was not able to play professional tennis for more than two years following the attack.

One 1994 study of the efficacy of victim impact statements found that sentencing decisions were rarely affected by them. In the words of the study: "These statements did not produce sentencing decisions that reflected more clearly the effects of crime on victims. Nor did we find much evidence that—with or without impact statements—sentencing decisions were influenced by our measures of the effects of crime on victims, once the charge and the defendant's prior record were taken into account."[82] The authors concluded that victim impact statements have little effect on courts because judges and other "officials have established ways of making decisions which do not call for explicit information about the impact of crime on victims."

The Constitutionality of Victim Impact Statements

In 1987, the constitutionality of victim impact statements was called into question by the U.S. Supreme Court in the case of *Booth* v. *Maryland*.[83] The case involved Irvin Bronstein, age 78, and his wife Rose, age 75, who were robbed and brutally murdered in their home in Baltimore, Maryland, in 1983. The killers were John Booth and Willie Reid, acquaintances of the Bronstein's, caught stealing to support heroin habits. After being convicted of murder, Booth decided to allow the jury (rather than the judge) to set his sentence. The jury considered, as required by state law, a victim impact statement which was part of a presentence report prepared by probation officers. The victim impact statement used in the case was a powerful one, describing the wholesome personal qualities of the Bronsteins and the emotional suffering their children had experienced as a result of the murders.

After receiving a death sentence, Booth appealed to the U.S. Supreme Court. The Court overturned his sentence, reasoning that victim impact statements, at least in capital cases, violate the Eighth Amendment ban on cruel and unusual punishments. In a close (5-to-4) decision, the majority held that information in victim impact statements leads to the risk that the death penalty might be imposed in an arbitrary and capricious manner.

In a complete about face, affected in no small part by the gathering conservative majority among its justices, the Supreme Court held in the 1991 case of *Payne* v. *Tennessee*[84] that the *Booth* ruling had been based on "a misreading of precedent."[85] The *Payne* case began with a 1987 double murder, in which a 28-year-old mother and 2-year-old daughter were stabbed to death in Millington, Tennessee.[86] A second child, 3-year-old Nicholas Christopher, himself severely wounded in the incident, witnessed the deaths of his mother and young sister. In a trial following the killings, the prosecution claimed that Pervis Tyrone Payne, a 20-year-old retarded man, had killed the mother and child after the woman resisted his sexual advances. Payne was convicted of both murders. At the sentencing phase of the trial, Mary Zvolanek, Nicholas's grandmother, testified that the boy continued to cry out daily for his dead sister. Following *Booth*, Payne's conviction was upheld by the Tennessee supreme court in an opinion which Justice Thurgood Marshall said did little to disguise the Tennessee court's contempt for the precedent set by *Booth*.

Victim Impact Statement.
The in-court use of victim- or survivor-supplied information by sentencing authorities wishing to make an informed sentencing decision.

This time, however, the Supreme Court agreed with the Tennessee justices, holding that "[v]ictim impact evidence is simply another form or method of informing the sentencing authority about the specific harm caused by the crime in question, evidence of a general type long considered by sentencing authorities." As Chief Justice Rehnquist wrote for the majority, "[c]ourts have always taken into consideration the harm done by the defendant in imposing sentence." In a concurring opinion, Justice Antonin Scalia held that "*Booth* significantly harms our criminal justice system..." and had been decided with "plainly inadequate rational support." Given the seemingly firm authority with which the Court's conservative majority now speaks, it is likely that the *Payne* decision will remain in place for a long time to come.

Traditional Sentencing Options

Sentencing is fundamentally a risk management strategy designed to protect the public while serving the ends of rehabilitation, deterrence, retribution, and restoration. Because the goals of sentencing are difficult to agree on, so too are sanctions. Lengthy prison terms do little for rehabilitation, whereas community release programs can hardly protect the innocent from offenders bent on continuing criminality.

Assorted sentencing philosophies continue to permeate state-level judicial systems. Each state has its own sentencing laws, and frequent revisions of those statutes are not uncommon. Because of huge variation from one state to another in the laws and procedures which control the imposition of criminal sanctions, sentencing has been called "the most diversified part of the Nation's criminal justice process."[87]

At least one common ground, however, can be found in the four traditional sanctions which continue to dominate the thinking of most legislators and judges. The four traditional sanctions are:

- ✔ Imprisonment
- ✔ Probation
- ✔ Fines
- ✔ Death

In the case of indeterminate sentencing, the first three options are widely available to judges. The option selected generally depends on the severity of the offense and the judge's best guess as to the likelihood of future criminal involvement by the defendant. Sometimes two or more options are combined, as when an offender might be fined and sentenced to prison, or placed on probation and fined in support of restitution payments.

Jurisdictions that operate under determinate sentencing guidelines generally limit the judge's choice to only one option and often specify the extent to which that option can be applied. Dollar amounts of fines, for example, are rigidly set, and prison terms are specified for each type of offense. The death penalty remains an option in a fair number of jurisdictions, but only for a highly select group of offenders.

Recently, the Bureau of Justice Statistics reported on the sentencing practices of state felony courts.[88] Highlights of the study, using data gathered by the National Judicial Reporting Program, showed that state courts annually convict about 900,000 persons of felonies (see Figure 9-2). Of these:

- ✔ Forty-five percent are sentenced to active prison terms.
- ✔ Thirty-three percent receive jail sentences, usually involving less than a year's confinement.
- ✔ Twenty-two percent are sentenced to probation (often with fines or other special conditions).
- ✔ The average prison sentence imposed on convicted felons is six years and six months.
- ✔ The average amount of time served in confinement for felons receiving active sentences will average about two and one-half years before release because of considerations for good time and other credits.

The same survey revealed that 48 percent of those convicted in state courts of drug trafficking were sentenced to prison. Twenty-five percent of drug trafficking convictions, however, resulted in probation, whereas 27 percent of convicted traffickers were sent to local jails for brief terms of imprisonment. Although the number of active sentences handed out to felons may seem low to some, the number of criminal defendants receiving active prison time has increased dramatically. Figure 9-3 shows that court-ordered prison commitments have increased nearly eightfold in the past 30 years.

Fines

The fine is one of the oldest forms of punishment, predating even the Code of Hammurabi.[89] Until recently, however, the use of fines as criminal sanctions suffered from built-in inequities and a widespread failure to collect them. Inequities arose when offenders with vastly different financial resources were fined similar amounts. A fine of $100, for example, can place a painful economic burden on a poor defendant, but is only laughable when imposed on a wealthy offender.

Today, fines are once again receiving attention as serious sentencing alternatives. One reason for the renewed interest is the stress placed on state resources by burgeoning prison populations. The extensive imposition of fines not only results

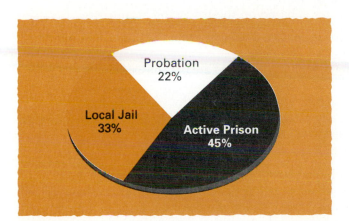

FIGURE 9-2

The sentencing of convicted felons in state courts by type of sentence. Source: Patrick A. Langan and Helen A. Graziadei, Felony Sentences in State Courts, 1992 (Washington, D.C.: Bureau of Justice Statistics, January 1995).

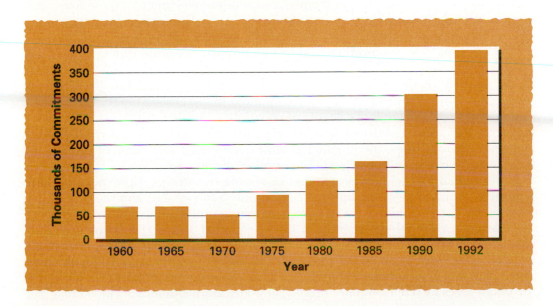

FIGURE 9-3

Court-ordered prison commitments, 1960–1992. Source: Patrick A. Langan and Helen A. Graziadei, Felony Sentences in State Courts, 1992 (Washington, D.C.: BJS, 1995), and other years.

in less crowded prisons but can contribute to state and local coffers and lower the tax burden of law-abiding citizens. Other advantages of the use of fines as criminal sanctions include the following:

✔ Fines can deprive offenders of the proceeds of criminal activity.
✔ Fines can promote rehabilitation by enforcing economic responsibility.
✔ Fines can be collected by existing criminal justice agencies and are relatively inexpensive to administer.
✔ Fines can be made proportionate to both the severity of the offense and the ability of the offender to pay.

A recent National Institute of Justice survey found that an average of 86 percent of convicted defendants in courts of limited jurisdiction receive fines as sentences, some in combination with another penalty.[90] Fines are also experiencing widespread use in courts of general jurisdiction, where the National Institute of Justice study found judges imposing fines in 42 percent of all cases which came before them for sentencing. Some studies estimate that more than $1 billion in fines are collected nationwide each year.[91]

Fines are often imposed for relatively minor law violations such as driving while intoxicated, reckless driving, disturbing the peace, disorderly conduct, public drunkenness, and vandalism. Judges in many courts, however, report the use of fines for relatively serious violations of the law, including assault, auto theft, embezzlement, fraud, and the sale and possession of various controlled substances. Fines are much more likely to be imposed, however, where the offender has both a clean record and the ability to pay.[92]

Opposition to the use of fines is based on the following arguments:

✔ Fines may result in the release of convicted offenders into the community, but do not impose stringent controls on their behavior.
✔ Fines are a relatively mild form of punishment and are not consistent with just deserts philosophy.
✔ Fines discriminate against the poor and favor the wealthy.
✔ Indigent offenders are especially subject to discrimination since they entirely lack the financial resources with which to pay fines.
✔ Fines are difficult to collect.

A number of these objections can be answered by procedures which make available to judges complete financial information on defendants. Studies have found, however, that courts of limited jurisdiction, which are the most likely to impose fines, are also the least likely to have adequate information on offenders' economic status.[93] Perhaps as a consequence, judges themselves are often reluctant to impose fines. Two of the most widely cited objections by judges to the use of fines are (1) fines allow more affluent offenders to "buy their way out" and (2) poor offenders cannot pay fines.[94]

A solution to both objections can be found in the Scandinavian system of day fines. The day-fine system is based on the idea that fines should be proportionate to the severity of the offense, but also need to take into account the financial resources of the offender. Day fines are computed by first assessing the seriousness of the offense, the defendant's degree of culpability, and his or her prior record as measured in "days." The use of days as a benchmark of seriousness is related to the fact that, without fines, the offender could be sentenced to a number of days (or months or years) in jail or prison. The number of days an offender is assessed is then multiplied by the daily wages that person earns. Hence, if two persons were sentenced to a five-day fine, but one earned only $20 per day, and the other $200 per day, the first would pay a $100 fine, and the second $1,000.

Recently, the National Institute of Justice reported on an experimental program conducted by the Richmond County Criminal Court in Staten Island, New York, which was designed to introduce and assess the use of day fines in the United States.[95] The Institute also reported on a similar 12-week experimental program involving the use of day fines by the Milwaukee Municipal Court. Both studies concluded that "the day fine can play a major…role as an intermediate sanction"[96] and that "the day-fine concept could be implemented in a typical American limited-jurisdiction court."[97]

Death: The Ultimate Sanction

Capital Punishment. Another term for the death penalty. Capital punishment is the most extreme of all sentencing options.

Capital punishment—the death penalty—has a long and gruesome history. Civilizations have almost always put criminals to death for a variety of offenses. As times changed, so did accepted methods of execution. Under the Davidic monarchy, biblical Israel institutionalized the practice of stoning convicts to death.[98] In that practice, the entire community could participate in dispatching the offender. As an apparent aid to deterrence, the convict's deceased body could be impaled on a post at the gates of the city or otherwise exposed to public view.[99]

Athenian society, around 200 B.C., was progressive by the standards of its day. The ancient Greeks restricted the use of capital punishment and limited the suffering of the condemned through the use of poison derived from the hemlock tree. Socrates, the famous Greek orator, accused of being a political subversive, died this way.

The Romans were far less sensitive. They used beheading most often although the law provided that arsonists should be burned alive and false witnesses thrown from a high rock.[100] Suspected witches were clubbed to death, and slaves were strangled. Even more brutal sanctions included drawing and quartering, and social outcasts, Christians, and rabble rousers were thrown to the lions.

After the fall of the Roman Empire, Europe was plunged into the Dark Ages, a period of superstition marked by widespread illiteracy and political turmoil. The Dark Ages lasted from 426 A.D. until the early 13th century. During the Dark Ages, executions were institutionalized through the use of ordeals designed to both judge and punish. Suspects were submerged in cold water, dumped in boiling oil, crushed under huge stones, forced to do battle with professional soldiers, or thrown into bonfires. Theological arguments prevalent at the time held that innocents, protected by God and heavenly forces, would emerge from any ordeal unscathed, whereas guilty parties would perish. Trial by ordeal was eliminated through a decree of the Fourth Lateran Council of 1215, under the direction of Pope Innocent III, after later evidence proved that many who died in ordeals could not have committed the crimes of which they were accused.[101]

Following the Fourth Lateran Council, trials, much as we know them today, became the basis for judging guilt or innocence. The death penalty remained in widespread use. As recently as a century and a half ago, 160 crimes were punishable in England by death.[102] The young received no special privilege. In 1801, a child of 13 was hanged in Tyburn, England, for stealing a spoon.[103]

Sophisticated techniques of execution were in use by the 19th century. One engine of death was the guillotine, invented in France around the time of the French Revolution. The guillotine was described by its creator, Dr. Joseph-Ignace Guillotin, as "a cool breath on the back of the neck"[104] and found widespread use in eliminating opponents of the Revolution.

In America, hanging became the preferred mode of execution. It was especially popular on the frontier since it required few special materials and was a relatively efficient means of dispatch. By the early 1890s, electrocution had replaced hanging as the preferred form of capital punishment in America. The appeal of electrocution was that it stopped the heart without visible signs of gross bodily trauma.

Executions: The Grim Facts

Since 1608, when records on capital punishment first became available, estimates are that more than 18,800 legal executions have been carried out in America.[105] Although capital punishment was widely used throughout the 18th and 19th centuries, the 20th century has seen a constant decline in the number of persons legally executed in the United States. Between 1930 and 1967, when the U.S. Supreme Court ordered a nationwide stay of pending executions, nearly 3,800 persons were put to death. The years 1935 and 1936 were peak years, with nearly 200 legal killings each year. Executions declined substantially every year thereafter. Between 1967 and 1977, a *de facto* moratorium existed, with no executions carried out in any U.S. jurisdiction. Following the lifting of the moratorium, executions increased. In 1993, 38 offenders were put to death, while "only" 31 were executed nationwide in 1994. 1995 set a modern record for executions, with 56 executions—19 in Texas alone.

In 1995, the state of New York reinstated the death penalty after a 30-year hiatus. Today, 38 of the 50 states and the federal government have capital punishment laws. All but New York permit execution for first-degree murder, whereas treason, kidnapping, the murder of a police or correctional officer, and murder while under a life sentence are punishable by death in selected jurisdictions.[106] New York allows for the imposition of a death sentence in cases involving the murder of law enforcement officers, judges, and witnesses and their families, and it applies the punishment to serial killers, terrorists, murderers-for-hire, and those who kill while committing another felony like robbery or rape.

The number of crimes punishable by death under federal jurisdiction increased dramatically with passage of the Violent Crime Control and Law Enforcement Act of 1994—and now includes a total of around 60 offenses. Of the 2,890 persons under sentence of death throughout the United States on January 1, 1995, 98 percent were male, 51 percent were white, 42 percent were black, and 5 percent were Hispanic. (Native Americans, Pacific Islanders, and "others" made up the remainder of groups reported in statistical tabulations.)[107]

Methods of imposing death vary by state. The majority of death penalty states authorize execution through lethal injection. Electrocution is the second most common means of dispatch, and hanging, the gas chamber, and firing squads have survived, at least as options available to the condemned, in a few states. In early 1996, for example, 49-year-old Billy Bailey was hanged at the Delaware Correctional Center for the 1979 murder of an elderly couple whose truck he stole. The day after Bailey died, 36-year-old John Albert Taylor was executed by a five-man firing squad in Utah. Taylor, a confirmed pedophile, died for raping, sodomizing, and strangling an 11-year-old girl in 1989. Both Bailey and Taylor were given the option of lethal injection, but declined.

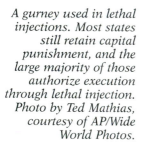

A gurney used in lethal injections. Most states still retain capital punishment, and the large majority of those authorize execution through lethal injection. Photo by Ted Mathias, courtesy of AP/Wide World Photos.

Opposition to Capital Punishment

Capital punishment is not without recognized problems. One serious difficulty centers on the fact that automatic review of all death sentences by appellate courts and constant legal maneuvering by defense counsel often lead to a dramatic delay between the time the sentence is passed and the time it is carried out. Such lengthy delays, compounded with uncertainty over whether a sentence will ever be finally imposed, directly contravene the generally accepted notion that punishment should be swift and certain.

Typical of delayed executions, on April 18, 1995, the Louisiana Supreme Court granted two-time killer Antonio James his 14th stay of execution just 4 hours before he was scheduled to die by lethal injection. The 39-year-old James had been sentenced to death 15 years earlier for shooting 70-year-old Henry Silver in the head during an armed robbery on New Year's Day 1979.[108] He was later sentenced to 99 more years in prison for killing Alvin Adams, 74, during an armed robbery 2 weeks after the Silver killing. In granting the stay, the Louisiana Supreme Court ruled that a state district court had erred a few days earlier by not granting a hearing on new evidence James's attorneys said could prove he was not the triggerman in either killing. Before the court's ruling, Governor Edwin Edwards had refused to block the execution. James has been on Louisiana's death row since 1981—longer than any other inmate still there.

Delays in the imposition of capital sanctions have been the source of much anguish for condemned prisoners as well as for the victims and the family members of both. In a recent speech before the American Bar Association, Chief Justice of the U.S. Supreme Court, William H. Rehnquist, called for reforms of the current federal *habeas corpus* system, which allows condemned prisoners constant opportunities for appeal. In the words of Rehnquist, "The capital defendant does not need to prevail on the merits in order to accomplish his purpose; he wins temporary victories by postponing a final adjudication."[109]

Although many death penalty appeals eventually reach the U.S. Supreme Court, the Court, contrary to popular belief, does not automatically review all death sentences. Commenting on the case of Curtis Lee Kyles, who had been on Louisiana's death row 11 years after being found guilty of the 1984 gunshot murder of a 60-year-old woman outside a New Orleans grocery store, U.S. Supreme Court Justice Antonin Scalia made clear the Court's position on appeals received from death row inmates: "The greatest puzzle of today's decision," wrote Scalia, "is what could have caused this capital case to be singled out. Perhaps it has been randomly selected as a symbol to reassure America that the U.S. Supreme Court is reviewing capital convictions to make sure no factual error has been made....If so, it is a false symbol, for we assuredly do not do that."[110]

Because of the strong emotions state-imposed death wrings from the hearts of many constituencies, many attempts have been made to abolish capital punishment since the founding of the United States. The first recorded effort to abolish the death penalty occurred at the home of Benjamin Franklin in 1787.[111] At a meeting on March 9 of that year, Dr. Benjamin Rush, a signer of the Declaration of Independence and leading medical pioneer, read a paper against capital punishment to a small but influential audience. Although his immediate efforts came to naught, his arguments laid the groundwork for many debates which followed. Michigan, widely regarded as the first abolitionist state, joined the Union in 1837 without a death penalty. A number of other states, including Massachusetts, West Virginia, Wisconsin, Minnesota, Alaska, and Hawaii, have since spurned death as a possible sanction for criminal acts. Many Western European countries have also rejected the death penalty. As noted earlier, it remains a viable sentencing option in 38 of the states and all federal jurisdictions. As a consequence, arguments continue to rage over its value.

Theory into Practice: Justice Blackmun's Pronouncement on the Death Penalty

On February 22, 1994, U.S. Supreme Court Justice Harry A. Blackmun used the Court's denial of an appeal by Bruce Edwin Callins, a Texas death row inmate, to explain why he would forever be opposed to the death penalty. Reproduced here are excerpts from his dissenting opinion in that case (*Callins* v. *Collins*). A Theory into Practice box on the facing page contains a contrasting opinion provided by Justice Antonin Scalia, writing for the Court's majority.

From this day forward, I no longer shall tinker with the machinery of death. For more than 20 years I have endeavored—indeed, I have struggled—along with a majority of this Court, to develop procedural and substantive rules that would lend more than the mere appearance of fairness to the death penalty endeavor. Rather than continue to coddle the Court's delusion that the desired level of fairness has been achieved and the need for regulation eviscerated, I feel morally and intellectually obligated simply to concede that the death penalty experiment has failed. It is virtually self-evident to me now that no combination of procedural rules or substantive regulations ever can save the death penalty from its inherent constitutional deficiencies. The basic question—does the system accurately and consistently determine which defendants "deserve" to die?— cannot be answered in the affirmative. It is not simply that this Court has allowed vague aggravating circumstances to be employed, see, *e.g.*, *Arave* v. *Creech*, (1993), relevant mitigating evidence to be disregarded, see, *e.g.*, *Johnson* v. *Texas*, (1993), and vital judicial review to be blocked, see, *e.g.*, *Coleman* v. *Thompson*, (1991). The problem is that the inevitability of factual, legal, and moral error gives us a system that we know must wrongly kill some defendants, a system that fails to deliver the fair, consistent, and reliable sentences of death required by the Constitution.

It is the decision to sentence a defendant to death—not merely the decision to make a defendant eligible for death—that may not be arbitrary. While one might hope that providing the sentencer with as much relevant mitigating evidence as possible will lead to more rational and consistent sentences, experience has taught otherwise. It seems that the decision whether a human being should live or die is so inherently subjective—rife with all of life's understandings, experiences, prejudices, and passions—that it inevitably defies the rationality and consistency required by the Constitution.

Perhaps one day this Court will develop procedural rules or verbal formulas that actually will provide consistency, fairness, and reliability in a capital-sentencing scheme. I am not optimistic that such a day will come. I am more optimistic, though, that this Court eventually will conclude that the effort to eliminate arbitrariness while preserving fairness "in the infliction of [death] is so plainly doomed to failure that it—and the death penalty—must be abandoned altogether." *Godfrey* v. *Georgia*, 446 U. S. 420, 442 (1980) (Marshall, J., concurring in the judgment). I may not live to see that day, but I have faith that eventually it will arrive. The path the Court has chosen lessens us all. I dissent.

QUESTIONS FOR DISCUSSION

1. Do you agree with Justice Blackmun's assessment of the death penalty as arbitrarily imposed? Why or why not?

2. If imposition of the death penalty is indeed arbitrary, as Justice Blackmun claims, how might it be made less so?

Today, four main rationales for abolishing capital punishment are heard:

1. The death penalty can and has been inflicted on innocent people.
2. Evidence has shown that the death penalty is not an effective deterrent.
3. The imposition of the death penalty is, by the nature of our legal system, completely arbitrary and even discriminatory.
4. Human life is sacred, and killing at the hands of the state is not a righteous act, but rather one which is on the same moral level as the crimes committed by the condemned.

The first three abolitionist claims are pragmatic; that is, they can be measured and verified by looking at the facts. The last claim is primarily philosophical and therefore not amenable to scientific investigation. Hence, we shall briefly examine only the first three.

Although some evidence does exist that a few innocent people have been executed, most research by far has centered on examining the deterrent effect of the

Theory into Practice: Justice Scalia's Rebuttal

Justice Blackmun dissents from the denial of certiorari in this case with a statement explaining why the death penalty "as currently administered," is contrary to the Constitution of the United States. That explanation often refers to "intellectual, moral, and personal" perceptions, but never to the text and tradition of the Constitution. It is the latter rather than the former that ought to control. The Fifth Amendment provides that "[n]o person shall be held to answer for a capital...crime, unless on a presentment or indictment of a Grand Jury,...nor be deprived of life...without due process of law." This clearly permits the death penalty to be imposed, and establishes beyond doubt that the death penalty is not one of the "cruel and unusual punishments" prohibited by the Eighth Amendment.

Convictions in opposition to the death penalty are often passionate and deeply held. That would be no excuse for reading them into a Constitution that does not contain them, even if they represented the convictions of a majority of Americans. Much less is there any excuse for using that course to thrust a minority's views upon the people. He chooses, as the case in which to make that statement, one of the less brutal of the murders that regularly come before us—the murder of a man ripped by a bullet suddenly and unexpectedly, with no opportunity to prepare himself and his affairs, and left to bleed to death on the floor of a tavern. The death-by-injection which Justice Blackmun describes looks pretty desirable next to that. It looks even better next to some of the other cases currently before us which Justice Blackmun did not select as the vehicle for his announcement that the death penalty is always unconstitutional—for example, the case of the 11-year-old girl raped by four men and then killed by stuffing her panties down her throat. See *McCollum* v. *North Carolina*, No. 93-7200, cert. now pending before the Court. How enviable a quiet death by lethal injection compared with that! If the people conclude that such more brutal deaths may be deterred by capital punishment; indeed, if they merely conclude that justice requires such brutal deaths to be avenged by capital punishment; the creation of false, untextual and unhistorical contradictions within "the Court's Eighth Amendment jurisprudence" should not prevent them.

QUESTIONS FOR DISCUSSION

1. Do you believe, as Justice Scalia seems to, that "justice requires...brutal deaths to be avenged by capital punishment"? Why or why not?

2. What recourse do opponents of the death penalty have in the face of constitutional support (Scalia mentions the Fifth Amendment) for the punishment itself?

---

death penalty. During the 1970s and 1980s,[112] the deterrent effect of the death penalty became a favorite subject for debate in academic circles. Studies[113] of states which had eliminated the death penalty failed to show any increase in homicide rates. Similar studies[114] of neighboring states, in which jurisdictions retaining capital punishment were compared with those which had abandoned it, also failed to demonstrate any significant differences. Although death penalty advocates remain numerous, few any longer argue for the penalty based on its deterrent effects. Deterrent studies continue, however. In 1988, for example, a comprehensive review[115] of capital punishment in Texas, which correlated executions since 1930 with homicide rates, failed again to find any support for the use of death as a deterrent. The study was especially significant because Texas had been very active in the capital punishment arena, executing 317 persons between 1930 and 1986.[116]

The abolitionist claim that the death penalty is discriminatory is harder to investigate. Although there may be past evidence that blacks and other minorities in the United States have been disproportionately sentenced to death,[117] the present evidence is not so clear. At first glance, as one study puts it, disproportionality seems apparent: 45 of the 98 prisoners executed between January 1977 and May 1988 were black or Hispanic; 84 of the 98 had been convicted of killing whites.[118] For an accurate appraisal to be made, however, any claims of disproportionality must go beyond simple comparisons with racial representation in the larger population and must somehow measure both frequency and seriousness of capital crimes between and within racial groups. Following that line of reasoning, the Supreme Court, in the 1987 case of *McCleskey* v. *Kemp*[119] held that a simple showing of racial discrepancies in the application of the death penalty does not constitute a constitutional violation.

Justifications for Capital Punishment

Justifications for the death penalty are collectively referred to as the retentionist position. The three retentionist arguments are (1) revenge, (2) just deserts, and (3) protection. Those who justify capital punishment as revenge attempt to appeal to the visceral feeling that survivors, victims, and the state are entitled to "closure." Only after execution of the criminal perpetrator, they say, can the psychological and social wounds engendered by the offense begin to heal.

The just deserts argument makes the simple and straightforward claim that some people deserve to die for what they have done. Death is justly deserved; anything less cannot suffice as a sanction for the most heinous crimes. As Justice Potter Stewart once wrote, "the decision that capital punishment may be the appropriate sanction in extreme cases is an expression of the community's belief that certain crimes are themselves so grievous an affront to humanity that the only adequate response may be the penalty of death."[120]

The third retentionist claim, that of protection, asserts that offenders, once executed, can commit no further crimes. Clearly the least emotional of the retentionist claims, the protectionist argument may also be the weakest since societal interests in protection can also be met in other ways such as incarceration. In addition, various studies have shown that there is little likelihood of repeat offenses among people convicted of murder and later released.[121] One reason for such results, however, may be that murderers generally serve lengthy prison sentences prior to release and may have lost whatever youthful propensity for criminality they previously possessed.

The Future of the Death Penalty

Because of the nature of the positions that both sides advocate, there is little common ground even for discussion between retentionists and abolitionists. Foes of the death penalty hope that its demonstrated lack of deterrent capacity will convince others that it should be abandoned. Their approach, based as it is on statistical evidence, appears on the surface to be quite rational. However, it is doubtful that many capital punishment opponents could be persuaded to support the death penalty even if statistics showed it to be a deterrent. Likewise, the tactics of death penalty supporters are equally instinctive. Retentionists could probably not be swayed by statistical studies of deterrence, no matter what they show, since their support is bound up with emotional calls for retribution.

The future of the death penalty rests primarily with state legislatures. Short of renewed Supreme Court intervention, the future of capital punishment may depend more on popular opinion than it does on arguments pro or con. Elected legislatures, because the careers of their members lie in the hands of their constituency, are likely to follow the public mandate. Hence, it may be that studies of public attitudes toward the death penalty may be the most useful in predicting the sanction's future.

National opinion polls conducted by the Gallup and Harris organizations detail massive support for capital punishment as far back as 1936, but show a gradual decline in backing until 1966, when a resurgence in support began.[122] The proportion of the American public which today endorses the death penalty in national polls is at an all-time high since record keeping began, surpassing even the support of 1936.[123] When asked if they would still favor the death penalty if evidence showed conclusively that it did not deter criminals, a slim majority of Americans still say yes.[124]

Demographic differences account for a considerable degree of variation in public opinion polls. Robert Bohm, for example, analyzing differences among respondents in nearly two dozen polls reports that[125] (1) "[i]n all 21 polls, the percentage of whites who favor the death penalty is greater than the percentage of blacks, while the percentage of blacks opposed and undecided is greater than the percentage of whites"; (2) "[i]n every year for which there are data, people in the top income or socioeconomic category have been more likely to support the death penalty and less likely to oppose it than people in the bottom category"; (3) "[i]n all 21 polls, the percentage of males who favor the death penalty exceeds the percentage of females, and the percentage of females opposed to the death penalty exceeds the percentage of males"; (4) "Democrats have shown the greatest opposition and the least support for the death penalty, Independents are less opposed and more supportive, and Republicans are least opposed and most supportive"; and (5) "...the South, surprisingly, has been the region least likely to support and most likely to oppose the death penalty." Other variables, such as age, religion, occupation, and city size, show less clear-cut relationships to self-avowed attitudes toward the death penalty.[126]

Some contemporary studies[127] have purported to show that support for capital punishment may be a relatively abstract form of endorsement. According to Frank P. Williams and Dennis Longmire, "A majority of citizens assert support for the general concept of the death penalty but their willingness to advocate execution as an acceptable sanction decreases as they are asked about its use in specific instances."[128] Even so, few legislators are apt to examine closely the results of polls which show such strong public leanings.

Changes in public opinion could conceivably come quickly, however. Citing the First Amendment to the U.S. Constitution, California television station KQED filed suit in 1990 in U.S. District Court in San Francisco asking that it be allowed to provide broadcast coverage of executions. The lawsuit claimed that the current state policy, of barring cameras at executions, "impedes effective reporting of executions which are events of major public and political significance."[129] Although the station's claims were denied by the court in a 1991 opinion, the station is appealing.

Capital Offense. A criminal offense punishable by death.

The Courts and the Death Penalty

The U.S. Supreme Court has served as a constant sounding board for issues surrounding the death penalty. One of the court's earliest cases in this area was *Wilkerson v. Utah* (1878),[130] which questioned shooting as a method of execution and raised Eighth Amendment claims that firing squads constituted a form of cruel and unusual punishment. The Court disagreed, however, contrasting the relatively civilized nature of firing squads with the various forms of torture often associated with capital punishment around the time the Bill of Rights was written.

In similar fashion, electrocution was supported as a permissible form of execution in *In re Kemmler* (1890).[131] In *Kemmler*, the Court defined cruel and unusual methods of execution as follows: "Punishments are cruel when they involve torture or a lingering death; but the punishment of death is not cruel, within the meaning of that word as used in the Constitution. It implies there something inhuman and barbarous, something more than the mere extinguishing of life."[132] Almost 60 years later, the Court ruled that a second attempt at the electrocution of a convicted person, when the first did not work, did not violate the Eighth Amendment.[133] The Court reasoned that the initial failure was the consequence of accident or unforeseen circumstances and not the result of an effort by executioners to be intentionally cruel.

It was not until 1972, however, in the landmark case of *Furman v. Georgia*,[134] that the Court recognized "evolving standards of decency"[135] which might necessitate a reconsideration of Eighth Amendment guarantees. In a 5-to-4 ruling, the *Furman* decision invalidated Georgia's death penalty statute on the basis that it allowed a jury unguided discretion in the imposition of a capital sentence. The majority of justices concluded that the Georgia statute, which permitted a jury to decide simultaneously issues of guilt or innocence while it weighed sentencing options, allowed for an arbitrary and capricious application of the death penalty.

Many other states with statutes similar to Georgia's were affected by the *Furman* ruling but moved quickly to modify their procedures. What evolved was a two-step procedure to be used in capital cases. As a consequence, death penalty trials today involve two stages. In the first stage, guilt or innocence is decided. If the defendant is convicted of a crime for which execution is possible, a second, or penalty, phase ensues. The penalty phase generally permits the introduction of new evidence that may have been irrelevant to the question of guilt, but that may be relevant to punishment, such as drug use or childhood abuse. Although in most death penalty jurisdictions, juries determine the punishment, the trial judge sets the sentence in the second phase of capital murder trials in Arizona, Idaho, Montana, and Nebraska. Alabama, Delaware, Florida, and Indiana allow juries only to recommend a sentence to the judge.

The two-step trial procedure was specifically approved by the Court in *Gregg* v. *Georgia* (1976).[136] In *Gregg*, the Court upheld the two-stage procedural requirements of Georgia's new capital punishment law as necessary for ensuring the separation of the highly personal information needed in a sentencing decision from the kinds of information reasonably permissible in a jury trial where issues of guilt or innocence alone are being decided. In the opinion written for the majority, the Court for the first time recognized the significance of public opinion in deciding on the legitimacy of questionable sanctions.[137] Its opinion cited the strong showing of public support for the death penalty following *Furman* to mean that death was still a socially and culturally acceptable penalty.

Post-*Gregg* decisions set limits on the use of death as a penalty for all but the most severe crimes. In 1977, in the case of *Coker* v. *Georgia*,[138] the Court struck down a Georgia law imposing the death penalty for the rape of an adult woman. The Court concluded that capital punishment under such circumstances would be "grossly disproportionate" to the crime. Somewhat later, in *Woodson* v. *North Carolina*,[139] a law requiring mandatory application of the death penalty for specific crimes was overturned.

In two 1990 rulings, *Blystone* v. *Pennsylvania*, and *Boyde* v. *California*, the Court upheld state statutes which had been interpreted to dictate that death penalties must be imposed where juries find a lack of mitigating factors that could offset obvious aggravating circumstances. Similarly, in the 1990 case of R. Gene Simmons, an Arkansas mass murderer convicted of killing 16 relatives during a 1987 shooting rampage, the Court granted inmates under sentence of death the right to waive appeals. Prior to the *Simmons* case, any interested party could file a brief on behalf of condemned persons—with or without their consent.

Recently, death row inmates, and those who file cases on behalf of such inmates as sounding boards to test the boundaries of statutory acceptability, have been busy bringing challenges to state capital punishment laws. Most such challenges focus on the procedures involved in sentencing decisions. In 1995, for example, in *Harris* v. *Alabama*,[140] the U.S. Supreme Court upheld Alabama's capital sentencing system, which allows juries to recommend sentences but judges to decide them. A challenge to the constitutionality of California's capital sentencing law, which requires the jury to consider, among other things, the circumstances of the offense, prior violent crimes by the defendant, and the defendant's age, was rejected in *Tuilaepa* v. *California* (1994).[141]

Today, an average of nine years and five months[142] passes between the time a sentence of death is imposed and the time it is carried out. In a strong move to reduce delays in the conduct of executions, the U.S. Supreme Court, in the case of *McCleskey* v. *Zandt* (1991),[143] limited the number of appeals a condemned person may lodge with the courts. Saying that repeated filings for the sole purpose of delay promotes "disrespect for the finality of convictions" and "disparages the entire criminal justice system," the Court established a two-pronged criterion for future appeals. According to *McCleskey*, in any petition beyond the first, filed with the federal court, capital defendants must demonstrate (1) good cause why the claim now being made was not included in the first filing and (2) how the absence of that claim may have harmed the petitioner's ability to mount an effective defense. Two months later, the Court reinforced *McCleskey*, when it ruled, in *Coleman* v.

Thompson,[144] that state prisoners could not cite "procedural default" such as a defense attorney's failure to meet a state's filing deadline for appeals as the basis for an appeal to federal court.

In 1995, in the case of *Schlup* v. *Delo*,[145] the Court continued to define standards for continued appeals from death row inmates under federal jurisdiction, ruling that before appeals based on claims of new evidence can be heard, "a petitioner must show that, in light of the new evidence, it is more likely than not that no reasonable juror would have found him guilty beyond a reasonable doubt."[146] A "reasonable juror" was defined as one who "would consider fairly all of the evidence presented and would conscientiously obey the trial court's instructions requiring proof beyond a reasonable doubt."

Observers noted that the Court's spate of decisions limiting the opportunity of convicted offenders to appeal would swiftly and dramatically increase the rate of executions across the nation. Shortly thereafter, Florida death row inmate Bobby Marion Francis became the first person put to death in the post-*McCleskey* period. Francis had been convicted of the 1975 torture death of a drug informant, Titus R. Walters. In an attempt to kill Walters, Francis injected him with Drano and battery acid, then shot him twice in the head. Still conscious, Walters was finally shot through the heart. Francis died in Florida's electric chair on June 25, 1991, at 7:07 A.M., 16 years after torturing and killing Walters.

Although at least one U.S. Supreme Court Justice has taken a strong position against the death penalty (see Theory into Practice box in this chapter), today's Court seems largely convinced of the constitutionality of a sentence of death. Open to debate, however, is the constitutionality of questionable *methods* for its imposition. In a 1993 hearing, *Poyner* v. *Murray*,[147] the U.S. Supreme Court hinted at the possibility of reopening questions first raised in *Kemmler*. The case challenged Virginia's use of the electric chair as a form of cruel and unusual punishment. Syvasky Lafayette Poyner, who originally brought the case before the Court, lost his bid for a stay of execution and was electrocuted in March 1993. Nonetheless, in *Poyner*, Justices Souter, Blackmun, and Stevens wrote: "The Court has not spoken squarely on the underlying issue since *In re Kemmler*...and the holding of that case does not constitute a dispositive response to litigation of the issue in light of modern knowledge about the method of execution in question." In a still more recent ruling, members of the Court questioned the constitutionality of hanging, suggesting that it may be a form of cruel and unusual punishment. In that case, *Campbell* v. *Wood* (1994),[148] the defendant, Charles Campbell, raped a woman, got out of prison, then came back and murdered her. His request for a stay of execution was denied since Washington state law (the state in which the murder occurred) offered Campbell a choice between various methods of execution and, therefore, an alternative to hanging.

Summary

The just deserts model, with its emphasis on retribution and revenge, is today the ascendant sentencing philosophy in the United States. Many citizens, however, still expect sentencing practices to provide for the general goals of deterrence, rehabilitation, incapacitation, and restitution. This ambivalence toward the purpose of sentencing reflects a more basic cultural uncertainty regarding the root causes of crime and the goals of the criminal justice system.

Determinate sentencing, embodied in the federal sentencing guidelines and in many state sentencing programs of today, is a child of the just deserts philosophy. The determinate sentencing model, however, although apparently associated with a reduction in biased and inequitable sentencing practices, may not be the panacea it once seemed. Inequitable practices under the indeterminate model may never have been as widespread as opponents of the model claimed them to be. Worse still, the determinate sentencing model may not reduce sentencing discretion, but simply move it out of the hands of judges and into the ever-widening sphere of plea bargaining. Doubly unfortunate, determinate sentencing, by its deemphasis of parole, weakens incentives among the correctional population for positive change and tends to swell prison populations until they're overflowing. Even so, as societywide sentiments and the social policies they support swing further in the direction of social responsibility, the interests of crime victims and the concerns of those who champion them can be expected to increasingly come to the fore.

 iscussion Questions

1. Outline the various sentencing rationales discussed in this chapter. Which of these rationales do you find most acceptable as the goal of sentencing? How might the acceptability of the choice you make vary with the type of offense? Can you envision any other circumstances which might make your choice less acceptable?
2. In your opinion, is the return to just deserts consistent with the determinate sentencing model? Why or why not?
3. Trace the differences between determinate and indeterminate sentencing. Which model holds the best long-term promise for crime reduction? Why?
4. What is a victim impact statement? Do you think victim impact statements should be admissible at the sentencing stage of criminal trials? If so, what material should they contain? What material should not be permitted in such reports? How could the information in victim impact statements be best verified?

 eferences

1. *Smith* v. *U.S.*, 113 S.Ct. 1178, 122 L.Ed. 2d 548 (1993).
2. For a thorough discussion of the philosophy of punishment and sentencing, see David Garland, *Punishment and Modern Society: A Study in Social Theory* (Chicago: University of Chicago Press, 1990); Ralph D. Ellis and Carol S. Ellis, *Theories of Criminal Justice: A Critical Reappraisal* (Wolfeboro, N.H.: Longwood Academic, 1989); and Colin Summer, *Censure, Politics, and Criminal Justice* (Bristol, Pa.: Open University Press, 1990).
3. The requirement for punishment is supported by the belief that social order (and the laws which represent it) could not exist for long if transgressions went unsanctioned.
4. "Back to the Chain Gang," *Newsweek*, October 17, 1994, p. 87.
5. Ibid.
6. Ibid.
7. For an excellent review of the new "get tough" attitudes influencing sentencing decisions, see: Tamasak Wicharaya, *Simple Theory, Hard Reality: The Impact of Sentencing Reforms on Courts, Prisons, and Crime* (Albany, N.Y.: State University of New York Press, 1995).
8. For a thorough review of the literature on deterrence, see Raymond Paternoster, "The Deterrent Effect of the Perceived Certainty and Severity of Punishment: A Review of the Evidence and Issues." *Justice Quarterly*, Vol. 4, no. 2 (June 1987), pp. 174–217.
9. Hugo Adam Bedau, "Retributivism and the Theory of Punishment," *Journal of Philosophy*, Vol. 75 (November 1978), pp. 601–620.
10. H. L. A. Hart, *Punishment and Responsibility: Essays in the Philosophy of Law* (Oxford: Clarendon Press, 1968).
11. Paul Gendreau and Robert R. Ross, "Revivification of Rehabilitation: Evidence from the 1980s." *Justice Quarterly*, Vol. 4, no. 3 (September 1987), pp. 349–408.
12. Gordon Bazemore and Mark S. Umbreit, *Balanced and Restorative Justice: Program Summary* (Washington, D.C.: OJJDP, October 1994), foreword.
13. 18 U.S.C. 3563 (a) (2).
14. See Joan Petersilia, *Expanding Options for Criminal Sentencing* (Santa Monica, Calif.: The Rand Corporation, 1987).
15. E-mail communications with the Office of Reparative Programs, Department of Corrections, State of Vermont, July 3, 1995.

16. Donna Hunzeker, "State Sentencing Systems and 'Truth in Sentencing,'" *State Legislative Report*, Vol. 20, no. 3 (Denver: National Conference of State Legislatures, 1995).

17. "Oklahoma Rapist Gets 30,000 Years," United Press International online, southwest edition, December 23, 1994.

18. Lawrence A. Greenfeld, "Prison Sentences and Time Served for Violence" (Washington, D.C.: Bureau of Justice Statistics, April 1995).

19. For a thorough consideration of alleged disparities, see G. Kleck, "Racial Discrimination in Criminal Sentencing: A Critical Evaluation of the Evidence with Additional Evidence on the Death Penalty," *American Sociological Review*, no. 46 (1981), pp. 783–805, and G. Kleck, "Life Support for Ailing Hypotheses: Modes of Summarizing the Evidence for Racial Discrimination in Sentencing," *Law and Human Behavior*, no. 9 (1985), pp. 271–285.

20. Donna Hunzeker, "State Sentencing Systems and 'Truth in Sentencing.'"

21. Lawrence A. Greenfeld, "Prison Sentences and Time Served for Violence," Bureau of Justice Statistics, *Selected Findings, No. 4*, April 1995.

22. *Arave v. Creech*, 113 S.Ct. 1534, 123 L. Ed. 2d 188 (1993). See also *Richmond v. Lewis*, 113 S.Ct. 538, 121 L. Ed. 2d 411 (1992).

23. For an early statement of this problem, see Franklin E. Zimring, "Making the Punishment Fit the Crime: A Consumer's Guide to Sentencing Reform," In Hawkins and Zimring, eds., *The Pursuit of Criminal Justice*, pp. 267–275.

24. Albert W. Alschuler, "Sentencing Reform and Prosecutorial Power: A Critique of Recent Proposals for 'Fixed' and 'Presumptive' Sentencing," in Sheldon L. Messinger and Egon Bittner, *Criminology Review Yearbook*, Vol. 1 (Beverly Hills, Calif.: Sage Publications, 1979), pp. 416–445.

25. Ibid., p. 422.

26. Christopher T. Link and Neal Shover, "The Origins of Criminal Sentencing Reforms," *Justice Quarterly*, Vol. 3, no. 3 (September 1986), pp. 329–342.

27. For a good discussion of such issues, see Hans Toch, "Rewarding Convicted Offenders," *Federal Probation* (June 1988), pp. 42–48.

28. As discussed later in this chapter, federal sentencing guidelines did not become effective until 1987 and still had to meet many court challenges.

29. U.S. Sentencing Commission, *Federal Sentencing Guidelines Manual* (Washington, D.C.: U.S. Government Printing Office, 1987), p. 2.

30. A maximum of 54 days per year of "good time" credit can still be earned.

31. Lawrence A. Greenfeld, "Prison Sentences and Time Served for Violence," Bureau of Justice Statistics, *Selected Findings*, No. 4, April 1995.

32. Bureau of Justice Statistics, "Prison Sentences and Time Served for Violence," (Rockville, Md.: BJS, 1995).

33. Thomas Martello, "Truth In Sentencing," the Associated Press, northern edition, April 26, 1994.

34. For an excellent review of the act and its implications see: Gregory D. Lee, "U.S. Sentencing Guidelines: Their Impact on Federal Drug Offenders," *FBI Law Enforcement Bulletin* (Washington, D.C.: FBI, May 1995), pp. 17–21.

35. U.S. Sentencing Commission, *Guidelines*, p. 10.

36. "Sentencing Panel Urges Parity for Crack and Powder Cocaine," *Criminal Justice Newsletter*, April 17, 1995, pp. 4–5.

37. Litigants claimed that Congress had violated constitutional guarantees of a separation of powers by including three judges on the Commission.

38. "Supreme Court Upholds Federal Sentencing Reforms," *Criminal Justice Newsletter*, Vol. 20, no. 3 (February 1, 1989), p. 1.

39. *Mistretta* v. *U.S.*, 488 U.S. 361, 371 (1989).

40. U.S. Sentencing Commission, *Guidelines*, p. 207.

41. *Deal* v. *U.S.*, 113 S.Ct. 1993, 124 L. Ed. 2d 44 (1993).

42. U.S. Sentencing Commission, *Guidelines*, p. 8.

43. "Sentencing Commission Chairman Wilkins Answers Questions on the Guidelines," National Institute of Justice, *Research in Action Report* (September 1987), p. 7.

44. James Eisenstein and Herbert Jacob, *Felony Justice* (Boston: Little, Brown, 1977).

45. Joan Petersilia, *Racial Disparities in the Criminal Justice System* (Santa Monica, Calif.: The Rand Corporation, 1983).

46. Anthony J. Ragona and John P. Ryan, *Beyond the Courtroom: A Comparative Analysis of Misdemeanor Sentencing—Executive Summary* (Chicago: American Judicature Society, 1983).

47. James H. Kuklinski and John E. Stanga, "Political Participation and Government Responsiveness: The Behavior of California Superior Courts," *American Political Science Review*, Vol. 73 (1979), pp. 1090–1099.

48. See Joseph Jacoby and Christopher Dunn, *National Survey on Punishment for Criminal Offenses—Executive Summary* (Washington, D.C.: Bureau of Justice Statistics, 1987). For a critique of this survey, see Barry Krisberg, "Public Attitudes About Criminal Sanctions," *The Criminologist*, Vol. 13, no. 2 (March–April 1988), pp. 12, 16.

49. Stephen P. Klein, Susan Turner, and Joan Petersilia, *Racial Equity In Sentencing* (Santa Monica, CA: The Rand Corporation, 1988).

50. Ibid., p. 11.

51. Ibid.

52. William Wilbanks, "Are Female Felons

Treated More Leniently by the Criminal Justice System?" *Justice Quarterly*, Vol. 3, no. 4 (December 1986), pp. 517–529.

53. Martha A. Myers and Susette M. Talarico, *The Social Contexts of Criminal Sentencing* (New York: Springer-Verlag, 1987).

54. Ibid., p. 170.

55. Martha A. Myers, "Sentencing Background and the Sentencing Behavior of Judges," *Criminology*, Vol. 26, no. 4 (1988), pp. 649–675.

56. Andrew Kelin, *Alternative Sentencing: A Practitioner's Guide* (Cincinnati, OH: Anderson, 1988), p. 23.

57. Ibid.

58. National Criminal Justice Information and Statistics Service, *Privacy and Security Planning Instructions* (Washington, D.C.: U.S. Government Printing Office, 1976).

59. U.S. Department of Justice, "State Criminal Records Repositories," Bureau of Justice Statistics, *Technical Report* (1985).

60. Privacy Act of 1974, 5, U.S.C.A. Section 522a, 88 Statute 1897, Public Law 93-579 (December 31, 1974).

61. Freedom of Information Act, 5 U.S.C. 522, and amendments. The status of presentence investigative reports has not yet been clarified under this act to the satisfaction of all legal scholars although generally state and federal courts are thought to be exempt from the provisions of the act.

62. Alexander B. Smith and Louis Berlin, *Introduction to Probation and Parole* (St. Paul, Minn.: West Publishing, 1976), p. 75.

63. Andrew Klein, *Alternative Sentencing: A Practitioner's Guide* (Cincinnati, Ohio: Anderson, 1988).

64. John Rosecrance, "Maintaining the Myth of Individualized Justice: Probation Presentence Reports," *Justice Quarterly*, Vol. 5, no. 2 (June 1988), pp. 237–256.

65. Ibid.

66. President's Task Force on Victims of Crime, *Final Report* (Washington, D.C.: U.S. Government Printing Office, 1982).

67. Peter Finn and Beverly N. W. Lee, *Establishing and Expanding Victim-Witness Assistance Programs* (Washington, D.C.: National Institute of Justice, August 1988).

68. Ibid.

69. President's Task Force on Victims of Crime, *Final Report*.

70. "Republican Policy Group Says Justice System Hurts Victims," *Criminal Justice Newsletter*, August 1, 1994, p. 4.

71. Office of Victims of Crime electronic update, August 3, 1995.

72. Public Law 97-291.

73. Dale G. Parent, Barbara Auerbach, and Kenneth E. Carlson, *Compensating Crime Victims: A Summary of Policies and Practices* (Washington, D.C.: National Institute of Justice, 1992), p. 39.

74. Robert J. McCormack, review of Robert Elias, *Victims Still: The Political Manipulation of Crime Victims* (Newbury Park, Calif.: Sage, 1993), in *Justice Quarterly*, Vol. 11, No. 4 (December 1994), pp. 725–727.

75. Proposition 8, California's Victim's Bill of Rights.

76. National Victim Center/Mothers Against Drunk Driving/American Prosecutors Research Institute, *Impact Statements: A Victim's Right to Speak: A Nation's Responsibility to Listen*, July 1994.

77. "Crazed Fan's Deadly 'Mission' Threat Terrified Actress." *The Fayetteville Observer-Times* (North Carolina), June 8, 1989, p. 11D.

78. Ibid.

79. Edwin Villmoare and Virginia V. Neto, "Victim Appearances at Sentencing Under California's Victim's Bill of Rights," National Institute of Justice, *Research in Brief* (August 1987).

80. Rick Atkinson, "Seles Says Attacker Has 'Ruined My Life'" Retrial of Parche Aims At Tougher Sentence," *The Washington Post*, March 22, 1995.

81. Rick Atkinson, "Suspended Sentence Upheld for Seles' Attacker." *The Washington Post*, April 4, 1995.

82. Robert C. Davis and Barbara E. Smith, "The Effects of Victim Impact Statements on Sentencing Decisions: A Test in an Urban Setting," *Justice Quarterly*, Vol. 11, no. 3 (September 1994), pp. 453–469.

83. *Booth v. Maryland*, 107 S.Ct. 2529 (1987).

84. *Payne v. Tennessee*, 501 U.S. 808 (1991).

85. "Supreme Court Closes Term with Major Criminal Justice Rulings," *Criminal Justice Newsletter* (July 1, 1991), Vol. 22, no. 13, p. 2.

86. See "What Say Should Victims Have?" *Time*, May 27, 1991, p. 61.

87. *Report to the Nation on Crime and Justice*, 2nd ed. (Washington, D.C.: U.S. Department of Justice, 1988), p. 90.

88. Patrick A. Langan and Helen A. Graziadei, *Felony Sentences in State Courts, 1992* (Washington, D.C.: Bureau of Justice Statistics, January 1995).

89. Sally T. Hillsman, Barry Mahoney, George F. Cole, and Bernard Auchter, "Fines as Criminal Sanctions," National Institute of Justice, *Research in Brief* (September 1987), p. 1.

90. Ibid., p. 2.

91. Sally T. Hillsman, Joyce L. Sichel, and Barry Mahoney, *Fines in Sentencing* (New York: Vera Institute of Justice, 1983).

92. Ibid., p. 2.

93. Ibid., p. 4.

94. Ibid.

95. Douglas C. McDonald, Judith Greene, and Charles Worzella, *Day Fines in American Courts: The Staten Island and Milwaukee Experiments* (Washington, D.C.: National Institute of Justice, 1992).

96. Ibid., p. 56.

97. Laura A. Winterfield and Sally T. Hillsman, *The Staten Island Day-Fine Project*

(Washington, D.C.: National Institute of Justice, 1993), p. 1.

98. Johnson, *History of Criminal Justice*, pp. 30–31.

99. Ibid., p. 31.

100. Ibid., p. 36.

101. Ibid., p. 51.

102. Arthur Koestler, *Reflections on Hanging* (New York: Macmillan, 1957), p. xi.

103. Ibid., p. 15.

104. Merle Severy, "The Great Revolution," *National Geographic* (July 1989), p. 20.

105. Capital Punishment Research Project, University of Alabama Law School.

106. U.S. Department of Justice, *Capital Punishment, 1993.* (Washington, D.C.: U.S. Government Printing Office, 1995).

107. National Institute of Justice, *Capital Punishment 1994*, (Washington, D.C.: NIJ, February 5, 1996).

108. "Killer Spared 14th Date with Execution in Louisiana," Reuter online, April 18, 1995.

109. "Chief Justice Calls for Limits on Death Row Habeas Appeals," *Criminal Justice Newsletter*, February 15, 1989, pp. 6–7.

110. Joan Biskupic, "Court Grants New Trial in Death Row Case," *The Washington Post* online, April 20, 1995.

111. Koestler, *Reflections on Hanging*, p. xii.

112. Studies include S. Decker and C. Kohfeld, "A Deterrence Study of the Death Penalty in Illinois: 1933–1980," *Journal of Criminal Justice*, Vol. 12, no. 4 (1984), pp. 367–379, and S. Decker and C. Kohfeld, "An Empirical Analysis of the Effect of the Death Penalty in Missouri," *Journal of Crime and Justice*, Vol. 10, no. 1 (1987), pp. 23–46.

113. See, especially, the work of W. C. Bailey, "Deterrence and the Death Penalty for Murders in Utah: A Time Series Analysis," *Journal of Contemporary Law*, Vol. 5, no. 1 (1978), pp. 1–20, and "An Analysis of the Deterrent Effect of the Death Penalty for Murder in California," *Southern California Law Review*, Vol. 52, No. 3 (1979), pp. 743–764.

114. B. E. Forst, "The Deterrent Effect of Capital Punishment: A Cross-State Analysis of the 1960's," *Minnesota Law Review*, Vol. 61 (1977), pp. 743–767.

115. Scott H. Decker and Carol W. Kohfeld, "Capital Punishment and Executions in the Lone Star State: A Deterrence Study," *Criminal Justice Research Bulletin*, Criminal Justice Center, Sam Houston State University, Vol. 3, no. 12 (1988).

116. Ibid.

117. As some of the evidence presented before the Supreme Court in *Furman* v. *Georgia* (408 U.S. 238, 1972) suggested.

118. *USA Today*, April 27, 1989, p. 12A.

119. *McCleskey* v. *Kemp*, 41 Crl 4107 (1987).

120. Justice Stewart, as quoted in *USA Today*, April 27, 1989, p. 12A.

121. Koestler, *Reflections on Hanging*, pp. 147–148, and Gennaro F. Vito and Deborah G. Wilson, "Back from the Dead: Tracking the Progress of Kentucky's Furman-Commuted Death Row Population," *Justice Quarterly*, Vol. 5, no. 1 (1988), pp. 101–111.

122. P. Harris, "Over-Simplification and Error in Public Opinion Surveys on Capital Punishment," *Justice Quarterly* (1986), pp. 429–455.

123. Ibid.

124. James O. Finckenauer, "Public Support for the Death Penalty: Retribution as Just Deserts or Retribution as Revenge?" *Justice Quarterly*, Vol. 5, no. 1 (March 1988), p. 83.

125. Robert M. Bohm, *The Death Penalty in America: Current Research* (Cincinnati, Ohio: Anderson, 1991), pp. 119–127.

126. Ibid., p. 135.

127. Frank P. Williams III, Dennis R. Longmire, and David B. Gulick, "The Public and the Death Penalty: Opinion as an Artifact of Question Type," a Sam Houston State University *Criminal Justice Research Bulletin*, Vol. 3, no. 8 (1988).

128. Ibid., p. 4.

129. *Criminal Justice Newsletter*, Vol. 21, no. 23 (December 3, 1990), p. 1.

130. *Wilkerson* v. *Utah*, 99 U.S. 130 (1878).

131. *In re Kemmler*, 136 U.S. 436 (1890).

132. Ibid., 447.

133. *Louisiana ex rel. Francis* v. *Resweber*, 329 U.S. 459 (1947).

134. *Furman* v. *Georgia*, 408 U.S. 238 (1972).

135. A position first ascribed to in *Trop* v. *Dulles*, 356 U.S. 86 (1958).

136. *Gregg* v. *Georgia*, 428 U.S. 153 (1976).

137. Ibid., 173.

138. *Coker* v. *Georgia*, 433 U.S. 584 (1977).

139. *Woodson* v. *North Carolina*, 428 U.S. 280 (1976).

140. *Harris* v. *Alabama* 115 S.Ct. 1031, 130 L. Ed. 2d 1004 (1995).

141. *Tuilaepa* v. *California* 114 S.Ct. 2630, 129 L. Ed. 2d 750 (1994).

142. James Stephen and Peter Brien, *Capital Punishment, 1993* (Washington, D.C.: Bureau of Justice Statistics, December 1994), p. 1.

143. *McCleskey* v. *Zandt*, 499 U. S. 467, 493–494 (1991)

144. *Coleman* v. *Thompson*, 501 U.S. 722 (1991).

145. *Schlup* v. *Delo*, 115 S.Ct. 851, 130 L. Ed. 2d 808 (1995).

146. Some Supreme Court watchers have concluded that *Schlup* v. *Delo* constitutes a relaxation of previous doctrine, under which the Court required prisoners to show "clear and convincing evidence" why their cases should be heard.

147. *Syvasky Lafayette Poyner* v. *Edward W. Murray, Ellis B. Wright, Jr.*, and *John Doe*, No. 92-7944. Decided May 17, 1993.

148. *Campbell* v. *Wood*, No. 93-7002 (1994).

PART 4

Corrections

INDIVIDUAL RIGHTS VERSUS SOCIAL CONCERNS

The Rights of the Convicted and Imprisoned

Common law, constitutional, and humanitarian rights of the convicted and imprisoned:

A Right Against Cruel or Unusual Punishment
A Right to Protection from Physical Harm
A Limited Right to Legal Assistance While Imprisoned
A Limited Right to Religious Freedom While Imprisoned
A Limited Right to Freedom of Speech While Imprisoned
A Right to Sanitary and Healthy Conditions of Confinement
A Right to Due Process Prior to Denial of Privileges

The individual rights listed must be effectively balanced against these community concerns:

Punishment of the Guilty
Safe Communities
The Reduction of Recidivism
Secure Prisons
Control over Convicts
The Prevention of Escape
Rehabilitation
Affordable Prisons

How does our system of justice work toward balance?

Punishment—that is justice for the unjust.

The great Christian apologist C. S. Lewis (1898–1963) once remarked that if satisfying justice is to be the ultimate goal of Western criminal justice, then the fate of offenders cannot be dictated merely by practical considerations. "The concept of desert is the only connecting link between punishment and justice," Lewis wrote. "It is only as deserved or undeserved that a sentence can be just or unjust," he concluded.

Once a person has been arrested, tried, and sentenced, the correctional process begins. Unlike Lewis's exhortation, however, the contemporary American correctional system—which includes probation, parole, jails, prisons, capital punishment, and a plethora of innovative alternatives to traditional sentences—is tasked with far more than merely carrying out sentences. We also ask of our correctional system that it ensure the safety of law-abiding citizens, that it select the best alternative from among the many available for handling a given offender, that it protect those under its charge, and that it guarantee fairness in the handling of all with whom it comes into contact.

This section of *Criminal Justice: A Brief Introduction* details the development of probation, parole, community corrections, and imprisonment as correctional philosophies; describes the nuances of prison and jail life; discusses special issues in contemporary corrections (including AIDS, geriatric offenders, and female inmates); and summarizes the legal environment which both surrounds and infuses the modern-day practice of corrections. Characteristic of today's correctional emphasis is a societywide push for harsher punishments. The culmination of that strategy, however, is dramatically overcrowded correctional institutions, the problems of which are also described. As you read through this section, encountering descriptions of various kinds of criminal sanctions, you might ask yourself: "When would a punishment of this sort be deserved?" In doing so, remember to couple that thought with another question: "What are the ultimate consequences (for society and for the offender) of the kind of correctional program we are discussing here?" Unlike Lewis, you may also want to ask: "Can we afford it?"

CHAPTER 10

Probation, Parole, *and* Community Corrections

—*PHOTO BY BOB DAEMMRICH/STOCK BOSTON*

*C*ommunity corrections is an integral part of the criminal justice system and should be fully implemented and promoted in order to save expensive and scarce jail and prison space for violent and serious offenders.[1]

—NATIONAL ASSOCIATION OF COUNTIES'
JUSTICE AND PUBLIC SAFETY STEERING COMMITTEE

*D*espite the "get tough" image of recent legislative initiatives, the United States relies primarily on a community-based system of sentencing.[2]

—JAMES M. BYRNE
UNIVERSITY OF LOWELL

*P*robation and parole services are characteristically poorly staffed and often poorly administered.[3]

—PRESIDENT'S COMMISSION ON LAW ENFORCEMENT
AND ADMINISTRATION OF JUSTICE

KEY CONCEPTS

probation	community corrections	parole
conditions of parole	conditions of probation	parole board
parole (probation) violation	parole (probation) revocation	revocation hearing
restitution	caseload	intermediate sanctions
split sentencing	shock probation	shock incarceration
mixed sentence	community service	intensive supervision
home confinement		

KEY CASES

Morrissey v. *Brewer*	*Gagnon* v. *Scarpelli*	*Bearden* v. *Georgia*
Greenholtz v. *Nebraska*	*Kelly* v. *Robinson*	*Black* v. *Ramano*
Minnesota v. *Murphy*	*Mempa* v. *Rhay*	

Introduction to Community Corrections

Fifteen years ago, Michael Kelley was convicted of raping two Massachusetts women. He was paroled in June 1991 after having spent 13 years in the Bridgewater Treatment Center for Sexually Dangerous Persons. His review board, three specialists, and a judge all declared him "not sexually dangerous." One year later, Kelley was back in custody, charged with the rape-murders of Colleen Coughlin, 21, and Debra Levangie, 24, both of Plymouth, Massachusetts.[4]

In 1992, 39-year-old Leslie Allen Williams, a parolee with a 20-year history of attacks on women, confessed to killing four teenage girls in Pontiac, Michigan. Williams confessed to the murders while jailed on charges he had abducted a young woman from a cemetery after she placed a wreath on her mother's grave. Before his 1992 arrest, Williams was paroled in 1990, having been in and out of prison for abducting and attacking women since 1971. Patrick Urbin, the father of 16- and 14-year-old sisters Michelle and Melissa Urbin—two of Williams's latest victims—said "[t]he system has failed us by letting this person out early…[w]e don't personally believe in the death penalty, but he should be behind bars for the rest of his life…[w]hy did they let him get so far and do so much in 20 years?"[5]

In 1995, the shocking case of Henry Marshall came to light during a television documentary[6] which detailed how the 36-year-old parolee viciously killed grill owner Dennis Griswold during a 1994 robbery of Griswold's business. Griswold's daughter, Danielle Griswold, a Tacoma, Washington, policewoman, investigated her father's murder and soon discovered that Marshall had been paroled early by Massachusetts authorities on a request from the FBI, with whom he had agreed to work as an informant. The FBI lost track of Marshall, and he crossed the country, traveling under his own name and ending up in Washington state where he shot Griswold—later bragging to acquaintances that he loved killing more than sex, and celebrating the murder with a steak cookout. Computerized background checks conducted by Officer Griswold quickly revealed that Marshall was extremely dangerous and had a lengthy record. Marshall had been charged with two attempted murders, claimed to be a hit man for a northeastern motorcycle gang, and had spent all but three months of his adult life either in prison, on parole, or out on bail awaiting trial. Prior to his early parole, in addition to the two attempted murder charges, Marshall had 23 previous criminal convictions.

Stories like these, appearing daily in papers across the country, have cast a harsh light on the early release of criminal offenders. This chapter takes a close look at the realities behind the practice of what we call "community corrections." **Community corrections**, also called community-based corrections, is a sentencing style that represents a movement away from traditional confinement options and an increased dependence on correctional resources which are available in the community. Community corrections can best be defined as the use of a variety of court-ordered programmatic sanctions permitting convicted offenders to remain in the community under conditional supervision as an alternative to active prison sentences. Community corrections includes a wide variety of sentencing options such as probation, parole, home confinement, the electronic monitoring of offenders, and other new and developing programs —all of which are covered in this chapter.

What Is Probation?

Probation, which is one aspect of community corrections, is "a sentence served while under supervision in the community."[7] Like other sentencing options, probation is a court-ordered sanction. Its goal is to allow for some degree

Community Corrections. (Also called Community-Based Corrections) A sentencing style that represents a movement away from traditional confinement options and an increased dependence on correctional resources which are available in the community.

Probation. A sentence of imprisonment that is suspended. Also, the conditional freedom granted by a judicial officer to an adjudicated adult or juvenile offender, as long as the person meets certain conditions of behavior.

of control over criminal offenders while using community programs to help rehabilitate them. Most of the alternative sanctions discussed later in this chapter are, in fact, predicated upon probationary sentences in which the offender is first placed on probation and then ordered to abide by certain conditions while remaining free in the community—such as participation in a specified program. Although probation can be directly imposed by the court in many jurisdictions, most probationers are technically sentenced first to confinement, but then immediately have their sentences suspended and are remanded into the custody of an officer of the court—the probation officer.

Probation has a long and diverse history. By the 1300s, English courts had established the practice of "binding over for good behavior,"[8] in which offenders could be entrusted into the custody of willing citizens. John Augustus (1784–1859), however, is generally recognized as the world's first probation officer. Augustus, a Boston shoemaker, attended sessions of criminal court in the 1850s and would offer to take carefully selected offenders into his home as an alternative to imprisonment.[9] At first, he supervised only drunkards, but by 1857, Augustus was accepting many kinds of offenders and devoting all of his time to the service of the court.[10] Augustus died in 1859, having bailed out more than 2,000 convicts during his lifetime. In 1878, the Massachusetts legislature enacted a statute which authorized the city of Boston to hire a salaried probation officer. Missouri (1897) followed suit, along with Vermont (1898) and Rhode Island (1899).[11] Before the end of the 19th century, probation had become an accepted and widely used form of community-based supervision. By 1925, all 48 states had adopted probation legislation. In the same year, the National Probation Act enabled federal district court judges to appoint paid probation officers and impose probationary terms.[12]

The Extent of Probation

Today, probation is the most commonly used form of criminal sentencing in the United States. Between 30 and 60 percent of all persons found guilty of crimes are sentenced to some form of probation.[13] Figure 10-1 shows that 57 percent of all persons under correctional supervision in the United States during 1995 were on probation. Not shown is the fact that the number of persons supervised yearly on probation has increased from slightly more than 1 million in 1980 to nearly 3 million today—almost a 300 percent increase.[14] This observation has caused some writers to call "probation crowding" an "immediate threat to the criminal justice process and to community protection."[15]

Even serious offenders stand about a 1-in-4 chance of receiving a probationary term, as Figure 10-2 shows. A 1995 Bureau of Justice Statistics study[16] of felony sentences in state courts found that 3 percent of people convicted of homicide were placed on probation, as were 13 percent of convicted rapists. Twelve percent of convicted robbers and 25 percent of burglars were similarly sentenced to probation rather than active prison time. In a recent example,[17] 47-year-old Carrie Mote of Vernon, Connecticut, was sentenced to probation for shooting her fiancé in the chest with a .38-caliber handgun after he called off their scheduled wedding. Ms. Mote, who faced a maximum of 20 years in prison, claimed to be suffering from diminished psychological capacity at the time of the shooting because of the emotional stress brought on by the canceled wedding.

At the beginning of 1995, a total of 2.9 million adults were on probation throughout the nation.[18] Individual states, however, made greater or lesser use of probation. North Dakota authorities, with the smallest probationary population, supervised only 2,006 people, whereas Texas reported 394,578 persons on probation (see Table 10-1). Fifty-nine percent of probationers successfully complete their probationary terms, about 2 percent abscond, and another 3 percent are convicted of new crimes while on probation.[19]

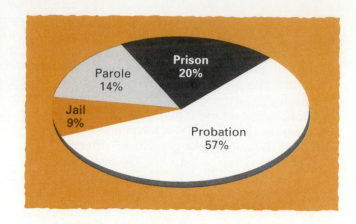

FIGURE 10-1
Persons under correctional supervision in the United States by type of supervision, 1995. Source: Bureau of Justice Statistics, Correctional Populations in the United States: Executive Summary (Washington, D.C.: BJS, 1995).

FIGURE 10-2
Percentage of convicted offenders receiving probation by type of crime. Source: Patrick A. Langan and Helen A. Graziadei, Felony Sentences in State Courts, 1992 (Washington, D.C.: BJS, 1995).

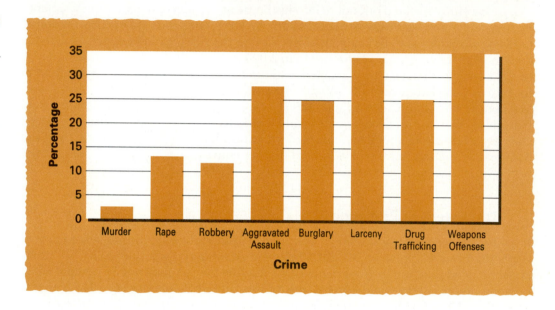

*C*onditions of Probation and Parole. The general (state-ordered) and special (court- or board-ordered) limits imposed on an offender who is released on either probation or parole. General conditions tend to be fixed by state statute, whereas special conditions are mandated by the sentencing authority and take into consideration the background of the offender and circumstances surrounding the offense.

Probation Conditions

Those sentenced to probation must agree to abide by court-mandated **conditions of probation**. Such conditions are of two types: general and specific. General conditions apply to all probationers in a given jurisdiction and usually include requirements that the probationer "obey all laws," "maintain employment," "remain within the jurisdiction of the court," "possess no firearm," "allow the probation officer to visit at home or at work," and so forth. Figure 10-3 shows a form that judges commonly use to impose general conditions of probation. Many probationers are also required to pay a fine to the court, usually in a series of installments that are designed to reimburse victims for damages and to pay lawyers' fees and other costs of court.

Special conditions may be mandated by a judge who feels that the probationary client is in need of particular guidance or control. Figure 10-3 also shows a number of special conditions that are routinely imposed on sizable subcategories of probationers. Special condition number 11, for example, is applicable in cases of driving under the influence, whereas number 12 is useful in dealing with thieves, burglars, and other property offenders. The judge may also add special conditions that are tailored specifically to individual probationers. In Figure 10-3, they would be indicated under number 18—"Other." Individualized conditions may prohibit a person from associating with named others (a codefendant, for example), they may require that the probationer be at home after dark, or they may demand that a particular treatment program be completed within a set period.

TABLE 10-1

Adults on Probation and Parole in the United States, January 1, 1995

Jurisdiction	Parolees	Probationers	Jurisdiction	Parolees	Probationers
U.S. TOTAL	**690,159**	**2,962,166**			
Federal	61,430	45,047	Montana	636	5,641
Alabama	6,729	36,024	Nebraska	771	17,554
Alaska	685	3,173	Nevada	3,529	9,410
Arizona	4,017	36,916	New Hampshire	835	4,323
Arkansas	4,036	18,598	New Jersey	41,820	106,921
California	80,845	285,105	New Mexico	1,505	8,670
Colorado	2,731	36,430	New York	53,832	164,589
Connecticut	1,000	53,453	North Carolina	21,027	89,889
Delaware	914	15,507	North Dakota	93	2,006
Florida	17,567	239,108	Ohio	7,180	105,953
Georgia	20,790	140,684	Oklahoma	2,604	26,484
Hawaii	1,541	12,515	Oregon	14,264	38,086
Idaho	837	5,153	Pennsylvania	70,355	99,524
Illinois	24,177	79,468	Rhode Island	528	18,179
Indiana	2,891	82,804	South Carolina	6,029	40,456
Iowa	2,339	15,504	South Dakota	661	3,410
Kansas	7,141	24,102	Tennessee	10,260	35,727
Kentucky	4,380	11,417	Texas	108,563	394,578
Louisiana	17,112	33,604	Utah	2,438	7,638
Maine[1]	40	8,669	Vermont	592	6,676
Maryland	14,795	76,940	Virginia	9,649	24,089
Massachusetts	4,533	46,672	Washington	1,650	111,450
Michigan	12,922	143,178	West Virginia	1,259	5,950
Minnesota	1,904	81,972	Wisconsin	7,065	45,901
Mississippi	1,517	9,041	Wyoming	362	3,382
Missouri	12,597	36,295	Washington, D.C.	6,574	8,325

1. Maine eliminated parole in 1976.

SOURCE: "The Nation's Correctional Population Tops 5 Million," U.S. Department of Justice press release, August 27, 1995.

Parole and probation are both forms of supervised release. Parole officers are shown here visiting a parolee (right) at his home. Photo by Warren Jorgensen, courtesy of AP Wide World Photos.

Parole. The status of an offender conditionally released from a prison by discretion of a paroling authority prior to expiration of sentence, required to observe conditions of parole, and placed under the supervision of a parole agency.

Parole Board. (Also called Parole Commission) A state paroling authority. Most states have parole boards which decide when an incarcerated offender is ready for conditional release and which may also function as revocation hearing panels.

What Is Parole?

Parole is the supervised early release of inmates from correctional confinement. It differs from probation in both purpose and implementation. Whereas probationers generally avoid serving time in prison, offenders who are paroled have already been incarcerated. While probation is a sentencing option available to a judge who determines the form probation will take, parole results from an administrative decision made by a legally designated paroling authority.

States differ in the type of parole decision-making mechanism they use, as well as the level at which it operates. Two major models prevail: (1) **Parole boards** grant parole based on their judgments and assessments. The parole board's decisions are termed "discretionary parole." (2) Statutory decrees produce "mandatory parole," with release dates usually near the completion of the inmate's prison sentence—minus time off for good behavior and other special considerations. While probation is a sentencing strategy, parole is a correctional strategy whose primary purpose is to return offenders gradually to productive lives. Parole, by making early release possible, can also act as a stimulus for positive behavioral change.

The use of parole in this country began with the Elmira Reformatory in 1876. As you may recall from Chapter 9, indeterminate sentences are a key part of a philosophy that stresses rehabilitation. The indeterminate sentence was made possible by an innovative New York law following the call of leading correctional innovators. Parole was a much-heralded tool of 19th-century corrections, whose advocates had been looking for a behavioral incentive to motivate youthful offenders to reform. Parole, through its promise of earned early release, seemed the ideal innovation.

Parolees comprise the smallest of the correctional categories shown in Figure 10-1 (other than "jail"). A growing reluctance to use parole seems due to the expanding realization that today's correctional routines have been generally ineffective at producing any substantial reformation among many offenders prior to their release back into the community. The abandonment of the rehabilitation goal, combined with a return to determinate sentencing in many jurisdictions, including the federal judicial system, has substantially reduced the amount of time the average correctional client spends on parole.

The Extent of Parole

Although time spent on parole is far less than it used to be, most inmates who are freed from prison are still paroled (about 75 percent) or are granted some other form of conditional release (about 5.5 percent).[20] Some states operating under determinate sentencing guidelines require that inmates serve a short time, such as 90 days, on reentry parole—a form of mandatory release. Mandatory releases have increased fivefold—from 6 percent of all releases in 1977 to more than 37 percent today.[21] As a result, determinate sentencing schemes have changed the face of parole in America, resulting in a dramatic reduction of the average time spent under postprison supervision, while having little impact on the number of released inmates who experience some form of parole.

At the beginning of 1995, more than 690,000 people were on parole throughout the United States (see Table 10-1). States vary considerably in the use they make of parole, influenced as they are by the legislative requirements of sentencing schemes. For example, in 1995, Maine, a state which is phasing out parole, reported only 40 people under parole supervision (the lowest of all the states), and North Dakota only 93, whereas Texas had a parole population

STATE OF NORTH CAROLINA

▶ *File No.*

_____ **County** _____ **Seat Of Court**

In The General Court Of Justice
☐ District ☐ Superior Court Division

NOTE:
(This form is not to be used for multiple offenses unless they are consolidated for judgment.)

STATE VERSUS	**JUDGMENT SUSPENDING SENTENCE**
Defendant	**AND**
	COMMITMENT ON SPECIAL PROBATION
	G.S. 15A-1341, 15A-1342, 15A-1343, 15A-1346

Race	*Sex*	*DOB*	

Attorney For State	*Def. Found* ☐ Not Indigent	*Def. Waived* ☐ Attorney	*Attorney For Defendant*	☐ Appointed	☐ Retained

The defendent ☐ pled guilty to: ☐ was found guilty by the Court of: ☐ was found guilty by a jury of: ☐ pled no contest to:

File No.(s) And Offense(s)	Date of Offense	G.S. No.	Fel./M.	Class	Max. Term	Presumptive

<table side-label="AGGRAVATING/ MITIGATING FACTORS">

The Court has considered the aggravating and mitigating factors in G.S. 15A-1340.4(a) and
☐ makes no written findings because the prison term imposed does not require such findings.
☐ makes no written findings because the prison term imposed is pursuant to a plea arrangement as to sentence.
☐ makes the Findings Of Factors In Aggravation And Mitigation Of Punishment set forth on the attached AOC-CR-303.

</table>

The Court, having considered evidence, arguments of counsel and statement of defendant, finds that the defendant's plea was freely, voluntarily, and understandingly entered, and Orders the above offenses be consolidated for judgment and the defendant be imprisoned.

for a term of	in the custody of the	☐ N.C. Dept. of Correction
		☐ Sheriff of _____ County

The defendant shall be given credit for _____ days spent in confinement prior to the date of this Judgment as a result of this charge, to be applied toward the ☐ sentence imposed above. ☐ imprisonment required for special probation below.

SUSPENSION OF SENTENCE

With the consent of the defendant and subject to the conditions set out below, the execution of this sentence is suspended and the defendant is placed on ☐ supervised probation for _____ years. ☐ unsupervised probation for _____ years.

☐ The above period of probation shall begin: ☐ when the defendant is paroled or otherwise released from incarceration in the case referred to below. ☐ at the expiration of the sentence in the case referred to below.
(NOTE: *List Case Number, Date, County And Court In Which Prior Sentence Imposed.)*

SPECIAL PROBATION – G.S. 15A-1351

<table side-label="SPECIAL PROBATION ORDER">

☐ As a condition of special probation, the defendant shall ☐ serve an active term of _____ ☐ days ☐ months in the custody of the ☐ N.C. DOC. ☐ Sheriff of this County. ☐ submit to IMPACT imprisonment per attached CR-302, Page Two. ☐ pay jail fees.
(NOTE: *This term shall NOT be reduced by good time, gain time or parole, or, unless provided above, by time in jail awaiting trial.)*

The defendant shall report in a sober condition to begin serving his term on:	Day	Date	Hour	☐ AM ☐ PM	and shall remain in custody until:	Day	Date	Hour	☐ AM ☐ PM

☐ The defendant shall again report in a sober condition to continue serving this term on the same day of the week for the next _____ consecutive weeks, and shall remain in custody during the same hours each week.

</table>

MONETARY CONDITIONS

The defendant shall pay to the Clerk of Superior Court the "Total Amount Due" shown below, plus the probation supervision fee set by law
☐ pursuant to a schedule determined by the probation officer. ☐ at the rate of $ _____ per _____ ,
beginning on _____ and continuing on the same day of each _____ thereafter until paid in full. ☐ Other:

Fine	Costs	Restitution*	Attorney's Fee	Community Service Fee	Total Amount Due
$	$	$	$	$	▶ $

*The name(s) and address(es) and amount(s) due the person(s) to receive this restitution are:

☐ All payments received by the Clerk shall first be disbursed pro rata among the persons entitled to restitution.
☐ Upon payment of the "Total Amount Due", the probation officer may transfer the defendant to unsupervised probation.

AOC-CR-302, Rev. 7/95   Material opposite unmarked squares is to be disregarded as surplusage.

(Continued on next page)

FIGURE 10-3
Probation agreement form. Courtesy of the North Carolina Administrative Office of the Courts and the North Carolina Department of Correction, Division of Adult Probation and Parole.

REGULAR CONDITIONS OF PROBATION – G.S. 15A-1343(b)

The defendant shall: 1. Commit no criminal offense in any jurisdiction. 2. Possess no firearm, explosive device or other deadly weapon listed in G.S. 14-269. 3. remain gainfully and suitably employed or faithfully pursue a course of study or of vocational training that will equip him for suitable employment. 4. Satisfy child support and family obligations, as required by the Court. If the defendant is on supervised probation, he shall also: 5. Remain within the jurisdiction of the Court unless granted written permission to leave by the Court or his probation officer. 6. Report as directed by the Court or his probation officer to the officer at reasonable times and places and in a reasonable manner, permit the officer to visit him at reasonable times, answer all reasonable inquiries by the officer, and obtain prior approval from the officer for, and notify the officer of, any change in address or employment. 7. Notify the probation officer if he fails to obtain or retain satisfactory employment. 8. At a time to be designated by his probation officer, visit with his probation officer at a facility maintained by the Division of Prisons. If the defendant is to serve an active sentence as a condition of special probation, he shall also: 9. Obey the rules and regulations of the Department of Correction governing the conduct of inmates while imprisoned. 10. Report to a probation officer in the State of North Carolina within 72 hours of his discharge from the active term of imprisonment.

SPECIAL CONDITIONS OF PROBATION – G.S. 15A-1343(b1), 143B-262(c)

The defendant shall also comply with the following special conditions which the Court finds are reasonably related to his rehabilitation:

☐ 11. Surrender his driver's license to the Clerk of Superior Court for transmittal to the Division of Motor Vehicles and not operate a motor vehicle for a period of _____ or until relicensed by the Division of Motor Vehicles, whichever is later.

☐ 12. Submit at reasonable times to warrantless searches by a probation officer of his person, and of his vehicle and premises while he is present, for the following purposes which are reasonably related to his probation supervision:
☐ stolen goods ☐ controlled substances ☐ contraband ☐ _____

☐ 13. Not use, possess, or control any illegal drug or controlled substance unless it has been prescribed for him by a licensed physician and is in the original container with the prescription number affixed on it; not knowingly associate with any known or previously convicted users, possessors, or sellers of any illegal drugs or controlled substances; and not knowingly be present at or frequent any place where illegal drugs or controlled substances are sold, kept, or used.

☐ 14. Supply a breath, urine, and/or blood specimen for analysis of the possible presence of a prohibited drug or alcohol, when instructed by his probation officer.

☐ 15. Successfully pass the General Education Development Test (G.E.D.) during the first _____ months of the period of probation.

☐ 16. Complete _____ hours of community or reparation service during the first _____ days of the period of probation, as directed by the community service coordinator, and pay the fee prescribed by G.S. 143B-475. 1(b) ☐ pursuant to the schedule set out under monetary conditions above. ☐ within _____ days of this Judgment and before beginning service.

☐ 17. Report for initial evaluation by_____ , participate in all further evaluation, counseling, treatment, or education programs recommended as a result of that evaluation, and comply with all other therapeutic requirements of those programs until discharged.

☐ 18. Other:

☐ 19. Comply with the Additional Conditions Of Probation which are set forth on AOC-CR-302, Page Two.

☐ A hearing was held in open court in the presence of the defendant at which time a fee, including expenses, was awarded the defendant's appointed counsel or assigned public defender.

ORDER OF COMMITMENT/APPEAL ENTRIES

☐ It is ORDERED that the Clerk deliver three certified copies of this Judgment and Commitment to the Sheriff or other qualified officer, and that the officer cause the defendant to be delivered with these copies to the custody of the agency named on the reverse to serve the sentence imposed or until he shall have complied with the conditions of release pending appeal.

☐ The defendant gives notice of appeal from the judgment of the District Court to the Superior Court. The current pretrial release order shall remain in effect. ☐ except that:

☐ The defendant gives notice of appeal from the judgment of the Superior Court to the Appellate Division. Appeal entries and any conditions of post conviction release are set forth on Form AOC-CR-350.

SIGNATURE OF JUDGE

Date	Name Of Presiding Judge (Type Or Print)	Signature Of Presiding Judge

CERTIFICATION

I certify that this Judgment and the attachment(s) marked below are true copies of the originals.
☐ Judgment Suspending Sentence, Page Two [Additional Conditions Of Probation (AOC-CR-302, Page Two)]
☐ Findings Of Factors In Aggravation And Mitigation Of Punishment (AOC-CR-303)

Date Of Certification	Date Certified Copies Delivered To Sheriff	Signature And Seal
		☐ Deputy CSC ☐ Assistant CSC ☐ Clerk Of Superior Court

NOTE: *Defendant signs the following statement in all cases except unsupervised probation without community or reparation service.*
I have received a copy of this Judgment which contains all of the conditions of my probation, and I agree to them. I understand that no person who supervises me or for whom I work while performing community or reparation service is liable to me for any loss or damage which I may sustain unless my injury is caused by that person's gross negligence or intentional wrongdoing.

Date Signed	Signature Of Defendant	Witnessed By:

AOC-CR-302, Side Two, Rev. 7/95   Material opposite unmarked squares is to be disregarded as surplusage.

FIGURE 10-3
(Continued)

PC -104a
10/92

STATE OF NORTH CAROLINA
PAROLE AGREEMENT BETWEEN THE NORTH CAROLINA PAROLE COMMISSION
AND

_____ , PAROLEE

In accepting this parole, I understand that the North Carolina Parole Commission may modify its terms. I also understand that I am under the legal custody of the Parole Commission until duly discharged by the Commission. I understand that should I violate parole, the Commission may cause me to be returned to custody for further action as provided by law. I understand that my term of parole shall be for no less than either (1) the remainder of the maximum term if the maximum term is less than one year, or (2) one year if the remainder of the maximum term is one year or more. I understand that I shall receive no credit for time spent on parole against the remainder of my sentence, and that in the event my parole is revoked I will be reimprisoned for the unserved portion of the maximum term of imprisonment imposed by the court. I understand that in the event of an alleged violation of parole, my parole time may be frozen at the time of the alleged violation. If my parole time is frozen, it may remain frozen until such time as the alleged violations are disposed of, even if it becomes necessary to extend my release date beyond its normal period. I further understand that if I abide by the terms and conditions of this parole, the Parole Commission will unconditionally discharge me no later than my maximum release date. In accepting this parole, I agree to abide by the following rules:

GENERAL CONDITIONS

1. I will report promptly to my Probation/Parole Officer when instructed to do so, and in the manner prescribed by my Probation/Parole Officer and the Parole Commission.
2. I will work steadily at an approved job, and not change my job or my residence without permission from my Probation/Parole Officer. If I am discharged from my job or evicted from my home, I will notify my Probation/Parole Officer. I will also support any persons dependent on me to the best of my ability.
3. I will obey all municipal, county, and state and federal laws, ordinances, and orders. If I am arrested or receive a citation to appear in court while on parole, I will report this fact to my Probation/Parole Officer within 24 hours of such arrest or citation.
4. I will not leave my county of residence without obtaining permission from my Probation/Parole Officer. I will not leave the State of North Carolina without permission from the Parole Commission or my Probation/Parole Officer.
5. I will not consume alcoholic beverages to excess or use or possess drugs in violation of state and federal laws.
6. I will not own or possess any firearms or deadly weapon without written permission from the Parole Commission.
7. I will notify my Probation/Parole Officer in writing three weeks in advance of any plans to alter my marital status (marriage, separation, divorce).
8. I will allow my Probation/Parole Officer to visit my home or place of employment at any time.
9. I do hereby waive extradition to the State of North Carolina from any state of the United States and also agree that I will not contest any effort by any state to return me to the State of North Carolina.
10. I will not enter into any agreement to act as an "informer" or special agent for any law enforcement agency without permission from the Parole Commission.
11. I will not assault, or harm, or threaten to assault or harm, any person.
12. I will comply with the following Special Conditions which have been imposed by the Parole Commission:

☐ In the event (1) I do not have a plan of employment at this time, or (2) my employment plan has been found to be only temporarily suitable, I understand and agree that I must diligently seek employment which is satisfactory to the Parole Commission, and I will use my best efforts to secure the same, and will report the progress of my efforts to my Probation/Parole Officer twice weekly until satisfactory employment is obtained. I further understand and agree that if I have not obtained satisfactory employment within 30 days from today, I may be returned to prison and my parole or conditional release may be revoked, in the discretion of the Commission.

☐ I, _____ , will pay to the Department of Correction the sum

of _____ per week/month to be used to make restitution to the following named payee(s) in the following amounts:

Name of Payee	Address	Amount to be Paid
_____	_____	_____
_____	_____	_____
_____	_____	_____

It shall be my responsibility to send my weekly/monthly payments to the Department of Correction at the following address: WORK RELEASE ACCOUNTING OFFICE, 831 West Morgan St., Raleigh, N.C. 27603.

PAYMENTS SHALL BE MADE EITHER BY CASHIER CHECK, CERTIFIED CHECK, OR POSTAL MONEY ORDER (NO PERSONAL CHECKS ACCEPTED). CHECKS SHALL BE MADE PAYABLE TO THE _DEPARTMENT OF CORRECTION_ AND INCLUDE THE NAME AND ADDRESS OF THE PAROLEE LISTED ABOVE.

(Continued on next page)

FIGURE 10-4
Parole agreement form. Courtesy of the North Carolina Parole Commission and the North Carolina Department of Correction, Division of Adult Probation and Parole.

I will accept counseling and/or treatment for drug and/or alcohol abuse at the discretion of the supervising officer.

I will not associate with known drug offenders, users, and/or pushers.

I will consent to a warrantless search of my person, premises, or any vehicle under my control by my supervising officer for any purpose reasonably related to parole supervision.

I will stay away from places where the selling and/or serving of alcohol is the primary business.

I will submit to any physical, chemical, or breathalyzer test when requested to do so by the Parole Commission, or by supervising PPO, for detection of alcohol and/or controlled substances, and pay costs thereof.

I will abide by curfew at discretion of PPO.

I will pay a parole supervision fee of $15 within 30 days after my release on parole and each month thereafter until my parole is terminated unless the Parole Commission relieves me of this obligation because of undue economic burden. I will send my parole supervision fee to the Clerk of Superior Court, Wake County, Raleigh, N.C.

I agree to:

1. Be under the Intensive Parole Supervision Program for a minimum of 6 months.

2. Obey any curfew imposed by the Parole Commission or by my Supervising Officer.

3. Submit to request for blood and urine samples for possible presence of drugs.

4. Attend and participate in counseling, treatment, or educational programs as directed by the Parole Commission or the Intensive/Parole Officer as approved by the Parole Commission, and abide by all rules, regulations, and directives of such programs.

5. Submit at reasonable times to warrantless searches by a Parole Officer of my person, vehicle, or premises while I am present for purposes which are reasonably related to parole supervision.

I will remain at ███████████████████████ School until completion of course.

I will have no contact with ███████████████████████████ (co-defendant).

If I violate any of the conditions or Special Conditions of parole, I may be arrested and held as a parole violator. In this event, I will be given a hearing at which time I may be represented by counsel and, if the Commission decides that I am in violation of one or more of the conditions of my parole, I may be returned to prison.

I have read or have had read to me the foregoing conditions of my parole. I fully understand them and will strictly follow them, and I understand and know what I am doing. No promises or threats have been made to me, and no pressure of any kind has been used against me at the time of signing this Parole Agreement.

DATE _____   SIGNED _____

DATE _____   WITNESS _____

DATE _____   WITNESS _____

NOTE TO CONVICTED FELONS: *The possession of a firearm by a convicted felon is a violation of both federal and state law. Also, the act of registering or voting is punishable by law until such time as these rights are restored.

FIGURE 10-4
(Continued)

in excess of 108,000, and California officials were busy supervising more than 80,000 persons.

Approximately 49 percent of parolees successfully complete parole, whereas about 26 percent are returned to prison for **parole violations**, and another 12 percent go back to prison for new offenses during their parole period. (Others may be transferred to new jurisdictions, abscond and not be caught, or die—bringing the total to 100 percent.)[22]

Parole Conditions

In those jurisdictions which retain discretionary parole, the **conditions of parole** remain very similar to the conditions agreed to by probationers. Figure 10-4 shows both sides of a typical parole agreement form, which parolees must sign before their release. The general conditions of parole are listed on the front of the form and include agreements not to willfully leave the state as well as a blanket agreement to extradition requests from other jurisdictions. Parolees must also periodically report to parole officers, and parole officers may visit parolees at their homes and places of business—often arriving unannounced.

The successful and continued employment of parolees is one of the major concerns of parole boards and their officers, and studies have found that successful employment is a major factor in reducing the likelihood of repeat offenses.[23] The importance of employment is stressed on the form in Figure 10-4, with the stricture that failure to find employment within 30 days may result in **revocation** of parole. As with probationers, working parolees can be ordered to pay fines and penalties. A provision for making **restitution** payments is included at the bottom of the first page with the names and addresses of recipients clearly specified.

Special parole conditions have been added to the form in Figure 10-4. One of them requires the parolee to pay a "parole supervisory fee of $15" every month, a requirement now being routinely imposed in some jurisdictions (although monetary amounts may vary). A relatively new innovation, parole supervision fees, shifts some of the expenses of community corrections to the offender.

Federal Parole

Federal parole decisions are made by the U.S. Parole Commission, which uses hearing examiners to visit federal prisons. Examiners typically ask inmates to describe why, in their opinion, they are ready for parole. The inmate's job readiness, home plans, past record, accomplishments while in prison, good behavior, and experiences on probation or parole form the basis for a report made by the examiners to the parole commission. The 1984 Comprehensive Crime Control Act, which mandated federal fixed sentencing and abolished parole for offenses committed after November 1, 1978, began a planned phase-out of the U.S. Parole Commission. Under the act, the Commission was to be abolished by 1992. However, action taken by Congress in late 1990 extended the life of the Commission until at least 1997.

Probation and Parole: The Pluses and Minuses

Advantages of Probation and Parole

Probation is used to meet the needs of offenders who require some correctional supervision short of imprisonment, while at the same time providing a reasonable degree of security to the community. Parole fulfills a similar purpose for

Probation (or Parole) Violation. An act or a failure to act by a probationer (or parolee) which does not conform to the conditions of probation (or parole).

Probation (or Parole) Revocation. The administrative action of a probation (or paroling) authority removing a person from probationary (or parole) status in response to a violation of lawfully required conditions of probation (or parole), including the prohibition against commission of a new offense, and usually resulting in a return to prison.

Restitution. A court requirement that an alleged or convicted offender pay money or provide services to the victim of the crime or provide services to the community.

offenders released from prison. Both probation and parole provide a number of advantages over imprisonment, including:

1. *Lower Cost.* Imprisonment is expensive. One study found that incarcerating a single offender in Georgia costs approximately $7,760 per year while the cost of intensive probation is as little as $985 per probationer.[24] The expense of imprisonment in some other states may be nearly three times as high as it is in Georgia. Not only do probation and parole save money, they may even help fill the public coffers. Some jurisdictions require that offenders pay a portion of the costs associated with their own supervision. Georgia, for example, charges clients between $10 and $50 per month while they are being supervised,[25] while Texas, in an innovative program which uses market-type incentives to encourage probation officers to collect fees,[26] has been able to annually recoup monies totaling more than half of the total that the state spends on probation services.

2. *Increased Employment.* Few people in prison have the opportunity to work. Work-release programs, correctional industries, and inmate labor programs operate in most states, but they usually provide only low-paying jobs and require few skills. At best, such programs include only a small portion of the inmates in any given facility. Probation and parole, on the other hand, make it possible for offenders under correctional supervision to work full time at jobs in the "free" economy. They can contribute to their own and their families' support, stimulate the local economy by spending their wages, and support government through the taxes they pay.

3. *Restitution.* Offenders who are able to work are candidates for court-ordered restitution. Society's interest in restitution (sometimes called "making the victim whole again") may be better served by a probationary sentence or parole than by imprisonment. Restitution payments to victims may help restore their standard of living and personal confidence while teaching the offender responsibility.

4. *Community Support.* The decision to release a prisoner on parole, or to sentence a convicted offender to a probationary term, is often partially based upon considerations of family and other social ties. Such decisions are made in the belief that offenders will be more subject to control in the community if they participate in a web of positive social relationships. An advantage of both probation and parole is that it allows the offender to continue personal and social relationships. Probation avoids splitting up families, while parole may reunite family members separated from each other by time in prison.

5. *Reduced Risk of Criminal Socialization.* Prison has been called a "school in crime." Probation insulates adjudicated offenders, at least to some degree, from the kinds of criminal values which permeate prison. Parole, by virtue of the fact that it follows time served in prison, is less successful than probation in reducing the risk of criminal socialization.

6. *Increased Use of Community Services.* Probationers and parolees can take advantage of services offered through the community, including psychological therapy, substance abuse counseling, financial services, support groups, church outreach programs, and social services. While a few similar opportunities may be available in prison, the community environment itself can enhance the effectiveness of treatment programs by reducing the stigmatization of the offender and allowing the offender to participate in the context of a more "normal" environment.

7. *Increased Opportunity for Rehabilitation.* Probation and parole can both be useful behavioral management tools. They reward cooperative offenders with freedom and allow for the opportunity to shape the behavior of offenders who may be difficult to reach through other programs.

Disadvantages of Probation and Parole

Any honest appraisal of probation and parole must recognize that they share a number of strategic drawbacks, such as:

1. *A Relative Lack of Punishment.* The just deserts model of criminal sentencing insists that punishment should be a central theme of the justice process. Although rehabilitation and treatment are recognized as worthwhile goals, the model suggests that punishment

serves both society's need for protection and the victim's need for revenge. Probation, however, is seen as practically no punishment at all and is coming under increasing criticism as a sentencing strategy. Parole is likewise accused of unhinging the scales of justice because (1) it releases some offenders early, even when they have been convicted of serious crimes, whereas other, relatively minor offenders, may remain in prison, and (2) it is dishonest because it does not require completion of the offender's entire sentence behind bars.

2. *Increased Risk to the Community.* Probation and parole are strategies designed to deal with convicted *criminal* offenders. The release into the community of such offenders increases the risk that they will commit additional offenses. Community supervision can never be so complete as to eliminate such a possibility entirely, and recent studies on parole have pointed to the fact that an accurate assessment of offender dangerousness is beyond our present capability.[27]

A 1992 Bureau of Justice Statistics study[28]—the nation's largest ever follow-up survey of felons on probation—found that 43 percent of probationers were rearrested for a felony within three years of receiving a probationary sentence and while still on probation. Half of the arrests were for a violent crime or a drug offense. An even greater percentage of probationers, 46 percent, were either sent to prison or jail or had absconded.

3. *Increased Social Costs.* Some offenders placed on probation and parole will effectively and responsibly discharge their obligations. Others, however, will become social liabilities. In addition to the increased risk of new crimes, probation and parole increase the chance that added expenses will accrue to the community in the form of child support, welfare costs, housing expenses, legal aid, indigent health care, and the like.

*T*he Legal Environment

Nine especially significant Supreme Court decisions provide a legal framework for probation and parole supervision. Among recent cases, that of *Griffin* v. *Wisconsin* (1987)[29] may be the most significant. In *Griffin,* the U.S. Supreme Court ruled that probation officers may conduct searches of a probationer's residence without need for either a search warrant or probable cause. According to the Court, "[a] probationer's home, like anyone else's, is protected by the Fourth Amendment's requirement that searches be 'reasonable.'" However, "[a] State's operation of a probation system…presents 'special needs' beyond normal law enforcement that may justify departures from the usual warrant and probable cause requirements." Probation, the Court concluded, is similar to imprisonment because it is a "form of criminal sanction imposed upon an offender after a determination of guilt."

Other court cases focus on the conduct of parole or probation **revocation hearings**. Revocation is a common procedure, and in 1993, 22 percent of adults on parole and 7.5 percent of those on probation throughout the United States had their conditional release revoked.[30] Revocation of probation or parole may be requested by the supervising officer if a client has allegedly violated the conditions of community release or has committed a new crime. The most frequent violations for which revocation occurs are (1) failure to report as required to a probation or parole office, (2) failure to participate in a stipulated treatment program, and (3) alcohol or drug abuse while under supervision.[31] Revocation hearings may result in an order that a probationer's suspended sentence be made "active" or that a parolee return to prison to complete his or her sentence in confinement.

In a 1935 decision (*Escoe* v. *Zerbst*)[32] which has since been greatly modified, the Supreme Court held that probation "comes as an act of grace to one convicted of a crime…" and that the revocation of probation without hearing or notice

*R*evocation Hearing. A hearing held before a legally constituted hearing body (such as a parole board) in order to determine whether or not a probationer or parolee has violated the conditions and requirements of his or her probation or parole.

CAREERS IN JUSTICE

Working for the Administrative Office of the U.S. Courts

TYPICAL POSITIONS: U.S. probation officer, pretrial services officer, statistician, defender services officer, and defense investigator.

EMPLOYMENT REQUIREMENTS: To qualify for the position of probation officer at the GS-5 level, an applicant must possess a bachelor's degree from an accredited college or university and have a minimum of two years of general work experience. General experience must have been acquired after obtaining the bachelor's degree, and cannot include experience as a police, custodial, or security officer unless work in such positions involved criminal investigative experience. In lieu of general experience, a bachelor's degree from an accredited college or university in an accepted field of study (including criminology, criminal justice, penology, correctional administration, social work, sociology, public administration, and psychology) will qualify an applicant for immediate employment at the GS-5 level providing that at least 32 semester hours or 48 quarter hours were taken in one or more of the accepted fields of study. One year of study qualifies applicants for appointment at the GS-7 level, whereas a master's degree in an appropriate field or a law degree may qualify the applicant for advanced placement.

OTHER REQUIREMENTS: Applicants must be less than 37 years of age at the time of hiring and be in excellent physical health.

SALARY: Appointees at the GS-5 level were earning $19,407 or more in mid-1995, and GS-7 appointees earned $24,030 or more. Experienced statisticians with bachelor's degrees earned between $33,000 and $60,000.

BENEFITS: U.S. probation and pretrial services officers are included in the federal hazardous-duty law enforcement classification and are covered by liberal federal health and life insurance programs. A comprehensive retirement program is available to all federal employees.

DIRECT INQUIRIES TO: Administrative Office of the U.S. Courts, Personnel Office, Washington, D.C. 20544. Phone: (202) 273-1297.

SOURCE: Administrative Office of the United States Courts.

to the probationer was acceptable practice. By 1967, however, the case of *Mempa* v. *Rhay*[33] found the Warren Court changing direction as it declared that both notice and a hearing were required. It also said that the probationer should have the opportunity for representation by counsel before a deferred prison sentence could be imposed.[34] Jerry Mempa had been convicted of riding in a stolen car at age 17 in 1959 and sentenced to prison, but his sentence was deferred and he was placed on probation. A few months later, he was accused of burglary. A hearing was held, and Mempa admitted his involvement in the burglary. An active prison sentence was then imposed. At the hearing, Mempa had not been offered the chance to have a lawyer represent him, nor was he given the chance to present any evidence or testimony in his own defense.

Two of the most widely cited cases affecting parolees and probationers are *Morrissey* v. *Brewer* (1972)[35] and *Gagnon* v. *Scarpelli* (1973).[36] In *Morrissey*, the Court declared a need for procedural safeguards in revocation hearings involving *parolees*. After *Morrissey*, revocation proceedings would require that (1) the parolee be given written notice specifying the alleged violation; (2) evidence of the violation be disclosed; (3) a neutral and detached body constitute the hearing authority; (4) the parolee have the chance to appear and offer a defense, including testimony, documents, and witnesses; (5) the parolee have the right to cross-examine witnesses; and (6) a written statement be provided to the parolee at the conclusion of the hearing that includes the hearing body's decision, the testimony considered, and reasons for revoking parole if such occurs.[37]

In 1973, the Court extended the procedural safeguards of *Morrissey* to *probationers* in *Gagnon* v. *Scarpelli* (1973). John Gagnon had pleaded guilty to armed robbery in Wisconsin and was sentenced to 15 years in prison. His sentence was suspended, and the judge ordered him to serve a 7-year probationary term. One month later, and only a day after having been transferred to the supervision of the Cook County, Illinois, Adult Probation Department, Gagnon was arrested by police in the course of a burglary. He was advised of his rights, but confessed to officers that he was in the process of stealing money and property when discovered. His probation was revoked without a hearing. Citing its own decision a year earlier in *Morrissey* v. *Brewer*, the Supreme Court ruled that probationers, because they face a substantial loss of liberty, were entitled to two hearings—the first, a preliminary hearing, to determine whether there is "probable cause to believe that he has committed a violation of his parole," and the second, "a somewhat more comprehensive hearing prior to the making of the final revocation decision." The Court also ruled that probation revocation hearings were to be held "under the conditions specified in *Morrissey* v. *Brewer*."

The Court also dealt with a separate question centered on Gagnon's indigent status. While being careful to emphasize the narrowness of the particulars in this case, the Court added to the protections granted under *Morrissey* v. *Brewer*, ruling that probationers have the right to a lawyer, even if indigent, provided they claimed that either (1) they had not committed the alleged violation or (2) they had substantial mitigating evidence to explain their violation. In *Gagnon* and later cases, however, the Court reasserted that probation and parole revocation hearings were not a stage in the criminal prosecution process, but a simple adjunct to it, even though they might result in substantial loss of liberty. The difference is a crucial one, for it permits hearing boards and judicial review officers to function, at least to some degree, outside the adversarial context of the trial court and with lessened attention to the rights of the criminally accused guaranteed by the Bill of Rights.

A more recent case, *Greenholtz* v. *Nebraska* (1979),[38] established that parole boards do not have to specify the evidence used in deciding to deny parole. The *Greenholtz* case focused on a Nebraska statute which required that inmates denied parole be provided with reasons for the denial. The Court held that reasons for parole denial might be provided in the interest of helping inmates prepare themselves for future review, but that to require the disclosure of evidence used in the review hearing would turn the process into an adversarial proceeding.

The 1983 Supreme Court case of *Bearden* v. *Georgia*[39] established that probation could not be revoked for failure to pay a fine and make restitution if it could not be shown that the defendant was responsible for the failure. The Court also held that alternative forms of punishment must be considered by the hearing authority and be shown to be inadequate before the defendant can be incarcerated. Bearden had pleaded guilty to burglary and had been sentenced to three years' probation. One of the conditions of his probation required that he pay a fine of $250 and make restitution payments totaling $500. Bearden successfully made the first two payments, but then lost his job. His probation was revoked, and he was imprisoned. The Supreme Court decision stated that "if the State determines a fine or restitution to be the appropriate and adequate penalty for the crime, it may not thereafter imprison a person solely because he lacked the resources to pay it."[40] The Court held that if a defendant lacks the capacity to pay a fine or make restitution, then the hearing authority must consider any viable alternatives to incarceration prior to imposing a term of imprisonment.

In another ruling affecting restitution, *Kelly v. Robinson* (1986),[41] the Court held that a restitution order cannot be vacated by a filing of bankruptcy. In the *Kelly* case, a woman convicted of illegally receiving welfare benefits was ordered to make restitution in the amount of $100 per month. Immediately following the sentence, the defendant filed for bankruptcy and listed the court-ordered restitution payment as a debt from which she sought relief. The bankruptcy court discharged the debt, and a series of appeals found the U.S. Supreme Court ruling that fines and other financial penalties ordered by criminal courts are not capable of being voided by bankruptcy proceedings.

A probationer's incriminating statements to a probation officer may be used as evidence if the probationer did not specifically claim a right against self-incrimination, according to *Minnesota v. Murphy* (1984).[42] Marshall Murphy was sentenced to three years' probation in 1980 on a charge of "false imprisonment" (kidnapping) stemming from an alleged attempted sexual attack. One condition of his probation required him to be entirely truthful with his probation officer "in all matters." Some time later, Murphy admitted to his probation officer that he had confessed to a rape and murder in conversations with a counselor. He was later convicted of first-degree murder, partially on the basis of the statements made to his probation officer. Upon appeal, Murphy's lawyers claimed that their client should have been advised of his right against self-incrimination during his conversation with the parole officer. Although the Minnesota supreme court agreed, the U.S. Supreme Court found for the state, saying that the burden of invoking the Fifth Amendment privilege against self-incrimination in this case lay with the probationer.

An emerging legal issue today surrounds the potential liability of probation officers and parole boards and their representatives for the criminal actions of offenders they supervise or whom they have released. Some courts have held that officers are generally immune from suit because they are performing a judicial function on behalf of the state.[43] Other courts, however, have indicated that parole board members who do not carefully consider mandated criteria for judging parole eligibility could be liable for injurious actions committed by parolees.[44] In general, however, most experts agree that parole board members cannot be successfully sued unless release decisions are made in a grossly negligent or wantonly reckless manner.[45] Discretionary decisions of individual probation and parole officers which result in harm to members of the public, however, may be more actionable under civil law, especially where their decisions were not reviewed by judicial authority.[46]

In 1995, for example, Pennsylvania state officials faced the possibility of lawsuits resulting from the release of Robert "Mudman" Simon by parole board officials. Mudman, a member of the Warlocks motorcycle gang, had been imprisoned for the murder of 19-year-old Beth Smith Dusenberg, who was shot in the face after she refused to let gang members rape her.[47] His release on parole after serving 12½ years on a 10- to 20-year sentence was approved by former Pennsylvania Board of Probation and Parole member Mary Ann Stewart and parole board chairman Allen Castor even though the sentencing judge recommended that Mudman not be released, and a psychiatrist wrote that "he was a sociopath, lacking in remorse, and prone to kill again."[48] Three months after he was set free, Mudman allegedly killed New Jersey policeman Ippolito "Lee" Gonzalez, shooting the officer twice in the face at point-blank range after a routine traffic stop. As hearings in the case progressed, the Pennsylvania legislature introduced a bill which in the future would require three parole board members to approve the release of any violent inmate and would give the sentencing judge in the case the power to veto any decision by the board.[49]

The Federal Probation System

The Federal Probation System is just over 70 years old.[50] In 1916, the U.S. Supreme Court in the *Killets* case[51] ruled that federal judges did not have the authority to suspend sentences and order probation. After a vigorous campaign by the National Probation Association, Congress finally passed the National Probation Act in 1925, authorizing the use of probation in federal courts. The bill came just in time to save a burgeoning federal prison system from serious overcrowding. The Mann Act, prohibition legislation, and the growth of organized crime had all led to increased arrests and a dramatic growth in the number of federal probationers in the early years of the system.

Although the 1925 act authorized one probation officer per federal judge, it allocated only $25,000 for officers' salaries. As a consequence, only 8 officers were hired to serve 132 judges, and the system came to rely heavily on voluntary probation officers. Some sources indicate that as many as 40,000 probationers were under the supervision of volunteers at the peak of the system.[52] By 1930, however, Congress provided adequate funding, and a corps of salaried professionals began to provide probation services to the U.S. courts.

In recent years, the work of federal probation officers has been dramatically affected by new rules of federal procedure. Presentence investigations have been especially affected. Revised Rule 32 of the *Federal Rules of Criminal Procedure*, for example, now mandates that federal probation officers who prepare presentence reports must:[53]

✔ Evaluate the evidence in support of facts.
✔ Resolve certain disputes between the prosecutor and defense attorney.
✔ Testify when needed to provide evidence in support of the administrative application of sentencing guidelines.
✔ Make use of an addendum to the report which, among other things, demonstrates that the report has been disclosed to the defense attorney, defendant, and government counsel.

Some authors have argued that these new requirements demand previously unprecedented skills from probation officers. Officers must now be capable of drawing objective conclusions based on the facts they observe, and they must be able to make "independent judgments in the body of the report regarding which sets of facts by various observers the court should rely upon in imposing sentence."[54] They must also be effective witnesses in court during the trial phase of criminal proceedings. Although in the past officers have often been called on to provide testimony during revocation hearings, the informational role now mandated throughout the trial itself is new.

The Job of a Probation/Parole Officer

Correctional personnel involved in probation/parole supervision totaled 43,198 (including approximately 2,500 federal officers) throughout the United States in 1990 according to the American Correctional Association (ACA).[55] Some 15,352 of these officers supervised probationers only, whereas 13,833 supervised both probationers and parolees. Salaries for entry-level parole officers were reported to be as low as $15,300 in 1993 although some states began officers at $35,600.[56] Probation officer salaries were within the same range. Chief parole officers in a few jurisdictions were earning as much as $107,700.

The tasks performed by probation and parole officers are often quite similar. Some jurisdictions combine the roles of both into one job. This section describes the duties of probation and parole officers, whether separate or performed by the same individuals. Probation/parole work consists primarily of four functions: (1) presentence investigations, (2) intake procedures, (3) needs assessment and diagnosis, and (4) the supervision of clients.

Where probation is a possibility, intake procedures may include presentence investigations, described in Chapter 9, which examine the offender's background in order to provide the sentencing judge with facts needed to make an informed sentencing decision. Intake procedures may also involve a dispute settlement process during which the probation officer works with the defendant and victim to resolve the complaint prior to sentencing. Intake duties tend to be more common among juvenile probation officers than they are in adult criminal court, but all officers may find themselves in the position of having to recommend to the judge what sentencing alternative would best answer the needs of the case.

Diagnosis refers to the psychological inventorying of the probation/parole client and may be done either on a formal basis involving the use of written tests administered by certified psychologists or through informal arrangements which typically depend on the observational skills of the officer. Needs assessment, another area of officer responsibility, extends beyond the psychological needs of the client to a cataloging of the services necessary for a successful experience on probation or parole.

Supervision of sentenced probationers or released parolees is the most active stage of the probation/parole process, involving months (and sometimes years) of periodic meetings between the officer and client and an ongoing assessment of the success of the probation/parole endeavor in each individual case.

One special consideration affecting the work of all probation/parole officers is the need for confidentiality. The details of the presentence investigation, psychological tests, needs assessment, conversations between the officer and client, and so on, should not be public knowledge. On the other hand, courts have generally held that communications between the officer and client are not privileged, as they might be between a doctor and patient.[57] Hence, incriminating evidence related by a client can be shared by officers with appropriate authorities.

Perhaps the biggest difficulty that probation and parole officers face is their need to walk a fine line between two conflicting sets of duties, one of which is to provide quasi–social work services and the other to handle custodial responsibilities. In effect, two conflicting images of the officer's role coexist. The social work model stresses a service role for officers and views probationers and parolees as "clients." Officers are seen as "caregivers," who attempt to assess accurately the needs of their clients and, through an intimate familiarity with available community services—from job placement, indigent medical care, and family therapy, to psychological and substance abuse counseling—match clients and community resources. The social work model depicts probation/parole as a "helping profession," wherein officers assist their clients in meeting the conditions imposed on them by their sentence.

The other model for officers is correctional. It sees probation/parole clients as "wards" whom officers are expected to control. This model emphasizes community protection, which officers are supposed to achieve through careful and close supervision. Custodial supervision means that officers will periodically visit their charges at work and at home, often arriving unannounced. It also means that they will be ready and willing to report clients for new offenses and for violations of the conditions of their release.

Most officers, by virtue of their personalities and experiences, probably identify more with one of the two models we have described than with the other. They think of themselves either primarily as caregivers or as correctional officers. Regardless of the emphasis which appeals most to individual officers, however, demands of the job are bound to generate role conflict at one time or another.

A second problem in probation/parole work is high **caseloads**. The President's Commission on Law Enforcement and the Administration of Justice recommended that probation/parole caseloads should average around 35 clients per officer.[58] However, caseloads of 250 clients are common in some jurisdictions. Various authors have found that high caseloads, combined with limited training, and time constraints forced by administrative and other demands, culminate in stopgap supervisory measures.[59] "Postcard probation," in which clients mail in a letter or card once a month to report on their whereabouts and circumstances, is an example of one stopgap measure that harried agencies with large caseloads use to keep track of their wards.[60]

Another difficulty with probation/parole work is the lack of opportunity for career mobility.[61] Probation and parole officers are generally assigned to small agencies, serving limited geographical areas, with one or two lead officers (usually called chief probation officers). Unless retirement or death claims the supervisors, there will be little chance for other officers to advance.

Intermediate Sanctions

Significant new sentencing options have become available to judges in innovative jurisdictions over the past few decades. Many such options are called **intermediate sanctions** because they employ sentencing alternatives which fall somewhere between outright imprisonment and simple probationary release back into the community. They are also called alternative sentencing strategies. Michael J. Russell, former director of the National Institute of Justice, says that:

> intermediate punishments are intended to provide prosecutors, judges, and corrections officials with sentencing options that permit them to apply appropriate punishments to convicted offenders while not being constrained by the traditional choice between prison and probation. Rather than substituting for prison or probation, however, these sanctions—which include intensive supervision, house arrest with electronic monitoring, and shock incarceration—bridge the gap between those options and provide innovative ways to ensure swift and certain punishment.[62]

A number of citizen groups and special interest organizations are working to widen the use of sentencing alternatives. One organization of special note is the Washington, D.C.–based Sentencing Project. The Sentencing Project was formed in 1986[63] through support from foundation grants.[64] The Project is dedicated to promoting a greater use of alternatives to incarceration and provides technical assistance to public defenders, court officials, and other community organizations.

The Sentencing Project and other groups like it have contributed to the development of more than 100 locally based alternative sentencing service programs. Most alternative sentencing services work in conjunction with defense attorneys to develop written sentencing plans. Such plans are basically well-considered citizen suggestions on what appropriate sentencing in a given instance might entail. Plans are often quite detailed and may include letters of support from employers, family members, the defendant, and even victims. Sentencing plans may be used in plea bargaining sessions or presented to judges following trial and conviction. A decade ago, for example, lawyers for country-and-western singer Willie Nelson successfully proposed an alternative option to tax court officials which allowed the singer to pay huge past tax liabilities by performing in concerts for that purpose. Lacking such an alternative, the tax court might have seized Nelson's property or even ordered the singer confined to a federal facility.

The basic philosophy behind intermediate sanctions is this: When judges can be offered well-planned alternatives to imprisonment, the likelihood of a prison sentence can be reduced. An analysis of alternative sentencing plans such as those sponsored by the Sentencing Project show that they are accepted by judges in up to 80 percent of the cases in which they are recommended and that as many as two-thirds of offenders who receive alternative sentences successfully complete them.[65]

Intermediate, or alternative, sanctions have three distinct advantages:[66] (1) They are less expensive to operate on a per offender basis than imprisonment; (2) they are "socially cost effective" because they keep the offender in the community, thus avoiding both the breakup of the family and the stigmatization which accompanies imprisonment; and (3) they provide flexibility in terms of resources, time of involvement, and place of service. Some of these new options we describe in the paragraphs that follow.

Split Sentencing

Split Sentence. A sentence explicitly requiring the convicted person to serve a period of confinement in a local, state, or federal facility followed by a period of probation.

In jurisdictions where **split sentencing** is an option, judges may impose a combination of a brief period of imprisonment and probation. Defendants sentenced under split sentencing are often ordered to serve time in a local jail rather than in a long-term confinement facility. "Ninety days in jail, together with two years of supervised probation," would be a typical split sentence. Split sentences are frequently used with minor drug offenders and serve notice that continued law violations may result in imprisonment for much longer periods.

Shock Probation/Shock Parole

Shock Probation. The practice of sentencing offenders to prison, allowing them to apply for probationary release, and enacting such release in surprise fashion. Offenders who receive shock probation may not be aware of the fact that they will be released on probation and may expect to spend a much longer time behind bars.

Shock probation bears a considerable resemblance to split sentencing. Again, the offender serves a relatively short time in custody (usually in a prison rather than jail) and is released on probation by court order. The difference is that shock probation clients must *apply* for probationary release from confinement and cannot be certain of the judge's decision. In shock probation, the court in effect makes a resentencing decision. Probation is only a statutory possibility and often little more than a vague hope of the offender as imprisonment begins. If probationary release is ordered, it may well come as a "shock" to the offender who, facing a sudden reprieve, may forswear future criminal involvement. Shock probation was first begun in Ohio in 1965[67] and is used today in about half of the United States.[68]

New Jersey runs a model modern shock probation program which is administered by a specially appointed Screening Board comprising correctional officials and members of the public. The New Jersey program has served as an example to many other states. It has a stringent set of selection criteria which allow only inmates serving sentences for nonviolent crimes to apply to the Screening Board for release.[69] Inmates must have served at least 30 days before applying. Those who have served more than 60 days are ineligible. Offenders must submit a personal plan describing what they will do when released, what their problems are, what community resources they need or intend to use, and what people can be relied on to provide assistance. Part of the plan involves a community sponsor with whom the inmate must reside for a fixed period (usually a few months) following release. The New Jersey program is especially strict because it does not grant outright release, but rather allows only a 90-day initial period of freedom. If the inmate successfully completes the 90-day period, continued release may be requested.

Shock probation lowers the cost of confinement, maintains community and family ties, and may be an effective rehabilitative tool.[70] Similar to shock probation is **shock parole**. Whereas shock probation is ordered by judicial authority, shock parole is an administrative decision made by a paroling authority. Parole boards or their representatives may order an inmate's early release, hoping that brief exposure to prison may have reoriented the offender's life in a positive direction.

A boot camp correctional officer greets a new arrival. Shock incarceration programs—also called boot camp prisons—*provide a sentencing alternative which is growing rapidly in popularity. Photo by R. Maiman, courtesy of Sygma.*

Shock Incarceration

Shock incarceration is the newest of the alternative sanctions discussed here.[71] Shock incarceration, designed primarily for young, first offenders, utilizes military-style "boot camp" prison settings to provide a highly regimented program involving strict discipline, physical training, and hard labor. Shock incarceration programs are of short duration, lasting for only 90 to 180 days. Offenders who successfully complete these programs are generally placed under community supervision. Program "failures" may be moved into the general prison population for longer terms of confinement.

The first shock incarceration program began in Georgia in 1983.[72] Since then, other programs have opened in Alabama, Arkansas, Arizona, Florida, Louisiana, Maryland, Michigan, Mississippi, New Hampshire, New York, Oklahoma, South Carolina, Texas, Massachusetts,[73] and other states. New York's program is the largest, with a capacity for 1,602 participants, whereas Tennessee's program can handle only 102.[74] There are other substantial differences between the states. About half provide for voluntary entry into their shock incarceration programs. A few allow inmates to decide when and whether they want to quit. Although most states allow judges to place offenders into such programs, some delegate that authority to corrections officials. Two states, Louisiana and Texas, authorize judges and corrections personnel joint authority in the decision-making process.[75] Some states, such as Massachusetts, have begun to accept classes of female inmates into boot camp settings. The Massachusetts program, which first accepted women in 1993, requires inmates to spend nearly four months undergoing the rigors of training.

The most comprehensive study of boot camp prison programs to date examined shock incarceration programs in eight states: Florida, Georgia, Illinois,

Shock Incarceration. A sentencing option which makes use of "boot camp" prisons in order to impress upon convicted offenders the realities of prison life.

Louisiana, New York, Oklahoma, South Carolina, and Texas. The report,[76] which was issued in 1995, found that boot camp programs are especially popular today because "they are...perceived as being 'tough on crime,'" and "have been enthusiastically embraced as a viable correctional option." The report concluded, however, that "the impact of boot camp programs on offender recidivism is at best negligible."

More limited studies, such as one which focused on shock incarceration in New York state, have found that boot camp programs save money in two ways: "first by reducing expenditures for care and custody" (since the intense programs reduce time spent in custody, and participation in them is the only way New York inmates can be released from prison before their minimum parole eligibility dates), and "second, by avoiding capital costs for new prison construction."[77] A 1995 study of Oregon's Summit boot camp program reached a similar conclusion. Although they did not study recidivism, Oregon researchers found that "the Summit boot camp program is a cost-effective means of reducing prison overcrowding by treating and releasing specially selected inmates earlier than their court-determined minimum period of incarceration."[78]

Mixed Sentencing and Community Service

Mixed sentences require that offenders serve weekends in jail and receive probation supervision during the week. Other types of mixed sentencing require participation in treatment or community service programs while a person is on probation. Community service programs began in Minnesota in 1972 with the Minnesota Restitution Program,[79] which gave property offenders the opportunity to work and turn over part of their pay as restitution to their victims. Courts throughout the nation quickly adopted the idea and began to build restitution orders into suspended-sentence agreements.

Community service is more an adjunct to, rather than a type of, correctional sentence. Community service is compatible with most other forms of innovation in probation and parole, except perhaps for home confinement (discussed later). Even there, however, offenders could be sentenced to community service activities which might be performed in the home or at a job site during the hours they are permitted to be away from their homes. Washing police cars, cleaning school buses, refurbishing public facilities, and assisting in local government offices are typical forms of community service. Some authors have linked the development of community service sentences to the notion that work and service to others are good for the spirit.[80] Community service participants are usually minor criminals, drunk drivers, and youthful offenders.

One problem with community service sentences is that authorities rarely agree on what they are supposed to accomplish. Most people admit that offenders who work in the community are able to reduce the costs of their own supervision. There is little agreement, however, over whether such sentences reduce recidivism, provide a deterrent, or act to rehabilitate offenders.

Intensive Supervision

Intensive probation supervision (IPS), first implemented by Georgia in 1982, has been described as the "strictest form of probation for adults in the United States."[81] The Georgia program involves a minimum of five face-to-face contacts between the probationer and supervising officer per week, mandatory curfew, required employment, a weekly check of local arrest records, routine and unannounced alcohol and drug testing, 132 hours of community service, and automatic notification of probation officers via the State Crime Information Network whenever an IPS client is arrested.[82] Caseloads of probation officers involved in IPS are much lower than the national average. Georgia officers work as a team with one probation officer and two surveillance officers supervising

Mixed Sentence. One which requires that a convicted offender serve weekends (or other specified periods) in a confinement facility (usually a jail) while undergoing probation supervision in the community.

Community Service. A sentencing alternative which requires offenders to spend at least part of their time working for a community agency.

Intensive Supervision. A form of probation supervision involving frequent face-to-face contacts between the probationary client and probation officers.

some 40 probationers.[83] IPS is designed to achieve control in a community setting over offenders who would otherwise have gone to prison.

North Carolina's Intensive Supervision Program follows the model of the Georgia program and adds a mandatory "prison awareness visit" within the first three months of supervision. North Carolina selects candidates for the Intensive Supervision Program on the basis of six factors: (1) the level of risk the offender is deemed to represent to the community; (2) assessment of the candidate's potential to respond to the program; (3) existing community attitudes toward the offender; (4) the nature and extent of known substance abuse; (5) the presence or absence of favorable community conditions, such as positive family ties, the possibility of continuing meaningful employment, constructive leisure-time activities, and adequate residence; and (6) the availability of community resources relevant to the needs of the case (such as drug treatment services, mental health programs, vocational training facilities, and volunteer services).[84] Some states have extended intensive supervision to parolees, allowing the early release of some who would otherwise serve lengthy prison terms.

Home Confinement and Electronic Monitoring

Home confinement, also referred to as house arrest, has been defined as "a sentence imposed by the court in which offenders are legally ordered to remain confined in their own residences."[85] They may leave only to attend to medical emergencies, go to their jobs, or buy household essentials. House arrest has been cited as offering a valuable alternative to prison for offenders with special needs. Pregnant women, geriatric convicts, offenders with special handicaps, seriously or terminally ill offenders, and the mentally retarded might all be better supervised through home confinement than traditional incarceration.

Florida's Community Control Program, authorized by the state's Correctional Reform Act of 1983, is the most ambitious home confinement program in the country.[86] On any given day in Florida as many as 5,000 offenders are restricted to their homes and supervised by community control officers who visit unannounced. Candidates for the program are required to agree to specific conditions, including

*H*ome Confinement. (Also called House Arrest) Individuals ordered confined in their homes are sometimes monitored electronically to be sure they do not leave during the hours of confinement. (Absence from the home during working hours is often permitted.)

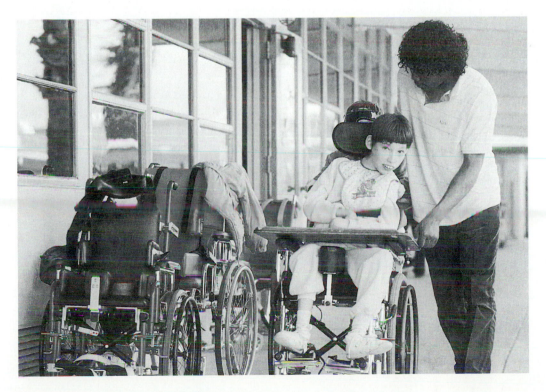

Via an alternative sentencing program, juvenile offenders in Bellflower, California, work with children who are physically challenged. Photo by Bart Bartholomew, courtesy of Black Star.

(1) restitution, (2) family support payments, and (3) supervisory fees (around $50 per month). They are also obligated to fill out daily logs about their activities. Community control officers have a minimum of 20 contacts per month with each offender. Additional discussions are held by the officer with neighbors, spouses, friends, landlords, employers, and others in order to allow the earliest possible detection of program violations or renewed criminality.

Florida's most serious home confinement offenders are monitored via a computerized system of *electronic bracelets*. Random telephone calls require the offender to insert a computer chip worn in a wrist band into a specially installed modem in the home, verifying his or her presence. More modern units make it possible to record the time a supervised person enters or leaves the home and whether the phone line or equipment has been tampered with, and to send or receive messages.[87] Electronic monitoring of offenders has undergone dramatic growth both in Florida and across the nation. A survey by the National Institute of Justice,[88] as the use of electronic monitoring was just beginning, showed only 826 offenders being monitored electronically in mid-1987. By 1989, only 2 years later, the number had jumped to around 6,500, and today it stands at 12,117.[89] Of these, 9,353 are serving probationary sentences, and 2,764 are parolees.

Many states view house arrest as a cost-effective response to the rising expense of imprisonment. Estimates show that traditional home confinement programs cost about $1,500 to $7,000 per offender per year, whereas electronic monitoring increases the costs by at least $1,000.[90] Advocates of house arrest argue that it is also socially cost-effective[91] since it provides no opportunity for the kinds of negative socialization which occur in prison. Opponents have pointed out that house arrest may endanger the public, that it may be illegal,[92] and that it may provide little or no punishment. Some years ago, for example, John Zaccaro, Jr., the son of former vice-presidential candidate Geraldine Ferraro, was sentenced to four months of house arrest for selling cocaine. His $1,500-a-month luxury apartment, with maid service, cable television, and many other expensive amenities, was in a building designed for expense-account businesspeople on short assignments to the Burlington, Vermont, area. Zaccaro's prosecutor observed, "This guy is a drug felon and he's living in conditions that 99.9 percent of the people of Vermont couldn't afford."[93]

Commonly called "house arrest," the electronic monitoring of convicted offenders appears to have the capacity to dramatically reduce correctional costs for nondangerous offenders. This photograph demonstrates the use of an electronic "ankle bracelet," capable of answering a computer's call to verify that the wearer is at home. Photo by Larry Downing, courtesy of Sygma.

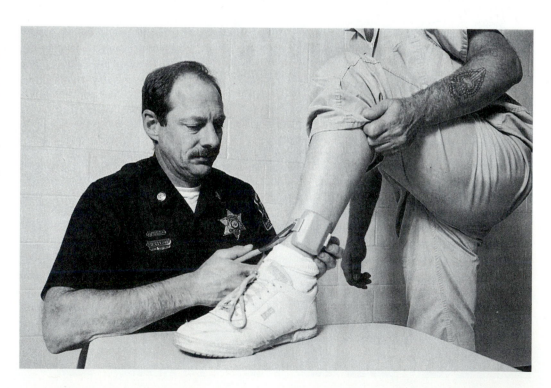

Questions About Alternative Sanctions

As prison populations continue to rise, some suggest that alternative sentencing strategies will become increasingly attractive. Many questions remain to be answered, however, before most alternative sanctions can be employed with confidence. These questions have been succinctly stated in a Rand Corporation study authored by Joan Petersilia.[94] Unfortunately, though the questions can be listed, few definitive answers are yet available. Some of the questions Petersilia identifies are as follows:

- ✔ Do alternative sentencing programs threaten public safety?
- ✔ How should program participants be selected?
- ✔ What are the long-term effects of community sanctions on people assigned to them?
- ✔ Are alternative sanctions cost-effective?
- ✔ Who should pay the bill for alternative sanctions?
- ✔ Who should manage stringent community-based sanctions?
- ✔ How should program outcomes be judged?
- ✔ What kinds of offenders benefit most from alternative sanctions?

The Future of Probation and Parole

Parole has been widely criticized in recent years. Citizen groups claim that it unfairly reduces prison sentences imposed on serious offenders. Academicians allege that parole programs can provide no assurance that criminals will not commit further crimes. Media attacks upon parole have centered on recidivism and have highlighted the so-called revolving prison door as representative of the failure of parole.

Some years ago, the case of Larry Singleton came to represent all that is wrong with parole. Singleton was convicted of raping 15-year-old Mary Vincent, then hacking off her arms and leaving her for dead on a hillside.[95] When an apparently unrepentant[96] Singleton was paroled after eight years in prison, public outcry was tremendous. Communities banded together to deny him residence, and he had to be paroled to the grounds of San Quentin prison.

Official attacks on parole have come from some powerful corners. Senator Edward Kennedy has called for the abolition of parole, as did former Attorney General Griffin Bell and former U.S. Bureau of Prisons Director Norman Carlson.[97] Prisoners have also challenged the fairness of parole, saying it is sometimes arbitrarily granted and creates an undue amount of uncertainty and frustration in the lives of inmates. Parolees have complained about the unpredictable nature of the parole experience, citing their powerlessness in the parole contract. Against the pressure of official attacks and despite cases like that of Singleton, parole advocates struggle to clarify and communicate the value of parole in the correctional process.

As more and more states move toward the elimination of parole, other voices call for moderation. A 1995 report by the Center for Effective Public Policy, for example, concludes that those states which have eliminated parole "have jeopardized public safety and wasted tax dollars." In the words of the report, "Getting rid of parole dismantles an accountable system of releasing prisoners back into the community and replaces it with a system that bases release decisions solely on whether a prison term has been completed."[98]

Probation, although it has generally fared better than parole, is not without its critics. The primary purpose of probation has always been rehabilitation. Probation is a powerful rehabilitative tool because, at least in theory, it allows the resources of a community to be focused on the offender. Unfortunately for advocates of probation, however, the rehabilitative ideal holds far less significance today than it has in the past. The contemporary demand for just deserts appears to have reduced the tolerance society as a whole feels for even relatively minor offenders. Further, the image of probation has not benefited from its all-too-frequent and inappropriate use with repeat or relatively serious offenders. Probation advocates themselves have been forced to admit that it is not a very powerful deterrent because it is far less punishing than a term of imprisonment. Arguments in support of probation have been weakened because some of the positive contributions probation had to offer are now being made available from other sources. Victims' compensation programs, for example, have taken the place of probationers' direct restitution payments to victims.

Acknowledging the complexities of the present situation, Vincent O'Leary has identified six trends bound to affect the future of both probation and parole.[99]

1. Increasing pressure to ensure that community supervision reflects the goals society has established for the handling of offenders.
2. The acknowledgment of risk control as an important function of the criminal justice system and the need to recognize that errors can be made in assessing risks.
3. The increased use of a variety of supervisory methods and variation in the size of caseloads supervised by one officer.
4. A clarification in the process by which offenders are moved from one level of supervision to another.
5. A greater emphasis on the accountability of individual officers as to the specific behavioral objectives to be achieved in working with clients.
6. The creation of information systems useful in judging effectiveness and in providing feedback on specific supervisory practices.

Probation will probably always remain a viable sentencing option if only because there will always be minor offenders for whom imprisonment is hard to justify. The return to determinate sentencing, however, which we discussed in Chapter 9, is a clear indication that parole, as it has existed for the last half century, is in for serious restructuring and may not survive in recognizable form. The overcrowded conditions of our nation's prisons, however, will probably work to continue at least a limited use of parole. Even states which have adopted determinate sentencing statutes still often depend upon a brief parole experience to successfully meet the basic needs of ex-offenders for finding housing, employment, and social services.

 Summary

Probation and parole are two of the most recent large-scale innovations in the long history of correctional supervision. They can be seen as either a blessing or a curse, depending upon which of their attributes are emphasized. Both probation and parole provide opportunities for the reintegration of offenders into the community through the use of resources not readily available in institutional settings. Unfortunately, however, increased freedom for criminal offenders also means some degree of increased risk for other members of society. Until and unless probation and parole solve the problems of accurate risk assessment, reduced recidivism, and adequate supervision, they will continue to be viewed with suspicion by clients and citizenry alike.

Discussion Questions

1. Probation is a sentence served while under supervision in the community. Do you believe that a person who commits a crime should be allowed to serve all or part of his or her sentence in the community? If so, what conditions would you impose on the offender?

2. Can you think of any other "general conditions" of probation or parole that you might add to the list of those found in the sample probation and parole forms in this chapter? If so, what would they be? Why would you want to add them?

3. Do you believe that ordering an offender to make restitution to his or her victim will teach the offender to be a more responsible person? Offer support for your opinion.

4. Do you believe that "role conflict" is a real part of most probation and parole officers' jobs? If so, do you see any way to reduce the role conflict experienced by probation and parole officers? How might you do it?

5. Do you think home confinement is a good idea? What do you think is the future of home confinement? In your opinion, does it discriminate against certain kinds of offenders? How might it be improved?

References

1. As quoted in *Criminal Justice Newsletter*, January 19, 1993, p. 1.

2. James M. Byrne, "Probation," a National Institute of Justice Crime File Series Study Guide (Washington, D.C.: U.S. Department of Justice, 1988), p. 1.

3. President's Commission on Law Enforcement and Administration of Justice, *The Challenge of Crime in a Free Society* (Washington, D.C.: U.S. Government Printing Office, 1967), p. 166.

4. "Paroled Rapist, Called 'Cured,' Charged with Murder of 2," *Fayetteville-Observer Times* (North Carolina), June 16, 1992, p. 4A.

5. "Parolee Confesses to Killing 4 Girls," *The Robesonian*, May 29, 1992, p. 1A.

6. ABC News, *Prime Time Live*, August 2, 1995.

7. *The Challenge of Crime in a Free Society*.

8. Alexander B. Smith and Louis Berlin, *Introduction to Probation and Parole* (St. Paul, Minn.: West Publishing, 1976), p. 75.

9. John Augustus, *John Augustus, First Probation Officer: John Augustus' Original Report on His Labors—1852* (Montclair, N.J.: Patterson-Smith, 1972).

10. Smith and Berlin, *Introduction to Probation and Parole*, p. 77.

11. Ibid., p. 80.

12. George C. Killinger, Hazel B. Kerper, and Paul F. Cromwell, Jr., *Probation and Parole in the Criminal Justice System* (St. Paul, Minn.: West Publishing, 1976), p. 25.

13. Joan Petersilia et al., *Granting Felons Probation* (Santa Monica, Calif.: The Rand Corporation, 1985).

14. Bureau of Justice Statistics, "Correctional Populations in the United States," *Executive Summary*, April 1995.

15. Byrne, "Probation," p. 1.

16. Patrick A. Langan and Helen A. Graziadei, *Felony Sentences in State Courts, 1992* (Washington, D.C.: BJS, 1995).

17. "Woman Gets Probation for Shooting Fiancee," *Fayetteville Observer Times* (North Carolina), April 16, 1992, p. 9A.

18. "Probation and Parole Caseloads Reach New Highs," BJS press release, August 24, 1995.

19. Tracy L. Snell, *Correctional Populations in the United States, 1992* (Washington, D.C.: BJS, 1995), p. 107.

20. Stephanie Minor-Harper and Christopher A. Innes, "Time Served in Prison and on Parole, 1984," Bureau of Justice Statistics Special Report (1987).

21. *Correctional Populations in the United States*, p. 29.

22. Ibid., p. 104.

23. "The Effectiveness of Felony Probation: Results from an Eastern State," *Justice Quarterly* (December 1991), pp. 525–543.

24. Byrne, "Probation."

25. Ibid., p. 3.

26. Peter Finn and Dale Parent, *Making the Offender Foot the Bill: A Texas Program* (Washington, D.C.: National Institute of Justice, 1992), and "Benefits of Probation Fees Cited in Texas Program," *Criminal Justice Newsletter*, January 19, 1993, p. 5.

27. See Andrew von Hirsch and Kathleen J. Hanrahan, *Abolish Parole?* (Washington, D.C.: Law Enforcement Assistance Administration, 1978).

28. Patrick A. Langan and Mark A. Cunniff, *Recidivism of Felons on Probation 1986–1989* (Washington, D.C.: Bureau of Justice Statistics, 1992).

29. *Griffin v. Wisconsin*, 483 U.S. 868, 107 S.Ct. 3164 (1987).

30. Jamie Lillis, "Twenty-two Percent of Adult Parole Cases Revoked in 1993," *Corrections Compendium*, August 1994, pp. 7–8.

31. Ibid.

32. *Escoe v. Zerbst*, 295 U.S. 490 (1935).

33. *Mempa v. Rhay*, 389 U.S. 128 (1967).

34. A deferred sentence involves postponement of the sentencing decision, which may be made at a later time, following an automatic review of the defendant's behavior in the interim. A suspended sentence requires no review unless the probationer violates the law or conditions of probation. Both may result in imprisonment.

35. *Morrissey* v. *Brewer*, 408 U.S. 471 (1972).

36. *Gagnon* v. *Scarpelli*, 411 U.S. 778 (1973).

37. Smith and Berlin, *Introduction to Probation and Parole*, p. 143.

38. *Greenholtz* v. *Inmate of Nebraska Penal and Correctional Complex*, 442 U.S. 1 (1979).

39. *Bearden* v. *Georgia*, 461 U.S. 660, 103 S.Ct. 2064, 76 L.Ed. 2d. 221 (1983).

40. Ibid.

41. *Kelly* v. *Robinson*, U.S. 107, S.Ct. 353, 93 L.Ed. 2d. 216 (1986).

42. *Minnesota* v. *Murphy*, U.S. 104, S.Ct. 1136, 79 L.Ed. 2d. 409 (1984).

43. *Harlow* v. *Clatterbuick*, 30 CLr. 2364 (VA S.Ct. 1986); *Santangelo* v. *State*, 426 N.Y.S. 2d. 931 (1980); *Welch* v. *State*, 424 N.Y.S. 2d. 774 (1980); and *Thompson* v. *County of Alameda*, 614 P. 2d. 728 (1980).

44. *Tarter* v. *State of New York*, 38 CLr. 2364 (NY S.Ct. 1986); *Grimm* v. *Arizona Board of Pardons and Paroles*; 115 Arizona 260, 564 P. 2d. 1227 (1977); and *Payton* v. *United States*, 636 F. 2d. 132 (5th Cir.).

45. Rolando V. del Carmen, *Potential Liabilities of Probation and Parole Officers* (Cincinnati, Ohio: Anderson, 1986), p. 89.

46. See, for example, *Semler* v. *Psychiatric Institute*, 538 F. 2d. 121 (4th Cir. 1976).

47. Mario F. Cattabiani, "Panel Opens Parole System Probe," *The Morning Call*, May 20, 1995, p. A6.

48. Ibid.

49. See, Megan O'Matz, "System Freed 'Mudman,' Panel Hears," *The Morning Call*, June 3, 1995, p. A6, and Pamela Sampson, "Carbon Judge Testifies at 'Mudman' Hearing," *The Times News*, p. 1A.

50. This section owes much to Sanford Bates, "The Establishment and Early Years of the Federal Probation System," *Federal Probation* (June 1987), pp. 4–9.

51. *Ex parte United States*, 242 U.S. 27.

52. Bates, "The Establishment and Early Years of the Federal Probation System," p. 6.

53. As summarized by Susan Krup Grunin and Jud Watkins, "The Investigative Role of the United States Probation Officer Under Sentencing Guidelines," *Federal Probation* (December 1987), pp. 43–49.

54. Ibid., p. 46.

55. American Correctional Association, *Vital Statistics in Corrections*, p. 55.

56. *The Corrections Yearbook: Probation and Parole 1993*.

57. *Minnesota* v. *Murphy*, U.S. 104, S.Ct. 1136, 1143 (1984).

58. National Advisory Commission on Criminal Justice Standards and Goals, *Task Force Report: Corrections* (Washington, D.C.: U.S. Government Printing Office, 1973).

59. James P. Levine, Michael C. Musheno, and Dennis J. Palumbo, *Criminal Justice in America: Law in Action* (New York: John Wiley, 1986), p. 548.

60. Ibid.

61. James A. Inciardi, *Criminal Justice*, 2nd ed. (New York: Harcourt Brace Jovanovich, 1987), p. 638.

62. From the introduction to James Austin, Michael Jones, and Melissa Bolyard, "The Growing Use of Jail Boot Camps: The Current State of the Art," (Washington, D.C.: National Institute of Justice, October 1993), p. 1.

63. Although now an independent nonprofit corporation, The Sentencing Project has its roots in a 1981 project of the National Legal Aid and Defender Association.

64. The Sentencing Project, *1989 National Directory of Felony Sentencing Services* (Washington, D.C.: The Sentencing Project, 1989).

65. The Sentencing Project, *Changing the Terms of Sentencing: Defense Counsel and Alternative Sentencing Services* (Washington, D.C.: The Sentencing Project, no date).

66. Joan Petersilia, *Expanding Options for Criminal Sentencing* (Santa Monica, CA: The Rand Corporation, 1987).

67. *Ohio Revised Code*, 2946.06.1, July 1965.

68. Lawrence Greenfield, Bureau of Justice Statistics, *Probation and Parole, 1984* (Washington, D.C.: U.S. Government Printing Office, 1986).

69. For a complete description of this program, see Petersilia, *Expanding Options for Criminal Sentencing*.

70. Harry Allen, Chris Eskridge, Edward Latessa, and Gennaro Vito, *Probation and Parole in America* (New York: The Free Press, 1985), p. 88.

71. For a good overview of such programs see: William N. Osborne, Jr., "Shock Incarceration and the Boot Camp Model: Theory and Practice," *American Jails*, July/August 1994, pp. 27–30.

72. Doris Layton MacKenzie and Deanna Bellew Ballow, "Shock Incarceration Programs in State Correctional Jurisdictions—An Update," *NIJ Reports* (May–June 1989), pp. 9–10.

73. "Boot Camp Prisons Grow in Scope and Number," *NIJ Reports* (November–December 1990), p. 6.

74. Ibid.

75. Ibid.

76. National Institute of Justice, *Multisite*

Evaluation of Shock Incarceration, (Washington, D.C.: NIJ, 1995).

77. Cherie L. Clark, David W. Aziz, and Doris L. MacKenzie, "Shock Incarceration in New York: Focus on Treatment," (Washington, D.C.: National Institute of Justice, August 1994), p. 8.

78. "Oregon Boot Camp Is Saving the State Money, Study Finds," *Criminal Justice Newsletter*, May 1, 1995, pp. 5–6.

79. Douglas C. McDonald, "Restitution and Community Service," National Institute of Justice *Crime File Study Guide* (1988).

80. Richard J. Maher and Henry E. Dufour, "Experimenting with Community Service: A Punitive Alternative to Imprisonment," *Federal Probation* (September 1987), pp. 22–27.

81. James P. Levine et al., *Criminal Justice in America: Law in Action* (New York: John Wiley, 1986), p. 549.

82. Billie S. Erwin and Lawrence A. Bennett, "New Dimensions in Probation: Georgia's Experience with Intensive Probation Supervision," National Institute of Justice *Research in Brief* (1987).

83. Ibid., p. 2.

84. North Carolina Department of Correction, *Intensive Supervision Manual* (Raleigh, N.C.: Division of Adult Probation and Parole, 1988), pp. 3–5.

85. Joan Petersilia, "House Arrest," National Institute of Justice *Crime File Study Guide* (1988).

86. Ibid.

87. Ibid.

88. Marc Renzema and David T. Skelton, *The Use of Electronic Monitoring by Criminal Justice Agencies, 1989*, Grant Number OJP-89-M-309 (Washington, D.C.: National Institute of Justice, 1990).

89. *Correctional populations in the United States, 1992.*

90. Petersilia, "House Arrest."

91. *BI Home Escort: Electronic Monitoring System*, advertising brochure, BI Incorporated, Boulder, Colorado (no date).

92. For additional information on the legal issues surrounding electronic home confinement, see Bonnie Berry, "Electronic Jails: A New Criminal Justice Concern," *Justice Quarterly*, Vol. 2, no. 1 (1985), pp. 1–22, and J. Robert Lilly, Richard A. Ball, and W. Robert Lotz, Jr., "Electronic Jail Revisited," *Justice Quarterly*, Vol. 3, no. 3 (September 1986), pp. 353–361.

93. "Zaccaro Serving Sentence in Luxury Apartment," *The Fayetteville Observer*, August 15, 1988, p. 10A.

94. Petersilia, "House Arrest."

95. "A Victim's Life Sentence," *People* Magazine, April 25, 1988.

96. Ibid., p. 40.

97. Inciardi, *Criminal Justice*, 2nd. ed.: p. 664.

98. The Center for Effective Public Policy, *Abolishing Parole: Why the Emperor Has No Clothes*, 1995.

99. See Vincent O'Leary and D. Clear, *Directions for Community Corrections in the 1990's* (Boulder, Colo.: National Institute of Corrections, 1984), and O'Leary, "Probation, A System in Change," *Federal Probation* (December 1987).

CHAPTER 11

Prisons *and* Jails

—*Photo by Richard Falco/Black Star*

*T*o put people behind walls and bars and do little or nothing to change them is to win a battle but lose a war. It is wrong. It is expensive. It is stupid.[1]

—FORMER CHIEF JUSTICE WARREN E. BURGER (1907–1995)

*I*nfinite are the nine steps of a prison cell, and endless is the march of him who walks between the yellow brick wall and the red iron gate, thinking things that cannot be chained and cannot be locked...

—ARTURO GIOVANNITTI (1884–1959)

*Y*ears ago I began to recognize my kinship with all living beings....I said then, and I say now, that while there is a lower class I am in it; while there is a criminal element, I am of it; while there is a soul in prison, I am not free.

—EUGENE V. DEBS
AMERICAN SOCIALIST LEADER (1855–1926)

KEY CONCEPTS

prison	ADMAX	jail
direct supervision	private prisons	privatization
count	regional jails	

Prisons Today

There are approximately 1,000 state and 80 federal **prisons** in operation across the country today although more are quickly being built, as both the states and the federal government scramble to fund and construct new facilities. America's prison population tripled in the 15 years following 1980, and by January 1995, the nation's prisons (combined state and federal populations) held just over one million inmates.[2] Six percent (or 64,403) of those imprisoned were women.[3]

Reflecting new "get-tough" attitudes now permeating society, prisons everywhere are crowded, and the incarceration rate for state and federal prisoners sentenced to more than a year has reached a record 387 prisoners per every 100,000 U.S. residents.[4] Male incarceration rates (which stand at 746 per 100,000 male residents), however, are 16 times higher than those of women (only 45 per every 100,000 females). Until 1996, the problem of overcrowding was worst in Texas, which has the nation's highest incarceration rate, with 545 of every 100,000 Texans behind prison bars. In 1996, Texas completed a $1.5 billion expansion program, moving more than 20,000 inmates into 28 new facilities across the state. The Texas prison system, which has been described as "by far the largest in the free world," is capable of housing 146,000 regular prison inmates.[5]

An examination of imprisonment statistics by race highlights the huge disparity between blacks and whites in prison. Whereas only 207 whites are imprisoned in the United States for every 100,000 white persons in the population, latest figures show an incarceration rate of 1,471 blacks for every 100,000 black residents.[6] Worse yet, the rate of growth in such figures shows the imprisonment of blacks increased dramatically over the past ten years, whereas the rate of white imprisonment has grown far less. Many of these statistics are displayed graphically in Figure 11-1.

Federal prisons tell a similar story. On January 1, 1995, federal prisons held 95,034 inmates in facilities originally designed to accommodate only 68,221.[7] Construction plans now nearing completion call for an additional 42,000 beds to be added to federal prisons in order to house a total inmate population of 102,000 persons by September 30, 1997. By then, however, even conservative estimates are that at least 104,300 prisoners will be held in federal correctional facilities—outstripping the ability of even the federal government to increase prison space to accommodate growing inmate populations.

The size of prison facilities varies greatly. One of every four state institutions is a large, maximum security prison, with a population approaching 1,000 inmates. A few exceed that figure, but the typical state prison is small, with an inmate population of fewer than 500, whereas community-based facilities average around 50 residents—such as halfway houses.

Most people sentenced to state prisons have been convicted of violent crimes (46 percent), whereas property crimes (23 percent) are the second most common category for which inmates have been sentenced, and drug crimes are the reason for which 22 percent of "active" sentences are imposed.[8] In contrast, prisoners sentenced for drug law violations are the single largest group of federal inmates (60 percent), and the increase in the imprisonment of drug offenders accounts for three-quarters of the total growth in the number of federal inmates since 1980.[9] The inmate population in general suffers from a low level of formal education, comes from a socially disadvantaged background, and lacks significant vocational skills.[10] Most adult inmates have served some time in juvenile correctional facilities.[11]

In a recent year, approximately 352,000 staff members were employed in corrections,[12] with the majority performing direct custodial tasks in state institutions. Females accounted for 20 percent of all correctional officers in 1992, with the proportion of women officers increasing at around 19 percent per year.[13] In an effort to

Prison. A state or federal confinement facility having custodial authority over adults sentenced to varying terms of confinement.

encourage the increased employment of women in corrections, the American Correctional Association formally adopted a statement[14] which reads: "Women have a right to equal employment. No person who is qualified for a particular position/assignment or for job-related opportunities should be denied such employment or opportunities because of gender." The official statement goes on to encourage correctional agencies to "ensure that recruitment, selection, and promotion opportunities are open to women."

According to a recent report by the American Correctional Association, 70 percent of correctional officers are white, 22 percent are black, and slightly more than 5 percent are Hispanic.[15] The inmate–custody staff ratio in state prisons averages around 4.1 to 1. Incarceration costs the states an average of $11,302 per inmate per year, whereas the federal government spends about $13,162 to house one inmate for a year.[16] The ACA reports[17] that in 1991, entry-level correctional officers were paid between $13,520 and $33,996, depending on the state in which they were hired. Salaries for systems administrators in adult correctional systems were as high as $131,731 (South Carolina), with institutional superintendents earning in the range of $26,436 to $93,693.

Security Levels

Carter, McGee, and Nelson[18] describe the typical state prison system (in relatively populous states) as consisting of:

✔ One maximum-security prison for long-term, high-risk cases
✔ One or more medium-security institutions for the bulk of offenders who are not high risks
✔ One institution for adult women
✔ One or two institutions for young adults (generally under age 25)
✔ One or two specialized mental hospital–type security prisons for mentally ill prisoners
✔ One or more open-type institutions for low-risk nonviolent populations

Maximum custody prisons are the institutions most often portrayed in movies and on television. They tend to be massive old prisons with large inmate populations. Some, like Central Prison in Raleigh, North Carolina, are much newer and incorporate advances in prison architecture to provide tight security without sacrificing building aesthetics. Such institutions provide a high level of security characterized by high fences, thick walls, secure cells, gun towers, and armed prison

FIGURE 11-1

U.S. Incarceration rates by race and sex. Source: U.S. Department of Justice, "State and Federal Prison Population Tops One Million," October 27, 1994.

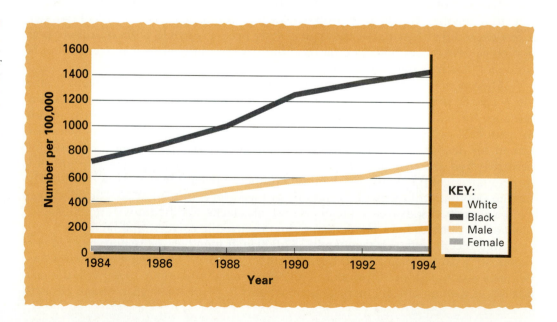

An Alabama chain gang sets out to work the roads. In 1995, reflecting a renewed societywide emphasis on punishment, Alabama became the first state to revive use of prison chain gangs. Photo courtesy of AP/Wide World Photos.

guards. Maximum custody prisons tend to locate cells and other inmate living facilities at the center of the institution and place a variety of barriers between the living area and the institution's outer perimeter. Technological innovations such as electric perimeters, laser motion detectors, electronic and pneumatic locking systems, metal detectors, X-ray machines, television surveillance, radio communications, and computer information systems are frequently used today to reinforce the more traditional maximum security strategies. These new technologies have helped lower the cost of new prison construction although some argue that prison electronic detection devices may be relied on too heavily and have not yet been adequately tested.[19] Death row inmates are all maximum security prisoners although the level of security on death row exceeds even that experienced by most prisoners held in maximum custody. Prisoners on death row must spend much of the day in single cells and are often permitted a brief shower only once a week under close supervision.

Most states today have one large centrally located maximum security institution. Some of these prisons combine more than one custody level and may be both

Theory into Practice: Prison Fashion in a "Get-Tough" Era

Alabama, which two weeks ago brought back prison chain gangs, will begin putting hot-pink uniforms on inmates who habitually masturbate in front of female guards. The garish garb is to elicit heckling from inmates and shame offenders into behaving. Nothing has deterred the men says prison spokesman Charlie Bodiford. "We've even taken...a picture of them and told them we were going to send it to their mothers. They don't care."

QUESTIONS FOR DISCUSSION

1. Do you think the kind of "punishment" described here might be effective? Why or why not?

2. If you were in charge of these prisoners, what steps might you take to control their behavior?

SOURCE: Nationline: "Prison Fashion," *USA Today*, May 19, 1995, p. 3A. Reprinted with permission.

maximum and medium security facilities. Medium security is a custody level that in many ways resembles maximum security. Medium security prisoners are generally permitted more freedom to associate with one another and can go to the prison yard, exercise room, library, and shower and bathroom facilities under less intense supervision than their maximum security counterparts. An important security tool in medium security prisons is the **count**, which is literally a headcount of inmates taken at regular intervals. Counts may be taken four times a day and usually require inmates to report to designated areas to be counted. Until the count has been "cleared," all other inmate activity must cease. Medium security prisons tend to be smaller than maximum security institutions and often have barbed-wire-topped chain-link fences in place of the more secure stone or concrete block walls found in many of the older maximum security facilities. Cells and living quarters tend to have more windows and are often located closer to the perimeter of the institution than is the case in maximum security. Dormitory-style housing, where prisoners live together in wardlike arrangements, may be employed in medium security facilities. Medium security facilities generally have more prison programs and opportunities for inmates to participate in recreational and other programs than do maximum custody facilities.

Minimum security institutions do not fit the stereotypical conception of prisons. Minimum security inmates are generally housed in dormitory-like settings and are free to walk the yard and visit most of the prison facilities. Some newer prisons provide minimum security inmates with private rooms which they can decorate (within limits) according to their tastes. Inmates usually have free access to a "canteen" which sells personal products like cigarettes, toothpaste, and candy bars. Minimum security inmates often wear uniforms of a different color from those of inmates in higher custody levels, and in some institutions, they may wear civilian clothes. They work under only general supervision and usually have access to recreational, educational, and skills training programs on the prison grounds. Guards are unarmed, gun towers do not exist, and fences, if they are present at all, are usually low and sometimes even unlocked. Many minimum security prisoners participate in some sort of work- or study-release program, and some have extensive visitation and furlough privileges. Counts may still be taken although most minimum security institutions keep track of inmates through daily administrative work schedules. The primary "force" holding inmates in minimum security institutions is their own restraint. Inmates live with the knowledge that minimum security institutions are one step removed from close correctional supervision and that if they fail to meet the expectations of administrators they will be transferred into more secure institutions, which will probably delay their release. Inmates returning from assignments in the community may be frisked for contraband, but body cavity searches are rare in minimum custody, being reserved primarily for inmates suspected of smuggling.

Upon entry into the prison system, most states assign prisoners to initial custody levels based on their perceived dangerousness, escape risk, and type of offense. Some inmates may enter the system at the medium (or even minimum) custody level. Inmates move through custody levels according to the progress they are judged to have made in self-control and demonstrated responsibility. Serious, violent criminals who begin their prison careers with lengthy sentences in maximum custody have the opportunity in most states to work their way up to minimum security although the process usually takes a number of years. Those who "mess up" and represent continuous disciplinary problems are returned to closer custody levels. Minimum security prisons, as a result, house inmates convicted of all types of criminal offenses.

The typical American prison today is medium or minimum custody. Some states have as many as 80 or 90 small institutions, which may originally have been located in every county to serve the needs of public works and highway maintenance. Medium and minimum security institutions house the bulk of the country's

Count. A headcount of inmates taken at regular intervals.

prison population and offer a number of programs and services designed to assist with the rehabilitation of offenders and to create the conditions necessary for a successful reentry of the inmate into society. Most prisons offer psychiatric services, academic education, vocational education, substance abuse treatment, health care, counseling, recreation, library services, religious programs, and industrial and agricultural training.[20]

The Federal Prison System

In 1895, the federal government opened a prison at Leavenworth, Kansas, for civilians convicted of violating federal law. Leavenworth had been a military prison, and control over the facility was transferred from the Department of the Army to the Department of Justice. By 1906, the Leavenworth facility had been expanded to a 1,200-inmate capacity, and another prison—in Atlanta, Georgia—had been built. McNeil Island Prison in Washington State was also functioning by the early 1900s. The first federal prison for women opened in 1927 in Alderson, West Virginia. With increasing complexity in the federal criminal code, the number of federal prisoners grew.[21]

On May 14, 1930, the Federal Bureau of Prisons (FBP) was created under the direction of Sanford Bates. The Bureau inherited a system which was dramatically overcrowded. Many federal prisoners were among the most notorious criminals in the nation, and ideals of humane treatment and rehabilitation were all but lacking in the facilities of the 1930s. Director Bates began a program of improvements to relieve overcrowding and to increase the treatment capacity of the system. In 1933, the Medical Center for Federal Prisoners opened in Springfield, Missouri, with a capacity of around 1,000 inmates. Alcatraz Island began operations in 1934.

The federal prison system classifies its institutions according to five[22] security levels: (1) administrative maximum (**ADMAX**); (2) high security; (3) medium security; (4) low security; and (5) minimum security. High security facilities are called United States Penitentiaries (USPs), medium and low security institutions are both called Federal Correctional Institutions (FCIs), and minimum security prisons are called Federal Prison Camps (FPCs).[23] Minimum security facilities (like Eglin Air Force Base, Florida, and Maxwell Air Force Base, Alabama) are essentially honor-type camps with barrackslike housing and have no fencing. Low security facilities in the federal prison system are surrounded by double chain-link fencing and employ vehicle patrols around their perimeters to enhance security. Medium security facilities (like those in Terminal Island, California; Lompoc, California; and Seagoville, Texas) make use of similar fencing and patrols, but supplement it with electronic monitoring of the grounds and perimeter areas. High security facilities (USPs such as those in Atlanta, Georgia; Lewisburg, Pennsylvania; Terre Haute, Indiana; and Leavenworth, Kansas) are architecturally designed to prevent escapes and to contain disturbances. They also make use of armed patrols and intense electronic surveillance. A separate federal prison category is that of Administrative Facility, consisting of institutions with special missions which are designed to house all types of inmates. Most administrative facilities are Metropolitan Detention Centers (MDCs). MDCs, which are generally located in large cities close to federal courthouses, are the jails of the federal correctional system and hold inmates awaiting trial in federal court. Another five administrative facilities are termed Medical Centers for Federal Prisoners (MCFPs) and function as hospitals.

As of fall 1995, the federal correctional system consisted of 82 facilities existing either as single institutions or as Federal Correctional Complexes (FCCs)—that is, sites consisting of more than one type of correctional institution (see Figure 11-2). The Federal Correctional Complex at Allenwood, Pennsylvania, for example, consists of a United States Penitentiary, a Federal Prison Camp, and two Federal Correctional Institutions (one low and one medium security), each with its own warden. Federal institutions can be classified by type as follows: 55 are Federal

ADMAX. Administrative maximum; the term used by the federal government to denote ultra-high security prisons.

Prison Camps (holding 31 percent of all federal prisoners); 17 are low security facilities (with 27 percent of the system's prisoners); 26 are medium security facilities (23 percent of the population); 8 are high security prisons (10 percent of prisoners); and 1 is an ADMAX facility (with 1 percent of the prison population).

One of the most recent additions to the system is the $60 million ultra-maximum security federal prison at Florence, Colorado—the federal system's only ADMAX unit. Dubbed by some "the Alcatraz of the Rockies," the new 575-bed facility is designed to be the most secure prison ever built by the government.[24] Opened in 1995, it holds mob bosses, spies, terrorists, murderers, and escape artists. Dangerous inmates are confined to their cells 23 hours per day and are not allowed to see or associate with other inmates. Electronically controlled doors throughout the institution channel inmates to individual exercise sessions, and educational courses, religious services, and administrative matters are conducted via closed-circuit television piped directly into the prisoners' cells. Remote-controlled heavy steel doors within the prison allow correctional staff to section off the institution in the event of rioting, and the system can be controlled from outside if the entire prison is compromised.

Twenty-one new federal prison facilities are scheduled to be in operation by 1998, including an FPC and FCI in Beckley, West Virginia; an FCC in Coleman, Florida; an FCC in Forrest City, Arkansas; an FCC in Yazoo City, Mississippi; an FDC (Federal Detention Center) in Seattle, Washington; an FDC in Honolulu, Hawaii; an FDC in Houston, Texas; an FDC in Philadelphia, Pennsylvania; and an FPC for women inmates in Scranton, Pennsylvania. Even with new facilities rapidly coming online, however, crowding in federal prisons is pervasive. The number of inmates held in federal prisons has risen from 24,000 in 1980 to 90,000 today.[25] Estimates are that, without changes, the federal prison population will exceed 116,000 inmates by 1999, with most of the increase due to lengthy sentences for drug offenders.

In an effort to combat rising expenses, the U.S. Congress recently passed legislation that imposes a "user fee" on federal inmates able to pay the costs associated with their incarceration.[26] Under the law, inmates may be assessed a dollar amount up to the cost of a year's incarceration—currently around $20,000. The statute, which was designed so as not to impose hardships on poor defendants or their dependents, directs that collected funds, estimated to soon total $48 million per year, are to be used to improve alcohol and drug abuse programs within federal prisons.

This new Federal Bureau of Prisons ADMAX facility in Florence, Colorado, opened in 1995. It is the only ultra-secure institution in the federal system. Photo by AFP, courtesy of Bettmann.

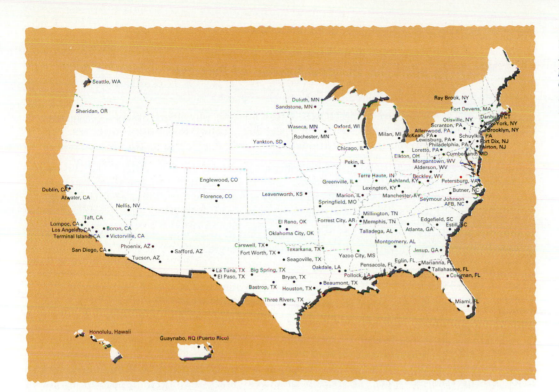

FIGURE 11-2

The federal correctional system, 1996 (includes facilities planned to open by 1998). Source: Federal Bureau of Prisons.

Recent Improvements

Amid frequent lawsuits, court-ordered changes in prison administration, and overcrowded conditions, outstanding prison facilities are being recognized through the American Correctional Association's program of accreditation. The ACA Commission on Accreditation has developed a set of standards which correctional institutions can use in self-evaluation. Those which meet the standards can apply for accreditation under the program. Unfortunately, accreditation of prisons has few "teeth." Although unaccredited universities would not long be in business, few prisoners can choose the institution they want to be housed in.

Another avenue toward improvement of the nation's prisons can be found in the National Academy of Corrections, the training arm of the National Institute of Corrections. The Academy, located in Boulder, Colorado, offers seminars and training sessions for state and local correctional managers, trainers, personnel directors, sheriffs, and state legislators.[27] Issues covered include strategies to control overcrowding, community corrections program management, prison programs, gangs and disturbances, security, and public and media relations, as well as many other topics.[28]

ails

Jails are short-term confinement facilities which were originally intended to hold suspects following arrest and pending trial. Today, jails also house those convicted of misdemeanors who are serving relatively short sentences, and felony offenders awaiting transportation to long-term confinement facilities. A 1995 report[29] by the National Institute of Justice found that the nation's jails held 434,838 men and 48,879 women, with approximately 6,725 people held in jails being younger than 18 years old. Numerically, 50 percent of jail inmates are pretrial detainees or are defendants involved in some stage of the trial process.[30] Whereas only a few years ago driving under the influence was the most common charge for jailed persons 45 years of age or older (accounting for 10 percent of all jail

Jail. A confinement facility administered by an agency of local government, typically a law enforcement agency, intended for adults but sometimes also containing juveniles, which holds persons detained pending adjudication or persons committed after adjudication (usually those committed on sentences of a year or less).

inmates),[31] persons charged with drug law violations now account for 25 percent of those in jail.[32] Bond has been set by the court, although not yet posted, for almost nine of ten jail inmates.[33] Significantly, one of the fastest-growing sectors of today's jail population consists of sentenced offenders serving time in local jails because overcrowded prisons cannot accept them.

A total of 3,304 jails are in operation throughout the United States today, staffed by approximately 165,500 correctional workers—the equivalent of about 1 employee for every 2.8 jail inmates.[34] Overall, the jail budget is huge, and facilities overflowing. Some $9.6 billion is spent every year by state and local governments to operate the nation's jails,[35] with more than $1 billion in additional monies earmarked for new jail construction and for facilities renovation. On average, according to a 1995 report, approximately $14,667 is spent yearly to house one jail inmate.[36]

Approximately 20 million people are admitted (or readmitted) to the nation's jails each year. Some jail inmates stay for as little as one day, whereas others serve extended periods of jail time. Most jails are small. Two of three were built to house 50 or fewer inmates. Most people who spend time in jail, however, do so in larger institutions.[37] According to a 1995 NIJ report, "about 6% of jail facilities housed more than half of all jail inmates…" in the nation.[38] Although there are many small and medium-sized jails across the country, a handful of "megajails" house thousands of inmates. The largest such facilities can be found in New York City's Riker's Island, Los Angeles County's Men's Central Jail, the Cook County jail in Chicago, Houston's Harris County Downtown Central Jail, the New Orleans Parish Prison System, and Los Angeles County's Pitchess Honor Ranch. The largest employer among these huge jails is the Cook County facility, with more than 1,200 personnel on its payroll.

Jails are busy places. The 1995 report by NIJ showed an average daily jail population of around half-a-million persons, and revealed that the number of jail inmates per 100,000 U.S. residents was 188—almost double what it had been ten years earlier. Not surprisingly, the nation's most populous states tend to have the most inmates. In 1995, for example, almost half of the nation's jail population was housed in the jails of five states:[39] California (with 62,298 jail inmates), Texas (55,395), Florida (34,183), New York (29,809), and Georgia (22,663). Some states, however, report a much higher rate of growth in the use of local confinement facilities than others. NIJ reports that jail populations in Texas grew by 264 percent in the ten years between 1985 and 1995, and increased 103 percent in Maryland—while growing only slightly in Maine, Missouri, Nebraska, and Wyoming. Some states, such as Louisiana (with 377 jail inmates per every 100,000 residents), Georgia (328 per 100,000), and Texas (307 per 100,000), show a high *rate* of jail usage, whereas other states, such as Iowa, Maine, and North Dakota (with only 57 jail inmates per 100,000 state residents), and Minnesota, Montana, and South Dakota (with around 81 per 100,000) make less use of jail.[40]

Most people processed through the country's jails are members of minority groups (61 percent), with 44 percent of jail inmates classifying themselves as black, 15 percent as Hispanic, and another 2 percent as minorities belonging to other races. Thirty-nine percent of jail inmates classify themselves as white. Ninety percent are male.[41]

Women and Jail

Although women compose only 10 percent of the country's jail population,[42] they are "virtually the largest growth group in jails nationwide."[43] Jailed women face a number of special problems. Only 25.7 percent of the nation's jails report having a classification system specifically designed to evaluate female inmates,[44] and, although "a large proportion of jurisdictions" report plans "to build facilities geared to the female offender,"[45] not all jurisdictions today even provide separate housing areas for female inmates. Educational levels are very low among jailed women, and fewer than half are high school graduates.[46] Pregnancy is another problem. Nationally, 4 percent of female inmates are pregnant at the time they come to jail,[47] but as much as 10 percent of the female population of urban jails is reported to be pregnant on any given day.[48] As a consequence, a few hundred children are born in jails each year. Jailed mothers are not only separated from their children, they may have to pay for their support. Twelve percent of all jails in one study group reported requiring employed female inmates to contribute to the support of their dependent children.

Drug abuse is another significant source of difficulty for jailed women. More than 30 percent of women who are admitted to jail have a substance abuse problem at the time of admission, and in some parts of the country, that figure may be as high as 70 percent.[49] Adding to the problem is the fact that substantive medical programs for female inmates, such as obstetrics and gynecological care, are often lacking. In planning medical services for female inmates into the next century, some writers have advised jail administrators to expect to see an increasingly common kind of inmate: "[a]n opiate-addicted female who is pregnant with no prior prenatal care having one or more sexually transmitted diseases, and fitting a high-risk category for AIDS (prostitution, IV drug use)."[50]

Female inmates are only half the story. Women working in corrections are the other. In a recent study,[51] Linda Zupan, one of the new generation of outstanding jail scholars, found that women composed 22 percent of the correctional officer force in jails across the nation. The deployment of female personnel, however, was disproportionately skewed toward jobs in the lower ranks. Although 60 percent of all support staff (secretaries, cooks, and janitors) were women, only one in every ten chief administrators was female. Zupan explains this pattern by pointing to the "token-status" of women staff members in some of the nation's jails.[52] Even so, Zupan did find that women correctional employees were significantly committed to their careers and that attitudes of male workers toward female coworkers in jails were generally positive. Zupan's study uncovered 626 jails in which more than 50 percent of the correction officer force consisted of women. On the opposite side of the coin, 954 of the nation's 3,316 jails have no female officers.[53] As Zupan notes, "[a]n obvious problem associated with the lack of female officers in jails housing females concerns the potential for abuse and exploitation of women inmates by male staff."[54]

Jails which do hire women generally accord them equal footing with male staffers. Although cross-gender privacy is a potential area of legal liability, few jails limit the supervisory areas which may be visited by female officers working in male facilities. In three quarters of the jails studied by Zupan, women officers were assigned to supervise male housing areas. Only one in four jails which employed women restricted their access to unscreened shower and toilet facilities used by men or to other areas such as sexual offender units.

Crowding in Jails

Jails have been called the "shame of the criminal justice system." Many are old, overcrowded, poorly funded, scantily staffed by underpaid and poorly trained employees, and given low priority in local budgets. Court-ordered caps on jail populations are increasingly common. A few years ago, for example, the Harris County Jail in Houston, Texas, was forced to release 250 inmates after missing a deadline for reducing its resident population of 6,100 people.[55] A nationwide survey, published by the Bureau of Justice Statistics in 1991, found that 46 percent of all jails were built more than 25 years ago, and of that percentage, over half were more than 50 years old.[56]

Overcrowded jails have become a critical issue throughout the justice system.[57] A 1983 national census revealed that jails were operating at only 85 percent

Children whose mothers are behind bars in a Rhode Island facility await their turn to visit. Women in jail face special problems, many of which are associated with child care. Photo by Gale Zucker, courtesy of Stock Boston.

of their rated capacity.[58] By 1990, however, the nation's jails were running at 108 percent of capacity, and new jails could be found on drawing boards and under construction across the country. By 1994, new facilities had opened, and overall jail occupancy was reported at 97 percent of rated capacity although some individual facilities were desperately overcrowded.[59] With square footage per inmate averaging only 58.3[60] in jails, managers still cite crowding and staff shortages as the two most critical problems facing jails today.[61]

The root cause of jail crowding can be found in a growing crime rate coupled with a punitive public attitude which has heavily influenced correctional practice. In 1995, for example, Maricopa County, Arizona, sheriff Joe Arpaio added 25 tents to 42 others he had ordered erected 2 years earlier in the desert outside Phoenix to relieve overcrowding in the county jail.[62] Arpaio, faced with 1,900 more inmates than his 3,900-capacity jail could handle, built the tent city with help from a volunteer posse, whose members work for free and pay for their own uniforms and guns. Temperatures in the desert jail, which is without air conditioning, soar to well over 100 degrees in the summertime, and wind-blown sand makes life difficult for inmates. In what some see as adding insult to injury, the tough-talking sheriff runs the desert jail frugally—replacing hot inmate meals with bologna sandwiches, and requiring inmates to cut one another's hair in order to save on barber's fees. He's also put an end to violent television, forcing inmates to watch shows like "Lassie" and "Donald Duck," rather than ones with shoot-em'-up themes.

Overcrowded prisons have also spilled over into jails. During the last few years, many states have begun using jails instead of prisons for the confinement of convicted felons, exacerbating the jail crowding problem still further. In 1993, for example, 34,200 inmates were being held in local jails because of crowding in state prisons. Another problem arises from the sentencing of individuals who are unable to make restitution, alimony, or child care payments to jail time—a practice which has made the local lockup at least partially a debtor's prison. Symptomatic of problems brought on by overcrowding, the National Institute of Justice reported 234 suicides in jails across the nation during a recent year.[63] Jail deaths from all causes (which totaled 647 nationwide in 1993) are shown in Figure 11-3.

Although the societal underpinnings of overcrowding are difficult to assess, some causes of jail crowding which can be immediately addressed include the following:[64]

✔ The inability of jail inmates to make bond because of institutionalized bail bond practices and lack of funding sources for indigent defendants
✔ Unnecessary delays between arrest and final case disposition
✔ Unnecessarily limited access to vital information about defendants which could be useful in facilitating court-ordered pretrial release
✔ The limited ability of the criminal justice system to handle cases expeditiously because of a lack of needed resources (judges, assistant prosecuting attorneys, and so on)

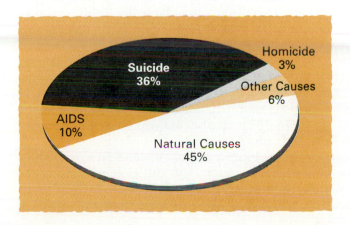

FIGURE 11-3
Causes of jail deaths, U.S. totals, 1993. Source: U.S. Department of Justice, "The Nation's Jails Hold Record 490,442 Inmates," NIJ press release (April 30, 1995).

✔ Inappropriate attorney delays in moving cases through court (motions to delay cases as part of an attorney's strategy, and so on)

✔ Unproductive statutes requiring that specified nonviolent offenders be jailed (including those requiring mandatory pretrial jailing of DWIs, minor drug offenders, second offense shoplifting, and so on)

Some innovative jurisdictions have already substantially reduced jail crowding. San Diego, California, for example, uses a privately operated detoxification reception program in order to divert many inebriates from the proverbial "drunk tank."[65] Officials in Galveston County, Texas, routinely divert mentally ill arrestees directly to a mental health facility.[66] Other areas use pretrial services and magistrates offices which are open 24 hours a day for the purpose of setting bail, making release possible.

*D*irect Supervision Jails. Temporary confinement facilities which eliminate many of the traditional barriers between inmates and correctional staff. Physical barriers in direct supervision jails are far less common than in traditional jails, allowing staff members the opportunity for greater interaction with, and control over, residents.

Direct Supervision Jails

Some authors have suggested that the problems found in many jails today stem from "mismanagement, lack of fiscal support, heterogeneous inmate populations, overuse and misuse of detention, overemphasis on custodial goals, and political and public apathy."[67] Others propose that environmental and organizational elements inherent in traditional jail architecture and staffing have given rise to today's difficulties.[68] Traditional jails, say these observers, were built on the assumption that inmates are inherently violent and potentially destructive. Hence, most of today's jails were constructed to give staff maximum control over inmates—through the use of thick walls, bars, and other architectural barriers to the free movement of inmates. Such institutions, however, also limit the correctional staff's visibility and access to many confinement areas. As a consequence, they tend to encourage just the kinds of inmate behavior that jails were meant to control. Inefficient hallway patrols and expensive video technology help in overcoming the limits that old jail architecture places on supervision.

In an effort to solve many of the problems which have dogged jails in the past, a new jail management strategy emerged during the 1980s. Called **direct supervision** (or podular/direct supervision, or PDS), this contemporary approach "joins podular/unit architecture with a participative, proactive management philosophy."[69] Often built in a system of "pods," or modular self-contained housing areas linked to one another, direct supervision jails eliminate the old physical barriers which separated staff and inmates. Gone are bars and isolated secure observation areas for officers. They are replaced by an open environment, in which inmates and correctional personnel mingle with relative freedom. In a growing number of such "new-generation" jails, large reinforced Plexiglas panels have supplanted walls and serve to separate activity areas, such as classrooms and dining halls, from one another. Soft furniture is often found throughout these institutions, and individual rooms take the place of cells, allowing inmates at least a modicum of personal privacy. In today's direct supervision jails, 16 to 46 inmates typically live in one pod, with correctional staffers present among the inmate population on an around-the-clock basis.

The first direct supervision jail opened in the 1970s in Contra Costa County, California. This 386-bed facility became a model for the nation, and other new-generation jails soon opened in Las Vegas; Portland; Reno; New York City; Bucks County, Pennsylvania; Vancouver, British Columbia; and Miami. The federal prison system opened PDS facilities in 1974–1975 in the Metropolitan Correctional Centers (MCCs) of San Diego, New York, and Chicago.

Direct supervision jails have been touted for their tendency to reduce inmate dissatisfaction and for their ability to deter rape and violence among the inmate population. By eliminating architectural barriers to staff–inmate interaction, direct supervision facilities are said to place officers back in control of institutions. Although these innovative facilities are still too new to assess fully, a number of studies have already demonstrated their success at reducing the likelihood of inmate victimization. One such study,[70] published in 1994, found that staff morale in direct supervision jails was far higher than in traditional institutions, while inmates reported reduced stress levels, and fewer inmate-on-inmate and inmate-on-staff assaults occurred in podular jails. Similarly, sexual assault, jail rape, suicide, and escape have all been found to occur far less frequently in direct supervision facilities than in traditional institutions.[71] Significantly, new-generation jails appear to reduce substantially the number of lawsuits brought by inmates and lower the incidence of adverse court-ordered judgments against jail administrators.

The most comprehensive study of direct supervision jails to date, which reported its results in April 1995, found that 114 confinement facilities across the country could be classified as direct supervision facilities.[72] The study, which attempted to survey all such jails, found that direct supervision jails:

1. Range in size from small jails with 24 inmates (and 12 officers on staff) to large facilities with 2,737 inmates (and 600 correctional officers).
2. Average 591 inmates and employ 148 officers, with an inmate-to-officer ratio of 16.8:1 during a given shift.
3. Are podular in design, with an average of 47 inmates and 1 officer per pod at any given time.
4. Hold local, state, and federal prisoners. About 45 percent of the institutions surveyed held only local inmates, whereas the rest held mixed groups of inmates.
5. Varied by security level. The majority (about 59 percent) mixed security levels, whereas 26 percent were maximum security jails. About 13 percent described themselves as medium security facilities, and another 2 percent fit within the minimum security category.
6. Were usually unionized. About 70 percent of direct supervision jails reported unionized staffs.

Although the number of direct supervision jails seems to be rapidly growing, such facilities are not without their problems. In 1993, for example, the 238-bed Rensselaer County PDS jail in Troy, New York, experienced a disturbance "that resulted in a total loss of control...removal of officers from the pods...and the escape of two inmates."[73] Somewhat later, the 700-bed San Joaquin County Jail in Stockton, California, experienced numerous problems, including the escape of 7 inmates.

Some authors[74] have recognized that new-generation jails are too frequently run by old-style managers and that correctional personnel sometimes lack the training needed to make the transition to the new style of supervision. Others[75] have suggested that managers of direct supervision jails, especially those at the midlevel, could benefit from clearer job descriptions and additional training. In the words of one Canadian advocate of direct supervision,[76] "training becomes particularly critical in direct supervision jails where relationships are more immediate and are more complex." Finally, recommendations from those tasked with hiring[77] say that potential new staff members should be psychologically screened and that intensive use be made of preemployment interviews, in order to determine the suitability of applicants for correctional officer positions in direct supervision jails.

Jails and the Future

In contrast to more visible issues confronting the justice system, such as the death penalty, gun control, the war on drugs, and big-city gangs, jails have received relatively little attention from the media and have generally escaped close public scrutiny. National efforts, however, to improve the quality of jail life are under way. Some changes involve adding crucial programs for inmates. A recent American Jail

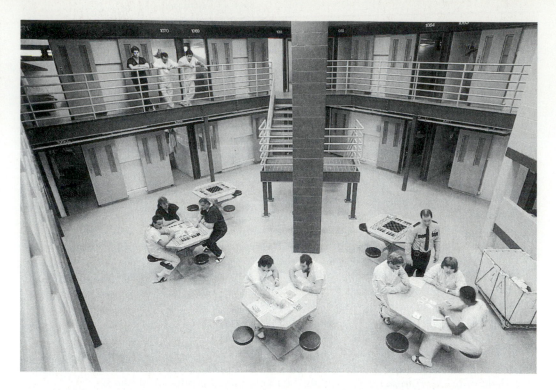

Inside a direct supervision jail. Inmates and officers can mingle in this Hillsborough County (New Hampshire) jail. Photo by Rick Friedman, courtesy of Black Star.

Association study of drug treatment programs in jails, for example, found that "a small fraction (perhaps less than 10 percent) of inmates needing drug treatment actually receive these services."[78] Follow-up efforts were aimed at developing standards to guide jails administrators in increasing the availability of drug treatment services to inmates.

Jail industries are another growing programmatic area. The best of them serve the community while training inmates in marketable skills.[79] In an exemplary effort to humanize its megajails,[80] for example, the Los Angeles County Sheriff's Department recently opened an inmate telephone answering service. Many calls are received by the Sheriff's Department daily, requesting information about a significant number of the county's 22,000 jail inmates. These requests for information were becoming increasingly difficult to handle because of the growing fiscal constraints facing local government. To handle the huge number of calls effectively without tying up sworn law enforcement personnel, the department began using inmates specially trained to handle incoming calls. Eighty inmates were assigned to the project, with groups of different sizes covering shifts throughout the day. Each inmate staffer went through a program designed to provide coaching in proper telephone procedures and to teach each operator how to run computer terminals containing routine data on the department's inmates. The new system is now fully in place and handles 4,000 telephone inquiries a day. The time needed to answer a call and provide information has dropped from 30 minutes under the old system to a remarkable 10 seconds today.

Another innovative program operates out of the Jackson County Detention Center (JCDC) in Kansas City, Missouri.[81] The JCDC began using citizen volunteers more than a decade ago. Today, 123 volunteers work in the facility—many of them as tutors in the general education program. Others offer substance abuse counseling, marriage counseling, and chaplain's services. Citizen volunteers have contributed 50,000 hours of service time during the past six years, at a value of more than half a million dollars.

Jail boot camps, like that run by the Harris County, Texas, probation department, are also growing in popularity. Boot camps in jail serve to give offenders who are sentenced to probationary terms a taste of confinement and the rigors of life behind bars. The Harris County CRIPP (Courts Regimented Intensive Probation Program) facility began operation in May 1991 and is located in Humble, Texas. Separate CRIPP programs are run for about 400 male and 50 female probationers.[82] The most recent study[83] of jail boot camps, which reported its findings in 1993, found only 10 such jail-based programs in the country although current numbers are probably higher.

Also capturing much recent attention are **regional jails**—that is, jails which are built and run using the combined resources of a variety of local jurisdictions and which have begun to replace smaller and often antiquated local jails in at least a few locations. One example of a regional jail is the Western Tidewater Regional Jail, serving the cities of Suffolk and Franklin, and the County of Isle of Wight in Virginia.[84] Regional jails, which are just beginning to come into their own, may develop more quickly in Virginia—where the state, recognizing the economies of consolidation, offers to reimburse localities up to 50 percent of the cost of building regional jails.

One final element in the unfolding saga of jail development should be mentioned: the emergence of state jail standards. Thirty-two states have set standards for municipal and county jails.[85] In 25 states, those standards are mandatory. The purpose of jail standards is to identify some basic minimum level of conditions necessary for inmate health and safety. On a national level, the Commission on Accreditation for Corrections, operated jointly by the American Correctional Association and the federal government, has developed its own set of jail standards,[86] as has the National Sheriff's Association. Both sets of standards are designed to ensure a minimal level of comfort and safety in local lockups. Increased standards, though, are costly. Local jurisdictions, already hard-pressed to meet other budgetary demands, will probably be slow to upgrade their jails to meet such external guidelines, unless forced to. Ken Kerle, in a study[87] of 61 jails which was designed to test compliance with National Sheriff's Association guidelines, discovered that in many standards areas—especially those of tool control, armory planning, community resources, release preparation, and riot planning—the majority of jails were sorely out of compliance. Lack of a written plan was the most commonly cited reason for failing to meet the standards.

In what may be one of the best set of recommendations for the development of jails which can serve into the next century, Joel A. Thompson and G. Larry Mays[88] suggest that (1) states should provide financial aid or incentives to local governments for jail construction and renovation, (2) all states must develop mandatory jail standards, (3) mandatory jail inspections should become commonplace in the enforcement of standards, (4) citizens should be educated about the function and significance of jails to increase their willingness to fund new jail construction, (5) all jails need to have written policies and procedures to be used in training and to serve as a basis for a defense against lawsuits, and (6) "[c]ommunities should explore alternatives to incarceration [because]…[m]any jail detainees are not threats to society and should not occupy scarce and expensive cell space."

Private Prisons

Some states have begun to supplement their prison resources through contracts with private firms to provide custodial and other correctional services. (Interest in the **privatization** of local jails is also on the increase although few privately run jails exist as of this writing.) The aim is to reduce overcrowding, lower operating expenses, and avoid lawsuits targeted at state officials and employees. Corrections Corporation of America (CCA) was one of the first companies to offer privately operated correctional facilities to states. In 1985, CCA made an unsuccessful bid to assume operation of the entire Tennessee prison system and now

Theory into Practice: American Jail Association
Code of Ethics for Jail Officers

As an officer employed in a detention/correctional capacity, I swear (or affirm) to be a good citizen and a credit to my community, state, and nation at all times. I will abstain from all questionable behavior which might bring disrepute to the agency for which I work, my family, my community, and my associates. My lifestyle will be above and beyond reproach and I will constantly strive to set an example of a professional who performs his/her duties according to the laws of our country, state, and community and the policies, procedures, written and verbal orders, and regulations of the agency for which I work.

ON THE JOB I PROMISE TO:

Keep
The institution secure so as to safeguard my community and the lives of the staff, inmates, and visitors on the premises.

Work
With each individual firmly and fairly without regard to rank, status, or condition.

Maintain
A positive demeanor when confronted with stressful situations of scorn, ridicule, danger, and/or chaos.

Report
Either in writing or by word of mouth to the proper authorities those things which should be reported, and keep silent about matters which are to remain confidential according to the laws and rules of the agency and government.

Manage
And supervise the inmates in an even-handed and courteous manner.

Refrain
At all times from becoming personally involved in the lives of the inmates and their families.

Treat
All visitors to the jail with politeness and respect and do my utmost to ensure that they observe the jail regulations.

Take
Advantage of all education and training opportunities designed to assist me to become a more competent officer.

Communicate
With people in or outside of the jail, whether by phone, written word, or word of mouth, in such a way so as not to reflect in a negative manner upon my agency.

Contribute
To a jail environment which will keep the inmate involved in activities designed to improve his/her attitude and character.

Support
All activities of a professional nature through membership and participation that will continue to elevate the status of those who operate our nation's jails.

Do my best through word and deed to present an image to the public at large of a jail professional, committed to progress for an improved and enlightened criminal justice system.

SOURCE: The American Jail Association, *Code of Ethics for Jail Officers* as adopted January 10, 1991. (Hagerstown, Md., The Association, 1991). Reprinted with permission.

operates a few dozen facilities across the country, including a halfway house for the Federal Bureau of Prisons.[89] In 1986, U.S. Corrections Corporation, another private firm, opened a 300-bed minimum security facility in Kentucky. By the late 1980s, more than 1,900 prisoners were held in privately operated secure correctional facilities.[90] The movement toward privatization of prisons rests on sound historical ground. State-run prisons have contracted with private industry for food, psychological testing, training, recreational, and other services in the past, and it is estimated that today more than three dozen states rely on private businesses to serve a variety of correctional needs.[91]

Many hurdles remain before the privatization movement can effectively provide large-scale custodial supervision. The Theory into Practice box on page 367 addresses some of the questions about the movement toward **private prisons**. One of the most significant barriers to privatization lies in the fact that some states have old laws which prohibit private involvement in correctional management. Other practical hurdles exist. States which do contract with private firms may face the

Theory into Practice: The Debate Over Private Prisons—Some Questions Which Remain

✔ Can the government delegate its powers to incarcerate persons to a private firm?

✔ Can a private firm deprive persons of their liberty and exercise coercive authority, perhaps through use of deadly force?

✔ Who would be legally liable in the event of lawsuits?

✔ Who would be responsible for maintaining the prison if the private employees go on strike?

✔ Would a private company have the right to refuse to accept certain types of inmates, for example, those with AIDS?

✔ If a private firm went bankrupt, who would be responsible for the inmates and the facility?

✔ Could a private company reduce staff salaries or hire nonunion members as a way of reducing costs?

✔ Would the "profit motive" operate to the detriment of the government or the inmates, either by keeping inmates in prison who should be released or by reducing services to a point at which inmates, guards, and the public were endangered?

✔ What options would a government with no facility of its own have if it became dissatisfied with the performance of the private firm?

✔ Is it appropriate for the government to circumvent the public's right to vote to increase its debt ceiling?

SOURCE: Bureau of Justice Statistics. *Report to the Nation on Crime and Justice,* 2nd ed. (Washington, D.C.: U.S. Department of Justice, 1988).

specter of strikes by guards, who do not come under state laws restricting the ability of employees to strike. Moreover, since responsibility for the protection of inmate rights still lies with the state, their liability will not transfer to private corrections.[92] In today's legal climate, it is unclear whether a state can shield itself or its employees through private prison contracting, but it would appear that such shielding is unlikely to be recognized by the courts. To limit liability, states will probably have to oversee private operations as well as set standards for training and custody.

Opponents of the movement toward privatization claim that cost reductions can be achieved only through lowered standards for the treatment of prisoners. They fear a return to the inhumane conditions of early jails, as private firms seek to turn prisons into profit-making operations. For states which do choose to contract with private firms, the National Institute of Justice recommends a "regular and systematic sampling" of former inmates to appraise prison conditions, as well as "on-site inspections at least every year" of each privately run institution. State personnel serving as monitors should be stationed in large facilities, and a "meticulous review" of all services should be conducted prior to the contract renewal date.[93]

Summary

"Doing time for crime" has become society's response to many who violate the criminal law. Even so, questions remain about the conditions of imprisonment in contemporary prisons and jails, and modern corrections is far from a panacea. The security orientation of correctional staff and administration leaves little room for capable treatment programs. Existing prisons are overcrowded, and new ones are expensive to build. An end to crowding is nowhere in sight, and a new "get tough" era influencing today's prison policy continues to swell prison populations even as it reduces inmate privileges. Studies demonstrating the likelihood of recidivism among prior correctional clients have called the whole correctional process into question, and the new get-tough era may reflect more a strategy of frustration than of hope.

Prisons today exist in a kind of limbo. As prison populations grow, uncertainties about the usefulness of treatment have left few officials confident of their ability to rehabilitate offenders. The return of prison industries, the interest in efficient technologies of secure imprisonment, and court-mandated reforms are all signs that society has given up any hope of large-scale reformation among inmate populations.

Discussion Questions

1. What do you think is the future of prisons? Describe the future you envision. On what do you base your predictions?
2. What do you see as the role of private prisons? What will be the state of private prisons two decades from now?
3. Explain the pros and cons of the emerging "get-tough" era in corrections. Do you believe that new rehabilitative models will be developed which will make get-tough policies a thing of the past? If so, on what will they be based?
4. What solutions, if any, do you see to the present overcrowded conditions of many prison systems? How might changes in the law help ease overcrowding? Are such changes a workable strategy? Why or why not?

References

1. As cited in the National Conference on Prison Industries, *Discussions and Recommendations* (Washington, D.C.: U.S. Government Printing Office, 1986), p. 23.
2. Allen J. Beck and Darrell K. Gilliard, *Prisoners in 1994* (Washington, D.C.: Bureau of Justice Statistics, August 1995).
3. Ibid.
4. Ibid.
5. "Prison Expansion Nears Completion," United Press International Southwest edition, online, June 12, 1995.
6. Allen J. Beck and Darrell K. Gilliard, *Prisoners in 1994* (Washington, D.C.: Bureau of Justice Statistics, August 1995).
7. Ibid.
8. Ibid.
9. Bureau of Justice Statistics, *National Corrections Reporting Program, 1985* (Washington, D.C.: BJS, December 1990), p. 14.
10. Ibid., p. 54.
11. Ibid.
12. American Correctional Association, *1993 Directory of Juvenile and Adult Correctional Departments, Institutions, Agencies, and Paroling Authorities* (Laurel, Md.: ACA, 1993).
13. American Correctional Association, "Correctional Officers in Adult Systems," *Vital Statistics in Corrections* (Laurel, Md.: ACA, 1991), p. 30.
14. Ibid., p. 73.
15. Ibid, p. 30. Note: "Other" minorities round out the percentages to a total of 100 percent.
16. U.S. Department of Justice, *Report to the Nation on Crime and Justice*, 2nd ed. (Washington, D.C.: U.S. Government Printing Office, 1988), p. 123.
17. American Correctional Association, "Correctional Officers in Adult Systems," *Vital Statistics in Corrections* (Laurel, MD: ACA, 1991), p.11.
18. Robert M. Carter, Richard A. McGee, and E. Kim Nelson, *Corrections in America* (Philadelphia: J. B. Lippincott, 1975), pp. 122–123.
19. George and Camille Camp, "Stopping Escapes: Perimeter Security," National Institute of Justice, *Construction Bulletin* (August 1987).
20. Adopted from Gloria A. Grizzle, et al., "Measuring Corrections Performance," NIJ Grant Number 78-NI-AX-0130, 1980, p. 31.
21. U.S. Bureau of Prisons.
22. An older system, in which the terms *Level 1*, *Level 2*, and so forth were used, was abandoned around 1990 and officially replaced with the new terminology used here.
23. Most of the information in this section comes from telephone conversations with and faxed information from the Federal Bureau of Prisons, August 25, 1995.
24. For additional information see Dennis Cauchon, "The Alcatraz of the Rockies," *USA Today*, November 16, 1994, p. 6A.
25. The Federal Bureau of Prisons daily count

stood at 89,856 on August 17, 1995. When all inmates for whom the Bureau is responsible were counted (including juveniles, those in jail, and inmates under home confinement) the total daily population under FBP control on August 17, 1995 was 100,315.

26. "Congress OKs Inmates Fees to Offset Costs of Prison," *Criminal Justice Newsletter*, October 15, 1992, p. 6.

27. National Institute of Corrections, "National Academy of Corrections: Outreach Training Programs" (July 1987).

28. National Institute of Corrections, "Correc-al Training Programs" (July 1987).

29. U.S. Department of Justice, "The Nation's Jails Hold Record 490,442 Inmates," National Institute of Justice Press release, April 30, 1995.

30. Craig A. Perkins, James J. Stephan, and Allen J. Beck, *Jails and Jail Inmates 1993-94* (Washington, D.C.: Bureau of Justice Statistics, April 1995).

31. U.S. Dept. of Justice, Bureau of Justice Statistics, *BJS Data Report, 1988* (Washington, D.C.: U.S. Government Printing Office, April 1989), p. 62.

32. Craig A. Perkins, James J. Stephan, and Allen J. Beck, *Jails and Jail Inmates 1993-94* (Washington, D.C.: Bureau of Justice Statistics, April 1995).

33. *BJS Data Report*, p. 63.

34. Craig A. Perkins, James J. Stephan, and Allen J. Beck, *Jails and Jail Inmates 1993-94* (Washington, D.C.: Bureau of Justice Statistics, April 1995).

35. Ibid.

36. Ibid.

37. U.S. Department of Justice, *Report to the Nation on Crime and Justice*, 2nd ed., p. 106.

38. Ibid.

39. U.S. Department of Justice, "The Nation's Jails Hold Record 490,442 Inmates."

40. Ibid.

41. Ibid.

42. Ibid.

43. William Reginald Mills and Heather Barrett, "Meeting the Special Challenge of Providing Health Care to Women Inmates in the '90's," *American Jails*, Vol. 4, no. 3. (September–October, 1990), p. 55.

44. American Correctional Association, *The Female Offender: What Does the Future Hold?* (Washington, D.C.: St. Mary's Press, 1990), p. 14.

45. Ibid., p. 21.

46. Ibid.

47. American Correctional Association, *Vital Statistics in Corrections*.

48. Mills and Barrett, "Meeting the Special Challenge," p. 55.

49. Ibid.

50. Ibid.

51. Linda L. Zupan "Women Corrections Officers in the Nation's Largest Jails," *American Jails* (January–February 1991), pp. 59–62.

52. Ibid., p. 11.

53. Linda L. Zupan, "Women Corrections Officers in Local Jails," paper presented at the annual meeting of the Academy of Criminal Justice Sciences, Nashville, Tennessee, March 1991.

54. Ibid., p. 6.

55. "Jail Overcrowding in Houston Results in Release of Inmates," *Criminal Justice Newsletter*, October 15, 1990, p. 5.

56. Bureau of Justice Statistics, *Census of Local Jails, 1988* (Washington, D.C.: BJS, 1991), p. 31.

57. Katherine M. Jamieson and Timothy J. Flanagan, eds., *Sourcebook of Criminal Justice Statistics, 1988* (Washington, D.C.: U.S. Government Printing Office, 1989).

58. Ibid.

59. U.S. Department of Justice, *The Nation's Jails Hold Record 490,442 Inmates.*

60. Bureau of Justice Statistics, *Census of Local Jails, 1988*, (Washington, D.C.: BJS, 1991), p. 15.

61. Randall Guynes, *Nation's Jail Managers Assess Their Problems* (Washington, D.C.: National Institute of Justice, 1988).

62. Carol J. Casteneda, "Arizona Sheriff Walking Tall, But Some Don't Like His Style," *USA Today*, May 26, 1995, p. 7A.

63. U.S. Department of Justice, "The Nation's Jails Hold Record 490,442 Inmates."

64. As identified in George P. Wilson and Harvey L. McMurray, *System Assessment of Jail Overcrowding Assumptions*, paper presented at the annual meeting of the Academy of Criminal Justice Sciences, Nashville, Tennessee, March 1991.

65. Andy Hall, *Systemwide Strategies to Alleviate Jail Crowding* (Washington, D.C.: National Institute of Justice, 1987).

66. Ibid.

67. Linda L. Zupan and Ben A. Menke, "The New Generation Jail: An Overview," in Joel A. Thompson and G. Larry Mays, eds., *American Jails: Public Policy Issues* (Chicago: Nelson-Hall, 1991), p. 180.

68. Ibid.

69. Herbert R. Sigurdson, Billy Wayson, and Gail Funke, "Empowering Middle Managers of Direct Supervision Jails," *American Jails* (Winter 1990), p. 52.

70. Byron Johnson, "Exploring Direct Supervision: A Research Note," *American Jails*, March–April 1994, pp. 63–64.

71. H. Sigurdson, *The Manhattan House of Detention: A Study of Podular Direct Supervision* (Washington, D.C.: National Institute of Corrections, 1985). For similar conclusions, see: Robert Conroy, Wantland J.

Smith, Linda L. Zupan, "Officer Stress in the Direct Supervision Jail: A Preliminary Case Study," *American Jails* (November–December 1991), p. 36.

72. Brian Dawe and James Kirby, "Direct Supervision Jails and Minimum Staffing," *American Jails*, (March–April 1995), pp. 97–100.

73. W. Raymond Nelson and Russell M. Davis, "Popular Direct Supervision: The First Twenty Years," *American Jails*, July–August 1995, p. 17.

74. Jerry W. Fuqua, "New Generation Jails: Old Generation Management," *American Jails* (March–April 1991), pp. 80–83.

75. Sigurdson, Wayson, and Funke, "Empowering Middle Managers."

76. Duncan J. McCulloch and Time Stiles, "Technology and the Direct Supervision Jail," *American Jails* (Winter 1990), pp. 97–102.

77. Susan W. McCampbell, "Direct Supervision: Looking for the Right People," *American Jails* (November–December 1990), pp. 68–69.

78. Robert L. May II, Roger H. Peters, and William D. Kearns "The Extent of Drug Treatment Programs in Jails: A Summary Report," *American Jails* (September–October 1990), pp. 32–34.

79. See, for example, John W. Dietler, "Jail Industries: The Best Thing That Can Happen to a Sheriff," *American Jails* (July–August 1990), pp. 80–83.

80. Robert Osborne, "Los Angeles County Sheriff Opens New Inmate Answering Service," *American Jails* (July–August 1990), pp. 61–62.

81. Nancy E. Bond and Dave Smith, "The Challenge: Community Involvement in Corrections," *American Jails* (November–December 1992), pp. 19–20.

82. Robert J. Hunter, "A Locally Operated Boot Camp," *American Jails*, July–August 1994, pp. 13–15.

83. James Austin, Michael Jones, and Melissa Bolyard, "The Growing Use of Jail Boot Camps: The Current State of the Art," (Washington, D.C.: National Institute of Justice, October 1993).

84. See J. R. Dewan, "Regional Jail—The New Kid on the Block," *American Jails*, May–June 1995, pp. 70–72.

85. Tom Rosazza, "Jail Standards: Focus on Change," *American Jails* (November–December 1990), pp. 84–87.

86. American Correctional Association, *Manual of Standards for Adult Local Detention Facilities*, 3rd ed. (College Park, Md.: ACA, 1991).

87. Ken Kerle, "National Sheriff's Association Jail Audit Review," *American Jails* (Spring 1987), pp. 13–21.

88. Joel A. Thompson and G. Larry Mays, "Paying the Piper but Changing the Tune: Policy Changes and Initiatives for the American Jail," in Joel A. Thompson and G. Larry Mays, eds. *American Jails: Public Policy Issues* (Chicago: Nelson-Hall, 1991), pp. 240–246.

89. John J. DiIulio, Jr., "Private Prisons," National Institute of Justice *Crime File Study Guide* (no date).

90. Ibid., p. 1.

91. Bureau of Justice Statistics, *Report to the Nation on Crime and Justice*, p. 119. See also Judith C. Hackett et al., "Contracting for the Operation of Prisons and Jails," National Institute of Justice *Research in Brief* (June 1987), p. 2.

92. For a more detailed discussion of this issue, see Ira Robbins, *The Legal Dimensions of Private Incarceration* (Chicago: American Bar Foundation, 1988).

93. Hackett et al., "Contracting for the Operation of Prisons and Jails," p. 6.

CHAPTER 12

Prison Life

—*Photo by Armineh Johannes/SIPA Press*

*O*ur policy of confining large numbers of offenders seems to have been ineffective in reducing the violent crime rate.

**—JOHN H. KRAMER, EXECUTIVE DIRECTOR
PENNSYLVANIA COMMISSION ON SENTENCING**

*T*he person of a prisoner sentenced to imprisonment in the State prison is under the protection of the law, and any injury to his person, not authorized by law, is punishable in the same manner as if he were not convicted or sentenced.

—CALIFORNIA PENAL CODE, SECTION 2650

*W*e must remember always that the doors of prisons swing both ways.[1]

**—MARY BELLE HARRIS
FIRST FEDERAL WOMAN WARDEN**

KEY CONCEPTS

total institutions	prison subculture	prisonization
prison argot	hands-off doctrine	civil death
grievance procedure	balancing test	*writ of habeas corpus*

KEY CASES

Pell v. *Procunier*	*Houchins* v. *KQED*	*Katz* v. *U.S.*
Block v. *Rutherford*	*Johnson* v. *Avery*	*Estelle* v. *Gamble*
Bounds v. *Smith*	*Newman* v. *Alabama*	*Wolff* v. *McDonnell*
Ruiz v. *Estelle*	*Hudson* v. *Palmer*	*Jones* v. *North Carolina*
Cruz v. *Beto*	*Helling* v. *McKinney*	*Prisoner's Union*
Sandin v. *Conner*		

Realities of Prison Life—The Male Inmate's World

For the first 150 years of their existence, prisons and prison life could be described by the phrase "out of sight, out of mind." Very few citizens cared about prison conditions, and those unfortunate enough to be locked away were regarded as lost to the world. By the mid-1900s, beginning with the treatment era, such attitudes started to change. Concerned citizens began to offer their services to prison administrations, neighborhoods began accepting work-release prisoners and halfway houses, and social scientists initiated a serious study of prison life.

This chapter describes the realities of prison life today, including prisoner lifestyles, prison subcultures, sexuality in prison, prison violence, and inmate "rights" and grievance procedures. We will discuss both the world of the inmate and the staff world. A separate section on women in prison details the social structure of women's prisons, daily life in such facilities, and the various types of female inmates. We turn now to early research on prison life and will quickly move on to a discussion of the inmate world.

Research on Prison Life—Total Institutions

Total Institutions. Enclosed facilities, separated from society both socially and physically, where the inhabitants share all aspects of their lives on a daily basis.

Hans Reimer, then chairman of the Department of Sociology at Indiana University, set the tone for studies of prison life in 1935 when he voluntarily served three months in prison as an incognito participant observer.[2] Reimer reported the results of his studies to the American Prison Association, stimulating many other, though less spectacular, efforts to examine prison life. Other early studies include Donald Clemmer's *The Prison Community* (1940),[3] Gresham M. Sykes's *The Society of Captives: A Study of a Maximum Security Prison* (1958),[4] Richard A. Cloward and Donald R. Cressey's *Theoretical Studies in Social Organization of the Prison* (1960), and Donald R. Cressey's *The Prison: Studies in Institutional Organization and Change* (1961).[5]

These studies and others focused primarily on maximum security prisons for men. They treated correctional institutions as formal or complex organizations and employed the analytical techniques of organizational sociology, industrial psychology, and administrative science.[6] As modern writers on prisons have observed: "[t]he prison was compared to a primitive society, isolated from the outside world, functionally integrated by a delicate system of mechanisms, which kept it precariously balanced between anarchy and accommodation."[7]

Another approach to the study of prison life was developed by Erving Goffman, who coined the term **total institutions** in a 1961 study of prisons and mental hospitals.[8] Goffman described total institutions as places where the same people work, play, eat, sleep, and recreate together on a daily basis. Such places include prisons, concentration camps, mental hospitals, seminaries, and other facilities in which residents are cut off from the larger society either forcibly or willingly. Total institutions are small societies. They evolve their own distinctive values and styles of life, and place pressures on residents to fulfill rigidly proscribed behavioral roles.

Generally speaking, the work of prison researchers built on findings of other social scientists who discovered that any group with similar characteristics, subject to confinement in the same place at the same time, develops its own subculture with specific components that govern hierarchy, behavioral patterns, values, and so on. Prison subcultures, described in the next section, also provide the medium through which prison values are communicated and expectations made known.

Prison Subcultures

Two social realities coexist in prison settings. One is the official structure of rules and procedures put in place by the wider society and enforced by prison staff. The other is the more informal, but decidedly more powerful, inmate world. The inmate world, best described by its pervasive immediacy in the lives of inmates, is controlled by **prison subculture**. The realities of prison life—including a large and often densely packed inmate population which must look to the prison environment for all its needs—mean that prison subculture is not easily subject to the control of prison authorities.

Prison subcultures develop independently of the plans of prison administrators, and inmates entering prison discover a social world not mentioned in the handbooks prepared by correctional staff. Inmate concerns, values, roles, and even language weave a web of social reality into which new inmates step, and in which they must participate. Those who try to remain aloof soon find themselves subjected to dangerous ostracism and may even be suspected of being in league with the prison administration.

The socialization of new inmates into the prison subculture has been described as a process of prisonization.[9] **Prisonization** refers to the learning of convict values, attitudes, roles, and even language. When the process is complete, new inmates have become "cons." The values of the inmate social system are embodied in a code whose violations can produce sanctions ranging from ostracism and avoidance to physical violence and homicide.[10] Sykes and Messinger[11] recognize five elements of the prison code:

1. Don't interfere with the interests of other inmates. Never rat on a con.
2. Don't lose your head. Play it cool and do your own time.
3. Don't exploit inmates. Don't steal. Don't break your word. Be right.
4. Don't whine. Be a man.
5. Don't be a sucker. Don't trust the guards or staff.

Stanton Wheeler closely examined the concept of prisonization in a study of the Washington State Reformatory.[12] Wheeler found that the degree of prisonization experienced by inmates tends to vary over time. He described changing levels of inmate commitment to prison norms and values by way of a "U-shaped" curve. When an inmate first enters prison, Wheeler said, the conventional values of outside society are of paramount importance. As time passes, the lifestyle of the prison is adopted. However, within the half-year prior to release, most inmates begin to demonstrate a renewed appreciation for conventional values.

Different prisons share aspects of a common inmate culture[13] so that prison-wise inmates who enter a new facility far from their home will already know the ropes. **Prison argot**, or language, provides one example of how widespread prison subculture can be. The terms used to describe inmate roles in one institution are generally understood in others. The word *rat*, for example, is prison slang for an informer. Popularized by crime movies of the 1950s, the term *rat* is understood today by members of the wider society. Other words common to prison argot are shown in the accompanying Theory into Practice box.

Some criminologists have suggested that inmate codes are simply a reflection of general criminal values. If so, they are brought to the institution rather than created there. Either way, the power and pervasiveness of the inmate code require convicts to conform to the world view held by the majority of prisoners.

The Evolution of Subcultures

Prison subculture is constantly changing. Like any other American subculture, it evolves to reflect the concerns and experiences of the wider culture, reacting to new crime control strategies and embracing novel opportunities for crime

Prison Subculture. The values and behavioral patterns characteristic of prison inmates. Prison subculture has been found to have surprising consistencies across the country.

Prisonization. The process whereby newly institutionalized individuals come to accept prison lifestyles and criminal values. Although many inmates begin their prison experience with only a modicum of values supportive of criminal behavior, the socialization experience they undergo while incarcerated leads to a much wider acceptance of such values.

Prison Argot. The slang characteristic of prison subcultures and prison life.

Theory into Practice: Prison Argot—The Language of Confinement

Writers who have studied prison life often comment on the use by prisoners of a special language or *argot*. This language generally refers to the roles assigned by prison culture to types of inmates as well as to prison activities. This box lists words identified in past studies by various authors. The first group of words are characteristic of male prisons; the last few words have been used in prisons for women.

Rat: An inmate who squeals (provides information about other inmates to the prison administration).

Gorilla: The inmate who uses force to take what he wants from others.

Merchant (or peddler): One who sells when he should give.

Fish: The newly arrived inmate.

Wolf: The male inmate who assumes the aggressive masculine role during homosexual relations.

Punk: The male inmate who is forced into a submissive or feminine role during homosexual relations.

Fag: The male inmate who is believed to be a "natural" or "born" homosexual.

Lemon Squeezer: The inmate who has an unattractive "girlfriend."

Screw: Guard.

Stud Broad (or Daddy): The female inmate who assumes the role of a male during lesbian relations.

Femme (or Mommy): The female inmate who plays the female role during lesbian relations.

Cherry (or Cherrie): The female inmate who has not yet been introduced to lesbian activities.

Fay Broad: A white female inmate.

Sources: Gresham Sykes, *The Society of Captives* (Princeton, N.J.: Princeton University Press, 1958); Rose Giallombardo, *Society of Women: A Study of a Woman's Prison* (New York: John Wiley, 1966); and Richard A. Cloward et al., *Theoretical Studies in Social Organization of the Prison* (New York: Social Science Research Council, 1960).

and its commission. The AIDS epidemic of the last two decades, for example, has brought about changes in prison sexual behavior, at least for a segment of the inmate population, and the emergence of a high-tech criminal group has further differentiated convict types. Because of such changes, John Irwin, by the time he was about to complete his now-famous study entitled *The Felon* (1970), expressed worry that his book was already obsolete.[14] *The Felon*, for all its insights into prison subculture, follows in the descriptive tradition of works by Clemmer and Reimer. Irwin recognized that by 1970 prison subcultures had begun to reflect cultural changes sweeping America. A decade later, other investigators of prison subculture were able to write: "It was no longer meaningful to speak of a single inmate culture or even subculture. By the time we began our field research…it was clear that the unified, oppositional convict culture, found in the sociological literature on prisons, no longer existed."[15]

Stastny and Tyrnauer, describing prison life at Washington State Penitentiary in 1982, discovered four clearly distinguishable subcultures: (1) official, (2) traditional, (3) reform, and (4) revolutionary. Official culture was promoted by the staff and by administrative rules of the institution. Enthusiastic participants in official culture were mostly correctional officers and other staff members although inmates were also well aware of the normative expectations official culture imposed on them. Official culture affected the lives of inmates primarily through the creation of a prisoner hierarchy based on sentence length, prison jobs, and the "perks" which cooperation with the dictates of official culture could produce. Traditional prison culture, described by early writers on the subject, still existed, but its participants spent much of their time lamenting the decline of the convict code among younger prisoners. Reform culture was unique at Washington State Penitentiary. It was the result of a brief experiment with inmate self-government during the early 1970s. Elements of prison life which evolved during the experimental period sometimes survived the termination of self-government and were eventually institutionalized in what Stastny and Tyrnauer call reform culture. Such elements included inmate participation in civic-style clubs, citizen involvement in the daily activities of the prison, banquets, and inmate speaking tours. Revolutionary culture built on the radical political rhetoric of the disenfranchised and found a ready audience among minority prisoners who saw themselves as victims of society's basic unfairness. Although they did not participate in it, revolutionary inmates understood traditional prison culture and generally avoided running afoul of its rules.

The Functions of Prison Society

How do social scientists and criminologists explain the existence of prison societies? Although people around the world live in groups and create their own cultures, in few cases does the intensity of human interaction approach the level found in prisons. As we discussed in Chapter 11, today's prisons are overcrowded places where inmates can find no retreat from the constant demands of staff and the pressures brought by fellow prisoners. Prison subculture, according to some authors, is fundamentally an adaptation to deprivation and confinement. It is a way of addressing the psychological, social, physical, and sexual needs of prisoners living within the context of a highly controlled and regimented institutional setting.

What are some of the deprivations prisoners experience? In *The Society of Captives*, Gresham Sykes calls felt deprivations the "pains of imprisonment."[16] The pains of imprisonment—the frustrations induced by the rigors of confinement—form the nexus of a deprivation model of prison culture. Sykes said that prisoners are deprived of (1) liberty, (2) goods and services, (3) heterosexual relationships, (4) autonomy, and (5) personal security, and that these deprivations lead to the development of subcultures intended to ameliorate the personal pains which accompany them.

In contrast to the deprivation model, the importation model of prison culture suggests that inmates bring with them values, roles, and behavior patterns from the outside world. Such external values, second nature as they are to career offenders, depend substantially on the criminal world view. When offenders are confined, these external elements shape the inmate social world.

The social structure of the prison, a concept that refers to accepted and relatively permanent social arrangements, is another element which shapes prisoner subculture. Donald Clemmer's early prison study recognized nine structural dimensions of inmate society. He said that prison society could be described in terms of:[17]

1. The prisoner/staff dichotomy
2. The three general classes of prisoners
3. Work gangs and cellhouse groups
4. Racial groups
5. Type of offense
6. The power of inmate "politicians"
7. Degree of sexual abnormality
8. The record of repeat offenses
9. Personality differences due to preprison socialization

Clemmer's nine structural dimensions are probably still descriptive of prison life today. When applied in individual situations, they designate an inmate's position in the prison "pecking order" and create expectations of the appropriate role for that person. Prison roles serve to satisfy the needs of inmates for power, sexual performance, material possessions, individuality, and personal pleasure—and to define the status of one prisoner relative to another. For example, inmate leaders, sometimes referred to as "real men" or "toughs" by prisoners in early studies, offer protection to those who live by the rules. They also provide for a redistribution of wealth inside prison and see to it that the rules of the complex prison-derived economic system—based on barter, gambling, and sexual favors—are observed.

Homosexuality in Prison

Homosexual behavior inside prisons is an important area which is both constrained and encouraged by prison subculture, and Sykes's early study of prison argot found many words describing homosexual activity. Among them were the terms *wolf, punk,* and *fag.* Wolves were aggressive men who assumed the masculine role in homosexual relations. Punks were forced into submitting to the female role, often by wolves. Fags described a special category of men who had a natural proclivity toward homosexual activity. Whereas both wolves and punks were fiercely committed to their heterosexual identity and participated in homosexuality only because of prison conditions, fags generally engaged in homosexual lifestyles before their entry into prison and continued to emulate feminine mannerisms and styles of dress once incarcerated.

Prison homosexuality depends to a considerable degree on the naiveté of young inmates experiencing prison for the first time. Older prisoners looking for homosexual liaisons may ingratiate themselves with new arrivals by offering cigarettes, money, drugs, food, or protection. At some future time these "loans" will be "called in," with payoffs demanded in sexual favors. Because the inmate code requires the repayment of favors, the "fish" who tries to resist may quickly find himself face to face with the brute force of inmate society.

Prison rape represents a special category of homosexual behavior behind bars. Estimates of the incidence of prison rape are both rare and dated. Those that are survey-based vary considerably in their findings. One such study found 4.7 percent of inmates in the Philadelphia prison system willing to report sexual assaults.[18] Another survey found that 28 percent of prisoners had been targets of sexual aggressors at least once during their institutional careers.[19]

Rape in prison is often the result of gang activity or of inmates working together to overcome the victim. Although not greatly different from other prisoners, a large proportion of sexual aggressors are characterized by low education and poverty, grew up in a broken home headed by the mother, and possess records for violent offenses. Victims of prison rape tend to be physically slight, young, white, nonviolent offenders from nonurban areas.[20] Lee Bowker, summarizing studies of sexual violence in prison,[21] provides the following observations:

1. Most sexual aggressors do not consider themselves to be homosexuals.
2. Sexual release is not the primary motivation for sexual attack.
3. Many aggressors must continue to participate in gang rapes in order to avoid becoming victims themselves.
4. The aggressors have themselves suffered much damage to their masculinity in the past.

As in cases of heterosexual rape, sexual assaults in prison are likely to leave psychological scars long after the physical event is over.[22] The victims of prison rape live in fear, may feel constantly threatened, and can turn to self-destructive activities.[23] At the very least, victims question their masculinity and undergo a personal devaluation. In some cases, victims of prison sexual attacks turn to violence. Frustrations, long bottled up through abuse and fear, may explode and turn the would-be rapist into a victim of prison homicide.

Prison Lifestyles and Inmate Types

Prison society is strict and often unforgiving. Even so, inmates are able to express some individuality through the choice of a prison lifestyle. John Irwin was the first well-known author to describe prison lifestyles, viewing them (like the subcultures of which they are a part) as adaptations to the prison environment.[24] Other writers have since elaborated on these coping mechanisms. Listed in the pages that follow are some of the types of prisoners described by commentators.

- *The Mean Dude.* Some inmates adjust to prison by being mean. They are quick to fight, and when they fight, they fight like wild men (or women). They give no quarter and seem to expect none in return. Other inmates know that such prisoners are best left alone. The mean dude receives frequent write-ups and spends much time in solitary confinement.

  The mean dude role is supported by the fact that some prisoners occupy it in prison as they did when they were free. Similarly, certain personality types, such as the psychopathic, may feel a natural attraction to this role. On the other hand, prison culture supports the role of the mean dude in two ways: (a) by expecting inmates to be tough and (b) through the prevalence of a type of wisdom which says that "only the strong survive" inside prison.

  A psychologist might say that the mean dude is acting out against the fact of captivity, striking out at anyone he (or she) can. This type of role performance is more common in male institutions and in maximum security prisons. It tends to become less common as inmates progress to lower security levels.

- *The Hedonist.* Some inmates build their lives around the limited pleasures which can be had within the confines of prison. The smuggling of contraband, homosexuality, gambling, drug running, and other officially condemned activities provide the center of interest for prison hedonists. Hedonists generally have an abbreviated view of the future, living only for the "now." Such a temporal orientation is probably characteristic of the personality type of all hedonists and exists in many persons, incarcerated or not.

- *The Opportunist.* The opportunist takes advantage of the positive experiences prison has to offer. Schooling, trade-training, counseling, and other self-improvement activities are the focal points of the opportunist's life in prison. Opportunists are the "do-gooders" of the prison subculture. They are generally well liked by prison staff, but other prisoners shun and mistrust them because they come closest to accepting the role which the staff defines as "model prisoner." Opportunists may also be religious, a role adaptation worthy of a separate description (see "The Religious").

- *The Retreatist.* Prison life is rigorous and demanding. Badgering by the staff and actual or feared assaults by other inmates may cause some prisoners to attempt psychological retreat from the realities of imprisonment. Such inmates may experience neurotic or psychotic episodes, become heavily involved in drug and alcohol abuse, or even attempt suicide. Depression and mental illness are the hallmarks of the retreatist personality in prison. The best hope for the retreatist, short of release, is protective custody combined with therapeutic counseling.

- *The Legalist.* The legalist is the "jail house lawyer." Just like the mean dude, the legalist fights confinement. The weapons in this fight are not fists or clubs, however, but the legal "writ." Convicts facing long sentences, with little possibility for early release through the correctional system, are most likely to turn to the courts in their battle against confinement.

- *The Radical.* Radical inmates picture themselves as political prisoners. Society, and the successful conformists who populate it, are seen as oppressors who have forced criminality upon many "good people" through the creation of a system which distributes wealth and power inequitably. The radical inmate speaks a language of revolution and may be versed in the writings of the "great" revolutionaries of the past.

  The inmate who takes on the radical role is unlikely to receive much sympathy from prison staff. Radical rhetoric tends to be diametrically opposed to staff insistence on accepting responsibility for problematic behavior.

- *The Colonizer.* Some inmates think of prison as their home. They "know the ropes," have many "friends" inside, and may feel more comfortable institutionalized than on the streets. They typically hold either positions of power or respect (or both) among the inmate population. These are the prisoners who don't look forward to leaving prison. Most colonizers grow into the role gradually and only after already having spent years behind bars. Once released, some colonizers have been known to attempt new crimes in order to return to prison.

- *The Religious.* Some prisoners profess a strong religious faith. They may be born again Christians, committed Muslims, or even Hare Krishnas. Religious inmates frequently attend services, may form prayer groups, and sometimes ask the prison administration to allocate meeting facilities or create special diets to accommodate their claimed spiritual needs.

Although it is certainly true that some inmates have a strong religious faith, staff members are apt to be suspicious of the overly religious prisoner. The tendency is to view such prisoners as "faking it" in order to demonstrate a fictitious rehabilitation and thereby gain sympathy for an early release.

- *The Realist*. The realist is a prisoner who sees confinement as a natural consequence of criminal activity. Time spent in prison is an unfortunate "cost of doing business." This stoic attitude toward incarceration generally leads the realist to "pull his (or her) own time" and to make the best of it. Realists tend to know the inmate code, are able to avoid trouble, and continue in lives of crime once released.

ealities of Prison Life: The Staff World

The flip side of inmate society can be found in the world of the prison staff, which includes many more people and professions than guard. Staff roles encompass those of warden, psychologist, counselor, area supervisor, program director, instructor, and correctional officer—and in some large prisons, physician, and therapist. Officers, generally seen as at the bottom of the staff hierarchy, may be divided into cellbock and tower guards, but some are regularly assigned to administrative offices where they perform clerical tasks.

Like prisoners, correctional officers undergo a socialization process that helps them function by the official and unofficial rules of staff society. Lucien Lombardo has described the process by which officers are socialized into the prison work world.[25] Lombardo interviewed 359 correctional personnel at New York's Auburn prison and found that rookie officers had to quickly abandon preconceptions of both inmates and other staff members. According to Lombardo, new officers learn that inmates are not the "monsters" much of the public makes them out to be. On the other hand, rookies may be seriously disappointed in their experienced col-

A San Diego (California) inmate shows off his physique. Some inmates attempt to adapt to prison life by acting tough. Recent attempts by both the states and the federal government to ban weight lifting programs in prison, however, may soon put a crimp in such styles of adaptation. Photo by Armineh Johannes, courtesy of SIPA Press.

leagues when they realize that ideals of professionalism, often stressed during early training, are rarely translated into reality. The pressures of the institutional work environment, however, soon force most correctional personnel to adopt a united front in relating to inmates.

One of the leading formative influences on staff culture is the potential threat that inmates pose. Inmates far outnumber correctional personnel in any institution, and the hostility they feel for guards is only barely hidden even at the best of times. Correctional personnel know that however friendly inmates may appear, a sudden change in institutional climate—as can happen in anything from simple disturbances on the yard to full-blown riots—can quickly and violently unmask deep-rooted feelings of mistrust and hatred.

As in years past, prison staffers are still most concerned with custody and control. Society, especially under the emerging just deserts philosophy of criminal sentencing, expects correctional staff to keep inmates in custody as the basic prerequisite of successful job performance. Custody is necessary before any other correctional activities, such as instruction or counseling, can be undertaken. Control, the other major staff concern, ensures order, and an orderly prison is thought to be safe and secure. In routine daily activities, control over almost all aspects of inmate behavior becomes paramount in the minds of most correctional officers. It is the twin interests of custody and control that lead to institutionalized procedures for ensuring security in most facilities. The use of strict rules; body and cell searches; counts; unannounced shakedowns; the control of dangerous items, materials, and contraband; and the extensive use of bars, locks, fencing, cameras, and alarms all support the human vigilance of the staff in maintaining security.

Types of Correctional Officers

Staff culture, in combination with naturally occurring personality types, gives rise to a diversity of officer "types." Like the inmate typology we have already discussed, correctional staff can be classified according to certain distinguishing characteristics. Among the most prevalent types are:

- *The Dictator.* Some officers go by the book. Others go beyond it, using prison rules to enforce their own brand of discipline. The guard who demands signs of inmate subservience, from constant use of the word *sir* or *ma'am* to frequent free shoeshines, is one type of dictator. Another goes beyond legality, beating or "macing" inmates even for minor infractions or perceived insults. Dictator guards are bullies. They find their counterpart in the mean inmate described earlier.

  Dictator guards may have sadistic personalities and gain ego satisfaction through the feelings of near omnipotence which come from the total control of others. Some may be fundamentally insecure and employ a false bravado to hide their fear of inmates. Officers which fit the dictator category are the most likely to be targeted for vengeance should control of the institution temporarily revert to the inmates.

- *The Friend.* Friendly officers try to fraternize with inmates. They approach the issue of control by trying to be "one of the guys." They seem to believe that they can win inmate cooperation by being nice. Unfortunately, such guards do not recognize that fraternization quickly leads to unending requests for special favors—from delivering mail to bending "minor" prison rules. Once a few rules have been "bent," the officer may find that inmates have the upper hand through the potential for blackmail.

  Many officers have amiable relationships with inmates. In most cases, however, affability is only a convenience which both sides recognize can quickly evaporate. Friendly officers, as the term is being used here, are *overfriendly*. They may be young and inexperienced. On the other hand, they may simply be possessed of kind and idealistic personalities built on successful friendships in free society.

- *The Merchant.* Contraband could not exist in any correctional facility without the merchant officer. The merchant participates in the inmate economy, supplying drugs, pornography, alcohol, and sometimes even weapons to inmates who can afford to pay for them.

Probably only a very few officers consistently perform the role of merchant although a far larger proportion may occasionally turn a few dollars by smuggling some item through the gate. Low salaries create the potential for mercantile corruption among many otherwise "straight arrow" officers. Until salaries rise substantially, the merchant will remain an institutionalized feature of most prisons.

- *The Indifferent.* The indifferent type of officer cares little for what goes on in the prison setting. Officers who fit this category may be close to retirement, or they may be alienated from their jobs for various reasons. Low pay, the view that inmates are basically "worthless" and incapable of changing, and the monotonous ethic of "doing time" all combine to numb the professional consciousness of even young officers.

Inmates do not see the indifferent officer as a threat, nor is such an officer likely to challenge the status quo in institutions where merchant guards operate.

- *The Climber.* The climber is apt to be a young officer with an eye for promotion. Nothing seems impossible to the climber, who probably hopes eventually to be warden or program director or to hold some high-status position within the institutional hierarchy. Climbers are likely to be involved in schooling, correspondence courses, and professional organizations. They may lead a movement toward unionization for correctional personnel and tend to see the guard's role as a "profession" which should receive greater social recognition.

Climbers have many ideas. They may be heavily involved in reading about the latest confinement or administrative technology. If so, they will suggest many ways to improve prison routine, often to the consternation of other complacent staff members.

Like the indifferent officers, climbers turn a blind eye toward inmates and their problems. They are more concerned with improving institutional procedures and with their own careers than they are with the treatment or day-to-day control of inmates.

- *The Reformer.* The reformer is the "do-gooder" among officers, the person who believes that prison should offer opportunities for personal change. The reformer tends to lend a sympathetic ear to the personal needs of inmates and is apt to offer "arm-chair" counseling and suggestions. Many reformers are motivated by personal ideals, and some of them are highly religious. Inmates tend to see the reformer guard as naive, but harmless. Because the reformer actually tries to help, even when help is unsolicited, he or she is the most likely of all the guard types to be accepted by prisoners.

The Professionalization of Correctional Officers

Expectations of correctional officers have never been high. Prison staffers are generally accorded low status in occupational surveys. Guard jobs require minimal formal education and hold few opportunities for professional growth and advancement. They are low-paying, frustrating, and often boring. Growing problems in our nation's prisons, including emerging issues of legal liability, however, require a well-trained and adequately equipped professional guard force. As correctional personnel become more and more proficient, the old concept of *guard* is being supplanted by that of a professional *correctional officer*.

A few states and some large-city correctional systems make efforts to eliminate individuals with potentially harmful personalities from correctional officer applicant pools. New York, New Jersey, Ohio, Pennsylvania, and Rhode Island all use some form of psychological screening in assessing candidates for prison jobs.[26]

Although only some states utilize psychological screening, all make use of training programs intended to prepare successful applicants for prison work. New York, for example, requires trainees to complete 6 weeks of classroom-based instruction, as well as 40 hours of rifle range practice, followed by another 6 weeks of on-the-job training. Training days begin around 5 A.M. with a mile run and conclude after dark with study halls for students who need extra help. To keep pace with rising inmate populations, the state has often had to run a number of simultaneous training academies.[27]

On the federal level, a new model for correctional careers confronts many of the problems of correctional staffing head on. The Federal Bureau of Prisons' Career

Development Model stands as an example of what state departments of correction can do in the area of staff training and development. The model establishes five sequential phases for the development of career correctional officers:[28] Phase I, Career Assessment; Phase II, Career Path Development; Phase III, Career Enhancement and Management Development; Phase IV, Advanced Management Development; and Phase V, Senior Executive Service Development. Using a psychological personality inventory, the model seeks to identify the skills, abilities, and interests of officers and matches them with career opportunities in the federal correctional system.

The new federal model builds on the large number and diverse types of federal institutions which allow personnel a wide choice in the conditions of employment. Such a situation may not be possible to duplicate in state correctional systems. Small institutions often have few opportunities for added responsibility, and state systems offer neither the geographical nor the programmatic diversity of the Federal Bureau of Prisons.

 Theory into Practice: Code of Ethics—American Correctional Association Preamble

The American Correctional Association expects of its members unfailing honesty, respect for the dignity and individuality of human beings, and a commitment to professional and compassionate service. To this end we subscribe to the following principles:

- Members will respect and protect the civil and legal rights of all individuals.
- Members will treat every professional situation with concern for the person's welfare and with no intent of personal gain.
- Relationships with colleagues will be such that they promote mutual respect within the profession and improve the quality of service.
- Public criticisms of colleagues or their agencies will be made only when warranted, verifiable and constructive in purpose.
- Members will respect the importance of all disciplines within the criminal justice system and work to improve cooperation with each segment.
- Subject to the individual's rights to privacy, members will honor the public's right to know, and will share information with the public to the extent permitted by law.
- Members will respect and protect the right of the public to be safeguarded from criminal activity.
- Members will not use their positions to secure personal privileges or advantages.
- Members will not, while acting in an official capacity, allow personal interest to impair objectivity in the performance of duty.
- No member will enter into any activity or agreement, formal or informal, which presents a conflict of interest or is inconsistent with the conscientious performance of his or her duties.

- No member will accept any gift, service or favor that is or appears to be improper or implies an obligation inconsistent with the free and objective exercise of his or her professional duties.
- In any public statement, members will clearly distinguish between personal views and those statements or positions made on behalf of an agency or the Association.
- Each member will report to the appropriate authority any corrupt or unethical behavior where there is sufficient cause to initiate a review.
- Members will not discriminate against any individual because of race, gender, creed, national origin, religious affiliation, age or any other type of prohibited discrimination.
- Members will preserve the integrity of private information; they will neither seek data on individuals beyond that needed to perform their responsibilities, nor reveal nonpublic data unless expressly authorized to do so.
- Any member who is responsible for agency personnel actions will make all appointments, promotions, or dismissals in accordance with established civil service rules, applicable contract agreements and individual merit, and not in furtherance of partisan interests.

Adopted August 1975 at the 105th Congress of Correction. Revised August 1990 at the 120th Congress of Correction.

SOURCE: American Correctional Association, *Code of Ethics* (Laurel, Md.: American Correctional Association, 1990). Reprinted with permission.

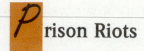

Prison Riots

The ten years between 1970 and 1980 have been called the "explosive decade" of prison riots.[29] The decade began with a massive uprising at Attica prison in New York state in September 1971. The Attica riot resulted in 43 deaths. More than 80 men were wounded. The "explosive decade" ended in 1980 at Santa Fe, New Mexico. There, in a riot at the New Mexico penitentiary, 33 inmates died, the victims of vengeful prisoners out to eliminate rats and informants. Many of the deaths involved mutilation and torture. More than 200 other inmates were beaten and sexually assaulted, and the prison was virtually destroyed.

Prison riots did not stop with the end of the explosive 1970s. For 11 days in 1987, the Atlanta (Georgia) Federal Penitentiary fell into the hands of inmates. The institution was "trashed," and inmates had to be temporarily relocated while it was rebuilt. The Atlanta riot followed closely on the heels of a similar, but less intense, disturbance at the federal detention center at Oakdale, Louisiana. Both outbreaks were attributed to the dissatisfaction of Cuban inmates, most of whom had arrived on the Mariel boat lift.[30] A two-night rampage in October 1989 left more than 100 people injured and the Pennsylvania prison at Camp Hill in shambles. At the time of the riot, the State Correctional Institution at Camp Hill was 45 percent over its capacity of 2,600 inmates.[31] Easter Sunday 1993 saw the beginning of an 11-day rebellion at the 1,800-inmate Southern Ohio Correctional facility in Lucasville, Ohio—one of the country's toughest maximum security prisons. The riot ended with nine inmates and one correctional officer dead. The officer had been hung. Paul W. Goldberg, executive director of the Ohio Civil Service Employees Association, told an Ohio senate panel that "[t]hose of us who deal with our prisons every day—the men and women on the front lines—know that overcrowding and understaffing are at the heart of Ohio's prison crisis....Lucasville is not an aberration....Every prison in Ohio is a powder keg."[32] The close of the riot—involving a parade of 450 inmates—was televised as prisoners had demanded. Among other demands were (1) no retaliation by officials, (2) review of medical staffing and care, (3) review of mail and visitation rules, (4) review of commissary prices, and (5) better enforcement against what the inmates called "inappropriate supervision."[33]

Causes of Riots

It is difficult to explain satisfactorily why prisoners riot, despite study groups which attempt to piece together the "facts" leading up to an incident. After the riot at Attica, the New York State Special Commission of Inquiry filed a report which recommended the creation of inmate advisory councils, changes in staff titles and uniforms, and other institutional improvements. The report emphasized "enhancing (the) dignity, worth, and self-confidence" of inmates. The New Mexico attorney general, in a final report on the violence at Santa Fe, placed blame upon a breakdown in informal controls and the subsequent emergence of a new group of violent inmates among the general prison population.[34]

A number of authorities[35] have suggested a variety of causes for prison riots. Among them are:

1. An insensitive prison administration and neglected inmates' demands. Calls for "fairness" in disciplinary hearings, better food, more recreational opportunities, and the like may lead to riots when ignored.
2. The lifestyles most inmates are familiar with on the streets. It should be no surprise that prisoners use organized violence when many of them are violent people anyway.
3. Dehumanizing prison conditions. Overcrowded facilities, the lack of opportunity for individual expression, and other aspects of total institutions culminate in explosive situations, of which riots are but one form.

4. The way that riots regulate inmate society and redistribute power balances among inmate groups. Riots provide the opportunity to "cleanse" the prison population of informers and rats and to resolve struggles between power brokers and ethnic groups within the institution.

5. "Power vacuums" created by changes in prison administration, the transfer of influential inmates, or court-ordered injunctions which significantly alter the informal social control mechanisms of the institution.

Although riots are difficult to predict in specific institutions, some state prison systems appear ripe for disorder. Texas, for example, has an overcrowded system that exhibits a number of characteristics listed earlier. Making matters worse, Texas prisons house a number of rapidly expanding gangs among whom turf violations can easily lead to widespread disorder. Gang membership among inmates in the Texas prison system, practically nonexistent in 1983, is now estimated at more than 1,200.[36] The Texas Syndicate, the Aryan Brotherhood of Texas, and the Mexican Mafia are probably the largest gangs functioning in the Texas prison system. Each has around 300 members.[37] Table 12-1 summarizes what is known about gangs in the Texas prison system.

Gangs in Texas grew rapidly in part because of the "power vacuum" created when a court ruling ended the "building tender" system.[38] Building tenders were tough inmates who were given an almost free reign by prison administrators in keeping other inmates in line, especially in many of the state's worst prisons. The end of the building tender system dramatically increased demands on the Texas Department of Corrections for increased abilities and professionalism among its guards and other prison staff.

A Broad River Correctional Institution (South Carolina) inmate is subdued following a riot there in 1995. A new rule requiring collar-length hair sparked the riot, which resulted in five staff members being stabbed. Three others were taken hostage. Photo by Jamie Francis, Pool, courtesy of AP/Wide World Photos.

The "real" reasons for any riot are probably institution specific and may not allow for easy generalization. However, it is no simple coincidence that the "explosive decade" of prison riots coincided with the growth of revolutionary prisoner subcultures referred to earlier. As the old convict code began to give way to an emerging perception of social victimization among inmates, it was probably only a matter of time until those perceptions turned to militancy. Seen from this perspective, riots are more a revolutionary activity undertaken by politically motivated cliques than spontaneous and disorganized expressions stemming from the frustrations of prison life.

Stages in Riots and Riot Control

Rioting cannot be predicted.[39] Riots are generally unplanned and tend to occur spontaneously, the result of some relatively minor precipitating event. Once the stage has been set, prison riots tend to evolve through five phases:[40] (1) explosion, (2) organization (into inmate-led groups), (3) confrontation (with authority), (4) termination (through negotiation or physical confrontation), and (5) reaction and explanation (usually by investigative commissions). Donald Cressey[41] points out that the early explosive stages of a riot tend to involve "binges" during which inmates exult in their newfound freedom with virtual orgies of alcohol and drug use or sexual activity. Buildings are burned, facilities are wrecked, and old grudges between individual inmates and inmate groups are settled, often through violence. After this initial explosive stage, leadership changes tend to occur. New leaders emerge who, at least for a time, may effectively organize inmates into a force that can confront and resist official's attempts to regain control of the institution. Bargaining strategies then develop, and the process of negotiation begins.

In the past, many correctional facilities depended on informal procedures to quell disturbances—and often drew on the expertise of seasoned correctional officers who were veterans of past skirmishes and riots. Given the large size of many of today's institutions, the rapidly changing composition of inmate and staff populations, and increasing tensions caused by overcrowding and the movement toward reduced inmate privileges, the "old guard" system can no longer be depended on to quell disturbances. Hence, most modern facilities have incident management procedures and systems in place which are designed to be implemented in the event of disturbances. Such systems remove the burden of riot control from the individual officer, depending instead on a systematic and deliberate approach developed to deal with a wide variety of correctional incidents.

TABLE 12-1

Prison Gangs and Gang Membership in the Texas Prison System, 1990

Name of Gang	Racial Composition	Membership	Year Formed
Texas Syndicate	Predominantly Hispanic	289	1975
Texas Mafia	Predominantly white	80	1982
Aryan Brotherhood of Texas	All white	170	1983
Mexican Mafia	All Hispanic	417	1984
Nuestro Carneles	All Hispanic	31	1984
Mandingo Warriors	All black	36	1985
Self-Defense Family	Predominantly black	76	1985
Hermanos De Pistolero	All Hispanic	75	1985
Total		1,174	

SOURCE: Robert S. Fong, Ronald E. Vogel, and S. Buentello "Prison Gang Dynamics: A Look Inside the Texas Department of Corrections," in A. V. Merlo and P. Menekos, eds., *Dilemmas and Directions in Corrections* (Cincinnati: Anderson, 1992).

ealities of Prison Life: Women in Prison

As Chapter 11 showed, 64,403 women are imprisoned in state and federal correctional institutions throughout the United States[42]—accounting for 6 percent of all prison inmates. A recent survey found that California has the largest number of female prisoners (6,747), exceeding even the federal government (6,399).[43] Figure 12-1 provides a breakdown of the total American prison population by gender and ethnicity. Most women inmates are housed in centralized state facilities known as "women's prisons," which are dedicated exclusively to the holding of female felons. Many states, however, particularly those with small populations, continue to keep women prisoners in special wings of what are otherwise institutions for men.

Although there are still far more men imprisoned across the nation than women (approximately 16 men for every woman), the number of female inmates is rising quickly.[44] A decade and a half ago—in 1981—women composed only 4 percent of the nation's overall prison population, but the number of female inmates nearly tripled during the 1980s—a rate of growth far greater than that shown by male inmates.

Women's prisons are overcrowded, as are men's. The California Institution for Women at Frontera, for example, was originally designed to hold 1,011 inmates. As of this writing, it holds more than 2,500 women. At Bedford Hills Correctional Facility in Westchester County, New York, double bunking is the rule, and conditions there are so crowded that inmates barely have the room necessary to turn around in their living quarters. Even well-managed prisons with nice facades, however, can have problems. One study of a pleasant-appearing women's prison in New York concluded that it was a place of "intense hostility, frustrations, and anger."[45]

Professionals working with imprisoned women attribute the rise in female prison populations largely to drugs. Figure 12-2 shows, in relative graphics, the proportion of men and women imprisoned for various kinds of offenses. Although the figure shows that approximately 33 percent of all women in prison are there explicitly for drug offenses, other estimates say that the impact of drugs on the imprisonment of women is far greater than a simple reading of the figure indicates. Warden Robert Brennan, of New York City's Rose M. Singer jail for women, estimates that drugs—either directly or indirectly—account for the imprisonment of around 95 percent of the inmates there. Drug-related offenses committed by women include larceny, burglary, fraud, prostitution, embezzlement, and robbery, as well as other crimes stimulated by the desire for drugs. In fact, incarcerated women most frequently list (1) trying to pay for drugs, (2) attempts to relieve economic pressures, and (3) poor judgment as the reasons for their arrest.[46]

Another reason for the rapid growth in the number of women behind bars may be the demise, over the last decade or two, of the "Chivalry Factor." The Chivalry Factor, so called because it was based on an archaic cultural stereotype that depicted women as helpless or childlike compared to men, allegedly lessened the responsibility of female offenders in the eyes of some male judges and prosecutors—resulting in fewer active prison sentences for women involved in criminal activity. Recent studies show that the Chivalry Factor is now primarily of historical interest. In jurisdictions examined, the gender of convicted offenders no longer affects sentencing practices except insofar as it may be tied to other social variables. B. Keith Crew,[47] for example, in a comprehensive study of gender differences in sentencing observes, "[a] woman does not automatically receive leniency because of her status of wife or mother, but she may receive leniency if those statuses become part of the official explanation of her criminal behavior (e.g., she was stealing to feed her children, or an abusive husband forced her to commit a crime)."

Although there may be no one "typical" prison for women, and no perfectly "average" female inmate, the American Correctional Association's 1990 report by the Task Force on the Female Offender found that women inmates and the institutions which house them could be generally described as follows:[48]

1. Most prisons for women are located in towns with fewer than 25,000 inhabitants.
2. A significant number of facilities were not designed to house female inmates.
3. The number of female offenders being sent to prison is rising.
4. Most facilities that house female inmates also house males.
5. Not many facilities for women have programs especially designed for female offenders.
6. Very few major disturbances or escapes are reported among female inmates.
7. Substance abuse among female inmates is very high.
8. Very few work assignments are available to female inmates.
9. The number of female inmates without a high school education is very high.

Statistics[49] show that the average age of female inmates is 29–30, most are black or Hispanic (57 percent), most come from single-parent or broken homes, and 50 percent have other family members who are incarcerated. The typical female inmate is a high school dropout (50 percent) who left school either because she was bored or because of pregnancy (34 percent). She has been arrested an average of two to nine times (55 percent) and has run away from home between one and three times (65 percent). Thirty-nine percent report using drugs to make them feel better emotionally, whereas 28 percent have attempted suicide at least once. Sixty-two percent were single parents with one to three children prior to incarceration, and many have been physically or sexually abused.[50]

Eighty percent of women entering prison are mothers, and 85 percent of those women retain custody of their children at the time of prison admission. One of four women entering prison has either recently given birth or is pregnant. Critics charge that women inmates face a prison system designed for male inmates and run by men. Hence, pregnant inmates, many of whom are drug users, malnourished, or sick, often receive little prenatal care—a situation that risks additional complications. Separation from their children is a significant deprivation facing incarcerated mothers. Although husbands or boyfriends may assume responsibility for the children of imprisoned spouses or girlfriends, such an outcome is the exception to the rule. Eventually, a large proportion of children are released by their imprisoned mothers into foster care or put up for adoption.

Some states do offer parenting classes for women inmates with children. In a national survey[51] of prisons for women, 36 states responded that they provide parenting programs which deal with caretaking, reducing violence toward children, visitation problems, and related issues. Some offer facilities as diverse as play areas complete with toys, whereas others attempt to alleviate difficulties attending mother–child visits. The typical program studied lasts from four to nine weeks, and provides for a meeting time of two hours per week.

Other meaningful prison programs for women are often lacking—perhaps because the ones which are in place were originally based on traditional models of female roles which left little room for substantive employment opportunities. Many trade-training programs still emphasize low-paying jobs such as cook, beautician, or laundry machine operator. Classes in homemaking are not uncommon.

Social Structure in Women's Prisons

Most studies of women's prisons have revealed a unique feature of such institutions: the way that women inmates construct organized families. Typical of such studies are Ward and Kassebaum's *Women's Prison: Sex and Social Structure*,[52] E. Heffernan's *Making It in Prison: The Square, The Cool, and the Life*,[53] and Rose Giallombardo's *Society of Women: A Study of Women's Prisons*.[54]

Giallombardo, for example, examined the Federal Reformatory for Women at Alderson, West Virginia, spending a year in gathering data (1962–1963). Focusing

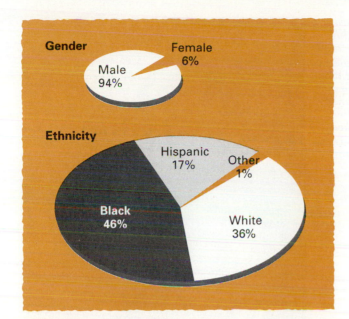

Gender

Male
94%

Female
6%

Ethnicity

Hispanic
17%

Other
1%

Black
46%

White
36%

FIGURE 12-1

Prison inmates by gender and ethnicity, state and federal prisons, 1995. Sources: BJS, Correctional Populations in the United States (Washington, D.C.: Bureau of Justice Statistics, 1995); and BJS press release, "State and Federal Prison Population Tops One Million," October 27, 1994.

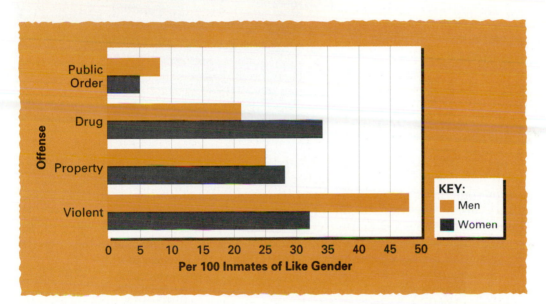

Offense

Public Order

Drug

Property

Violent

KEY:
Men
Women

0   5   10   15   20   25   30   35   40   45   50

Per 100 Inmates of Like Gender

FIGURE 12-2

Men and women in prison by type of offense. Source: Bureau of Justice Statistics, Survey of State Prison Inmates 1991 (Washington, D.C.: U.S. Government Printing Office, 1993).

closely on the formation of families, she entitled one of her chapters, "The Homosexual Alliance as a Marriage Unit." In it she describes in great detail the sexual identities assumed by women at Alderson and the symbols they chose to communicate those roles. Hair style, dress, language, and mannerisms were all used to signify "maleness" or "femaleness." Giallombardo details "the anatomy of the marriage relationship from courtship to 'fall out,' that is, from inception to the parting of the ways, or divorce."[55] Romantic love at Alderson was seen as of central importance to any relationship between inmates, and all homosexual relationships were described as voluntary. Through marriage, the "stud broad" became the husband, and the "femme" the wife.

Studies attempting to document the extent of inmate involvement in prison "families" produce varying results. Some have found as many as 71 percent of women prisoners involved in the phenomenon, whereas others have found none.[56] The kinship systems described by Giallombardo and others, however, extend beyond simple "family" ties to the formation of large, intricately related, groups involving a large number of nonsexual relationships. In these groups, the roles of

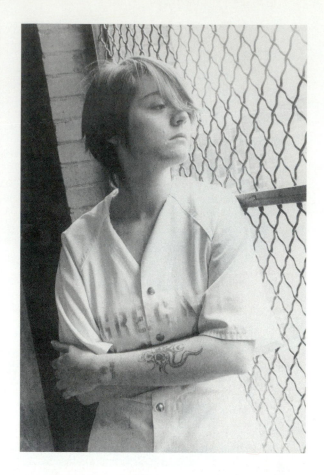

The number of women in prison is growing steadily. Because of disciplinary problems, this woman is housed in the segregation unit of a Rhode Island correctional facility. Photo by Gale Zucker, courtesy of Stock Boston.

"children," "in-laws," "grandparents," and so on, may be explicitly recognized. Even "birth order" within a family can become an issue for kinship groups.[57] Kinship groups sometimes occupy a common household—usually a prison cottage or dormitory area. The description of women's prisons provided by authors like Giallombardo show a closed society in which social interaction—including expectations, normative forms of behavior, and emotional ties—is regulated by an inventive system of artificial relationships which mirror the outside world.

Some authors have suggested that this emphasis on describing family structures in women's prisons is unfortunate because it tends to deny other structural features of those institutions.[58] The family emphasis may, in fact, be due to traditional explanations of female criminality which were intertwined with narrow understandings of the role of women in society.

Types of Female Inmates

As in institutions for men, the subculture of women's prisons is multidimensional. Esther Heffernan, for example, found that three terms used by women prisoners she studied—the "square," the "cool," and the "life"—were indicative of three styles of adaptation to prison life.[59] Square inmates had few early experiences with criminal lifestyles and tended to sympathize with the values and attitudes of conventional society. Cool prisoners were more likely to be career offenders. They tended to keep to themselves and were generally supportive of inmate values. Women who participated in the "life" subculture were quite familiar with lives of crime. Many had been arrested repeatedly for prostitution, drug use, theft, and so on. "Life" group members were full participants in the economic, social, and familial arrangements of the prison. Heffernan believed that the "life" offered an alternative lifestyle to women who had experienced early and constant rejection by conventional society. Within the

Six women live in the one-story red-brick bungalow set on the grounds of the Mountain View Unit of the Texas Department of Criminal Justice in picturesque Coryell County, Texas. The bungalow is home to the Texas prison system's female death row inmates, dubbed "the Mountain View Six." The six women have freedoms unheard of among the 399 condemned male inmates in Texas. A vegetable garden grows by one side of their neatly kept cottage, and a volleyball net stretches across the front yard. The women spend time together in a day room where a television set plays soap operas and movie thrillers during waking hours. They eat many of their meals together at a table and sew and paint dolls in a special cottage workshop—laboring to meet a long waiting list of orders. The Mountain View Six are:

- Cathy Lynn Henderson: a former baby-sitter, under sentence of death for the January 1994 abduction and murder of a 3-month-old baby boy.
- Erica Yvonne Sheppard: sentenced to die for the June 1993 robbery-murder of a Houston woman.
- Frances Elaine Newton: a former housewife convicted of the April 1987 killing of her husband and two children (aged 7 years and 21 months) for insurance monies.
- Betty Lou Beets: shot her fifth husband to death in 1993 near Gun Barrel City, Texas, in a bid to collect insurance monies.
- Karla Faye Tucker: axed at least one person to death during a burglary in Houston in 1983.
- Pamela Lynn Perillo: killed 26-year-old Bob Skeens in Houston during a 1980 robbery.

SOURCE: Michael Graczyk, "Life on Death Row: One of Small Comforts for Texas Women," Associated Press wire services, August 27, 1995.

"life," women could establish relationships, achieve status, and find meaning in their lives. The "square," the "life," and the "cool" represented subcultures to Heffernan because individuals with similar adaptive choices tended to closely relate to one another and to support the lifestyle characteristic of that type.

"Square" inmates are definitely in the minority in prisons for both men and women. Perhaps for that reason they have rarely been studied. In an insightful self-examination, however, one such inmate, Jean Harris, published her impressions of prison life after more than seven years in the maximum security Bedford Hills (New York) Correctional Facility. Harris was convicted of killing the "Scarsdale Diet Doctor," Herman Tarnower, over a romance gone sour. A successful socialite in her early 50s at the time of the crime, Harris had an eye-opening experience in prison. Her book, *They Always Call Us Ladies*,[60] argues hard for prison reform. Sounding like the "square" she was, Harris says other inmates are "hard for you and me to relate to"[61] and describes them as "childlike women without social skills."[62] Speaking to a reporter, Harris related, "There's really nobody for me to talk to here."[63] Harris was granted clemency by New York Governor Mario Cuomo on December 29, 1992—after having served 12 years in prison.[64]

Recently, the social structure of women's prison has become dichotomized by the advent of "crack kids," as they are called in prison argot. Crack kids, whose existence highlights generational differences among female offenders, are streetwise young women with little respect for traditional prison values, for their elders, or even for their own children. Known for frequent fights, and for their lack of even simple domestic skills, these young women quickly estrange many older inmates, some of whom call them "animalescents."

Violence in Women's Prisons

Some authors have suggested that violence in women's prisons is less frequent than it is in institutions for men. Bowker observes that "[e]xcept for the behavior of a few 'guerrillas,' it appears that violence is only used in women's prisons to settle questions of dominance and subordination when other manipulative strategies fail to achieve the desired effect."[65] It appears that few homosexual liaisons are forced, perhaps representing a general aversion among women to such victimization in wider society. At least one study, however, has shown the use of sexual violence in women's prisons as a form of revenge against inmates who are overvocal in their condemnation of such practices among other prisoners.[66]

Not all abuse occurs at the hands of inmates. On November 15, 1992, 14 correctional officers, 10 men and 4 women, were indicted for the alleged abuse of female inmates at the 900-bed Women's Correctional Institute in Hardwick, Georgia. The charges resulted from affidavits filed by 90 female inmates alleging "rape, sexual abuse, prostitution, coerced abortions, sex for favors, and retaliation for refusal to participate"[67] in such activities. One inmate, who was forced to have an abortion after becoming pregnant by a male staff member, said "[a]s an inmate, I simply felt powerless to avoid the sexual advances of staff and to refuse to have an abortion."[68]

The Task Force on the Female Offender[69] recommends a number of changes in the administration of prisons for women. Among them are:

1. Substance abuse programs should be available to women inmates.
2. Women inmates need to acquire greater literacy skills, and literacy programs should form the basis on which other programs are built.
3. Female offenders should be housed in buildings independent of male inmates.
4. Institutions for women should develop programs for keeping children in the facility in order to "fortify the bond between mother and child."
5. To ensure equal access to assistance, institutions should be built to accommodate programs for female offenders.

 risoner Rights

Until the 1960s, American courts took a neutral approach—commonly called the **hands-off doctrine**—toward the running of prisons. Judges assumed that prison administrators were sufficiently professional in the performance of their duties to balance institutional needs with humane considerations. The hands-off doctrine rested on the belief that defendants lost most of their rights on conviction, suffering a kind of **civil death**. Many states defined the concept of civil death through legislation which denied inmates the right to vote, hold public office, or even marry. Some states made incarceration for a felony a basis for uncontested divorce at the request of the noncriminal spouse.

The hands-off doctrine ended in 1969 when a federal court declared the entire Arkansas prison system unconstitutional after hearing arguments that it constituted a form of cruel and unusual punishment.[70] The court's decision resulted from what it judged to be pervasive overcrowding and primitive living conditions. Stories about the system by longtime inmates claimed that a number of other inmates had been beaten or shot to death by guards and buried over the years in unmarked graves on prison property. An investigation did unearth some skeletons in old graves, but their origin was never resolved.

Detailed media coverage of the Arkansas prison system gave rise to suspicions about correctional institutions everywhere. Within a few years, federal courts intervened in the running of prisons in Florida, Louisiana, Mississippi, New York City, and Virginia.[71] In 1975, in a precedent-setting decision, U.S. District Court Judge Frank M. Johnson issued an order which banned the Alabama Board of Corrections from accepting any more inmates. Citing a population which was more than double the capacity of the state's system, Judge Johnson enumerated 44 standards to be met before additional inmates could be admitted to prison. Included in the requirements

Hands-Off Doctrine. A historical policy of nonintervention with regard to prison management which American courts tended to follow until the late 1960s. For the past 30 years, the doctrine has languished as judicial intervention in prison administration has dramatically increased, although there is now growing evidence of a return to a new hands-off doctrine.

Civil Death. The legal status of prisoners in some jurisdictions who are denied the opportunity to vote, hold public office, marry, or enter into contracts by virtue of their status as incarcerated felons. Although civil death is primarily of historical interest, some jurisdictions still place limits on the contractual opportunities available to inmates.

were specific guidelines on living space, staff–inmate ratios, visiting privileges, the racial makeup of staff, and food service modifications.

The Legal Basis of Prisoners' Rights

In 1974, the Supreme Court case of *Pell* v. *Procunier*[72] established a **balancing test** which, although it was at the time addressed only to First Amendment rights, served to define a guideline generally applicable to all prison operations. In *Pell*, the Court ruled that the "prison inmate retains those First Amendment rights that are not inconsistent with his status as a prisoner or with the legitimate penological objectives of the corrections system."[73] In other words, inmates have rights much the same as people who are not incarcerated, provided that the legitimate needs of the prison for security, custody, and safety are not compromised. Other court decisions have declared that order maintenance, security, and rehabilitation are all legitimate concerns of prison administration, but that financial exigency and convenience are not. As the balancing test makes clear, we see reflected in prisoner rights a microcosm of the due process versus social order dilemma found in wider society.

Prisoner rights, because they are constrained by the legitimate needs of imprisonment, are more conditional rights than they are absolute rights. The Second Amendment to the U.S. Constitution, for example, grants citizens the right to bear arms. The right to arms is, however, necessarily compromised by the need for order and security in prison, and we would not expect a court to rule that inmates have a right to weapons. Conditional rights, because they are subject to the exigencies of imprisonment, bear a strong resemblance to privileges, which should not be surprising since "privileges" were all that inmates officially had until the modern era. The practical difference between a privilege and a conditional right stems from the fact that privileges exist only at the convenience of granting institutions and can be revoked at any time for any reason. The rights of prisoners, on the other hand, have a basis in the Constitution and in law external to the institution. Although the institution may change them for legitimate correctional reasons, they may not be infringed without good cause that can be demonstrated in a court of law.

The past two decades have seen many lawsuits brought by prisoners challenging the constitutionality of some aspect of confinement. Suits filed by prisoners with the courts are generally called **writs of habeas corpus** and formally request that the person detaining a prisoner bring him or her before a judicial officer to determine the lawfulness of imprisonment. The American Correctional Association says that most prisoner lawsuits have been based on: "1. the Eighth Amendment prohibition against cruel and unusual punishment; 2. the Fourteenth Amendment prohibition against the taking of life, liberty, or property without due process of law; and 3. the Fourteenth Amendment provision requiring equal protection of the laws."[74] Aside from appeals by inmates which question the propriety of their convictions and sentences, such constitutional challenges represent the bulk of legal action initiated by those imprisoned. State statutes and federal legislation, however, including Section 1983 of the Civil Rights Act of 1871, provide other bases for challenges to the legality of specific prison conditions and procedures.

Precedents in Inmate Rights

To date, the Supreme Court has not spoken with finality on many questions of inmate rights, and there is some evidence of a trend back to a modified "hands-off doctrine."[75] However, High Court decisions of the last few decades can be interpreted along with a number of lower court findings to enumerate the conditional

Balancing Test. A principle developed by the courts, and applied to the corrections arena by the 1974 case of *Pell* v. *Procunier*, which attempts to weigh the rights of an individual as guaranteed by the Constitution, against the authority of states to make laws or otherwise restrict a person's freedom in order to protect its interests and its citizens.

Writ of Habeas Corpus. The writ which directs the person detaining a prisoner to bring him or her before a judicial officer to determine the lawfulness of the imprisonment.

TABLE 12-2

The Conditional Rights of Inmates

<u>Religious Freedom</u>
The Right of Assembly for Religious Services and Groups
The Right to Attend Services of Other Religious Groups
The Right to Receive Visits from Ministers
The Right to Correspond with Religious Leaders
A Right to Observe Religious Dietary Laws
The Right to Wear Beards and Religious Insignia
    <u>Freedom of Speech</u>
The Right to Meet with Members of the Press[1]
The Right to Receive Publications Directly from the Publisher
The Right to Communicate with Nonprisoners
    <u>Access to Legal Assistance</u>
A Right of Access to the Courts
A Right to Visits from Attorneys
A Right to Mail Communications with Lawyers[2]
A Right to Communicate with Legal Assistance Organizations
A Right to Consult "Jail House Lawyers"[3]
A Right to Assistance in Filing Legal Papers, which should include *one* of the following:
    Access to an Adequate Law Library
    Paid Attorneys
    Paralegal Personnel or Law Students
    <u>Medical Treatment</u>
A Right to Sanitary and Healthy Conditions
A Right to Medical Attention for Serious Physical Problems
A Right to Needed Medications
A Right to Treatment in Accordance with "Doctor's Orders"
    <u>Protection</u>
A Right to Food, Water, and Shelter
A Right to Protection from Foreseeable Attack
A Right to Protection from Predictable Sexual Abuse
A Right to Protection Against Suicide
    <u>Institutional Punishment and Discipline</u>
An Absolute Right Against Corporal Punishments (unless *sentenced* to such punishments)
A Right to Due Process Prior to Punishment, including:
    Notice of Charges
    A Fair and Impartial Hearing
    An Opportunity for Defense
    A Right to Present Witnesses
    A Written Decision

---

1. But not beyond the opportunities afforded for inmates to meet with members of the general public.

2. Mail communications are generally designated as privileged or nonprivileged. Privileged communications include those between inmates and their lawyers or court officials, and cannot legitimately be read by prison officials. Nonprivileged communications include most other written communications.

3. Jail house lawyers are inmates with experience in the law, usually gained from filing legal briefs on their own behalf or on the behalf of others. Consultation with jail house lawyers was ruled permissible in the Supreme Court case of *Johnson v. Avery*, 393 U.S. 483 (1968) unless inmates are provided with paid legal assistance.

rights of prisoners shown in Table 12-2. A number of especially significant Court decisions are discussed in the following pages.

Communications

As previously mentioned, the rights listed in Table 12-2 are not absolute, but must be balanced against the security, order maintenance, and treatment needs of the institution. The Supreme Court has indicated that institutional exigency can in fact abbreviate any right. In the case of *Procunier* v. *Martinez* (1974),[76] for example, the Court ruled that a prisoner's mail may be censored if it is necessary to do so for security purposes. On the other hand, mere institutional convenience does not provide a sufficient basis for the denial of rights. In *McNamara* v. *Moody* (1979),[77] a federal court upheld the right of an inmate to write vulgar letters to his girlfriend in which he made disparaging comments about the prison staff. The court reasoned that the letters may have been embarrassing to prison officials but that they did not affect the security or order of the institution. However, libelous materials have generally not been accorded First Amendment protection in or out of institutional contexts.

Concerning inmate publications, legal precedent has held that prisoners have no inherent right to publish newspapers or newsletters for use by other prisoners although many institutions do permit and finance such periodicals.[78] Publications originating from outside prison, such as newspapers, magazines, and special interest tracts, have generally been protected when mailed directly from the publisher although magazines which depict deviant sexual behavior can be banned according to *Mallery* v. *Lewis* (1983)[79] and other precedents. Nudity by itself is not necessarily obscene, and federal courts have held that prisons cannot ban nude pictures of inmates' wives and girlfriends.[80]

Religious Practice

The early Supreme Court case of *Cruz* v. *Beto* (1972)[81] established that inmates must be given a "reasonable opportunity" to pursue their faith, even if it differs from traditional forms of worship. Meeting facilities must be provided for religious use when those same facilities are made available to other groups of prisoners for other purposes,[82] but no group can claim exclusive use of a prison area for religious reasons.[83] The right to assemble for religious purposes, however, can be denied to inmates who use such meetings to plan escapes or who take the opportunity to dispense contraband. Similarly, prisoners in segregation do not have to be permitted the opportunity to attend group religious services.[84]

Although prisoners cannot be made to attend religious services,[85] records of religious activity can be maintained in order to administratively determine dietary needs and eligibility for passes to religious services outside the institution.[86] In *Dettmer* v. *Landon* (1985),[87] a federal court held that an inmate who claimed to practice witchcraft must be provided with the artifacts necessary for his worship services. Included were items such as sea salt, sulfur, a quartz clock, incense, candles, and a white robe without a hood. However, drugs and dangerous substances have not been considered permissible even when inmates claimed they were a necessary part of their religious services.[88] Prison regulations prohibiting the wearing of beards, even those grown for religious reasons, were held acceptable for security considerations in the 1985 federal court case of *Hill* v. *Blackwell*.[89]

Visitation

Visitation and access to the news media are other areas which have come under court scrutiny. Maximum security institutions rarely permit "contact" visits, and some have on occasion suspended all visitation privileges. In the case of *Block* v. *Rutherford* (1984),[90] the Supreme Court upheld the policy of the Los Angeles County Central Jail which prohibited all visits from friends and relatives. The Court agreed that the large jail population and the conditions under which visits might take place could combine to threaten the security of the jail.

In *Pell* v. *Procunier* (1974),[91] cited in the balancing test, the Court found in favor of a California law which denied prisoners the opportunity to hold special meetings with members of the press. The Court reasoned that media interviews could be conducted through regular visitation arrangements and that most of the information desired by the media could be conveyed through correspondence. In *Pell*, the Court also held that any reasonable policy of media access was acceptable so long as it was administered fairly and without bias.

In a later case, the Court ruled that news personnel cannot be denied correspondence with inmates, but also ruled that they have no constitutional right to interview inmates or to inspect correctional facilities beyond the visitation opportunities available to others.[92] This equal access policy was set forth in *Houchins* v.

KQED, Inc. (1978) by Justice Stewart who wrote that "The Constitution does no more than assure the public and the press equal access once government has opened its doors."[93]

Legal Access to the Courts

A well-established right of prisoners is access to the courts[94] and to legal assistance. The right of prisoners to petition the court was recognized in *Bounds* v. *Smith* (1977),[95] a far-reaching Supreme Court decision. While attempting to define "access," the Court imposed on the states the duty of assisting inmates in the preparation and filing of legal papers. Assistance could be provided through trained personnel knowledgeable in the law or via law libraries in each institution, which all states have since built.

In the earlier case of *Johnson* v. *Avery* (1968),[96] the Court had ruled that persons under correctional supervision have a right to consult "jail house lawyers," for advice when assistance from trained professionals is not available. Other court decisions have established that inmates have a right to correspond with their attorneys[97] and with legal assistance organizations. Such letters, however, can be opened and inspected for contraband[98] (but not read) by prison authorities in the presence of the inmate. The right to meet with hired counsel for reasonable lengths of time has also been upheld.[99] Indigent defendants must be provided with stamps for the purpose of legal correspondence,[100] and inmates cannot be disciplined for communicating with lawyers or requesting legal help. Conversations between inmates and their lawyers can be monitored although any evidence obtained through such a process cannot be used in court.[101] Inmates do not, however, have the right to an appointed lawyer, even when indigent, if no judicial proceedings against them have been initiated.[102]

Medical Care

The historic Supreme Court case of *Estelle* v. *Gamble* (1976)[103] specified prison officials' duty to provide for inmates' medical care. In *Estelle*, the Court concerned itself with "deliberate indifference" among the staff toward a prisoner's need for serious medical attention. Deliberate indifference can mean a wanton disregard for the health of inmates. Hence, though poor treatment, misdiagnosis, and the like may constitute medical malpractice, they do not necessarily constitute deliberate indifference.[104]

 Theory into Practice: Religious Assembly

The following statements, excerpted from prison "rule books" of two different states, capture the essence of the court-created balancing test as it weighs prison administrative and security concerns against the right to freedom of religion which is guaranteed by the U.S. Constitution:

Religious Services. Religious services, speeches, or addresses by inmates other than those approved by the Superintendent or designee are prohibited.

Source: Standards of Inmate Behavior, All Institutions, State of New York, Department of Correctional Services (1988).

Freedom of Religion. Inmates will be able to practice their religion in keeping with the security needs of each unit. Ministers and other religious counselors will be allowed to visit inmates. The time, place, and method of such visits are controlled by the custody and security needs of each unit.

SOURCE: *Rules and Procedures Governing the Management and Conduct of Inmates Under the Control of the Division of Prisons,* North Carolina Division of Prisons (1983).

More recently, in *Farmer* v. *Brennan* (1994),[105] the Court clarified the concept of deliberate indifference by holding that it required both actual knowledge and disregard of risk of harm. The case involved Dee Farmer, a preoperative transsexual with obvious feminine characteristics who had been incarcerated with other males in the federal prison system. Farmer was sometimes held in the general prison population but was more often in segregation. While mixing with other inmates, however, Farmer was beaten and raped by a fellow prisoner. Subsequently, he sued correctional officials, claiming that they had acted with deliberate indifference to his safety because they knew that the penitentiary had a violent environment as well as a history of inmate assaults, and because they should have known that Farmer would be particularly vulnerable to sexual attack.

The Court sent Farmer's case back to a lower court for rehearing, after clarifying what it said was necessary to establish deliberate indifference. "Prison officials," wrote the justices, "have a duty under the Eighth Amendment to provide humane conditions of confinement. They must ensure that inmates receive adequate food, clothing, shelter, and medical care, and they must protect prisoners from violence at the hands of other prisoners. However, a constitutional violation occurs only where...the official has acted with 'deliberate indifference' to inmate health or safety." The Court continued: "A prison official may be held liable under the Eighth Amendment for acting with 'deliberate indifference' to inmate health or safety only if he knows that inmates face a substantial risk of serious harm and disregards that risk by failing to take reasonable measures to abate it."[106]

Two other cases, *Ruiz* v. *Estelle* (1982)[107] and *Newman* v. *Alabama* (1972),[108] have had substantial impact concerning the rights of prisoners to medical attention. In *Ruiz,* the Texas Department of Corrections was found lacking in its medical treatment programs. The court ordered an improvement in record keeping, physical facilities, and general medical care while it continued to monitor the progress of the department. In *Newman,* Alabama's prison medical services were found so inadequate as to be "shocking to the conscience." Problems with the Alabama program included:[109]

- ✔ Not enough medical personnel
- ✔ Poor physical facilities for medical treatment
- ✔ Poor administrative techniques for dispersal of medications
- ✔ Poor medical records
- ✔ A lack of medical supplies
- ✔ Poorly trained or untrained inmates who provided some medical services and performed minor surgery
- ✔ Medically untrained personnel who determined the need for treatment

Part of the issue of medical treatment is the question of whether inmates can be forced to take medication or can refuse to eat. A 1984 federal court case held that inmates could be medicated in emergency situations against their wills.[110] The court did recognize that unwanted medications designed to produce only psychological effects, such as tranquilizers, might be refused more readily than life-sustaining drugs.[111] Similarly, other courts have held that inmates do not have a right to starve themselves to death.

In 1993, the Court gave indication that environmental conditions of prison life which pose a threat to inmate health may have to be corrected. In *Helling* v. *McKinney,*[112] Nevada inmate William McKinney claimed that exposure to secondary cigarette smoke circulating in his cell was threatening his health in violation of the Eighth Amendment's prohibition on cruel and unusual punishment. The Court, in ordering that a federal district court provide McKinney with the opportunity to prove his allegations, held that "[a]n injunction cannot be denied to inmates who plainly prove an unsafe, life-threatening condition on the ground that nothing yet has happened to them." In effect, the *Helling* case gave notice to prison officials that they are responsible not only for "inmates' current serious health problems," but also for maintaining environmental conditions under which health problems might be prevented from developing.

Privacy

Many court decisions, including the Tenth Circuit case of *U.S.* v. *Ready* (1978)[113] and the U.S. Supreme Court decisions of *Katz* v. *U.S.* (1967)[114] and *Hudson* v. *Palmer* (1984),[115] have held that inmates cannot have a reasonable expectation to privacy while incarcerated. Palmer, an inmate in Virginia, claimed that Hudson, a prison guard, had unreasonably destroyed some of his personal (noncontraband) property following a cell search. Palmer's complaint centered on the lack of due process which accompanied the destruction. The Court disagreed, saying that the need for prison officials to conduct thorough and unannounced searches precludes inmate privacy in personal possessions.

In *Block* v. *Rutherford*, (1984)[116] the Court established that prisoners do not have a right to be present during a search of their cells. Some lower courts, however, have begun to indicate that body cavity searches may be unreasonable unless based on a demonstrable suspicion or conducted after prior warning has been given to the inmate.[117] They have also indicated that searches conducted simply to "harass or humiliate" inmates are illegitimate.[118] These cases may be an indication that the Supreme Court will soon recognize a limited degree of privacy in prison cells searches, especially those which uncover legal documents and personal papers prepared by the prisoner.[119]

Grievance Procedures. Formalized arrangements, usually involving a neutral hearing board, whereby institutionalized individuals have the opportunity to register complaints about the conditions of their confinement.

Disciplinary and Grievance Procedures

A major area of inmate concern is the hearing of grievances. Complaints may arise in areas as diverse as food service (quality of food or special diets for religious purposes or health regimens), interpersonal relations between inmates and staff, denial of privileges, and accusations of misconduct levied against an inmate or a guard. By the early 1970s, prisoners quickly began to capitalize on the courts' abandonment of the hands-off doctrine. Whereas only about 2,000 petitions per year concerning inmate problems were being filed with the courts in 1961, by 1975 the number of filings had increased to around 17,000. Today, the number is even greater.

In 1972, the National Council on Crime and Delinquency developed a Model Act for the Protection of Rights of Prisoners, which included the opportunity for grievances to be heard, and the 1973 National Advisory Commission on Criminal Justice Standards and Goals called for the establishment of responsible practices for the hearing of inmate grievances. Finally, in 1977, in the case of *Jones* v. *North Carolina Prisoners' Labor Union, Inc.*,[120] the Supreme Court held that prisons must establish some formal opportunity for the airing of inmate grievances. Soon, formal grievance plans were established in prisons in an attempt to divert inmate-originated grievances away from the courts.

Today, all sizable prisons have an established **grievance procedure** whereby an inmate files a complaint with local authorities and receives a mandated response. Modern grievance procedures range from the use of a hearing board comprised of staff members and inmates to a single staff appointee charged with the resolution of complaints. Inmates who are dissatisfied with the handling of their grievance can generally appeal beyond the level of the local prison unit. The accompanying Theory into Practice box outlines the procedures to be followed in the filing of grievances in the New York state correctional system.

Disciplinary actions by prison authorities may also require a formalized hearing process, especially when staff members bring charges of rule violations against inmates which might result in some form of punishment being imposed on them. In a precedent-setting decision, the Supreme Court decided, in the case of *Wolff* v.

McDonnell (1974),[121] that sanctions could not be levied against inmates without appropriate due process. The *Wolff* case involved an inmate who had been deprived of previously earned "good-time" credits because of misbehavior. The Court established that good-time credits were a form of "state-created right(s)," which, once created, could not be "arbitrarily abrogated."[122] *Wolff* was especially significant because it began an era of court scrutiny of what came to be called "state-created liberty interests." State-created liberty interests were said to be based on the language used in published prison regulations, and were held, in effect, to confer due process guarantees on prisoners. Hence, if a prison regulation said that disciplinary hearing should be held before a prisoner could be sent to solitary confinement, and that such a hearing should permit a discussion of the evidence for and against the prisoner, courts interpreted that regulation to mean that the prisoner had a state-created right to a hearing, and sending him or her to solitary confinement in violation of the regulation was a violation of a state-created liberty interest. State-created rights and privileges were also called "protected liberties" in later court decisions and were interpreted to include any significant change in a prisoner's status.

In the interest of due process, and especially where written prison regulations governing the hearing process exist, courts have generally held that inmates going before disciplinary hearing boards are entitled to (1) notice of the charges brought against them, (2) the chance to organize a defense, (3) an impartial hearing, and (4) the opportunity to present witnesses and evidence on their behalf. A written statement of the hearing board's conclusions should be provided to the inmate.[123] More recently, in the case of *Ponte v. Real* (1985),[124] the Supreme Court held that prison officials must provide an explanation to inmates who are denied the opportunity to have a desired witness at their hearing. The case of *Vitek v. Jones* (1980) extended the requirement of due process to inmates about to be transferred from prisons to mental hospitals.[125]

So that inmates can know what is expected of them as they enter prison, the American Correctional Association recommends: "A rulebook that contains all chargeable offenses, ranges of penalties and disciplinary procedures [be] posted in a conspicuous and accessible area; [and] a copy…given to each inmate and staff member."[126] A list of "major" and "minor" rule violations, typical of many prisons, is shown in a Theory into Practice box on the next page.

Theory into Practice: Procedures for the Filing of Inmate Grievances in the State of New York

1. Inmate grievance forms shall be made available to any inmate through the facility's duty office within 24 hours of a request. The grievance complaint form shall be filled out by the inmate with the assistance of any other inmate or staff member of the inmate's choice.

2. The completed grievance form shall be transmitted to the designated staff person who shall attempt to help resolve the grievance informally.

3. If the grievance cannot be resolved informally within four working days, the designated staff shall convene an IGRC (Inmate Grievance Review Committee) hearing within seven working days from the date the grievance was received by that staff person. The IGRC shall be composed of two staff representatives appointed by the superintendent, two inmates selected by the grievant, and the nonvoting chairperson designated by the superintendent or his or her designee.

4. At the IGRC hearing, the inmate, the advisor, and the other parties shall hear the grievance and the IGRC shall render a recommendation (to the superintendent).

SOURCE: State of New York, Department of Correctional Services, Directive 4041, *Inmate Grievance Program Modification Plan.*

Theory into Practice: Typical Rules Governing the Conduct of Prisoners' Major and Minor Offenses

1.00   All Penal Law offenses are prohibited and may be referred to law enforcement agencies for prosecution through the courts.

100.10   Inmates shall not assault, inflict or attempt to inflict bodily harm upon any other inmate.

100.11   Inmates shall not assault, inflict or attempt to inflict bodily harm upon any staff member.

100.13   Inmates shall not engage in fighting.

101.10   Inmates shall not engage in, encourage, solicit or attempt to force others to engage in sexual acts.

101.21   Physical contact between inmates, including but not limited to kissing, embracing or hand holding, is prohibited.

104.11   Inmates shall not engage in any violent conduct or conduct involving the threat of violence.

105.10   The unauthorized assembly of inmates in groups is prohibited.

105.11   Religious services, speeches or addresses by inmates other than those approved by the superintendent or designee are prohibited.

106.10   All orders of facility personnel will be obeyed promptly and without argument.

108.10   Inmates shall not escape, attempt to escape, conspire to, or be an accessory to an escape.

113.10   Inmates shall not make, possess, sell or exchange any item of contraband that may be classified as a weapon by description, use, or appearance.

113.12   Inmates shall not make, possess, use, sell or exchange any narcotic, narcotic paraphernalia, or controlled substance.

SOURCE: Excerpted from State of New York, Department of Correctional Services, *Standards of Inmate Behavior, All Institutions*, revised June 1988.

A Return to the Hands-Off Doctrine?

Many state-created rights and "protected liberties" may soon be a thing of the past. In June 1991, an increasingly conservative U.S. Supreme Court signaled the beginning of what appears to be at least a partial return to the hands-off doctrine of earlier times. The case, *Wilson* v. *Seiter*,[127] involved a 1983 suit brought against Richard P. Seiter, director of the Ohio Department of Rehabilitation and Correction, and Carl Humphreys, warden of the Hocking Correctional Facility (HCF) in Nelsonville, Ohio. In the suit, Pearly L. Wilson, a felon incarcerated at HCF, alleged that a number of the conditions of his confinement—specifically, overcrowding, excessive noise, insufficient locker storage space, inadequate heating and cooling, improper ventilation, unclean and inadequate restrooms, unsanitary dining facilities and food preparation, and housing with mentally and physically ill inmates—constituted cruel and unusual punishment in violation of the Eighth and Fourteenth Amendments to the U.S. Constitution. Wilson asked for a change in prison conditions and sought $900,000 from prison officials in compensatory and punitive damages.

Both the federal district court in which Wilson first filed affidavits and the Sixth Circuit Court of Appeals held that no constitutional violations existed because the conditions cited by Wilson were not the result of malicious intent on the part of officials. The U.S. Supreme Court agreed, noting that the "deliberate indifference" standard applied in *Estelle* v. *Gamble*[128] to claims involving medical care is similarly applicable to other cases in which prisoners challenge the conditions of their confinement. In effect, the Court created a standard which effectively means that all future challenges to prison conditions by inmates, which are brought under the Eighth Amendment, must show deliberate indifference by the officials responsible for the existence of those conditions before the Court will hear the complaint.

The written opinion of the Court in *Wilson* v. *Seiter* is telling. Writing for the majority, Justice Scalia observed that "if a prison boiler malfunctions accidentally during a cold winter, an inmate would have no basis for an Eighth Amendment claim, even if he suffers objectively significant harm. If a guard accidentally stepped on a prisoner's toe and broke it, this would not be punishment in anything remotely like the accepted meaning of the word."

Although the criterion of deliberate indifference is still evolving, it is likely that such indifference could be demonstrated by petitioners able to show that prison administrators have done nothing to alleviate life-threatening prison conditions after those conditions had been called to their attention. Even so, critics of *Wilson* are concerned that the decision may excuse prison authorities from the need to improve living conditions within institutions on the basis of simple budgetary constraints. Four of the justices themselves recognized the potential held by *Wilson* for a near-return to the days of the hands-off doctrine. Although concurring with the Court's majority, Justices White, Marshall, Blackmun, and Stevens noted their fear that "[t]he ultimate result of today's decision, [may be] that 'serious deprivations of basic human needs'…will go unredressed due to an unnecessary and meaningless search for 'deliberate indifference.'"

In the 1995 case of *Sandin* v. *Conner*,[129] the U.S. Supreme Court took a much more definitive stance in favor of a new type of hands-off doctrine, and voted 5–4 to reject the argument that any state action taken for a punitive reason encroaches upon a prisoner's constitutional due process right to be free from the deprivation of liberty. The Court effectively set aside substantial portions of earlier decisions such as *Wolff* v. *McDonnell* (1974)[130] and *Hewitt* v. *Helms* (1983)[131] which, wrote the justices, focused more on procedural issues than on those of "real substance." As a consequence, the majority opinion held, past cases such as these have "impermissibly shifted the focus" away from the *nature* of a due process deprivation to one based on the language of a particular state or prison regulation. "This shift in focus," the justices wrote, "has encouraged prisoners to comb regulations in search of mandatory language on which to base entitlements to various state-conferred privileges." As a result, the Court said, cases such as *Wolff* and *Hewitt* "created disincentives for States to codify prison management procedures in [order to avoid lawsuits by inmates], and…led to the involvement of federal courts in the day-to-day management of prisons."

In *Sandin*, Demont Conner, an inmate at the Halawa Correctional Facility in Hawaii, was serving an indeterminate sentence of 30 years to life for numerous crimes, including murder, kidnapping, robbery, and burglary. Conner alleged in a lawsuit in federal court that prison officials had deprived him of procedural due process when a hearing committee refused to allow him to present witnesses during a disciplinary hearing and then sentenced him to segregation for alleged misconduct. An appellate court agreed with Conner, concluding that an existing prison regulation which instructed the hearing committee to find guilt in cases where a misconduct charge is supported by substantial evidence meant that the committee could not impose segregation if it did not look at all the evidence available to it.

The Supreme Court, however, reversed the decision of the appellate court, holding that although "such a conclusion may be entirely sensible in the ordinary task of construing a statute defining rights and remedies available to the general public, [i]t is a good deal less sensible in the case of a prison regulation primarily designed to guide correctional officials in the administration of a prison." The Court concluded that "such regulations [are] not designed to confer rights on inmates," but are meant only to provide *guidelines* to prison staff members. Hence, based on *Sandin*, it appears that inmates in the future will have a much more difficult time challenging the administrative regulations and procedures imposed upon them by prison officials, even when stated procedures are not explicitly followed. "The *Hewitt* approach," wrote the majority in *Sandin*, "has run counter to the view expressed in several of our cases that federal courts ought to afford appropriate deference and flexibility to state officials trying to manage a volatile environment....The time has come" said the Court, "to return to those due process principles that were correctly established and applied in" earlier times.

Issues Facing Prisons Today

Prisons are society's answer to a number of social problems. They house outcasts, misfits, and some highly dangerous people. Although prisons provide a part of the answer to the question of crime control, they also face problems of their own. We describe a few of those special problems next.

AIDS

An earlier chapter discussed the steps being taken by police agencies to deal with health threats represented by AIDS. In 1993, the Centers for Disease Control reported confirming 11,565 cases of AIDS among inmates of the nation's prisons[132]—an increase of more than fivefold since 1987. By the time of the survey, more than 3,500 inmate deaths had been attributed to HIV infection throughout prisons and jails across the nation. Recent surveys,[133] one conducted in 1995, have estimated the number of HIV-infected inmates in the nation's prisons at much higher levels—some as high as 80,000 inmates.[134] Positive seroprevalence rates have been found to vary from region to region—ranging between 2.1 and 7.6 percent of all men entering prison and between 2.5 and 14.7 percent of women. Some states have especially high rates. New York, for example, recently reported that 20 percent of all inmates it houses are HIV positive, with slightly less than 10 percent of those exhibiting symptoms of AIDS.

Men account for 95 percent of all inmates affected by AIDS. Blacks, at 58 percent, compose the largest racial/ethnic category; 32 percent of those infected are white, and 10 percent are Hispanic.

The incidence of HIV infection among the general population stands at 8.6 cases per 100,000 according to a recent report by the Centers for Disease Control. Among inmates, however, the incidence rate of reported HIV infection is 2,200 cases per 100,000[135]—many times as great, and AIDS has become the leading cause of death among prison inmates.[136] The fact that inmates tend to have histories of high-risk behavior, especially intravenous drug use, probably explains the huge difference in infection rates.

Contrary to popular opinion, AIDS transmission inside prisons appears minimal. In a test of inmates at a U.S. Army military prison, 542 prisoners who, on admission had tested negative for exposure to the AIDS virus, were retested two years later. None showed any signs of exposure to the virus.[137] On the other hand, some authorities suggest that it is only a matter of time before intravenous drug abuse and homosexual activity inside prisons begin to make a visible contribution to the spread of AIDS.[138] Similarly, prison staffers fear infection from AIDS through routine activities, such as cell searches, responding to fights, performing body searches, administering CPR, and confiscating needles or weapons.

A recent report by the National Institute of Justice[139] suggests that two types of strategies are available to correctional systems to reduce the transmission of AIDS. One strategy relies on medical technology to identify seropositive inmates and segregate them from the rest of the prison population. Mass screening and inmate segregation, however, may be prohibitively expensive. They may also be illegal. Some states specifically prohibit HIV antibody testing without the informed consent of the person tested.[140] The related issue of confidentiality may be difficult to manage, especially where the purpose of testing is to segregate infected inmates from others. In addition, civil liability may result where inmates are falsely labeled infected or where inmates known to be infected are not prevented from spreading the disease. Although, as of 1995, only two state prison systems[141] segregated all known HIV-infected inmates, more limited forms of separation can be practiced. In 1994, for example, a federal appeals court upheld a California prison policy which bars inmates who are HIV-positive from working in food service jobs.[142]

Many state prison systems routinely deny HIV-positive inmates jobs, educational opportunities, visitation privileges, conjugal visits, and home furloughs, causing some researchers to conclude that "inmates with HIV and AIDS are routinely discriminated against and denied equal treatment in ways that have no accepted medical basis."[143] Theodore Hammett, the nation's leading researcher on AIDS in prison, says, "the point is, people shouldn't be punished for having a certain medical condition."[144] The second strategy is one of prevention through education. Educational programs teach both inmates and staff members about the dangers of high-risk behavior, and offer suggestions on how to avoid HIV infection. An NIJ model program[145] recommends the use of simple straightforward messages presented by knowledgeable and approachable trainers. Alarmism, says NIJ, is to be avoided. A 1994 survey[146] found that 98 percent of state and federal prisons provide some form of AIDS/HIV education and that 90 percent of jails do as well—although most such training is oriented toward correctional staff rather than inmates.

In anticipation of court rulings which will likely prohibit the mass testing of inmates for the AIDS virus, the second strategy seems best. A third, but controversial, strategy involves issuing condoms to prisoners. Although this alternative is sometimes rejected because it implicitly condones sexual behavior among inmates, six correctional systems within the United States report that they make condoms available to inmates on request.[147]

Geriatric Offenders

As determinate sentencing and the just deserts model take greater hold, and more and more criminals are sentenced to longer prison terms, there will be increasing numbers of older prisoners among the general prison population. Although some prisoners grow old behind bars, others are old before they get there.

Geriatric inmates are becoming a large part of the inmate population. Here Jonathan Turley, founder of the Project for Older Prisoners (POPS), speaks with two Angola, Louisiana, inmates. Photo by Mark Sultz, courtesy of AP/Wide World Photos.

American prisons, serving an aging population, are seeing more geriatric prisoners than ever before. Authorities estimate that whereas 20 percent of today's prisoners are over 50 years old, around 40 percent will fall into that category by the year 2000.[148]

The "graying" of America's prison population is due to a number of causes: (1) increasing crime among those over 50, (2) the gradual aging of the society from which prisoners come, (3) a trend toward longer sentences, especially for violent offenders with previous records (for example, the "three-strikes" laws of many states), and (4) the gradual accumulation of older habitual offenders in prison.[149]

Crimes of violence are what bring most older inmates into the correctional system. According to one study, 52 percent of inmates who were over the age of 50 at the time they entered prison had committed violent crimes, compared with 41 percent of younger inmates.[150] Ronald Wikberg and Burk Foster provide a snapshot of long-termers in their recent study of Angola prison.[151] Wikberg and Foster described 31 inmates at the Louisiana State Penitentiary at Angola who had served a continuous sentence of 25 years or longer, as of early 1988. They found the typical long-termer to be black (27 of 31), with many of them sentenced for raping or killing a white. Inmate ages ranged from 42 to 71. A common thread linking most of these inmates was that their release was opposed by victims' families and friends. Some had a record as prison troublemakers, but a few had been near-model prisoners.

Long-termers and geriatric inmates have special needs. They tend to suffer from handicaps, physical impairments, and illnesses not generally encountered among their more youthful counterparts. Unfortunately, few prisons are equipped to deal adequately with the medical needs of aging offenders. Some large facilities have begun to set aside special sections to care for elderly inmates with "typical" disorders such as Alzheimer's disease, cancer, or heart disease. Unfortunately, such efforts have barely kept pace with problems. The number of inmates requiring round-the-clock care is expected to increase dramatically over the next two decades.[152]

Even the idea of rehabilitation takes on a new meaning where geriatric offenders are concerned. What kinds of programs are most likely to be useful in providing the older inmate with the needed tools for success on the outside? Which counseling strategies hold the greatest promise for introducing socially acceptable behavior patterns into the long-established lifestyles of elderly offenders about to be released? There are few answers to these questions. To date, no in-depth federal studies to answer such questions have been done which might help prepare the nation's prison system for handling the needs of older inmates.[153]

Mentally Ill Inmates

The mentally ill are another inmate category with special needs. Some inmates are neurotic or have personality problems which increase tension in prison. Others have serious psychological disorders which may have escaped earlier diagnosis (at trial) or which did not provide a legal basis for the reduction of criminal responsibility. A fair number of offenders develop psychiatric symptoms while in prison. Some news accounts of modern prisons have focused squarely on the problem: "raging mental illness is so common it's ignored," wrote a *Newsweek* staffer visiting a women's prison.[154]

Unfortunately, few states have any substantial capacity for the psychiatric treatment of mentally disturbed inmates. In 1982, Hans Toch described the largely ineffective practice of bus therapy, whereby disturbed inmates are shuttled between mental health centers and correctional facilities.[155] In February 1990, the U.S. Supreme Court, in the case of *Washington State* v. *Harper*, ruled that mentally ill inmates could be required to take antipsychotic drugs, even against their wishes. The ruling stipulated that such a requirement would apply where "the inmate is dangerous to himself or others, and the treatment is in the inmate's medical interest."

Mentally deficient inmates constitute still another group with special needs. Some studies estimate the proportion of mentally deficient inmates at about 10 percent.[156] Retarded inmates are less likely to complete training and rehabilitative programs successfully than are other inmates. They also evidence difficulty in adjusting to the routines of prison life. As a consequence, they are likely to exceed the averages in proportion of sentence served.[157] Only seven states report special facilities or programs for the mentally retarded inmate.[158] Other state systems "mainstream" such inmates, making them participate in regular activities with other inmates.

Texas, one state which does provide special services for retarded inmates, began a Mentally Retarded Offender Program (MROP) in 1984. Inmates in Texas are given a battery of tests that measure intellectual and social adaptability skills, and prisoners who are identified as retarded are housed in special satellite correctional units. The Texas MROP program provides individual and group counseling, along with training in adult life skills.

Summary

Prisons are small societies, and studies of prison life have detailed the existence of prison subcultures, replete with inmate values, social roles, and lifestyles. Prison subcultures are very influential and must be reckoned with by both inmates and staff.

Complicating life behind bars are the numerous conflicts of interest between inmates and staff. Lawsuits, riots, violence, and frequent formal grievances are symptoms of these differences. The conditional rights of prisoners, which have been repeatedly defined by the U.S. Supreme Court, mandate professionalism among prison administrators and require vigilance in the provision of correctional services.

Problems which exist in conventional society are mirrored and often magnified inside prison. HIV-infected inmates, geriatric offenders, and the mentally ill all constitute special groups within the inmate population which require additional care.

Crime does not stop at the prison door, nor does rehabilitation automatically begin. If we expect prisons to meet the demands of rehabilitation and reformation, in addition to those of retribution, punishment, and deterrence, we must be willing to solve the problems of prison first.

Discussion Questions

1. Explain the concept of prison subcultures. What purpose do you think such subcultures serve? Why do they develop?
2. What does "prisonization" mean? Describe the U-shaped curve developed by Wheeler as it relates to prisonization. Why do you think the curve is U-shaped?
3. What is prison argot? What purpose does it serve?
4. What are the primary concerns of prison staff? Do you agree that those concerns are important? What other goals might staff focus on?
5. What does the term *state-created rights* mean within the context of corrections? What do you think might be the future of such state-created rights?
6. Explain the "balancing test" established by the Supreme Court in deciding issues of prisoners' rights. How might such a test apply to the emerging area of inmate privacy?
7. What are some of the special problems facing prisons today which are discussed in this chapter? What new problems do you think the future might bring?

References

1. Joseph W. Rogers, "Mary Belle Harris: Warden and Rehabilitation Pioneer," *Criminal Justice Research Bulletin*, Vol. 3, no. 9 (Huntsville, Tex.: Sam Houston State University, 1988), p. 8.

2. Hans Reimer, "Socialization in the Prison Community," *Proceedings of the American Prison Association, 1937*, (New York: American Prison Association, 1937), pp. 151–155.

3. Donald Clemmer, *The Prison Community* (Boston: Christopher, 1940).

4. Gresham M. Sykes, *The Society of Captives: A Study of a Maximum Security Prison* (Princeton, N.J.: Princeton University Press, 1958).

5. Donald R. Cressey, ed., *The Prison: Studies in Institutional Organization and Change* (New York: Holt, Rinehart and Winston, 1961).

6. Lawrence Hazelrigg, ed., *Prison Within Society: A Reader in Penology* (Garden City, N.Y.: Anchor Books, 1969), preface.

7. Charles Stastny and Gabrielle Tyrnauer, *Who Rules the Joint? The Changing Political Culture of Maximum-Security Prisons in America* (Lexington, Mass.: Lexington Books, 1982), p. 131.

8. Erving Goffman, *Asylums: Essays on the Social Situation of Mental Patients and Other Inmates* (Garden City, N.Y.: Anchor Books, 1961).

9. The concept of prisonization is generally attributed to Clemmer, *The Prison Community*, although Quaker penologists of the late 1700s were actively concerned with preventing "contamination" (the spread of criminal values) among prisoners.

10. Gresham M. Sykes and Sheldon L. Messinger, "The Inmate Social System," in Richard A. Cloward et al., *Theoretical Studies in Social Organization of the Prison* (New York: Social Science Research Council, 1960), pp. 5–19.

11. Ibid., p. 5.

12. Stanton Wheeler, "Socialization in Correctional Communities," *American Sociological Review*, Vol. 26 (October 1961), pp. 697–712.

13. Sykes, *The Society of Captives*, p. xiii.

14. Stastny and Tyrnauer, *Who Rules the Joint?* p. 135.

15. Ibid.

16. Sykes, *The Society of Captives*.

17. Donald Clemmer, *The Prison Community* (New York: Holt, Rinehart and Winston, 1940), pp. 294–296.

18. Alan J. Davis, "Sexual Assaults in the Philadelphia Prison System and Sheriff's Vans," *Trans-Action*, Vol. 6 (December 1968), pp. 8–16.

19. Daniel Lockwood, "Sexual Aggression Among Male Prisoners," unpublished dissertation, (Ann Arbor, Mich.: University Microfilms International, 1978).

20. Lee H. Bowker, *Prison Victimization* (New York: Elsevier, 1980).

21. Ibid., p. 42.

22. Ibid., p. 1.

23. Hans Toch, *Living in Prison: The Ecology of Survival* (New York: The Free Press, 1977), p. 151.

24. John Irwin, *The Felon* (Englewood Cliffs, N.J.: Prentice Hall, 1970).

25. Lucien X. Lombardo, *Guards Imprisoned: Correctional Officers at Work* (New York: Elsevier, 1981), pp. 22–36.

26. Leonard Morgenbesser, "NY State Law Prescribes Psychological Screening for CO Job Applicants," *Correctional Training* (Newsletter of the American Association of Correctional Training Personnel, Winter 1983), p. 1.

27. "A Sophisticated Approach to Training Prison Guards," *Newsday*, August 12, 1982.

28. Rosalie Rosetti, "Charting Your Course: Federal Model Encourages Career Choices," *Corrections Today* (August 1988), pp. 34–38.

29. Stastny and Tyrnauer, *Who Rules the Joint?* p. 1.

30. See Frederick Talbott, "Reporting from Behind the Walls: Do It Before the Siren Wails," *The Quill* (February 1988), pp. 16–21.

31. "Prison Riot Leaves Injuries," *The Fayetteville Observer-Times* (North Carolina), October 28, 1989, p. 1A.

32. Lee Leonard, "Lucasville Guards Were Outnumbered 50–1 Before Riot," *Columbus Dispatch*, May 12, 1993.

33. "Ohio Prison Rebellion Is Ended," *USA Today*, April 22, 1993, p. 2A.

34. *Report of the Attorney General on the February 2 and 3, 1980 Riot at the Penitentiary of New Mexico* (two parts), June and September 1980.

35. See, for example, American Correctional Association, *Riots and Disturbances in Correctional Institutions* (College Park, Md.: ACA, 1981); Michael Braswell et al., *Prison Violence in America* (Cincinnati: Anderson, 1985); and R. Conant, "Rioting, Insurrectional and Civil Disorderliness," *American Scholar*, Vol. 37 (Summer 1968), pp. 420–433.

36. Robert S. Fong, Ronald E. Vogel, and S. Buentello, "Prison Gang Dynamics: A Look Inside the Texas Department of Corrections," in A. V. Merlo and P. Menekos, eds., *Dilemmas and Directions in Corrections* (Cincinnati, OH: Anderson, 1992).

37. Ibid.

38. *Ruiz* v. *Estelle*, 503 F.Supp. 1265 (S.D. Texas, 1980).

39. S. Dillingham and R. Montgomery, J., "Prison Riots: A Corrections Nightmare Since 1774," in Braswell et al., *Prison Violence in America*, pp. 19–36.

40. Vernon Fox, "Prison Riots in a Democratic Society," *Police*, Vol. 26, no. 12 (December 1982), pp. 35–41.

41. Donald R. Cressey, "Adult Felons in Prison," in Lloyd E. Ohlin, ed., *Prisoners in America* (Englewood Cliffs, N.J.: Prentice Hall, 1972), pp. 117–150.

42. Bureau of Justice Statistics, *Prisoners in 1994* (Washington, D.C.: BJS, 1995).

43. Ibid.

44. This section owes much to the American Correctional Association, Task Force on the Female Offender, *The Female Offender: What Does the Future Hold?* (Washington, D.C.: St. Mary's Press, 1990), and "The View from Behind Bars," *Time*, Fall 1990 (special issue), pp. 20–22.

45. James C. Fox, "Women's Prison Policy, Prisoner Activism, and the Impact of the Contemporary Feminist Movement: A Case Study," *The Prison Journal*, Vol. 64, no. 1 (Spring–Summer 1984), pp. 15–36.

46. American Correctional Association, *The Female Offender*.

47. B. Keith Crew, "Sex Differences in Criminal Sentencing: Chivalry or Patriarchy?" *Justice Quarterly*, Vol. 8, no. 1 (March 1991), pp. 59–83.

48. American Correctional Association, *The Female Offender*.

49. Ibid.

50. Mary Jeanette Clement, "National Survey of Programs for Incarcerated Women," paper presented at the Academy of Criminal Justice Sciences annual meeting, Nashville, Tennessee, March 1991.

51. Ibid., pp. 8–9.

52. D. Ward and G. Kannebaum, *Women's Prison: Sex and Social Structure* (London: Weidenfeld and Nicolson, 1966).

53. Esther Heffernan, *Making It in Prison: The Square, the Cool and the Life* (London: Wiley-Interscience, 1972).

54. Rose Giallombardo, *Society of Women: A Study of Women's Prisons* (New York: John Wiley, 1966).

55. Ibid., p. 136.

56. For a summary of such studies (including some previously unpublished), see Bowker, *Prisoner Subcultures*, p. 86.

57. Giallombardo, *Society of Women*, p. 162.

58. Russell P. Dobash, P. Emerson Dobash, and Sue Gutteridge, *The Imprisonment of Women* (Oxford: Basil Blackwell, 1986), p. 6.

59. Heffernan, *Making It in Prison*.

60. Jean Harris, *They Always Call Us Ladies* (New York: Scribners, 1988).

61. "The Lady on Cell Block 112A," *Newsweek*, September 5, 1988, p. 60.

62. Ibid.

63. Ibid.

64. "Scarsdale Diet Doctor's Killer Given Clemency," *USA Today*, December 30, 1992, p. 3A.

65. Bowker, *Prison Victimization*, p. 53.

66. Giallombardo, *Society of Women*.

67. "Georgia Indictments Charge Abuse of Female Inmates," *USA Today*, November 16, 1992, p. 3A.

68. Ibid.

69. American Correctional Association, *The Female Offender*, p. 39.

70. *Holt* v. *Sarver*, 309 F.Supp. 362 (E.D. Ark 1970).

71. Vergil L. Williams, *Dictionary of American Penology: An Introduction* (Westport, Conn.: Greenwood, 1979), pp. 6–7.

72. *Pell* v. *Procunier*, 417 U.S. 817, 822 (1974).

73. Ibid.

74. American Correctional Association, *Legal Responsibility and Authority of Correctional Officers: A Handbook on Courts, Judicial Decisions and Constitutional Requirements* (College Park, Md.: ACA, 1987), p. 8.

75. According to the ACA, *Legal Responsibility*, p. 57, "A trend may be developing in favor of less intrusive remedial orders in conditions cases in favor of allowing institutional official an opportunity to develop and implement relief with as little court involvement as possible." For further information on this and other issues in the area of prisoners' rights, see Barbara B. Knight and Stephen T. Early, Jr., *Prisoner's Rights in America* (Chicago: Nelson-Hall, 1986).

76. *Procunier* v. *Martinez*, 416 U.S. 396 (1974).

77. *McNamara* v. *Moody*, 606 F.2d 621 (5th Cir. 1979).

78. *The Luparar* v. *Stoneman*, 382 F.Supp. 495 (D. Vt. 1974).

79. *Mallery* v. *Lewis*, 106 Idaho 227 (1983).

80. See for example, *Pepperling* v. *Crist*, 678 F.2d 787 (9th Cir. 1981).

81. *Cruz* v. *Beto*, 405 U.S. 319 (1972).

82. *Aziz* v. *LeFevre*, 642 F.2d 1109 (2nd Cir. 1981).

83. *Glasshofer* v. *Thornburg*, 514 F.Supp. 1242 (E.D. Pa. 1981).

84. See, for example, *Smith* v. *Coughlin*, 748 F.2d 783 (2d Cir. 1984).

85. *Campbell* v. *Cauthron*, 623 F.2d 503 (8th Cir. 1980).

86. *Smith* v. *Blackledge*, 451 F.2d 1201 (4th Cir. 1971).

87. *Dettmer* v. *Landon*, 617 F.Supp. 592, 594 (D.C. Va. 1985).

88. *Lewellyn (L'Aquarius)* v. *State*, 592 P.2d 538 (Okla. Crim. App. 1979).

89. *Hill* v. *Blackwell*, 774 F.2d 338, 347 (8th Cir. 1985).

90. *Block* v. *Rutherford*, 486 U.S. 576 (1984).

91. *Pell* v. *Procunier*, 417 U.S. 817, 822 (1974).

92. *Houchins* v. *KQED, Inc.*, 438 U.S. at 11 (1978).

93. Ibid.

94. For a Supreme Court review of the First Amendment right to petition the courts, see *McDonald* v. *Smith*, 105 S.Ct. 2787 (1985).

95. *Bounds* v. *Smith*, 430 U.S. 817, 821 (1977).

96. *Johnson* v. *Avery*, 393 U.S. 483 (1968).

97. *Bounds* v. *Smith*.

98. *Taylor* v. *Sterrett*, 532 F.2d 462 (5th Cir. 1976).

99. *In re Harrell*, 87 Cal. Rptr. 504, 470 P.2d 640 (1970).

100. *Guajardo* v. *Estelle*, 432 F.Supp. 1373 (S.D. Texas, 1977).

101. *O'Brien* v. *United States*, 386 U.S. 345 (1967); and *Weatherford* v. *Bursey*, 429 U.S. 545 (1977).

102. *U.S.* v. *Gouveia*, 104 S.Ct. 2292, 81 L.Ed. 2d 146 (1984).

103. *Estelle* v. *Gamble*, 429 U.S. 97 (1976).

104. Ibid., pp. 105–106

105. *Farmer* v. *Brennan*, 114 S.Ct. 1970, 128 L. Ed. 2d 811 (1994).

106. Ibid.

107. *Ruiz* v. *Estelle*, 679 F.2d 1115 (5th Cir. 1982).

108. *Newman* v. *Alabama*, 349 F.Supp. 278 (M.D. Ala. 1972).

109. Adapted from American Correctional Association, *Legal Responsibility and Authority of Correctional Officers*, pp. 25–26.

110. *In re Caulk*, 35 CrL 2532 (New Hampshire S.Ct. 1984).

111. Ibid.

112. *Helling* v. *McKinney*, 113 S.Ct. 2475, 125 L. Ed. 2d 22 (1993).

113. *U.S.* v. *Ready*, 574 F.2d 1009 (10th Cir. 1978).

114. *Katz* v. *U.S.*, 389 U.S. 347, 88 S.Ct. 507, 19 L.Ed. 2ed 576 (1967).

115. *Hudson* v. *Palmer*, 468 U.S. 517 (1984).

116. *Block* v. *Rutherford*, 104 S.Ct. 3227, 3234–35 (1984).

117. *U.S.* v. *Lilly*, 576 F.2d 1240 (5th Cir. 1978).

118. *Palmer* v. *Hudson*, 697 F.2d 1220 (4th Cir. 1983).

119. William H. Erickson et al., *United States Supreme Court Cases and Comments* (New York: Matthew Bender, 1987), Section 10.02 2 (c), pp. 10–38.

120. *Jones* v. *North Carolina Prisoners' Labor Union, Inc.*, 433 U.S. 119, 53 L.Ed. 2d 629, 641 (1977).

121. *Wolff* v. *McDonnell*, 94 S.Ct. 2963 (1974).

122. Ibid.

123. Ibid.

124. *Ponte* v. *Real*, U.S. 105 S.Ct. 2192 L.Ed. 2d (1985).

125. *Vitek* v. *Jones*, 445 U.S. 480 (1980).

126. American Correctional Association, Standard 2-4346. See ACA, *Legal Responsibility and Authority of Correctional Officers*, p. 49.

127. *Wilson* v. *Seiter* 501 U.S. 294 (1991).

128. *Estelle* v. *Gamble*, 429 U.S. 97, 106 (1976).

129. *Sandin* v. *Conner*, 63 U.S.L.W. 4601 (1995).

130. *Wolff* v. *McDonnell*, 94 S.Ct. 2963 (1974).

131. *Hewitt* v. *Helms*, 459 U. S. 460 (1983).

132. Cheryl A. Crawford, "Health Care Needs in Corrections: NIJ Responds," *National Institute of Justice Journal*, November 1994, p. 31.

133. National Research Council, *The Social Impact of AIDS in the United States* (Washington, D.C.: National Academy Press, 1993), p. 180.

134. Dennis Cauchon, "AIDS in Prison: Locked Up and Locked Out," *USA Today*, March 31, 1995, p. 6A.

135. Bureau of Justice Statistics, *1992 Update: HIV/AIDS in Correctional Facilities* (Washington, D.C.: U.S. Department of Justice, 1993), p. 54.

136. "AIDS in Prison: Locked Up and Locked Out."

137. Theodore M. Hammett, *AIDS in Correctional Facilities: Issues and Options*, 3ed. (Washington, D.C.: National Institute of Justice, 1988), p. 29.

138. M. A. R. Kleiman and R. W. Mockler, "AIDS, the Criminal Justice System, and Civil Liberties," *Governance: Harvard Journal of Public Policy* (Summer–Fall 1987), pp. 48–54.

139. Hammett, *AIDS in Correctional Facilities*, p. 37.

140. At the time of this writing, California, Wisconsin, Massachusetts, New York, and the District of Columbia were among such jurisdictions.

141. Cheryl A. Crawford, "Health Care Needs in Corrections: NIJ Responds."

142. See "Court Allows Restriction on HIV-Positive Inmates," in *Criminal Justice Newsletter*, Vol. 25, no. 23 (December 1, 1994), pp. 2–3.

143. "AIDS in Prison: Locked up and Locked Out."

144. Hammett, *AIDS in Correctional Facilities*.

145. Hammett, *AIDS in Correctional Facilities*, pp. 47–49.

146. Darrell Bryan, "Inmates, HIV and the Constitutional Right to Privacy: AIDS in Prison Facilities," *Corrections Compendium*, Vol. 19, no. 9 (September 1994), pp. 1–3.

147. Cheryl A. Crawford, "Health Care Needs in Corrections: NIJ Responds."

148. Sol Chaneles, "Growing Old Behind Bars,"

Psychology Today (October 1987), pp. 47–51.

149. Ronald Wikbert and Burk Foster, "The Longtermers: Louisiana's Longest Serving Inmates and Why They've Stayed So Long," paper presented at the annual meeting of the Academy of Criminal Justice Sciences, Washington, D.C., 1989.

150. Lincoln J. Fry, "The Older Prison Inmate: A Profile," *The Justice Professional*, Vol. 2, no. 1 (Spring 1987), pp. 1–12.

151. Wikberg and Foster, "The Longtermers."

152. Ibid., p. 51.

153. Chaneles, "Growing Old Behind Bars," p. 51.

154. "The Lady in Cell Block 112A," *Newsweek*, September, 5, 1988, p. 60.

155. Hans Toch, "The Disturbed Disruptive Inmate: Where Does the Bus Stop?" *The Journal of Psychiatry and Law*, Vol. 10 (1982), pp. 327–349.

156. Robert O. Lampert, "The Mentally Retarded Offender in Prison," *The Justice Professional*, Vol. 2, no. 1 (Spring 1987), p. 61.

157. Ibid., p. 64.

158. George C. Denkowski and Kathryn M. Denkowski, "The Mentally Retarded Offender in the State Prison System: Identification, Prevalence, Adjustment, and Rehabilitation," *Criminal Justice and Behavior*, Vol. 12 (1985), pp. 55–75.

Appendix

he Bill of Rights

Articles in Addition to, and Amendments of, the Constitution of the United States of America, Proposed by Congress, and Ratified by the Legislatures of the Several States, Pursuant to the Fifth Article of the Original Constitution.

AMENDMENT I. (1791)

Congress shall make no law respecting an establishment of religion, or prohibiting the free exercise thereof; or abridging the freedom of speech, or of the press; or the right of the people peaceably to assemble, and to petition the Government for a redress of grievances.

AMENDMENT II. (1791)

A well regulated Militia, being necessary to the security of a free State, the right of the people to keep and bear Arms, shall not be infringed.

AMENDMENT III. (1791)

No Soldier shall, in time of peace be quartered in any house, without the consent of the Owner, nor in time of war, but in a manner to be prescribed by law.

AMENDMENT IV. (1791)

The right of the people to be secure in their persons, houses, papers, and effects, against unreasonable searches and seizures, shall not be violated, and no Warrants shall issue, but upon probable cause, supported by Oath or affirmation, and particularly describing the place to be searched, and the persons or things to be seized.

AMENDMENT V. (1791)

No person shall be held to answer for a capital, or otherwise infamous crime, unless on a presentment or indictment of a Grand Jury, except in cases arising in the land or naval forces, or in the Militia, when in actual service in time of War or public danger; nor shall any person be subject for the same offence to be twice put in jeopardy of life or limb; nor shall be compelled in any criminal case to be a witness against himself, nor be deprived of life, liberty, or property, without due process of law; nor shall private property be taken for public use, without just compensation.

AMENDMENT VI. (1791)

In all criminal prosecutions, the accused shall enjoy the right to a speedy and public trial, by an impartial jury of the State and district wherein the crime shall have been committed, which district shall have been previously ascertained by law, and to be informed of the nature and cause of the accusation; to be confronted with the witnesses against him; to have compulsory process for obtaining Witnesses in his favor, and to have the Assistance of Counsel for his defence.

AMENDMENT VII. (1791)

In Suits at common law, where the value in controversy shall exceed twenty dollars, the right of trial by jury shall be preserved, and no fact tried by a jury, shall be otherwise reexamined in any Court of the United States, than according to the rules of the common law.

AMENDMENT VIII. (1791)

Excessive bail shall not be required, nor excessive fines imposed, nor cruel and unusual punishments inflicted.

AMENDMENT IX. (1791)

The enumeration of the Constitution, of certain rights, shall not be construed to deny or disparage others retained by the people.

AMENDMENT X. (1791)

The powers not delegated to the United States by the Constitution, nor prohibited by it to the States, are reserved to the States respectively, or to the people.

Case
Index

Name
Index

McCormack, William U., 185
McCormick, Kenneth L. J., 193
McCummings, Bernard, 183
McDonald, Steven, 178
McEwen, J. Thomas, 121
McGee, Jim, 95
McInnis, Mac, 281
Mackay, Peta, 171
Mack, John, 96
McLaren, Roy Clinton, 191
McNulty, Paul, 10
McVeigh, Timothy, 241, 245–46, 247
Maguire, Kathleen, 59, 187
Manson, Charles, 37
Marshall, Henry, 322
Marshall, John, 220
Marshall, Thurgood, 148, 151–52, 154, 223, 261, 399
Martinez, Roberto, 159
Martin, William, 229
Mauro, Tony, 75
Mays, G. Larry, 365
Meddis, Sam Vincent, 10, 115, 117
Meese, Edwin III, 117, 158
Menendez, Lyle and Erik, 98, 270
Michaelson, Dick, 178
Milano, Peter, 65
Miller, Glenn, 63
Miller, Neal, 211, 212
Milloy, Courtland, 95
Mills, James, 174, 180–81
Miranda, Ernesto, 157–58
Montesquieu, 69
Moore, Mark H., 112, 118
Moore, Richter, 198
Moreno, Jaime, 15
Morgan, Joe, 131
Morris, Allison, 53
Morse, Stephen J., 100
Moss, Desda, 115, 117
Muraskin, Roslyn, 26, 27
Murphy, Patrick V., 105, 123, 169
Myers, Martha, 294

Negron, Guadalupe, 83
Neighbors, William D., 142
Nelson, Willie, 339
Niederhoffer, Arthur, 170
Nixon, Walter L., Jr., 238
Nolan-Haley, Jacqueline M., 71, 82
Nolan, Joseph R., 71, 82

O'Connor, Sandra Day, 144, 268
Oran, Daniel, 78
Osby, Daimion, 13–14, 95–97
Ouderkirk, John, 271
Owens, Compton, 174
Owens, Dan, 285

Packer, Herbert, 24, 25
Parche, Guenter, 301
Parker, Larry, 177
Parker, William H., 26
Peak, Ken, 113
Peel, Sir Robert, 85
Pellicano, Anthony, 99
Perez, Jacob, 226
Petersilia, Joan, 345
Pike, Albert, 234
Pinizzotto, Anthony J., 177
Pinkerton, Allan, 195
Politan, Nicholas H., 11
Pollak, Otto, 57–58
Powell, Laurence, 130, 133–34
Prenzler, Tim, 171
Preszler, Alan, 186
Price, Niko, 95, 98
Pryor, Donald E., 226
Puente, Maria, 97
Pugsley, Robert, 98
Puro, Steven, 137

Radelet, Louis A., 111
Radovcich, Joel, 31
Rankin, A., 225
Reagan, Ronald, 9, 87, 249
Reaves, Brian A., 226
Rehnquist, William H., 140, 223, 264, 302, 307
Reimer, Hans, 372, 374
Reno, Janet, 9, 193
Richardson, James, 12
Richter, Geraldine, 89
Ricksgers, Michael, 100
Robinson, Charles Scott, 285
Rodriguez, Matt L., 116
Rogan, Dennis P., 122
Rosenhan, David, 99–100
Rothstein, Paul, 97
Rottman, David B., 211
Rubin, H. Ted, 216
Rush, Benjamin, 307

Saizow, Hildy, 211, 212
Saldana, Theresa, 300
Salvi, John III, 70
Samaha, Joel, 171
Sapp, Allen D., 188, 191
Sauls, John Gales, 144
Scalia, Antonin, 264, 307, 309
Scarfo, Nicodemo, 64
Scheidegger, Kent, 100, 223
Schoenberg, Ronald L., 93, 94
Schofield, Daniel L., 185
Schultz, Dorothy Moses, 193
Seles, Monica, 301
Seneca, 278

Subject Index